Cover Photo: **The Evolving Face of Nursing**

Mural by Meg Seligman

Photo by Steven Weinik

For years, the most popular mural in Philadelphia, the "city of murals," was the nursing mural ("A Tribute to Nursing") on the side of a building at Broad and Vine Streets. That mural focused on the history of nursing rather than its future. When the wall became compromised, the city enlisted the support of the Independence Foundation and others to commission a new nursing mural by internationally known muralist Meg Seligman. After interviewing many nurses who spoke about the various dimensions of their current work and opportunities for innovations in health care, Seligman designed a mural that focused on contemporary nursing with links to its past and future. Titled "The Evolving Face of Nursing," the 6,500 square foot mural incorporates the faces of nurses and key images that convey the intellectual, creative, and emotional work of nursing through images and symbols. This dynamic mural changes color and emphasis at night through the use of LED lighting—a feature that Seligman used for the first time in this mural. The mural was unveiled on October 6, 2010. The cover photograph by Philadelphia-based photographer, Steven Weinik, shows its location within the community, symbolizing the work of diverse nurses with individuals, families, and communities.

THE NURSING PROFESSION

Development, Challenges, and Opportunities

EDITORS

**DIANA J. MASON, RN, PhD, FAAN
STEPHEN L. ISAACS, JD
DAVID C. COLBY, PhD**

FOREWORD BY
RISA LAVIZZO-MOUREY, MD, MBA

JOSSEY-BASS
A Wiley Imprint
www.josseybass.com

Published by Jossey-Bass
A Wiley Imprint
989 Market Street, San Francisco, CA 94103-1741—www.josseybass.com

Readers should be aware that Internet Web sites offered as citations and/or sources for further information may have changed or disappeared between the time this was written and when it is read.

Limit of Liability/Disclaimer of Warranty: While the publisher and author have used their best efforts in preparing this book, they make no representations or warranties with respect to the accuracy or completeness of the contents of this book and specifically disclaim any implied warranties of merchantability or fitness for a particular purpose. No warranty may be created or extended by sales representatives or written sales materials. The advice and strategies contained herein may not be suitable for your situation. You should consult with a professional where appropriate. Neither the publisher nor author shall be liable for any loss of profit or any other commercial damages, including but not limited to special, incidental, consequential, or other damages.

Jossey-Bass books and products are available through most bookstores. To contact Jossey-Bass directly call our Customer Care Department within the U.S. at 800-956-7739, outside the U.S. at 317-572-3986, or fax 317-572-4002.

Jossey-Bass also publishes its books in a variety of electronic formats. Some content that appears in print may not be available in electronic books.

Library of Congress Cataloging-in-Publication Data

The nursing profession : development, challenges, and opportunities / editors, Diana J. Mason, Stephen L. Isaacs, David C. Colby ; foreword by Risa Lavizzo-Mourey. — 1st ed.
p. ; cm. — (Robert Wood Johnson foundation health policy series) Complements: The future of nursing / Committee on the Robert Wood Johnson Foundation Initiative on the Future of Nursing, at the Institue of Medicine. c2011.
Includes bibliographical references.
ISBN 978-1-118-02881-0 (pbk.); 978-1-118-12220-4 (e-bk.); 978-1-118-12221-1 (e-bk.); 978-1-118-12222-8 (e-bk.)
1. Nursing—Practice—United States.   2. Nursing—United States.   3. Leadership—United States.
I. Mason, Diana J., 1948-   II. Isaacs, Stephen L.   III. Colby, David C.   IV. Committee on the Robert Wood Johnson Foundation Initiative on the Future of Nursing, at the Institute of Medicine. Future of nursing.   V. Series: Robert Wood Johnson Foundation series on health policy.
[DNLM: 1. Nursing—trends—United States—Collected Works.   2. Nurse's Role—United States—Collected Works. WY 16 AA1]
RT82.N8684   2011
610.73—dc22

2011006933

Printed in the United States of America
FIRST EDITION

PB Printing   10 9 8 7 6 5 4 3 2 1

CONTENTS

health care system must include an adequate supply of well-trained professionals who can deliver care to all Americans. Nurses are at the center of this discussion."[2] I am pleased and proud that the Robert Wood Johnson Foundation has played an important role in nursing's development and will continue to do so in the future.

Risa Lavizzo-Mourey, MD, MBA
President and CEO
The Robert Wood Johnson Foundation
Princeton, New Jersey
May 2011

NOTES

1. Isaacs, S. L., & Knickman, J. R., (Eds). *Generalist medicine and the U.S. health system.* San Francisco: Jossey-Bass, 2004; Lear, J. G., Isaacs, S. L., & Knickman, J. R. (Eds). *School health services and programs.* San Francisco: Jossey-Bass, 2006; Warner, K. E., Isaacs, S. L., & Knickman, J. R. *Tobacco control policy.* San Francisco: Jossey-Bass, 2008; Meier, D. E., Isaacs, S. L., & Hughes, R. G., (Eds). *Palliative care: Transforming the care of serious illness.* San Francisco: Jossey-Bass, 2010.

2. Rother, J., & Lavizzo-Mourey, R. Addressing the nursing shortage: A critical element in health reform. *Health Affairs* 28, w260–w264 (2009).

FOREWORD

Like the other four books in the Robert Wood Johnson Foundation Health Policy Series,[1] *The Nursing Profession: Development, Challenges, and Opportunities* focuses on a discipline or profession that has been a Foundation priority for many years. Strengthening the nursing profession has been of central importance to the Robert Wood Johnson Foundation over its nearly forty-year existence, and we have devoted more than $200 million to the growth and improvement of nursing education and practice. Our dedication to nursing continues the legacy of our founder. In his personal philanthropy and as the head of his own New Brunswick-based foundation, Robert Wood Johnson was genuinely interested in improving nursing, and gave generously to amplify the role of nurses in improving health. The foundation that bears his name has sustained that commitment.

As far back as 1973, the Foundation awarded a series of grants to develop an emerging field—nurse practitioners—an idea that was, at the time, untested and controversial. These grants demonstrated that nurse practitioners could provide high-quality primary care services in remote rural areas and underserved inner cities. Since that time, the Robert Wood Johnson Foundation has invested in:

- Strengthening nursing school faculty and leadership
- Addressing nursing shortages
- Improving the nursing workforce
- Conducting research on nursing
- Developing public health nursing
- Establishing nurse-run school health centers
- Improving hospital nursing

And this is only a partial list.

The Nursing Profession: Development, Challenges, and Opportunities begins with a comprehensive review of the nursing field by Diana Mason, the Rudin Professor of Nursing at the Hunter-Bellevue School of Nursing, City University of New York, and former editor-in-chief of the *American Journal of Nursing.* Mason's chapter is followed by reprints of twenty-four of the most influential or significant articles on nursing—some of them classic pieces dating back to Florence Nightingale, others presenting more current thinking on critical issues. This source material is rarely found in one place.

The Robert Wood Johnson Foundation Initiative on the Future of Nursing at the Institute of Medicine (IOM) issued its report in October 2010. It sets forth a blueprint for nursing that can guide policymakers and those in the health care professions. We hope that *The Nursing Profession: Development, Challenges, and Opportunities* will be a worthy companion to the IOM report. Both publications illustrate our dedication to improving a field that is so critical to the nation's health and are especially timely, because "a reformed

We dedicate this book to the memory of C. Patrick Crow, who died shortly after editing its lead chapter. Over the course of the past fifteen years, Pat edited both the Robert Wood Johnson Foundation *Anthology* and its Series on Health Policy. He was an extraordinary editor and, even more important, an exemplary human being. We shall miss him.

SLI, DCC, DJM

PREFACE

SUSAN B. HASSMILLER

May we hope that, when we are all dead and gone, leaders will arise who have been personally experienced in the hard, practical work, the difficulties, and the joys of organizing nursing reforms, and who will lead far beyond anything we have done!

—Florence Nightingale

The Robert Wood Johnson Foundation and Institute of Medicine (IOM) became partners in 2008 to develop the Robert Wood Johnson Foundation Initiative on the Future of Nursing at the IOM. A core product of the Initiative was an IOM report called *The Future of Nursing: Leading Change, Advancing Health,* which was issued in October 2010.[1] The report examined the capacity of the nursing workforce to meet the demands of a newly reformed health care system, keeping in mind the needs of an aging population and the emphasis on care in the community. It made a series of recommendations that address a range of public policy and system changes, including vital roles for nurses in designing and implementing a more effective and efficient health care system. The committee's ultimate goal was to improve patient care and health care outcomes.

The Robert Wood Johnson Foundation has continued the Future of Nursing Initiative by partnering with AARP to facilitate a national campaign to encourage the adoption of the recommendations, and as stakeholders in the nursing and policy communities feel the need, come up with additional recommendations or priority areas on which to work. We will continue to raise the notion of the value to society of investing in a strong, well-educated, and empowered nursing workforce. Partners in this campaign include leaders from government, business, policy, academia, medicine, and of course, nursing. A National Summit on Advancing Health through Nursing was held in Washington, DC, at the end of November 2010, to mark the official start of the campaign.

The IOM committee working on the report was heavily influenced by the best thinking of those who study and practice nursing, including authors of the articles reprinted in *The Nursing Profession: Development, Challenges, and Opportunities.* I can think of no better place for those who are interested in or touched by nursing to gain an understanding of the history of the current issues facing the nursing profession than this anthology. It is my sincere hope that readers of this book will be inspired by the authors—both past and present—who influenced the field.

Together, *The Future of Nursing: Leading Change, Advancing Health* report and *The Nursing Profession: Development, Challenges, and Opportunities* lay the groundwork for understanding where the field has been, where it stands currently, and where it needs to go in the future in order to address the issues facing nursing and improve the health of all Americans.

NOTE

1. http://www.iom.edu/Reports/2010/The-Future-of-Nursing-Leading-Change-Advancing-Health.aspx

Susan B. Hassmiller, PhD, RN, FAAN, serves as the Robert Wood Johnson Foundation Special Adviser on Nursing and Director of the Initiative on the Future of Nursing.

EDITORS' INTRODUCTION

DIANA J. MASON, STEPHEN L. ISAACS, AND DAVID C. COLBY

This book is designed to be a resource for those who are interested in or touched by nursing. We have tried to capture the field in a single volume and to share the best thinking of those who study and practice it. Readers—whether researchers or practitioners, foundation or government officials, students, or simply laypeople interested in nursing—should use this volume to gain a better understanding of the nursing profession and the issues with which those in the field and related fields are grappling.

An initial challenge for the editors was determining how to present the wealth of information in an engaging, readable way—one that would satisfy both those deeply knowledgeable in the field as well as those less familiar with nursing. This challenge was relatively easy to overcome because *The Nursing Profession: Development, Challenges, and Opportunities* is the fifth volume in a series whose format, according to the reviews, appears to be working. We adopted that format, one that consists of a comprehensive review article, followed by reprints of the twenty-four or so most influential or important articles in the field.

Finding a knowledgeable, highly respected expert on nursing—one who is a good writer to boot—to do a comprehensive review of the field presented a second challenge. Fortunately, one of us—Diana Mason—met all of the requisites, and she has written the lead chapter, which covers the field in its entirety (with the exception of the specifics of clinical nursing). Among the topics that Dr. Mason covers are:

- The history of nursing
- The nursing profession
- Current issues and challenges, including the nursing shortage, educating and training nurses, utilizing advanced practice nurses to their fullest, quality and cost, long-term care, community-based care, gender and power, and new areas for nursing
- A vision for the future

The most daunting challenge, not surprisingly, turned out to be selecting the articles or book chapters for reprint. How to choose twenty-four that represent the most important or influential in a field with such an extensive, high-quality literature? As a first step, we asked more than thirty experts for their top picks. From their suggestions, plus those gleaned from our own experience and literature reviews, we compiled an initial list of roughly 200 articles or book chapters that were potential reprint candidates.

The three editors discussed each of the articles and winnowed the list gradually. We wanted to be sure to include pieces that were of historical importance (such as a selection from Florence Nightingale's *Notes on Nursing* and the *Goldmark Report*), that influenced the field (such as Mary Mundinger's article on nurse practitioners in the *Journal of the American Medical Association* and Linda Aiken's article, also in *JAMA*, on hospital nursing), that captured basic aspects of the profession (such as Susan Reverby's article on womanhood and nursing and Claire Fagin and Donna Diers' short commentary, *Nursing as Metaphor*), and that synthesized issues in a clear and compelling manner (for example, the articles by Peter Buerhaus and colleagues on the nursing shortage and by Connie Mullinex and Dawn Bucholtz on nurse practitioners). We organized the reprints by topic, roughly following the major themes presented in Mason's review chapter and tried, though with only partial success, to strike an equitable balance in the number of reprints within each category.

We realize that many worthy pieces are not included in the twenty-four that are reprinted in the book. It is likely that another team of editors would have come up with a somewhat different list of reprints. We believe, however, that the final list represents a fair sample of the most important and influential articles in the nursing field.

As Risa Lavizzo-Mourey observed in her foreword, this book is designed in part to complement the report by the Institute of Medicine on the future of nursing. In that regard, we are honored to have a preface by Susan Hassmiller, the executive director of the IOM's Initiative on the Future of Nursing, and an afterword by Donna Shalala and Linda Burnes Bolton, the chair and vice chair of IOM committee that prepared the report.

With the passage of Patient Protection and Affordable Care Act in 2010 and its implications for the way health services are delivered, the condition of nursing in our nation will be more important than ever. The combination of the IOM report and this book will, we hope, promote greater understanding of the nursing field; educate the nursing, health care, student, and policy communities, as well as the interested public; and help inform a nursing agenda that will lead to improving the health and well-being of all Americans.

ACKNOWLEDGMENTS

We are particularly grateful to David Keepnews for his in-depth, detailed reviews of two drafts of the opening chapter to the book. He also recommended writings for us to consider, as did the following people: Patricia Archbold, Geraldine "Polly" Bednash, Patricia Benner, Amy Berman, Peter Buerhaus, Mary Chaffee, Sally Cohen, Donna Diers, Claire Fagin, Patty Franklin, Kristine Gebbie, Catherine Gilliss, Charlene Harrington, Susan Hassmiller, Maureen "Shawn" Kennedy, Christine Kovner, Ellen Kurtzman, Afaf Meleis, Mathy Mezey, Mary Naylor, Susan Reinhard, Marla Salmon, Ellen Sanders, Nancy Sharp, Julie Sochalski, Virginia Tilden, Marita Titler, Antonia Villarruel, Colleen Conway-Welch, and Patricia Yoder-Wise. The final decision on which articles to reprint was made solely by the editors, taking into consideration the guidance of these experts.

At the Robert Wood Johnson Foundation, we wish to acknowledge David Morse and Fred Mann for their wise counsel, Sarah Pickell for her research and editorial assistance, Mary Beth Kren for locating source materials, Rose Littman for facilitating communications among the editors, Hope Woodhead and Sherry DeMarchi for overseeing the book's distribution, Mimi Turi for managing the budget and contract arrangements, and Risa Lavizzo-Mourey for her support and guidance.

We also recognize the work of Shirley Tiangsing in translating printed text of the reprints into an electronic format.

Elizabeth Dawson, research and editorial director at Health Policy Associates, did outstanding work in conducting research, overseeing the production process, proofreading, and resolving with great aplomb all of the problems that arose. We are very appreciative of her efforts.

DJM, SLI, DCC

REVIEW OF THE NURSING FIELD

An Original Article

Diana J. Mason, "The Nursing Profession: Development, Challenges, and Opportunities"

THE NURSING PROFESSION: DEVELOPMENT, CHALLENGES, AND OPPORTUNITIES

DIANA J. MASON

CHAPTER CONTENTS

Nursing has a long and important legacy. Nurses have served as advocates for a better, safer, more humanistic health care system, and for public policies that promote the health of the nation throughout the profession's history.

- Lillian Wald in 1893 founded the Henry Street Settlement that provided home care to New York City's poor immigrants on the Lower East Side of Manhattan when no other providers would serve them.[1]

- Margaret Sanger was a public health nurse whose fight for the reproductive rights of women from 1916, when she established the nation's first birth control clinic, to her death in 1966 changed the nation's policies on access to birth control information and services.[2]

- Ruth Watson Lubic, the first nurse to receive the John A. and Catherine D. MacArthur Foundation's "Genius Award," has spent the last half century as a leader in reframing childbearing as a "normal" life experience rather than a disease. She founded one of the first freestanding, nurse-midwife-run childbearing centers in the nation and spread her model to the South Bronx and Washington, D.C., where she has improved outcomes for mothers and babies.

- Connie Hill is a pediatric nurse manager on a respiratory unit at Chicago's Children's Hospital, where she refused to accept the notion that her urban community could not muster the resources to support long-term ventilator-dependent children and their families after hospital discharge. She formed a coalition of stakeholders to bring about the policy, system, and financial changes needed to accomplish this.[3]

The legacy of nurses such as these continues to be enriched by those who follow their example and refuse to be bound by others' views of their profession or of women's place in society and the health care system. Nurses are expert clinicians, researcher-scientists, policymakers, chief executive officers of hospitals and their own organizations, primary care providers, independent practitioners, deans of schools of nursing in research-intensive universities, heads of foundations, and leaders in every segment of society. Every day, nurses innovate to keep people alive, prevent pressure ulcers and infections, reduce pain and suffering, and ease the transition from life to death. They screen schoolchildren's ability to see and hear, teach older adults and their family caregivers how to manage illnesses such as congestive heart failure, provide outreach to the homeless, counsel those with mental illness, and are otherwise present during some of the most intense, joyous, painful, difficult, and profound times of people's lives.

Yet nurses face significant barriers to providing the care that people need, and they are often excluded from policymaking in workplaces, boardrooms, and government entities. Legal and regulatory barriers to the full utilization of nurses persist, limiting the nation's ability to use its health care workforce efficiently and effectively. Other barriers are not specific to nurses but impede them from fully using their expertise. For example, nurses are skilled in managing chronic illness and coordinating care, but most payers do not cover these services.

Most policy discussions about nursing have focused on nursing shortage—a focus that overlooks the innovations and perspectives nurses can offer to improve both the way health care is delivered and the overall well-being of Americans. Certainly, the shortage is a complex problem of supply and demand. With the doubling of the nursing workforce over the past 25 years, it has become clear that the demand is outpacing the nation's ability to educate and retain enough nurses. In fact, the demand part of the equation speaks to how valuable nurses are to the nation's health care system. But there are two pitfalls that should be avoided in addressing the shortage. First, much of the focus has been on how to recruit more new nurses, with insufficient regard for how to retain and better utilize qualified nurses and decrease unnecessary demands on their time. Second, although nurses are part of most discussions about the health care workforce, they are often excluded from discussions of how to transform health care. Meeting these challenges requires an understanding of the complex realities of nursing and the important policy issues that confront the nation.

A BRIEF HISTORY OF NURSING

In her insightful discussion of the gradual professionalization of nursing during the nineteenth century and the first half of the twentieth, historian Susan Reverby describes the inherent tension between duties and rights that increased as nursing emerged from traditional "women's work":

> Nursing was organized under the expectation that its practitioners would accept a duty to care rather than demand a right to determine how they would satisfy this duty. Nurses were expected to act out of an obligation to care, taking on caring more as an identity than as work, and expressing altruism without thought of autonomy either at the bedside or in their profession. Thus, nurses, like others who perform what is defined as "women's work" in our society, have had to contend with what appears as a dichotomy between the duty to care for others and the right to control their own activities in the name of caring.[4]

These tensions between rights and duties continue to haunt nursing to this day.

The Beginnings of Modern Nursing

Prior to Florence Nightingale, daughters and wives were expected to care for infirm relatives. It wasn't until the Crimean War (1853–1856) that Nightingale, regarded by many as the mother of modern nursing, performed the work that indelibly marked the profession and the development of health care delivery, leaving a legacy of data-driven, altruistic practice.

Nightingale violated prevailing tenets of the privileged class of England in the early 1800s to become a nurse. Her work at the British military hospital at Scutari, begun in November 1854, was groundbreaking. She collected data on the causes of death among the soldiers and demonstrated that a significant number were due to poor nutrition and unsanitary, toxic environmental conditions at the hospital. The changes she instigated in the hospital dramatically improved clinical outcomes.[5,6]

Her treatise, *Notes on Nursing: What It Is and What It Is Not*,[7] defined nursing as creating the conditions for nature to take its course in healing a person—conditions such as a clean and nontoxic environment, fresh air, good nutrition, comfort, rest, and emotional support. While ostensibly deferring to the military surgeons at the hospital in keeping with gendered role expectations of the day, she used her connection with a reporter at the *London Times* to get front-page coverage of the problems at the hospital. The reports sparked public outrage, and she got the supplies, equipment, and support that she needed. Nightingale went on to transform the British, Indian, and military health services.

Nightingale also upgraded and formalized nursing education and the role of nurses. She transformed the image of the drunken, untrustworthy nurse immortalized as Sarah Gamp in Charles Dickens's *Martin Chuzzlewit*, to that of an educated, ethical, caring "lady." Indeed, Nightingale was referred to as "the *lady* with the lamp," because of her habit of making rounds night and day, tending to ill soldiers, and overseeing her nursing staff with a comportment that challenged the Gamp stereotype of nurses. She established the Nightingale School of Nursing at what is now St. Thomas Hospital in England, and replaced physician oversight of nursing services with an independently funded women's nursing organization. This work coincided with other experiments in modern nursing in Germany and France and became the model for educating nurses in Western countries.[8,9]

In the United States, the Civil War had demonstrated the need for trained nurses, although both men and women tended to wounded soldiers on both sides of the conflict. Walt Whitman was among these untrained nurses, as were Harriet Tubman and Sojourner Truth, two women born into slavery and committed to promoting freedom and human rights as conditions necessary for a healthy nation.[10] After the war, urbanization disrupted family relationships and gender roles, opening new opportunities for women and leading to the emergence of more formalized nursing education and practice.

The Professionalization of Nursing

By the late 1800s, the professionalization of nursing was well under way. In 1873, New York City's Bellevue Hospital became the first in the country to establish a program of nursing education based on the Nightingale model. New Haven Hospital and Massachusetts General Hospital quickly followed. Between 1890 and 1900, about 400 training schools for nurses opened across the country.[11] These hospital programs offered diplomas in nursing and an apprentice-style education in which students cared for patients in hospitals under the tutelage of a nursing supervisor. Later viewed as an exploitation of women, these students worked long hours, six days a week.

Once they graduated, most of the new nurses sought employment in private homes. This situation persisted until the Great Depression stripped families of their ability to hire nurses. Later, the Hill-Burton Act of 1946 boosted the numbers of hospital nurses by providing funds for the construction of new hospitals across the country, giving acute care preeminence in the American health care system and initiating an unquenchable demand for hospital nurses that continues to this day.[12]

In the early years of this professionalization, Isabel Hampton Robb, who in 1889 became the first head of the Johns Hopkins School of Nursing, promoted the idea that nurses were motivated by altruism and the moral responsibility to care for and promote the health of others, regardless of the setting.[13] Motivated by this vision of the mission of nursing, nurses began venturing into poor communities to educate women about home hygiene, healthy living, and nutrition. The most noteworthy of these nurses was Lillian Wald.

Wald was born into a well-off family in Cincinnati, Ohio, that later moved to Rochester, New York, where she attended a boarding school. She decided to dedicate her life to nursing and enrolled in the New York Hospital Training Program in 1889. She coined the name "public health nursing" for nurses who served poor and middle-class families in their homes and communities. She taught classes in health promotion and disease prevention. In 1893, Wald founded the Nurses Settlement, which became known as the Henry Street Settlement, to better address the horrific living conditions and poor health of immigrants living on the Lower East Side of Manhattan. In addition to providing health and hygiene classes, she and a group of nurses made home visits, often navigating unsafe, unclean environments, as immortalized in the famous photograph of a Henry Street nurse going from one tenement to another across the rooftops, which also saved them time.

Wald also started the Visiting Nurse Service of New York, occupational health nursing, and school health nursing. Before the phrase was coined, she recognized what we now know as "the social determinants of health," arguing that preventing illness was cheaper than caring for the ill. She understood that children cannot be healthy without having an opportunity to play under safe conditions, so she started the first playground in the city. At a time when there was a bureau for the protection of animals but no comparable federal oversight for the welfare of children, she became a leading advocate for the first federal Children's Bureau. She also knew that the arts can enrich the emotional lives of people worried about how to provide the next meal for a family, so she opened a theater as part of the settlement house. She believed that war does not create health, so she actively opposed the nation's involvement in the First World War.[14] Although social work also claims her, nurses view Wald as

Source: Visiting Nurse Service of New York, www.vnsny.org; c. 1905

an exemplar of the profession's promise of innovation, altruism, and reformation and its understanding of the family and community context of individual health.

But not all nurses were as well educated—or as visionary—as Wald. In fact, the lack of standardization among the hospital training programs that had mushroomed in the late 1800s prompted a movement to secure legal registration of nurses. North Carolina became the first state to enact a registration law, doing so in 1903, followed by New York, New Jersey, and Virginia. By 1917, 45 states had passed nurse practice acts, most of which authorized boards of examiners to ensure, among other things, that an applicant to become a registered nurse met the necessary criteria. These included graduation from an approved training program.[15,16]

Throughout the ensuing decades, states refined their legal definitions of nursing. Legal scholar Barbara Safriet documented that early medical practice acts were written so broadly that they precluded other professions from claiming health care roles that were independent of physician supervision.[17] This issue has been central to nursing's battle for independence and authority over its own practice.

War and the Development of Nursing

Wartime has provided opportunities for nurses to make significant advances in both science and professional status. The American Red Cross, founded in 1905 by congressional mandate to ensure the availability of relief and aid during national crises, formed its nursing services under the leadership of the nurse Jane Delano in 1909. The Red Cross played a critical role in providing nurses at military and Red Cross hospitals during World War I. To ensure a continuing supply of nurses during the war, the Army School of Nursing was established, along with a "training camp" at Vassar College that set the stage for nursing education to move into universities.[18] Following both World Wars, the skills and knowledge that nurses needed to care for the wounded expanded and were carried into civilian nursing practice.

The Vietnam War also advanced nurses' roles and responsibilities. Nurses were essential providers of emergency, trauma, and rehabilitative care, but their contributions to the war went largely unrecognized until Morley Safer focused a segment of *60 Minutes* on the post-traumatic stress disorder experienced by many nurse veterans of that war.[19]

Nonetheless, the military has been a place for nurses to advance their careers and the profession. To this day, when a flood of wounded and dying soldiers comes through the door of a military hospital, an "all hands on deck" attitude prevails, and legal barriers to what nurses and other health care professionals do melt away. A recent example is that of Rear Admiral Kathleen Martin, a nurse who commanded Bethesda's National Naval Medical Center in 1999 and 2000. In 2007, another nurse, Major General Gale Pollack, served as the Acting Surgeon General of the United States Army for nine months following media reports of poor care at Walter Reed Medical Center. She was the first woman and nonphysician to serve as Army Surgeon General. Both of these nurses also served as chief of the Army Nurse Corps.

Modern Nursing: Education, Specialization, and Certification

After World War I, the nation confronted a shortage of nurses and continuing problems with the lack of standards for nursing education. Nurses had died while caring for people who took ill during the influenza epidemic of 1918, and hospitals expanded diploma nursing programs with little regard for the quality of the education. In 1919, the Rockefeller Foundation funded a Committee for the Study of Nursing Education. The Committee's report, issued in 1923 and known as the Goldmark Report, was critical of hospital training programs and called for a separation of education from service and moving nursing education into universities.[20]

Since the Goldmark Report was issued, nursing education and practice have been studied repeatedly by national commissions, all of which have reached remarkably similar conclusions.[21] After the Second World War, the Carnegie Corporation provided partial funding for what became known as the Brown Report (after staff member Esther Lucille Brown, a social scientist), published in 1948.[22] Its recommendations on nursing education echoed those in the Goldmark Report, but also called for a differentiation between "professional" and "technical" nursing and the expansion of nursing practice in community settings.

The recommendation was taken up in the 1950s by Mildred Montag, founder and director of the first nursing program at Adelphi University in New York in 1942 and subsequently a professor at Columbia University's Teacher's College. Montag developed a proposal that was funded by the W. K. Kellogg Foundation to educate *technical* nurses in associate degree programs at seven junior colleges and a hospital.[23] Thus began a continuing debate about the appropriate roles and education of nurses, as associate degree nursing programs proliferated without adoption of the "technical nurse" moniker. Most important, the Brown Report and Montag's work led to an end of the dominance of hospitals in the education of nurses. Thereafter, most hospital diploma nursing programs either closed or partnered with community colleges and universities. As of 2008, there were only 69 diploma nursing programs left in the country.

Following World War II, more women (and a few men), often from families of little means, enrolled in universities to be educated as nurses. They were supported, in part, by the GI Bill and, later, by the federal Nurse Training Act of 1964.[24] The funding enabled them to enter a profession—and the middle class. There was also a need for nurses with a stronger foundation in the sciences. As the education of nurses moved into colleges and universities, nursing faculty had to meet academic standards. In the 1960s, the federal nurse-scientist program provided support for postgraduate nurses to obtain doctorates in fields such as physiology, psychology, anthropology, and sociology.[25] These nurse-scientists led the profession's efforts to build its scientific base.

The number of baccalaureate schools of nursing increased, and in 1956 Columbia University opened the country's first graduate program in a clinical nursing specialty. The women's movement and social upheavals of the 1960s and 1970s encouraged nurses to seek the education and authority commensurate with their greater responsibilities. Baccalaureate and master's degree programs prepared registered nurses who resisted the outdated role of the nurse as the physician's handmaiden and aimed at claiming control over their profession. They carved out their own sphere of practice and developed new roles, including clinical nurse specialists and nurse practitioners.

The development of this latter role has been particularly significant. In 1966, pediatrician George Silver and University of Colorado nursing dean Loretta Ford developed a postbaccalaureate program to prepare nurses, in collaboration with pediatricians, to provide primary care to underserved children.[26] The program was so successful that nurse practitioner certificate programs proliferated as a way to address the shortage of primary care physicians. These programs moved from being affiliated with schools of medicine to being full-fledged graduate programs in schools of nursing.

Just as medicine evolved from a generalist to a specialist focus, nursing specialties emerged over the years. Since the late 1800s, nurses had specialized in public health, midwifery, and anesthesia. But it wasn't until the late 1960s, with the expansion of intensive care units, that subspecialties took hold. To meet the need for nurses capable of exercising assessment and monitoring skills in high-tech environments, nursing developed subspecialties in critical care, such as neonatal, cardiac, and neurosurgical. Other subspecialties arose around specific diseases and clinical conditions, clinical settings and services, procedures, and populations.

The first certification examination for a specialty was offered by the American Association of Nurse Anesthetists in 1945, after more than a half century of nurse-administered anesthesia.[27] In 1991, the American Nurses Association (ANA) formed the American Nurses Credentialing Center to promote excellence in practice. To date, it has certified over 250,000 nurses in various specialties. Specialty nursing organizations realized that providing certification is a revenue-generating activity, and many have developed their own certification programs.

The American Nurses Credentialing Center also developed a designation for hospitals that demonstrate excellence in nursing practice—the Magnet Recognition Program. The nursing shortage of the 1980s led to widespread reports of poor working conditions that were undermining nurses' ability to deliver safe patient care and causing nurses to leave practice. Some hospitals had no trouble recruiting and retaining highly qualified nurses. These hospitals had reputations for excellence in nursing care, and nurses considered them to be good places to work. A group of nurse-researchers who were fellows of the American Academy of Nursing examined best practices for ensuring excellence in nursing in 41 hospitals from around the country that fit this description.[28] Interviews with the hospitals' chief nursing officers and staff nurses revealed the key elements. These were further refined and used to evaluate hospitals that apply for Magnet designation. This designation has driven changes in nursing practice and hospital environments.

Throughout the years, nursing practice has evolved along with advances in science and technology. Nurses have been key to making modern, high-tech hospitals more hospitable. It can be argued, however, that caring for patients has shifted from creating conditions for patients to heal—the purpose of nursing as defined by Nightingale—to tending to machines that monitor patients and deliver therapies. In fact, the worst of hospital nursing today loses sight of the patient in the maelstrom of modern-day medical and technological complexity. The best of nursing keeps the patient as the focal point and seeks to integrate the various technologies that have become markers of acute care institutions.

THE NURSING PROFESSION

Defining Nursing

Health care used to be defined as the province of physicians who diagnosed and treated disease—a perspective that left nurses and other providers struggling to define their roles. Was nursing more than what physicians wanted nurses to do? Did nurses have any specialized knowledge and skill that was different from that of physicians? Could nursing exist apart from medicine? Did it have its own intrinsic value? Full utilization of nurses requires an understanding of the answers to these questions.

Caring in a nursing context demands expert knowledge about, and the ability to integrate, the physical, psychological, emotional, and social dimensions of health; skill in administering supportive care; superb critical thinking and clinical judgment; honed assessment skills; proficiency in coordinating care and advocacy, and more.[29]

There are three classic definitions of nursing. Nightingale viewed nursing as activities "to put the patient in the best condition for nature to act upon him."[30] One hundred years later, Virginia Henderson, an influential thinker at Columbia University Teachers College and the Yale School of Nursing, provided a definition that was adopted by the International Council of Nurses and published by the *American Journal of Nursing*. Hers was the first to clearly articulate nurses' independent functions:

> The unique function of the nurse is to assist the individual, sick or well, in the performance of those activities contributing to health or its recovery (or a peaceful death) that he would perform unaided if he had the necessary strength, will or knowledge. And to do this in such a way as to help him gain independence as rapidly as possible. This aspect of her work, this part of her function, she initiates and controls; of this she is a master.[31]

Henderson's definition differentiated nurses' unique sphere of practice ("independent" functions) versus the commonly understood "dependent" functions—those that depended upon a physician's order or prescription. Henderson even defined the role of the nurse in relation to physicians and the medical regimen with a patient focus: "In addition, she *helps the patient* [italics added] carry out the therapeutic plan as initiated by the physician." And, for the first time, Henderson's definition clearly articulated the legitimacy of two important health care roles that nurses had long fulfilled: caring for people at the end of life, when recovery is not possible, and promoting the health of people who are not ill.

The third important definition of nursing was included in the landmark New York State Nurse Practice Act of 1972. Because the definition was contained in a statute, it provided legal support for nurses' independent practice:

> The practice of the profession of nursing as a registered professional nurse is defined as diagnosing and treating human responses to actual or potential health problems through such services as casefinding, health teaching, health counseling, and provision of care supportive to or restorative of life and well-being, and executing medical regimens prescribed by a licensed physician, dentist or other licensed health care provider legally authorized under this title and in accordance with the commissioner's regulations. A nursing regimen shall be consistent with and shall not vary any existing medical regimen.[32]

The last sentence was written to allay the concerns of physicians who claimed that fully independent nurses could destroy physicians' authority over patients' medical care.[33] It remains in the state's practice act.

The New York State law became a model for other states. It enabled nurses to claim a body of knowledge apart from medicine and to have authority over their own practices. The language in the legislation referring to "diagnosing and treating human responses" reflected a movement among nurses to develop nursing diagnoses that centered on the patients' responses to health problems and were distinct from disease-centered medical diagnoses. Including "potential health problems" in the definition reinforced the importance of disease prevention and health promotion. In contemporary terms, the work defined in this practice act entails care coordination, chronic care management, disease prevention, and health promotion.

In 1980, to help nurses, policymakers, health care administrators, and others conceptualize more clearly the scope of professional nursing, the ANA published *Nursing: A Social Policy Statement*.[34] This document articulated a social context for nursing, describing nurses' responsibilities to patients and society, and validating an advocacy role for nursing. The most recent version of *Nursing's Social Policy Statement* defines the role of the profession as:

> the protection, promotion, and optimization of health and abilities, prevention of illness and injury, alleviation of suffering through the diagnosis and treatment of human response, and advocacy in the care of individuals, families, communities, and populations.[35]

The Nursing Workforce

The nursing workforce is large and diverse. It includes registered nurses (RNs), licensed practical or vocational nurses (LPNs, LVNs), advanced practice registered nurses (APRNs), and direct care workers, such as nursing assistants and home health aides (who are seldom discussed in nursing workforce studies, as they are unlicensed).

Direct Care Workers

Direct care workers include nursing assistants, home health aides, and personal care assistants. The majority work in home and community settings and are key to keeping disabled and elderly people in their own homes. They provide the bulk of care in long-term care facilities and augment the nursing staff in many hospitals. They increasingly care for people who may have severe dementia, paralytic stroke, or other debilitating conditions that are challenging even to professional health care providers.

Although they are not licensed by the states, direct care workers who work in Medicare- and Medicaid-certified facilities or home care agencies are required by the federal government to be certified. The requirements for designating a provider as a certified nursing assistant are completion of 75 hours of training and competence to provide assistance in activities of daily living (such as bathing, feeding, toileting, and ambulating) and to perform certain nursing procedures under the supervision of an LPN or RN.[36]

Today, there are more than 3 million direct care workers in the United States.[37] Almost half are self-employed or work for private households, 42% have some college education, and 88% are women.[38] The average direct care worker's salary is less than $25,000 per year and 45% of direct care workers live in households with an annual income that is less than 200% of the poverty level.[39] These positions frequently are low-paid and lack health insurance and other benefits.[40]

Licensed Practical or Vocational Nurses (LPNs)

As the education of nurses moved from the hospital to the university and community colleges, the role of the LPN (also referred to as vocational nurse in some states) evolved as someone with technical skill—from bathing a patient to administering medications or changing dressings—but without the education for independently assessing patients, diagnosing health problems, developing interventions, and evaluating outcomes. LPNs function under the supervision of a registered nurse, physician, dentist, or other licensed provider. Their education varies from about nine months to two years in length, and is provided largely by vocational training programs.

There are approximately 890,000 LPNs in the United States.[41] Ninety-seven percent are women. Two-thirds (67%) are white, one-quarter (26%) are black, and 3% are Hispanic. Fourteen percent have no more than a high school education; 34% have "some" college education; 45%, an associate's degree; and 5%, a baccalaureate or higher degree. Their average annual salary in 2008 was just over $40,000.[42] Approximately one-quarter work in hospitals, 28% in "nursing and personal care facilities," and 12% in physicians' offices.[43] Twenty-four percent of RNs worked as LPNs prior to their first RN position.[44]

Registered Nurses

In 2008, there were 3,063,163 RNs in the United States—an increase of 5.3% since 2004. More than 84% are employed in nursing, and this is the highest proportion recorded (see Figure 1).

Although nurses' real earnings remained flat in the 1990s, this has now changed. Nurses' average annual salary in 2008 was $66,973, an increase of over 15% since 2004.[45]

RNs remain predominantly women (94.2%).[46] The RN workforce has aged from 1980 to 2008; in 2008, the average age of an RN was 47 years, illustrating the imperative to increase the pipeline of new nurses as older ones approach retirement.[47]

Regarding ethnicity, 83.2% of RNs are non-Hispanic white, a drop of over four percentage points since 2000; 5.4% are black or African American; 5.8% are Asian; and 3.6% Hispanic or Latino.[48]

To qualify as an RN, one of several possible educational programs must be completed: a diploma hospital program; an associate degree program (usually provided by community colleges); a college or university baccalaureate program; or a direct-entry master's degree program that bypasses the baccalaureate degree for people with bachelor's degrees in other fields. Graduates from any of these programs are eligible to sit for the RN licensing exam, the NCLEX-RN, required by all states. Over 45% of today's RNs began their education in associate degree programs; however, only 5.8% of associate degree (ADN) graduates between 1970 and 1994 went on to obtain a master's degree in nursing or a doctorate by 2004, compared with 19.7% of RNs whose initial nursing education was a bachelor of science in nursing (BSN).[49] Nonetheless, the educational preparation of nurses is improving, as illustrated in Figure 2.

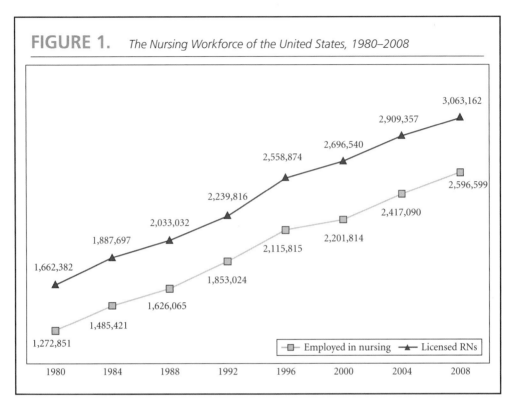

FIGURE 1. *The Nursing Workforce of the United States, 1980–2008*

Source: U.S. Department of Health and Human Services, Health Resources and Services Administration. (2010). *The Registered Nurse Population: Initial Findings from the 2008 National Sample Survey of Registered Nurses.*

In 2008, 36.8% of all RNs held baccalaureate degrees and 13.2% had a master's or doctoral degree in nursing.[50] Between 1980 and 2008, the percentage of nurses with only a diploma decreased from 54.7% to 13.9%. Among those with advanced degrees, 375,794 had master's degrees and 28,369 had doctorates.

Advanced Practice Registered Nurses

Advanced practice registered nurses (APRNs) are RNs who have received additional education to expand their scope of practice. They make up 8.2% of the RN population. As of 2008, there were 250,527 APRNs in the United States, an increase of 4.2% since 2004. The demand for APRN services has spread from primary care to all settings. There are four types of APRNs:

- Nurse practitioners (NPs), 63.2% of all APRNs (158,348), whose practice may include the assessment, diagnosis, and treatment of disease, albeit with a nursing lens that focuses on patient needs, health promotion, and self-care management.

- Clinical nurse specialists (59,242), who concentrate on nursing care specific to a population, setting, disease, type of care, or clinical problem; they provide direct care

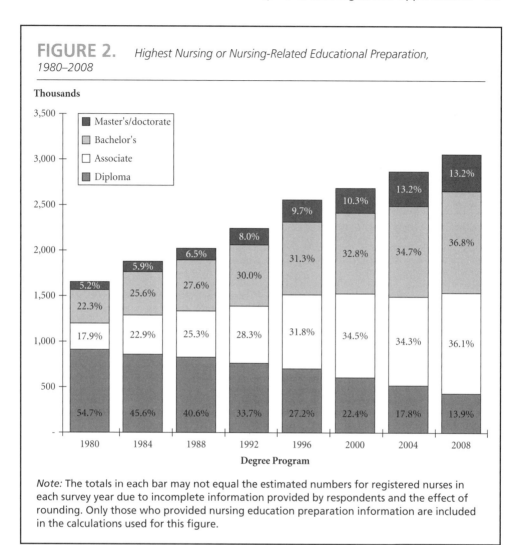

FIGURE 2. *Highest Nursing or Nursing-Related Educational Preparation, 1980–2008*

Note: The totals in each bar may not equal the estimated numbers for registered nurses in each survey year due to incomplete information provided by respondents and the effect of rounding. Only those who provided nursing education preparation information are included in the calculations used for this figure.

Source: U.S. Department of Health and Human Services, Health Resources and Services Administration. (2010). *The Registered Nurse Population: Initial Findings from the 2008 National Sample Survey of Registered Nurses.*

to patients, assist with delineating best practices in care, and teach nurses and other health care workers how to improve the care they deliver to a population; their numbers are declining—by 22.4% since 2004—as nurses increasingly seek preparation as nurse practitioners.

- Certified nurse anesthetists (38,821) who provide the full range of perianesthesia services, including pain management.

- Certified nurse midwives (18,492), who focus on women's health, including child-birthing and gynecologic care for women of all ages.[51]

Entry into these roles now requires a master's degree. However, the American Association of Colleges of Nursing has called for the Doctor of Nursing Practice (DNP) to be the educational route for APRNs by 2015.

Others Providing Nursing Care

Hospitals and other health care organizations have often responded to the shortage of licensed nurses by developing new categories of workers, such as "patient care technicians" and "patient care associates," often nursing assistants or medical technicians who receive additional training by the facility to take on more advanced technical aspects of acute care, such as dressing changes. These workers generally function under the supervision of licensed nurses (RNs or LPNs). In ambulatory care and the operating room, one can find patient care technicians and surgical first assistants who function under the supervision of physicians. Professional nursing organizations have resisted efforts to create new categories of workers who provide nursing care without supervision or oversight by licensed nurses, but the 2009 Institute of Medicine report, *Retooling for an Aging America: Building the Health Care Workforce*, encourages flexibility in developing new roles for health care workers to care for an increasing number of older adults.[52]

Additionally, family members provide nursing care that even health care providers find challenging, such as dressing complex wounds or bathing loved ones with dementia.[53] There are over 44 million family caregivers over the age of 18 in the United States, providing care that has been valued at $375 billion annually.[54] Nurses are increasingly involved in addressing the needs of family caregivers, advocating public policies that will support family caregivers, and partnering with social workers and other health care professionals to reform the health care system in ways that will better prepare family members to provide care in the home.

Although this chapter is confined to the licensed nursing workforce, there is an urgent need to understand and develop the capacity of unlicensed providers as well.

Nurses' Employment: Where Nurses Work (and What They Do)

The majority (62.2%) of RNs worked in hospitals in 2008.[55] This percentage will decline if the nation shifts from an emphasis on acute care to health promotion and chronic care management. Of RNs, 11% work in ambulatory care; 11% in public health or community health settings, including home care; 7% in long-term care facilities; 3% in school health; 3% in nursing education; almost 2% in "insurance claims and benefits"; less than 1% in occupational health; and about 0.4% in a policy, planning, regulatory, or licensing agency.[56] These settings have different educational requirements.

Hospital Nursing

Nursing care is the core business of hospitals—people are seldom hospitalized unless they need nursing care. In hospitals, nurses assess patients with complex, often life-threatening health problems, monitor changes in patients' conditions that could lead to complications, administer medications and check for adverse reactions, prevent hospital-acquired infections, provide emotional support and teaching to patients and families, record the patient's reactions to care, and participate in interdisciplinary team efforts to prepare the patient for discharge. Patients who only a few years ago would have been in intensive care units are now cared for on regular units (or "floors"), presenting challenges to so-called "floor nurses" who must have unprecedented knowledge and skills in managing complex care for seriously ill patients.

In 2004, almost 30% of all hospital nurses worked on a general or specialty inpatient unit and 17% in critical care.[57] Some hospitals have all-RN staff. Others continue to use some LPNs, although the percentage of LPNs working in hospitals has declined in recent years.[58,59] The clinical nurse leader—a new nursing role conceived in 2004 at a meeting of the American Association of Colleges of Nursing—is a master's level staff nurse who has the additional training to examine quality-of-care outcomes and develop evidence-based practice for a clinical unit or a population of patients. Clinical nurse leaders are now used extensively by the Veterans Health Administration.

In the hospital setting, APRNs serve as nurse-midwives; surgical first assistants in the operating room; clinical nurse specialists who provide specialty consultation on diabetes, wounds, and myriad other clinical conditions; nurse anesthetists who provide perianesthesia care in both inpatient and outpatient departments; and nurse practitioners throughout the hospital.

Nurse managers or administrators oversee patient care units (formerly called nursing units) and are responsible for managing scores of staff members and multimillion-dollar budgets for personnel, supplies, and equipment. Increasingly, nurse managers have one or more master's degrees in nursing, business, or health care administration. They focus on improving the quality and safety of care and use data to monitor and improve clinical and financial performance.

The hierarchy of nursing management usually includes a clinical director of nursing or a director of clinical services to whom a number of nurse managers report, and a chief nursing officer who is often the vice president for patient care services, responsible for interdisciplinary clinical services as well as nursing. Because of their clinical, management, and business acumen, nurses can be found in the roles of chief operating officer or chief executive officer in hospitals and health systems. Nurses also hold key positions in quality and performance improvement departments, infection control, employee health, and other departments. This description of nurse administrators applies to other health care settings as well.

Primary and Ambulatory Care

In primary and ambulatory care, nurses' roles vary by educational preparation. Licensed practical nurses may conduct basic assessments of patients, administer medications, collect specimens, and provide basic teaching. RNs can do these tasks, as well as conduct higher-level assessments of the less obvious patient health needs, conduct common examinations, counsel patients and families about illnesses and their management, and provide telephone follow-up as needed.

Nurse practitioners perform comprehensive health assessments, diagnose and treat disease, suture wounds and do other technical procedures, and engage in all of the activities described for the RN. In 1999, there were 45,200 NPs in primary care; by 2005, the number was 82,622. Between the mid-1990s and mid-2000s, NPs were the fastest growing group of primary care providers, with an annual increase in the number of NPs per capita of 9.4%, compared with 3.89% for physician assistants and 1.17% for primary care physicians.[60]

Home Care

Nurses often describe the difference between hospital and home nursing in terms of who is in control. In hospitals, patients and families have little power, but in their own homes they are in control. In the home, as compared with the hospital, the nurse is a guest and becomes more of a partner with the patient and family. Obviously, home care does not provide the same on-site supports as hospital care, so nurses must be prepared to function independently while collaborating remotely with other providers of care. In patients' homes, nurses conduct comprehensive assessments of patients, family members, and the living environment; reconcile multiple medications that could have adverse interactions; provide treatments such as complex dressing changes and administration of intravenous therapies; teach patients and family caregivers to manage their own care; communicate with other health care providers about patients' conditions and coordination of care; and oversee the need for and performance of unlicensed home health aides.[61]

Hospice care includes an in-home component, and nurses are its backbone. They work with patients and family members to define the goals and priorities of care; manage symptoms, including pain; provide counseling about end-of-life options and palliative care; and offer emotional support, which extends to surviving family members after the patient dies.

Public Health and Community Nursing

Public health nurses have often served as the bridge between an individual or family and a population or community, just as they did in Lillian Wald's day. They provide personal and illness care to the uninsured and Medicaid populations, conduct maternal–child health screenings, make follow-up home visits to at-risk patients, run clinics to screen for and treat infectious diseases and collaborate with other workers to stop their spread, provide immunizations, provide essential emergency services in natural and man-made disasters, and work with community leaders and government officials to design programs and policies that can promote the health of residents. Public health nurses also run community health programs and clinics. They comprise 30% of public health agencies' staff and are the senior executive in 34% of the agencies.[62,63]

School Health

Although school nurses may be known for tending to playground injuries and taking temperatures of febrile students, these are only small parts of what school nurses do. For the most part, they have a role in injury prevention and treatment, screening for and responding to undiagnosed health problems, and providing case management and direct care. They provide health education for students and teachers, advocate for children and families, and develop health promotion strategies and programs such as nutrition and obesity prevention and management. School nurses also play a crucial leadership role in schools and as first responders during disasters.[64] For example, Mary Pappas, a school nurse in New York City, reported to the health department a sudden and dramatic increase in students with symptoms of the flu. This was the first outbreak of H1N1 in the city; her swift action helped contain the spread of the virus.[65]

Long-Term Care

Only 6.3% of RNs work in nursing homes or extended-care facilities.[66] LPNs and certified nursing assistants are the mainstay of providers in long-term care facilities.[67] Almost 33% of LPNs work in long-term care.[68] However, federal law requires a registered nurse to be the chief nursing officer, responsible for ensuring that standards of care in long-term care facilities are being met.

Continuing problems with the quality of care in long-term care facilities have led to calls for better training and supervision of nursing staff and for better enforcement of governmental standards for staffing.[69] In recent years, nurses have been integral to the operation of community and home-based models that have become more popular ways to provide long-term care.

Other Settings

Occupational health nurses provide a variety of services to employees. As employers recognize the economic value of keeping employees healthy, nurses have played key roles in developing and providing on-site wellness programs. Nurses also work as educators in academia, researchers in clinical and academic settings, case managers in all health care settings, key providers of telehealth services, clinical educators for pharmaceutical and other product companies, policymakers, lawyers and legal nurse consultants who are highly sought after in medical malpractice cases, forensic experts, and journalists. Nurses work in almost every sector of society.

Organized Nursing

Joan Lynaugh, professor emerita at the University of Pennsylvania School of Nursing, has summarized the enduring conflicts that have resulted from a continuing need for more nurses:

1. Nurse leaders' efforts to upgrade preparation for practice and to restrict numbers often compete with social desires to contain cost in providing nursing care.

2. Differentiation of nursing practice to improve quality through specialization conflicts with institutional needs for flexible generalist nursing staffs.

3. Nurse-controlled practice and differentiated practice, such as that of nurse practitioners and nurse-midwives, create fears of competition among physicians.[70]

These conflicts have been a major focus of organized nursing, from the movement to secure registration for nurses in the early 1900s to current efforts to improve nurses' working conditions and remove barriers to full utilization of advanced practice registered nurses.

Nurses have organized themselves in both professional organizations and unions, sometimes with one organization combining these dual missions. The Nurses Associated

Alumnae was formed in 1900 and was the precursor to the American Nurses Association, founded in 1911. Other national nursing organizations emerged in the early 1900s, often around the registration movement, but only for whites. In 1908, the National Association of Colored Graduate Nurses formed, and it continued until 1952 when the ANA admitted nurses of color. In 1971, it reorganized under the name of the National Black Nurses Association because black nurses felt that the ANA was not meeting their interests and some state nursing associations had continued to discriminate against black nurses.[71] Today, there are other nursing organizations dedicated to representing the interests and needs of specific ethnic nursing groups, such as the Philippine Nurses Association of America and the Hispanic Nurses Association.

As nurses specialized, so did nursing organizations. Today, there are over 100 national nursing associations. Two national organizations are devoted to advancing nursing education: the National League for Nursing, an organization that focuses on nursing education in general, and the American Association of Colleges of Nurses, which addresses baccalaureate and higher degree education. Both have organizational arms that accredit schools of nursing. Two national organizations represent nurse practitioners as a whole: the American College of Nurse Practitioners and the American Academy of Nurse Practitioners. Other organizations represent advanced practice registered nurses in specific roles, such as the National Organization of Nurse Practitioner Faculties, the American College of Nurse-Midwives, the National Association of Clinical Nurse Specialists, and the American Association of Nurse Anesthetists. Still other organizations are defined by clinical specialties, such as associations for nurses who focus on pain management, hospice and palliative care, plastic surgery, and intravenous therapy. There are also several organizations devoted to advancing nursing research.

Nurses have also organized into labor unions. Nurses' frustrations with their working conditions led the ANA, in 1946, to encourage affiliated state nurses associations to serve as the exclusive collective bargaining agent for nurses. By 1972, over twenty unions unaffiliated with the ANA were organizing nurses. The unionization of nurses has often created rifts in the profession between pro-union and anti-union nurses, staff nurses and nurse administrators, and state nurses associations that embrace a role in collective bargaining and those that reject it. The ANA has struggled with its identify as a labor organization. It doesn't engage in collective bargaining directly but has endorsed it as a necessary option to ensure the economic and general welfare of nurses.

Because of the ANA's commitment to remaining a multipurpose professional organization, some of its member state nurses associations viewed the ANA's support of collective bargaining as insufficient. Beginning in 1993 with the California Nurses Association, the largest state nurses' association in the country, at least six state nurses' associations have disaffiliated from the ANA in order to redirect dues into the state association's own collective bargaining efforts. The ANA formed a union arm, the United American Nurses, in 1999 after a contentious fight with nonunion association members in right-to-work states. Two years later, the ANA affiliated with the AFL-CIO and secured a seat on its executive council. Then, in December 2007, the ANA ended its relationship with United American Nurses. These battles have taken a toll on organized nursing's ability to increase its membership and present a united front. In 2010, only about 6% of the nation's nurses were members of the ANA.

Other unions representing nurses include the Service Employees International Union, the United Federation of Teachers, and the American Federation of State, County and Municipal Employees. Approximately one-fifth of nurses are members of unions, a percentage that has remained constant since the 1990s.[72] Despite the existence of a consortium of over 70 national nursing organizations called the Nursing Organization Alliance that focuses primarily on networking and sharing information, the profession has largely been unable to coalesce around many issues of great importance to nursing and the nation's health. Notable exceptions have been the solid opposition to organized medicine on three fronts: its unilateral attempts to turn nurses into physician assistants in the 1960s; to define a new provider of nursing care who would be supervised by physicians (a "registered care technician") during the shortage of the 1990s; and, more recently, to restrict the scope of advanced practice registered nurses. Early indicators suggest that national nursing organizations are also coalescing around the implementation of recommendations put forth in the 2010 Institute of Medicine report, *The Future of Nursing.*

Nursing Research

One of the agendas advanced by organized nursing has been building the profession's scientific basis—an agenda first defined by Nightingale. Early nursing research focused on nurses and nursing education rather than nursing care.[73,74] With the demand for more nursing faculty and federal support for the development of nurse scientists in the 1960s, formalized nursing research began to be generated, mostly by academics with doctorates.

Nursing Research, the first nursing journal devoted to research, was launched in 1952. A decade later, the American Nurses Foundation had established a small research grants program. Research from the post–World War II years through the early 1960s included studies on end-of-life issues, post-operative vomiting, patient education, breastfeeding, and pain relief; but studies of nurses' characteristics, attitudes, and behaviors proliferated. Leaders in the profession began to speak about an imperative for research that focused on practice.

Susan Gortner, former head of nursing research in the Division of Nursing of the Department of Health, Education, and Welfare, refers to the "transition years" for nursing research as the period between 1965 and 1985 when the number of nurses with PhDs increased, as did the federal financial support for nursing research.[75] The Division of Nursing in what is now called the Health Resources and Services Administration (HRSA) of the Department of Health and Human Services provided grants for nursing research training programs, as well as for research projects. The ANA established a Commission on Research in 1971 and a Council of Nurse Researchers in 1972. With support from the Division of Nursing, they provided the impetus for developing nursing research priorities.

But funding nursing research through the Division removed it from the domain of National Institutes of Health (NIH) and relegated it to the shadows of the scientific community.[76] By the 1980s, nurse researchers were submitting grant proposals to the NIH but becoming frustrated with repeated rejections. These nurse researchers documented that the high NIH rejection rate was due largely to a poor match between the kinds of questions nurses wanted to explore and the NIH's disease-oriented research agenda.

In December 1984, an NIH Task Force Report on Nursing Research concluded that the mission of the NIH encompassed the goals and methods of nursing research. This provided nursing organizations with a rationale for the creation of a National Center for Nursing Research at the NIH, which was proposed as part of the NIH's reauthorizing legislation in 1986. After a series of political battles, including overriding President Reagan's veto, Congress authorized creation of the National Center for Nursing Research. In 1993, the Center was given the status of an institute within NIH—the National Institute of Nursing Research (NINR). The Institute's research focus encompasses health promotion and disease prevention, quality of life, health disparities, and end-of-life care. In 2008, the NINR was budgeted $137.48 million, or 0.4% of the NIH annual budget of over $29 billion.[77]

CURRENT ISSUES AND CHALLENGES

The Nursing Shortage

Numbering more than three million, nurses are the largest group of health providers in the United States. There are more nurses today than ever before. Since 1980, the number of RNs has increased more than 90%.[78] (See Figure 1.) But projections indicate that the United States will have half a million fewer full-time RNs than it needs by 2025.[79]

In 1987, professors Linda Aiken, from the University of Pennsylvania School of Nursing, and Connie Mullinix, from East Carolina University College of Nursing, documented that prior shortages of nurses were cyclical, responding to market forces.[80] Their article was written during a significant shortage, and they cautioned that the current shortage and future ones were likely to be different from prior cycles. Because the demand for nurses was escalating with the aging of the country's population, they correctly predicted a continuing shortage that would override the cyclical pattern of prior years. In fact, the demand for nurses is projected to increase by 2–3% a year for the next 20 years.[81]

Peter Buerhaus, a nurse and professor at the Vanderbilt University Medical Center, and his colleagues developed a model for forecasting the future size of the nursing workforce and have revised their estimates over time, as changes occur in the variables that affect how many people enter and stay in nursing.[82] In 2008, they projected a shortfall of 500,000 RNs by 2025. This will be the largest shortage of nurses in history and will occur despite an easing of the current nursing shortage because of the recession. A community that becomes complacent about the temporary abatement in the shortage of nurses will be faced with a crisis if steps are not taken now to meet the future demand.

The nursing shortage affects all sectors of health care but has hit some areas harder than others. One of the most enduring shortages is in long-term care, which has experienced annual turnover rates of nursing personnel that exceed 100%. The 2008 Institute of Medicine report, *Retooling for an Aging America,* issued a number of recommendations related to ensuring a future workforce that is prepared to care for a growing population of older adults.[83] Since 1995, the John A. Hartford Foundation has invested $75 million to develop the capacity of nurses and direct care workers to care for older adults.

Another area of concern is community-based nursing. As the United States looks for ways to shift the focus of health care from acute care to health promotion, disease prevention, and chronic care management, the demand for nurses in community-based settings is expected to increase. Public health and home care agencies struggle to compete with acute care facilities in attracting nurses because of poorer wages and benefits.[84]

Factors Contributing to the Shortage

A number of factors have been identified as contributing to the shortage.

The Aging of the Nursing Workforce.   The average age of a nurse is now 47 years and, as Figure 3 illustrates, is increasing, largely because of the drop-off in new recruits to the

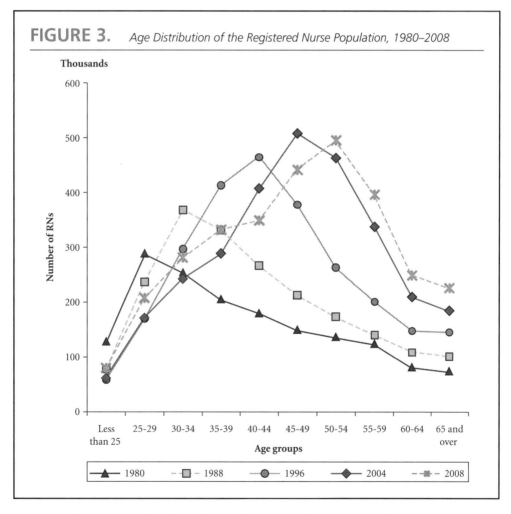

FIGURE 3.   *Age Distribution of the Registered Nurse Population, 1980–2008*

Source: U.S. Department of Health and Human Services, Health Resources and Services Administration. (2010). *Registered Nurse Population: Initial Findings from the 2008 National Sample Survey of Registered Nurses.*

profession during the 1990s and the increasing age of t̶h̶e̶ ̶average nursing student. Fifty-five percent of nurses who responded to the 2004 National Sample Survey of Registered Nurses said they intend to retire between 2011 and 2020.[85]

Staff nursing is physically demanding, and this becomes an increasingly significant problem for older nurses. One time-motion study of hospital staff nurses found that they walked between one and five miles per 10-hour-day shift.[86] Nurses are at risk for back and other injuries from lifting patients; exposure to infectious agents such as MRSA, HIV, and the H1N1 influenza virus, and hazardous substances such as radiation and chemotherapy drugs; adverse effects of shift work, whether working nights or rotating shifts; injuries from the violent behavior of patients and others; and secondary post-traumatic stress disorder from witnessing trauma, child abuse, and other horrific conditions.[87] The cumulative effects of these over two or more decades can take its toll.

Difficulty of Recruiting People into Nursing. Making nursing a more attractive career option means enhancing the public perception of nurses and the work they do, as well as ensuring good wages and job security. Particularly during economic downturns, people think about preparing for jobs that pay decently and are relatively secure, making nursing a good choice. When the economy weakens, nursing jobs are usually among those least threatened.

A severe shortage occurred in the 1980s as applicants and enrollments to schools of nursing declined dramatically. But by 2008, schools of nursing were turning away an estimated 99,000 qualified applicants to pre-licensure programs—almost 40% of those who applied—and more than 49,000 qualified applicants were turned away from baccalaureate and graduate programs.[88,89] What changed?

One change is the public perception of nursing. From Sarah Gamp to sex object to physician's handmaiden, accurate portrayals of nurses doing the intellectually and emotionally demanding work of nursing have been rare.[90] Studies of nursing shortages repeatedly included recommendations that nurses change this image, although few of these studies dealt with the real factors that contributed to the cyclical shortages, such as low wages and poor working conditions.[91] Nonetheless, by the twenty-first century, nurses viewed their profession's image as an unnecessary and inaccurate barrier to ensuring an adequate supply of nurses.

In 2000, Johnson & Johnson launched a major initiative to promote nursing as a career—an unprecedented commitment by an American corporation. Called the Campaign for Nursing's Future, J&J launched a Web site on nursing careers (www.discovernursing.com) and a major advertising campaign, Dare to Care—a theme that coincides with Reverby's contention that nurses are duty-bound to care in a society that refuses to value caring.[92] It has helped change the public's image of nursing.[93]

A Shortage of Faculty. With pressure on the profession to increase the numbers of new nurses, new schools of nursing have opened and existing schools have expanded their program offerings and capacity. But the supply of nurses qualified to fill faculty positions is inadequate to meet the demand. The faculty vacancy rate for the 2009–2010 academic year was 6.6%,[94] but this figure reflects budgeted positions and doesn't adequately capture the degree to which nursing programs could expand capacity to meet the demand for more nurses. In fact, more than half of the baccalaureate, master's, and doctoral nursing programs in the country could expand enrollments if they could hire more faculty.[95]

The shortage of nursing faculty is related to three factors: the supply of available faculty, their educational preparation, and productivity.[96]

Supply of Faculty. The average age of nursing faculty is 53.5 years,[97] so retirement is looming for many and promises to exacerbate the faculty shortage. Their salaries often pale in comparison with those of nurses in clinical settings, as well as with what faculty in medicine, law, and business earn.[98]

Education. Even if faculty salaries are improved, an insufficient number of graduate-level nurses are prepared to fill existing vacancies, and the pool of baccalaureate-prepared nurses who may eventually obtain advanced degrees is insufficient to ensure adequate numbers of qualified faculty in the future.[99]

Foundations and private donors, such as the Gordon and Betty Moore Foundation in California and the Donald and Barbara Jonas Center for Nursing Excellence in New York City, are providing scholarships for the doctoral education of nurses willing to commit to teaching. Private philanthropy, however, will not be sufficient to ensure that the nation has enough nursing faculty.

Productivity. Changing how nurses are educated could improve the productivity and efficiency of nursing faculty. Nursing's approach to educating students has changed little over the last half century.[100] Clinical experiences require a faculty member to supervise no more than eight to ten undergraduate nursing students, making this part of the curriculum expensive and faculty-intensive.

Some schools are exploring more productive approaches to clinical education. For example, the University of Portland School of Nursing has developed several "dedicated education units" (DEUs)—partnerships between the nursing school and clinical settings (particularly hospitals) where nursing students learn under the supervision of established clinicians. A clinical faculty coordinator from the school of nursing can be responsible for up to 28 students, working with a number of staff nurses from the DEUs who serve as clinical instructors to one or two students on an ongoing basis.[101]

Limited Clinical Capacity. Nursing schools' access to the myriad clinical settings needed for a generalist nursing education is quite competitive in some areas of the country. Strategies to address this problem have included DEUs that can accommodate students on all shifts and simulation laboratories. The labs, however, are too expensive for some schools.

A new model of integrated nursing education that establishes collaborative partnerships between associate and baccalaureate degree programs provides another approach to reducing the competition among schools for limited clinical sites. Developed by professor of nursing Christine Tanner at the Oregon Health Sciences University's School of Nursing, the so-called Oregon Model identifies the knowledge and competencies shared by associate and baccalaureate nurses, provides some courses that both groups take, and permits associate degree students to pursue the baccalaureate degree with fewer credits than are required by the usual RN-to-BSN programs.[102,103] This model is being replicated in North Carolina, New York, and elsewhere.

Difficulty of Retaining Nurses.   Nursing will never be able to attract and retain enough nurses unless fundamental improvements are made in work environments, staffing ratios, and nurses' roles. This is particularly true for hospitals and long-term care facilities. In a study of nurses' intentions to stay in their jobs, Aiken and colleagues found that 23% of a sample of Pennsylvania nurses intended to leave nursing within a year, but fully one-third of those younger than 30 planned to do so.[104] In 2000, the percentage of nurses with active RN licenses who worked in nursing decreased for the first time by one point (to 81.7%), which equates to 27,000 nurses.[105,106]

Even new nurses may not last long in hospitals. Almost 88% of all nurses start their careers in hospitals, regardless of future ambitions.[107] Hospitals are seen as the place for gaining the necessary experiential knowledge of practice. But a new graduate is hardly prepared for the realities of practice.[108] Christine Kovner and Carol Brewer, professors of nursing at New York University and the University of Buffalo, respectively, are conducting a multistate, longitudinal study of new nurses' turnover rates, attitudes, and intentions regarding their first professional nursing jobs. Among the early findings: new nurse turnover is 18% within one year and 26% within two years of starting their jobs.[109] This is lower than previous estimates but still costly to hospitals. The cost of replacing one staff nurse has been estimated at about $64,000,[110,111] but the cost of replacing new nurses is higher because of the additional supervisory and training costs.[112]

Factors associated with new nurses' dissatisfaction with their jobs include high patient caseloads, mandatory overtime, and shift work.[113,114,115] Twenty-six percent of new nurses find it difficult to do their jobs because of insufficient supplies and equipment.

Some nurses who leave their jobs will not seek another job in nursing. In 2004, approximately 4% of nurses worked outside of nursing and another 12% were unemployed; both groups reported dissatisfaction with the workplace (for example, burnout, the physical demands of the job, scheduling problems) as the driving force behind their leaving nursing.[116] Although the economic recession has reduced the number of nurses leaving the profession, this is likely to change once nurses are financially able to retire or to leave high-paying hospital jobs. Among the reasons why it is difficult to retain nurses are these.

Poor Staffing and Overtime.   Nurses become dissatisfied and have higher rates of burnout when their caseloads are too high and patient safety is jeopardized.[117] In Aiken and her colleagues' study of nurses' experience of working in hospitals, inadequate staffing was a major concern among the American nurses, with only about 34% reporting that staffing was adequate.[118] Some hospitals have responded to shortages of RNs by increasing the use of nonnurses or using other staffing strategies that may have untoward immediate and long-term effects, including causing more nurses to leave their jobs and jeopardizing patient safety.

A particularly egregious example of short-sighted staffing policies is the use of mandatory overtime, the practice of forcing nurses to work additional hours beyond the scheduled shift. Supervisors and administrations often pressure nurses to work long hours under threat of disciplinary action, up to and including termination.

Despite many state boards of nursing having adopted policies stating that the refusal of mandatory overtime does not constitute patient abandonment, hospitals have threatened to report nurses refusing to work overtime to the state board for patient abandonment. During the shortage of the 1980s and 1990s, some hospitals—instead of creating working conditions that would attract and retain nurses, as Magnet hospitals were doing—relied on mandatory overtime. Recent studies show the percentages of nurses who worked mandatory overtime ranging from 13% of new nurses to 16.7% of all nurses.[119,120] In the latter study, 24% of nurses who were single parents reported that they worked at jobs that had mandatory overtime.

Research has demonstrated that nurses working more than 12 hours a day or 40 hours a week have a far greater likelihood of making an error.[121] Even though two-thirds of overtime hours are voluntary,[122] they should be restricted to protect the health of both nurses and patients.

Unions and state nurses associations have led efforts to ban mandatory overtime and set minimum nurse staffing levels. In 1999, the California Nurses Association and the Service Employees International Union led a successful campaign to mandate minimum nurse-patient staffing ratios in California—the only state to do so. In 2004, California hospitals were required to have no more than six patients for each licensed nurse (RN or LPN) on a medical or surgical unit. The ratio decreased to five patients per nurse in 2005.

The evidence to date of the lower ratios' impact on outcomes of care and nurse satisfaction has been equivocal.[123,124] Anecdotal reports indicate that some hospitals are meeting these mandates by hiring more temporary staff and reducing unit support staff, such as nursing assistants and unit secretaries, leaving nurses to do work that someone with less education could perform for lower pay. Obviously, this undermines the purpose of increasing the licensed nursing staff. Some hospitals, especially public hospitals, may also be reducing services and expenditures on other essential services.[125] Nonetheless, a comparative study of staffing and patient outcomes in California, New Jersey, and Pennsylvania two years after the California ratios were implemented found that the California nurses cared for one to two patients fewer than RNs in the other states and this improved staffing was associated with lower rates of patient mortality, nurse burnout, and job dissatisfaction.[126]

Conditions of hospital participation in Medicare require that the nursing service must have "adequate numbers" of licensed registered nurses, licensed practical (vocational) nurses, and other personnel to provide nursing care to all patients as needed, but this language is vague. Some states, such as Oregon, now require hospitals to involve nurses in setting unit-specific staffing ratios and have regulations mandating minimum nurse–patient staffing ratios in specialty areas; but attempts to replicate the California model have been unsuccessful.[127]

Hospitals and long-term care facilities have also relied upon foreign nurses to improve staffing. Foreign-born nurses make up approximately 14% of the RN workforce in the United States, up from 5.1% in 1998, although not all of these were trained in foreign countries.[128,129] Critics have challenged the recruitment of foreign nurses as a way of alleviating the nursing shortage for a number of reasons:

■ Cultural differences may result in care that is technically proficient but lacking in the expected psychosocial dimension.

■ Filling vacant positions with immigrant nurses relieves the institution of its responsibility to create working conditions that will be effective in recruiting and retaining American nurses. In addition, foreign nurses are often afraid to speak out about poor working conditions or to join union or advocacy activities because of fear that they will be deported. Their American colleagues sometimes become resentful of colleagues who will not stand with them in fighting for improved working conditions for all nurses.

■ Recruitment of nurses from underdeveloped countries may worsen shortages in the home country and has been framed as immoral unless some exchange is made for the home country's investment in training the nurse.

■ Some institutions or recruiting agencies have exploited immigrant nurses, providing them with pay and benefits that are lower than their American counterparts, inadequate housing, and other treatment that has resulted in accusations that poor recruiting practices can lead to a kind of human trafficking.[130,131]

Wages.   In 2009, the U.S. Department of Labor reported a median annual salary for RNs of $62,450 in 2008, with the lowest 10% earning less than $43,410 and the highest 10% earning more than $92,240.[132] Nurses' wages have increased over time, but they have often lagged behind what one would expect with an increase in demand during shortages. This may signify biases against women's work and possible collusion among hospitals to suppress wages.[133] Indeed, in 2006 anti-trust class action suits were filed against health systems in Albany, Chicago, Memphis, Detroit, and San Antonio for such collusion. In 2009, Northeast Health in Albany settled the suit and agreed to pay nurses $1.25 million in back wages.[134]

Increasing nurses' pay will probably not suffice to retain all nurses. One estimate concluded that to end the nursing shortage solely by means of offering better pay, inflation-adjusted wages would have to increase between 3.2% to 3.8% a year until 2016.[135] Given the current pressure to decrease health care costs during an economic downturn, such pay increases are unlikely.

Other Factors.   There are other ways to create supportive work environments, such as offering child care services and flexible scheduling options to ease the conflict that nurses often feel when job demands compete with the needs of their families.[136,137] Supportive work environments also advance nurse–physician communication by treating frontline nurses as equal members of an interdisciplinary team, giving nurses authority that matches their responsibility for the lives of patients, and engaging nurses in decision making within their organizations.[138,139]

Potential Solutions to the Nursing Shortage

Hospitals and other health care organizations responded to nursing shortages through a variety of strategies, ranging from increasing the use of staffing agencies and foreign nurses to investing in the education of new nurses; these efforts met with varying degrees of success.[140] Several strategies are highlighted below.

Creating Environments for Excellence in Nursing: Magnet Designation. The development of the Magnet program by the American Nurses Credentialing Center was based on research conducted under the auspices of the American Academy of Nursing that identified 14 factors that support the development of excellence in nursing within an institution, including:

■ A participative management style that encourages staff participation in decision making at all levels

■ A chief nursing officer who is visible and accessible at the highest levels of the organization, including the board of trustees

■ A pervasive sentiment among top administrators that nurses are key to the hospital's success

■ High-quality, well-educated nurses as leaders throughout the organization

■ Decentralized organizational structure and local decision making

■ Favorable nurse–patient ratios and recruitment of well-educated nurses

■ Personnel policies that include competitive salaries and benefits for nurses, work schedules that meet the needs of the personal lives of staff, and opportunities for nurses to be promoted with identifiable career ladders

■ The primacy of high-quality patient care and staffing

■ The use of professional practice models that give nurses the authority and autonomy to match their responsibility and encourage them to innovate

■ Excellent nurse–physician relationships, along with well-tuned interdisciplinary teams that accord equal status to nurses

■ Investments in nursing staff development, continuing education, career development, and orientation[141]

Nearly seven years after the original research identifying workplace characteristics that promote excellence in nursing, the American Nurses Credentialing Center developed criteria for hospitals to apply for "Magnet designation" for excellence in nursing.[142] The Magnet designation can be acquired by long-term care facilities, and efforts are underway to develop criteria for home care agencies. Today, more than 350 health care organizations in the United States and internationally have Magnet recognition and many other hospitals are pursuing the "Magnet journey."

Some, including this author, believe that the Magnet program, although not perfect, has been one of nursing's best tools for spurring workplace changes necessary to retain nurses and promote safe, high-quality care. The research on Magnet hospitals is complicated because Magnet designation is a proxy for specific characteristics that may be shared with hospitals that have not pursued the designation. Nonetheless, studies have found that Magnet hospitals have a 4.6% to 7.7% lower mortality rate, higher patient satisfaction, and lower levels of staff burnout and job dissatisfaction than non-Magnet hospitals.[143,144,145,146,147] Hospitals have found that the designation makes good business sense. They refer to their Magnet status in marketing efforts, and it helps them save money on risk payouts and reduce spending on nurse recruitment and orientation.[148] Today, *U.S. News and World Report* includes Magnet status in its scoring of America's best hospitals.[149]

Engaging Nurses in Redesigning Work Processes: Transforming Care at the Bedside (TCAB).

In its effort to address the nursing shortage, the Robert Wood Johnson Foundation recognized that some of the most neglected nurses were those on medical-surgical units of hospitals—the "floors" or units that usually account for the greatest proportion of a hospital's beds. The Foundation contracted with the Institute for Healthcare Improvement to design a program that would empower nurses on medical-surgical units as change agents. The program is called Transforming Care at the Bedside.

Transforming Care at the Bedside requires support from the top levels of the organization, including the chief executives and board of trustees, but it is not a top-down approach. Rather, it empowers staff at the unit level to identify issues that impede safe, satisfying, efficient care, and provides them with tools for engaging in "rapid-cycle change": it trains them in generating ideas to address the issues, testing them on a small scale, evaluating them, and determining whether to abort, adapt, or maintain and spread the change.

Examples of changes made by program's units include developing a color-coded system for identifying when conditions on the unit had become unsafe for new admissions and transfers,[150] reducing the time nurses spend "hunting and gathering" supplies and equipment by moving commonly used items into patients' rooms,[151] and using laptop computers at the patient's bedside to communicate with off-unit physicians via video.[152]

UCLA professor and researcher Jack Needleman and his colleagues evaluated Transforming Care at the Bedside and concluded that it was effective in reducing the turnover rate of nurses, making care safer, improving patient satisfaction, and increasing the time that nurses spend in direct patient contact.[153,154,155] Nursing leader Linda Burnes Bolton and research scientist Harriet Aronow, both of Cedars-Sinai Medical Center in Los Angeles, have made a business case for the program by looking at the cost of conducting the program and the savings from improved outcomes and reduced turnover of nurses.[156] In 2010, there were over 300 U.S. hospitals and other countries engaged in Transforming Care at the Bedside.

Retaining Nurses: Internships, Residencies, and Retraining.

To attempt to retain new nurses, hospitals have developed internships and residency programs that provide mentorship, education, and greater support, usually for the first year of practice.[157,158,159] However, these programs vary tremendously in quality, focus, and duration, depending on the hospital's resources. For example, if the residency includes assigning the new nurse a smaller caseload for a substantial period of time, the hospital will need more nurses to provide care during the residency period.

Colleen Goode, professor at the University of Colorado College of Nursing, and her colleagues have argued that new graduates should not be expected to move into full-time clinical practice without some continued training and support.[160] They propose that nurse residency programs be standardized, much as medicine has done. The Commission on Collegiate Nursing Education, the accrediting arm of the American Association of Colleges of Nursing, has approved standards for accrediting postbaccalaureate residency programs.

Initiatives are also needed to reduce the physical demands of hospital nursing and to provide alternative work situations for aging nurses (along with the education and training needed to shift their work roles). Ergonomic changes in the workplace can ameliorate the stress of working in demanding environments—for example, redesigning units to reduce the amount of walking, using available technology and equipment for safe patient handling, and flexible scheduling that permits 8-hour instead of 12-hour shifts.

In addition, older nurses from acute care, ambulatory care, or home health settings would be well suited for positions in telehealth that focus on care coordination and chronic disease management. Nursing for Life is a career transition program provided online by the College of Nursing at Michigan State University to help nurses move into these more age-friendly roles. Launched in 2008 with grants from Blue Cross Blue Shield of Michigan and the Robert Wood Johnson Foundation, the program strives to keep in the workforce those nurses who may consider leaving because of the physical challenges of acute care or dissatisfaction with the work. Nurses complete self-paced modules and a supervised clinical experience in one of four areas: home, ambulatory, hospice and palliative, or long-term care (other areas will be added). As of January 2010, 43 nurses had completed or enrolled in the program. Eighty percent of those who have completed the program found a position in the area they studied.[161]

Expanding Educational Capacity. The Nurse Training Act, Title VIII of the Public Health Service Act, which was signed into law in 1964 and today is administered by the Health Resources and Services Administration (HRSA), provides the largest source of federal funding for the education, recruitment, and retention of nurses. In fiscal year 2010, this support amounted to nearly $244 million. Table 1 shows the various nursing initiatives funded under Title VIII from 2005 to 2010.

Funding for Title VIII was flat until 2010, with a decline in real dollars and 21% and 28% decreases in the numbers of students supported in 2007 and 2008, respectively. In 2002, Congress passed the Nurse Reinvestment Act that includes faculty educational loan forgiveness and continues as part of Title VIII. But the funding increase was modest, at best.

Other sources of support for nurses' education, training, and workforce development are Title VII of the 1963 Public Health Act, which was enacted to encourage a primary care workforce (its funding level today is one-tenth of what it was in the mid-1970s, having decreased from $2.5 billion per year to $222 million),[162] the National Health Service Corps, which supports health care providers, including nurses, who agree to work in underserved areas, and the American Recovery and Reinvestment Act—the economic stimulus package signed by President Obama in 2009—that included $500 million for various health care shortages, of which $200 million was designated for nursing.

On the whole, funding for nursing education pales in comparison with funding for medical education. For example, Medicare funding for Graduate Medical Education (GME) has included only a small percentage for nursing education, and that has been restricted to the dwindling number of hospital diploma schools of nursing.

TABLE 1. **Title VIII Nursing Programs—Funding from FY 2005–2010**

	FY 2005	FY 2006	FY 2007	FY 2008	FY 2009	FY 2010
Advanced Education Nursing	58,160	57,061	57,061	61,875	64,438	64,438
Nurse education, practice and retention	36,468	37,291	37,291	36,640	37,291	39,896
Workforce diversity	16,270	16,107	16,107	15,826	16,107	16,107
Loan Repayment and Scholarship	31,482	31,055	31,055	30,512	37,128	93,864
Comprehensive geriatric education	3,450	3,392	3,392	3,333	4,567	4,567
Nursing faculty loan program	4,831	4,773	4,773	7,860	11,500	25,000
Total, Title VIII Nursing	**150,661**	**149,679**	**149,679**	**156,046**	**171,031**	**243,872**

Note: The year-long CR passed by the House Dec. 8 included $633 million for Titles VII and VIII. No program-specific funding amounts have been provided.

Adapted from President's Budget, HRSA Budget Justification, P.L. 111-117, Senate Report No. 111-243.

Moreover, there is concern that the federal government's approach to funding for healthcare workforce development is outdated. Federal spending for medical education through Medicare GME funds alone is $12 billion annually (FY 2009), whereas nursing and all other health professions collectively receive only $524 million from HRSA for education and development in primary care, general dentistry, nursing, and for providers to work in medically underserved communities and in shortage specialties. Only $171 million of the HRSA money is specific to nursing workforce development.[163]

The Affordable Care Act of 2010 authorizes increased funding for nursing education under Title VIII of the Public Health Service Act, as well as expansion of the National Health Service Corps and other programs to increase the supply of nurses, particularly those delivering primary care. It authorizes a Medicare Graduate Nurse Education Demonstration Program that provides funding to five hospitals that partner with schools of nursing and community-based clinics for the clinical training of APRNs.

However, whether Congress will appropriate funding for these activities remains to be seen. Regardless, the nation cannot rely solely on federal support to build its educational capacity. An example of a nongovernmental effort is the Center for Championing Nursing in America. In 2008, the Robert Wood Johnson Foundation awarded $10 million to AARP over a five-year period to create the center. Its initial work has targeted the development of multisector partnerships in key states to build educational capacity in various ways, such as funding scholarships and expanding educational sites.

Hospitals and other health care organizations have supported faculty positions, provided loans and scholarships to students, and invested in creative initiatives to address the shortage. But they are unlikely to be able to invest more.[164] With the passage of health care reform, there are opportunities—and perhaps a mandate—for hospitals to rethink how they use nurses.

Reducing the Demands on Nurses' Time.   As noted earlier, there are more nurses today than ever before, and still there are not enough. What can be done to reduce the demand for nurses or make more efficient use of them?

In 2004, the Robert Wood Johnson Foundation funded the Center for Health Design to examine the evidence linking hospital design and patient outcomes, patient satisfaction, staff satisfaction, and staff efficiency. Its review of over 600 rigorously designed studies found that good design can reduce staff stress and fatigue, increase efficiency and effectiveness in delivering care, promote patient safety, and improve outcomes and overall health care quality.

For example, hospital staff nurses spend almost one-third of their time walking; another third is spent on documentation.[165,166] Only about 30% of medical-surgical nurses' time is spent in the patients' rooms. This allocation of time and focus depends upon the layout of the unit, the available technology (including whether an electronic medical record is accessible in each patient's room), and the way care processes are designed.

Technology, which is becoming more pervasive in all health care settings, is often assumed to expedite or facilitate care delivery and make care safer. But these assumptions have been questioned in a technology project undertaken by the American Academy of Nursing's Workforce Commission.[167] The Technology Drill Down project examined the workflow of nurses in more than 200 units in 25 hospitals. Nurses reported equipment malfunctions, problems with interoperability of various systems, inefficient technology (including bar coding), and a lack of availability of hardware (whether computers or so-called smart pumps for intravenous infusions) that impeded their work. They also identified how technology could help them in their work, generating nearly 600 ideas.

In 2008, The Joint Commission released its *Guiding Principles for the Development of the Hospital of the Future,* which contains principles on matters such as staffing, safe patient handling, and physical design that could make hospitals and other health care facilities safer and more efficient.[168] A new Hill-Burton Act could stimulate the redesign of hospitals in ways that would improve nurses' job satisfaction, with The Joint Commission guidelines serving as criteria for public grants for infrastructure development and modification or enhanced payment by public and private payers—but only with nurses at decision-making tables every step of the way.

Building an Educated Workforce to Meet Contemporary and Future Needs

The rise of collegiate nursing programs and decline of hospital diploma programs has been a deliberate change recommended by many national councils and commissions.[169] Figure 4, which illustrates the 40-year trend in graduations from diploma, associate degree, and baccalaureate degree nursing programs, also shows that enrollments in schools of nursing are at an all-time high. Although some have challenged the need for increasing the number of new nurses,[170,171,172] the figure reinforces the argument that the supply of nurses is unable to keep up with the demand.

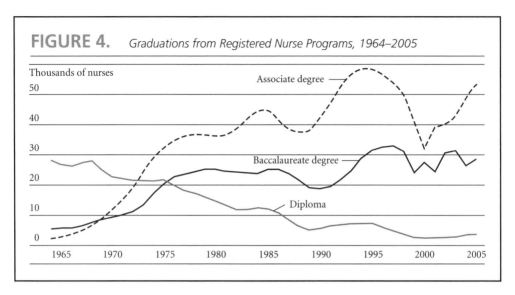

FIGURE 4.   *Graduations from Registered Nurse Programs, 1964–2005*

Source: Used with permission of Project Hope/*Health Affairs* from Aiken, L. H., Cheung, R. B., & Olds, D. M. (2009). Education policy initiatives to address the nurse shortage in the United States. *Health Affairs, 28*(4), p. w648; permission conveyed through Copyright Clearance Center, Inc. The published article is archived and available online at www.healthaffairs.org.

Educational Requirements for Entry into Practice

For years, the nursing community has argued over whether the entry point into professional practice should be the bachelor of science in nursing (BSN) or the associate degree in nursing (ADN). Arguments in favor of the BSN include:

- Contemporary professional nursing practice requires the breadth of education, especially in humanities and social sciences, that only a baccalaureate degree can provide.

- Nurses will not have parity with other health professionals without this minimum preparation (pharmacists, physical therapists, and other clinicians are required to have a clinical doctorate).

- Baccalaureate programs give nurses the basic knowledge of research needed to meet the current mandate for evidence-based practice.

- Baccalaureate programs also provide nurses with needed leadership skills.

Arguments against the BSN as the entry level into professional practice include:

- New nurses from ADN programs do as well, if not better, than BSN graduates on the licensing exam (NCLEX).

- Community colleges provide affordable access to a high-quality education that may be, but does not have to be, the end point in a nurse's career path.

- The nation needs more nurses than baccalaureate programs can produce.

The so-called "1985 Proposal" by the ANA and the New York State Nurses Association was an attempt to require professional nurses to hold a baccalaureate degree. It failed. Only North Dakota passed such legislation, but it was later reversed.[173]

There is some evidence that hospitals with a higher proportion of nurses holding baccalaureate or higher degrees have better clinical outcomes.[174,175,176] This has led hospitals and other health care organizations to look for nurses with the BSN, particularly since 2009 when the recession eased the nursing shortage in some communities. The push for Magnet designation has also contributed to hiring preferences for nurses with more education.

Certainly, nursing has one of the best career and educational ladders of any health profession. Many potential students are unable to afford the cost of a four-year BSN education.[177] Those with an ADN can get a BSN in two years or less through RN Pathway programs that many schools of nursing in universities now offer. Employers often underwrite, to some degree, nurses who want to continue their formal education. Although nursing's educational ladder should lead to significant numbers of ADN nurses moving on to the BSN and BSN nurses acquiring a graduate degree, the number who have actually done so has been disappointing.[178]

The BSN in 10 is a new approach to increasing the number of nurses with baccalaureate degrees, whereby states would require associate degree and diploma graduates to secure a BSN within ten years of their initial graduation in order to continue practicing as a registered nurse. Resistance has come primarily from community colleges, but opposition may lessen if creative approaches are developed to implement the BSN in 10—for example by having community colleges offer baccalaureate degrees, as is happening in Florida, or by expanding online programs for registered nurses seeking the BSN, such as the Multi-State Approach to the Preparation of Registered Nurses provided by the Western Governors University.[179]

Others argue for graduate preparation for nurses who want to stay in practice. A 2010 report by the Carnegie Foundation for the Advancement of Teaching, *Educating Nurses: A Call for Radical Transformation,* recommends an MSN in 10, calling for entry into professional nursing practice to be at the baccalaureate level, accompanied by the expectation that graduates will obtain the MSN to continue to practice.[180] Shortly after the report was released, the American Association of Community Colleges issued a statement opposing this recommendation, noting that, because associate degree programs produce the majority of new nurses, this change would "constrict the pipeline," exacerbate the shortage, and limit access to nursing care needlessly.[181] The National League for Nursing, which promotes excellence in nursing education at all levels, echoed this criticism,[182] whereas the American Association of Colleges of Nursing, which represents baccalaureate and higher degree nursing education, supported the report's recommendation.

Increasing the number of nurses with higher degrees may not, by itself, be sufficient to ensure a well-prepared nursing workforce. Increasingly, health care analysts and visionaries recognize that nurses are key to a high-functioning, complex health care system; and nursing education may have to change the way it prepares nurses to work in this system. The 2010 Carnegie report acknowledges the difficulties in teaching the large amount of material that nurses may need. It recommends a shift toward a patient-centered (rather than setting-centered) approach that focuses on the development of reasoning and judgment needed in specific clinical situations. This can be done only if there is better integration of the theory and clinical aspects of nursing education. The Carnegie report is expected to spur experimentation in nursing education.

Advanced Practice Registered Nursing Education

State statutes and regulations define the scope of practice of APRNs in different ways; as a result, an inconsistent patchwork of policies governing APRN education, licensure, and practice has evolved. For example, APRNs in New York do not need national certification to practice, but they do in Iowa. Nurse practitioners in New York must work under a formal collaborative practice agreement with a physician, whereas those in Iowa can practice without such an agreement. The National Council of State Boards of Nursing recognized that this lack of uniformity is confusing to the public, restricts mobility of APRNs across state lines, and limits federal approaches to removing barriers to APRN practice. Working with organizations representing the licensure, accreditation, certification, and education of APRNs, the council developed a consensus document that state boards of nursing and other concerned parties will use to develop uniform approaches to regulating APRNs.[183,184] The proposed regulatory model includes:

- All advance practice nurses will be referred to as advanced practice registered nurses (APRNs).
- The credential will be "APRN, CNP" for certified nurse practitioners.
- Each APRN will declare a focus on one of six populations: neonatal, pediatrics, women's health or gender related, adult-gerontology, individuals across the lifespan or families, or mental health.
- APRNs must complete an accredited graduate-level educational program in the specific APRN role that includes core courses in physiology/pathophysiology, health assessment, and pharmacology.
- APRNs must successfully complete a national certification exam.
- Additional certification in a specialty can be attained in areas such as oncology.
- Existing advanced practice registered nurses will be grandfathered in.

The time line for implementation is 2015. The challenge in doing so will be securing statutory and regulatory changes at the state level. As of 2010, 17 state boards of nursing reported having plans to implement the consensus model.[185]

Recently, a debate has arisen around the preparation of APRNs. In 2004, the American Association of Colleges of Nursing proposed a new entry-level credential for APRNs: the doctor of nursing practice, or DNP. It did this for a couple of reasons. First, the amount of time APRNs spend acquiring the master's degree often exceeds the hours that other disciplines, such as physical therapists, spend in acquiring a clinical doctorate. Other health care disciplines have moved to the clinical doctorate; why shouldn't nursing? Second, master's programs for APRNs focus primarily on providing care to individual patients. For APRNs to serve as clinical leaders, they need a better grounding in aggregate-level analyses in order to evaluate evidence of best practices for specific populations and engage in translational efforts to improve care.

Arguments against the DNP have included the following:

- Given the cost and longer course of study, the number of nurses who will pursue advanced practice nursing will decrease.

■ Some schools of nursing are in colleges that are not authorized to grant doctorates so the number of programs available to prepare advanced practice registered nurses will decrease.

■ Fewer nurses will pursue the PhD, undermining gains that nurses have made in academia and the ability of the profession to produce the research needed to define best clinical practices.

■ The gulf between academicians (PhD) and clinicians (DNP) will widen.[186]

One particularly controversial development was initiated by the Council for the Development of Comprehensive Care, an interdisciplinary group affiliated with the Columbia University School of Nursing whose mission is "to develop and promulgate the clinical doctoral role and measurable standards of practice through certification." It negotiated with the National Board of Medical Examiners to develop a certification examination in comprehensive care that is based upon Part III of the U.S. Medical Licensing Exam (50% of the first cohort of DNP graduates who sat for the exam passed it). This step brought fierce objections from organized medicine. Moreover, physicians objected to nurses being referred to as "doctor" and have proposed state legislation to restrict the use of the title to physicians, osteopaths, dentists, and, in some cases, psychologists.[187]

Despite concerns from within the nursing profession about whether the DNP should be a research degree and whether there should be a residency or other practice requirement, DNP programs have proliferated. As of 2010, there were over 120 DNP programs and an estimated 161 more are under development. The DNP is here to stay, but continued refinement of the curriculum, certification standards and methods, and experience or residency expectations are likely.

Funding Support for a Better-Educated Nursing Workforce

The path to a better-educated nursing workforce will require the improved public and private financial support outlined earlier in this chapter. Through their grant making, HRSA and private foundations can stimulate innovations in nursing pedagogy. State licensing boards will need to develop regulatory flexibility to permit experimentation with curricula that deviate from traditional approaches.

Some state nursing boards are ready to be flexible. For example, Christine Tanner and colleagues who are part of the Oregon Consortium for Nursing Education negotiated with the Oregon State Board for Nursing to try a new curriculum.[188] The curriculum is being replicated elsewhere. The Jonas Center for Nursing Excellence and the Robert Wood Johnson Foundation's Partners in Nursing initiative have provided funding for schools in New York City and North Carolina to replicate or adapt the Oregon model.

Full Utilization of Advanced Practice Registered Nurses

As the education and roles of APRNs evolved and changes in state nurse practice acts permitted greater degrees of independent practice, physicians became concerned about losing control, and they challenged APRNs on the grounds of patient safety and quality of care.[189,190] The challenges continue. In 2009, the American Medical Association circulated a series of documents on the scope of practice of other health care professionals, whom they referred to as "limited licensed providers."[191]

The series, called the *AMA Scope of Practice Data Series: A Resource Compendium for State Medical Associations and National Medical Specialty Societies*, targets nurse practitioners, nurse-midwives, and nurse anesthetists, as well as nonnurse professionals who have gained greater independence from physicians, such as optometrists, podiatrists, physical therapists, and family therapists. The last document in the series claimed, despite the evidence to the contrary, that nurse practitioners must be supervised by physicians in order to ensure safe, quality patient care.

Clinical Outcomes and Advanced Practice Nursing

So what is the evidence on the outcomes of care provided by APRNs? Scores of studies, including several systematic reviews and meta-analyses, report remarkably consistent findings.[192,193,194,195] As long ago as 1986, the U.S. Office of Technology Assessment conducted an analysis of the care provided by nurse practitioners, nurse-midwives, and physician assistants; it concluded that they provided care comparable to that of physicians and were often better at communicating with patients.[196]

Subsequent studies have demonstrated that nurse practitioners have clinical outcomes comparable to those of physicians for the primary care services that they are able to provide (which the Office of Technology Assessment estimated to be up to 90% of primary care in 1986). A 1995 meta-analysis of 38 studies of nurse practitioners and nurse-midwives— which met rigorous criteria—found that nurse practitioners provide care that is comparable to physicians, they are better on health promotion, and they elicit higher patient satisfaction.[197]

One study comparing the outcomes of patients cared for by nurse practitioners and by physicians in five primary care practices in New York attracted great attention because of its randomized design and its publication in the *Journal of the American Medical Association*. Mary Mundinger, former Dean of the Columbia University School of Nursing, and her colleagues found that the two professions' practices were comparable in terms of resource utilization, clinical outcomes, and patient satisfaction over six months and two years.[198,199] Despite these findings, calls for more research confirming the safety and quality of nurse practitioners continued, as did organized medicine's opposition to unsupervised nurse practitioner practice.[200]

In 2004, the Cochrane Collaboration published a systematic review of 16 studies that compared the outcomes of APRNs and physicians providing similar primary care services.[201] The nurse practitioners and physicians were similar in patient outcomes, care processes, resource utilization, and cost of care. The review questioned whether the presence of the nurse practitioners actually increases access to care and thereby increases costs, despite the lower pay of nurse practitioners compared with physicians.

This question highlights the limitations in current cost analyses conducted by the Congressional Budget Office. When asked to evaluate the financial impact of federal policies that would improve access to APRNs, the Congressional Budget Office generally assumes that increasing access to any group of health care providers will result in increased costs because more people will use the services.[202] This assumption seems unwarranted as the nation expands health insurance coverage for millions of Americans and as evidence mounts that expanding primary care can reduce the use and cost of emergency and acute care.[203]

In brief summary, the evidence shows that:

■ APRNs improve access to care for homebound elderly,[204] nursing home patients,[205] low-income pregnant women,[206] and people living in rural areas.[207] They reduce length of stay and cost of postoperative cardiovascular care[208] and neonatal care.[209] Clinical nurse specialists have reduced the rate of smoking among people with respiratory disease.[210]

■ Nurse anesthetists provide most of the anesthesia care to underserved populations in rural America and augment the surgical capacity of major academic medical centers in all areas of the country.[211,212] Studies of outcomes of anesthesia provided by nurse anesthetists with and without anesthesiologist supervision have shown mixed results.[213,214,215,216]

■ The maternal and child outcomes of care provided by certified nurse-midwives are comparable to or better than those of obstetricians when caring for low-risk women. A systematic review published in 2009 by the Cochrane Collaboration of 11 studies with over 12,000 deliveries concluded that nurse-midwifery care was associated with lower rates of fetal loss before 24 weeks gestation, hospitalization, regional anesthesia, episiotomies, and use of forceps or other instruments during childbirth; higher rates of spontaneous vaginal delivery, breastfeeding; and no adverse outcomes.[217]

These are only highlights of some of the overwhelming evidence documenting the safety and quality of APRN practice.

Barriers to Full Utilization of APRNs

Is physician supervision of APRN practice necessary to attain these outcomes? When APRNs practice in rural areas or underserved urban communities, the "supervision" may be miles away and amount to someone with whom the APRN can consult or refer difficult cases. But knowing when to consult another colleague is a hallmark of any wise health care professional. When laws or regulations require on-site supervision or otherwise restrict APRN practice, access to and the cost of health services may be affected adversely.

In 1992, Nichols estimated that it was costing the nation between $6 and $8 billion for inefficient and underutilization of APRNs.[218] Two Institute of Medicine studies recommended removing the barriers to full utilization of APRNs so the nation can meet the need for primary care and other health care services—a need that will be increased by the Affordable Care Act's expansion of insurance coverage.[219,220]

Scope of Practice. In the early years of the APRN movement, NPs were certified and practiced under the direction of or in collaboration with a physician. Their educational preparation was limited to programs ranging in length from six weeks to one year, until the profession recognized that these APRNs were providing advanced *nursing care* and needed to be educated in graduate nursing programs. As APRN education, knowledge, and independence evolved, nursing redefined its scope of practice in state statutes or regulations to protect APRNs from charges of practicing medicine without a license. In 1992, then Yale University law professor Barbara Safriet wrote a landmark analysis of the challenges that APRNs confronted as a result of medical practice acts written so broadly that they encompassed all health care and provided physicians with authority over all other health care providers.[221] APRNs and other health care professionals have waged an ongoing battle to change legal definitions of their scopes of practice to reflect their education and actual practice, and to stave off efforts by medical societies to control their practice. Nonetheless, APRNs have been able to make headway at the state and federal levels.

The first legal authority for NPs to practice was created in 1972 in Idaho. Over time, a patchwork of state laws governing NP practice evolved, such that NPs in one state practice independently but NPs in a bordering state can practice only under on-site physician supervision. There are two primary issues with how state practice acts define APRNs: (1) the extent to which a relationship with physicians is defined, and (2) whether the act includes prescriptive authority and the type of pharmaceutical agents that can be prescribed (for example, opioids and other controlled medications). As can be seen in Figures 5 and 6, the western rural states are among those with the most permissive state laws. Nurse practitioners in Washington, Oregon, Wyoming, Montana, Idaho, Utah, Arizona, and New Mexico, for example, can practice without any legal mandate for physician supervision, direction, or collaboration and can prescribe any medication without such mandates.[222]

Authorization for independent practice does not mean that APRNs don't collaborate with physicians and other health care providers. To the contrary, nursing and APRNs embrace an interdisciplinary team approach to care;[223] but particularly in rural areas, the APRN may be the sole provider.

The American Medical Association and other medical societies have repeatedly launched campaigns to stop advances in APRNs' authority to practice and to roll back laws and regulations that removed physician supervision requirements. One strategy for ensuring physician authority over APRNs has been to include it in federal Medicare and Medicaid law and regulations. For example, Medicare requires physician supervision of nurse practitioners and nurse anesthetists in Critical Access Hospitals and for hospitals that seek Medicare's Centers of Excellence designation.

Nurse anesthetists face additional oversight. At the close of its second term, the Clinton Administration, with the support of the American Hospital Association and the National Rural Health Association, dropped a federal requirement for physician supervision (not necessarily anesthesiologists) of certified registered nurse anesthetists in hospitals that receive Medicare funding. Less than one year later, the Bush Administration reversed this ruling despite the fact that the majority of states don't require physician supervision of these nurse anesthetists.[224] Because certified registered nurse anesthetists are the only anesthesia provider in many rural areas and underserved urban communities,[225] the new ruling included a provision for states to apply for a waiver, providing the governor first consults with the boards of medicine and nursing. If a state permits independent practice by a certified registered nurse anesthetist and it has not opted for a waiver of the Medicare requirement for physician supervision, the federal policy overrules the state policy and the nurse anesthetist must be supervised.

The local variation in scopes of practice for APRNs, whether from state practice acts or federal regulations, reflects differences in the demand for health care providers and in the relative political power of nursing and medicine, rather than evidence-based policy. The *Consensus Model for APRN Regulation: Licensure, Accreditation, Certification and*

FIGURE 5. *Summary of APRN Legislation: Legal Authority for Scope of Practice*

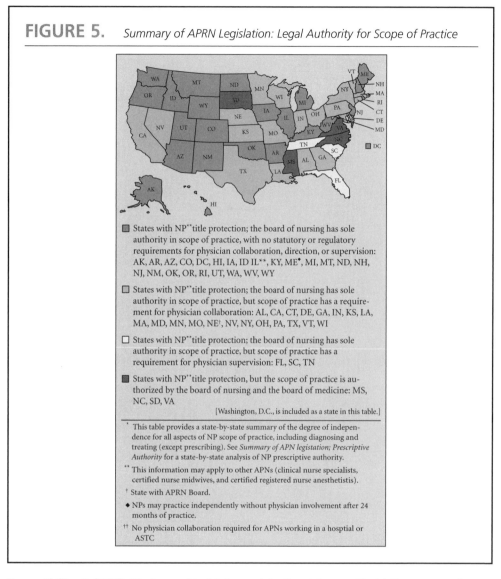

States with NP**title protection; the board of nursing has sole authority in scope of practice, with no statutory or regulatory requirements for physician collaboration, direction, or supervision: AK, AR, AZ, CO, DC, HI, IA, ID IL**, KY, ME*, MI, MT, ND, NH, NJ, NM, OK, OR, RI, UT, WA, WV, WY

States with NP**title protection; the board of nursing has sole authority in scope of practice, but scope of practice has a requirement for physician collaboration: AL, CA, CT, DE, GA, IN, KS, LA, MA, MD, MN, MO, NE†, NV, NY, OH, PA, TX, VT, WI

States with NP**title protection; the board of nursing has sole authority in scope of practice, but scope of practice has a requirement for physician supervision: FL, SC, TN

States with NP**title protection, but the scope of practice is authorized by the board of nursing and the board of medicine: MS, NC, SD, VA

[Washington, D.C., is included as a state in this table.]

* This table provides a state-by-state summary of the degree of independence for all aspects of NP scope of practice, including diagnosing and treating (except prescribing). See *Summary of APN legislation; Prescriptive Authority* for a state-by-state analysis of NP prescriptive authority.

** This information may apply to other APNs (clinical nurse specialists, certified nurse midwives, and certified registered nurse anesthetists).

† State with APRN Board.

◆ NPs may practice independently without physician involvement after 24 months of practice.

†† No physician collaboration required for APNs working in a hosptial or ASTC

Education developed by the nursing community in recognition of the need to standardize state and federal rules and regulations regarding the legal authority to practice can serve to explain to policymakers the specifics of the changes needed to improve access to these important providers of health care.[226]

What's the harm of requiring physician supervision of APRNs? Nursing organizations argue that unnecessary supervision is costly (requiring two providers to see a patient) and

FIGURE 6.   *Summary of APRN Legislation: Prescriptive Authority*

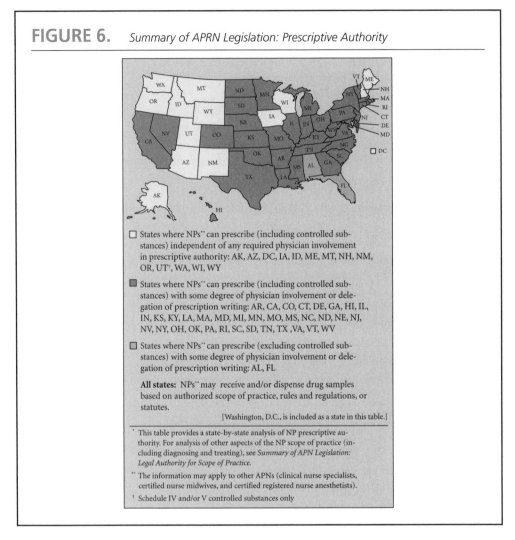

☐ States where NPs** can prescribe (including controlled substances) independent of any required physician involvement in prescriptive authority: AK, AZ, DC, IA, ID, ME, MT, NH, NM, OR, UT†, WA, WI, WY

■ States where NPs** can prescribe (including controlled substances) with some degree of physician involvement or delegation of prescription writing: AR, CA, CO, CT, DE, GA, HI, IL, IN, KS, KY, LA, MA, MD, MI, MN, MO, MS, NC, ND, NE, NJ, NV, NY, OH, OK, PA, RI, SC, SD, TN, TX ,VA, VT, WV

☐ States where NPs** can prescribe (excluding controlled substances) with some degree of physician involvement or delegation of prescription writing: AL, FL

All states: NPs** may receive and/or dispense drug samples based on authorized scope of practice, rules and regulations, or statutes.

[Washington, D.C., is included as a state in this table.]

* This table provides a state-by-state analysis of NP prescriptive authority. For analysis of other aspects of the NP scope of practice (including diagnosing and treating), see *Summary of APN Legislation: Legal Authority for Scope of Practice.*

** The information may apply to other APNs (clinical nurse specialists, certified nurse midwives, and certified registered nurse anesthetists).

† Schedule IV and/or V controlled substances only

harmful to patients if important services are delayed or unavailable. In underserved rural areas, such supervision can impede APRNs from opening their own practices to provide access to primary care.

Exclusive and Inclusive Language.   There are multiple governmental restrictions on what APRNs can do despite statutory authority in state practice acts. For example:

■   Medicare prohibits APRNs from certifying home health services for patients and hospice care.

- Medicare does not include APRNs as providers who can order respiratory therapy.

- Under Medicare's hospital "conditions of participation," practice privileges are granted to physicians by the medical staff; APRNs are not defined in the regulations as eligible for privileges.

- Medicare requires skilled nursing facilities to complete a comprehensive physical examination on all new admissions but will not pay for the stay unless a physician does the examination.

- Clinical nurse specialists are not included as authorized providers of services in federally funded rural health clinics.

- Under U.S. Code Title 5, nurse practitioners and nurse-midwives are prohibited from doing physicals for workers' compensation cases and signing off on claims.

- Medicaid allows states to decide whether to recognize nurse practitioners and nurse-midwives as primary care providers. Medicaid managed care plans are not required to include these APRNs.

When Massachusetts expanded health coverage to all residents, it quickly realized that it didn't have the capacity to meet the new demand for primary care. To remedy the situation, Massachusetts passed a law in 2008 that named nurse practitioners as primary care providers. The 2008 law did not change nurse practitioners' legal scope of practice. In fact, organized nursing deliberately chose not to seek amendment of the state's nurse practice act in order to reduce physicians' fears that nurse practitioners were seeking greater independence.[227]

Payment.   Although payment for APRN services has improved, APRNs are not consistently paid at the full physician rate for the same service. Federal Medicaid law requires states to pay only family and pediatric nurse practitioners—not all nurse practitioners—under the fee-for-service arrangement; but some states have decided to reimburse all nurse practitioners. Medicare pays nurse practitioners and clinical nurse specialists 85% of what a physician is paid for the same service if it is provided independent of physician oversight; if the APRN service is billed under the "incident-to" billing provision of Medicare, the physician must directly supervise the care, the bill is under the physician's Medicare number, and the payment is at the full physician rate.

Certified nurse-midwives had been paid 65% of physician payments under Medicare Part B. This was increased to 100% under the Affordable Care Act of 2010. State Medicaid payments for midwifery care vary but are likely to increase along with the new Medicare payment rate. However, Medicare does not include payment for resident training if a certified nurse midwife or other APRN supervises that training, leaving academic medical centers reluctant to hire nurse-midwives.

Certified registered nurse anesthetists are not included in the list of providers who can be paid for evaluation and management services under Medicare.[228] In addition, Medicare doesn't recognize nurse anesthetists' on-call costs that are covered for anesthesiologists under Medicare's provisions for Critical Access Hospitals and other rural health programs. The American Association of Nurse Anesthetists has argued that any provider who is qualified to provide specific Medicare services should be reimbursed for them and at an equal rate.

"Equal pay for same service" continues to be a goal for APRNs. But simply being paid at all by private insurers can be a challenge. A 2006 study of 112 managed care organizations in 49 states and the District of Columbia found that only 33% credentialed nurse practitioners as primary care providers and of those that did so, only 52% paid the NPs the same rate as primary care physicians.[229]

Removing Barriers

In 2010, the Josiah Macy Jr. Foundation issued a report on primary care that was the result of an interprofessional group cochaired by Linda Cronenwett, former dean of the University of North Carolina School of Nursing, and Victor Dzau, a physician and Duke University's Chancellor for Health Affairs. Titled *Who Will Provide Primary Care and How Will They Be Trained?*, the report recommended that:

> state and national legal, regulatory, and reimbursement policies should be changed to remove barriers that make it difficult for nurse practitioners and physician assistants to serve as primary care providers and leaders of patient-centered medical homes or other models of primary care delivery. All primary care providers should be held accountable for the quality and efficiency of care as measured by patient outcomes.[230]

This recommendation is notable given that 33 of the group of 49 national health care leaders were physicians.

In 2010, AARP made the removal of barriers to full utilization of nurses and all primary care providers, as well as unlicensed personnel, one of its legislative priorities, providing a powerful consumer voice to the policy debates.[231]

Additional options for removing the barriers include:

- A federal directive, modeled on the approach taken with military and VA facilities and the Indian Health Service, overriding state restrictions on the scope of practice of APRNs practicing in federally qualified health centers and facilities participating in Medicare or Medicaid.

- A national scope of practice law that governs the practice of nurses, including APRNs.

- Providing states with monetary incentives under Medicaid to remove barriers to APRN scope of practice and payment.

Quality and Costs in Acute Care

Nurses are sometimes described as being the last barrier between an error and the patient. But nurses can also cause errors, particularly in systems of care that have failed to adopt and integrate the kinds of redundant safeguards that are expected in banks and airlines. Simply put, nurses are key to quality and safety in care.[232] Fortunately, a great deal is known about the relationship between nursing and patient safety and costs. In 2008, the Agency for Healthcare Research and Quality released a two-volume compilation of the evidence base and strategies for safe, quality nursing care.[233]

Nurse Staffing and Clinical Outcomes

The nursing shortage of the 1980s dissipated in the 1990s as the penetration of managed care into major markets led to layoffs of nurses and their replacement with unlicensed personnel with comparatively little training. Nurses knew intuitively that patients were being harmed and launched public relations campaigns around "Every Patient Deserves an RN."[234] The publicity about nurses' concerns for patient safety attracted the attention of Congress, resulting in the Institute of Medicine conducting a study of nurse staffing in hospitals and nursing homes. Its report, *Nursing Staff in Hospitals and Nursing Homes: Is It Adequate?*, concluded that there was sufficient evidence on the impact of nurse staffing on nursing home outcomes to recommend improved staffing in long-term care facilities. Noting that the evidence linking nurse staffing with patient outcomes in hospitals was largely anecdotal, the report also called for research that would fill the gap.[235]

Among the first studies to respond to this challenge, two were particularly significant and garnered considerable attention. The first, by UCLA professor Jack Needleman and his colleagues, was published in the *New England Journal of Medicine* in 2002 and examined nursing care hours per patient day, differentiating between registered nurses, licensed practical nurses, and nurses' aides.[236] The authors reported that a higher *number* of overall nursing care hours and a higher *proportion* of nursing care hours provided by RNs resulted in shorter lengths of stay, lower rates of gastrointestinal bleeding and urinary tract infections. The higher proportion of RN hours regardless of overall nursing care hours was associated with lower rates of cardiac arrest, shock, sepsis, pneumonia, and deep vein thrombosis. These associations were not present for licensed practical nurses or nurses' aides.

Shortly afterwards, Linda Aiken, professor at the University of Pennsylvania School of Nursing, and her colleagues published a study in the *Journal of the American Medical Association* on the link between hospital nurse staffing and patient deaths, complications, nurse burnout, and job dissatisfaction. The study found that the addition of one patient to the average nurse's caseload increased the risk of a patient dying within 30 days of admission by 7% and increased the odds of nurse burnout by 23% and job dissatisfaction by 15%.[237]

Study after study has linked nursing care and adequate nurse staffing to improved clinical outcomes. Of 21 studies published between 2002 and 2006 included in a literature review, only three failed to find a significant relationship between nurse staffing and patient outcomes.[238] In 2007, the federal Agency for Healthcare Quality and Research released a review of 94 studies of nurse staffing between 1990 and 2006, and a meta-analysis of the association between staffing and clinical and financial outcomes. The review confirmed that nurse staffing affects patient mortality and "nurse sensitive" outcomes. An increase of one RN full-time equivalent in ICUs and surgical and medical units was associated with lower rates of patient mortality, hospital-acquired pneumonia, cardiac arrest, failure to rescue, unplanned extubations, and respiratory failure; and it shortened length of stay by 24% in ICUs and 31% in surgical patients. Although an increase in RN hours was associated with a reduced mortality rate, an increase in LPN hours actually increased the mortality rate.[239]

Patient satisfaction with care has become an important indicator of quality. Harvard School of Public Health professor Ashish Jha and his colleagues found that the ratio of nurses to patient days predicted patient ratings of the adequacy of pain management, communications about medications, and discharge, as well as the extent to which they would recommend the hospital to others, although they could not determine whether the relationship was causal.[240]

Nurse Staffing and Financial Outcomes

Hospital administrators, however, questioning the impact of improved nurse staffing on financial outcomes, claimed that they could not afford to hire more RNs. This is not an easy issue to address. Charges for nursing care in hospitals are not separately accounted for by billing but rather are included in the bundled cost of care for a specific diagnosis. In addition, *charges* for care may not be an accurate reflection of actual *costs*[241] and not all of the services that RNs provide can be captured in monetary terms.[242] What is the value of emotional support of a dying patient or their family?

Researchers have developed models and analytic techniques to measure nursing costs related to the care of patients,[243] including for specific conditions such as heart failure[244] or for specific treatments such as pain management.[245] But the challenge of studying the financial outcomes of nurse staffing may have resulted in relatively few researchers including this variable in their studies. A review of 117 studies on nurse staffing between 1983 and 2007 found that only 18 addressed financial outcomes.[246]

Nevertheless, the evidence in these 18 studies suggests that better nurse staffing may save money, depending upon how "better nurse staffing" is defined. For example, a study by Michael McCue, professor of health administration at Virginia Commonwealth University, and his colleagues found that a 1% increase in RN FTEs was associated with a 0.25% increase in operating costs but *without* a decrease in profits; whereas a 1% increase in non-RN FTEs increased operating costs only 0.18% but *reduced* profits by 0.21%.[247]

Using a different approach, Needleman and his colleagues examined the costs associated with three different models of improving nurse staffing: increasing the overall nursing care hours, increasing the proportion of nursing care hours provided by RNs, or doing both. They found that all three reduced length of stay, adverse events, and deaths. But increasing the proportion of nursing care hours provided by RNs actually lowered costs.[248]

Michael Rothberg, a physician and professor at Tufts University, and his colleagues compared the cost-effectiveness of various nurse staffing ratios (ranging from 4:1 patients per RN to 8:1) with other "safety interventions" for averting death. Although an HIV blood test was the most cost-effective intervention, 5:1 and 4:1 patient-to-nurse ratios were more cost-effective than thrombolytics for treatment of myocardial infarctions and Pap testing, leading the researchers to conclude that "[c]onsidered as a patient safety intervention, improved nurse staffing has a cost-effectiveness that falls comfortably within the range of other widely accepted interventions."[249]

By itself, the reduction in length of stay that is associated with higher proportions of RN staffing can account for these findings.[250,251] In addition, an increase in adverse events that is associated with reduced RN staffing hours can prolong length of stay and increase treatment costs.[252] These costs are expected to increase with payment rules promulgated in 2008 by the Centers for Medicare & Medicaid (CMS) stating that the federal government will no longer pay for treatment of hospital-acquired, preventable occurrences, such as certain infections and pressure ulcers. Private insurers are following suit. Many of these occurrences can be prevented by good nursing care.

Defining what "adequate nurse staffing" looks like for specific settings is challenging. The educational level of the nursing staff has been shown to be a factor in this definition; hospitals with a high proportion of RNs with a baccalaureate or higher degree are associated with better outcomes.[253] Aiken and her colleagues demonstrated that a 10% increase in the proportion of RNs with a baccalaureate or master's degree reduced the risk of mortality and failure to rescue by 5% each.[254]

In addition, the impact of *improving* nurse staffing depends upon an institution's existing level and mix of staffing.[255] Adding an RN to a unit that is well staffed may have a marginal impact on patient outcomes and end up having a negative effect on the unit's financial margin. On the other hand, adding that RN to a poorly staffed unit can reduce deaths, length of stay, adverse outcomes, and nurse turnover—all of which can improve the unit's financial picture.

Improving and Using Data on Nursing and Quality

Definitions and standardization of measures are crucial when studying nurse staffing and clinical outcomes; they are controversial as well. Needleman and colleagues measured nurse staffing in hours of care per patient day,[256] whereas Aiken and colleagues used mean caseload of patients for nurses providing hands-on care.[257] Some studies measured nurse staffing at the unit level and others at the hospital level, making comparisons suspect.

At the same time, researchers have refined the variables thought to be sensitive to nursing care. For example, "failure to rescue" became an important measure of the adequacy of the surveillance capacity of nurses. Defined as the "number of deaths in patients who developed an adverse occurrence among the number of patients who developed an adverse occurrence,"[258] the measure reflects whether staffing levels permit nurses to be in the presence of acutely ill patients for a long enough period of time to witness, evaluate, and respond to deteriorations in patients' conditions.

The development of nurse-sensitive outcomes has been essential for ongoing research and public reporting on the quality and safety of nursing care. The ANA has developed a National Database of Nursing Quality Indicators. It contains unit-level data from over 1,700 hospitals nationwide. The indicators, which are endorsed by the National Quality Forum, include: patient falls with and without injury; pressure ulcers whether community-, hospital- or unit-acquired; nursing skill mix; nursing hours per patient day; RN job satisfaction; RN perceptions of their practice environments; RN education and certification; pediatric pain assessment; pediatric IV filtration rate; psychiatric patient assault rate; use of restraints; nurse turnover; and nosocomial infections, such as ventilator-assisted pneumonia, central line–associated bloodstream infection, and catheter-associated urinary tract infections.[259]

The National Quality Forum has also been defining key indicators of quality in inpatient nursing care. In 2003, it released the "NQF 15", a set of process and outcome measures that are affected or provided by nursing personnel, and it called for public reporting on these measures.[260] In 2006, the Robert Wood Johnson Foundation launched the Nursing Quality Interdisciplinary Research Initiative to address the gaps in knowledge about nursing's effect on quality and identify opportunities for further research on the topic.

The Lewin Group's Timothy Dall and his colleagues argue that "the economic value of nursing is greater for payers than for individual healthcare facilities" because the impact of good hospital nursing care extends beyond the hospitalization.[261] Patients who are discharged with fewer complications, better prepared for self-care management, and with higher levels of functioning will have shorter recovery periods and less need for additional services.

Long-Term Care

An estimated 10.9 million people residing in the United States, half of them non-elderly, suffer from cognitive and mobility impairment and need help with activities of daily living.[262] Most receive assistance from unpaid family caregivers, but 13% receive long-term care services in their homes or communities from paid providers, largely through Medicare and Medicaid. Another 1.8 million people receive long-term care services in nursing homes. Whether in the community or a nursing home, long-term care is more likely to be provided by paid workers as the person ages and functional impairment increases.

Long-term care is largely nursing care delivered by providers ranging from family caregivers and personal care assistants who help with activities of daily living to advanced practice registered nurses who manage disabling conditions through medications and other interventions. Reports of poor outcomes, including injuries and deaths, in long-term care facilities led to federal and state regulations to improve staffing and other factors related to quality of care. The 1987 federal Nursing Home Reform Law required facilities to "protect and promote the rights of each resident," including the right to be protected from abuse and care that harms. The regulations set minimum nurse staffing standards that address skill mix and a minimum number of nursing care hours per resident.[263] However, enforcement of these regulations has been sorely lacking.[264] In 2008, the Inspector General of the Department of Health and Human Services reported that the percentage of nursing homes that had been cited for safety and health violations in 2007 ranged from 88.4% for non-profit homes to 93.5% for for-profit homes.[265]

Long-term care facilities rely heavily on certified nursing assistants and licensed practical nurses, but RNs are also needed. In many cases, the care is not as technically complex as that in acute care, but it can make the difference between life and death, disability and independence. Adequate nursing staff in skilled nursing facilities is associated with lower rates of death, dehydration, pressure ulcers, urinary tract infections, and antibiotic use, as well as more discharges to home and higher levels of functioning.[266] Although this finding does not just apply to RNs, the evidence is strongest for RN staffing.

Three Institute of Medicine reports have recommended improved nurse staffing in nursing homes.[267,268,269] But payment for care in long-term care facilities is unlikely to be sufficient to dramatically improve RN staffing beyond the 45 minutes per resident per day already called for in federal regulations. This includes managerial and administrative time, however, and research has found dramatic improvements in outcomes when RNs spend 30–40 minutes in direct patient care (see Figure 7).[270]

Charlene Harrington, a nurse and a professor emerita at the University of California, San Francisco, has argued that poor staffing in long-term care facilities is related to problems with payment; furthermore, the need to make a profit in investor-owned facilities can compromise staffing and quality of care.[271] The investor-ownership model has been found to have worse nurse staffing and poorer outcomes than nonprofit or public facilities.[272] The Affordable Care Act calls for transparency in nursing home ownership.

FIGURE 7. *Outcomes Associated with Average RN Time per Resident per Day*

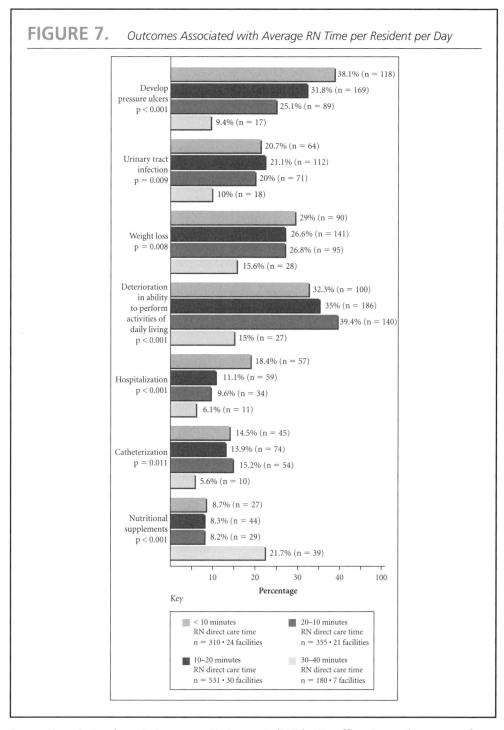

Source: Horn, S., Buerhaus, P., Bergstrom, N., Smout, R. (2005). RN staffing time and outcomes of long-stay nursing home residents. *American Journal of Nursing,105*(11), p. 61. Copyright © 2005 *American Journal of Nursing.* Used with permission. All rights reserved.

The aging of the U.S. population will increase the need for skilled care but the solution is not an all-RN nursing staff. Rather, there needs to be a mix that includes RNs, licensed practical nurses, and certified nursing assistants. In long-term care settings, RNs have been reluctant to expand the job responsibilities of unlicensed personnel, also referred to as direct-care workers; but if these personnel are adequately trained, have sufficient oversight and support, have reasonable caseloads, and are paid a decent wage with standard benefits and opportunities for promotion, excellence in long-term care is possible.[273]

In 2005, an expert consensus panel funded by the John A. Hartford Foundation called for increasing the use of APRNs in nursing homes. APRNs have been instrumental in developing home- and community-based models of long-term care that have improved quality of life and functionality for older people and led to fewer complications, at a cost that is comparable to or less than that of institutionalization. The cost savings are partly attributable to reductions in emergency department usage and hospitalizations. This has particular significance for health care costs given that emergency department usage between 1993 and 2003 increased by 34% for people aged 65 to 74 years and by 93% for blacks in this age group.[274]

Keeping older adults healthy with high levels of independent functioning and chronic care management is exemplified in these community-based models of long-term care developed by nurses:

LIFE. The University of Pennsylvania School of Nursing founded Living Independently for Elders (LIFE), a program to keep older adults out of nursing homes by providing comprehensive care with the primary site being an adult day-care center; however, the nurse practitioners, who are the primary care providers, follow the patients across settings, including in the home or a nursing home. Using an interdisciplinary team approach, the program has improved rates of falls, pressure ulcers, depression, and other adverse outcomes; reduced use of psychotropic medications; reduced nursing home admissions, lengths of stay and ER visits; and produced sound financial outcomes. It qualifies for capitated payment under Medicare and Medicaid as a PACE program, or Programs of All-Inclusive Care for the Elderly.[275,276]

Evercare. This program of Ovations/UnitedHealthcare was developed in 1987 by two nurse practitioners to provide care coordination for older adults across settings. Now in 35 states and adapted in the United Kingdom, Evercare uses nurse practitioners as key providers on an interdisciplinary team that focuses on helping older adults and their families to better manage their care, intervening early when signs of deteriorating health emerge, maintaining functioning and independence, and reducing mortality rates and health care costs. Evercare saves over $100,000 per nurse practitioner annually.[277,278]

Senior ASSIST. Assisting Seniors to Stay Independent through Services and Teaching is a Nebraska program started in 1987 for frail elderly who do not qualify for home care under Medicare but need more care than a primary care or physician's office can provide. Serving older adults who may have cognitive impairment and complex medical problems, the program has high patient and physician satisfaction, decreases hospital admissions and emergency room visits, and saves money.[279]

All of these alternatives use APRNs within a multidisciplinary team that may be led by the nurse. The efficient use of APRNs in long-term care settings requires removing barriers to full utilization and payment of APRNs, access to health information technology, integrating APRNs into accountable care organizations, and investing to scale-up the new models of long-term care.

Community-Based Care

The new models of community-based long-term care developed by nurses mark a shift away from the institutional models that have proved to be costly and mostly incompatible with a patient-centered, individualized philosophy of care. Just as society was seduced into thinking that high-tech care in institutions would cure all ills, so too was nursing. Acute care has dominated the nursing curriculum and few new graduates think of beginning their career anywhere except a hospital, if only for a year. Nonetheless, nursing has been the core of community-based care—from home health to public health to school health. The challenge is to prepare more nurses to shift from acute to community care and to push community-based health organizations to create the space for this shift.

Consider public health. Despite the rich history of public health nursing that began at the turn of the twentieth century with Lillian Wald, the role of public health nurses is threatened today. Escalating costs, unstable revenue streams, and funding silos for individual care can threaten the population-focused activities of public health departments.[280]

Many public health departments have ended or restricted programs that provided individual personal or illness care to the poor or uninsured, except when a problem threatens the whole community, as with infectious diseases that continue to be addressed through immunization programs.[281] The Wald model of nurses being *in* the community to provide individual care that informs population-based interventions to promote health is at risk of being lost.

Interestingly, the clinical aspects of public health agencies that encompass screening, treatments, maternal-child health, prevention, and personal care services are more likely to be included in an agency if a nurse is the senior executive. If a nonnurse or nonclinician is the senior executive or if there is a relatively low percentage of nurses on staff, the regulatory role and environmental health functions of a public health agency are more likely to dominate.[282]

Kevin Grumbach, a primary care physician and health policy expert at the University of California, San Francisco, and his colleagues studied public health nurses in California and concluded that they were not adequately addressing population- and community-level needs.[283] Nonetheless, caring for individuals in the community can provide important information for nursing the community as a whole as illustrated by the following examples:

Neighborhood Nursing

Visiting Nurse Services often assist with public health functions. In the 1990s, the Visiting Nurse Service of Central Jersey recognized that funding streams forced its nurses to function in programmatic silos rather than with a community focus. In the 1990s, it developed Neighborhood Nursing to foster a community focus to the work of its nurses who were already working in a community location. Nurses were assigned to be *the* nurse for a community and to work with the community to address its health-related priorities, whether fire safety, housing for the homeless, or educating community groups about HIV/AIDS prevention.[284]

Nurse-Managed Health Centers

Over the past three decades, more than 250 nurse-managed health centers have emerged to serve vulnerable and underserved populations across the country, usually as initiatives of schools of nursing, with initial funding support from HRSA's Division of Nursing. Most are interdisciplinary centers that combine primary care and aggregate-level assessments and interventions, with physicians serving as consultants or employees. Nurses manage and lead the centers, provide most of the primary care, and work with community boards to develop programs to promote the health of the community. An example is the Eleventh Street Family Health Service, affiliated with Drexel University and founded and directed by public health nurse Patricia Gerrity, which serves as the health home for over 6,000 residents of North Philadelphia. It combines interprofessional primary care with interventions such as a community garden tended by youth, cooking classes to teach culturally relevant approaches to better nutrition, and other services guided by a community advisory board. Nurse-managed health centers such as this one hold promise for expanding the nation's infrastructure of community health centers.

The Nurse-Family Partnership

The Nurse Family Partnership is another model of public health that is spreading across the country and was showcased in a 2006 *New Yorker* story, "Swamp Nurse," about the work of Luwana Marts, a nurse who works in the program in Louisiana.[285] The aim of the program is to reduce the risk of at-risk, poor, first-time mothers and their infants. The program follows pregnant women and their newborns through the age of two.[286] Nurses visit the women in their homes, assess their physical and psychosocial health status and resources, assess the newborns' health, examine ways to improve mother–baby bonding and parenting skills, and counsel the women on self-care issues that aim to empower them to make better life and health decisions. Its focus is primarily on the care of individuals and families rather than the community as a whole; but public health departments such as New York City's are viewing the program as a way to reduce the health risks associated with poverty.

The outcomes of the Nurse-Family Partnership programs include reduced second pregnancies, child abuse, and arrests; and increased likelihood of education and employment of the mother, the father being present in the home, and more time between pregnancies. The average return on every dollar spent on the program is estimated to be $5.70 for higher-risk mothers and $1.26 for lower-risk mothers.[287]

Whether non-RNs can provide the same quality of care as RNs is a subject of debate. Federal support to spread such home visitation programs doesn't specify that nurses provide this care. But the Nurse-Family Partnership's founders, David Olds and Harriet Kitzman, a nurse, have argued that the model relies upon nurses' expertise and skill and have provided supporting evidence.[288]

School Health Nursing

Nurses are the mainstay of school health services. School nursing has existed for over a century but suffers from a lack of research documenting its impact and from inadequate and unstable funding that is characteristic of school health in general.[289,290] When state and local budgets are restricted, school nurse positions are likely to be cut. Even during financially stable times, school nurse positions may be insufficient for doing more than mandatory screening and first aid.

There are over 75,000 school nurses in the country; but over 37% of these work part-time, and 50% of public schools have no full-time registered nurse.[291,292] The National Association of School Nurses recommends the following nurse-to-student ratios:

- 1:750 for students in the general population

- 1:225 in the student populations that may require daily professional school nursing services or interventions

- 1:125 in student populations with complex health care needs

- 1:1 may be necessary for individual students who require daily and continuous professional nursing services[293]

Few school systems meet these ratios.[294] Some schools are expecting teachers to provide the routine health care that is needed by children who may have chronic illnesses or be disabled—a population that has grown since the federal and state governments removed barriers to disabled children attending public schools. This care can be complex and time-consuming, and school nurses are essential for managing and preventing the growing prevalence of asthma, diabetes, obesity, and other conditions among school-aged children.

APRNs may be school nurses but sometimes are not able to practice to the full scope of their practice because the school district does not want the additional liability that accompanies diagnosing illnesses and prescribing first-level treatment before referring. If APRNs were able to practice to the full scope of the law, they could provide underserved families with access to health care, bill for their services, and generate revenues to cover the cost of care.

Experimentation with different models of school health services is needed. In recognition that the school may provide the only point of access to health care for some children and their families, the National Nursing Center Consortium has proposed expanding nurse-managed health centers to schools. School-based health centers already exist in some communities and provide an infrastructure for expanding access to primary care.[295,296] Telehealth may enable some school systems to improve services despite understaffing of nurses or physicians.[297]

Gender and Power

In 1983, Claire Fagin and Donna Diers, then deans of the schools of nursing at the University of Pennsylvania and Yale University, respectively, wrote a commentary in the *New England Journal of Medicine* about the visibly discomforting and disturbing reactions that some people had at cocktail parties when someone was introduced as a nurse.[298] Such a pronouncement is a conversation stopper, they argued, probably because nursing is a metaphor for notions such as motherhood (nurturing and caring—not an appropriate topic for business or professional discussions in mixed company), class struggles (most nurses work in hierarchical settings where the top dogs are physicians or administrators), unseemly intimacy ("Nurses do for others publicly what healthy persons do for themselves privately"), equality (treating all patients the same regardless of their station in life rather than embracing a hierarchy of power and position), and conscience (reminding physicians of their fallibility). Despite the discomfort that these metaphors can create in some venues, Fagin and Diers suggested that the metaphors may represent the very reasons why some people are drawn to the profession. And yet, although few physicians would fail to clearly identify themselves as such, contemporary nurses may hide their identity because of the reactions they encounter.

These reactions are socially constructed and framed by nursing traditionally and currently being a predominantly female profession. As noted earlier, society has expected women and nurses to do nursing work but refused to value it sufficiently, as reflected in low status, poor pay, and subservient views of the role. Columbia University professor Sheila Rothman has pointed out that as long as women worked in places with meager wages and few resources, no one cared. Once they started to receive better pay, authority, and power in their positions, the work became more attractive to men. In the early 1900s, nurses held sufficient power to advocate safe care in hospitals and forge new initiatives in the community and home setting, where they functioned independently.[299,300] It was not uncommon for a nurse to direct a hospital, as Sophia Palmer did at the Rochester General Hospital before becoming editor-in-chief of the *American Journal of Nursing* in 1900. As hospitals proliferated with funding from the Hill Burton Act in 1946, they became complex organizations with extensive resources at their command and nurse leaders were often replaced with men who were physicians and, later, business executives.

Rothman provides another example of this shift in power and control. In the early 1900s, nurses were providing care to the poor on the Lower East Side of Manhattan when no health services were available to the community. Few physicians cared, as the nurses were paid meager wages mostly through donations from private philanthropists. In 1921, Congress passed the Sheppard-Towner Act to reduce maternal and infant mortality. It provided support for prenatal and child health clinics that used nurses to deliver care that emphasized hygiene, nutrition, and health education. As the success of this reform movement took hold, physicians expanded their private practices to include these services for individuals and Sheppard-Towner was ended. Rothman concludes: "The defeat of Sheppard-Towner marked the end of female expertise in the field of health care and, at the same time, shifted the provision of preventive health services from the public to the private sector."[301]

Today, this shift in power and control continues. For example, nurses have been involved in integrative or holistic health care since the days of Nightingale and more so since the 1970s when Martha Rogers, director of the nursing program at New York University, developed a theory of nursing that was based upon quantum physics and provided a framework for modalities such as therapeutic touch, imagery, and movement therapy.[302,303] In the 1990s, some insurers began to pay for alternative or integrative health services. Today, integrative health services are headed by physicians and many have no nurses on staff.

Nurses were highly respected in their communities until the women's movement of the 1960s when feminists viewed nursing (and other female-dominated professions) as something that smart, savvy women didn't do.[304] Nurses took on a mantle of a powerless and oppressed group, despite their being more educated than ever before, taking on more complex roles, and becoming scientists.[305] In fact, nursing became committed to ensuring that it met the criteria for being deemed a "profession" by prevailing standards. At the same time, the women's movement emboldened many nurses to challenge society's diminished view of their work. They persisted in power struggles within and outside of the profession to advocate better education of nurses, control of their practice without undue restrictions and barriers, and challenging others to value nursing and its importance in the health care system—struggles that continue today.

The classic example of how this power struggle has been played out is in the nurse-physician relationship—a longstanding point of contention that persists. In 1967, physician Leonard Stein wrote about the "Doctor-Nurse Game" in the *Archives of General Psychiatry*—a bold physician pointing out to his colleagues that the communication games nurses had to play to assuage the position and egos of some physicians didn't serve either profession or patients well.[306] Nurses who knew what was wrong with a patient or what medication needed to be ordered could not forthrightly share their recommendations without being viewed as insubordinate or offensive. Instead, they would make "suggestions" or pose a question to the physician. It was deemed inappropriate for a nurse to assume that she had more knowledge or wisdom than a physician. The deference of nurses to physicians also took the form of nurses standing up for physicians who arrived on the unit and even giving them their seats.

Thirty-five years later, physician Alan Rosenstein and VHA colleague Michelle O'Daniel reported on what had become a consequence of nurses' evolving unwillingness to continue to play this game: the abusive behavior by physicians was perceived by both groups as being a threat to the safety of patients and affecting the retention of nurses.[307,308] The issue was serious enough for The Joint Commission (the accrediting body for hospitals and other health care facilities) to issue a directive requiring facilities to establish "zero tolerance" policies and procedures on abusive behavior among employees and anyone authorized to practice under the facilities' auspices.[309]

Class issues also come into play in shaping society's views of nurses, since nurses rarely come from upper-class families. Nurses historically have engaged in intimate work that breaks down class boundaries at the bedside—nurses care for people of all socio-economic classes and hold an ethic that rejects class-bound differences in the care they provide. Regardless of the patient's social class, gender, race, ethnicity, or religious prefer-ence, the nurse controls the encounter. Once nurses leave the bedside, however, this ethic of classlessness and control no longer operates in the same way. Whether in relation to physicians, hospital administrators, policymakers or others in positions of power, relatively few nurses have been able to muster the authority to break through class boundaries and become full participants in the negotiations that determine the fate of their profession.

In 1973, Jane Ashley, a professor at Boston College's Connell School of Nursing, wrote about the continuing power struggles that nurses encountered in trying to break out of ste-reotypical views: "Although many nurses hold positions of potential leadership and power and engage in constant decision making, few are recognized as appropriate participants in policy decisions."[310] Unfortunately, this view continues to resonate with contemporary nursing, forcing nurses to grapple with the gendered, historical context of the profession. Today, this context frames many issues, including:

- Nursing remains a predominantly female profession with nursing school enrollments being 90% women; women now constitute half of the enrollees in medical schools in the nation.[311]

- There continue to be calls for more evidence of nurses' worth, despite overwhelming evidence in support of their impact on the outcomes of care.

■ Nurses' relative invisibility in society has extended to the media. In 1997, the Woodhull Study on Nursing and the Media, commissioned by Sigma Theta Tau International Nursing Honorary Society to examine nursing's representation by news media, found that nurses were included in relevant news stories only 4% of the time. Captions for photos that included nurses often failed to name the nurse. Worse, health care trade publications such as *Modern Healthcare* used nurses as sources only 1% of the time.[312] Since this report, journalists have increasingly turned to nurses as expert sources, and news media are somewhat more willing to report on studies published in the *American Journal of Nursing* and other nursing journals.

■ Nurses are underrepresented on governing boards of health-related organizations, including hospitals. Lawrence Prybil, professor emeritus at the University of Iowa College of Public Health, and his colleagues studied 123 nonprofit, community hospital systems and found that only 2.3% of hospital board members were nurses; 22.6% were physicians. Only 0.8% of chief nursing officers were voting members of the board, compared with 5.1% of vice presidents for medical affairs and 42.7% of chiefs of staff.[313,314]

■ Nurses continue to struggle to be included at key policymaking and advisory bodies. During the first decade of this century, not a single nurse served on the New York City HIV/AIDS Commission despite the call for such an appointment from the nursing community and the availability of nurses who were experts on HIV/AIDS.

These are not simply matters of parity. During a time when the nation is focused on how to make health care more accessible, safe, cost-effective, and relevant to people's needs, society loses when it fails to tap into the expertise of its largest health profession.

Why haven't nurses made more progress in creating social conditions that enable their expertise to be tapped? Although gender- and class-bound views of nursing may account for society's biases about nurses' place in decision making about health care, nurses have to own their fate. A 2010 Gallup survey of the perceptions of health care opinion leaders regarding nursing's leadership in health care reform noted that too many nurses don't want to assume the mantle of leaders in health care and that nursing seldom presents a single unified voice on policy matters.[315] With over 120 national nursing organizations, unity is no easy feat. Most nursing curricula now include content on health policy and politics, helping to raise nurses' expectations for full participation in health care decision-making.

But nursing's views of and effectiveness in political action and shaping health policy have waxed and waned over the years. Sally Cohen, a professor in the University of New Mexico College of Nursing and senior fellow at the University's Robert Wood Johnson Center for Health Policy, and her colleagues described various stages of nursing's political development that ranged from becoming aware of the importance of politics and power for the profession's self-interests to leading on addressing the broader health and social issues of the day. The authors noted that the profession's movement through these stages has been uneven, probably owing to an internalization of its historical, second-class role in health care.[316]

Cohen and her colleagues and others outside the nursing profession, such as the 1995 Pew Health Professions Commission, have argued that the profession needs to do a better job of preparing nurses to lead.[317] Efforts are under way to do so. For over 25 years, the Wharton Business School has offered a program to give senior nursing executives the administrative and leadership knowledge to become more effective leaders. In 1997, the Robert Wood Johnson Foundation created the Nurse Executive Fellows program to train mid-career leaders. The American Academy of Nursing has created several fellowships for nurse leaders, including one at the Institute of Medicine and another at AARP. Nurse Leaders in the Boardroom, supported by the Robert Wood Johnson Foundation in partnership with AARP's Center for Championing Nursing in America, assists nurses in acquiring appointments to nonprofit boards and other influential advisory positions at the state level.

Real gains in tapping nurses' expertise will arise from partnerships between nursing and the public. The AARP Center for Championing Nursing in America has created an innovative partnership between nurses and consumers that promises to support this quest for advancing nursing's interests and leadership role in health care. In early 2010, AARP's Public Policy Institute announced that the organization had included in its policy agenda removing barriers to APRNs' practice. In 1987, Susan Reverby concluded her classic study of caring, womanhood, and nursing with these thoughts:

> If nursing can achieve the power to practice altruism with autonomy, all of us have much to gain. Nursing has always been a much conflicted metaphor in our culture, reflecting all the ambivalences we give to the meaning of womanhood. Perhaps in the future it can give this metaphor and, ultimately, caring, new value in all our lives.[318]

This will only happen through the vision and concerted action of nurses and others concerned with access to high-quality, affordable health care.

OPPORTUNITIES: A VISION FOR THE FUTURE

The underlying premise of this chapter is that nurses and their work are essential for the health of the nation. This should be intuitive, but the profession has had to prove it over and over again. An overwhelming body of evidence demonstrates the benefits of adequate nurse staffing and APRN care. Moreover, the innovative models of care that nurses have developed speak to their understanding of the health needs of people and their vision for meeting those needs.

Innovative Models of Care

In 2006, the American Academy of Nursing initiated the Raise the Voice Campaign, funded in part by the Robert Wood Johnson Foundation, to identify and make visible innovative models of care developed by nurses for which there are positive clinical and financial outcome data. Those nurse-innovators who developed the models are called Edge Runners. As of 2010, there were close to 50 Edge Runners. Whether designated as Edge Runners or not, nurses have been in the forefront of developing innovative models of care. Some of these models have been discussed already, including Senior ASSIST, Evercare, and LIFE. Others include:

Childbirthing Centers
Freestanding childbirthing centers were developed by certified nurse midwives to provide a "normal" delivery experience, enabling women and families to labor and birth in

a home-like setting without fetal monitoring, epidurals, and unnecessary episiotomies. Only low-risk women are eligible, and the centers have hospital backup for those women and babies at high risk. Women are educated and empowered to be in charge of their birthing experiences, to attend to their own health through nutrition and exercise, to breastfeed, and to prepare for the new addition to the family.

Today, there are over 195 childbirthing centers in the country. Two Cochrane Collaboration reviews have concluded that midwifery care, including childbirthing centers, improves outcomes for mother and infants, including higher rates of breastfeeding, reduced hospitalization rates, and reduced infant mortality.[319,320] Childbirthing centers have been endorsed by the American College of Obstetricians and Gynecologists. The National Association of Childbirthing Centers reviews and accredits childbirthing centers, thus attesting to their quality. Childbirthing centers could be the frontline maternity service for women if payment were at a sustainable level.

Transitional Care
When patients are about to be discharged from a hospital, they and their family caregivers may feel frightened and unprepared to manage symptoms that may worsen. Although hospitals give lip service to discharge planning, the reality is that payment for preparing patients and family caregivers for the transition to home is minimal or nonexistent, offering little incentive to spend time on it. This can lead to patients returning to the hospital. Twenty percent of all Medicare discharges from hospitals result in readmission within 30 days; 67% of patients with medical conditions and 51% of those who had surgery were readmitted or died within a year of the hospitalization. The cost of these rehospitalizations was estimated at $17.4 billion in 2004.[321]

Over 20 years ago, Mary Naylor, a nurse, researcher, and professor at the University of Pennsylvania, and her colleagues at the school of nursing began to test what is now known as the Transitional Care Model that uses nurse practitioners to ease the transition from hospital to home. Initially, the model targeted low-birthweight infants' transition to home. Subsequently, Naylor adapted the model for older adults with multiple chronic illnesses.[322] The nurse practitioner clarifies the patient's and family member's health needs, priorities, and goals during the hospitalization, evaluates and reconciles medications, coordinates multiple specialty services, and prepares the patient and family caregiver for managing care at home. Once the patient is discharged, the nurse practitioner makes a home visit within 48 hours—a crucial period when patients and family caregivers become concerned about symptoms that may worsen from the stress of the discharge day. The nurse practitioner continues to visit the patient and family, guiding them in managing both the remnants of the acute illness and the daily challenges of living with a chronic illness. The duration of the service varies with the needs of the patient and family caregiver, but usually last no more than 90 days.

Naylor and colleagues have documented that the Transitional Care Model improves the quality of life and physical functioning, increases the time from discharge to first readmission or death, and decreases readmission rates. Looking at all costs during a year except out-of-pocket patient expenses and medications, a conservative cost analysis showed a savings of $5,000 per Medicare beneficiary.[323]

Aetna and Kaiser Permanente have been testing variations on the services and providers (for example, baccalaureate-prepared RN versus APRN). AARP recognized that transitional care is valuable for its members and worked to ensure that the Affordable Care Act of 2010 included support for demonstration projects on transitional care.

Nurse-Managed Centers

The nation has 1,067 community health centers that operate 6,700 clinics for medical, dental, and mental health care to about 16 million low-income and uninsured people. President Obama sees their expansion as key to providing access to primary care for the growing number of people who will be insured after the Affordable Care Act.[324] That act authorizes funding to expand and evaluate nurse-managed centers, which could be a model for increasing access to primary care; however, the funding still has to be appropriated by Congress.

For over two decades, HRSA has offered grants to schools of nursing to establish nurse-managed clinics for underserved populations. These could also serve as clinical teaching sites. Today, there are over 250 nurse-managed clinics across the nation providing interdisciplinary health services to individuals, families, and communities.

Nurse-managed centers vary in their level of sophistication and success. Some have struggled to get paid by Medicaid managed care plans and private insurers that may not credential APRNs. Some have closed while others have gone on to become federally qualified health centers, providing them with enhanced payments. Some of the best centers don't have this status but could if the following changes were made:

1. *Removing the requirement that federally qualified health centers be governed by a 51% consumer-majority board.* Most centers fall under the governance structure of a university, which is not dominated by community members. This criterion could be modified for university-affiliated health centers. Another alternative would be for the federal government to develop regulations that treat nurse-managed centers as the safety net provider that most are, paying them more but without the same governance requirement.

2. *Payment for APRN services, credentialing by insurers, and being designated as qualified to lead a health or medical home.* Eleven nurse managed centers in Pennsylvania applied for medical home designation by the National Commission on Quality Assurance in 2009. The designation was denied because they met all of the criteria except one: the centers were not physician-led—despite their having physicians as consultants or employees. In 2010, The Joint Commission announced that it would be competing with NCQA to grant medical home designation and its criteria did not include that the home be physician-led. Subsequently, NCQA granted the medical home designation belatedly to the nurse-managed centers that had applied in 2009.

3. *Providing the center with financial support for infrastructure development*, including health information technology.

Convenient Care Clinics

Retail, or convenient care, clinics have emerged as a way to increase people's access to services that focus on the diagnosis and treatment of common conditions, such as upper respiratory infections and influenza, without appointments and at convenient hours for working families. Staffed primarily by nurse practitioners, there are now approximately 1,200 retail clinics serving over 3.5 million people.

Retail clinics came under attack by physicians who claimed that they provided inferior care, interfered with patients' relationships with primary care providers, missed opportunities for preventive care such as immunizations, and didn't save money since they probably resulted in more prescriptions being written to be filled at the retail stores' pharmacies. Ateev Mehrotra, a physician and policy analyst at RAND, and his colleagues have refuted these charges in papers published in *Health Affairs* and the *Annals of Internal Medicine.*[325,326] Despite this, there continue to be efforts to restrict the practice of retail clinics.[327]

Promoting Health and Wellness

A number of nursing innovations focus on prevention and wellness:

- *The Chicago Parent Program.* This program was developed by Deborah Gross, a professor of nursing at Johns Hopkins University, and an interdisciplinary team in collaboration with African American and Latino parents with funding from the National Institute of Nursing Research. It provides a culturally specific 12-week training course on parenting for low-income, ethnic minority parents delivered in day-care centers. It uses videotaped vignettes to illustrate children's behavioral problems and ways that parents can address them, along with group discussions of the principles and applications of the approaches. A parent group advised on the design of the training, scenarios for videotaping, and other aspects of the program.[328,329,330]

  A study that compared baseline and one-year outcomes of the program with a control group found that the program benefited both parents and their children. At an estimated cost of under $300 per child, it has produced more than a 900% return on that investment. Although the program needs longer follow-up, its outcomes to date speak to the potential for interdisciplinary teams to help people to improve their parenting skills and give children a better start. The model has been adopted by the Mayo Clinic and Chicago Head Start.

- *Health InterConnexions.* This program uses nurses as coaches to help employees change their health behaviors and monitor their health outcomes. Targeting the 60–80% of employees who are considered to have unhealthy lifestyles, the program engages employees in assessing and monitoring their health risk using online tools and objective measures of their health status (such as weight and body mass index), identifies actual or potential health problems, sets health goals with employees, and provides in-person coaching sessions to help them change their health habits. The program has reduced employer and employee health care costs, reduced employees' health risk, and reduced sick leave.[331]

- *Sister-to-Sister HIV Risk Reduction.* Based upon multiple NIH-funded studies, Loretta Sweet Jemmott and John Jemmott from the University of Pennsylvania School of Nursing and Annenberg School for Communication, respectively, have developed a 20-minute intervention provided by nurses and other health care providers to help women visiting health centers develop the knowledge and skills to reduce their HIV risk. Sister-to-Sister emphasizes negotiated condom use and knowledge about HIV transmission and prevention using videos, exercises, and discussion and uses African American nurses to provide the intervention at primary care clinics.

The program's outcomes include increased condom use, reduced incidence of unprotected sex and of sexually transmitted diseases.[332] It was selected by the Centers for Disease Control and Prevention as a "best-evidence" HIV prevention intervention.

These and other nurse-led innovations hold promise for the nation's mandate to reduce the burden of illness in financial and humans terms. But they are challenged to fulfill this promise for several reasons.

First, they often lack the kind of visibility that will bring the work to the attention of policymakers. Second, regulations developed to protect the public against unsafe care present barriers to nurses (and others) who try to innovate with new models of care delivery. Third, financial support is needed to scale-up many of these innovations. Fourth, the American Academy of Nursing's Raise the Voice Campaign discovered that some nurse-led innovations lacked the clinical and financial outcome data necessary for spreading beyond a single site. An investment is needed in developing nurses' knowledge and skill in defining and selecting key outcome measures, designing data-collection and analysis systems and procedures, and conducting controlled clinical trials.

Ensuring that the Nation Fully Utilizes Its Nursing Workforce

In 1991, over 60 national nursing organizations signed onto *Nursing's Agenda for Health Care Reform*, a statement of nursing's beliefs about what the U.S. health care system should look like.[333] The agenda included an emphasis on community-based primary care services using the most cost-effective providers and interventions and supporting consumer responsibility for self-care and personal health. In 2008, the ANA reaffirmed the agenda.

This vision of the 60 national nursing organizations is not one that puts technology and acute care first. Rather, trusting, knowing relationships between people and their health care providers—whether nurses, APRNs, social workers, physicians, nursing assistants, or family caregivers—are primary. Nurses excel at building these relationships in order to promote health, whether that means helping people to change their behaviors, assisting the sick to recover, or allowing the dying to experience a peaceful death.

What is needed to ensure that the nation is fully utilizing the talents of the nursing workforce?

1. *Ensure an adequate supply of well-prepared nurses in ways that go beyond simply increasing their numbers. This should entail clearly redefining nurses' roles according to their educational preparation, developing data-driven strategies for workforce development and deployment, transforming nursing education, and requiring residency programs in all settings for new nurses.*

   Although a growing number of states have offices or centers that analyze nursing workforce data and promote workforce development, inconsistencies in the types of data and how they are collected have challenged national and state planning efforts. A Forum of State Nursing Workforce Centers was developed in 2005 to share workforce information and strategies; as of 2009, 33 states were participating. The Forum has developed a Minimum Dataset Project to set standards for consistent data definition and collection and to serve as a central repository for nursing workforce data. Expanding this capacity across all states is essential to inform both state and national workforce strategies. HRSA could take a leading role in supporting such efforts as it addresses national objectives and policies for ensuring an adequate nursing and health care workforce.

As the nursing workforce becomes more educated, it becomes more diverse in its capabilities. The number of nurses with clinical or research doctorates will increase. Although the proportion of nurses with baccalaureate degrees is likely to increase, the demand for nurses will continue to support associate degree preparation as one route of entry into practice. The BSN in 10 or even the MSN in 10 are opportunities to provide educational support for people who may not be able to afford four years of undergraduate education. Such statutory requirements may not be necessary if employers give preferential hiring to nurses with baccalaureate and higher degrees, as has occurred since the 2008 recession; but when the demand for nurses increases beyond the supply, this solution will fall short as employers struggle to fill vacant positions.

We'll end up with either unsafe care or underutilization of well-prepared nurses if we fail to differentiate among the practice roles and responsibilities of nurses with differing levels of educational preparation and experience. As the need for nurses grows with the aging population and the nation puts more emphasis on primary care and chronic care management, we must weave a new tapestry of health care provider roles and responsibilities. Such redefinitions must consider how to capitalize on the knowledge and skills of registered nurses, advanced practice registered nurses, certified nursing assistants, and family caregivers, as well as those of physicians and other health care providers.

This will also require that nursing get rid of its own traditional barriers to full utilization of LPNs and nursing assistants and adopt a competency-based approach to their roles and functions. This is unlikely to occur without movement toward dismantling the barriers between nursing and medicine. As AARP champions improved access to affordable, high-quality care, its support of removing barriers to APRNs is accompanied by calls for better use of LPNs and nursing assistants, which represents a smart move forward for nursing and consumers.

Redefining and developing competency-based approaches to all health care providers' roles could be priorities of the new National Workforce Commission that is part of the Affordable Care Act of 2010. The Commission should seek to align the health care workforce with needed shifts in health care delivery. Such redefinition could also occur within hospitals, home care agencies, community health centers, occupational health offices, and all health care organizations. The availability of funding for demonstration projects that explore modified roles for health care providers as prioritized by the Commission could stimulate such local discussions and tests of change. In addition, the Commission could evaluate, test, and disseminate best practices for recruiting, preparing, and retaining more ethnic minority, low-income, and rural providers, and, for nursing, more men. But a visionary approach by this Commission will require that its membership include workforce leaders in the various health care disciplines, including nursing, along with individuals who are not vested in traditional models of professional education and practice. In 2010, nurse Peter Buerhaus was appointed to chair the Commission, but Congress had not appropriated its funding.

Preparing this workforce requires new approaches to nursing education. The 2010 Carnegie report on nursing education provides direction for better integrating clinical and didactic education and developing the clinical judgment and reasoning skills in new nurses across settings. As the health care system shifts to a greater emphasis on primary care, chronic care management, and population-based care, nursing education will need support to innovate with curricula. With Congressional support through Title VIII funding, HRSA can target resources to stimulate such innovation, as it has in the past through its Division of Nursing.

But it's also unrealistic to expect that any new graduate can withstand the first year of practice and function fully without additional guidance and support. Residencies should be required of all new nurses and these should be available in all clinical settings, rather than continuing the expectation that nurses must cut their teeth in the acute care setting. Similar approaches could also help experienced nurses transition to new settings, return to practice after a hiatus, or move into new roles after obtaining graduate preparation as APRNs.

2. *Create and maintain supportive work environments for nurses in which their authority matches their responsibilities, ensuring that they are key members of the health care team, and lead the team when it is appropriate for them to do so.*

The Magnet Recognition program and Transforming Care at the Bedside have shown how to retain nurses and engage them fully in professional nursing work, but too few hospitals and other facilities have acquired the Magnet designation or seek to do so. The new Medicare and Medicaid Center for Innovation could fund multisite comparative studies of the outcomes of Magnet facilities. Magnet designation could be associated with enhanced reimbursement under Medicare and Medicaid. Although some data on the impact of Magnet status on provider retention and quality of care are available, more is needed to substantiate an investment of public monies to stimulate other facilities to pursue the qualities and characteristics that mark the designation. Long-term care facilities and home care agencies could be encouraged to apply for Magnet status with enhanced Medicaid and Medicare reimbursement rates as incentives. Better teamwork among nurses, physicians, and other health care providers will only come with team education within universities and health care organizations. Its relationship to patient safety suggests that an investment in teamwork by health care organizations, insurers, and government would reap benefits by improving clinical outcomes and reducing errors and preventable facility-acquired conditions. Interprofessional team education may also help to reduce the longstanding tensions between nursing and medicine.

The leadership of these teams should be driven by the needs of the population being served and the skills and knowledge of the team members. For example, a master's-prepared social worker with substantial clinical experience may be the best person to lead an interdisciplinary team that is caring for the chronically mentally ill.

3. *Shift funding for research from continuing to demonstrate what we already know— that nursing care produces good clinical and financial outcomes—to delineating the best nursing skill mix for specific populations and settings and including nursing interventions in comparative effectiveness research.*

There continue to be calls for more data to substantiate nursing's specific contribution to improving clinical outcomes in all settings. But nursing is being held to a different standard to prove its worth. Consider the case of hospitalists. Hospitalists are physicians who are hired by hospitals to manage inpatient hospital care for a specific group of patients, such as patients on an oncology unit. Today, there are over 20,000 hospitalists and the demand exceeds the supply. But there is a paucity of research on the outcomes of their practice. In 2007, Peter Lindenauer, the director of the Baystate Medical Center, and his colleagues published in the *New England Journal of Medicine* the first multisite study of the clinical and financial outcomes of hospitalist compared with general internists and family physicians at 45 hospitals. Hospitalists decreased length of stay by an average of 0.4 days and reduced the cost of care by $125 per patient. There was no change in mortality rate or hospital readmissions.[334] Despite these modest outcomes, Laurence McMahon, professor of health policy and management at the University of Michigan School of Public Health, in a commentary in the same issue of the journal, wrote, "The field of hospital medicine is here to stay, so we need to move past studies of costs and outcomes and focus on relevant patient care and systems questions. . . ."[335] It's time for the same to be said about nursing.

Certainly, refining our understanding of the dose and type of nursing care that is needed for specific outcomes could be helpful in shaping what nurses do and how they are used, and more research is needed on how to improve staffing when there are limited financial and human resources.[336] Research on determining the best skill mix to deliver care and scaling-up nursing innovations in care should be high priorities if we are to shift the focus of health care from acute care to health promotion and prevention.

Nursing research is focused squarely on the most important challenges facing our health care system today—promoting health and managing symptoms and chronic conditions. As such, the National Institute for Nursing Research budget should be increased at least ten-fold. This funding should support investigation of the important clinical questions that are likely to be asked by researchers from many disciplines, including by a growing cadre of doctorate-prepared nurses.

4. *Develop a national standard for scope of practice, education, and credentialing of advanced practice registered nurses and remove statutory and regulatory barriers to full utilization of APRNs.*

Given that APRNs, working independently in some states, provide care of comparable safety and quality to physicians, Medicare and Medicaid should set a consistent evidence-based standard of APRN practice. The Consensus Document on Licensure, Accreditation, Certification, and Education developed by the National Council of State Boards of Nursing and other national nursing organizations provides a blueprint for standardizing these four areas related to APRN practice. Although the standards can be adopted state by state, a national scope of practice law could eliminate or minimize the political conflicts that will undoubtedly ensue with an individual state strategy. The state boards of nursing would retain the responsibility for ensuring that APRNs practicing within their borders have the federally prescribed education and credentials and for handling complaints and disciplinary action.

A national scope of practice law is likely to be accompanied by its own political battles. It would have to reflect the most progressive state nurse practice acts. Otherwise, there is a risk that the law could erect new barriers to the practice of nurses in states that permit independent practice. A federal directive could accomplish much the same until state laws are rectified. Such a directive would specify that any health care organization receiving funding from Medicare or Medicaid must follow a federal definition of APRN scope of practice, effectively overriding state laws, much as occurs now in the Indian Health Service, military facilities, and the Veterans Health Administration.

In addition to addressing how APRN practice is defined, CMS can quickly correct regulatory language that serves to exclude APRNs from functioning within the full range of their scope of education and practice, such as including APRNs as providers who can order home health and hospice services. And in lieu of other federal action, financial incentives under Medicaid or through workforce development funds from HRSA could be provided to states that adopt national standards for licensure, accreditation, certification, and education and remove state barriers to APRN practice.

5. *Develop private and public support for evaluating, sustaining, and spreading nursing innovations in care.*

The Affordable Care Act leaves much work to be undertaken in order to reform health care into accessible, affordable, equitable, high-quality approaches to promoting the health of individuals, families, and communities. It fails to cover all who live in this country, ensuring the continuing need for safety-net health care services such as nurse-managed centers and retail clinics. The Center for Innovation established by the Act provides an opportunity to expand nursing innovations and explore their operations in concert with accountable care organizations and bundled payments for care across settings. Nursing care and nurses' roles should be addressed in any proposal submitted for funding by the Center for Innovation or justification provided for its exclusion. It should no longer be acceptable for national and state foundations and government-sponsored demonstration projects to exclude nurse-led models of care simply because they are nurse-led, as CMS did with medical home demonstration projects.

The National Health Insurance Exchange that will be established under the Act should require that all applicant insurers credential APRNs and pay them for their services at the full physician rate.

6. *Include nurses on every health-related advisory group at the local, state, and national level.*

Few advisory groups on health care—whether governing boards of nonprofit healthcare organizations, workforce commissions, payment reform commissions, public health committees or boards of health—would operate without physician members. Why would they operate without nurses, since these essential providers can bring so much to the table?

It is not sufficient to have a token nurse on such advisory groups. Nurses are a diverse group whether by clinical role, specialty practice, setting, education, or other characteristic. Merely seeking parity in numbers with physicians would turn this aim into a numbers game; it should not be. Rather, the aim of nursing membership should be to capture different and creative perspectives on health matters.

■ ■ ■

Building local support for nursing can help to identify and develop nurse leaders prepared to be at the table. The Robert Wood Johnson Foundation, in partnership with Northwest Foundation, developed the Partners Investing in Nursing's Future program to stimulate and direct local philanthropic support for nursing. Although usually thought of in terms of financial support, local foundations are often influential members of their communities and have the opportunity to open doors for nurses, ask why nurses are not appointed to an advisory group, and provide support for helping nurses in their communities develop the skills to be knowledgeable advisers.

Consumers can also advocate better nursing representation on advisory groups. Whether as part of the local AARP chapter or parent-teachers association, consumers can support calls for the participation of nurses in health care deliberations. But nurses can't wait for others to advocate for them. It's incumbent upon nurses at all levels to develop the infrastructure for ensuring that nurses possess the skills in policy advisement, identify opportunities for appointments, and develop a list of those nurses who are ready, willing, and able to serve.

Nurses can and will build upon a rich legacy of innovations and commitment to promoting the health of individuals, families, and communities. At this opportune time in reforming the U.S. health care system, the nation can afford no less.

NOTES

1. Siegel, B. (1983). *Lillian Wald of Henry Street.* New York: MacMillan.

2. Chesler, E. (1992). *Woman of valor: Margaret Sanger and the birth control movement in America.* New York: Simon and Schuster.

3. Osterlund, H. (2006). Helping them get home: A Chicago nurse makes a difference for children with complex medical needs. *American Journal of Nursing, 106*(6), pp. 102–103.

4. Reverby, S. (1987). A caring dilemma: Womanhood and nursing in historical perspective. *Nursing Research, 36*(1), pp. 5–11.

5. Dossey, B. (2009). *Florence Nightingale: Mystic, visionary, healer.* Philadelphia: F.A. Davis.

6. Woodham-Smith, C. (1983). *Florence Nightingale, 1820–1910.* New York: Atheneum.

7. Nightingale, F. (1860). *Notes on nursing: What it is and what it is not.* London: D. Appleton and Company, reprinted by Dover Publications, New York, 1969.

8. Lynaugh, J. (2001). Nursing's history: Looking backward and seeing forward. In E. Baer, P. D'Antonio, S. Rinker & J. Lynaugh (Eds.), *Enduring issues in American nursing* (pp. 10–24). New York: Springer.

9. James, J. (2001). Isabel Hampton and the professionalization of nursing in the 1980s. In E. Baer, P. D'Antonio, S. Rinker, & J. Lynaugh (Eds.), *Enduring issues in American nursing* (pp. 42–84). New York: Springer.

10. Carnegie, M. (1995). *Path we tread: Blacks in nursing worldwide, 1854–1994.* New York: Jones and Bartlett.

11. Birnbach, N. (1999). Commentary: Registration. In T. Schorr & M. Kennedy (Eds.), *100 years of American nursing: Celebrating a century of caring* (pp. 17–22). Philadelphia: Lippincott.

12. Lynaugh, J. (2001). Nursing's history: Looking backward and seeing forward. In E. Baer, P. D'Antonio, S. Rinker & J. Lynaugh (Eds.), *Enduring issues in American nursing* (pp. 10–24). New York: Springer.

13. Robb, I. (1903). The quality of thoroughness in nurses' work. *American Journal of Nursing, 4*(3), pp. 169–176.

14. Siegel, B. (1983). *Lillian Wald of Henry Street.* New York: MacMillan.

15. Birnbach, (1999). Commentary: Registration. In T. Schorr & M. Kennedy (Eds.), *100 years of American nursing: Celebrating a century of caring* (pp. 17–22). Philadelphia: Lippincott.

16. Pollitt, P., & Miller, W. (2010). North Carolina: Pioneer in American nursing. *American Journal of Nursing, 110*(2), pp. 70–71.

17. Safriet, B. (1992). Health care dollars and regulatory sense: The role of advanced practice nursing. *Yale Journal on Regulations, 417*, pp. 442–445.

18. Schorr, T., & Kennedy, M. (Eds.). *100 years of American nursing: Celebrating a century of caring.* Philadelphia: Lippincott.

19. Evans, D. (2002). Transforming vision into reality: The Vietnam Women's Memorial. In D. Mason, J. Leavitt, & M. Chaffee (Eds.), *Policy and politics in nursing and health care* (4th Ed.). St. Louis: Saunders.

20. Goldmark, J. (1923). *Nursing and nursing education in the United States: Report of the Committee for the Study of Nursing Education.* New York: Macmillan.

21. Gebbie, K. (2009). 20th-century reports on nursing and nursing education: What difference did they make? *Nursing Outlook, 57*, pp. 84–92.

22. Brown, L. (1948). *Nursing for the future: A report prepared for the National Nursing Council.* New York: Russell Sage Foundation.

23. Montag, M. (1959). *Community college education for nursing.* New York: McGraw-Hill.

24. Lynaugh, J. (2008). Nursing the Great Society: The impact of the Nurse Training Act of 1964. *Nursing History Review, 16*, pp. 13–28.

25. Hutchinson, S. (2001). The development of qualitative health research: Taking stock. *Qualitative Health Research, 11*(4), pp. 505–521.

26. Fairman, J. (2009). *Making room in the clinic: Nurse practitioners and the evolution of modern health care.* New Brunswick, NJ: Rutgers University Press.

27. American Association of Nurse Anesthetists. (2009). *The history of nurse anesthesia practice.* Accessed on February 20, 2010, at http://www.aana.com/crnahistory.aspx.

28. McClure, M., Poulin, M., Sovie, M., & Wandelt, M. (1983). *Magnet hospitals: Attraction and retention of professional nurses.* Washington, DC: American Nurses Association.

29. Benner, P. (1984). *From novice to expert: Excellence and power in clinical nursing practice.* Menlo Park, CA: Addison-Wesley.

30. Nightingale, F. (1860). *Notes on nursing: What it is and what it is not.* London: D. Appleton and Company, reprinted by Dover Publications, New York, 1969.

31. Henderson, V. (1964). The nature of nursing. *American Journal of Nursing, 64*(8), 62–68.

32. New York State Education Department, Office of Health Professions. (n.d.). *Education Law, Title VIII, Article 139.* Accessed on February 14, 2010, at http://www.op.nysed.gov/prof/nurse/article139.htm.

33. Driscoll, V. (1976). *Legitimizing the profession of nursing: The distinct mission of the New York State Nurses Association.* Guiderland, NY: The Foundation of the New York State Nurses Association.

34. American Nurses Association. (1980). *Nursing: A social policy statement.* Kansas City, MO: American Nurses Association

35. American Nurses Association. (2010). *Nursing's social policy statement: The essence of the profession* (p. 10). Washington, DC: American Nurses Association.

36. Kelly, M. (1989). The Omnibus Budget Reconciliation Act of 1987. A policy analysis. *Nursing Clinics of North America, 24*(3), pp. 791–794.

37. Bureau of Labor Statistics. (2009a). *May 2008 national occupational and employment wage estimates, United States.* Accessed on February 26, 2010, at http://www.bls.gov/oes/2008/may/oes_nat.htm#b31–0000.

38. Paraprofessional Healthcare Institute. (2009). *PHI Fact. No. 3.* Accessed on February 26, 2010 at http://www.directcareclearinghouse.org/download/NCDCW%20Fact%20Sheet-1.pdf.

39. Bureau of Labor Statistics. (2009a). *May 2008 national occupational and employment wage estimates, United States.* Accessed on February 26, 2010, at http://www.bls.gov/oes/2008/may/oes_nat.htm#b31–0000.

40. National Center for Health Workforce Analyses (2004). *Nursing aides, home health aides, and related health care occupations—National and local workforce shortages and associated data needs.* U.S. Department of Health and Human Services Health Resources and Services Administration Bureau of Health Professions. Accessed on August 30, 2010, at http://bhpr.hrsa.gov/healthworkforce/reports/nursinghomeaid/nursinghome.htm.

41. Bureau of Health Professions. (2004a). *Supply, demand, and use of licensed practical nurses.* Accessed on February 26, 2010, http://bhpr.hrsa.gov/healthworkforce/reports/nursing/lpn/c2.htm.

42. Bureau of Labor Statistics. (2009a). *May 2008 national occupational and employment wage estimates, United States.* Accessed on February 26, 2010, at http://www.bls.gov/oes/2008/may/oes_nat.htm#b31–0000.

43. Bureau of Labor Statistics. (2009b). Licensed practical and licensed vocational nurses. *Occupational outlook handbook, 2010–2011.* Accessed on February 27, 2010, at http://www.bls.gov/oco/ocos102.htm.

44. Bureau of Health Professions. (2004a). *Supply, demand, and use of licensed practical nurses.* Accessed on February 26, 2010, http://bhpr.hrsa.gov/healthworkforce/reports/nursing/lpn/c2.htm.

45. Bureau of Health Professions. (2010). *The registered nurse population: Initial findings from the 2008 National Sample Survey of Registered Nurses.* Rockville, MD: Health Resources and Services Administration. Accessed on April 3, 2010, at http://bhpr.hrsa.gov/healthworkforce/rnsurvey/initialfindings2008.pdf.

46. Bureau of Health Professions. (2004b). *The registered nurse population: Findings from the 2004 National Sample Survey of Registered Nurses.* Rockville, MD: Health Resources and Services Administration. Available at http://bhpr.hrsa.gov/healthworkforce/rnsurvey04/3.htm, accessed on January 12, 2010.

47. Bureau of Health Professions. (2010). *The registered nurse population: Initial findings from the 2008 National Sample Survey of Registered Nurses.* Rockville, MD: Health Resources and Services Administration. Accessed on April 3, 2010, at http://bhpr.hrsa.gov/healthworkforce/rnsurvey/initialfindings2008.pdf.

48. Bureau of Health Professions. (2010). *The registered nurse population: Initial findings from the 2008 National Sample Survey of Registered Nurses.* Rockville, MD: Health Resources and Services Administration. Accessed on April 3, 2010, at http://bhpr.hrsa.gov/healthworkforce/rnsurvey/initialfindings2008.pdf.

49. Aiken, L., Cheung, R., & Olds, D. (2009). Education policy initiatives to address the nurse shortage in the United State. *Health Affairs, 28*(4), pp. w646–w656.

50. Bureau of Health Professions. (2010). *The registered nurse population: Initial findings from the 2008 National Sample Survey of Registered Nurses.* Rockville, MD: Health Resources and Services Administration. Accessed on August 30, 2010, at http://bhpr.hrsa.gov/healthworkforce/rnsurvey/initialfindings2008.pdf.

51. Bureau of Health Professions. (2010). *The registered nurse population: Initial findings from the 2008 National Sample Survey of Registered Nurses.* Rockville, MD: Health Resources and Services Administration. Accessed on April 3, 2010, at http://bhpr.hrsa.gov/healthworkforce/rnsurvey/initialfindings2008.pdf.

52. Institute of Medicine. (2008). *Retooling for an aging America: Building the health care workforce.* Washington, DC: National Academies Press.

53. Reinhard, S., Brooks-Danso, A., & Kelly, K. (Eds.) (2008). State of the science: Professional partners supporting family caregiving. *American Journal of Nursing, 108*(9 supp), pp. 1–93.

54. Gibson, M. & Houser, A. (2008). *Valuing the invaluable: The economic value of family caregiving.* Washington, DC: AARP.

55. Bureau of Health Professions. (2010). *The registered nurse population: Initial findings from the 2008 National Sample Survey of Registered Nurses.* Rockville, MD: Health Resources and Services Administration. Accessed on April 3, 2010, at http://bhpr.hrsa.gov/healthworkforce/rnsurvey/initialfindings2008.pdf.

56. Bureau of Health Professions. (2004b). *The registered nurse population: Findings from the 2004 National Sample Survey of Registered Nurses.* Rockville, MD: Health Resources and Services Administration. Accessed on January 12, 2010, at http://bhpr.hrsa.gov/healthworkforce/rnsurvey04/3.htm.

57. Bureau of Health Professions. (2004b). *The registered nurse population: Findings from the 2004 National Sample Survey of Registered Nurses.* Rockville, MD: Health Resources and Services Administration. Accessed on January 12, 2010, at http://bhpr.hrsa.gov/healthworkforce/rnsurvey04/3.htm.

58. Estabrooks, C., Midodzi, W., Cummings, G., Ricker, K., & Giovannetti, P. (2005). The impact of hospital nursing characteristics on 30-day mortality. *Nursing Research, 54*(2), pp. 74–84.

59. Aiken, L., Clarke, S., Cheung, R., Sloane, D., & Silber, R. (2003). Educational levels of hospital nurses and patient mortality. *Journal of the American Medical Association, 290*(12), pp. 1617–1623.

60. Government Accounting Office (GAO). (2008). *Primary care professionals: Recent supply trends, projections, and valuation of services.* Testimony presented before the Health, Education, Labor, and Pensions Committee, U.S. Senate, February 12.

61. Buhler-Wilkerson, K. (2003). *No place like home: A history of nursing and home care in the United States.* Baltimore: Johns Hopkins University Press.

62. Bekemeier, B., & Jones, M. (2010). Relationships between local public health agency functions and agency leadership and staffing. *Journal of Public Health Management and Practice, 16*(2), E8-E16. Accessed on February 27, 2010, at http://www.ncbi.nlm.nih.gov.proxy.wexler.hunter.cuny.edu/pubmed/20150786?itool=EntrezSystem2. PEntrez.Pubmed.Pubmed_ResultsPanel.Pubmed_RVDocSum&ordinalpos=3.

63. Association of State and Territorial Directors of Nursing, Public Health Preparedness Committee. (2007). *The role of public health nurses in emergency preparedness and response.* Accessed on February 27, 2010, at http://www .astdn.org/downloadablefiles/ASTDN%20EP%20Paper%20final%2010%2029%2007.pdf.

64. American Academy of Pediatrics. (2008). *Role of the school nurse in providing school health services.* Accessed on February 27, 2010, at http://aappolicy.aappublications.org/cgi/reprint/pediatrics;121/5/1052.pdf.

65. Jacobson, J. (2009). School nurses nationwide respond to Influenza A (H1N1) outbreak. *American Journal of Nursing, 109*(6), p. 19.

66. Bureau of Health Professions. (2004b). *The registered nurse population: Findings from the 2004 National Sample Survey of Registered Nurses.* Rockville, MD: Health Resources and Services Administration. Accessed on January 12, 2010 at http://bhpr.hrsa.gov/healthworkforce/rnsurvey04/3.htm.

67. Seago, J., Spetz, J., Chapman, S., & Dyer, W. (2006). Can the use of nurses alleviate the nursing shortage? *American Journal of Nursing, 106*(7), pp. 40–49.

68. Bureau of Health Professions. (2004a). *Supply, demand, and use of licensed practical nurses.* Accessed on February 26, 2010, http://bhpr.hrsa.gov/healthworkforce/reports/nursing/lpn/c2.htm.

69. Harrington, C. (2011). Long-term care policy issues. In D. Mason, J. Leavitt, M. Chaffee (Eds.), *Policy and politics in nursing and health care* (6th Ed). St. Louis: Elsevier.

70. Lynaugh, J. (2001). Nursing's history: Looking backward and seeing forward. In E. Baer, P. D'Antonio, S. Rinker & J. Lynaugh (Eds.), *Enduring issues in American nursing* (pp. 10–24). New York: Springer.

71. Carnegie, M. (1995). *Path we tread: Blacks in nursing worldwide, 1854–1994.* New York: Jones and Bartlett.

72. Lovell, V. (2006). *Solving the nursing shortage through higher wages.* Washington, DC: Institute for Women's Policy Research.

73. Diers, D. (1979). *Research in nursing practice.* New York: Lippincott.

74. Gortner, S. (2000). Knowledge development in nursing: Our historical roots and future opportunities. *Nursing Outlook, 48*(2), 60–67.

75. Gortner, S. (2000). Knowledge development in nursing: Our historical roots and future opportunities. *Nursing Outlook, 48*(2), 60–67.

76. Kjervik, D. (2006). Creation of the National Institute of Nursing Research: Talking the walk for nursing research. *Journal of Professional Nursing, 22*(1), pp. 5–6.

77. American Association of Colleges of Nursing. (2008). *Support the Mission of the National Institute of Nursing Research in FY 2009.* Accessed on April 23, 2010, at http://www.aacn.nche.edu/Government/pdf/08NINRFS .pdf.

78. Bureau of Health Professions. (2004b). *The registered nurse population: Findings from the 2004 National Sample Survey of Registered Nurses.* Rockville, MD: Health Resources and Services Administration. Accessed on January 12, 2010 at http://bhpr.hrsa.gov/healthworkforce/rnsurvey04/3.htm.

79. Buerhaus, P. (2008). Current and future state of the U.S. nursing workforce. *Journal of the American Medical Association, 300*(20), pp. 2422–2424.

80. Aiken, L., & Mullinix, C. (1987). The nurse shortage: Myth or reality? *New England Journal of Medicine*, 317(10), pp. 641–646.

81. Buerhaus, P. Auerbach, D., & Staiger, D. (2009). The recent surge in nurse employment: Causes and implications. *Health Affairs, 28*(4), pp. w657–w668.

82. Auerbach, D., Buerhaus, P., & Staiger, D. (2007). Better late than never: Implications of a later entry into nursing. *Health Affairs, 26*(1), pp. 178–185.

83. Institute of Medicine. (2008). *Retooling for an aging America: Building the health care workforce.* Washington, DC: National Academies Press.

84. Rosati, R., Marren, J., Davin, D., & Morgan, C. (2009). The linkage between employee and patient satisfaction in home healthcare. *Journal of Healthcare Quality, 31*(2), pp. 44–53.

85. Bureau of Health Professions. (2004b). *The registered nurse population: Findings from the 2004 National Sample Survey of Registered Nurses.* Rockville, MD: Health Resources and Services Administration. Accessed on January 12, 2010, at http://bhpr.hrsa.gov/healthworkforce/rnsurvey04/3.htm.

86. Hendrich, A., Chow, M., Skierczynski, B., & Lu, Z. (2008). A 36-hour time and motion study: How do medical-surgical nurses spend their time? *The Permanente Journal, 12*(3), pp. 25–34.

87. Trinkoff, A., Geiger-Brown, J., Caruso, C., Lipscomb, J., Johantgen, M., Nelson, A., Sattler, B. & Selby, V. (2008). Personal safety for nurses. In R. Hughes (Ed.), *Patient safety and quality: An evidence-based handbook for nurses.* Chapter 39. Rockville, MD: Agency for Healthcare Quality and Research.

88. National League for Nursing. (2009a). *Annual nursing review documents: Application, admission, enrollment, and graduation rates for all types of prelicensure nursing programs.* Accessed January 12, 2010, at http://www.nln.org/newsreleases/annual_survey_031609.htm.

89. American Association of Colleges of Nursing. (2009c). *Student enrollment expands at U.S. nursing colleges and universities for the 9th year despite financial challenges and capacity restraints.* Accessed on February 27, 2010, http://www.aacn.nche.edu/Media/NewsReleases/2009/StudentEnrollment.html.

90. Summers, S., & Summers, H. (2009). *Saving lives: Why the media's portrayal of nurses puts us all at risk.* New York: Kaplan.

91. Friss, L. (1994). Nursing studies laid end to end form a circle. *Journal of Health Politics, Policy and Law, 19*(3), 587–631.

92. Reverby, S. (1987). A caring dilemma: Womanhood and nursing in historical perspective. *Nursing Research, 36*(1), pp. 5–11.

93. Donelan, K., Buerhaus, P., DesRoches, C., Dittus, R., & Dutwin, D. (2008). Public perceptions of nursing careers: The influence of media and nursing shortages. *Nursing Economic$, 26*(3), pp. 1–9.

94. Fang, D., & Tracy, C. (2010). Special survey on vacant faculty positions for academic year 2009–2010. Accessed on February 27, 2010, at http://www.aacn.nche.edu/IDS/pdf/vacancy09.pdf.

95. National League for Nursing. (2009b). *Notable findings from an annual survey of schools of nursing.* Accessed on February 27, 2010, at http://www.nln.org/newsreleases/annual_survey_2010.htm.

96. Yordy, K. (2006). *The nursing faculty shortage: A crisis for health care.* Princeton, NJ: Robert Wood Johnson Foundation. Accessed on February 27, 2010, at http://www.rwjf.org/files/publications/other/NursingFacultyShortage071006.pdf.

97. American Association of Colleges of Nursing. (2009b). *Nursing faculty shortage fact sheet.* Accessed on January 13, 2010, at http://www.aacn.nche.edu/Media/FactSheets/FacultyShortage.htm.

98. Kaufman, K. (2007). Introducing the NLN/Carnegie national survey of nurse educators: Compensation, workload, and teaching practice. *Nursing Education Perspectives, 28*(3), pp. 164–167.

99. Bevill, J., Cleary, B., Lacey, L., & Mooney, J. (2007). Educational mobility of RNs in North Carolina: Who will teach tomorrow's nurses? *American Journal of Nursing, 107*(5), pp. 60–70.

100. Tanner, C., Gubrud-Howe, P., & Shores, L. (2008). The Oregon Consortium for Nursing Education: A response to the nursing shortage. *Policy, Politics and Nursing Practice, 9*(3), pp. 203–209.

101. Moscato, S., Miller, J., Logsdon, K., Weinberg, S., & Chorpenning, L. (2007). Dedicated Education Unit: An innovative clinical partner education model. *Nursing Outlook, 55*, pp. 31–37.

102. Tanner, C., Gubrud-Howe, P., & Shores, L. (2008). The Oregon Consortium for Nursing Education: A response to the nursing shortage. *Policy, Politics and Nursing Practice, 9*(3), pp. 203–209.

103. Tanner, C. (2006). Thinking like a nurse: A research-based model of clinical judgment in nursing. *Journal of Nursing Education, 45*(6), pp. 204–211.

104. Aiken, L., Clarke, S., Sloane, D., Sochalski, J., Busse, R., Clarke, H., Giovannetti, P., Hunt, J., Rafferty, A., & Shamian, J. (2001). Nurses' reports on hospital care in five countries. *Health Affairs, 20*(3), pp. 43–53.

105. Brewer, C., & Kovner, C. (2001). Research questions about the nursing labor supply: Participation, wages, and pipeline issues. *Applied Nursing Research, 14*(3), 117–118.

106. Bureau of Health Professions. (2001). *National sample survey of registered nurses—March 2000.* Rockville, MD: Health Services and Resources Administration.

107. Kenward, K., & Zhong, E. (2006). *Report of findings from the practice and professional issues survey, fall 2004.* Chicago: National Council of State Boards of Nursing.

108. Kramer, M. (1974). *Reality shock: Why nurses leave nursing.* St. Louis, MO: Mosby.

109. Kovner, C., & Brewer, C. (2010). Newly licensed registered nurses study. Accessed on August 26, 2010, at http://www.rnworkproject.org/.

110. Jones, C. (2005). The costs of nurse turnover, Part 2. *Journal of Nursing Administration, 35*(1), pp. 41–49.

111. Advisory Board Company. (1999). A misplaced focus: Reexamining the recruiting/retention trade-off. *Nurse Watch, 11,* pp. 1–14.

112. Goode, C., Lynn, M., Krsek, C., & Bednash, G. (2009). Nurse residency programs: An essential requirement for nursing. *Nursing Economic$, 27*(3), pp. 141–147.

113. Kovner, C. T., Brewer, C. S., Greene, W., & Fairchild, S. (2009). Understanding new registered nurses' intent to stay at their jobs. *Nursing Economics, 27*(2), pp. 81–98.

114. Kovner, C., Brewer, C., Fairchild, S., Poornima, S., Kim, H., & Djukic, M. (2007). Newly licensed RNs' characteristics, work attitudes, and intentions to work. *American Journal of Nursing, 107*(9), pp. 58–70.

115. Kovner, C., Brewer, C., Wu, Y., Cheng, Y., & Suzuki, M. (2006). Factors associated with work satisfaction of registered nurses. *Journal of Nursing Scholarship, 38*(1), pp. 71–79.

116. Black, L., Spetz, J., & Harrington, C. (2008). Nurses working outside of nursing: Societal trend or workplace crisis? *Policy, Politics & Nursing Practice, 9*(3), pp. 143–157.

117. Aiken, L., Clarke, S., Sloane, D., Sochalski, J., & Silber, J. (2002). Hospital nurse staffing and patient mortality, nurse burnout, and job dissatisfaction. *JAMA, 288*(16), pp. 1987–1993.

118. Aiken, L., Clarke, S., Sloane, D., Sochalski, J., Busse, R., Clarke, H., Giovannetti, P., Hunt, J., Rafferty, A.M., & Shamian, J. (2001). Nurses' reports on hospital care in five countries. *Health Affairs, 20*(3), pp. 43–53.

119. Kovner, C., Brewer, C., Fairchild, S., Poornima, S., Kim, H., & Djukic, M. (2007). Newly licensed RNs' characteristics, work attitudes, and intentions to work. *American Journal of Nursing, 107*(9), pp. 58–70.

120. Trinkoff, A., Geiger-Brown, J., Brady, B., Lipscomb, J., & Muntaner, C. (2006). How long and how much are nurses working? *American Journal of Nursing, 106*(4), pp. 60–71.

121. Rogers, A., Hwang, W.-T., Scott, L., Aiken, L., & Dinges, D. (2004). The working hours of hospital staff nurses and patient safety. *Health Affairs, 23*(4), pp. 202–212.

122. Bureau of Health Professions. (2004b). *The registered nurse population: Findings from the 2004 National Sample Survey of Registered Nurses.* Rockville, MD: Health Resources and Services Administration. Accessed on January 12, 2010, at http://bhpr.hrsa.gov/healthworkforce/rnsurvey04/3.htm.

123. Bolton, L., Aydin, C., Donaldson, N., Brown, D., Sandhu, M., Fridman, M., & Aronow, H. (2007). Mandated nurse staffing ratios in California: A comparison of staffing and nursing-sensitive outcomes pre- and postregulation. *Policy, Politics, & Nursing Practice, 8*(4), pp. 238–250.

124. Spetz, J., Chapman, S., Herrera, C., Kaiser, J., Seago, J., & Dower, C. (2009). *Assessing the impact of California's nurse staffing ratios on hospitals and patient care.* California Health Care Foundation. Accessed on January 14, 2010, at http://www.chcf.org/topics/view.cfm?itemID=133857.

125. Conway, P., Konetzha, R., Shu, J., Volpp, K., & Sochalski, J. (2008). Nurse staffing ratios: Trends and policy implications for hospitalists and the safety net. *Society of Hospital Medicine, 3*(3), pp. 193–199.

126. Aiken, L., Sloane, D., Cimiotti, J., Clarke, S., Flynn, L., Seago, J., Spetz, J., & Smith, H. (2010). Implications of the California nurse staffing mandate for other states. *Health Services Research.* DOI: 10.1111/j.1475–6773.2010.01114. Accessed on July 7, 2010, at http://www3.interscience.wiley.com.proxy.wexler.hunter.cuny.edu/cgi-bin/fulltext/123346354/PDFSTART.

127. American Nurses Association. (2010b). *Safe staffing saves lives.* Accessed on April 1, 2010, at www.safestaffingsaveslives.org.

128. Brush, B., Sochalski, J., & Berger, A. (2004). Imported care: Recruiting foreign nurses to U. S. health care facilities. *Health Affairs, 23*(3), pp. 78–87.

129. Auerbach, D., Buerhaus, P., & Staiger, D. (2007). Better late than never: Implications of a later entry into nursing. *Health Affairs, 26*(1), pp. 178–185.

130. Kingma, M. (2006). *Nurses on the move: Migration and the global health care economy.* Ithaca, NY: Cornell University Press.

131. Nichols, B., Davis, C., & Richardson, D. (2011). Global nurse migration. In D. Mason, J. Leavitt, & M. Chaffee (Ed.), *Policy and politics in nursing and health care.* (6th Ed.) St. Louis: W. B. Saunders/Elsevier.

132. U.S. Department of Labor. (2009). *Occupational outlook handbook, 2010–2011.* Accessed on March 6, 2010, at http://www.bls.gov/oco/ocos083.htm#oes_links.

133. Lovell, V. (2006). *Solving the nursing shortage through higher wages.* Washington, DC: Institute for Women's Policy Research.

134. Healthcare Finance News. *New York nurses win $1.25 million class-action wage settlement.* (2009, April 3). Accessed on February 27, 2010, at http://www.healthcarefinancenews.com/news/new-york-nurses-win-125m-class-action-wage-settlement.

135. Spetz, J., & Given, R. (2003). The future of the nurse shortage: Will wage increases close the gap? *Health Affairs, 22*(6), 1 pp. 99–206.

136. Dickerson, S., Brewer, C., Kovner, C., & Way, M. (2007). Giving voice to registered nurses' decisions to work. *Nursing Forum, 42*(3), 1 pp. 32–143.

137. Kovner, C., Brewer, C., Greene, W., & Fairchild, S. (2009). Understanding new registered nurses' intent to stay at their jobs. *Nursing Economics, 27*(2), pp. 81–98.

138. Rosenstein, A. (2002). Nurse-physician relationships: Impact on nurse satisfaction and retention. *American Journal of Nursing, 102*(6), pp. 26–34.

139. Aiken, L. (2002). Superior outcomes for magnet hospitals: The evidence base. In M. McClure, A. S. Hinshaw (Eds.), *Magnet hospitals revisited.* (pp. 61–82). Washington, DC: American Nurses Publishing.

140. May, J., Bazzoli, G., & Gerland, A. (2006). Hospitals' responses to nurse staffing shortages. *Health Affairs, 26,* pp. w316–w323.

141. McClure, M., Poulin, M., Sovie, M., & Wandelt, M. (1983). *Magnet hospitals: Attraction and retention of professional nurses.* Washington, DC: American Nurses Association.

142. American Nurses Credentialing Center (ANCC). (n.d.). Magnet recognition program overview. Accessed on January 18, 2010, at http://nursecredentialing.org/Magnet/ProgramOverview.aspx.

American Public Health Association, Public Health Nursing Sections. (1996). *The definition and role of public health nursing.* Washington, DC: APHA.

143. Aiken, L., Haven, D., & Sloane, D. (2000). The Magnet services recognition program. *American Journal of Nursing, 100*(3), pp. 26–35.

144. Kramer, M., & Schmalenberg, C. (2002). Staff nurses identify essentials of magnetism. In M. McClure, A.S. Hinshaw, A.S. (Eds.), *Magnet hospitals revisited.* (pp. 25–60). Washington, DC: American Nurses Publishing.

145. Scott, J., Sochalski, J., & Aiken, L. (1999). Review of magnet hospital research: findings and implications for professional nursing practice. *Journal of Nursing Administration, 29*(1), pp. 9–19.

146. Aiken, L., Smith, H., & Lake, E. (1994). Lower Medicare mortality among a set of hospital known for good nursing care. *Medical Care, 32*(8), pp. 771–787.

147. Aiken, L., Clarke, S., Sloane, D., Lake, E., & Cheney, T. (2008). Effects of hospital care environment on patient mortality and nurse outcomes. *Journal of Nursing Administration, 38*(5), pp. 223–229.

148. McClure, M., & Hinshaw, A. (Eds.). (2002). *Magnet hospitals revisited.* Washington, DC: American Nurses Publishing.

149. American Nurses Credentialing Center (ANCC). (n.d.). *Magnet recognition program overview.* Accessed on January 18, 2010, at http://nursecredentialing.org/Magnet/ProgramOverview.aspx.

150. Merryman, T., & Concordia, E. (2007). Transforming care at the bedside: Shadyside Hospital's code red. In D. Mason, J. Leavitt, M. Chaffee (Eds.), *Policy and politics in nursing and health care* (5th ed.), pp. 497–499. St. Louis, MO: Elsevier.

151. Stefancyk, A. (2009). High-use supplies at the bedside. *American Journal of Nursing, 109*(2), pp. 33–35.

152. Hain, P., Ng, C., Aronow, H., Swanson, J., & Bolton, L. (2009). Improving communication with bedside video rounding. *American Journal of Nursing, 109*(11 Suppl), pp. 18–20.

153. Needleman, J., Parkerton, P., Pearson, M., Soban, L., Upenieks, V., & Yee, T. (2009). Overall effect of TCAB on initial participating hospitals. *American Journal of Nursing, 109*(11 Suppl), pp. 59–65.

154. Parkerton, P., Needleman, J., Pearson, M., Upenieks, V., Soban, L., & Yee, T. (2009). Lessons from nursing leaders on implementing TCAB. *American Journal of Nursing, 109*(11 Suppl), pp. 71–76.

155. Pearson, M., Needleman, J., Parkerton, P., Upenieks, V., Soban, L., & Yee, T. (2009). Participation of unit nurses. *American Journal of Nursing, 109*(11 Suppl), pp. 66–70.

156. Bolton, L., & Aronow, H. (2009).The business case for TCAB. *American Journal of Nursing, 109*(11 Suppl), pp. 77–80.

157. Newhouse, R., & Hoffman, J. (2007). Evaluating an innovative program to improve new nurse graduate socialization into the acute healthcare setting. *Nursing Administration Quarterly, 31*(1), pp. 50–60.

158. Pine, R., & Tart, K. (2007). Return on investment: Benefits and challenges of a baccalaureate nurse residency program. *Nursing Economic$, 25*(1), pp. 13–18.

159. Halfer, D. (2007). A magnetic strategy for new graduate nurses. *Nursing Economic$, 25*(1), pp. 6–12.

160. Goode, C., Lynn, M., Krsek, C., & Bednash, G. (2009). Nurse residency programs: An essential requirement for nursing. *Nursing Economic$, 27*(3), pp. 141–147.

161. Terri Wehrwein, personal communication, February 15, 2010.

162. Derksen, D., & Whelan, E. (2009). *Closing the healthcare workforce gap: Reforming federal health care workforce policies to meet the needs of the 21st century.* Washington, DC: Center for American Progress.

163. Derksen, D., & Whelan, E. (2009). *Closing the healthcare workforce gap: Reforming federal health care workforce policies to meet the needs of the 21st century.* Washington, DC: Center for American Progress.

164. Aiken, L., & Cheung, R. (2008). Nursing workforce challenges in the United States: Implications for policy. *OECD Health Working Papers*, No. 35, Organisation of Economic Co-operation and Development Publishing.

165. Ulrich, R., Quan, X., Simring, C., Joseph, A., & Choudhary, R. (2004). *The role of the physical environment in the hospital of the 21st century: A once-in-a-lifetime opportunity.* The Center for Health Design. Accessed on January 11, 2010, at http://www.healthdesign.org/research/reports/physical_environ.php.

166. Hendrich, A., Chow, M., Skierczynski, B., & Lu, Z. (2008). A 36-hour time and motion study: How do medical-surgical nurses spend their time? *The Permanente Journal, 12*(3), pp. 25–34.

167. Bolton, L., Gassert, C., & Cipriano, P. (2008). Smart technology, enduring solutions. *Journal of Health Information and Management, 22*(4), pp. 24–30.

168. The Joint Commission. (2008). *Health care at the crossroads: Guiding principles for the development of the hospital of the future.* Chicago: The Joint Commission.

169. Gebbie, K. (2009). 20th-century reports on nursing and nursing education: What difference did they make? *Nursing Outlook, 57,* pp. 84–92.

170. Donley, R. (2005). Challenges for nursing in the 21st century. *Nursing Economic$, 23*(6), pp. 312–318.

171. Benner, P., Sutphen, M., Leonard, V., & Day, L. (2010). *Educating nurses: A call for radical transformation.* San Francisco: Jossey-Bass.

172. Pew Health Professions Commission. (1995). *Critical challenges: revitalizing the health professions for the twenty-first century.* Accessed on March 11, 2010, at http://futurehealth.ucsf.edu/Content/29/1995–12_Critical_Challenges_Revitalizing_the_Health_Professions_for_the_Twenty-First_Century.pdf.

173. Mooney, M. (2007). Hog-housed: The life and death of bachelor of science in nursing entry into practice in North Dakota. In D. Mason, J. Leavitt, M. Chaffee (Eds.), *Policy and politics in nursing and health care* (5th Ed.), pp. 731–734. St. Louis, MO: Elsevier.

174. Aiken, L., Clarke, S., Cheung, R., Sloane, D., & Silber, R. (2003). Educational levels of hospital nurses and patient mortality. *Journal of the American Medical Association, 290*(12), pp. 1617–1623.

175. Estabrooks, C., Midodzi, W., Cummings, G., Ricker, K., & Giovannetti, P. (2005). The impact of hospital nursing characteristics on 30-day mortality. *Nursing Research, 54*(2), 7 pp. 4–84.

176. Aiken, L., Clarke, S., Sloane, D., Lake, E., & Cheney, T. (2008). Effects of hospital care environment on patient mortality and nurse outcomes. *Journal of Nursing Administration, 38*(5), pp. 223–229.

177. Baum, S., & Ma, J. (2007). *Trends in college pricing.* Trends in Higher Education Series. College Board. Accessed on March 11, 2010, at http://www.careercornerstone.org/pdf/universities/tuition07.pdf.

178. Bevill, J., Cleary, B., Lacey, L., & Mooney, J. (2007). Educational mobility of RNs in North Carolina: Who will teach tomorrow's nurses? *American Journal of Nursing, 107*(5), pp. 60–70.

179. Cleary, B., McBride, A., McClure, M., & Reinhard, S. (2009). Expanding the capacity of nursing education. *Health Affairs, 28*(4), pp. w634–w645.

180. Benner, P., Sutphen, M., Leonard, V., & Day, L. (2010). *Educating nurses: A call for radical transformation.* San Francisco: Jossey-Bass.

181. American Association of Community Colleges. (2010). Constricting nursing pipeline would exacerbate shortages, reduce access. Accessed on January 13, 2010, at http://www.aacc.nche.edu/newsevents/News/articles/Documents/nursign010810.pdf.

182. Malone, B. (2010). Choosing sides. *Inside Higher Ed.* Accessed on March 11, 2010, at http://www.insidehighered.com/views/2010/01/14/malone.

183. Stanley, J. (2009). Reaching consensus on a regulatory model: What does this mean for APRNs? *Journal for Nurse Practitioners, 5*(2), pp. 99–104.

184. National Council of State Boards of Nursing, *Consensus model for APRN regulation: Licensure, accreditation, certification, and education.* (2007). Accessed on March 27, 2010, at http://www.aacn.nche.edu/Education/pdf/APRNReport.pdf.

185. Phillips, S. (2010). 22nd annual legislative update: Regulatory and legislative successes for APNs. *The Nurse Practitioner, 35*(1), pp. 24–47.

186. Dracup, K., Cronenwett, L., Meleis, A., & Benner, P. (2005). Reflections on the doctorate of nursing practice. *Nursing Outlook, 53*(4), pp. 177–182.

187. Croasdale, M. (2008). Medical testing board to introduce doctor of nursing certification, *Amednews.com.* Accessed on March 28, 2010, at http://www.ama-assn.org/amednews/2008/06/16/prl10616.htm.

188. Tanner, C., Gubrud-Howe, P., & Shores, L. (2008). The Oregon Consortium for Nursing Education: A response to the nursing shortage. *Policy, Politics and Nursing Practice, 9*(3), pp. 203–209.

189. Mason, D., Vaccaro K., & Fessler, M. (2000). Early views of nurse practitioners: A Medline search. *Clinical Excellence for Nurse Practitioner, 4*(3), pp. 175–183.

190. Mullinix, C., & Bucholtz, D. (2009). Role and quality of nurse practitioner practice: A policy issue. *Nursing Outlook, 57,* pp. 93–96.

191. American Medical Association. (2009). *AMA scope of practice data series: Nurse practitioners.* Chicago: American Medical Association.

192. Sox, H. (1979). Quality of patient care by nurse practitioners and physician's assistants: A ten-year perspective. *Annals of Internal Medicine, 91*(3), pp. 459–468.

193. Feldman, M., Ventura, M., & Crosby, F. (1987). Studies of nurse practitioner effectiveness. *Nursing Research, 36*(5), pp. 303–308.

194. Brown, S., & Grimes, D. (1995). A meta-analysis of nurse practitioners and nurse midwives in primary care. *Nursing Research, 44*(6), pp. 332–339.

195. Laurant, M., Reeves, D., Hermens, R., Braspenning, J., Grol, R., & Sibbald, B. (2004). Substitution of doctors by nurses in primary care. *Cochrane Database of Systematic Reviews, Issue 4.* Accessed on January 16, 2010 at http://mrw.interscience.wiley.com.proxy.wexler.hunter.cuny.edu/cochrane/clsysrev/articles/CD001271/pdf_fs.html.

196. U.S. Congress, Office of Technology Assessment. (1986). *Nurse practitioners, physician assistants, and certified nurse-midwives: A policy analysis* (Health Technology Case Study 37), OTA-HCS-37. Washington, DC: U.S. Government Printing Office.

197. Brown, S., & Grimes, D. (1995). A meta-analysis of nurse practitioners and nurse midwives in primary care. *Nursing Research, 44*(6), pp. 332–339.

198. Mundinger, M., Kane, R., Lenz, E., Totten, A., Tsai, W., Cleary, P., Friedewald, W., Siu, A., & Shelanski, M. (2000). Primary care outcomes in patients treated by nurse practitioners and physicians: A randomized trial. *Journal of the American Medical Association, 283*, pp. 59–68.

199. Lenz, E., Mundinger, M., Kane, R., Hopkins, S., & Lin, S. (2004). Primary care outcomes in patients treated by nurse practitioners or physicians: Two-year follow-up. *Medical Care Research and Review, 61*(3), pp. 332–51.

200. Herrick, T. (2000). *JAMA* reports patient outcomes comparable for NPs, MDs: Study may signal shift in physician attitudes. *Clinician News, 1*, pp. 6–7.

201. Laurant, M., Reeves, D., Hermens, R., Braspenning, J., Grol, R., & Sibbald, B. (2004). Substitution of doctors by nurses in primary care. *Cochrane Database of Systematic Reviews*, Issue 4. Accessed on January 16, 2010, at http://mrw.interscience.wiley.com.proxy.wexler.hunter.cuny.edu/cochrane/clsysrev/articles/CD001271/pdf_fs.html.

202. P. Reinecke, personal communication, September 10, 2009.

203. Jenkins, M., & Torrisi, D. (1995). Marketing and management: NPs, community nurse centers, and contracting for managed care. *Journal of the American Academy of Nurse Practitioners, 7*(3), pp. 119–123.

204. Restrepo, A., Davitt, C., & Thompson, S. (2001). House calls: Is there an APN in the house? *Journal of the American Academy of Nurse Practitioners, 13*(12), pp. 560–564.

205. Aigner, M., Drew, S., & Phipps, J. (2004). A comparative study of nursing home resident outcomes between care provided by nurse practitioners/physicians versus physicians only. *Journal of the American Medical Directors Association, 5*(1), pp. 16–23.

206. Klima, C., Norr, K., Vonderheid, S., & Handler, A. (2009). Introduction of CenteringPregnancy in a public health clinic. *Journal of Midwifery and Women's Health, 54*(1), pp. 27–34.

207. Seibert, E., Alexander, J., & Lupien, A. (2004). Rural nurse anesthesia practice: a pilot study. *AANA Journal, 72*(3), pp. 181–90.

208. Meyer, S., & Miers, L. (2005).Cardiovascular surgeon and acute care nurse practitioner: collaboration on postoperative outcomes. *AACN Clinical Issues, 16*(2), pp. 149–158.

209. Brooten, D., Kumar, S., Brown, L., Butts, P., Finkler, S., Bakewell-Sachs, S., Gibbons, A., Delivoria-Papadopoulos, M. (1986). A randomized clinical trial of early hospital discharge and home follow-up of very-low-birth-weight infants. *New England Journal of Medicine, 315*(15), pp. 934–939.

210. DeJong, S., & Veltman, R. (2004). The effectiveness of a CNS-led community-based COPD screening and intervention program. *Clinical Nurse Specialist,18*(2), pp. 72–79.

211. Fallacaro, M. (1997). The practice and distribution of Certified Registered Nurse Anesthetists in federally designated nurse shortage areas. *CRNA: The Clinical Forum for Nurse Anesthetists, 8*(2), pp. 55–61.

212. Seibert, E., Alexander, J., & Lupien, A. (2004). Rural nurse anesthesia practice: a pilot study. *AANA Journal, 72*(3), pp. 181–190.

213. Silber, J., Kennedy, S., Even-Shoshan, O, Chen, W., Koziol, L., Showan, A., & Longnecker, D. (2000). Anesthesiologist direction and patient outcomes. *Anesthesiology, 93*(1), pp. 152–163.

214. Pine, M., Holt, K., & Lou, Y. (2003). Surgical mortality and type of anesthesia provider. *AANA Journal, 71,* pp. 109–116.

215. Smith, A., Kane, F., & Milne, R. (2004). Comparative effectiveness and safety of physician and nurse anaesthetists: A narrative systematic review. *British Journal of Anaesthesia, 93,* pp. 540–545.

216. Needleman, J., & Minnick, A. (2008). Anesthesia provider model, hospital resources, and maternal outcomes. *Health Services Research, 44*(2), pp. 464–482.

217. Hatem, M., Sandall, J., Devane, D., Soltani, H., & Gates, S. (2008). Midwife-led versus other models of care for childbearing women. *Cochrane Database of Systematic Reviews, 4,* CD004667. Accessed on April 5, 2010, at http://www.mrw.interscience.wiley.com.proxy.wexler.hunter.cuny.edu/cochrane/clsysrev/articles/CD004667/pdf_standard_fs.html.

218. Nichols, L. (1992). Estimating costs of underusing advanced practice nurses. *Nursing Economics, 10*, pp. 343–351.

219. Institute of Medicine, Committee on the Status of Primary Care. (1996). *Primary care: America's health in a new era.* Washington, DC. National Academies Press.

220. Institute of Medicine. (2010). *The future of nursing: Leading change; advancing health.* Washington, DC: National Academies Press.

221. Safriet, B. (1992). Health care dollars and regulatory sense: The role of advanced practice nursing. *Yale Journal on Regulations, 417,* pp. 442–445.

222. Phillips, S. (2010). 22nd annual legislative update: Regulatory and legislative successes for APNs. *The Nurse Practitioner, 35*(1), pp. 24–47.

223. Cronenwett, L., & Dzau, V. (2010). Chairman's summary of the conference. In B. Culliton (Ed.), *Who will provide primary care and how will they be trained?* New York: Josiah Macy, Jr. Foundation.

224. Inglis, T. (2003). Nurse anesthetists: One step forward, one step back. *American Journal of Nursing, 103*(1), pp. 91–93.

225. American Association of Nurse Anesthetists. (2009). *The history of nurse anesthesia practice.* Accessed on February 20, 2010 at http://www.aana.com/crnahistory.aspx.

226. Stanley, J. (2009). Reaching consensus on a regulatory model: What does this mean for APRNs? *Journal for Nurse Practitioners, 5*(2), pp. 99–104.

227. Craven G., & Ober, S. (2009). Massachusetts nurse practitioners step up as one solution to the primary care access problem: A political success story. *Policy, Politics and Nursing Practice, 10*(2), pp. 94–100.

228. CMS, *Medicare Claims Processing Manual.* (2009). Chapter 12. Accessed on March 30, 2010, at http://www.cms.gov/manuals/Downloads/clm104c12.pdf.

229. Hansen-Turton, T., Ritter, A., Rothman, N., & Valdez, R. (2006). Insurer policies create barriers to health care access and consumer choice. *Nursing Economics, 24*(4), pp. 204–211.

230. Cronenwett, L., & Dzau, V. (2010). Chairman's Summary of the Conference. In B. Culliton (Ed.), *Who will provide primary care and how will they be trained?* New York: Josiah Macy, Jr. Foundation.

231. AARP. (2010). *AARP 2010 policy supplement: Scope of practice of advanced practice registered nurses.* Washington, DC: AARP.

232. Draper, D., Felland, L., Liebhaber, A., & Melichar, L. (2008). The role of nurses in hospital quality improvement. *Research Briefs, No. 3.* Washington, DC: Center for Studying Health System Change.

233. Hughes, R. (2008). *Patient safety and quality: An evidence-based handbook for nurses.* Rockville, MD: Agency for Healthcare Quality and Research.

234. Sheridan-Gonzalez, J., & Wade, M. (1998). Every patient deserves a nurse. In D. Mason, J. Leavitt (eds.), *Policy and politics in nursing and health care* (3rd ed.), pp. 235–240.

235. Wunderlich, G., Sloan, F., & Davis, C. (1996). *Nursing staff in hospitals and nursing homes: Is it adequate?* Washington, DC: National Academy Press.

236. Needleman, J., Buerhaus, P., Mattke, S., Stewart, M., & Zelevinsky, K. (2002). Nurse staffing levels and the quality of care in hospitals. *New England Journal of Medicine, 346*(22), pp. 1715–1722.

237. Aiken, L., Clarke, S., Sloane, D., Sochalski, J., & Silber, J. (2002). Hospital nurse staffing and patient mortality, nurse burnout, and job dissatisfaction. *JAMA, 288*(16), 1987–1993.

238. Unruh, L. (2008). Nurse staffing and patient, nurse, and financial outcomes. *American Journal of Nursing, 108*(1), pp. 62–71.

239. Kane, R., Shamliyan, T., Mueller, C., Duval, S., & Wilt, T. (2007). *Nurse staffing and the quality of patient care.* Rockville, MD: Agency for Healthcare Research and Quality. Accessed on January 14, 2010, at http://www.ahrq .gov/downloads/pub/evidence/pdf/nursestaff/nursestaff.pdf.

240. Jha, A., Orav, E., Zheng, J., & Epstein, A. (2008). Patients' perception of hospital care in the United States. *New England Journal of Medicine, 359*(18), pp. 1921–1931.

241. Finkler, S. (1982). The distinction between cost and charges. *Annals of Internal Medicine, 96,* 102–109.

242. Dall, T., Chen, Y., Siefert, R., Maddox, P. & Hogan, P. (2009). The economic value of professional nursing. *Medical Care, 47*(1), 97–104.

243. Needleman, J., Buerhaus, P., Stewart, M., Zelevinsky, K., & Mattke, S. (2006). Nurse staffing in hospitals: Is there a business case for quality? *Health Affairs, 25*(1), pp. 204–211.

244. Titler, M., Jensen, G., Dochterman, J., Xie, X.-J., Kanak, M., Reed, D., & Shever, L. (2007). Cost of hospital care for older adults with heart failure: Medical, pharmaceutical, and nursing costs. *HSR: Health Services Research, 43*(2), 635–655.

245. Brooks, J., Titler, M., Ardery, G., & Herr, K. (2008). Effect of evident-based acute pain management practices on inpatient costs. *HSR: Health Services Research, 44*(1), pp. 245–263.

246. Unruh, L. (2008). Nurse staffing and patient, nurse, and financial outcomes. *American Journal of Nursing, 108*(1), pp. 62–71.

247. McCue, M., Mark, B., & Harless, D. (2003). Nurse staffing, quality, and financial performance. *Journal of Health Care Finance, 29*(94), pp. 54–76.

248. Needleman, J., Buerhaus, P. Stewart, M., Zelevinsky, K., & Mattke, S. (2006). Nurse staffing in hospitals: Is there a business case for quality? *Health Affairs, 25*(1), pp. 204–211.

249. Rothberg, M., Abraham, I., Lindenauer, P., & Rose, D. (2005). Improving nurse-to-patient staffing ratios as a cost-effective safety intervention. *Medical Care, 43*(8), pp. 785–791.

250. Unruh, L. (2008). Nurse staffing and patient, nurse, and financial outcomes. *American Journal of Nursing, 108*(1), pp. 62–71.

251. Needleman, J., Buerhaus, P., Stewart, M., Zelevinsky, K., & Mattke, S. (2006). Nurse staffing in hospitals: Is there a business case for quality? *Health Affairs, 25*(1), pp. 204–211.

252. Cho, S.-H., Ketefian, S., Barkauskas, V., & Smith, D. (2003). The effects of nurse staffing on adverse events, morbidity, mortality, and medical costs. *Nursing Research, 52*(2), pp. 71–79.

253. Estabrooks, C., Midodzi, W., Cummings, G., Ricker, K., & Giovannetti, P. (2005). The impact of hospital nursing characteristics on 30-day mortality. *Nursing Research, 54*(2), pp. 74–84.

254. Aiken, L., Clarke, S., Cheung, R., Sloane, D., & Silber, R. (2003). Educational levels of hospital nurses and patient mortality. *Journal of the American Medical Association, 290*(12), pp. 1617–1623.

255. Mark, B., Harless, D., McCue, M., & Xu, Y. (2004). A longitudinal examination of hospital registered nurse staffing and quality of care. *HSR: Health Services Research, 39*(2), pp. 279–300.

256. Needleman, J., Buerhaus, P., Mattke, S., Stewart, M., & Zelevinsky, K. (2002). Nurse staffing levels and the quality of care in hospitals. *New England Journal of Medicine, 346*(22), pp. 1715–1722.

257. Aiken, L., Clarke, S., Sloane, D., Sochalski, J., & Silber, J. (2002). Hospital nurse staffing and patient mortality, nurse burnout, and job dissatisfaction. *JAMA, 288*(16), pp. 1987–1993.

258. Kane, R., Shamliyan, T., Mueller, C., Duval, S., & Wilt, T. (2007). *Nurse staffing and the quality of patient care.* Rockville, MD: Agency for Healthcare Research and Quality. Accessed on January 14, 2010, at http://www.ahrq .gov/downloads/pub/evidence/pdf/nursestaff/nursestaff.pdf.

259. American Nurses Association. (2010a). *National Database of Nursing Quality Indicators (NDNQI)®.* Accessed on March 10, 2010, at http://www.www.safestaffingsaveslives.org/WhatisSafeStaffing/OneMinuteEssays/NDNQI .aspx.

260. National Quality Forum. (2007). Nursing performance measurement and reporting: A status report. *Navigating Quality Forward,* Issue Brief No. 5, pp. 104. Accessed on January 15, 2010, at http://www.qualityforum.org/Publications/2007/07/Nursing_Performance_Measurement_and_Reporting.aspx.

261. Dall, T., Chen, Y., Siefert, R., Maddox, P., & Hogan, P. (2009). The economic value of professional nursing. *Medical Care, 47*(1), pp. 97–104.

262. Kaye, H., Harrington, C., LaPlante, M. (2010). Long-term care: Who gets it, who provides it, who pays, and how much? *Health Affairs, 29*(1), pp. 11–21.

263. Harrington, C., Kovner, C., Mezey, M., Kayser-Jones, J., Burger, S., Morhler, M., Burke, R., & Zimmerman, D. (2000). Experts recommend minimum nurse staffing standards for nursing facilities in the United States. *The Gerontologist, 40*(1), pp. 5–16.

264. Harrington, C. (2011). Long-term care policy issues. In D. Mason, J. Leavitt, & M. Chaffee (Eds.), *Policy and politics in nursing and health care* (6th ed). St. Louis: Elsevier.

265. Office of the Inspector General, U.S. Department of Health and Human Services. (2008). *Memorandum Report: "Trends in Nursing Home Deficiencies and Complaints," OEI-02–08–00140.* Accessed on April 23, 2010, at http://graphics8.nytimes.com/packages/pdf/national/nursinghome.pdf.

266. Harrington, C. (2011). Long-term care policy issues. In D. Mason, J. Leavitt, M. Chaffee (Eds.), *Policy and politics in nursing and health care* (6th ed). St. Louis: Elsevier.

267. Wunderlich, G., & Kohler, P. (2001). *Improving the quality of long-term care.* Washington, DC: National Academy Press.

268. Wunderlich, G., Sloan, F., & Davis, C. (1996). *Nursing staff in hospitals and nursing homes: Is it adequate?* Washington, DC: National Academy Press.

269. Institute of Medicine. (2008). *Retooling for an Aging America: Building the Health Care Workforce.* Washington, DC: National Academies Press.

270. Horn, S., Buerhaus, P., Bergstrom, N., & Smout, R. (2005). RN staffing time and outcomes of long-stay nursing home residents. *American Journal of Nursing, 105*(11), pp. 58–70.

271. Harrington, C. (2011). Long-term care policy issues. In D. Mason, J. Leavitt, M. Chaffee (Eds.), *Policy and politics in nursing and health care* (6th ed). St. Louis: Elsevier.

272. Harrington, C., Woolhandler, S., Mullan, J., Carrillo, H., & Himmelstein, D. (2001). Does investor ownership of nursing homes compromise the quality of care? *American Journal of Public Health, 91*, pp. 1452–1455.

273. Mason, D. (2009). Contrasts in long-term care. *American Journal of Nursing, 109*(1), pp. 50–51.

274. Robert, D., McKay, M., & Shaffer, A. (2008). Increasing rates of emergency department visits for elderly patients in the United States, 1993 to 2003. *Annals of Emergency Medicine, 51*(6), pp. 769–774.

275. Sullivan-Marx, E., Bradway, C., & Barnsteiner, J. (2010). Innovative collaborations: a case study for academic owned nursing practice. *Journal of Nursing Scholarship, 42*(1), pp. 50–57.

276. Kane, R., Homyak, P., Bershadsky, B., & Flood, S. (2006). Variations on a theme called PACE. *Journal of Gerontology, Series A: Biological Sciences and Medical Sciences, 61*(7), pp. 689–693.

277. Kane, R., Keckhafer, G., Flood, S., Bershadsky, B., & Siadaty, M. (2003). The effect of Evercare on hospital use. *Journal of the American Geriatrics Society, 51*, pp. 1427–1434.

278. American Academy of Nursing. (n.d.-b). *Evercare: putting nurse practitioners and care manager at the heart of care delivery.* Accessed on February 27, 2010, at http://www.aannet.org/files/public/Evercare_template.pdf.

279. American Academy of Nursing. (n.d.-e). *Senior ASSIST: Bridging a gap in services for community dwelling elderly.* Accessed on February 27, 2010, at http://www.aannet.org/files/public/Senior%20Assist_template.pdf.

280. Gebbie, K. (1995). Follow the money: Funding streams and public health nursing. *Journal of Public Health Management Practice, 1*(3), pp. 23–28.

281. The Quad Council of Public Health Nursing Organization. (2007). *The public health nursing shortage: a threat to the public's health.* Accessed on December 28, 2010, at http://www.resourcenter.net/images/ACHNE/Files/QCShortagePaperFinal2-07.pdf.

282. Bekemeier, B., & Jones, M. (2010). Relationships between local public health agency functions and agency leadership and staffing. *Journal of Public Health Management and Practice, 16*(2), E8–E16. Accessed on February

27, 2010, at http://www.ncbi.nlm.nih.gov.proxy.wexler.hunter.cuny.edu/pubmed/20150786?itool=EntrezSystem2 .PEntrez.Pubmed.Pubmed_ResultsPanel.Pubmed_RVDocSum&ordinalpos=3.

283. Grumbach, K., Miller, J., Mertz, E., & Finocchio, L. (2004). How much public health in public health nursing? *Public Health Nursing, 21*(3), pp. 266–276.

284. Reinhard, S., Christopher, M., Mason, D., McConnell, K., Rusca, P., & Toughill, E. (1996). Promoting healthy communities through neighborhood nursing. *Nursing Outlook, 44*(5), 223–228.

285. Boo, K. (2006, February 6). Swamp nurse. *New Yorker*, pp. 54–64.

286. Eckenrode, J., Campa, M., Luckey, D., Henderson, C., Cole, R., Kitzman, H., Anson, E., Sidora-Arcoleo, K., Powers, J., & Olds, D. (2010). Long-term effects of prenatal and infancy nurse home visitation on the life course of youths 19-year follow-up of a randomized trial. *Archives of Pediatric and Adolescent Medicine, 164*(1), pp. 9–15.

287. Karoly, L., Killburn, M., & Cannon, J. (2005). *Early childhood interventions: Proven results, future promise.* Arlington, VA: RAND Corporation. Accessed on April 1, 2010, at http://www.rand.org/pubs/monographs/2005/ RAND_MG341.pdf.

288. Olds, D., Robinson, J., O'Brien, R., Luckey, D., Pettitt, L., Henderson, C., Ng, R., Sheff, K., Korfmacher, J., Hiatt, S. & Talmi, A. (2002). Home visiting by paraprofessionals and by nurses: A randomized controlled trial. *Pediatrics, 110* (3), pp. 486–496.

289. Hootman, J. (2002). The importance of research to school nurses and school nursing practice. *Journal of School Nursing, 18*(2), pp. 18–24.

290. Costante, C. (2001). School health nursing: Framework for the future, part I. *Journal of School Nursing, 17*(1), pp. 3–11.

291. National Association of School Nurses. (2009). *Student-to-School Nurse Ratio Improvement Act of 2009, H.R. 2730.* Accessed on February 27, 2010, at http://www.nasn.org/Portals/0/legislation/HR2730_Ratio_Support_Bill.pdf.

292. Bureau of Health Professions. (2004b). *The registered nurse population: Findings from the 2004 National Sample Survey of Registered Nurses.* Rockville, MD: Health Resources and Services Administration. Accessed on January 12, 2010, at http://bhpr.hrsa.gov/healthworkforce/rnsurvey04/3.htm.

293. National Association of School Nurses. (2006). *School nurse management of students with chronic health conditions.* Accessed on February 27, 2010, at http://www.nasn.org/Default.aspx?tabid=351.

294. Gutta, M., Engelke, M., & Swanson, M. (2004). Does the school nurse-to-student ratio make a difference? *Journal of School Health, 74*(1), pp. 6–9.

295. Hansen-Turton, T., Bailey, D., & Torres, M. (2010). Nurse-managed centers: The key to a healthy future. *American Journal of Nursing, 110*(9): 23–26.

296. National Association of School Nurses. (2001). *The role of the school nurse in school-based health centers.* Accessed on February 27, 2010, at http://www.nasn.org/Default.aspx?tabid=245.

297. Costante, C. (2001). School health nursing: Framework for the future, part I. *Journal of School Nursing, 17*(1), pp. 3–11.

298. Fagin, C., & Diers, D. (1983). Nursing as metaphor. *New England Journal of Medicine, 309*(2), pp. 116–117.

299. Rothman, S. (1978). *Woman's proper place: A history of changing ideals and practices, 1870 to the present.* New York: Basic Books.

300. Ashley, J. (1973). This I believe about power in nursing. *Nursing Outlook, 21,* pp. 637–641.

301. Rothman, S. (1978). *Woman's proper place: A history of changing ideals and practices, 1870 to the present.* New York: Basic Books.

302. Rogers, M. (1970). *An introduction to the theoretical basis of nursing.* Philadelphia: F. A. Davis.

303. Dykeman, M., & Loukissa, D. (1993). The science of unitary human beings: An integrative review. *Nursing Science Quarterly, 6*(4), pp. 179–188.

304. Vance, C., Talbott, S., McBride, A., & Mason, D. (1985). An uneasy alliance: Nursing and the women's movement. *Nursing Outlook, 33*(6), pp. 281–285.

305. Roberts, S. (1983). Oppressed group behavior and the implications for nursing. *Advances in Nursing Science, 5*(4), 2 pp. 1–30.

306. Stein, L. (1967). The doctor-nurse game. *Archives of General Psychiatry, 16*(6), pp. 699–703.

307. Rosenstein, A., & O'Daniel, M. (2008). A survey of the impact of disruptive behavior and communication defects on patient safety. *The Joint Commission Journal on Quality and Patient Safety, 34*(8), pp. 464–471.

308. Rosenstein, A., & O'Daniel, M. (2005). Disruptive behavior and clinical outcomes: Perceptions of nurses and physicians. *American Journal of Nursing, 105*(1), pp. 54–64.

309. The Joint Commission. (2009). *Code of conduct.* Chicago: The Joint Commission.

310. Ashley, J. (1973). This I believe about power in nursing. *Nursing Outlook, 21,* pp. 637–641.

311. American Association of Colleges of Medicine. (2009). *U.S. medical school applicants and students, 1982–1983 and 2009–2010.* Accessed on March 30, 2010, at http://www.aamc.org/data/facts/charts1982to2010.pdf.

312. The Woodhull Study on Nursing and the Media. (1997). *Health care's invisible partner: Final report.* Indianapolis, IN: Sigma Theta Tau International Honor Society of Nursing.

313. Prybil, L., Levey, S., Peterson, R., Heinrich, D., Brezinski, P., Zamba, G., Amendola, A, Price, J., & Roach, W. (2009). *Governance in high-performing community health systems: A report on Trustee and CEO views.* Chicago: Grant Thorton, LLP.

314. Pynes, J. (2000). Are women underrepresented as leaders of nonprofit organizations? *Review of Public Personnel Administration, 20*(2), pp. 35–49.

315. Gallup. (2010). *Nursing leadership from bedside to boardroom: Opinion leaders' perception.* Accessed on March 25, 2010, at http://newcareersinnursing.org/sites/default/files/file-attachments/Top%20Line%20Report.pdf.

316. Cohen, S., Mason, D., Kovner, C., Leavitt, J., Pulcini, J., & Sochalski, J. (1996). Stages of nursing's political development: Where we've been and where we ought to go. *Nursing Outlook, 44*(6), 2 pp. 59–266.

317. Pew Health Professions Commission. (1995). *Critical challenges: revitalizing the health professions for the twenty-first century.* Accessed on March 11, 2010, at http://futurehealth.ucsf.edu/Content/29/1995–12_Critical_Challenges_Revitalizing_the_Health_Professions_for_the_Twenty-First_Century.pdf.

318. Reverby, S. (1987). A caring dilemma: Womanhood and nursing in historical perspective. *Nursing Research, 36*(1), pp. 5–11.

319. Hatem, M., Sandall, J., Devane, D., Soltani, H., & Gates S. (2008). Midwife-led versus other models of care for childbearing women. *Cochrane Database of Systematic Reviews, 4,* CD004667. Accessed on April 5, 2010, at http://www.mrw.interscience.wiley.com.proxy.wexler.hunter.cuny.edu/cochrane/clsysrev/articles/CD004667/pdf_standard_fs.html.

320. Hodnett, E., Gates, S., Hofmey, G., & Sakala, C. (2007). Continuous support for women during childbirth. *Cochrane Database of Systematic Reviews, 3,* CD003766. Accessed on April 4, 2010, http://www.mrw.interscience.wiley.com.proxy.wexler.hunter.cuny.edu/cochrane/clsysrev/articles/CD003766/pdf_standard_fs.html.

321. Jencks, S., Williams, M., & Coleman, E. (2009). Rehospitalizations among patients in the Medicare fee-for-service program. *New England Journal of Medicine, 360*(14), pp. 1418–1428.

322. Brooten, D., Naylor, M., York, R., Brown, L., Munro, B., Hollingsworth, A., Cohen, S., Finkler, S., Deatrick, J., & Youngblut, J. (2002). Lessons learned from testing the quality cost model of advanced practice nursing (APN) transitional care. *Journal of Nursing Scholarship, 34*(4), pp. 369–375.

323. Naylor, M., Brooten, D., Campbell, R., Maislin, G., McCauley, K., & Schwartz, J. (2004). Transitional care of older adults hospitalized with heart failure: A randomized, controlled trial. *Journal of the American Geriatrics Society, 52*(5), pp. 675–684.

324. Kaiser Family Foundation. (2009). *House Majority Whip James Clyburn introduces bill to quadruple number of community health center in the U. S.* Accessed on January 11, 2010, at http://www.kaiserhealthnews.org/Daily-Reports/2009/March/03/dr00057260.aspx?referrer=search.

325. Mehrotra, A., Liu, H., Adams, J., Wang, M., Lave, J., Thygeson, N. M., Solberg, L., & McGlynn, E. (2009). The costs and quality of care for three common illnesses at retail clinics as compared to other medical settings. *Annals of Internal Medicine, 151*(5), pp. 321–328.

326. Mehrotra, A., Wang, M., Lave, J., Adams, J., & McGlynn, E. (2008). Retail clinics, primary care physicians, and emergency departments: A comparison of patients' visits. *Health Affairs (Millwood), 27*(5), pp. 1272–1282.

327. Dolan, P. (2009, March 4). Retail clinics attracting legislator interest. *amednews.com.* Accessed on December 21, 2009, at http://www.ama-assn.org/amednews/2009/03/02/bisg0304.htm.

328. Gross, D., Garvey, C., Julion, W., Fogg, L., Tucker, S., & Mokros, H. (n.d.). The Chicago Parent Program: Evaluating effectiveness with low-income multi-ethnic parents of young children. Accessed on April 2, 2010, at http://www.chicagoparentprogram.org/blog/wp-content/uploads/cpp_prevention_science.pdf.

329. Breitenstein, S., Gross, D., Ordaz, I., Julion, W., Garvey, C., & Ridge, A. (2007). Promoting mental health in early childhood programs serving families from low-income neighborhoods. *Journal of the American Psychiatric Nurses Association, 13,* p. 313.

330. American Academy of Nursing. (n.d.-a). *Chicago Parenting Program: Teaching better ways to address difficult children's behavioral problems.* Accessed on April 23, 2010, at http://www.aannet.org/files/public/Chicago%20 Parent_template.pdf.

331. American Academy of Nursing. (n.d.-d). *Health InterConnexions: Reducing health care costs by encouraging healthier lifestyle choices.* Accessed on April 3, 2010, at http://www.aannet.org/files/public/HealthInterx _template.pdf.

332. Jemmott, L., Jemmott, J., III, & O'Leary, A. (2007). Effects on sexual risk behavior and STD rate of brief HIV/ STD prevention interventions for African American women in primary care settings. *American Journal of Public Health, 97,* pp. 1034–1040.

333. American Nurses Association. (1991). *Nursing's agenda for health care reform.* Washington, DC: ANA.

334. Lindenauer, P., Rothberg, M., Pekow, P., Kenwood, C., Benjamin, E., & Auerbach, A. (2007). Outcomes of hospitalists, general internists, and family physicians. *New England Journal of Medicine, 357*(25), pp. 2589–2600.

335. McMahon, L. (2007). The hospitalist movement—Time to move on. *New England Journal of Medicine, 357*(25), pp. 2627–2629.

336. Mitchell, P., & Mount, J. (2009). *Nurse staffing—A summary of current research opinion and policy.* Pullman: The William D. Ruckelshaus Center, University of Washington.

THE HISTORY OF NURSING AND THE ROLE OF NURSES

Reprints of Key Articles

Florence Nightingale, "Notes on Nursing: What It Is, And What It Is Not"

Virginia Henderson, "The Nature of Nursing"

Susan Reverby, "A Caring Dilemma: Womanhood and Nursing in Historical Perspective"

Claire M. Fagin and Donna Diers, "Nursing as Metaphor"

Sally Solomon Cohen, Diana J. Mason, Christine Kovner, Judith K. Leavitt, Joyce Pulcini, and Julie Sochalski, "Stages of Nursing's Political Development: Where We've Been and Where We Ought to Go"

Susan R. Gortner, "Knowledge Development in Nursing: Our Historical Roots and Future Opportunities"

NOTES ON NURSING: WHAT IT IS, AND WHAT IT IS NOT

FLORENCE NIGHTINGALE

This chapter originally appeared as Nightingale, F. (1860). *Notes on nursing: What it is, and what it is not*. New York: D. Appleton and Company.

EDITORS' NOTE

This historic book was the first to describe the elements of nursing. Nightingale wrote it for women who were not trained as nurses but were expected to care for family members. Some nursing theorists view *Notes on Nursing* as evidence that Nightingale was the first nurse theorist—one who had a holistic view of health that included the environment. The excerpt that follows is taken from the opening chapter.

■ ■ ■

Shall we begin by taking it as a general principle—that all disease, at some period or other of its course, is more or less a reparative process, not necessarily accompanied with suffering: an effort of nature to remedy a process of poisoning or of decay, which has taken place weeks, months, sometimes years beforehand, unnoticed, the termination of the disease being then, while the antecedent process was going on, determined?

If we accept this as a general principle, we shall be immediately met with anecdotes and instances to prove the contrary. Just so if we were to take, as a principle—all the climates of the earth are meant to be made habitable for man, by the efforts of man—the objection would be immediately raised—will the top of Mount Blanc ever be made habitable? Our answer would be, it will be many thousands of years before we have reached the bottom of Mount Blanc in making the earth healthy. Wait till we have reached the bottom before we discuss the top.

In watching diseases, both in private houses and in public hospitals, the thing which strikes the experienced observer most forcibly is this, that the symptoms or the sufferings generally considered to be inevitable and incident to the disease are very often not symptoms of the disease at all, but of something quite different—of the want of fresh air, or of light, or of warmth, or of quiet, or of cleanliness, or of punctuality and care in the administration of diet, of each or of all of these. And this quite as much in private as in hospital nursing.

The reparative process which Nature has instituted and which we call disease, has been hindered by some want of knowledge or attention, in one or in all of these things, and pain, suffering, or interruption of the whole process sets in.

If a patient is cold, if a patient is feverish, if a patient is faint, if he is sick after taking food, if he has a bed-sore, it is generally the fault not of the disease, but of the nursing.

I use the word nursing for want of a better. It has been limited to signify little more than the administration of medicines and the application of poultices. It ought to signify the proper use of fresh air, light, warmth, cleanliness, quiet, and the proper selection and administration of diet—all at the least expense of vital power to the patient.

It has been said and written scores of times, that every woman makes a good nurse. I believe, on the contrary, that the very elements of nursing are all but unknown.

By this I do not mean that the nurse is always to blame. Bad sanitary, bad architectural, and bad administrative arrangements often make it impossible to nurse. But the art of nursing ought to include such arrangements as alone make what I understand by nursing, possible.

The art of nursing, as now practiced, seems to be expressly constituted to unmake what God had made disease to be, viz., a reparative process.

To recur to the first objection. If we are asked, Is such or such a disease a reparative process? Can such an illness be unaccompanied with suffering? Will any care prevent such a patient from suffering this or that?—I humbly say, I do not know. But when you have done away with all that pain and suffering, which in patients are the symptoms not of their disease, but of the absence of one or all of the above-mentioned essentials to the success of Nature's reparative processes, we shall then know what are the symptoms of and the sufferings inseparable from the disease.

Another and the commonest exclamation which will be instantly made is—Would you do nothing, then, in cholera, fever, etc.?—so deep-rooted and universal is the conviction that to give medicine is to be doing something, or rather everything; to give air, warmth, cleanliness, etc., is to do nothing. The reply is, that in these and many other similar diseases the exact value of particular remedies and modes of treatment is by no means ascertained, while there is universal experience as to the extreme importance of careful nursing in determining the issue of the disease.

The very elements of what constitutes good nursing are as little understood for the well as for the sick. The same laws of health or of nursing, for they are in reality the same, obtain among the well as among the sick. The breaking of them produces only a less violent consequence among the former than among the latter—and this sometimes, not always.

It is constantly objected—"But how can I obtain this medical knowledge? I am not a doctor. I must leave this to doctors."

Oh, mothers of families! You who say this, do you know that one in every seven infants in this civilized land of England perishes before it is one year old? That, in London, two in every five die before they are five years old? And, in the other great cities of England, nearly one out of two?* "The life duration of tender babies" (as some Saturn, turned analytical chemist, says) "is the most delicate test" of sanitary conditions. Is all this premature

---

*Upon this fact the most wonderful deductions have been strung. For a long time an announcement something like the following has been going the round of the papers:—"More than 25,000 children die every year in London under 10 years of age; therefore we want a Children's Hospital." This spring there was a prospectus issued, and divers other means taken to this effect:—"There is a great want of sanitary knowledge in women; therefore we want a Women's Hospital." Now, both the above facts are too sadly true. But what is the deduction? The causes of the enormous child mortality are perfectly well known; they are chiefly want of cleanliness, want of ventilation, want of white-washing; in one word, defective *household* hygiene. The remedies are just as well known; and among them is certainly not the establishment of a Child's Hospital. This may be a want; just as there may be a want of hospital room for adults. But the Registrar-General would certainly never think of giving us as a cause for the high rate of child mortality in (say) Liverpool that there was not sufficient hospital room for children; nor would he urge upon us, as a remedy, to found an hospital for them.

suffering and death necessary? Or did Nature intend mothers to be always accompanied by doctors? Or is it better to learn the piano-forte than to learn the laws which subserve the preservation of offspring?

Again, women, and the best women, are woefully deficient in sanitary knowledge; although it is to women that we must look, first and last, for its application, as far as *household* hygiene is concerned. But who would ever think of citing the institution of a Women's Hospital as the way to cure this want?

We have it, indeed upon very high authority that there is some fear lest hospitals, as they have been *hitherto,* may not have generally increased, rather than diminished, the rate of mortality—especially of child mortality.

Macaulay somewhere says, that it is extraordinary that, whereas the laws of the motions of the heavenly bodies, far removed as they are from us, are perfectly well understood, the laws of the human mind, which are under our observation all day and every day, are no better understood than they were two thousand years ago.

But how much more extraordinary is it that, whereas what we might call the coxcombries of education—e.g., the elements of astronomy—are now taught to every school-girl, neither mothers of families of any class, nor school-mistresses of any class, nor nurses of children, nor nurses of hospitals, are taught anything about those laws which God has assigned to the relations of our bodies with the world in which He has put them. In other words, the laws which make these bodies, into which He has put our minds, healthy or unhealthy organs of those minds, are all but unlearnt. Not but that these laws—the laws of life—are in a certain measure understood, but not even mothers think it worth their while to study them—to study how to give their children healthy existences. They call it medical or physiological knowledge, fit only for doctors.

Another objection.

We are constantly told—"But the circumstances which govern our children's healths are beyond our control. What can we do with winds? There is the east wind. Most people can tell before they get up in the morning whether the wind is in the east."

To this one can answer with more certainty than to the former objections. Who is it who knows when the wind is in the east? Not the Highland drover, certainly, exposed to the east wind, but the young lady who is worn out with the want of exposure to fresh air, to sunlight, etc. Put the latter under as good sanitary circumstances as the former, and she too will not know when the wind is in the east.

2

THE NATURE OF NURSING

VIRGINIA HENDERSON

EDITORS' NOTE

At a time when the profession was struggling to define itself apart from medicine, Virginia Henderson provided a clear definition of nursing that delineated an independent dimension. It provided the language for nurses to articulate what was uniquely nursing, including its role in health and illness, recovering and dying.

■ ■ ■

It is self-evident that an occupation, and especially a profession whose services affect human life, must define its function. Nursing's attempt to do so has a long, and still unfinished, history. Inevitably, we go back to Florence Nightingale. In her *Notes on Nursing: What It Is and What It Is Not,* she says, in essence, that what nursing has to do is to ". . . put the patient in the best condition for nature to act upon him."[1] There is no doubt that Miss Nightingale's concept influenced the development of modern nursing more than any other. Some nurses still cite this as the definition they find most helpful.

But with the passage of the nurse registration act in England and state nurse practice acts in the United States around the turn of the century, it became necessary to describe nursing in such a way as to protect the public and the nurse. The definitions at this time were necessarily concerned with what the nurse was legally empowered to do and, as most nurses were then working as private practitioners in homes and hospitals, most of the legal definitions implied that the nurse operated under the supervision of a physician. They failed to identify that aspect of her work that was independent or self-directed.

The idea of the nurse as merely the physician's assistant, however, has never been satisfying to the occupation as a whole or to many of its individual members. For example, in 1933 and 1934, Effie J. Taylor defined nursing as "adapting prescribed therapy and preventive treatment to the specific physical and psychic needs of the individual"[2,3]. She also added, "the real depths of nursing can only be made known through ideals, love, sympathy, knowledge, and culture, expressed through the practice of artistic procedures and relationships." In these statements, made 30 years ago, Miss Taylor anticipated some of the current emphasis on patient-centered care and a liberal education for the nurse.

Immediately after World War II, the rumblings of dissatisfaction with the ambiguous position of nursing heard during the first half of the century, developed into a major explosion of discontent. In 1946, the American Nurses' Association asked certain nursing leaders to formulate *their* definitions of nursing and devoted a session at that year's convention to the subject.[4]

About this time, Esther Lucile Brown was asked by the National Nursing Council to study the needs of society for nursing. Included in her report is a definition of nursing developed by a group of nurse experts—an excellent statement, but so general any health worker might claim it also applies to his field.[5]

Three regional conferences were also held in connection with Miss Brown's study. At one of these a small committee, of which I was a member, developed a definition that was much more specific than the one previously referred to; it represented, in fact, my point of view modified by the thinking of others in the group. Although this statement was included in the report of the regional conferences, it has never been cited directly.[6]

Another approach to defining nursing was the American Nurses' Association's five-year investigation of the nurse's function. Studies were made in 17 different states, and the results summarized in *Twenty Thousand Nurses Tell Their Story.*[7] And, following this, the various ANA sections developed statements on the functions, standards, and qualifications for practice in the fields of nursing represented.

Whether or not these research efforts give us a satisfying description of the nursing function is open to question, but certainly they throw considerable light on what nurses were actually doing in the 1950s, and on what they consider their proper functions.

Now, just as at the turn of the century, the necessity for a legal definition of nursing practice remains. The most recent official statement (1962) on the subject, was designed for inclusion in nurse practice acts.[8] This statement, although still very general and inclusive, suggests that the nurse can observe, care for, and counsel the patient and can supervise other health personnel without herself being supervised by the physician. It implies a more independent function for the nurse than did previous official statements.[9]

While the official statements on nursing may serve the purpose for which they are intended, there is abundant evidence that they have not satisfied everyone. And, in recent years, with the development of varying types and grades of nursing personnel, the difficulty of defining function has been compounded. Probably the effort of organized nursing to formulate a statement of its function will always be unfinished business since conditions change from one era to the next and with the culture or nature of a society. But so long as available definitions are unsatisfying to nurses, or too general to guide practice, research, and education, individuals will continue to search for statements that fulfill their needs.

DEVELOPMENT OF A CONCEPT

My interpretation of the nurse's function is the synthesis of many influences, some positive and some negative. Before discussing it, however, and identifying the most significant experiences leading to its formulation, I should first make clear that I do not expect everyone to agree with me. Rather, I would urge every nurse to develop her own concept; otherwise, she is merely imitating others or acting under authority. In my own case I felt as though I was steering an uncharted course until I resolved certain doubts about my true function as a nurse.

My basic training was largely in a general hospital where, for the nurse, technical competence, speed of performance, and a "professional" (actually an impersonal) manner were stressed. We were introduced to nursing as a series of almost unrelated procedures, beginning with making an unoccupied bed and progressing to, say, aspiration of body cavities. In this era, ability to catheterize a patient seemed to qualify a student for "night duty" where, without any previous experience in the administration of a service, she might have the entire care of 30 sick souls and bodies.

An authoritarian type of medicine and nursing were practiced in this hospital. Teaching was based on the textbook. Not even lip service was given "patient-centered care," "family health service," "comprehensive care" or "rehabilitation."

But there was, for me, an influence in these early student days that tended to negate this mechanistic approach to patient care. Annie W. Goodrich was dean of my school, the Army School of Nursing, and whenever she visited our unit she lifted our sights above techniques and routines. She saw nursing as a "world-wide social activity," a creative and constructive force in society, and, having a powerful intellect and boundless compassion for humanity, she never failed to infect us with "the ethical significance of nursing."[10] It is to her that I attribute my early discontent with the regimentalized patient care in which I participated and the concept of nursing as merely ancillary to medicine. But while Miss Goodrich presented us with the highest aim for nursing she left us to translate it into concrete acts. I needed someone to "show me"—as Liza Doolittle sang, when words had ceased to be enough for her. I seldom, if ever, saw graduate nurses practice nursing; never my teachers. Their teaching was in a classroom.

A positive nursing experience, however, was a summer spent, when I was still a student with the Henry Street Visiting Nurse Agency. Here I began to discard the formal approach to patients approved in the general hospital. In fact, I acquired a skepticism of medical care in hospitals that remains with me. Seeing the sick return to their homes following hospitalization, I began to realize that the seemingly successful institutional regimen nevertheless often failed to change the factors in the patient's way of living that had hospitalized him in the first place. Even today I question whether our traditional hospital routines and practices can really prepare a patient for a return to health. Nowhere during my entire student experience, it seems to me, did I have the opportunity to see or practice individualized care—to acquire the human relations skills that I needed. My psychiatric nursing affiliation concentrated on disease entities and their treatment, not on how the nurse might help the individual patient. And although, during my pediatric nursing affiliation, I first experienced the satisfaction—and saw the superiority—of a "case" as opposed to a "functional" assignment, the care was too mechanistic to teach me the true value of patient-centered care.

With this background and after a year of visiting nurse work I became the only full-time instructor in a school of nursing. Here I was forced to learn as I taught. I at least sensed the need for more knowledge and clarification of my ideas and, fortunately for all concerned, I went back to school.

Except for a brief period of clinical supervision and teaching at the Strong Memorial Hospital, I remained at Teachers College, Columbia University—as student and teacher—for some 2 years, and during this time my concept of nursing was not so much changed as clarified. It is impossible to identify all the persons and experiences that brought this about, but a few stand out.

Caroline Stackpole based her teaching of physiology on Claude Bernard's dictum that health depends upon keeping the lymph constant around the cell.[11] This emphasis on the unit structure taught me relationships in what were, up to that time, unrelated laws of health. Miss Stackpole was a master teacher who was never satisfied until the student answered his own question. Jean Broadhurst, a microbiologist, had this same concept of teaching. Primarily from those two, I acquired an analytic approach to all aspects of care and treatment.

Now, as I read reports of malnutrition from therapeutic diets, emotional and physiological crises from endocrine therapy, drug-induced skin lesions, and the varied complications from cortisone administration, I think to myself: "the constancy of the intercellular fluids has been dangerously reduced." Ever since I grasped this danger I have believed that a definition of nursing should imply an appreciation of the principle of physiological balance. It makes so vivid the importance of forcing fluids, of feeding the comatose, or of relieving oxygen want.

Dr. Edward Thorndike's work in psychology, also at Teachers College, provided some parallel generalizations, or fixed points, in the psychosocial realm. His study of the fundamental needs of man made me realize that illness all too often places a person in a setting where shelter from the elements is almost the only fundamental need that is fully met. In most hospitals the patient cannot eat as he wishes, his freedom of movement is curtailed, his privacy is invaded; he is put to bed in strange nightclothes, making him feel as unattractive as a punished child; he is separated from the objects of his affection; he is deprived of almost every diversion and of his work, and is reduced to dependence on persons who are often younger than he is, and sometimes less intelligent and courteous.

From the time I saw hospitalization in this light I have questioned every nursing routine or restriction that is in conflict with the individual's fundamental need for shelter, food, communication with others, and the company of those he loves; for opportunity to win approval, to dominate and be dominated, to learn, to work, to worship, and to play. In other words, I have since conceived it to be the aim of nursing to keep the individual's day as normal as possible—to keep him in "the stream of life" to the extent that it is consistent with the physician's therapeutic plan.

Soon after this enlightenment I saw the work of Dr. George G. Deaver and the physical therapists associated with him at the Institute for the Crippled and Disabled in New York City. It seemed to me that in their work I was witnessing the implementation of many ideas I had been accumulating. And I saw that much of the effort of rehabilitation went into building the patient's independence—the independence of which hospital personnel had unwittingly deprived him or had, at least, failed to encourage. Nothing has made my concept of nursing more concrete than the insistence of these workers on individualized programs with constant evaluation of the patient's needs and progress toward the goal of independence.

My participation in preparing the 1937 *Curriculum Guide,* in the work of the NLNE's special committee on postgraduate clinical courses, and in the regional conferences associated with Miss Brown's study, all forced me to express in writing these evolving concepts of nursing. It was not until the 1940s, however, that I could test my ideas in actual practice, when we developed at Teachers College a unique—at least, for that time—type of advanced study in medical-surgical nursing.

This course was unique because it was organized around nursing problems rather than medical diagnoses and diseases of body systems. The associated field experience gave the graduate nurse student an opportunity, for example, to increase her competence in helping a patient to cope with such problems as long-term illness, impending surgery, the relative isolation necessitated by a communicable disease, or the depression following the loss of an arm or a leg. It was one of the first advanced clinical courses where students actually nursed patients and conducted nursing clinics and interdisciplinary conferences around the care of the patients they nursed.

Exchanging views with the able nurses associated with me in planning or teaching this course, and with the students, who were often experienced and expert, was of immeasurable benefit to me in clarifying my ideas. Therefore, in the 1955 revision of Harmer and Henderson's *The Principles and Practice of Nursing,* I was able to present what seemed to me a tested and specific definition of nursing.[12]

Since that time the writings of psychiatric nurses, particularly those of Gwen Tudor (Will) and Ida Orlando (Pelletier) have made me realize how easily the nurse can act on misconceptions of the patient's needs if she does not check her interpretation of them with him.[13,14] The continuing work of faculty and students at the Yale University School of Nursing has reinforced Miss Orlando's conclusions, and further convinced me, that the most effective nursing involves a continuous analysis and validation of the nurse's interpretation of the patients' needs.

UNIQUE FUNCTION

In 1958 the nursing service committee of the International Council of Nurses asked me to describe my concept of basic nursing. The resulting statement published in pamphlet form by the ICN in 1961, was an adaptation of the definition of nursing in Harmer and Henderson and represented the final crystallization of my ideas on the subject.[15]

It is my contention that the nurse is, and should be legally, an independent practitioner, so long as she is not diagnosing or treating disease or making a prognosis, for these functions fall in the physician's realm. But the nurse is *the* authority on basic nursing care. And, by basic nursing care, I mean helping the patient with the following activities or providing conditions under which he can perform them unaided:

1. Breathe normally
2. Eat and drink adequately
3. Eliminate body wastes
4. Move and maintain desirable posture
5. Sleep and rest
6. Select suitable clothes—dress and undress
7. Maintain body temperature within normal range by adjusting clothing and modifying the environment
8. Keep the body clean and well groomed and protect the integument
9. Avoid dangers in the environment and avoid injuring others
10. Communicate with others in expressing emotions, needs, fears, et cetera
11. Worship according to one's faith
12. Work in such a way that there is a sense of accomplishment
13. Play, or participate in various forms of recreation
14. Learn, discover, or satisfy the curiosity that leads to "normal" development and health and use the available health facilities.

In helping the patient with these activities the nurse has infinite need for knowledge of the biological and social sciences and of the skills based on them. There are few more complex arts than that of keeping a patient well nourished and his mouth healthy during a long comatose period; or of helping the depressed, mute psychotic re-establish normal human relations. There is no worker but the nurse who can and will devote herself so consistently day and night to these ends.

This unique function of the nurse I see as a complex service. But, in emphasizing this basic function, I do not mean to disregard the nurse's therapeutic role. She is in most situations the patient's prime helper in carrying out the physician's prescriptions.

If we put total medical care in the form of a pie graph we might assign wedges of different sizes to members of what we now refer to as "the team." The wedge must differ in size for each member according to the problem facing the patient; in some situations certain members of the team have no part of the pie at all. The patient always has a slice, although that of the newborn infant or the unconscious adult is only a sliver; his very life depends on others, but most particularly on the nurse.

In contrast, where an otherwise healthy adult is suffering from a skin condition such as acne, he and his physician compose the team and they can divide the whole pie between them. If the problem is an orthopedic disability, the largest slice may go to the physical therapist; when a sick child is cared for at home by the mother, then the latter's share may be by far the largest. But of all the members of the team, excepting the patient and the physician, the nurse has most often a piece of the pie and, next to theirs, hers is usually the largest share.

In talking about nursing we tend to stress promotion of health and prevention and cure of disease; we rarely speak of the inevitable end of life. Critics of our culture say we are prone to shrink from the thought and sight of old age and death. The nurse, however, cannot do this if she is to fulfill her unique function as I see it. There is a great deal that the nurse can do to keep the environment in which death occurs an esthetic one, and to relieve the patient's discomfort with nursing measures. Even more important, in my concept of nursing, is the nurse's effort to assist the patient toward a "peaceful death" by facing it with him honestly and courageously, thus lending it dignity and even an awesome beauty.

In essence, then, I see nursing as *primarily complementing the patient by supplying what he needs in knowledge, will, or strength to perform his daily activities and also to carry out the treatment prescribed for him by the physician.* What are the implications of such a concept for nursing practice, research, and education?

NURSING PRACTICE

The nurse who sees herself as reinforcing the patient where he lacks will, knowledge, or strength must make an effort to know him, to understand him, to "get inside his skin," as we have said. She will listen to him, his family, and his friends with interest. She will be especially aware of her relation with the patient and will try to make it a constructive, or therapeutic one realizing that this demands self-understanding. Finally, and most important, she will give of herself to the patient.

She will be willing, even anxious, to help the patient perform the functions we have just enumerated. In cooperation with the patient, his family, and other members of the health team, and according to the situation, she will make some sort of individualized plan, or a daily regimen that meets the whole range of human needs. She will not be satisfied to provide merely shelter, sanitary facilities, three meals a day, and the treatments prescribed by the physician.

But just as the nurse seeks to meet the patient's needs during a period of dependency, so she also tries to shorten this period. Before she commits any act for the patient, she asks herself what part of it he could himself perform. If he is unable to act at all, she identifies what he lacks and she helps to supply this lack as rapidly as she can. She evaluates her success with each patient according to the degree to which he establishes independence in all the activities that make up for him, a normal day. The rehabilitation of *all* patients, in the hands of such a nurse, begins with her first service to them.

This primary function of the practicing nurse must, of course, be performed in such a way that it promotes the physician's therapeutic plan. That means helping the patient carry out prescribed treatments or administering the treatment herself. Again, she will consider herself more successful if she assists the patient than if she acts for him.

Now, in certain situations, the nurse may find it necessary to assume the role of a physician—in hospitals with no resident physician, for instance, or in emergency conditions. First aid, which has elements of diagnosis and therapy, is expected of all informed citizens under certain circumstances.

As long as nurses are better prepared than any other member of the health team to act as a physician surrogate they will be tempted, in the interests of the patient, to assume this role. But it is not, in my judgment, their *true role*. In assuming it they not only practice skills in which they are ill prepared but rob themselves of the time needed for the performance of their primary role. Inevitably it forces nurses to delegate their primary function to inadequately prepared personnel. In my opinion, the social pressures that have called for a phenomenal increase in nurses has also demanded a proportionate increase in doctors.

This brings us to the question of the coordinating, managerial, and teaching functions that now consume so much of the professional nurse's time. Nurses must, of course, administer nursing services and teach nursing, but whether they should coordinate the services of the entire medical team is questionable. I, for one, applaud the investigations on non-nursing coordinators and administrators of clinical units.[16,17] I am impressed, too, with the emphasis that Dorothy Smith has recently placed on developing a system in which the nurse can function as effectively as she knows how.[18]

The nurse who sees her primary function as a direct service to the patient will find an immediate reward in his progress toward independence through this service. To the extent that her practice offers this reward, it will be satisfying; to the extent that the situation deprives her of it, she will be dissatisfied. And she will use whatever influence she possesses to foster conditions that make the social rewards for practice at least commensurate with those for teaching and administration.

NURSING RESEARCH

When a nurse operates under a definition of nursing that specifies an area in which she is pre-eminently qualified, she automatically imposes on herself the responsibility for designing the methods she uses in her area of expertness. Studies of nursing functions have shown that, of the hundreds of specific acts performed by nurses, many are non-nursing in nature and could be assigned to other personnel; others are medically prescribed procedures for the design of which the physician is partially responsible. But if the nurse carries out the latter procedures and is liable, in the legal sense, for harmful effects on the patient, then she *must* share the responsibility for the design of the procedure with the physician.

The activities with which I am mainly concerned, however, are those having to do with nursing care itself. Most of these procedures—in fact, most aspects of basic nursing, including the nurse's approach to the patient and what she may and may not say or do for him—are based on tradition or authority, learned by imitation, and taught with little, if any, scientific backing. It is my contention that methods in this all-important area will remain static and invalidated if the nurse fails to study them.

In a survey and assessment of nursing research, Leo W. Simmons and I have pointed out the preponderance of education and occupational studies over clinical investigations.[19] We tried to identify the conditions that discouraged patient-centered research and found: that the major energies of the occupation have gone into improving preparation for nursing and into learning how to recruit and hold sufficient numbers of workers in the occupation; that the demand for administrators and teachers almost exhausts the supply of degree holders, with the result that nurses with a university background tend to study administrative and educational problems; and that those few nurse practitioners prepared to study nursing practice often fail to get the support they need from hospital administrators, nursing service administrators, and physicians.

But if, by definition, nursing has an area of independent professional practice, is not clinical nursing research as necessary, if not more so, than research into other professional problems? Do we not deny our function when we fail to investigate it?

The Surgeon General's Consultant Group on Nursing says, "Nursing research must be stimulated. Research in nursing has just begun to yield the body of knowledge needed as a basis or the improvement of nursing care. . . . Much greater support is required for patient-oriented studies in line with the changing patterns of nursing care."[20]

It is not only in this country that the need for research in nursing practice is recognized. Margaret Jackson, a British physician, has expressed some of these ideas simply and directly:

> Research into nursing methods and appliances possibly began with Eve. Miss Nightingale and the generation of nurses trained under her aegis took it, of course, immeasurably further; but since their day it seems to have come to a dead end of evolution, like the frog. The basic techniques of bed-making, blanket-bathing, giving an enema, administering medicines, and the like, seems hardly to have changed within the memory of woman; and few nurses seem to pause and ask themselves whether their methods and equipment are the best possible, or whether in fact they might be better.[21]

It is my belief that on every clinical service of a hospital a medical research committee and a nursing research committee are needed—both devoted to the ultimate and common goal of improving patient care. The medical research committee would study those problems lying wholly in the realm of medical practice; the nursing research committee would investigate procedures or problems that lie wholly within the realm of nursing practice. But still another committee—a joint one which would include not only doctors and nurses but other specialists as indicated—is also needed to study such treatments or diagnostic tests as are prescribed by the physician and carried out entirely or partially by the nurse.

In this era, research is the name we attach to the most reliable type of analysis. It is based on the full use of scientific findings and is the most reasonable approach man has invented to the solution of his problems. No profession, occupation, or industry can, in this age, adequately evaluate or improve its practice without research. Nursing, if it is truly to represent an area of independent practice, must therefore assume responsibility for validating and improving the methods it uses.

NURSING EDUCATION

A definition staking out an area of health and human welfare in which the nurse is the expert and an independent practitioner calls for education rather than training: a liberalizing education, a grounding in the physical, biological, and social sciences, and the ability to use analytic processes. The curriculum must be organized around the nurse's major function rather than that of the physician, as it has been in the past.

Early emphasis must be given to fundamental human needs, to patients' daily activities, and to the development of the nurse's ability to assess them properly and help the person meet them. In the next stage of the professional curriculum the student might then be introduced to the modifications in nursing care demanded by chronological and intellectual age, sex, emotional balance, state of consciousness, nutritional balance, and other conditions common to all patients and found on any clinical service. This content might constitute the core of the clinical curriculum. Finally, the student would be helped to study the particular needs of each patient, both in relation to these more general conditions and to those stemming from his specific disease, handicap, or condition.

Since the turn of the century, prominent American nurses—conspicuous among them, Miss Goodrich and Miss Watting—and physicians have said that nursing schools should be developed within the educational system—not within the service institutions—of this country. But it is not only in this country that this need has been recognized. Informed physicians and educators throughout the world expressed this opinion.

A revision of established patterns of nursing education calls for strong leadership. At a meeting 20 years ago when someone was bemoaning the fact that there were no leaders in nursing coming along to take the place of our great women of the past, Miss Goodrich rose to protest. She said that the conditions were passing that demanded the militant personalities of earlier years; the idea—not the individual—should lead, she said. She believed firmly that what she called "the complete nurse"—the woman with social experience and a thorough education—had proved her worth, not only as administrator and teacher but more particularly as a practitioner. Therefore she saw as inevitable, rather than as something we must fight for, the preparation of nurses, within the colleges and universities.

I think that the professional quality of nursing service and the appropriateness of a professional preparation have been grasped in many countries, but the means by which these ideas can be implemented are slow in developing. It is up to us who share this faith in the social value of nursing to speed this process.

SUMMARY

The function we believe the nurse performs is primarily an independent one—that of acting for the patient where he lacks knowledge, physical strength, or the will to act for himself. We see this function as complex and creative, as offering unlimited opportunity for the application of the physical, biological, and social sciences, and the development of skills based on them. We believe society wants and expects this service from the nurse and no other worker is as able, or willing, to give it.

If a nurse believes that she is preeminent in an area of health practice, she will try to develop a working milieu in which she can realize her potential value to the person served. She will also recognize her responsibility for the validation and improvement of methods she uses, or for clinical nursing research.

In order to practice as an expert in her own right and to use the scientific approach to the improvement of practice, the nurse needs the kind of education that, in our society, is available only in colleges and universities. Educational programs operated on funds pinched from the budgets of service agencies cannot provide the preparation she needs. Her work demands self-understanding and a universal sympathy for and understanding of, diverse human beings. The "liberalizing" effect of a general education must be recognized, for the personality of the nurse is possibly the most important intangible in measuring the effect of nursing care. As Clare Dennison herself once said, "Finally and fundamentally the quality of nursing care depends upon the quality of those giving care."[22]

NOTES

1. Nightingale, F. *Notes on Nursing: What it is and What it is Not.* Philadelphia, J. B. Lippincott Co., 1946.

2. Smith, M. A concept of nursing. *Amer.J.Nurs. 33:*565, June 1933.

3. Taylor, E. Of what is the nature of nursing? *Amer.J.Nurs. 34:*476, May 1934.

4. The biennial. *Amer.J.Nurs. 46:*728–746, Nov. 1946.

5. Brown, E. *Nursing for the Future.* New York, Russell Sage Foundation, 1948.

6. National Nursing Council. *A Thousand Think Together: a Report of Three Regional Conferences Held in Connection with the Study of Schools of Nursing.* New York, The Council, 1948.

7. Hughes, E., and others. *Twenty Thousand Nurses Tell Their Story.* Philadelphia, J. B. Lippincott Co., 1958.

8. American Nurses' Association. ANA board approves a definition of nursing practice. *Amer.J.Nurs. 55:*1474, Dec. 1955.

9. ———. Professional nursing defined. *Amer.J.Nurs. 37:*518, May 1957.

10. Goodrich, A. *The Social and Ethical Significance of Nursing.* New York: Macmillan Co., 1932.

11. Kimber, D., and others. *Anatomy and Physiology.* 14th ed. New York, Macmillan Co., 1961.

12. Harmer, B. *Textbook of the Principles and Practice of Nursing,* rev. by Virginia Henderson. 5th ed. New York, Macmillan Co., 1955.

13. Tudor, G. A sociopsychiatric nursing approach to intervention in a problem of mutual withdrawal on a mental hospital ward. *Psychiatry 15:*193–217, May 1952.

14. Orlando, I. *The Dynamic Nurse-Patient Relationship: Function, Process and Principles.* New York, G. P. Putnam's Sons, 1961.

15. Henderson, V. *Basic Principles of Nursing Care.* London, International Council of Nurses, 1960.

16. Yankauer, R., and Levine, E. The floor manager position—does it help the nursing unit? *Nurs.Res. 3:*4–10, June 1954.

17. Henderson, C. Freeing the nurse to nurse. *Amer.J.Nurs. 64:*72–77, Mar. 1964.

18. Smith, D. Myth and method in nursing practice. *Amer.J.Nurs. 64:*68–72, Feb. 1964.

19. Simmons, L., and Henderson, V. *Nursing Research: a Survey and Assessment.* New York, Appleton-Century-Crofts, 1964.

20. U.S. Public Health Service. *Toward Quality in Nursing: Needs and Goals. Report of the Surgeon General's Consultant Group on Nursing.* (Publication No. 992) Washington, D.C., U.S. Government Printing Office, 1963.

21. Jackson, M. Where should the nurse be trained? 2. In long-stay hospitals. *Nurs.Times 51:*560–561, May 20, 1955.

22. Dennison, C. Maintaining the quality of nursing service in the emergency. *Amer.J.Nurs. 42:*774–784, July 1942.

3

A CARING DILEMMA: WOMANHOOD AND NURSING IN HISTORICAL PERSPECTIVE

SUSAN REVERBY

This article originally appeared as Reverby, S. (1987). A caring dilemma: Womanhood and nursing in historical perspective. *Nursing Research, 36*(1), pp. 5–11. Copyright © 1987. All rights reserved. Reprinted with permission.

EDITORS' NOTE

This article is based upon historical research by a non-nurse and Harvard professor, Susan Reverby. First published as a book, *Ordered to Care: The Dilemma of American Nursing,* the ideas in this article helped nurses and others to understand the roots of nursing's central paradox: being committed to caring in a society that has not valued this work.

■ ■ ■

"Do not undervalue [your] particular ability to care," students were reminded at a recent nursing school graduation.[1] Rather than merely bemoaning yet another form of late twentieth-century heartlessness, this admonition underscores the central dilemma of American nursing: The order to care in a society that refuses to value caring. This article is an analysis of the historical creation of that dilemma and its consequences for nursing. To explore the meaning of caring for nursing, it is necessary to unravel the terms of the relationship between nursing and womanhood as these bonds have been formed over the last century.

THE MEANING OF CARING

Many different disciplines have explored the various meanings of caring.[2] Much of this literature, however, runs the danger of universalizing caring as an element in female identity, or as a human quality, separate from the cultural and structural circumstances that create it. But as policy analyst Hilary Graham has argued, caring is not merely an identity; it is also work. As she notes, "Caring touches simultaneously on who you are and what you do."[3] Because of this duality, caring can be difficult to define and even harder to control. Graham's analysis moves beyond seeing caring as a psychological trait; but her focus is primarily on women's unpaid labor in the home. She does not fully discuss how the forms of caring are shaped by the contexts under which they are practiced. Caring is not just a subjective and material experience; it is a historically created one. Particular circumstances, ideologies, and power relations thus create the conditions under which caring can occur, the forms it will take, the consequences it will have for those who do it.

The basis for caring also shapes its effect. Nursing was organized under the expectation that its practitioners would accept a duty to care rather than demand a right to determine how they would satisfy this duty. Nurses were expected to act out of an obligation to care, taking on caring more as an identity than as work, and expressing altruism without thought of autonomy either at the bedside or in their profession. Thus, nurses, like others who perform what is defined as "women's work" in our society, have had to contend with what appears as a dichotomy between the duty to care for others and the right to control their own activities in the name of caring. Nursing is still searching for what philosopher Joel Feinberg argued comes prior to rights, that is, being "recognized as having a claim on rights."[4] The duty to care, organized within the political and economic context of nursing's development, has made it difficult for nurses to obtain this moral and, ultimately, political standing.

Because nurses have been given the duty to care, they are caught in a secondary dilemma: forced to act as if altruism (assumed to be the basis for caring) and autonomy (assumed to be the basis for rights) are separate ways of being. Nurses are still searching for a way to forge a link between altruism and autonomy that will allow them to have what philosopher Larry Blum and others have called "caring-with-autonomy," or what psychiatrist Jean Baker Miller labeled "a way of life that includes serving others without being subservient."[5] Nursing's historical circumstances and ideological underpinnings have made creating this way of life difficult, but not impossible, to achieve.

CARING AS DUTY

A historical analysis of nursing's development makes this theoretical formulation clearer. Most of the writing about American nursing's history begins in the 1870s when formal training for nursing was introduced in the United States. But nursing did not appear de novo at the end of the nineteenth century. As with most medical and health care, nursing throughout the colonial era and most of the nineteenth century took place within the family and the home. In the domestic pantheon that surrounded "middling" and upper-class American womanhood in the nineteenth century, a woman's caring for friends and relatives was an important pillar. Nursing was often taught by mother to daughter as part of female apprenticeship, or learned by a domestic servant as an additional task on her job. Embedded in the seemingly natural or ordained character of women, it became an important manifestation of women's expression of love of others, and was thus integral to the female sense of self.[6] In a society where deeply felt religious tenets were translated into gendered virtues, domesticity advocate Catharine Beecher declared that the sick were to be "commended" to a "woman's benevolent ministries."[7]

The responsibility for nursing went beyond a mother's duty for her children, a wife's for her husband, or a daughter's for her aging parents. It attached to all the available female family members. The family's "long arm" might reach out at any time to a woman working in a distant city, in a mill, or as a maid, pulling her home to care for the sick, infirm, or newborn. No form of women's labor, paid or unpaid, protected her from this demand. "You may be called upon at any moment," Eliza W. Farrar warned in *The Young Lady's Friend* in 1837, "to attend upon your parents, your brothers, your sisters, or your companions."[8] Nursing was to be, therefore, a woman's duty, not her job. Obligation and love, not the need of work, were to bind the nurse to her patient. Caring was to be an unpaid labor of love.

THE PROFESSED NURSE

Even as Eliza Farrar was proffering her advice, pressures both inward and outward were beginning to reshape the domestic sphere for women of the then-called "middling classes." Women's obligations and work were transformed by the expanding industrial economy and changing cultural assumptions. Parenting took on increasing importance as notions of "moral mothering" filled the domestic arena and other productive labor entered the cash nexus. Female benevolence similarly moved outward as women's charitable efforts took increasingly institutional forms. Duty began to take on new meaning as such women were advised they could fulfill their nursing responsibilities by managing competently those they hired to assist them. Bourgeois female virtue could still be demonstrated as the balance of labor, love, and supervision shifted.[9]

An expanding economy thus had differing effects on women of various classes. For those in the growing urban middle classes, excess cash made it possible to consider hiring a nurse when circumstances, desire, or exhaustion meant a female relative was no longer available for the task. Caring as labor, for these women, could be separated from love.

For older widows or spinsters from the working classes, nursing became a trade they could "profess" relatively easily in the marketplace. A widow who had nursed her husband till his demise, or a domestic servant who had cared for an employer in time of illness, entered casually into the nursing trade, hired by families or individuals unwilling, or unable, to care for their sick alone. The permeable boundaries for women between unpaid and paid labor allowed nursing to pass back and forth when necessary. For many women, nursing thus beckoned as respectable community work.

These "professed" or "natural-born" nurses, as they were known, usually came to their work, as one Boston nurse put it, "latterly" when other forms of employment were closed to them or the lack of any kind of work experience left nursing as an obvious choice. Mehitable Pond Garside, for example, was in her fifties and had outlived two husbands—and her children could not, or would not, support her—when she came to Boston in the 1840s to nurse. Similarly Alma Frost Merrill, the daughter of a Maine wheelwright, came to Boston in 1818 at nineteen to become a domestic servant. After years as a domestic and seamstress, she declared herself a nurse.[10]

Women like Mehitable Pond Garside and Alma Frost Merrill differed markedly from the Sairey Gamp character of Dickens's novel, *Martin Chuzzlewit*. Gamp was portrayed as a merely besotted representative of lumpenproletarian womanhood, who asserted her autonomy by daring to question medical diagnosis, to venture her own opinions (usually outrageous and wrong) at every turn, and to spread disease and superstition in the name of self-knowledge. If they were not Gamps, nurses like Garside and Merrill also were not the healers of some more recent feminist mythology that confounds nursing with midwifery, praising the caring and autonomy these women exerted, but refusing to consider their ignorance.[11] Some professed nurses learned their skills from years of experience, demonstrating the truth of the dictum that "to make a kind and sympathizing nurse, one must have waited, in sickness, upon those she loved dearly."[12] Others, however, blundered badly beyond their capabilities or knowledge. They brought to the bedside only the authority their personalities and community stature could command: Neither credentials nor a professional identity gave weight to their efforts. Their womanhood, and the experience it gave them, defined their authority and taught them to nurse.

THE HOSPITAL NURSE

Nursing was not limited, however, to the bedside in a home. Although the United States had only 178 hospitals at the first national census in 1873, it was workers labeled "nurses" who provided the caring. As in home-based nursing, the route to hospital nursing was paved more with necessity than with intentionality. In 1875, Eliza Higgins, the matron of Boston's Lying-In Hospital, could not find an extra nurse to cover all the deliveries. In desperation, she moved the hospital laundress up to the nursing position, while a recovering patient took over the wash. Higgins' diaries of her trying years at the Lying-In suggest that such an entry into nursing was not uncommon.[13]

As Higgins' reports and memoirs of other nurses attest, hospital nursing could be the work of devoted women who learned what historian Charles Rosenberg has labeled "ad hoc professionalism," or the temporary and dangerous labor of an ambulatory patient or hospital domestic.[14] As in home-based nursing, both caring and concern were frequently demonstrated. But the nursing work and nurses were mainly characterized by the diversity of their efforts and the unevenness of their skills.

Higgins' memoirs attest to the hospital as a battleground where nurses, physicians, and hospital managers contested the realm of their authority. Nurses continually affirmed their right to control the pace and content of their work, to set their own hours, and to structure their relationships to physicians. Aware that the hospital's paternalistic attitudes and practices toward its "inmates" were attached to the nursing personnel as well, they fought to be treated as workers, "not children," as the Lying-In nurses told Eliza Higgins, and to maintain their autonomous adult status.[15]

Like home-based nursing, hospital nurses had neither formal training nor class status upon which to base their arguments. But their sense of the rights of working-class womanhood gave them authority to press their demands. The necessity to care, and their perception of its importance to patient outcome, also structured their belief that demanding the right to be relatively autonomous was possible. However, their efforts were undermined by the nature of their onerous work, the paternalism of the institutions, class differences between trustees and workers, and ultimately the lack of a defined ideology of caring. Mere resistance to those above them, or contending assertions of rights, could not become the basis for nursing authority.

THE INFLUENCE OF NIGHTINGALE

Much of this changed with the introduction of training for nursing in the hospital world. In the aftermath of Nightingale's triumph over the British army's medical care system in the Crimea, similar attempts by American women during the Civil War, and the need to find respectable work for daughters of the middling classes, a model and support for nursing reform began to grow. By 1873, three nursing schools in hospitals in New York, Boston, and New Haven were opened, patterned after the Nightingale School at St. Thomas' Hospital in London.

Nightingale had envisioned nursing as an art, rather than a science, for which women needed to be trained. Her ideas linked her medical and public health notions to her class and religious beliefs. Accepting the Victorian idea of divided spheres of activity for men and women, she thought women had to be trained to nurse through a disciplined process of honing their womanly virtue. Nightingale stressed character development, the laws of health, and strict adherence to orders passed through a female hierarchy. Nursing was built on a model that relied on the concept of duty to provide its basis for authority. Unlike other feminists at the time, she spoke in the language of duty, not rights.

Furthermore, as a nineteenth-century sanitarian, Nightingale never believed in germ theory, in part because she refused to accept a theory of disease etiology that appeared to be morally neutral. Given her sanitarian beliefs, Nightingale thought medical therapeutics and "curing" were of lesser importance to patient outcome, and she willingly left this realm to the physician. Caring, the arena she did think of great importance, she assigned to the nurse. In order to care, a nurse's character, tempered by the fires of training, was to be her greatest skill. Thus, to "feminize" nursing, Nightingale sought a change in the class-defined behavior, not the gender, of the work force.[16]

To forge a good nurse out of the virtues of a good woman and to provide a political base for nursing, Nightingale sought to organize a female hierarchy in which orders passed down from the nursing superintendent to the lowly probationer. This separate female sphere was to share power in the provision of health care with the male-dominated arenas of medicine. For many women in the Victorian era, sisterhood and what Carroll Smith-Rosenberg has called "homosocial networks" served to overcome many of the limits of this separate but supposedly equal system of cultural division.[17] Sisterhood, after all, at least in its fictive forms, underlay much of the female power that grew out of women's culture in the nineteenth century. But in nursing, commonalities of the gendered experience could not become the basis of unity since hierarchical filial relations, not equal sisterhood, lay at the basis of nursing's theoretical formulation.'

Service, Not Education. Thus, unwittingly, Nightingale's sanitarian ideas and her beliefs about womanhood provided some of the ideological justification for many of the dilemmas that faced American nursing by 1900. Having fought physician and trustee prejudice against the training of nurses in hospitals in the last quarter of the nineteenth century, American nursing reformers succeeded only too well as the new century began. Between 1890 and 1920, the number of nursing schools jumped from 35 to 1,775, and the number of trained nurses from 16 per 100,000 in the population to 141.[18] Administrators quickly realized that opening a "nursing school" provided their hospitals, in exchange for training, with a young, disciplined, and cheap labor force. There was often no difference between the hospital's nursing school and its nursing service. The service needs of the hospital continually overrode the educational requirements of the schools. A student might, therefore, spend weeks on a medical ward if her labor was so needed, but never see the inside of an operating room before her graduation.

Once the nurse finished her training, however, she was unlikely to be hired by a hospital because it relied on either untrained aides or nursing student labor. The majority of graduate nurses, until the end of the 1930s, had to find work in private duty in a patient's home, as the patient's employee in the hospital, in the branches of public health, or in some hospital staff positions. In the world of nursing beyond the training school, "trained" nurses still had to compete with the thousands of "professed" or "practical nurses who continued to ply their trade in an overcrowded and unregulated marketplace. The title of nurse took on very ambiguous meanings.[19]

The term, "trained nurse," was far from a uniform designation. As nursing leader Isabel Hampton Robb lamented in 1893, "the title 'trained nurse' may mean then anything, everything, or next to nothing."[20]

The exigencies of nursing acutely ill or surgical patients required the sacrifice of coherent educational programs. Didactic, repetitive, watered-down medical lectures by physicians or older nurses were often provided for the students, usually after they finished ten to twelve hours of ward work. Training emphasized the "one right way" of doing ritualized procedures in hopes the students' adherence to specified rules would be least dangerous to patients.[21] Under these circumstances, the duty to care could be followed with a vengeance and become the martinet adherence to orders.

Furthermore, because nursing emphasized training in discipline, order, and practical skills, the abuse of student labor could be rationalized. And because the work force was almost entirely women, altruism, sacrifice, and submission were expected, encouraged, indeed demanded. Exploitation was inevitable in a field where, until the early 1900s, there were no accepted standards for how much work an average student should do or how many patients she could successfully care for, no mechanisms through which to enforce such standards. After completing her exhaustive and depressing survey of nursing training in 1912, nursing educator M. Adelaide Nutting bluntly pointed out: "Under the present system the school has no life of its own."[22] In this kind of environment, nurses were trained. But they were not educated.

Virtue and Autonomy. It would be a mistake, however, to see the nursing experience only as one of exploitation and the nursing school as a faintly concealed reformatory for the wayward girl in need of discipline. Many nursing superintendents lived the Nightingale ideals as best they could and infused them into their schools. The authoritarian model could and did retemper many women. It instilled in nurses idealism and pride in their skills, somewhat differentiated the trained nurse from the untrained, and protected and aided the sick and dying. It provided a mechanism for virtuous women to contribute to the improvement of humanity by empowering them to care.

For many of the young women entering training in the nineteenth and early twentieth centuries, nursing thus offered something quite special: both a livelihood and a virtuous state. As one nursing educator noted in 1890: "Young strong country girls are drawn into the work by the glamorer [*sic*] thrown about hospital work and the halo that sanctifies a Nightingale."[23] Thus, in their letters of application, aspiring nursing students expressed their desire for work, independence, and womanly virtue. As with earlier, nontrained nurses, they did not seem to separate autonomy and altruism, but rather sought its linkage through training. Flora Jones spoke for many such women when she wrote the superintendent of Boston City Hospital in 1880, declaring, "I consider myself fitted for the work by inclination and consider it a womanly occupation. It is also necessary for me to become self-supporting and provide for my future."[24] Thus, one nursing superintendent reminded a graduating class in 1904: "You have become self-controlled, unselfish, gentle, compassionate, brave, capable—in fact, you have risen from the period of irresponsible girlhood to that of womanhood."[25] For women like Flora Jones, and many of nursing's early leaders, nursing was the singular way to grow to maturity in a womanly profession that offered meaningful work, independence, and altruism.[26]

Altruism, Not Independence. For many, however, as nursing historian Dorothy Sheahan has noted, the training school, "was a place where . . . women learned to be girls."[27] The range of permissible behaviors for respectable women was often narrowed further through training. Independence was to be sacrificed on the altar of altruism. Thus, despite hopes of aspiring students and promises of training school superintendents, nursing rarely united altruism and autonomy. Duty remained the basis for caring.

Some nurses were able to create what they called "a little world of our own." But nursing had neither the financial nor the cultural power to create the separate women's institutions that provided so much of the basis for women's reform and rights efforts.[28] Under these conditions, nurses found it difficult to make the collective transition out of a woman's culture of obligation into an activist assault on the structure and beliefs that oppressed them. Nursing remained bounded by its ideology and its material circumstances.

THE CONTRADICTIONS OF REFORM

In this context, one begins to understand the difficulties faced by the leaders of nursing reform. Believing that educational reform was central to nursing's professionalizing efforts and clinical improvements, a small group of elite reformers attempted to broaden nursing's scientific content and social outlook. In arguing for an increase in the scientific knowledge necessary in nursing, such leaders were fighting against deep-seated cultural assumptions about male and female "natural" characteristics as embodied in the doctor and the nurse. Such sentiments were articulated in the routine platitudes that graced what one nursing leader described as the "doctor homilies" that were a regular feature at nursing graduation exercises.[29]

Not surprisingly, such beliefs were professed by physicians and hospital officials whenever nursing shortages appeared, or nursing groups pushed for higher educational standards or defined nursing as more than assisting the physician. As one nursing educator wrote, with some degree of resignation after the influenza pandemic in 1920: "It is perhaps inevitable that the difficulty of securing nurses during the last year or two should have revived again the old agitation about the 'over-training' of nurses and the clamor for a cheap worker of the old servant-nurse type."[30]

First Steps Toward Professionalism. The nursing leadership, made up primarily of educators and supervisors with their base within what is now the American Nurses' Association and the National League for Nursing, thus faced a series of dilemmas as they struggled to raise educational standards in the schools and criteria for entry into training, to register nurses once they finished their training, and to gain acceptance for the knowledge base and skills of the nurse. They had to exalt the womanly character, self-abnegation, and service ethic of nursing while insisting on the right of nurses to act in their own self-interest. They had to demand higher wages commensurate with their skills, yet not appear commercial. They had to simultaneously find a way to denounce the exploitation of nursing students, as they made political alliances with hospital physicians and administrators whose support they needed. While they lauded character and sacrifice, they had to find a way to measure it with educational criteria in order to formulate registration laws and set admission standards. They had to make demands and organize, without appearing "unlady-like." In sum, they were forced by the social conditions and ideology surrounding nursing to attempt to professionalize altruism without demanding autonomy.

Undermined by Duty. The image of a higher claim of duty also continually undermined a direct assertion of the right to determine that duty. Whether at a bedside, or at a legislative hearing on practice laws, the duty to care became translated into the demand that nurses merely follow doctors' orders. The tradition of obligation almost made it impossible for nurses to speak about rights at all. By the turn of the century necessity and desire were pulling more young women into the labor force, and the women's movement activists were placing rights at the center of cultural discussion. In this atmosphere, nursing's call to duty was perceived by many as an increasingly antiquated language to shore up a changing economic and cultural landscape. Nursing became a type of collective female grasping for an older form of security and power in the face of rapid change. Women who might have been attracted to nursing in the 1880s as a womanly occupation that provided some form of autonomy, were, by the turn of the century, increasingly looking elsewhere for work and careers.

A DIFFERENT VISION

In the face of these difficulties, the nursing leadership became increasingly defensive and turned on its own rank and file. The educators and supervisors who comprised leadership lost touch with the pressing concern of their constituencies in the daily work world of nursing and the belief systems such nurses continued to hold. Yet many nurses, well into the twentieth century, shared the nineteenth-century vision of nursing as the embodiment of womanly virtue. A nurse named Annette Fiske, for example, although she authored two science books for nurses and had an M.A. degree in classics from Radcliffe College before she entered training, spent her professional career in the 1920s arguing against increasing educational standards. Rather, she called for a reinfusion into nursing of spirituality and service, assuming that this would result in nursing's receiving greater "love and respect and admiration."[31]

Other nurses, especially those trained in the smaller schools or reared to hold working-class ideals about respectable behavior in women, shared Fiske's views. They saw the leadership's efforts at professionalization as an attempt to push them out of nursing. Their adherence to nursing skill measured in womanly virtue was less a conservative and reactionary stance than a belief that seemed to transcend class and educational backgrounds to place itself in the individual character and work-place skills of the nurse. It grounded altruism in supposedly natural and spiritual, rather than educational and middle-class, soil. For Fiske and many other nurses, nursing was still a womanly art that required inherent character in its practitioners and training in practical skills and spiritual values in its schools. Their beliefs about nursing did not require the professionalization of altruism, nor the demand for autonomy either at the bedside or in control over the professionalization process.

Still other nurses took a more pragmatic viewpoint that built on their pride in their work-place skills and character. These nurses also saw the necessity for concerted action, not unlike that taken by other American workers. Such nurses fought against what one 1888 nurse, who called herself Candor, characterized as the "missionary spirit . . . [of] self-immolation" that denied that nurses worked because they had to make a living.[32] These worker-nurses saw no contradiction between demanding decent wages and conditions for their labors and being of service for those in need. But the efforts of various groups of these kinds of nurses to turn to hours' legislation, trade union activity, or mutual aid associations were criticized and condemned by the nursing leadership. Their letters were often edited out of the nursing journals, and their voices silenced in public meetings as they were denounced as being commercial, or lacking in proper womanly devotion.[33]

In the face of continual criticism from nursing's professional leadership, the worker-nurses took on an increasingly angry and defensive tone. Aware that their sense of the nurse's skills came from the experiences of the work place, not book learning or degrees, they had to assert this position despite continued hostility toward such a basis of nursing authority.[34] Although the position of women like Candor helped articulate a way for nurses to begin to assert the right to care, it did not constitute a full-blown ideological counterpart to the overwhelming power of the belief in duty.

The Persistence of Dilemmas. By midcentury, the disputes between worker-nurses and the professional leadership began to take on new forms, although the persistent divisions continued. Aware that some kind of collective bargaining was necessary to keep nurses out of the unions and in the professional associations, the ANA reluctantly agreed in 1946 to let its state units act as bargaining agents. The nursing leadership has continued to look at educational reform strategies, now primarily taking the form of legislating for the B.S. degree as the credential necessary for entry into nursing practice, and to changes in the practice laws that will allow increasingly skilled nurses the autonomy and status they deserve. Many nurses have continued to be critical of this educational strategy, to ignore the professional associations, or to leave nursing altogether.

In their various practice fields nurses still need a viable ideology and strategy that will help them adjust to the continual demands of patients and an evermore bureaucratized, cost-conscious, and rationalized work setting. For many nurses it is still, in an ideological sense, the nineteenth century. Even for those nurses who work as practitioners in the more autonomous settings of health maintenance organizations or public health offices, the legacy of nursing's heritage is still felt. Within the last two years, for example, the Massachusetts Board of Medicine tried to push through a regulation that health practitioners acknowledge their dependence on physicians by wearing a badge that identified their supervising physician and stated that they were not doctors.

Nurses have tried various ways to articulate a series of rights that allow them to care. The acknowledgment of responsibilities, however, so deeply ingrained in nursing and American womanhood, as nursing school dean Claire Fagin has noted, continually drown out the nurse's assertion of rights.[35]

Nurses are continuing to struggle to obtain the right to claim rights. Nursing's educational philosophy, ideological underpinnings, and structural position have made it difficult to create the circumstances within which to gain such recognition. It is not a lack of vision that thwarts nursing, but the lack of power to give that vision substantive form.[36]

BEYOND THE OBLIGATION TO CARE

Much has changed in nursing in the last forty years. The severing of nursing education from the hospital's nursing service has finally taken place, as the majority of nurses are now educated in colleges, not hospital-based diploma schools. Hospitals are experimenting with numerous ways to organize the nursing service to provide the nurse with more responsibility and sense of control over the nursing care process. The increasingly technical and machine-aided nature of hospital-based health care has made nurses feel more skilled.

In many ways, however, little has changed. Nursing is still divided over what counts as a nursing skill, how it is to be learned, and whether a nurse's character can be measured in educational criteria. Technical knowledge and capabilities do not easily translate into power and control. Hospitals, seeking to cut costs, have forced nurses to play "beat the clock" as they run from task to task in an increasingly fragmented setting.[37]

Nursing continues to struggle with the basis for, and the value of, caring. The fact that the first legal case on comparable worth was brought by a group of Denver nurses suggests nursing has an important and ongoing role in the political effort to have caring revalued. As in the Denver case, contemporary feminism has provided some nurses with the grounds on which to claim rights from their caring.[38]

Feminism, in its liberal form, appears to give nursing a political language that argues for equality and rights within the given order of things. It suggests a basis for caring that stresses individual discretion and values, acknowledging that the nurses' right to care should be given equal consideration with the physician's right to cure. Just as liberal political theory undermined more paternalistic formulations of government, classical liberalism's tenets applied to women have much to offer nursing. The demand for the right to care questions deeply held beliefs about gendered relations in the health care hierarchy and the structure of the hierarchy itself.

Many nurses continue to hope that with more education, explicit theories to explain the scientific basis for nursing, new skills, and a lot of assertiveness training, nursing will change. As these nurses try to shed the image of the nurse's being ordered to care, however, the admonition to care at a graduation speech has to be made. Unable to find a way to "care with autonomy" and unable to separate caring from its valuing and basis, many nurses find themselves forced to abandon the effort to care, or nursing altogether.

ALTRUISM WITH AUTONOMY

These dilemmas for nurses suggest the constraints that surround the effectiveness of a liberal feminist political strategy to address the problems of caring and, therefore, of nursing. The individualism and autonomy of a rights framework often fail to acknowledge collective social need, to provide a way for adjudicating conflicts over rights, or to address the reasons for the devaluing of female activity.[39] Thus, nurses have often rejected liberal feminism, not just out of their oppression and "false consciousness," but because of some deep understandings of the limited promise of equality and autonomy in a health care system they see as flawed and harmful. In an often inchoate way, such nurses recognize that those who claim the autonomy of rights often run the risk of rejecting altruism and caring itself.

Several feminist psychologists have suggested that what women really want in their lives is autonomy with connectedness. Similarly, many modern moral philosophers are trying to articulate a formal moral theory that values the emotions and the importance of relationships.[40] For nursing, this will require the creation of the conditions under which it is possible to value caring and to understand that the empowerment of others does not have to require self-immolation. To achieve this, nurses will have both to create a new political understanding for the basis of caring and to find ways to gain the power to implement it. Nursing can do much to have this happen through research on the importance of caring on patient outcome, studies of patient improvements in nursing settings where the right to care is created, or implementing nursing control of caring through a bargaining agreement. But nurses cannot do this alone. The dilemma of nursing is too tied to society's broader problems of gender and class to be solved solely by the political or professional efforts of one occupational group.

Nor are nurses alone in benefiting from such an effort. If nursing can achieve the power to practice altruism with autonomy, all of us have much to gain. Nursing has always been a much conflicted metaphor in our culture, reflecting all the ambivalences we give to the meaning of womanhood.[41] Perhaps in the future it can give this metaphor and, ultimately, caring, new value in all our lives.

NOTES

1. Gregory Wticher, "Last Class of Nurses Told: Don't Stop Caring," *Boston Globe,* May 13, 1985, pp. 17–18.

2. See, for examples, Larry Blum et al., "Altruism and Women's Oppression," in *Women and Philosophy,* eds. Carol Gould and Marx Wartofsy (New York: G.P. Putnam's, 1976), pp. 222–247; Nel Noddings, *Caring.* Berkeley: University of California Press, 1984; Nancy Chodorow, *The Reproduction of Mothering.* Berkeley: University of California Press, 1978; Carol Gilligan, *In a Different Voice.* Cambridge: Harvard University Press, 1982; and Janet Finch and Dulcie Groves, eds., *A Labour of Love, Women, Work and Caring.* London and Boston: Routledge, Kegan Paul, 1983.

3. Hilary Graham, "Caring: A Labour of Love," in *A Labour of Love,* eds. Finch and Groves, pp. 13–30.

4. Joel Feinberg, Rights, *Justice and the Bounds of Liberty* (Princeton: Princeton University Press, 1980), p. 141.

5. Blum et al., "Altruism and Women's Oppression," p. 223; Jean Baker Miller, *Toward a New Psychology of Women* (Boston: Beacon Press, 1976), p. 71.

6. Ibid; see also Iris Marion Young, "Is Male Gender Identity the Cause of Male Domination," in *Mothering: Essays in Feminist Theory,* ed. Joyce Trebicott (Totowa, NJ: Rowman and Allanheld, 1983), pp. 129–146.

7. Catherine Beecher, *Domestic Receipt-Book* (New York: Harper and Brothers, 1846), p. 214.

8. Eliza Farrar, *The Young Lady's Friend—By a Lady* (Boston: American Stationer's Co., 1837), p. 57.

9. Catherine Beecher, *Miss Beecher's Housekeeper and Healthkeeper.* New York: Harper and Brothers, 1876; and Sarah Josepha Hale, *The Good Housekeeper.* Boston: Otis Brothers and Co., 7th edition, 1844. See also Susan Strasser, *Never Done: A History of Housework.* New York: Pantheon, 1982.

10. Cases 2 and 18, "Admissions Committee Records," Volume I, Box 11, Home for Aged Women Collection, Schlesinger Library, Radcliffe College, Cambridge, Mass. Data on the nurses admitted to the home were also found in "Records of Inmates, 1858–1901," "Records of Admission, 1873–1924," and "Records of Inmates, 1901–1916," all in Box 11.

11. Charles Dickens, *Martin Chuzzlewit.* New York: New American Library, 1965, original edition, London: 1865; Barbara Ehrenreich and Deirdre English, *Witches, Nurses, Midwives: A History of Women Healers.* Old Westbury: Glass Mountain Pamphlets, 1972.

12. Virginia Penny, *The Employments of Women: A Cyclopedia of Women's Work* (Boston: Walker, Wise and Co., 1863), p. 420.

13. Eliza Higgins, Boston Lying-In Hospital, Matron's Journals, 1873–1889, Volume I, January 9, 1875, February 22, 1875, Rare Books Room, Countway Medical Library, Harvard Medical School, Boston, Mass.

14. Charles Rosenberg, "'And Heal the Sick': The Hospital and the Patient in 19th Century America," *Journal of Social History 10* (June 1977):445.

15. Higgins, Matron's Journals, Volume II, January 11, 1876, and July 1, 1876. See also a parallel discussion of male artisan behavior in front of the boss in David Montgomery, "Workers' Control of Machine Production in the 19th Century," *Labor History 17* (Winter 1976):485–509.

16. The discussion on Florence Nightingale is based on my analysis in *Ordered to Care,* chapter 3. See also Charles E. Rosenberg, "Florence Nightingale on Contagion: The Hospital as Moral Universe," in *Healing and History,* ed. Charles E. Rosenberg. New York: Science History Publications, 1979.

17. Carroll Smith-Rosenberg, "The Female World of Love and Ritual," Signs: *Journal of Women in Culture and Society 1* (Autumn 1975):1.

18. May Ayers Burgess, Nurses, *Patients and Pocketbooks.* New York: Committee on the Grading of Nursing, 1926, reprint edition (New York: Garland Publishing Co, 1985), pp. 36–37.

19. For further discussion of the dilemmas of private duty nursing, see Susan Reverby, "'Neither for the Drawing Room nor for the Kitchen': Private Duty Nursing, 1880–1920," in *Women and Health in America,* ed. Judith Walzer Leavitt. Madison: University of Wisconsin Press, 1984, and Susan Reverby, "'Something Besides Waiting': The Politics of Private Duty Nursing Reform in the Depression," in *Nursing History: New Perspectives, New Possibilities,* ed. Ellen Condliffe Lagemann. New York: Teachers College Press, 1982.

20. Isabel Hampton Robb, "Educational Standards for Nurses," in *Nursing of the Sick 1893* (New York: McGraw-Hill, 1949), p. 11. See also Janet Wilson James, "Isabel Hampton and the Professionalization of Nursing in the 1890s," in *The Therapeutic Revolution,* eds. Morris Vogel and Charles E. Rosenberg. Philadelphia: University of Pennsylvania Press, 1979.

21. For further discussion of the difficulties in training, see JoAnn Ashley, Hospitals, *Paternalism and the Role of the Nurse.* New York: Teachers College Press, 1976, and Reverby, Ordered to Care, chapter 4.

22. Educational Status of Nursing, *Bureau of Education Bulletin Number 7,* Whole Number 475 (Washington, D.C.: Government Printing Office, 1912), p. 49.

23. Julia Wells, "Do Hospitals Fit Nurses for Private Nursing," *Trained Nurse and Hospital Review 3* (March 1890):98.

24. Boston City Hospital (BCH) Training School Records, Box 4, Folder 4, Student 4, February 14, 1880, BCH Training School Papers, Nursing Archives, Special Collections, Boston University, Mugar Library, Boston, Mass. The student's name has been changed to maintain confidentiality.

25. Mary Agnes Snively, "What Manner of Women Ought Nurses to Be?" *American Journal of Nursing 4* (August 1904):838.

26. For a discussion of many of the early nursing leaders as "new women," see Susan Armeny, "'We Were the New Women': A Comparison of Nurses and Women Physicians, 1890–1915." Paper presented at the American Association for the History of Nursing Conference, University of Virginia, Charlottesville, Va., October 1984.

27. Dorothy Sheahan, "Influence of Occupational Sponsorship on the Professional Development of Nursing." Paper presented at the Rockefeller Archives Conference on the History of Nursing, Rockefeller Archives, Tarrytown, NY, May 1981, p. 12.

28. Estelle Freedman, "Separatism as Strategy: Female Institution Building and American Feminism, 1870–1930," *Feminist Studies 5* (Fall 1979):512–529.

29. Lavinia L. Dock, *A History of Nursing, volume 3* (New York: G.P. Putnam's, 1912), p. 136.

30. Isabel M. Stewart, "Progress in Nursing Education during 1919," *Modern Hospital 14* (March 1920):183.

31. Annette Fiske, "How Can We Counteract the Prevailing Tendency to Commercialism in Nursing?" Proceedings of the 17th Annual Meeting of the Massachusetts State Nurses' Association, p. 8, Massachusetts Nurses Association Papers, Box 7, Nursing Archives.

32. Candor, "Work and Wages," Letter to the Editor, Trained Nurse and Hospital Review 2 (April 1888):167–168.

33. See the discussion in Ashley, Hospitals, Paternalism and the Role of the Nurse, pp. 40–43, 46–48, 51, and in Barbara Melosh, "The Physician's Hand": *Work Culture and Conflict in American Nursing* (Philadelphia: Temple University Press, 1982), passim.

34. For further discussion see Susan Armeny, "Resolute Enthusiasts: The Effort to Professionalize American Nursing, 1880–1915." PhD dissertation, University of Missouri, Columbia, Mo., 1984, and Reverby, Ordered to Care, chapter 6.

35. Feinberg, Rights, pp. 130–142; Fagin, "Nurses' Rights," *American Journal of Nursing 75* (January 1975):82.

36. For a similar argument for bourgeois women, see Carroll Smith-Rosenberg, "The New Woman as Androgyne: Social Disorder and Gender Crisis," in *Disorderly Conduct* (New York: Alfred Knopf, 1985), p. 296.

37. Boston Nurses' Group, "The False Promise: Professionalism in Nursing," *Science for the People 10* (May/June 1978):20–34; Jennifer Bingham Hull, "Hospital Nightmare: Cuts in Staff Demoralize Nurses as Care Suffers," *Wall Street Journal,* March 27, 1985.

38. Bonnie Bullough, "The Struggle for Women's Rights in Denver: A Personal Account," *Nursing Outlook 26* (September 1978):566–567.

39. For critiques of liberal feminism see Allison M. Jagger, *Feminist Politics and Human Nature* (Totowa, NJ: Rowman and Allanheld, 1983), pp. 27–50, 173, 206; Zillah Eisenstein, *The Radical Future of Liberal Feminism.* New York and London: Longman, 1981; and Rosalind Pollack Petchesky, *Abortion and Women's Choice* (Boston: Northeastern University Press, 1984), pp. 1–24.

40. Miller, Toward a New Psychology; Jane Flax, "The Conflict Between Nurturance and Autonomy in Mother-Daughter Relationships and within Feminism," *Feminist Studies 4* (June 1978):171–191; Blum et al., "Altruism and Women's Oppression."

41. Claire Fagin and Donna Diers, "Nursing as Metaphor," *New England Journal of Medicine 309* (July 14, 1983):116–117.

4

NURSING AS METAPHOR

CLAIRE M. FAGIN
DONNA DIERS

EDITORS' NOTE

At a time when traditional roles for women were eschewed by feminists, the deans of the schools of nursing at the University of Pennsylvania and Yale University wrote about what many nurses experienced when they told others their work was nursing. It connected the nurse's work to social constructs associated with the word "nursing." This essay was first published in the *New England Journal of Medicine* then reprinted in the *American Journal of Nursing*.

■ ■ ■

For some time now we have been curious about the reactions elicited in social situations when we tell people we are nurses. First reactions include the comment, "I never met a nurse socially before"; stories about the person's latest hospitalization, or childbearing experiences; the question "How can you bear handling bedpans (vomit, blood)?" or the remark, "I think I need another drink." We believe the statements reflect the fact that nursing evokes disturbing and discomforting images that many educated, middle-class, upwardly mobile Americans find difficult to handle. As nurses, we are educated to give comfort, so it is something of a paradox when we make ourselves and others uncomfortable socially.

It is easy to say that some reactions are based on an underlying attitude toward nurses that we tend to think of as a stereotype. But labeling the attitude does not help us explain it or escape it. Perhaps we can deal with the social perception by examining the metaphors that underlie the concept of "nurse"—metaphors that influence not only language but also thought and action.

Nursing is a metaphor for mothering. Nursing has links with nurturing, caring, comforting, the laying on of hands, and other maternal types of behavior. Even the thought of the vertical nurse over the horizontal patient evokes regressed feelings. Adults do not like to be reminded of the child who remains inside all of us.

Nursing is a metaphor for class struggle. Not only does nursing represent women's struggles for equality, but its position in the health world is that of the classic underdog, struggling to be heard, approved, and recognized. Nurses constitute the largest occupational group in the health-care system (1.6 million). They work predominantly in settings that are dominated by physicians and in which physicians represent the upper and controlling class. Dominant groups yield ground reluctantly, especially to those whom others regard as having simply settled for a job.

Nursing is a metaphor for equality. Little social distance separates the nurse from the patient or the patient from other patients in the nursing-care setting, no matter what the social class of each. Nurses themselves make little distinction in rank among persons with widely varying amounts of education. Nurses are perceived as members of the working class, and although this perception is valuable to the patient when he or she is ill and wants to be comforted, it may be awkward to encounter one's nurses at a black-tie reception.

Among physicians, nursing may be a metaphor for conscience. Nurses see all that happens in the name of health care—the neglect as well as the cures, the reasons for failure as well as those for success. The anxiety, not to mention the guilt, engendered by what nurses may know can be considerable. Nurses recognize that many of the physician's attempts to conquer death do not work. They are an uncomfortable reminder of fallibility.

Nursing is a metaphor for intimacy. Nurses are involved in the most private aspects of people's lives, and they cannot hide behind technology or a veil of omniscience. Nurses do for others publicly what healthy persons do for themselves privately. Nurses, as trusted peers, are there to hear secrets, especially the ones born of vulnerability. Nurses are treasured when these interchanges are successful; but most often people do not wish to remember their vulnerability or loss of control, and nurses are indelibly identified with those times.

Thanks to the worst of this kind of thinking, nursing is a metaphor for sex. Having seen and touched the bodies of strangers, nurses are perceived as willing and able sexual partners. Knowing and experienced, they, unlike prostitutes, are thought to be safe—a quality suggested by the cleanliness of their white uniforms and their professional aplomb.

Something like the sum of these images makes up the psychological milieu in which nurses live and work. Little wonder, then, that some of us have been badgered (at least in our earlier days) about our choice of career. Little wonder, then, that nurses have had to develop a resilience required of few other professionals. Little wonder, too, that it is so difficult for us to reply to our detractors. One may wonder why any self-respecting, reasonably intellectual man or woman chooses nursing as a lifelong career. Our students at Pennsylvania and Yale are regularly asked "Why are you becoming a nurse? You have the brains to be a (doctor, lawyer, other)." All of them, long before entering schools such as ours, must answer this question for themselves and their questioners in a way that permits them to begin and to continue nursing. Their responses and ours frequently focus on the role of the nurse or the variety and mobility possible in a nursing career. But that kind of answer doesn't get to the heart of the problem. The right answer has to address the metaphors. The answer must convey the feeling of satisfaction derived from the caring role; indifference to power for its own sake; the recognition that one is a doer who enjoys doing for and with others; but most of all, the pleasure associated with helping others from the position of a peer rather than from the assumed superordinate position of some other professions.

Why not turn the metaphors around? Intimacy—why shrink from the word, even while we educate our listeners about its finer meaning—equality, conscience, and the many qualities of motherhood (another word that can usefully be separated from its stereotype) are exactly what draw people into nursing and keep them there.

If we could manage to be wistfully amused by the reactions we evoke rather than defensive, life would be easier. Educated, middle-class, upwardly mobile—we are indeed the peers of others at social gatherings. We are peers informed about disease prevention, the promotion of health, and rehabilitation. We are not disinterested experts but advocates, even for those who misinterpret us. Others may be only dimly aware of our role, but it is rooted deep in our history and exemplified by the great nursing leaders who have moved society forward: Lavinia Dock, so active in pursuing women's rights; Lillian Wald, who developed the Henry Street Settlement and educated all of us in understanding and approaching health and social problems; Margaret Sanger, who faced disdain, ignominy, and imprisonment in her struggle to educate the public about birth control; and Sister Kenny, who was once the only hope for polio victims.

So much for the metaphors of others. For ourselves? We think of ourselves as Florence Nightingales—tough, canny, powerful, autonomous, and heroic.

5

STAGES OF NURSING'S POLITICAL DEVELOPMENT: WHERE WE'VE BEEN AND WHERE WE OUGHT TO GO

SALLY SOLOMON COHEN

DIANA J. MASON

CHRISTINE KOVNER

JUDITH K. LEAVITT

JOYCE PULCINI

JULIE SOCHALSKI

This article originally appeared as *Nursing Outlook, 44*(6), Cohen S.S., Mason D.J., Kovner C., Leavitt J.K., Pulcini J., & Sochalski J., Stages of nursing's political development: Where we've been and where we ought to go, pp. 259–266.

EDITORS' NOTE

Many ask why the nation's largest health care profession doesn't have more clout. This article provides a framework for viewing nursing's movement through various stages of political involvement and sophistication and sheds some light on what is needed for the profession to have more influence in policy matters.

■ ■ ■

The nursing profession has a long history of political activism that has been heightened in recent years through the politics of health care reform. However, although a plethora of articles, speeches, and monographs address the importance of political activism for nurses, no attempts have been made to systematically analyze the evolution of nursing as a body politic. In this article we identify four stages of nursing's political development and recommend strategies for implementing the fourth and most complex stage. These stages are based on information gathered in a review of the literature of nursing's political activism and analyses of nursing's political involvement.

Usually the vehicle for collective action is a professional organization, which in this case is the American Nurses Association (ANA). Although nurses have been politically active through many organizations, the ANA has been the major voice for nursing at the federal level. At the state level, state nurses associations typically take the lead in determining preferred policy and lobbying on most issues of concern to nursing. Most of the discussion of political activism in this article will be in reference to the ANA.

Table 5.1 illustrates the four stages of the profession's recent political development. Stage 1, the "buy-in" stage, represents the profession's recognition of the importance of political activism. In stage 2, the "self interest" stage, nursing develops and uses its political expertise as it relates to the profession's self-interests. In stage 3, the "political sophistication" stage, the profession goes beyond self-interest and recognizes the importance of activism on behalf of the public while attaining increased sophistication in its political strategies. Stage 4 is proposed as the "leading the way" stage, in which the profession is envisioned as providing true political leadership on broader health care issues that speak to the public's interests. Stage 4 is not necessarily the final stage in nursing's political development, but is as far as we have taken this model. Subsequent stages of this model may well be identified as nursing moves into the next century.

Some general perspectives about these stages include the following: First, the stages of nursing's political activism are not time bound; nursing has straddled more than one stage of political development at a time. Depending on the issues, there may be movement back and forth among stages. Second, the first stages are no less meaningful or of less value than later ones. There may be times when it is in the profession's interest to pursue

TABLE 5.1. **The Progress of Nursing Through Four Stages of Political Development**

	Stage 1 (Buy-in)	Stage 2 (Self-interest)	Stage 3 (Political sophistication)	Stage 4 (Leading the way)
Nature of action	Reactive, with a focus on nursing issues	Reactive to nursing issues (e.g., funding for nursing education) and broader issues (e.g., long-term care and immunizations	Proactive on nursing and other health issues (e.g., Nursing's Agenda for Health Care Reform)	Proactive on leadership and agenda-setting for a broad range of health and social policy issues
Language	Learning political language	Using nurse jargon (e.g., caring, nursing diagnosis)	Using parlance and rhetoric common to health policy deliberations	Introducing terms that reorder the debate
Coalition building	Political awareness; occasional participation in coalitions	Coalition forming among nursing organizations	Coalition forming among nursing groups; active and significant participation in broader health care groups (e.g., Clinton task force on health care reform)	Initiating coalitions beyond nursing for broad health policy concerns
Nurses as policy shapers	Isolated cases of nurses being appointed to policy positions, primarily because of individual accomplishments	Professional associations get nurses into nursing-related positions	Professional organizations get nurses appointed to health-related policy positions (e.g., nurse position on ProPAC)	Many nurses sought to fill nursing and health policy positions because of value of nursing expertise and knowledge

the strategies of some of the earlier stages. Third, the events that characterize each stage of nursing's political activism are ongoing and are not intended to end or be replaced by those of other stages. Fourth, individual nurses or groups may progress through the various stages at different rates, resulting in different groups or individuals being at different stages. Finally, the last stage is a culmination of previous stages and contains strands from each.

STAGE 1

The first stage of political activism, the "buy-in" stage, encompasses activities that encourage and promote the political awareness of nurses, typically at the time that nurses have their first policy or political experience in relation to their professional goals. This stage can be linked to the late 1970s and early 1980s, when the first of many books and articles were published about the importance of nurses becoming involved in the political arena.[1–10] These publications are noteworthy because they identified linkages between nursing clinical practice and political activism, whether in institutional, community, or government settings; they were also a call to arms to fellow nurses. Several major themes emerged from these publications. The first theme emphasized the importance of nurses becoming politically active to advance the profession in the political arena or risk being excluded from important political decisions that would affect the practice of nursing. Leading early proponents of these views included Archer and Goehner,[3] Diers,[4] and Kalisch and Kalisch.[7]

A second theme emerging from these publications related to the difficulties that nursing faced in obtaining power within political and institutional circles. Many of the publications discussed the importance of power and the need for nurses to obtain more of it.[11] At times, consciousness-raising was approached from a gender-based context. In the words of the late nurse activist Jo Ann Ashley, "Coming to grips with the damaging effects of patriarchy is necessary before nurses can begin to visualize new ways of thinking, acting, and being at home and at work."[12]

A third theme that characterizes the literature on nursing and political activism during stage 1 is the identification of ways in which nurses can become politically active and involved. This includes Maraldo's[9] appeal to the human side of politics, the comprehensive discussion by Davis et al.[2] of ways for nurses to expand their role in the policy-making process, the political action handbook by Mason and Talbott,[13] and anecdotal reports of how nursing leaders, many of whom were nurse educators, worked to demystify politics in attempts to increase the numbers of nurses engaged with politics at national, state, local, or institutional levels.[1,13,14]

The political awakening of nursing included a recognition of the importance of health policy in nursing curricula. Several nurses called on their colleagues to "recognize that there are far-reaching implications for the inclusion of political matters in our classrooms."[15,16–19]

During this initial "buy-in" stage, only a handful of nurses held legislative or policy positions. One of the pioneers in this area was Sheila Burke, who started her tenure with Senator Robert Dole in the late 1970s and served for several years as his chief of staff.[20] Some individual nurses develop politically at different stages in a manner distinct from the development of the profession as a whole. These nurses often serve as role models, not necessarily through the efforts of their professional organizations. Once in key policy positions, their links to organized nursing are important for motivating and assisting nurses in their political endeavors.

STAGE 2

The second stage of the political development of the nursing profession is the "self-interest" stage, during which the profession develops its identity and focus as a special interest. This stage encompasses the activities that enhance the nursing profession's identity as a special interest in the political arena. During stage 2, the profession moves beyond the heightened awareness that characterizes stage 1 to political activism, wherein nursing begins to develop its own sense of uniqueness.

In general, this stage is characterized by the reaction of nursing to proposed or established policies, in contrast to subsequent stages, when proactivism and defining the agenda become more prevalent. For example, during one "self-interest" stage, most of nursing's attention at the federal level focused on lobbying for legislation to authorize and fund nursing education and research in the face of the continued insistence of presidents from Nixon through Bush to underbudget for, and, in the case of Carter, to rescind previously appropriated funds for nursing education and research.[8,21]

It is important to distinguish between self-interest and selfishness. Self-interest is often necessary for movement into the later stages because it fosters self-understanding. Acting in one's self-interest can also benefit others in society or a community.[22] Thus self-interest is not inherently bad and can also work to improve the well-being of others.

As nursing diversified clinically, resulting in a proliferation of specialty organizations, the number of nursing groups interested in becoming politically active increased. By the mid 1980s, the ANA was no longer the only nursing organization with Washington representatives and lobbyists. As a result, the need for coordination among nursing interests became acute. A major difference between the first and second stages is the growing acknowledgment of the importance of nurses working together, or at least showing a united front, despite differences of opinion among individuals and groups.

Stage 2 is characterized by a new sense of identity emanating from the development of nursing coalitions and the building of nursing's political case. This new sense of identity enabled the profession to lobby for and eventually succeed in getting Congress to establish the National Center for Nursing Research in 1985, which Congress upgraded to the National Institute of Nursing Research in 1993. Lobbying for the new nursing research entity in the mid 1980s is also an example of how nursing had to overcome internal differences as it worked toward an important political goal.[23]

The formation of nursing coalitions in the legislative arena illustrates the type of coordinating and activism that typifies stage 2. In addition to the Tri-Council for Nursing (consisting of the ANA, American Colleges of Nursing, National League for Nursing, and American Organization of Nurse Executives), other examples of these coalitions included state alliances of nurse practitioners, the American College of Nurse Practitioners (formed in 1993), and the expansion of the National Federation of Specialty Nursing Organizations (formed in 1981).[24] Whatever the differences among these organizations and despite conflicts over competition and the claiming of credit, the ability to forge coalitions and compromises symbolized a new level of maturity for the profession.

The second stage also entails nurses speaking in their own language. In arguing for the importance of federal funding for nursing education and research, nurses emphasized the contributions they make to the care of patients, which required explaining the nursing component of care in health care delivery. Similarly, in lobbying for changes for state nurse practice acts to include "diagnosing and treating human responses to actual and potential health problems," nurses had to explain to legislators the meaning of nursing diagnosis. This in turn required defining terms such as nursing diagnosis and delineating the differences between nursing and medicine. Nurses also found themselves explaining other issues facing the profession to nonnurses, such as the difference between nurse practitioners and clinical specialists, the many pathways for becoming a registered professional nurse, and the challenges and conflicts these options created within the profession.

This need to explain nursing jargon did not always result in a step forward for the profession. In retrospect, it often impeded nursing's ability to move its agenda forward and be part of important health policy discussions. The language of stage 2 contrasts with the language of subsequent stages, when nurses individually and collectively, become more fluent in the parlance of mainstream health policy circles, thereby facilitating political advancement.

The development of nursing as a special interest also included the growth of ANA's political activities. For example, the proliferation of ANA's congressional district coordinators and senate coordinators across the United States enabled nurses to organize within their congressional districts and states, thereby increasing their visibility, access to legislators, and influence in the political process.

Another example of a strategy used in stage 2 is the work of nurses at the state level who organized and successfully lobbied for changes in laws and regulations that promoted the advanced practice of nursing. Their achievements included prescriptive authority for advanced practice registered nurses (APRNs) and the enactment of laws and promulgation of regulations that recognized the unique aspects of APRN practice.[25,26]

A significant event during stage 1 was the formation of the first political action committee for nursing. As Rothberg[27] recounted, in 1971 "a small group of troubled nurses met in New York State to determine how the nursing profession might exert greater influence over health care in the country." During the next few years they formed the group Nurses for Political Action (NPA), intending it to be the "political arm of organized nursing—specifically of ANA."[27] Its board members acknowledged the importance of NPA being linked with ANA, and they reached out to the national association. In 1974, after extensive negotiating, NPA disbanded and was replaced by Nurses' Coalition for Action in Politics (N-CAP), under the auspices of the ANA. That year ANA allocated $50,000 to establish N-CAP, whose purposes included educating nurses about political issues and working with nurses in states and local areas for grassroots organizing.[8,28]

Contributions to the American Nurses Association Political Action Committee (ANA-PAC), which was the new name for N-CAP, increased significantly, reaching more than $1 million in 1994.[29] Between the 1992 and 1993 election cycles, ANA-PAC had the second largest increase in contributions to federal candidates of all PACs in the United States. By 1994 it ranked third among health-related PACs (surpassed by the American Medical Association and the American Dental Association) in contributions made to federal candidates. (The American Hospital Association ranked fourth.)[30] This tremendous growth, largely as a result of telemarketing, marked a new type of political sophistication for ANA and its members.

STAGE 3

The third stage in the political development of the nursing profession is "political sophistication" in which nursing develops more complex and sophisticated methods of political activism and involvement than in previous stages. As a result other health policy leaders, including government officials, recognize the talents of individual nurses and acknowledge the expertise that the profession, collectively, can offer to health policy decision making. This stage is characterized by nursing getting beyond its own language.

One of the most important activities characterizing the transformation between stages 2 and 3 was the drafting and development of *Nursing's Agenda for Health Care reform,*[31] which marks a milestone for the profession in terms of consensus-building and collaboration among organizations. The vision of this agenda and the acceptance it gained within nursing and other policy circles reflects a new level of political maturity for the nursing body politic. For the first time the entire profession, not just an organization (as was the case with the ANA social policy statement), had a document that depicted the values that nursing stands for in terms of health policy and quality patient care. These same elements enhance the ability of nurses—individually and collectively—to represent themselves to legislators and others during deliberations on health care reform.

A second achievement that exemplifies stage 3 development is the appointment of nurses to federal panels and agencies, ranging from the Prospective Payment Assessment Commission to the Agency for Health Care Policy Research (AHCPR), where nurses have been active in the development of many of the clinical guidelines issued in areas such as pain management, urinary incontinence, depression in primary care, and pressure sores.[32] Certain nurses and organizations, such as the ANA, realized the importance of "working the system" to lobby the appointment of nurses as co-chairs of the clinical guidelines panels. Although the nurses appointed to these and other important panels make important contributions to policy analyses and recommendation, the behind-the-scenes work of the professional organizations, mostly ANA, in getting them appointed characterizes the overlap between stages two and three. The lobbying or negotiating needed to ensure that nursing is represented as a special interest typifies stage 2, whereas the knowledge that these nurses have to offer fits under stage 3, because they are recognized as experts beyond the nursing profession in broader health policy circles.

Similarly, the many nurses who were selected as The Robert Wood Johnson Foundation Health Policy or White House Fellows and subsequently became leaders in health policy also illustrate the growing sophistication of the profession characterized by stage 3. Each of these appointments reflects the expert status that nursing is acquiring—collectively and individually—beyond the more self-serving interest that characterizes stages 1 and 2.

Stage 3 has also been marked by a proliferation of nurses elected or appointed to positions at the federal and state levels of government. By 1996, 71 nurses held elected positions in state legislatures, and many more were members of legislative staffs in Congress or state governments (personal communication, ANA, April 1996). As nurses became more adept at working political systems, they also improved their ability to navigate the increasingly complex webs of health care institutions.

Another characteristic of stage 3 is that nurses have become increasingly savvy in areas such as campaign financing laws, election strategies, and public relations techniques.[33] For example, in 1994, during the health care reform debate, ANA established a cadre of nurses with knowledge of the media through a grassroots program called Nurses Strategic Action Team (N-STAT). In addition to mobilizing nurses to respond quickly to congressional decisions, N-STAT provided media training to hundreds of nurses who could use the media to influence the public and policy makers. Nurses participating in N-STAT learn how to hold press conferences, speak on television and radio, and mobilize letters to the editor.

Stage 3 activities have also included an increase in the number of graduate nursing programs and courses that focus on health policy, as well as new strategies for teaching health policy.[34-41] These ideas build on similar themes of stage 1 but take them to a more sophisticated level, including the notion of a nurse policy analyst as a new type of advanced practice role.[42] Many publications on health policy authored or co-authored by nurses, yet focusing beyond the implications for nursing, are testimony to nursing's widening vistas on health policy.[43–46]

Finally, stage three also includes an increase in what Donna Diers described as "friends in all places."[47] That is, as a result of the clout that nursing acquired politically and in other professional arenas, many nonnurses such as Barbara Safriet[48] and Suzanne Gordon[49] were reaching their own conclusions regarding the advantages of nursing practice. The broadened scope of nursing's political involvement and sophistication, augmented by the political activities of stages 1 and 2, facilitated the entry of nurses into important political circles, such as President Clinton's task force on health care reform.

STAGE 4

The fourth stage in the development of the profession's political identity can be described as "leading the way," or the agenda-setting stage. Nursing has only just begun to enter this phase, during which the profession builds on the sophistication of stage 3 and begins to set the agenda for health policy beyond issues that would be more traditionally defined as relevant to nursing.

The major difference between stages 3 and 4 is that the expertise that nurses have to offer in stage 4 is more than contributory, as it is in stage 3. Instead, in stage 4 nurses become the initiators of crucial health policy ideas and innovations as instigators, leaders, or formulators of health policy.

The fourth stage is based on the conviction that it is important for nurses to participate in policy making, not only for self-interests, but because of how nursing values can improve the health and health care of people. MacPherson[50] and others[51,52] have discussed nursing's special value orientation—one that embraces concepts such as caring, health promotion, informed and supported self-care, and holism—that is not often represented at policy tables.

During this phase, the profession is recognized for its leadership in agenda-setting for a broad range of health and social policy issues, such as AIDS, school-based health centers, women's concerns, human rights and health care, and international health. Nursing also can contribute its perspective to broader public issues related to prevention and health promotion, but beyond what has heretofore been considered priority for nursing's political agenda. Quality education of children, adequate housing, promotion of nonviolent methods of conflict management, or meaningful work at an adequate wage can all be viewed as primary prevention strategies to promote healthy lifestyles and prevent unnecessary injuries, stress, or illnesses.

The fourth phase of political development also includes the appointment of nurses to high-level political positions within health policy, government, academic, and other circles. In recent years nurses have been appointed as university presidents and vice provosts and to high-level health and other policy positions in local, state, and federal governments. It is important to note that what makes these accomplishments characteristic of stage four is that these nurses are typically appointed without the suggestion or recommendation of the nursing profession or organized nursing. Rather, these talented nurses reach these high-level positions mainly through their own accomplishments. In addition, by nature of their positions, these nurses are accountable to constituencies that extend beyond nursing, demonstrating the influence that nurses can bring to many different types of policy arenas. Unlike in stage 1, where such nurses were few and far between, in stage 4, many nurses have these influential positions.

IN PURSUIT OF STAGE 4

The move to stage 4 must be deliberately pursued if the perspective and values of nursing are to help reshape our health care system. The further the profession is able to move into this stage, the more the public will benefit from nursing's expertise and the advocacy that nurses can provide on behalf of the public. Activism on broader health and social issues does not preclude continued vigilance on professional issues that are more directly related to nursing practice, such as reimbursement of advanced practice nurses. Indeed, stage 4 does not rule out pursuit of self-interests; it merely does so within a context that emphasizes the larger public good.

At a time when uncertainty regarding the reorganization of health care delivery prevails, the present and immediate future can be viewed as a critical time of transition to move toward stage 4. Blumenthal[53] is one of many who contend that increasing public dissatisfaction with accessing health care, limitations on provider choice and overall benefits, and erosion of "care" brought on by cost constraints under managed care will present a great opportunity and challenge for true health care reform in the future. Nursing can play an important role in this process. Leading the way in developing an antidote that "puts the care back into health care" in a cost-effective way could establish the profession as a more prominent player in policy and political circles.

Pursuit of stage 4 can be enhanced in the following ways:

Building coalitions and constituencies. Building coalitions around health and social issues takes on increasing importance in stage 4 of the model. At a time when special interest groups have proliferated, grassroots mobilization is seen as key to making a difference in many public policy decisions.[54] Issue-based collaboration is often needed to formulate and implement public policy. Whereas this collaboration usually occurs with the leadership of organizations and groups, leaders need a constituency supporting their actions.

Building a constituency first involves identifying an existing or potential constituency or target population and then connecting that group's values, interests, and beliefs to the issue at hand. However, it is not enough to focus only on nurses as constituents. Nursing needs to reach audiences that extend beyond its members. The profession will be propelled further into stage 4 when the expertise it has acquired in organizing and mobilizing its own members is applied to other groups; this calls for nursing to take the lead by mobilizing other groups, such as senior citizens and advocates for the young, to support our issues. For instance, nursing could take the initiative on debates around Medicaid and Medicare, not only to support issues such as reimbursement for advanced practice nurses, but also to speak forcefully about how communities can develop new ways to work together to meet the health needs of underserved populations. In addition, nursing needs to reach out to groups that have opposed some of our issues in the past and find common ground for support.

Leadership development. Reaching stage 4 also requires that nursing seek out, develop, and support its visionaries and risk-takers. The collective will almost always lag behind individual visionaries, but the collective can be moved by the visionaries.[55] Today's visionaries must actively cultivate and educate the next generation about the workings of the legislative, judicial, and executive branches of government.

To enhance leadership development, the ANA or other nursing organizations might consider sponsoring political "mentorships." Under such a mentorship program, which would be similar in concept to an internship, nurses could apply to spend time with a nurse political leader. These leaders could include nurses who are lobbyists, appointed or elected public officials, coalition leaders, executive directors, deans, researchers, or clinicians who are involved in some notable way in the shaping of health and public policy.

Mobilizing nurses for campaigns. To promote the election of nurses to public offices, organized nursing needs to educate and mobilize nurses for campaign involvement and ensure that nurse candidates will have the financial resources to successfully pursue elected office. Not all nurse candidates will get the support of nursing PACs, but we yearn for the day when nursing's diversity is represented among a large number of nurses who hold public office.

Organized nursing might consider the example of the Women's Political Caucus in many states. This group actively seeks out women candidates and provides them with technical assistance to run campaigns, financial backing, and political support. The Women's Political Caucus runs seminars on campaign management that are targeted for all women candidates, even those running for local offices. The group recognizes that this type of support will pay off in the end, because election at the local level is usually the precursor to higher office and because local politics can be important in their own right (e.g., school policy and public health). Another strategy would be to promote the enrollment of nurses in programs such as the Women's Campaign School at Yale University that are established to encourage women to enter and flourish in the political process.

New integration of health policy into curricula. Educators should integrate health policy and politics into the curriculum in such a way that it is no longer seen as an add-on. Buerhaus[35] argues that a separate course, rather than sporadic lectures on policy issues, is needed to enable students to develop an adequate understanding of health and public policies and policy-making processes. The connections between health, nursing practice, and policy and political activism must be explicit.[18] In addition, the connection to the broader social issues of the times must be evident. The inclusion of policy content on certification examinations is another way to enhance the linkages among practice, education, and policy.

Developing public media expertise. The importance of the media in influencing public policy debates was evident in the derailing of Clinton's health care reform effort by the "Harry and Louise" commercials sponsored by the Health Insurance Association of America,[53] and should not be underestimated by nursing. We will not move to stage 4 without having sophisticated skills in making use of the media to communicate with the public. N-STAT is a good starting point for preparing nurses to develop media expertise, and more of such activities will be necessary to attain stage 4.

To foster better access to media and provide opportunities for media training, some nurses are creating their own radio or television programs or are writing health columns for community newspapers. In New York City, "Healthstyles" is a weekly live radio program on health and health policy that is produced and moderated by the Nursing and Health

Resource Network, a collective of nurses for WBAI-Pacifica Radio, in collaboration with the New York Counties Registered Nurses Association (District 13 of the New York State Nurses Association). The program provides a training ground for nurses who are not experienced in the media and a forum for nursing perspectives on health care. "Healthstyles" has developed a reputation as a unique voice in health journalism[56] and received media awards from the Public Health Association of New York City and the American Academy of Nursing. The Network has helped nurses across the United States and in Canada to begin and sustain similar programs. This network is an example of how nurses can use the media and take the lead on a wide range of issues, which characteristic of stage 4.

Publishing in nonnursing journals and in the popular press can enhance nursing's visibility on policy matters within the health care and public communities. For example, Linda Aiken's publication on the nursing shortage in *The New England Journal of Medicine*[57] and, more recently, her publications on the impact of professional nursing on morbidity and mortality outcomes in *Medical Care*[58] brought these issues to the attention of policy makers in government and workplaces to an extent that would not have occurred through publication in nursing journals alone. In the public press, Ellen Baer and Suzanne Gordon have published several op-ed pieces for major newspapers on topics such as feminism and nursing, the replacement of registered nurses with technicians, and home health care.[59-62] These publications have presented a nursing viewpoint to a wide spectrum of readers.

Increased sophistication in policy analysis and related research. We need to develop our level of sophistication in conducting policy analysis, policy research, and nursing research with policy implications. The work of Brooten et al.[63] on the effects of nurse specialist transitional care on outcomes and cost is an example of the type of research and its dissemination that combines nurses' expertise in these areas. The American Academy of Nursing's recent cosponsorship with the Agency for Health Care Policy and Research of a senior nurse scholar is one example of how to foster such scholarship.

Doctoral nursing programs should provide more opportunities for students to learn some of these skills. Every graduate of a doctoral program in nursing should be able to articulate the policy relevance of his or her research.

Policy analysis should also be valued as a career choice for nurses and not just a by-product of one's educational program. Although the case can be made that nurses interested in this role should pursue education through established nonnursing graduate programs in public policy, select nursing doctoral programs can help build the profession's expertise in this regard.

CONCLUSION

It is our belief that moving into stage 4 requires an examination of preconceived notions about "appropriate" political behavior bringing new vision to political action.[55] Nursing's values can serve to transform political processes and public policy. For example, if nursing is to get more nurses into elected policy-making positions, we must question whether existing political rules that support incumbency will further this objective. Nursing's voice in campaign finance reform thus takes on great importance.

The recommendations presented here require that professional nursing organizations continue to value the gains that will be made by collaborating with each other and with nonnursing organizations to move the profession into stage 4. One of the most exciting potential collaborations has begun between the National Advisory Council on Nursing Education and Practice, which advises the Secretary of Health and Human Services, and the Council of Graduate Medical Education, which advises Congress on health policy issues pertaining to medical education. The groups have collaborated on a study of primary care and are working together on issues of collaboration in medical and nursing education. Not only do these two bodies set national policy for funding of health personnel, but they also serve as models for collaboration between the two professions in all areas of policy development.[64] As equal partners in these endeavors, nursing can demonstrate its credibility and expertise about all aspects of health care delivery, including health workforce issues.

The ideas presented here are by no means intended to be exhaustive. We hope that they stimulate critical analyses and additional ideas for promoting nursing's political development. As rapid changes in health care continue, the time continues to be ripe for nursing's values to undergird new health policy initiatives that will inevitably evolve in the future.

This article has outlined a scheme for understanding the development of nursing as a body politic and strategies for moving the profession to stage 4 of this scheme. Nursing can use this framework to understand where the profession falls on the spectrum and then work collectively and individually to promote the expertise and knowledge that nursing has to offer in policy arenas. In many ways, this means sustaining a level of political participation that spans all four stages.

REFERENCES

1. Cowart ME. Teaching the legislative process. *Nurs Outlook* 1977;25(12):777–80.

2. Davis CK, Oakley D, Sochalski JA. Leadership for expanding nursing influence on health policy. *J Nurs Adm* 1982;12(1):15–21.

3. Archer S, Goehner PA. Acquiring political clout: guidelines for nurse administrators. *J Nurs Adm* 1981;11(11–12):49–55.

4. Diers D. A different kind of energy: nurse power. *Nurs Outlook* 1978;26(1):51–5.

5. Hott JR. The struggles inside nursing's body politic. *Nurs Forum* 1976;15(4):325–40.

6. Hughes E, Proulx J. Learning about politics. *Am J Nurs* 1979;79(3):494–5.

7. Kalisch B, Kalisch P. A discourse on the politics of nursing. *J Nurs Adm* 1976;6(3):29–34.

8. Kalisch B, Kalisch P. *The politics of nursing.* Philadelphia: J B Lippincott, 1982.

9. Maraldo P. Politics: a very human matter. *Am J Nurs* 1982;82(7):1104–5.

10. Mullane MK. Nursing care and the political arena. *Nurs Outlook* 1975;23(11):699–701.

11. Ashley JA. This I believe about power in nursing. *Nurs Outlook* 1973;21(10):637–41.

12. Ashley JA. Power in structured misogyny: implications for the politics of care. *Adv Nurs Sci* 1980;2(4):3–22.

13. Mason DJ, Talbott SW, editors. *Political action handbook for nurses: changing the workplace, government, organizations and community.* Menlo Park (CA): Addison-Wesley, 1985.

14. Jones L. Students participate in the legislative process. *Nurs Outlook* 1980;28(7):438–40.

15. Fagin CM, Maraldo PJ. Janforum: health policy in the nursing curriculum: why do we need it? *J Adv Nurs* 1981;6(1):71–4.

16. Diers D. Health policy and nursing curricula—a natural fit. *Nurs Health Care* 1985;6(10):421–33.

17. Leininger M. Political nursing: essential for health service and education systems of tomorrow. *Nurs Adm Q* 1978;2(3):1–16.

18. Solomon SB, Roe SC. *Integrating public policy into the curriculum.* New York: National League for Nursing, 1986. Publication No. 15–1995.

19. Schutzenhofer KK, Cannon SB. Moving nurses into the political process. *Nurs Educ* 1986;11(2):26–8.

20. DeParle J. Sheila Burke is the militant feminist Commie peacenik who's telling Bob Dole what to do. *New York Times* 1995 Nov 12;Sect 6:32–8, 90, 100–5(col. 1).

21. Kalisch P, Kalisch B. The nurse shortage, the president, and the congress. *Nurs Forum* 1980;19(2):138–64.

22. Stone D. *Policy, paradox and political reason.* New York: HarperCollins, 1988:13–4.

23. Dumas RG, Felton G. Should there be a National Institute of Nursing? *Nurs Outlook* 1984;32(1):16–22.

24. Kelly LY, Joel LA. *Dimensions in professional nursing.* 7th ed. New York: McGraw-Hill, 1995:618–21.

25. Birkholz G, Walker D. Strategies for state statutory language changes granting fully independent nurse practitioner practice. *Nurs Pract* 1994;19(1):54–8.

26. Pearson LJ. Annual update of how each state stands on legislative issues affecting advanced nurse practice. *Nurs Pract* 1996;21(1):10–70.

27. Rothberg JS. The growth of political action in nursing. *Nurs Outlook* 1985;33(3):133–5.

28. West N. An idea is born: the beginning of nursing PACs. In: Mason D, Talbott S, editors. *Political action handbook for nurses: changing the workplace, government, organizations and community.* Menlo Park (CA): Addison-Wesley, 1985:484–9.

29. ANA-PAC tops $1 million, endorses more than 180 candidates to date. *Am Nurse* 1994;(Sept):30.

30. Federal Election Commission. *Report of Federal Election Commission: end of year 1994.* Washington (DC): The Commission, 1995.

31. *Nursing's agenda for health care reform.* Kansas City (MO): American Nurses' Publishing, 1993.

32. Jacox AK, Carr DB. Clinical practice guidelines. *Nurs Econ* 1991;9(2):118–20.

33. Mason DJ, Talbott S, Leavitt JK, editors. *Politics and policy for nurses: action and change in the workplace, government, organizations and community.* 2nd ed. Philadelphia: W B Saunders, 1990.

34. Andreoli KG, Musser LA, Otto DA. Health policy in nursing curriculum. *J Nurs Educ* 1987;26(6):239–43.

35. Buerhaus PI. Teaching health care public policy. *Nurs Health Care* 1992;13(6):304–9.

36. Landsberger BH, Landsberger HA. Health policy opinions of graduate students in nursing. *Int J Nurs Stud* 1986;23(2)159–76.

37. Martin EJ, White JE, Hansen MM. Preparing students to shape health policy. *Nurs Outlook* 1989;37(2):89–93.

38. McGivern DO. Teaching nurses the language of the marketplace. *Nurs Health Care* 1988;9(3):126–30.

39. Raudonis BM, Griffith G. Model for integrating health services research and health care policy formation. *Nurs Health Care* 1991;12(1):89–93.

40. Thomas PA, Shelton CR. Teaching students to become active in public policy. *Public Health Nurs* 1994;11(2):75–9.

41. Williams DM. Policy at the grassroots: community-based participation in health care policy. *J Prof Nurs* 1991;7(5):271–6.

42. Stimpson M, Hanley B. Nurse policy analyst: advanced practice role. *Nurs Health Care* 1991;12(1):10–5.

43. Aiken LH. Evaluation research and public policy: lessons from the National Hospice Study. *J Chronic Dis* 1986;39(1):1–4.

44. Freeman HE, Aiken LH, Blendon RJ, Corey CR. Uninsured working-age adults: characteristics and consequences. *Health Serv Res* 1990;24(6):811–23.

45. Harrington C, Grant LA. The delivery, regulation and politics of home care: a California case study. *Gerontologist* 1990;30(4):451–61.

46. Kovner CT. Mental disorders, DRGs, and the elderly. *Nurs Econ* 1989;7(1):25–31.

47. Diers D. Friends in all places. *J Prof Nurs* 1993;9(2):70.

48. Safriet BJ. Health care dollars and regulatory sense: The role of advanced practice nursing. *Yale J Reg* 1992;9(2):417–88.

49. Gordon S. *Prisoners of men's dreams: striking out for a new feminine future.* Boston: Little, Brown and Company, 1991.

50. MacPherson KI. Health care values, policy and nursing. *Adv Nurs Sci* 1987;9(3):1–11.

51. Backer B, Mason DJ, Nickitas DC, McBride AB, Vance C. Feminist perspectives on policy and politics. In: Mason DJ, Talbott S, Leavitt JK, editors. *Policy and politics for nurses: action and change in the workplace, government, organizations and community.* 2nd ed. Philadelphia: W B Saunders, 1993:18–35.

52. Reverby S. *Ordered to care: the dilemma of American nursing.* Cambridge: Cambridge University Press, 1987.

53. Blumenthal D. Health care reform—past and future. *N Engl J Med* 1955;332(7):465–468.

54. Faucheux R. The grassroots explosion. *Campaigns and Elections* 1995;(Dec/Jan):20–25.

55. Mason DJ, Leavitt JK. Political activism: the individual versus the collective. *J New York State Nurs Assoc* 1995;26(1):46–7.

56. Lipsyte R. Nurse radio: out of the medical wilderness. *New York Times* 1994 Dec 11; Sect. 13:1.

57. Aiken L, Mullinix C. The nurse shortage: myth or reality? *New Engl J Med* 1987;317(10):641–6.

58. Aiken L, Smith HL, Lake ET. Lower Medicare mortality among a set of hospitals known for good nursing care. *Med Care* 1994;32(8):771–87.

59. Baer ED. The feminist disdain for nursing. *New York Times* 1991 Feb 23; Sect. 1:25(col. 2).

60. Baer ED, Gordon S. The gender battle in nursing. *Boston Globe* 1994 Dec 28;15.

61. Baer ED, Gordon S. Home health care is fraught with danger. *Philadelphia Inquirer* 1995 Apr 10; Sect. A:9(col. 1).

62. Gordon S, Baer ED. Fewer nurses to answer the buzzer. *New York Times* 1994 Dec 6; Sect. A:23(col. 2).

63. Brooten D, Naylor M, York R, Brown L, Roncoli M, Hollingsworth A, et al. Effects of nurse specialist transitional care on patient outcomes and cost: results of five randomized trials. *Am J Managed Care* 1995;1(1):45–51.

64. Bureau of Health Professions, Health Resources and Services Administration. *Final report from the workgroup on primary care workforce projections.* Washington (DC): Government Printing Office, 1995.

ACKNOWLEDGMENTS

The views in this article are those of the authors and do not necessarily reflect those of the Agency for Health Care Policy and Research.

We thank Joyce Shea for research and technical assistance in preparing this manuscript.

6

KNOWLEDGE DEVELOPMENT IN NURSING: OUR HISTORICAL ROOTS AND FUTURE OPPORTUNITIES

SUSAN R. GORTNER

This article originally appeared as *Nursing Outlook, 48*(2), Gortner, S., Knowledge development in nursing: Our historic roots, pp. 60–67. Copyright © 2000 with permission from Elsevier. All rights reserved.

EDITORS' NOTE

Few non-nurses realize that nursing has developed an impressive body of research that has changed health care, beginning with Florence Nightingale—nursing's first researcher. But it took decades for American nurses to pursue scholarly endeavors that would define it as a profession and academic discipline. This article describes the historical development of nursing's scientific endeavors, including the evolution of federal support for nursing research.

■ ■ ■

The purpose of this article is to provide an historical overview of nursing research in the past century and to offer projections on where our science will be headed in the 21st century. For the overview, a number of reviews were drawn upon[1-4] with reliance on the last citation, which surveyed published nursing literature from 1900 to 1975. In the last 2 decades, other analyses of published research have been carried out,[5-7] including an impressive first encyclopedia of nursing research.[8] Research agendas and priorities have been developed by the American Nurses Association Commission[9] and Cabinet on Nursing Research,[10] the American Academy of Nursing Ad Hoc Group on Knowledge Generation,[11,12] and by consultant groups to the division of Nursing's research program,[13,14] and to the former National Center for Nursing Research.[15] Recent research publications of the nursing schools at the University of California–Los Angeles (UCLA), University of California–San Francisco (UCSF), and the University of Maryland[16-18] were used to formulate contemporary research questions. As such, they are illustrative rather than representative. Projections for the 21st century have been drawn from the author's reflections on our science,[14,19-22] from Donaldson's seminal paper at the 25th anniversary of the American Academy of Nursing,[23] and from the latest research agenda of the National Institute of Nursing Research.[24] Comments will be made on how our practice has been affected through research, and where applications did not occur, when perhaps they should have. Examples will be from projects personally known to the author.

THE EARLY YEARS

Nursing practice and issues arising from practice have influenced research topics since the time of Nightingale.

While practice issues have varied since then, some early concerns regarding quality of care and qualified caregivers transcend the 19th and 20th centuries into the 21st century. It is no accident that the development of formal programs of nursing education was seen as the means to improve practice. Historical perspectives on nursing and nursing research may be depicted as follows: in the early 1900s, concern was for improvement of the public's health; major communicable diseases of childhood and adulthood were prevalent; maternal/child health had yet to benefit from prenatal care and improved obstetrical practices. Most surgery was done in the home. The literature in our professional journals addressed problems associated with tuberculosis, meningitis, scarlet fever, etc. In 1913, the committee on public health nursing of the National League for Nursing Education discussed its concern about infant mortality, prevention of blindness, and the problem of unlicensed midwives. The committee believed that the nursing profession should recognize its role in the prevention of unnecessary deaths among infants and in prevention of unnecessary blindness, and that intelligent care of the sick must involve "some knowledge of the scientific approach to disease . . . causes and prevention . . . ."[4]

During the 1920s, the first case studies appeared; they were used both as a teaching tool for students and as a record of patient progress; nursing care plans for specific patient groups and procedures appeared (e.g., use of turpentine stupes), and continued until recently as a means to standardize and improve practice, medical as well as nursing. The case approach as a major research and teaching model in clinical nursing practice paralleled the use of case studies in medical practice and research. These case studies were used to describe unusual patient situations or symptoms and to report on the effects of nursing and medical therapies with groups of patients. According to personal interviews with the late Lucile Petry Leone,* the need for systematic evaluations of nursing procedures had its origins in the post-Depression years. The Depression forced the graduate nurse out of the home and into the hospital and, at the same time, the first postgraduate nursing programs began to develop.[4]

The war years prompted the collection of national data on nursing needs and resources (types, numbers, and uses of nurses). In the immediate postwar years, the federal government, assisted by professional nursing organizations and foundations, provided funds and staff to establish resources for nursing, one such being the Division of Nursing Resources of the United States Public Health Service created in 1948. Its staff carried out studies on nurse supply and distribution, job satisfaction and turnover, requirements for public health nursing services, personnel costs, and costs for collegiate nursing education. These studies were widely used throughout the United States, frequently in conjunction with federal staff consultation and training. A 5-year study of nursing functions and activities was begun by the American Nurses Association in 1950, resulting in functions, standards, and qualifications for practice,[25] as well as the publication *Twenty Thousand Nurses Tell Their Story.*[26] Also noteworthy during this time was the W. K. Kellogg Foundation Nursing Service Administration Research Project, in which faculty from 12 universities worked with Finer at the University of Chicago to determine needs for administrative science and skills in nursing.[27] Thus the period between 1930 and 1960 concentrated on the components of professional nursing practice and how best to secure them.

Focus on the organization and delivery of nursing services was given a boost when the Division of Nursing Resources initiated a small competitive research grants and

---

*Lucille Petry Leone spent many hours with the author and the late Helen Nahm in the writing of the overview of nursing research. She died on Thanksgiving Day, 1999.

fellowship program in 1955. Lucile Petry Leone, former director of the cadet nurse corps and then chief nurse officer and assistant surgeon general in the Public Health Service, convinced the surgeon general and the director of the National Institutes of Health to allocate $500,000 for grants and $125,000 for fellowships from the NIH budget. These programs were the precursors to the National Center for Nursing Research and the current National Institute for Nursing Research.[4] In 1952, the journal *Nursing Research* came into being; the first few issues contained a section entitled the "Research Reporter," in which areas suitable for research were noted; guest editorials emphasized the need for grassroots support of nursing research by hospitals, agencies, and schools. Lucile Petry Leone's editorial in the Fall 1955 issue summarized the types of studies needed in nursing, based on a staff paper she had prepared earlier. These types included studies of nursing care most essential to patient recovery; the nature of the therapeutic relationship; analysis and optimal use of nursing skills; and efforts to reduce staff turnover rates and student drop-out rates. Her thinking provided a visionary public platform for nursing research.[28]

Virginia Henderson's 1956 guest editorial noted that studies of the nurse outnumbered studies of practice 10 to 1, that more than half of the doctoral theses were carried out in the field of education, and that "responsibility for designing its methods is often cited as an essential characteristic of a profession . . . ."[29] Six years later, the first Nurse Scientist Graduate Training Grants were awarded to universities offering resources in one or more basic science departments for preparation through the doctorate. The first grant awards were to Boston University School of Nursing for training in biology, psychology, and sociology, and to the University of California School of Nursing for training in sociology. The next fiscal year, 3 additional grants were awarded, one to the UCLA School of Nursing for study in sociology; one to the University of Washington School of Nursing for graduate study in anthropology, microbiology, physiology and sociology, and the third to Western Reserve University School of Nursing for study in biology, physiology, psychology, and sociology.* Subsequently, grants were made to schools of nursing at the University of Kansas, Teachers College–Columbia University, University of Pittsburgh, University of Arizona, University of Colorado, University of Illinois, and briefly, New York University (the grant program was terminated in 1975). Required interdepartmental seminars helped to define the boundaries of nursing science for the early grantees. It is not surprising that nurse scientist graduate training settings later developed into PhD programs in nursing.[22]

In the early 1960s, establishment of the American Nurses Foundation grants program helped to address the demand for more practice-related studies. The foundation published the priorities that would guide funding: effects of performance of nursing acts on the patient (i.e., nursing procedures and outcomes); effects on nursing of changing patterns of nursing care and changing health needs, and nursing in different illness categories.[30]

---

*The first Doctor of Nursing Science program (in psychiatric nursing) was offered by Boston University; the next was at the University of California San Francisco. The first PhD program in nursing was begun by New York University, to be followed by the University of Pittsburgh.

Ellwynne Vreeland, the first chief of the federal nursing research branch, wrote chief nurse officer Lucile Petry Leone in 1959 that studies were needed to further development of nursing theory by identifying the scientific content of nursing, by seeking and experimenting with new concepts of nursing (e.g., motivation—"finding out why nurses can 'bring back' patients who have given up and who fail to respond to careful medical treatment"), and by careful study of the nursing care given by expert practitioners (the specifics of expert nursing, etc.).[31]

Soon the specifics of expert nursing became apparent as several university schools of nursing undertook studies of the nursing process, patient responses to care, and behavioral phenomena. The Yale study of nursing effects on postoperative vomiting became widely cited because of its experimental design and findings suggesting that nurse counseling had a positive effect.[32] UCLA nursing investigators studied recovery stages from myocardial infarction[33] (interviews with cardiologists revealed no clear demarcation of stages appropriate for nursing detection), breastfeeding,[34] rooming-in,[35] and pain relief.[36] These became among the first practice-related studies to be published in the new journal, *Nursing Research.*

At UCSF, sociologists Strauss and Glaser combined talents with nurse investigator Quint to study hospital personnel's views on death and dying.[37] Quint's seminal study of the experiences of women undergoing radical mastectomies[38] was to launch a scientific career that Donaldson has termed "pathfinding."[23] Studies at the University of Washington in the early 1960s focused on nursing services for psychiatric, tubercular, alcoholic, and maternity patients; variables included professional attitudes, activities, and accountability for patient care.[4] Batey's later expertise in research resource development was an outgrowth of her study with Julian of organizational patterns in psychiatric settings.[39] One of the earliest controlled attempts to document the effects of nursing intervention on the clinical progress of chronically ill adults was carried out by nursing investigators.[40]

At Presbyterian-University of Pennsylvania Medical Center, a project carried out between 1963 and 1967 in a special facility, the coronary care unit, demonstrated significant reductions in patient morbidity and mortality through continuous monitoring and prompt treatment by expert nurses.[41] This project had been supported by the fledgling research grants program of the Division of Nursing Resources; it was to become the model of coronary care nursing nationwide. It was also among the first reports of nursing research to be published in the *Journal of the American Medical Association.*

Thus the real thrust of nursing research began in the 1960s, a function of the vision of nursing leaders such as Lulu Wolf Hassenplug, Helen Nahm, Mary Tschudin, Hildegard Peplau, Virginia Henderson, Lucile Petry Leone, Ellwynne Vreeland, Faye Abdellah, and Jessie Scott, and the availability of public as well as private funds to support the studies and train nurses in research. I joined the division staff in 1966 to aid in the review of the Nurse Training Act of 1964, and in 1967 was appointed executive secretary to the Research in Patient Care Review Committee, the outside group of scientists charged with determining the scientific merit of research proposals submitted from throughout the United States. During my time as staff scientist and later as branch chief for research grants and fellowships, we attempted to nourish the growing enterprise of nursing research nationwide through staff consultation, conferences, research development grants, nurse scientist graduate training grants, and individual research fellowships.

We publicized the grant programs,[42] urged scientific accountability for the profession[43] as a practice profession[44] and early on attempted to show the contributions of research to patient care with a proposed classification, which named nursing research a "science of practice."[45]

To recapitulate, knowledge development in nursing began in earnest only 40 years ago, primarily in university schools of nursing where nurse scientist graduate training was ongoing in alliance with other disciplines, but also in medical centers such as the City of Hope, where Geraldine Padilla was director of research, at Luther Hospital in Eau Claire, Wisconsin, where Carol Lindeman was in charge, and at the Loeb Center for Nursing at Montefiore under the direction of Genrose Alfano. The Loeb Center for Nursing, which demonstrated that cost-effective care could be rendered to elders in a nursing center, was not seen as an innovation until such practice innovations were publicized by the American Academy of Nursing. Why the lag in impact of this research?

Annual research conferences sponsored by the American Nurses Association and later by the regional nursing research societies provided forums for investigators to present their findings and learn the importance of public scrutiny.[4] The art of the critique developed gradually, communality and collegiality joined communication and publication as hallmarks of our research efforts, and greater sophistication among nursing's investigators and clinicians resulted in greater intradisciplinary and interdisciplinary collaboration.

THE TRANSITION YEARS

I have termed the period from 1965 to 1985 "transitional," because professional nursing took on major leadership activities to influence federal policy for nursing education and research. The American Nurses Association established a Commission on Research in 1971; the Council of Nurse Researchers was created in 1972. In a paper presented at the first program meeting of the council in 1973, I described the increasing concern that research financed by the federal government be related to major health priorities, stating that ". . . there is no mistaking the trend toward greater legislative specification of science in the health fields."[46] The scientist audience was urged to develop research priorities for nursing research.

In response, Lindeman undertook a Delphi survey of priorities in clinical nursing research through the Western Interstate Commission on Higher Education, with Division of Nursing support.[2] Respondents identified items on the quality of care, nursing role, nursing process, and the research process. Patient welfare concerns, particularly items related to nursing interventions to mitigate stress, pain, and to provide patient education and support to frail elders also were cited.[47]

When the late President Nixon impounded Nurse Training Act, research, and fellowship funds in 1973, all federal support for fellowships and training grants was halted. The president was taken to court by a coalition of nursing organizations and forced to release the funds in 1974. The Division of Nursing held several invitational conferences on nurse scientist graduate training and doctoral personnel needs. Commission members traveled to Washington, DC, in 1975 to meet with legislators and federal program staff, the first such contacts to be made by what was later to become the nursing research advocacy group. In my capacity as branch chief, I was asked to meet with commissioners to present program needs, vital information for program development and funding that had been embargoed as a result of closure of all public information offices in 1971. Although we could not publish grant and fellowship information, we could respond to requests for information about the programs. To their credit, grantees understood this constraint and found opportunities to request program information. Thus the commission was able to develop priorities for research training and research and set goals for accomplishing them including funding levels.[9]

Health science research training authorization was restored with the passage of the National Research Service Awards Act in 1974; 2 years later, primarily through Connie Holleran's efforts, the Division of Nursing research training programs were included.[48] Publication of a review of research grants awarded[1] was followed by 2 historical overviews of nursing research;[2,3] 2 new research journals, *Research in Nursing and Health* and *The Western Journal of Nursing Research* appeared in 1978. The 94th Congress specified $5 million for research projects in nursing and $1 million for research fellowships to be spent during 1977 and 1978, the first time funds for nursing research had been earmarked in the appropriation. Until then and since 1964, nursing research funds had been allocated along with Nurse Training Act funds, although that act dealt exclusively with training to address the quality and quantity of professional nurses.[48]

This somewhat awkward allocation process and the difficulty health manpower legislation was experiencing In the 1970s led to open discussions by nurse scientists and educators regarding the need to locate the nursing research programs within the research environment of the National Institutes of Health. The discussions were frank and heated; well-respected deans worried that such a relocation would fracture federal nursing; others worried that nursing research could not mature if not nourished within the institute structure. Legislators were sympathetic and passed legislation (Public Law 99–158) authorizing a new center at the National Institutes of Health; it came into being in 1986 after a successful override of a presidential veto in main attributed to nurse scientist lobbying efforts, including the persuasive efforts of the entire membership of the American Heart Association Council on Cardiovascular Nursing which was meeting in Washington, DC, at the time. Council Chairperson Marie Cowan adjourned us to go on the Hill. We did, and the entire California delegation was visited (including the senate office of then Senator Pete Wilson was voted to override the veto).

Coincidental with establishment of the national center was the continuing work both of the American Nurses Association Cabinet on Nursing Research and the scientist group in the American Academy of Nursing. The cabinet published *Directions for Nursing Research: Toward the 21st Century* in 1985, setting goals, priorities, and strategies with dollar amounts to achieve them.[10] The next year the American Academy of Nursing held its annual meeting in Kansas City, with the program theme "Nursing in the Year 2000: Setting the Agenda for Knowledge Generation and Utilization." Stevenson and Woods provided a synthesis of the focus group priorities both for the new national center and also for research in the next 2 decades.[12] These specified fundamental knowledge development about clinical problems, followed by clinical therapeutics to test interventions, and increasing emphasis on health promotion, health status and functioning, on the family, and on vulnerable populations and age groups. Scientific knowledge synthesis was aided by the beginning of a series of annual reviews of nursing research under the direction of Werley and Fitzpatrick.

Oberst,[11] at the same Academy conference, provided a thoughtful insight for a possible Year 2000 research agenda:

> The heart of the problem may lie in the almost total absence of basic research into the nature of the phenomena we wish to influence. We know very little about patterns of fatigue and sleep or about the nature of immobility, confusion, or anorexia. We cannot expect to intervene to prevent or control a problem such as incontinence, for instance, without basic knowledge of the natural history of that condition in a variety of contexts.

Oberst also spoke to the extreme biophysical derangement associated with organ transplantation, microsurgery, aggressive chemotherapy protocols, asking whether health providers know the short-term and long-term physical and psychological effects of these events and their meaning for patients and families. This problem has continued to interest investigators. Mishel and Murdaugh studied an opportunistic sample of heart transplantation patients and families; this study is one of the finest examples of grounded theory methodology published.[49] Jenkins is among others studying the effects of aggressive protocols on quality of life.[18]

The transition years also saw the development of research on primary care and evaluation of nurse practitioner programs. Research was directed toward: (1) understanding the influence of structural variables on nurse practitioner performance (e.g., access to settings), (2) identifying personal and professional characteristics contributing to successful performance as a nurse practitioner, and (3) specifying the nature of clinical judgments used by nurse practitioners and physicians working collaboratively in patient care management to assign patients either to a nurse or physician and then reassign responsibilities as changes in health status occur. How do the management plans differ? This last question addresses the elusive nature of the nurse-patient encounter (the initial plan, examination, questioning, priority setting, treatment, and evaluation).[48] Ford and Silver evaluated the posttraining activities of skilled pediatric nurses and found that these nurses could handle independently three fourths of clinical visits in a rural station with high patient satisfaction regarding counseling and health monitoring.[50]

Lewis and Resnik evaluated the use of adult nurse practitioners at the University of Kansas medical clinic with similar findings[51]; to their disappointment, the program was discontinued after grant funding ceased. Veterans Administration (VA) South Hill clinic in Los Angeles became the site of a second attempt to demonstrate the effectiveness of nurse practitioners in managing adult chronic conditions, this time those of veterans. Charles Lewis had just come to UCLA; Theresa Cheyovich was a visionary nursing chief at the clinic, and I represented the "Feds" in the first interagency agreement signed by the VA with another federal agency. Two UCLA-trained PRIMEX nurses (UCLA was the original PRIMEX training site), one a former VA clinic nurse, undertook caseloads released by then 33 VA physicians, who had been painstakingly persuaded by Lewis to participate in the project. One nurse in particular was able to realize major changes in health status and outcomes of her veteran case load. Examining her encounters, we discovered she "contracted" with patients on a weekly basis, and used social persuasion and professional skills to bolster patient confidence in their own health management.[52] Further, the experiment was so successful that the VA proceeded thereafter to train and place nurse practitioners in many of its settings. Here is still another example of how nursing research has impacted practice.

NURSING RESEARCH BECOMES NURSING SCIENCE

What occurred also during this transition period was a shift in thinking from *research* to *science,* a recognition that what we had thought was nursing science was really research, the tool of science. Nursing science was depicted as a human science that had the additional requirement of intervention or clinical therapy. Nursing research was redefined "as the discrete and aggregated investigations that constitute the professions modes and foci of inquiry. . . ."[19] The phenomena of interest to nursing were already being documented through research to become tentative propositions about human health and illness, vulnerable population groups (the aged, the chronically ill, women, children, infants), and illness recovery processes and risk factors. The seminal essay by Donaldson and Crowley on "The Discipline of Nursing"[53] clarified our thinking on what might become our knowledge domains and syntax. Meleis' inaugural Helen Nahm lecture on nursing scholarship heralded both the scientific and theoretical developments that were to occur in the next 2 decades.[54] Clinical science was seen as focusing on human problems and treatment modalities; fundamental science was characterized as having no immediate utility but devoted to understanding basic processes across a wide variety of disciplines.[19]

The last period of knowledge development in this century witnessed an explosion of fundamental and clinical science activities in nursing. How these phenomena came about is described next.

Nursing Science Comes of Age

Our science came into maturity during the past decade and a half as a result of several factors. First, emphasis began to shift from discrete studies to aggregates of studies, the precursors of programs of research. The shift initially was encouraged by the Division of Nursing's Nursing Research Emphasis Grant Program, in which areas of concentration, such as vulnerable populations and health across the life span, were suggested as topics to be coupled with graduate education.[55] The program at UCSF concentrated on two of these areas, and solicited proposals from faculty that would both extend knowledge and involve and excite graduate students; we were funded and renewed for 5 years. Second, schools of nursing began to recruit doctorally prepared faculty with excellent research preparation and programmatic interests that fit with concentrations of research within the school. University nursing schools featured "centers of excellence," in which faculty effort and talent were aggregated, acknowledging that selectivity was required to achieve excellence. Third, educational programs in many universities maintained sufficient stability that faculty time and effort could be redirected toward research. That is, curriculum revisions seemed to reach a plateau. Collaboration and colleagueship began to replace competitiveness and solo investigations. Fourth, external competition for research support increased as grant success was forthcoming from both public and private agencies; in the university systems, extramural support is one criterion for advancement up the faculty ranks. At UCSF initially, successful investigators received a bottle of champagne; later beer, and then soda sufficed. Fifth, arguments over appropriate methods, whether experimentation, description and/or interpretation, waxed heatedly and then seemed to wane, as many of us put our energies into substance activities, whether empirical investigations or philosophic musings, or both, as was the case with me. Sixth, scientists such as Lindsey, Cowan, Donaldson, Woods, Shaver, Brooten, Norbeck, and Dracup, to name but a few, took the brave step of becoming deans, thus reinforcing the science enterprise in their settings. With this momentum and influx of prepared scientist nurses, some of whom had been exposed to philosophers in their graduate programs, came debate about the nature of nursing science, what should be the prevailing world view and research approach. We spent a great deal of time speaking and writing to empiricism, phenomenology (later hermeneutics), critical theory, and feminism, to name but a few. Postpostivists, of which I am one, were maligned for speaking to the components of "good science" such as credibility, reproducibility, and rigor.[22]

The knowledge development group at the American Academy of Nursing program meeting in 1986 attempted to draw a cease-fire between the received and perceived views of science, endorsing pluralism.[56] Meleis called for a "passion for substance" rather than a passion for method[57]; and I attempted to formulate a philosophy of science for nursing that would embrace values.[58] Notions about nursing research and its substantive activity also have been formulated throughout the years by Ellis,[59] Batey,[60] Barnard,[61] and Shaver.[62] The following represents but one definition of nursing science, drawing on Barnard[13,61] and Donaldson and Crowley[23]:

> Nursing science as a form of human science, has as its object of analysis the human organism, with particular reference to human response states in health and illness and health across the life span. Its aim is to generate a body of knowledge that can define patterns of behavior associated with normal and critical life events such as catastrophic illness; depict changes in health status and predict how these are brought about; and along with other scientific fields, determine the principles and laws governing life states and processes.[20]

In the decades of knowledge development documented in this review, nursing has identified with tasks and technology and has characterized itself as a compassionate human service; it has taken as its subject matter the ecology of human health and human responses to health illness. While these conceptualizations may appear sequential, based on historical literature, in reality they are concurrent.

The researchable components of human health across the life span comprise indicators of health status, biological, and behavioral factors contributing to health and illness, culture, environment, and treatment outcomes. These components were displayed in the National Center for Nursing Research national nursing research agenda, developed after an invitational conference on research priorities in nursing science at which 50 nurse scientists were present.[15] To establish the agenda, priorities were selected on the basis of the existing knowledge base, opportunities, areas of low emphasis in other institutes, marketability, and available scientific personnel. These priorities were staged as follows: I—"HIV Positive Clients, Partners and Families," and "Prevention and Care of Low Birth Weight Infants"; II—"Long Term Care and Symptom Management and Information Systems"; and III—"Health Promotion" (in which the "most critical issues for study are the fundamental psychosocial mechanisms underlying maintenance of health promotion behaviors . . ."), and "Technology Dependency Across the Lifespan."[15]

Ten years later, the National Institute of Nursing Research (NINR) distributed a statement on strategic planning for the 21st century with this definition of research (not science!):

> Nursing research addresses the issues that examine the core of patients and families personal encounters with illness, treatment, disease prevention. NINR's primary activity is clinical research and most studies involve patients. The basic science is linked to patient problems.
>
> . . . Nursing research is essential in defining and confronting the compelling health and illness challenges of the 21st Century.[24]

These challenges include risk reduction, promotion of healthy lifestyles, enhanced quality of life for persons with chronic conditions, and care for persons at the end of life. These areas are familiar; they have remained persistent for more than 30 years. The National Institute for Nursing Research stated the following *scientific goals* for the next 5-year period:

1. Identify research opportunities that will achieve scientific distinction within the scientific and practice communities and within NIH as a result of their significant contributions to health:

    End of life/palliative care research

    Chronic illness experiences

    Quality of life and quality of care issues

    Health promotion and disease prevention

    Telehealth interventions

    Implications of genetic advances

    Cultural and ethnic consideration to decrease health disparities

2. Identify future opportunities for high-quality cost-effective care for patients and contribute to the scientific base of nursing practice through research on:

    Chronic illness (arthritis, diabetes) and long-term care including family care

    Health promotion and risk behaviors

    Cardiopulmonary health and critical care

    Neurofunction and sensory conditions

    Immune response and oncology

    Reproductive and infant health

3. Communicate research findings.

4. Enhance research training opportunities.

These initiatives are already displayed in the research programs of many university schools of nursing. I reviewed the research publications from the schools of nursing at the UCLA,[16] UCSF,[17] and the University of Maryland[18] in preparation for the original presentation on which this article is based. The scientific topics in these settings include vulnerable populations, cardiovascular and other illnesses, symptom management, chronic pain, health promotion/illness prevention, risk reduction, quality of life, the family in health and illness, women's health, and nursing therapeutics (including intensive cardiac monitoring, coaching for recovery, and "kangaroo care"). As examples:

- Is pain relief universal or are there gender differences? Miakowski & Levine, UCSF

- Does an ischemia monitoring protocol result in improved patient outcomes? Drew et al, UCSF

- What is the relationship between daytime fatigue and sleep disturbance in women? Lee, UCSF

- Does a collaborative intervention (advanced practice nurses and community peer advisors) improve outcomes for cardiac elders? Rankin, UCSF

- What is the role of exercise in heart failure patients? Dracup, Woo, Cowan, Vredevoe, Padilla, Doering et al., UCLA

- Can an intervention with low income adolescent mothers reduce HIV risk and improve health outcomes? Koniak-Griffin, UCLA

- What chromosomal abnormalities result from environmental toxins and affect reproductive health? Robbins, UCLA

- What is the quality of life experience of women with differing stages of lung cancer? Sarna, UCLA

- Can kangaroo care be as effective in ventilated infants as in premature infants? Ludnington, University of Maryland

- What are the effects of estrogen on platelet function after cerebral ischemia? Kearney, University of Maryland

- How do aggressive treatment modalities affect health status and quality of life? Jenkins, University of Maryland

In the study write-ups, investigators often revealed how their interests originated. Many investigators were and are advanced practice nurses. As such they have credibility both as clinicians as well as scientists. Not surprisingly then research findings have had an impact on practice by encouraging family sensitive care in several settings,* by enhancement of patient self-confidence and self-efficacy through coaching, counseling, and performance,[†] by advocating improved critical care heart monitoring procedures,[‡] by early discharge of low-birth-weight infants,* and by sensory stimulation of the neonate including skin-to-skin contact.[†]

---

*Suzanne Feetham, Kathleen Dracup, and Catherine Gilliss are among the pioneers in family nursing research, along with Lorraine Wright of Canada. Sally Rankin, Maribelle Leavitt, and Kit Chesla are among others who have studied families in acute and chronic illness.

[†]Louise Jenkins and Susan Gortner were among the first to employ self-efficacy as a variable in patient recovery; Sally Rankin, Diane Carroll, Mariead Hickey, Virginia Carrieri, and Marylin Dodd are among others who have studied self-efficacy in clinical populations.

[‡]Barbara Drew has been the pioneering investigator in this aspect of critical care nursing.

*Eileen Hasselmeyer, Mary Neal, and Kathryn Barnard were the original pioneers in studies of neonate stimulation, followed by Anderson, Whalberg, and Lundington, among others.

[†]Dorothy Brooten is credited for demonstrating the cost-effectiveness of low-birth-weight infants.

Whereas nursing investigators have not always received the publicity given medical investigators, this bias is changing slowly as more nurses are appointed and elected to public office and as more become members of scientific and governmental advisory groups. The media recognition awards given annually by the American Academy of Nursing also have been instrumental in raising the veil of public ignorance. Schorr and Kennedy's[63] splendid pictorial of 100 years of American nursing, just released, is a cause for celebration!

Where the areas of concentration some 20 years ago tended to reflect one dominant knowledge domain, for example, the psychosocial, now the biophysical, particularly biology and genetics, are reflected in the investigations noted above and elsewhere. This phenomenon may have been encouraged by the report of the National Center for Nursing Research biological task force, which stated: "the implications for the interface of nursing science with the biological sciences as a basis for research and its subsequent findings for practice are tremendous."[64] It also may be a natural development of better understanding that nursing problems cannot be solved within one knowledge domain; most involve multiple and complex factors.[20,21]

FUTURE OPPORTUNITIES

In preparing for this last section, I queried several colleagues throughout the United States to inquire where the future might lead us. Invariably, the response was (1) to reexamine the impact of organizational structures on nursing effectiveness, (2) to continue to examine fundamental processes underlying human responses to health and illness, (3) to take the lead with family health, (4) to continue study of end-of-life and palliative care, and (5) to have an impact on health policy. I would add one more to which I would give considerable urgency: (6) to identify the biobehavioral factors (in epidemiologic terms, the host factors) that explain much of illness and associated behavior. These factors will frame why questions (e.g., why is it that personal recovery beliefs are such a powerful predictor of cardiac surgical outcomes along with the usual pathophysiologic markers?) that will bring our science into increasing respect within the greater medical science community at the National Institutes of Health and elsewhere.

Donaldson's "Breakthroughs in Nursing Research" given at the 25th Anniversary of the American Academy of Nursing in 1998, identified "pathfinders" who created a new realm of nursing research or reconceptualized an existing realm of nursing research.[23] Many were already working in the above areas 30 years ago. Noting that nursing has the "brilliance in family health," she encouraged us to know well the human genotype project, the environment as the social context for health, and to strengthen the bridge between public health and person/family health. To these I would add: and strengthen collaboration (between nursing and other disciplines and within nursing) and continue to address fundamental problems at the biobehavioral interface.

Two additional opportunities need mentioning. Nursing has a proud heritage of safe and effective midwifery service that has affected health legislation for Medicaid and rural health but still has not removed barriers to hospital practice.[65] What may be needed here are collaborative teams of obstetrical fellows and midwives in some forward-thinking health science settings that will become "pacesetters" in collaborative practice.

Fagin's[66] guest editorial in *Nursing Outlook* on the changing burden of care brought on by managed care pleads with us in academia to *know* what it is like at the bedside. Without documentation of the effects of management on the burden of care, we may not save our workforce. Burden of care has been an issue for us and for housestaff all of this century. To become clinically refreshed, I undertook a day of practice 20 years ago on a cardiovascular surgery unit. I had forgotten what it was like to leave a lunch half eaten in the staff room. What made this experience bearable was the professional support provided by my mentors, 2 cardiovascular clinical nurse specialists, with whom I collaborated in clinical research on cardiac surgery recovery.*

In conclusion, tribute is paid to readers who are pacesetters in clinics, hospitals, private practice, public health, and academia every day of their professional lives. Those of us now white-haired are grateful that you are where you are and doing what you do. The future is really ours, as it was years ago!

REFERENCES

1. Abdellah FG. Overview of nursing research 1955–1968. *Nurs Research* 1970;19:6–17, 151–62, 239–52.

2. Lindeman CA. Delphi survey of priorities in nursing research. *Nurs Research* 1975;24:434–41.

3. DeTornyay R. *Nursing research in the Bicentennial year.* Boulder (CO): Western Interstate Commission for Higher Education; 1976.

4. Gortner SR, Nahm H. An overview of nursing research in the United States. *Nurs Research* 1977;26:10–32.

5. Brown JS, Tanner CA, Padrick KP. Nursing's search for scientific knowledge. *Nurs Research* 1983;32:29–32.

6. Jacobsen BS, Meininger JC. The designs and methods of published nursing research: 1956–1983. *Nurs Research* 1985;34:306–12.

7. Moody LE, Wilson ME, Smythe K, Schwartz R, Tittle M, VanCott ML. Analysis of a decade of nursing practice research: 1977–1986. *Nurs Research* 1988;37:374–9.

8. Fitzpatrick JJ, editor-in-chief. *Encyclopedia of nursing research.* New York: Springer; 1998.

9. American Nurses Association Commission on Nursing Research. *Nursing research: toward a science of health care. Priorities for research in nursing.* Kansas City: American Nurses Association; 1976.

10. American Nurses Association Cabinet on Nursing Research. *Directions for nursing research: toward the twenty-first century.* Kansas City: American Nurses Association; 1985.

11. Oberst MT. Nursing in the year 2000: setting the agenda for knowledge generation and utilization. In: Sorenson G, editor. *Setting the agenda for the year 2000: knowledge development in nursing.* Kansas City: American Academy of Nursing; 1986.

12. Stevenson JS, Woods NF. Strategies for the year 2000: synthesis and projections. In: Sorenson G, editor. *Setting the agenda for the year 2000: knowledge development in nursing.* Kansas City: American Academy of Nursing; 1986.

13. Barnard KE. Knowledge for practice: directions for the future. *Nurs Research* 1980;29:208–12.

14. Gortner SR. Nursing research: out of the past and into the future. *Nurs Research* 1980;29:204–7.

15. National Center for Nursing Research. Report of the national nursing research agenda for the participants in the conference on research priorities in nursing science, January 27–29, 1988 [unpublished]. Prepared by D. Bloch. Bethesda: National Center for Nursing Research; 1988.

16. *Research spanning the life cycle.* Vol. 15. Los Angeles: University of California, Los Angeles School of Nursing; Fall 1998.

*The author is indebted to Patricia Sparacino, cardiovascular surgery nurse specialist at the Medial Center, University of California, San Francisco, and Julie Shinn, clinical coordinator in cardiovascular surgical nursing at Stanford University Medical Center. Both are internationally known clinician/scholars and Academy members.

17. *The science of caring*. Vol. 11. San Francisco: University of California, San Francisco School of Nursing; Spring 1999.

18. *Advancing the science of nursing*. Vol. 11. Baltimore: University of Maryland School of Nursing; 1997–1999.

19. Gortner SR. Nursing science in transition. *Nurs Research* 1980;29:180–3.

20. Gortner SR. Knowledge development in a practice discipline: philosophy and pragmatics. In: Williams C, editor. *Nursing research and policy formation: the case of prospective payment*. Kansas City: American Academy of Nursing; 1984.

21. Gortner SR, Schultz PR. Approaches to nursing science methods. Image *J Nurs Sch* 1988;20:22–4.

22. Gortner SR. Historical development of doctoral programs: shaping our expectations. *J Prof Nurs* 1991;7:45–53.

23. Donaldson S. Breakthroughs in nursing research. Invited presentation. Proceedings of the 25th Anniversary of the American Academy of Nursing; 1998; Acapulco, Mexico.

24. Grady P. Strategic planning for the 21st century. Proceedings of the National Institute for Nursing Research State of the Science Congress; 1999 Sept 16–18; Washington, DC.

25. American Nurses Association. *Functions, standards and qualifications for practice*. New York: The Association; 1959.

26. Hughes EC, et al. *Twenty thousand nurses tell their story*. Philadelphia: JB Lippincott Co; 1958.

27. Finer H. *Administration and the nursing services*. New York: Macmillan Co; 1952.

28. Leone LP. The ingredients of research. *Nurs Research* 1955;4:51.

29. Henderson V. Research in nursing practice—When? *Nurs Research* 1956;4:99.

30. American Nurses Foundation. Research-pathway to future progress in nursing care. *Nurs Research* 1960;9:4–7.

31. Vreeland E. Memorandum to Lucile Petry Leone, chief nurse officer. Some frontiers for nursing research. Feb 1959.

32. Dumas RG, Leonard RC. The effect of nursing on the incidence of postoperative vomiting. *Nurs Research* 1963;12:12–5.

33. Coston HM. Myocardial infarction: stages of recovery and nursing care. *Nurs Research* 1960;9:178–84.

34. Disbrow MA. Any mother who really wants to nurse her baby can do so. *Nurs Forum* 1963;2:39–48.

35. Ringholz S, Morris M. A test of some assumptions about rooming-in. *Nurs Research* 1961;10:196–9.

36. Moss FT, Myer B. The effects of nursing interaction upon pain relief in patients. *Nurs Research* 1966;15:303–6.

37. Glaser BG, Strauss, AL. *Awareness of dying* (Observation Series). Chicago: Aldine Publishing Co; 1965.

38. Quint J. *The nurse and the dying patient*. New York: Macmillan Co; 1967.

39. Batey M, Julian J. Staff perceptions of state psychiatric hospital goals. *Nurs Research* 1963;12:89–92.

40. Little DE, Carnevali D. Nurse specialist effect on tuberculosis: report on a field experiment. *Nurs Research* 1967;16:321–6.

41. Meltzer LE, Pinneo R, Ferrigan MM, Kitchell JR, Ipsen J, Bearman J. *Intensive coronary care; an analysis of the system and the acute phase of myocardial infarction*. New York: Charles Press; 1969.

42. Gortner SR. Research in nursing. The federal interest and grant program. *Am J Nurs* 1973;73:1052–3.

43. Gortner SR. Scientific accountability in nursing. *Nurs Outlook* 1974;22:764–8.

44. Gortner SR. Research for a practice profession. *Nurs Research* 1974;24:193–7.

45. Gortner SR, Bloch D, Phillips, TP. Contributions of nursing research to patient care. *J Nurs Admin* 1976;6:22–8.

46. Gortner SR. The relations of scientists with professional and sponsoring organizations and with society. In: Batey M, editor. *Issues in research: social, professional, and methodological*. Selected papers from the first American Nurses Association Council of Nurse Researchers program meeting. Kansas City: The Association; 1974.

47. Lindeman CA. Priorities in clinical nursing research. Nurs Outlook 1975;23:693–8.

48. Gortner SR. Trends and historical perspective. In: Downs FS, Fleming JW. *Issues in nursing research*. New York: Appleton-Century-Crofts; 1979.

49. Mishel M, Murdaugh C. Family adjustment to heart transplantation. *Nurs Research,* 1987;36:332–8.

50. Silver HK, Ford LC, Day LR. The pediatric nurse practitioner program: expanding the role of the nurse to provide increased health care for children. *JAMA* 1968;204:298–302.

51. Lewis CE, Resnik BA. Nurse clinics and progressive ambulatory patient care. *N Eng J Med* 1967;277:1236–41.

52. Cheyovich TK, Lewis CE, Gortner SR. *The nurse practitioner in an adult outpatient clinic.* Washington (DC): Health Resources Administration. HEW Publication No (HRA) 76–29; 1976.

53. Donaldson S, Crowley D. The discipline of nursing. *Nurs Outlook* 1978;26:113–20.

54. Meleis AI. The age of nursing scholarliness: now is the time. The inaugural Helen Nahm Research Lecture. San Francisco: University of California, San Francisco School of Nursing; 1980.

55. Holzemer WL, Gortner SR. Evaluation of the nursing research emphasis/grants for doctoral programs in nursing grant program 1979–1984. *J Prof Nurs* 1988;4:381–6.

56. Stevenson JS, Woods NF. Nursing science and contemporary science. Emerging paradigms. In: Sorenson G, editor. *Setting the agenda for the year 2000: knowledge development in nursing.* Kansas City: American Academy of Nursing; 1986.

57. Meleis AI. ReVisions in knowledge development: a passion for substance. *Sch Inquiry Nurs Pract Int J* 1987;1:5–19.

58. Gortner SR. Nursing values and science: toward a science philosophy. *Image J Nurs Sch* 1990;22:101–5.

59. Ellis R. Values and vicissitudes of the scientist nurse. *Nurs Research* 1970;19:440–5.

60. Batey M. Conceptualizing the research process. *Nurs Research* 1971;20:296–301.

61. Barnard K. The research cycle: nursing, the profession, the discipline. In: *Communicating Nursing Research. Vol. 15: nursing science in perspective.* Boulder: Western Interstate Commission for Higher Education; 1982.

62. Shaver J. A biopsychosocial view of human health. *Nurs Outlook* 1985;33:187–91.

63. Schorr T, Kennedy MS. *100 years of American nursing. Celebrating a century of caring.* Philadelphia: Lippincott Williams Wilkins; 1999.

64. Hinshaw AS, Sigmon HD, Lindsey AM. Interfacing nursing and biologic science. *J Prof Nurs* 1991;7:264.

65. Diers D, Burst HV. Effectiveness of policy related research: nurse-midwifery as case study. *Image J Nurs Sch* 1983;15:68–74.

66. Fagin C. Nursing research and the erosion of care [guest editorial]. *Nurs Outlook* 1998;46:259–60.

ACKNOWLEDGMENTS

I gratefully acknowledge the contribution of Rebecca Wilson-Loots, academic program analyst, Department of Family Health Care Nursing, University of California–San Francisco, for her assistance with the original paper and slide preparation.

NURSING EDUCATION AND TRAINING

Reprints of Key Articles

7

THE GOLDMARK REPORT

COMMITTEE ON NURSING EDUCATION

This report originally appeared as Committee on Nursing Education. (1922). The Goldmark Report: The Report of the Committee on Nursing Education. *The Nation's Health, 4*(7).

EDITORS' NOTE

The Goldmark Report was the first of many national reports on the profession with an emphasis on the education of nurses. This landmark report's recommendations included moving nursing education from hospitals to universities. They remain relevant today as some hospital diploma programs continue and unaccredited proprietary programs are proliferating in some states.

■ ■ ■

The Committee which presents the following report was first appointed by the Rockefeller Foundation in January, 1919, to conduct a study of "the proper training of public health nurses."

It was, therefore, the pressing need for more, and for better, nurses in the field of public health that first suggested the desirability of such an investigation. It soon became clear, however, that the entire problem of nursing and of nursing education, relating to the care of the sick as well as to the prevention of disease, formed one essential whole and must be so considered if sound conclusions were to be attained. A year later, in February, 1920, the Foundation requested us to broaden the scope of our inquiry to include "a study of general nursing education, with a view to developing a program for further study and for recommendation of further procedure." We have attempted therefore to survey the entire field occupied by the nurse and other workers of related type; to form a conception of the tasks to be performed and the qualifications necessary for their execution; and on the basis of such a study of function to establish sound minimum educational standards for each type of nursing service for which there appears to be a vital social need.

Since it was the obvious need for more adequate nursing service in the field of public health which brought to a head the demand for a comprehensive study of nursing education—long felt and first voiced by the official organization of nurses—it seems natural to begin with a consideration of this phase of the broader problem.

It is obvious that the public health movement has passed far beyond its earlier objectives of community sanitation and the control of the contact-borne diseases by isolation and the use of sera and vaccines. Many major health problems of the present day, such as the control of infant mortality and tuberculosis, can be solved only through personal hygiene—an alteration in the daily habits of the individual—and through the establishment of new contacts with the public—contacts which shall permit the application of the resources of medical science at a stage in disease when they can produce a maximum effect. Such changes in the daily habits of the people and in their relation to their medical advisors, can be accomplished by but one means—education. In its present phase of emphasis on personal hygiene, the public health movement has thus become during the past two decades preeminently a campaign of popular education.

THE NURSE IN PUBLIC HEALTH

The new educational objectives of the health administrator may be approached to a limited extent by mass methods. The printed page, the public lecture, the exhibit, the cinematograph, the radiogram, help to prepare the ground and to make success easier. The ultimate victory over ignorance is, however, rarely attained in such ways. Direct personal contact with the conditions of the individual life is essential to success in a matter so truly personal as hygiene. We have sought during the past twenty years for a missionary to carry the message of health into each individual home; and in America we have found this messenger of health in the public health nurse. In order to meet generally accepted standards we should have approximately fifty thousand public health nurses to serve the population of the United States—as against eleven thousand now in the field. All public health authorities will probably agree that the need for nurses is the largest outstanding problem before the health administrator of the present day.

In view of this fact, public health authorities, both in this country and abroad, have naturally considered the possibility of finding a short way out of their difficulties by the employment of women trained in some less rigorous fashion than that involved in the education of the nurse. It was therefore to the question of the necessary and desirable equipment of the teacher of hygiene in the home that we first directed our attention. There are at present two distinct types of public health nursing practise in the United States—that in which the nurse confines herself to the teaching of hygiene, and that in which such instructive work is combined with the actual care of the sick. A third type of visiting nursing, in which bedside care is given with no educational service, may be observed in individual instances. It results, however, from temporary limitations rather than considered policy, since practically all visiting nurse associations, in theory at least, stress hygienic education in their official program.

The question whether the public health nurse should or should not also render bedside care has been hotly debated during the past few years. The arguments for purely instructive service rest mainly on two grounds, the administrative difficulties involved in the conduct of private sick nursing by official health agencies and the danger that the urgent demands of sick nursing may lead to the neglect of preventive educational measures which are of more basic and fundamental significance. Both these objections are real and important ones. Yet the observations made in the course of our survey indicate that both may perhaps ultimately be overcome. Several municipal health departments have definitely undertaken to provide organized nursing service for bedside care combined with health teaching, while in other instances instructive nurses, under public auspices, combine a certain amount of emergency service with their fundamentally educational activities. So far as the neglect of instructive work is concerned it results from numerical inadequacy of personnel and can be avoided by a sufficiently large nursing staff.

On the other hand, the plan of instructive nursing divorced from bedside care suffers from defects which if less obvious than those mentioned above are in reality more serious, because they are inherent in the very plan itself and therefore not subject to control. In the first place—the introduction of the instructive but non-nursing field worker creates at once a duplication of effort since there must be a nurse from some other agency employed in the same district to give bedside care. In the second place, the field worker who attempts health education without giving nursing care is by that very fact cut off from the contact which gives the instructive bedside nurse her most important psychological asset. The nurse who approaches a family where sickness exists, and renders direct technical service in mitigating the burden of that sickness, has an overwhelming advantage, then and thereafter, in teaching the lessons of hygiene. With an adequate number of nurses per unit of population, we believe that the combined service of teaching and nursing will yield the largest results. Nurses employed by state health departments and others whose work is largely stimulative and supervisory in nature may not of course be in position to render direct bedside care.

Nurse Best Health Educator

There are other messengers who may be sent into the field to fulfil other functions. The task of the trained social worker for example is to diagnosticate and repair maladjustments in social relationships, a correlated but quite distinct vocational field. Even public health agencies may employ other field workers of an allied type, such as clinic messengers. It is obvious, however, that where health instruction is combined with bedside care the fully trained nurse is the only possible type of health educator; and such a combination represents the one type of service which it is feasible to supply in rural districts. Even purely instructive work if conducted on the generalized district plan, calls for an ability to detect the early signs of contagious disease, to discern symptoms which suggest tuberculosis, to give counsel as to infant care or the feeding of older children, which can scarcely be attained without a wide training. The relative lack of nursing personnel in Europe has there led to the attempt to train health visitors of the purely instructive type for dealing with special individual problems, such as tuberculosis or child welfare, by training courses much shorter than those required for the preparation of the nurse. Opinion as to the result of such experiments in Europe varies widely; but for conditions as they exist in the United States we are convinced that the teacher of hygiene in the home should be equipped with no less rigorous training than that accorded to the bedside nurse, further supplemented by special studies along the lines of public health and social service.

That an improvement in quality, as well as an increase in the number of public health nurses is fundamental to the complete success of the public health movement, is a point on which we find all competent authorities to be substantially agreed. Miss Goldmark's report of an intensive study of the daily work of 164 public health nurses, representing forty-seven different organizations, gives glimpses of women whose constructive service and compelling personal inspiration seem to touch the highest possibilities of social achievement. Such a nurse establishes herself in the confidence of her community, so that she becomes its trusted advisor and best friend, caring for the sick, securing medical aid, counseling as to hygiene, resolving difficulties of a hundred sorts with the touch of a practised hand.

Nearly half of the nurses observed in our survey were classed as definitely successful in their work and less than one-fourth as definitely unsuccessful—a showing perhaps better than would be made by a random sampling of most professions. Yet it remains true that either from a lack of knowledge of preventive measures or of teaching methods, from failure to effect contact with physicians or with social agencies, a substantial proportion of public health nurses do fail to realize the possibilities of their profession. Administrative policies, overloading and inadequate supervision, are sometimes at the root of the trouble;

yet it is obvious that such a calling as public health nursing demands in the first place a high degree of natural capacity and in the second place a sound and a broad education.

Essential Qualifications

We are convinced, therefore, that the teacher of hygiene in the home should possess in the first place the fundamental education of the nurse and that this should be supplemented by a graduate course in the special problems of public health. The latter point will be discussed in detail in a succeeding paragraph but we believe that the general considerations so far discussed warrant the following conclusion:

> *Conclusion 1.—That, since constructive health work and health teaching in families is best done by persons: (a) capable of giving general health instruction, as distinguished from instruction in any one specialty, and (b) capable of rendering bedside care at need, the agent responsible for such constructive health work and health teaching in families should have completed the nurses' training. There will of course be need for the employment in addition to the public health nurse of other types of experts such as nutrition workers, social workers, occupational therapists, and the like.*
>
> *That as soon as may be practicable all agencies, public or private, employing public health nurses should require as a prerequisite for employment the basic hospital training, followed by a post-graduate course, including both class work and field work, in public health nursing.*

Before considering the basic demand for nurses to function in the routine care of the sick we must point out that it is by no means only in the field of public health nursing, that the need for women of high natural qualifications and fundamental training is now manifest. The modern hospital and the modern dispensary represent social forces of enormous and growing magnitude. The technical complexity of their operation increases with every passing year; and, aside from the problem of the staff nurses required for the ordinary routine of such institutions, which will be discussed in a succeeding paragraph, there is perhaps no more urgent problem for the hospital administrator than that of obtaining nursing superintendents and supervisors adequate for the performance of their difficult tasks. The development, both of public health nursing and of administrative hospital nursing, involves and demands a corresponding development in nursing education which constitutes another inviting field for women.

The defective preparation and qualifications of many instructors in schools of nursing in both practical and theoretical branches is very marked. Yet in the training school the instructor is often called upon to teach six or eight different subjects, far more than would be demanded even of the teacher in a country high school. It should be noted, however, that the appointment of any full-time instructors is a very recent development and has marked a signal educational advance.

Nursing the Sick

With the development of nursing education which we visualize in the future, and particularly with the growth of University Schools of Nursing, to be discussed in a succeeding paragraph, the field for well-qualified teachers of nursing should prove an increasingly attractive one. We believe we may safely advance as

Conclusion 2.—That the career open to young women of high capacity in public health nursing or in hospital supervision and nursing education is one of the most attractive fields now open, in its promise of professional success and of rewarding public service; and that every effort should be made to attract such young women into this field.

We may pass next to the urgent and fundamental problem of providing nursing care for the sick of the community. Here we find far less unanimity of sentiment in regard either to the quantitative or the qualitative adequacy of nursing service under existing conditions. An appalling shortage of nurses existed during the war; but conditions have materially changed during the past three years. The census reports show an increase in trained registered nurses, male and female, from 82,327 in 1910 to 149,128 in 1920, a truly phenomenal increase of 83 per cent. Some eleven thousand of these are employed as public health nurses and approximately the same number in hospitals and other institutions, leaving over 120,000 for private duty service, of whom, however, many are not in the active practise of their profession. This 1920 figure gives us a ratio of one trained nurse to seven hundred persons for the country as a whole. The majority of trained nurses are concentrated in the larger cities so that the rural districts in many states are wholly lacking in service of this kind. The evidence is that at present in the cities the supply of trained nurses is adequate to existing demands in normal times. The reason why many persons who need nursing care in hospitals and in the homes of the poor fail to receive it is to be sought in economic factors, rather than in a shortage of nurses.

In regard to the quality of the nursing service available at the present day we find even more radical differences of opinion. Private physicians, frequently express the view that for ordinary nursing, even the graduate of the existing training school is "over-trained," that the service which she renders is too costly, and that a woman with a very brief training in bedside routine would be as satisfactory, or perhaps more satisfactory, than the average registered nurse. As a result of this feeling there have been persistent and vigorous efforts in certain quarters to break down the standards of nursing education which have been laboriously built up during the past twenty years.

Insofar as these efforts would remove the safeguards which guarantee to the patient suffering from acute disease, and to the physician caring for such a patient, the quality of service necessary for safety, we feel that they constitute a real danger to the cause of public health. Nurses, physicians, hospital authorities and legislators, in erecting these safeguards, have been inspired by a just sense of the vital dangers to life which may result from the unskilled nursing of a critical case and of the grave responsibility incurred by both the medical and the nursing professions when such malpractice occurs. We would therefore record our conviction in regard to this point as:

Conclusion 3.—That for the care of persons suffering from serious and acute disease the safety of the patient and the responsibility of the medical and nursing professions demand the maintenance of the standards of educational attainment now generally accepted by the best sentiment of both professions and embodied in the legislation of the more progressive states and that any attempt to lower these standards would be fraught with real danger to the public.

Subsidiary Nursing Service

When we find that certain private physicians, like the public health administrators, demand nurses of a higher quality than those now in the field, while others desire merely "hands for the physician" with a minimum of education below the present standard, it seems probable that there is reason on both sides and that the apparent conflict is due to a difference in the objectives to be met. For the care of acute and serious illness and for public health work it seems certain that we need high natural qualifications and sound technical education; for the care of mild and chronic and convalescent illness it may well be that a different type of capacity and training may be necessary.

It seems clear to the Committee, however, that, if two types of nursing service are desirable, the distinction should be drawn not on economic grounds but according to the type of illness involved. We are even somewhat doubtful as to the possibility of attaining very substantial economies by the introduction of a subsidiary type of private duty nurse. Our survey of the situation does not indicate that the income of the private duty nurse is at present generally an exorbitant one, when we take into account the amount of unemployment— amounting in a typical group of 118 nurses to a week each month during the busy winter season. If this factor be allowed for, the margin between the average annual income of the private duty nurse and that of the domestic servant is not so great as to permit of the existence of an intermediate grade on a salary level very much below that of the present Registered Nurse. The solution of the economic problem which confronts the family of low income must probably be sought along the line of cost distribution through some form of community organization or along the line of group insurance such as that now being experimentally tested in New York City.

In any event, a pneumonia case, a diphtheria case, a grave cardiac case will require the highest grade of nursing obtainable whether it occurs in a palace or a hovel. It is the mild and chronic and convalescent case which offers a field for the partially trained worker, and the exact extent of this field has never yet been fully surveyed. In our own study we have secured careful estimates from 118 graduate nurses which indicate that during a period of three months one quarter of their time was spent on cases which could have been cared for by an attendant of the partially trained type. A somewhat similar estimate was obtained from forty-eight practicing physicians, twenty-one believing that trained nurses were unnecessarily employed for less than a quarter of their cases, seventeen placing the figures between half and three-quarters and ten at over three-quarters.

In considering the problem of subsidiary nursing service it must be remembered that we are dealing with no new development. Of the three hundred thousand male and female nurses in the United States in 1920, slightly more than half were of grades below the standard of the graduate nurse. The "practical nurse" the "trained attendant," is an existing fact; and in the opinion of a large group of the medical profession who utilize her services she fills a real place in the complex problem of caring for the sick. If we include with the trained and registered nurses (149,128) the student nurses in hospitals (54,953) and to these add the number of attendants and practical nurses, (151,996) as constituting the entire body of persons occupied in caring for the sick we have altogether one nurse, trained or untrained, in every 294 well persons. This would seem to give an adequate supply if numbers alone are considered, provided a proper distribution could be secured.

On the other hand the dangers in the existence of a loosely-defined and unregulated group of partially trained workers, in the same field with a more highly educated type, constitutes a real and a serious complication. The nursing profession has discharged a fundamental duty to the public in stimulating the development of registration laws which define and limit the practice of that profession and protect the community against fraud and exploitation by those who collect fees and assume responsibilities to which their qualifications do not entitle them. In addition to the registration of the trained nurse it is essential that the lower grade of nursing service should also be defined and registered; and the states of New York, Missouri, California, Michigan, and Maryland have taken definite steps in enacting legislation toward this end. The name to be selected for the subsidiary group is a difficult problem. As is often the case the root of disagreement lies largely in nomenclature. The title "attendant," embodied in three of the laws mentioned above, is distasteful to those who bear it and tends to discourage the enlistment of those who may desire to enter this field. On the other hand the term "practical nurse" assumes a most unfortunate antithesis between education and practice; and the splendid professional and public service rendered by "the nurse" in war and in peace, entitles her to the protection of her existing professional status. We are inclined to believe that the term "nursing aide" or "nursing attendant" best meets the need for clear differentiation, while providing the subsidiary worker with a suitable name.

With two distinct grades of service available, the individual physician would be responsible for the choice of a trained nurse or a nursing attendant or nursing aide in a given instance. The public can only be safeguarded in these matters by state legislation providing for licensing of nursing registries and requiring explicit statement as to the license qualifications of each nurse or nursing aide furnished. We believe that by this means the maximum increase of nursing service possible under existing economic conditions could be attained; and we would therefore recommend as

Conclusion 4.—That steps should be taken through state legislation for the definition and licensure of a subsidiary grade of nursing service, the subsidiary type of worker to serve under practising physicians in the care of mild and chronic illness and convalescence and possibly to assist under the direction of the trained nurse in certain phases of hospital and visiting nursing.

Our survey of the actual field of nursing service has thus led us to the conclusion that the good of the community demands (a) the recruiting for public health nursing, hospital nursing, and the care of the acutely ill of a larger number of young women and the provision for such women of a sound and effective education; and (b) the development and standardization of a subsidiary nursing service of a different grade for the care of mild and chronic disease. We may next pass to the second part of our problem—a consideration of existing educational facilities for the training of the two types of workers indicated as desirable.

So far as the trained nurse is concerned, whether she is to function in private duty, in public health, or in institutional service, it is clear that her basic professional education must be acquired in the hospital training school. We have therefore devoted a major part of the present investigation to a somewhat detailed study of existing conditions and future possibilities in hospital training.

HOSPITAL TRAINING SCHOOL

The development of the hospital training school for nurses constitutes a unique chapter in the history of education. In almost all fields of professional life education has begun on a basis of apprentice training. The first law schools and the first medical schools were the outgrowth of the lawyer's and the physician's office. In nearly all other fields than that of nursing, however, even in such relatively new professions as journalism and business and advertising, education has outgrown the apprentice stage and leadership has passed into the hands of independent institutions, organized and endowed for a specifically educational purpose. The training of nurses, on the other hand, is still in the main, actually if not technically, directed by organizations created and maintained for the care of disease, rather than for professional education.

The progress which has been accomplished in nursing education, under such anomalous conditions, is such as to reflect high credit upon both hospital administrators and the leaders of the nursing profession. The hospitals have in many instances been inspired by a broad and constructive vision of training school possibilities; while the devotion with which nursing directors have labored for high standards, often against almost insuperable obstacles, calls for the warmest admiration. Yet the conflict of interests between a policy of hospital administration, which properly aims to care for the sick at a minimum cost, and a policy of nursing education which with equal propriety aims to concentrate a maximum of rewarding training into a minimum time, is a real and vital one.

The fact that a field so tempting as that of modern nursing, with its remarkable possibilities of service in public health, in institutional management and in teaching, fails to attract students in the number and of the quality we should desire, strongly suggests that there is some shortcoming in the established avenues of approach to the nursing profession. The hospitals themselves, depending as they do so largely upon student nurses for their routine operation, have in past years found themselves seriously handicapped by the small number of applicants, and many a superintendent will testify to the fact that the difficulty of securing a high quality of nursing is one of the gravest which he has to meet. The phenomenally rapid growth in the number of hospitals has created within a brief period a demand for a large number of students and the requirements for admission have therefore been kept at a very low level, thus resulting in a reduction in the proportion of well-educated applicants. For the good of the hospital, as well as for that of the nursing profession and of the public at large, a careful and dispassionate appraisal of the adequacy of the present day training school would seem to be urgently desirable.

Training Schools Studied

An extensive survey of the vast field of hospital training schools (there are over 1,800 such schools in the United States) was obviously beyond the possible resources of our committee. It was therefore decided to select a small group of schools, of reasonably typical character, for intensive study. Twenty-three such schools were finally chosen, representing large and small, public and private, general and special hospitals, in various sections of the United States. These schools were undoubtedly well above the median grade and their average may, we believe, be taken as fairly representative of the best current practice in nursing education. Each school was studied in detail by two types of investigators, one a practical expert in nursing education and the other an experienced educator from outside the nursing field. By this means we aimed, on the one hand to secure competent criticism of nursing procedures, and on the other a broad viewpoint of general educational standards. The detailed results of this investigation, as presented in Miss Goldmark's report will, we believe, prove highly enlightening to the student of this problem.

The training of the nurse involves a certain basic knowledge of the fundamental chemical and biological sciences, theoretical instruction in the principles of nursing and above all, supervised practical training in actual nursing procedures. In all three phases of this work Miss Goldmark's report reveals conspicuous successes and equally conspicuous failures; and the remarkable thing is that successes and failures so often appear side by side in the same institution.

Thus, we may find in a training school with a good ward service that the fundamental science courses fail because of wholly inadequate laboratory equipment. In another school, the theoretical instructor may show a hopeless lack of teaching ability (as in the case of class presentation which consisted in the dictation of questions and answers from a prehistoric notebook); or she may be so handicapped by other duties as to leave no time for the proper conduct of her classes. Lectures by physicians may be informative and inspiring in one department of a hospital, irregular in delivery, careless, and dull in content in another. Ward assignments are in many cases largely dictated by the need for hospital service rather than by the educational requirements of the students. This is clearly evidenced by the astonishing irregularity of the time spent on different services by individual students and by the marked deviation between all the time assignments actually performed and those scheduled in the official program of the course. Thus in one school where seven and a half months were assigned to surgical service the members of a single class had actually worked on this service for from seven to thirteen and three-quarter months. Of the twenty-three schools surveyed by us one made no adequate provision for obstetrical service, while five gave no training in pediatrics, seven, no experience in communicable disease, and eighteen, none in mental disease. In view of the difficulties in making affiliations in some of these subjects, notably in communicable and mental disease, some of these omissions are scarcely to be wondered at.

The supervision of work on the wards was in certain instances notably inadequate. In only a few brilliantly exceptional cases was the ward work purposefully correlated with theoretical instruction. The lack of an intelligently planned progressive training was obvious in a large number of the hospitals studied, first year students often being found in positions of responsibility for which they were wholly unprepared, while seniors in another ward were repeating an educationally idle and profitless routine. Most striking of all, was the factor of time wasted in procedures, essential to the conduct of the hospital, but of no educational value to the student concerned. Hours and days spent in performing the work of a ward maid, in putting away linen, in sterilizing apparatus, in mending rubber gloves, in running errands, long after any important technique involved had become second nature, accounted in one typical hospital where this problem was specially studied for a clear wastage of between one-fourth and one-fifth of the student's working day.

The total amount of time assigned to ward service under the conditions which obtain in many hospitals is, in itself, a fairly complete obstacle to educational achievement. Our selected group of hospitals, surely in this respect far above the general average, shows a median day of 8.5 hours on ward duty alone, and unproductive night duty is the rule rather than the exception. Crowded and unattractive living conditions tend, in certain hospitals, to impair the morale of the student body and an atmosphere of autocratic discipline frequently prevents the development of a psychological atmosphere favorable to effective cooperative effort.

The foregoing paragraphs present, we are aware, a somewhat gloomy picture. In presenting them, we would emphasize two points which are of major importance. In the first place, such shortcomings as have been pointed out are not fairy chargeable to deliberate neglect on the part of hospital authorities or nursing superintendents. In so far as they exist, they are due to the inherent difficulty of adjusting the conflicting claims of hospital management and nursing education, under a system in which nursing education is provided with no independent financial endowments for its specific ends. The difficulties involved in the task of resolving this conflict are perhaps illustrated by the fact that out of 144 registered training schools in New York State, 60 changed superintendents during a single recent year.

In the second place it is encouraging to note, by reference to Miss Goldmark's report, that every one of the shortcomings in hospital training discussed above has been corrected, with substantially complete success, in one or more of the training schools studied by our investigators. The difficulties are not insuperable. Each of them has been overcome in some schools and most of them in some of the best schools. Training schools exist today in which the student receives a sound and an inspiring education, with a minimum of sacrifice to the exigencies of hospital administration. Yet such schools are still the exception; and we are convinced that the progress we desire can come only through a frank facing of the truth. The following statement is, we believe, thoroughly justified by such facts as we have been able to obtain:

> *Conclusion 5.—That, while training schools for nurses have made remarkable progress, and while the best schools of today in many respects reach a high level of educational attainment, the average hospital training school is not organized on such a basis as to conform to the standards accepted in other educational fields; that the instruction in such schools is frequently casual and uncorrelated; that the educational needs and the health and strength of students are frequently sacrificed to practical hospital exigencies; that such shortcomings are primarily due to the lack of independent endowments for nursing education; that existing educational facilities are on the whole in the majority of schools inadequate for the preparation of the high grade of nurses required for the care of serious illness, and for service in the fields of public health nursing and nursing education, and that one of the chief reasons for the lack of sufficient recruits, of a high type, to meet such needs lies precisely in the fact that the average hospital training school does not offer a sufficiently attractive avenue of entrance to this field.*

Recommendations Made

Recommendations for the improvement of the hospital training school are therefore made on the basis of these conditions. Miss Goldmark's study has not stopped short with a revelation of the defects which are commonly found in the conduct of nursing education.

It makes clear that only the coordination and standardization of the best existing practice is necessary in order to place nursing education on the plane where it belongs.

In the first place we believe that a training school which aims to educate nurses capable of caring for acute disease or of going on into public health nursing or supervisory and teaching positions must require for entrance the completion of a High School course or its equivalent. Nearly one-third of all the training schools in the United States now make this requirement and with 150,000 girls graduating from High Schools every year it should be possible for well-organized courses to attract an ample number of candidates.

The course should begin with a preliminary term of four months' training in the basic sciences and in elementary nursing procedures with appropriate ward practice but without regular service, as outlined in Miss Goldmark's report. The necessary teaching personnel and laboratory equipment for the former may in many instances be secured by the smaller hospitals through the establishment of a central training course or by cooperation with High Schools, Normal Schools, or Junior Colleges.

There should then follow a period of twenty-four months (including two months for vacation) devoted to a carefully graded and progressive course in the theory and practice of nursing, with lectures and ward practice so correlated as to facilitate intelligent case study and with the elimination of routine duties of no educational value. Hospital and dispensary services in medicine, surgery, pediatrics, obstetrics, communicable diseases and mental diseases should be provided through appropriate affiliation. Teachers and equipment should be of such a grade as would be acceptable in a reputable college or normal school.

We regard it as fundamental that the working day for the student nurse, including ward work and classroom periods, should not exceed eight hours. The working week should not exceed forty-eight hours and preferably forty-four hours. Training School experience, as well as a comparison with that accumulated in other educational fields, makes it clear that a longer period of scheduled work for the student is incompatible, either with educational attainment or with the maintenance of health.

By such an organization of the course of study, and particularly by the elimination of unrewarding routine service, we are convinced that the period of training may be safely shortened from the present standard of three years to twenty-eight months. Such a saving would mean an increase of over 20 per cent in the potential output of the training school through the saving of time alone. The shortening of the course would, in itself, prove an attraction to the prospective student; but the main consideration to be kept in view is that the shorter course projected would not imply a lowering but a raising of educational standards. Miss Goldmark's analysis of the situation makes it clear that the intensively planned course of 28 months would involve no substantial sacrifice in a single service as compared with the actual median practice of the present day and would supply other services now almost universally neglected. It is the experience in every other field of education that the way to attract students is to raise standards, not to lower them. In medicine, in law, in engineering, in teaching, the schools which raise requirements are the ones from which students must be turned away; and even in nursing the success of the better schools furnishes convincing testimony to the same basic principle. It is the higher standing of the course here outlined quite as much as its lessened length which we are confident would insure an increase in the number of students, as well as an improvement in their quality.

Post-Graduate Education

There are, we believe, two fundamental essentials to the success of a training school planned on the suggested lines. It must first of all be directed by a board or a committee, organized more or less independently for the primary purposes of education. The interests of hospital management and of educational policy must necessarily at times conflict and unless the educational viewpoint is competently represented the training school will infallibly suffer in the end. In the second place, it is fundamental to the success of nursing education that adequate funds should be available for the educational expenses of the school itself, and for the replacement of student nurses by graduate nurses and hospital help in the execution of routine duties of a non-educational character. A satisfactory relationship between school and hospital demands careful cost-accounting and a clear analysis of the money value of services rendered by the school to the pupil and the hospital, by the pupil to the hospital, and by the hospital to the pupil and the school. The cost of adequate education must in any case be a paramount consideration, to which we shall return in a succeeding paragraph. Assuming its essential importance, the following conclusion seems to be justified:

> *Conclusion 6.—That, with the necessary financial support, and under a separate board or training-school committee, organized primarily for educational purposes, it is possible with completion of a high school course or its equivalent as a prerequisite, to reduce the fundamental period of hospital training to 28 months and at the same time, by eliminating unessential, non-educational routine, and adopting the principles laid down in Miss Goldmark's report to organize the course along intensive and coordinated lines with such modifications as may be necessary for practical application; and that courses of this standard would be reasonably certain to attract students of high quality in increasing numbers.*

The course of twenty-eight months discussed above would furnish the complete education for a student desiring to practice as a bedside nurse in private duty or in hospitals and other institutions; and its completion should entitle her to the Diploma in Nursing and to state registration. For the nurse who desires to specialize along either of the more advanced lines, of public health nursing, or hospital supervision and nursing education, a further period of post-graduate training is obviously desirable.

Teachers College of Columbia University has played the part of pioneer in preparing graduate nurses for hospital supervision and nursing education and certain of the newer University Schools of Nursing are already offering attractive courses along the same line. The development of graduate courses in public health nursing has made even more notable progress. The first organized course of this type was offered in Boston in 1906 and by 1920 there were twenty such courses in operation, under the auspices of Universities, Public Health Nursing Associations or Schools of Social Work.

The activities of sixteen of these schools of public health nursing have been studied in the course of our investigation and the results achieved in this new field are in general deserving of high praise. The course is apparently in process of standardization at a length of about eight months, four devoted to theoretical instruction in public health, public health nursing, educational psychology and social problems, and four to supervised field work with a public health nursing organization. The courses at present offered are in many instances tentative and lacking in assured financial status. With the development of the University School of Nursing, (to be discussed in succeeding paragraphs) they may be expected to fall within its sphere of influence and to develop an increasing stability and usefulness.

Conclusion 7.—Superintendents, supervisors, instructors, and public health nurses should in all cases receive special additional training beyond the basic nursing course.

For advanced training, the development of the University School of Nursing has been perhaps the most notable feature in the progress of nursing education during the past ten years. As long ago as 1899 Teachers College of Columbia University admitted properly qualified nurses to its junior class, thus giving two years of college credit for the three years of nursing training. Since 1916, no less than thirteen different colleges and universities have provided combined courses, through which students may acquire both a nurse's training and a college degree.

University School of Nursing

The combined course, in such schools for example, involves two years of ordinary college work including besides work of a liberal nature certain of the fundamental sciences basic in nursing education. Then follow two years of intensive training in the hospital and finally, a fifth year of post-graduate education in one of the higher specialties of nursing, public health, institutional supervision, or nursing education. At the close of training, the student receives a diploma in nursing and the bachelor's degree in nursing or in science.

This type of School of Nursing should in the judgment of the Committee be a separate and independent department of the University, cognate in rank and organization with the School of Medicine or the School of Law. It should have direct responsibility for all instruction given during the years of hospital training and the post-graduate nursing year.

A definite affiliation with one or more hospitals must in any case be established, along the line of those agreements now in force between medical schools and hospitals. The school supplies student nursing service and assumes a definite responsibility for a larger or smaller share of ward supervision and perhaps of graduate service. The hospital, on the other hand, provides maintenance for the nursing staff and conforms to the standards held by the University to be essential for the realization of its educational ideals. A University Hospital will of course offer the most promising field for a University School of Nursing; but in default of such an institution there seems no reason why a University School should not establish satisfactory working agreements with various adjacent hospitals, provided only that the maintenance of adequate standards in the practice field remains in its own hands.

If its present practical function be clearly understood the University School of Nursing possesses unique advantages in respect to both of the essentials for success in nursing education, to which reference has been made in a preceding paragraph. It possesses the power of independent educational leadership and is grounded on the solid foundations of educational ideals, to a degree which a training-school committee, ultimately responsible to a board of hospital trustees, can seldom hope to realize; and it is likely to obtain financial resources of a more nearly adequate extent. Furthermore, through its university contacts the University School of Nursing has unique opportunities to attract students of the type so greatly needed for the fulfilment of the higher tasks in the nursing of the future.

It should be made quite clear that the Committee does not recommend that nursing schools in general should work toward the establishment of courses of a character that a University would accept for a degree. We realize that the numerical proportion of the nursing profession to be contributed by the University School will perhaps always be a relatively small one. Yet we believe that the importance of this portion of the educational structure would be difficult to overestimate. The value that we see at present in the University Schools is that they will furnish a body of leaders who have the fundamental training essential in administrators, teachers, and the like. One of the greatest, if not the greatest of the reasons for the imperfections in the present training of private duty nurses is that great numbers of schools have developed without any coincident development of adequate numbers of persons properly trained to guide the pupils during their course. Unless well taught they cannot be well trained. The University School of Nursing should be the keystone of the entire arch. It will not only train leaders and develop and standardize procedures for all other schools. It will, by its permeating influence, give inspiration and balance to the movement as a whole and gradually but steadily improve the efficiency of every institution for the training of nurses of whatever type. We would therefore urge as

> *Conclusion 8.—That the development and strengthening of university schools of nursing of a high grade for the training of leaders is of fundamental importance in the furtherance of nursing education.*

We have pointed out in a preceding section of this report that there appears to be a real place for nursing service of a subsidiary type, to be used in the institution and in the home, for the routine care of patients suffering from disease of a mild or chronic type or in convalescence. We have also pointed out that this subsidiary service is an existing fact, whether we like it or not.

Existing facilities for the training of the subsidiary worker are today of the most limited type. It is obvious that courses in home nursing of a few weeks duration, such as those conducted under the auspices of the American Red Cross, while most useful in disseminating the sort of knowledge which all girls and women should possess, in no way suffice as preparation for the practice of a profession. When they are advertised as adequate for this latter end, such courses may do far more harm than good—as evidenced by the fact that "graduates" of such courses after forty-eight hours of instruction have practiced as qualified nurses and received $5 a day for their services.

Training of Subsidiary Workers

Courses for the training of nursing aides offered by the Household Nursing Association of Boston and by local Young Women's Christian Associations in various parts of the country and those stimulated by the Bureau for the Home Care of the Sick under the Thomas Thompson Trust are on a wholly different basis. The number of graduates from such courses is, however, small and their control after graduation loose and unsatisfactory. Since the existence of the subsidiary nursing group is a concrete fact, and in view of the valuable results to be derived from the service of this group in a definitely restricted field, it seems obvious that specific provision should be made for the training of workers of this type.

The field for the training of nursing aides would seem to be an ample one. The special hospital, not served by affiliation with a school of nursing, and the small general hospital whose facilities are inadequate for the maintenance of a nursing school of standard grade might be considered as training grounds. In the large general hospital whose opportunities are not fully utilized by student nurses there is no valid objection to the training of the subsidiary group, provided that it is conducted in separate and distinct wards so that the sacrifice of the interests of either of the two groups of pupils may be avoided. The requirements for entrance should be a grammar school course or its equivalent and the period of training eight or nine months. Suggestions of great value in regard to the safeguarding of such a course for "attendants" will be found in a recent report issued by the Board of Regents of the University of the State of New York.

It is essential in providing for this new type of education that hospital patients should be protected from malpractice and students from exploitation by an adequate graduate nursing service for the care of acute illness and for supervision of the students. Again, therefore, we must assume a reasonable financial support before this, or any other, educational enterprise can be honestly undertaken. Furthermore, we believe that a useful development in the training of nursing aides can only be expected when the standards of the schools for such aides and their activities after graduation are controlled by a properly safeguarded system of state legislation, such as now exists in Missouri.* With these assumptions we would recommend as

> *Conclusion 9.—That when the licensure of a subsidiary grade of nursing service is provided for, the establishment of training courses in preparation for such service is highly desirable; that such courses should be conducted in special hospitals, in small unaffiliated general hospitals or in separate sections of hospitals where nurses are also trained; provided the standards of such schools be approved by the same educational board which governs nursing training schools; and that the course should be of eight or nine months duration.*

The Financial Problem

We believe that the educational plan which has been outlined above is, according to existing information, necessary and sufficient for the solution of the problems involved in securing an adequate nursing service of all essential types. The school for nursing aides would provide the subsidiary worker needed for the care of the mild and chronic and convalescent case. The hospital training school, with adequate funds and an independent educational organization, would attract more candidates and better candidates and would prepare them adequately for the nursing of acute disease. The University School of Nursing would prepare the leaders in public health nursing, in hospital supervision and nursing education and

---

*The Missouri net is unusually effective in providing that "no person shall practice as a nurse for hire or engage in the care of the sick as an attendant for hire unless licensed by the Board as hereinafter provided."

would inspire and standardize the entire movement. Progress must be made gradually, of course, building up for the future, step by step, upon the basis of existing facilities.

It is clear, however, that the attainment of these ends requires financial support, and requires it at all points along the line. The training of nursing aides will cost more money; the University School will require endowment on a reasonably generous scale. The hospital, in its operation of the training school has for generations been trying to make bricks without straw, in the upbuilding of an educational system on an apprentice basis and without independent educational resources. It has made every possible effort—except the effort to secure educational endowment; it is time that the hospital should be relieved from the dilemma of exploiting student nurses on the one hand, or of diverting funds given for the care of the sick on the other, by the provision of endowments specifically devoted to the purposes of education.

We are well aware that many of those who have taken counsel with us in regard to this matter have cherished the hope that the Committee would find some magic pathway out of the maze of nursing education; but such hopes are vain. There is no short cut to the end which we all have in view. The establishment of a sound educational policy is the one essential to attracting students in quantity and of quality; and a sound educational policy requires specific financial support. If the community needs and desires the service of competent nurses for the care of the sick and the prosecution of the campaign of public health, it must pay for their education, as it pays for every other conceivable kind of education—either through taxes or through voluntary contributions or through the generosity of its great philanthropic foundations. No broadly conceived and systematic effort to obtain such financial support for nursing education has ever yet been made; when it is made we are convinced that it will not fail. In institutions where nursing education has been even partially endowed, as in the first school of nursing at St. Thomas' Hospital, London, and the Department of Nursing and Health at Teachers' College, New York, substantial achievements in the better education of nurses have been rendered possible.

It is obvious that the plan recommended for improvement of the education of nurses cannot be adequately put into effect in any hospital training school without additional funds for this purpose. The strategic position which the University Schools of Nursing will occupy in regard to the whole movement indicates their development as of special importance. An adequate endowment for a group of such University schools would establish centers of influence which could safely be trusted to exert a profound influence upon nursing education. We, therefore, urge as the final conclusion from our study of this problem:

Conclusion 10.—That the development of nursing service adequate for the care of the sick and for the conduct of the modern public health campaign demands as an absolute prerequisite the securing of funds for the endowment of nursing education of all types; and that it is of primary importance, in this connection, to provide reasonably generous endowment for University Schools of Nursing.

8

CAREER PATHWAYS IN NURSING: ENTRY POINTS AND ACADEMIC PROGRESSION

C. FAY RAINES

M. ELAINE TAGLAIRENI

This article appeared originally as Raines, C. F., & Taglaireni, M. E. (2008). Career pathways in nursing: Entry points and academic progression. *The Online Journal of Issues in Nursing, 13*(3), Manuscript 1. Copyright © 2008 American Nurses Association. All rights reserved. Reprinted with permission. (www.nursingworld.org/ojin.)

EDITORS' NOTE

There are multiple routes to becoming a registered nurse. This is a strength since one can argue that nursing has the best career ladder of any profession. But it has also challenged the profession to find ways to improve the educational preparation of its workforce. This article provides a clear description of the educational pathways to nursing.

■ ■ ■

The national dialogue about the nursing shortage has helped to underscore the critical role nurses play in healthcare delivery. The national dialogue about the nursing shortage has helped to underscore the critical role nurses play in healthcare delivery. First noted in 1998, the current shortfall in the number of nurses needed to provide care in the United States (U.S.) is expected to increase to more than 500,000 by the year 2025 according to the latest projections by workforce analysts (Buerhaus, Staiger, & Auerbach, 2008). A growing body of research confirms that registered nurses (RNs) are indeed essential to patient safety; too few nurses have been linked to diminishing the overall quality of care in hospitals and other settings (Agency for Healthcare Research and Quality [AHRQ], 2007). Stakeholders at the federal and state levels have made addressing the nursing shortage a priority and are moving to enact legislation and launch programs both to increase capacity in nursing education programs and to provide funding to prepare the additional faculty needed to teach future generations of nurses.

 . . . nursing has . . . become an attractive option for career changers looking to transition into the healthcare workforce and add new meaning to their professional pursuits. Fortunately, today's nursing shortage *cannot* be attributed to a lack of interest in nursing careers. Both the American Association of Colleges of Nursing (AACN) and the National League for Nursing (NLN) have reported steady increases in enrollment in entry-level nursing programs over the past few years, with the latest numbers showing about five percent growth in the number of students enrolled in both 2006 and 2007 (AACN, 2008; NLN, 2008). Applications to nursing programs are up across the board and competition for limited enrollment slots is intensifying. In addition to strong interest among new high school graduates, nursing has also become an attractive option for career changers looking to transition into the healthcare workforce and add new meaning to their professional pursuits.

 What is driving this resurgence of interest in nursing careers? The media spotlight on the RN shortage has served to showcase nursing as a lucrative, secure field that offers a variety of practice opportunities beyond traditional roles. With 2.4 million nurses in the workforce in 2006, RNs comprise the largest segment of professionals (28%) working in the healthcare industry and one of the largest segments of the U.S. workforce as a whole (Dohm & Shniper, 2007). Looking forward, government analysts project that more than

587,000 new nursing positions will be created through 2016 making nursing the nation's top profession in terms of projected job growth.

In addition to offering a high level of job security, nurse employers are increasingly offering more attractive levels of compensation in an effort to appeal to new recruits and retain working RNs in the profession. Registered nurses, in fact, are among the highest paid practitioners of any "large occupation" as classified by the U.S. Bureau of Labor Statistics (2007). Nearly 57% of RNs today work in general medical and surgical hospitals where salaries average $60,970 per year. Salaries for new nurses are somewhat lower, but it is not uncommon to hear that new clinicians are offered salaries in the $45,000 to $50,000 range. Nurses with advanced practice preparation, including nurse practitioners and clinical nurse specialists, currently command salaries of $80,000 and upwards (Mee, 2006).

. . . today's nursing shortage cannot be attributed to a lack of interest in nursing careers . . . many career seekers see nursing as a dynamic profession that brings many rewards and great potential for advancement. With a career horizon brimming with opportunities, many career seekers see nursing as a dynamic profession that brings many rewards and great potential for career advancement. Beyond the high demand for nurses to provide direct care, nurses are also needed as researchers, healthcare administrators, educators, policy analysts, nurse executives, and independent practitioners. The latest developments from the field promise new nurses virtually unlimited opportunities for progression to advanced degrees in nursing practice, as well as opportunities for teaching. With salaries climbing, opportunities expanding, and the demand for nursing services on the rise, now is an exciting time to consider a career in nursing.

During the past decade new and innovative pathways to prepare nurses for an increasingly complex, uncertain, healthcare environment have emerged. Nursing continues to offer multiple ways for students to enter the profession and has consistently advocated for creative and innovative opportunities for academic progression that meet the needs of a student population that is diverse along numerous dimensions. The focus of this article is on a discussion of the current pathways available to enter the nursing profession and the wide-ranging models available for students to achieve advanced educational preparation within nursing. While it is certainly possible to change goals and directions, early consideration of the desired end point can provide helpful direction in selecting the most efficient and effective path to reaching career goals.

TRADITIONAL ENTRY POINTS INTO NURSING

Though the subject of much debate, the nursing profession in the U.S. recognizes three traditional routes to becoming an RN: a diploma program most often administered in hospitals; an associate degree program usually offered at community colleges; and a baccalaureate degree program offered at senior colleges and universities. Graduates of all three programs sit for the National Council Licensing Examination for RNs (NCLEX-RN©) which measures minimum technical competency for entry-level nursing practice. The National Council of State Boards of Nursing (NCSBN) administers the NCLEX examination and publishes data each year on the number of new nurses by entry point. In 2007, the breakdown of newly minted RNs included 58.4% from associate degree programs, 38.4% with baccalaureate degrees, and 3.1% from diploma programs (NCSBN, 2008).

Diploma Programs

Using an apprenticeship model, hospital-based diploma programs prepare graduates to deliver direct patient care in a variety of settings. Diploma programs may partner with colleges and universities to offer credit courses for co-requisite course work, but, graduates do not receive a nursing degree upon graduation. According to the latest data from the *National Sample Survey of Registered Nurses* (Health Resources and Services Administration [HRSA], 2007), approximately 25.2% of practicing nurses completed their initial RN education in diploma programs. The number of diploma programs has declined sharply since 1965 when the American Nurses Association called for moving hospital-based RN programs into the college and university system (Donley & Flaherty, 2002).

Associate Degree Programs

Typically offered in community colleges, Associate Degree in Nursing (ADN) programs provide an efficient, economical pathway to becoming a registered nurse. Approximately 42.2% of the RN workforce received their basic education in ADN programs (HRSA, 2007). Graduates are prepared with the clinical competence and technical proficiency needed to practice safely in multiple settings and to fully assume the RN role (Mahaffey, 2002). The number of ADN programs has grown considerably since first introduced in 1958 with about 940 programs now enrolling students nationwide. With more than 600 of these programs offered in the U.S. community-college system, ADN educators are committed to offering quality programs that are "continually evolving to reflect local community needs and current and emerging healthcare delivery systems" (National Organization for Associate Degree Nursing [NOADN], 2007).

Baccalaureate Programs

Offered at four-year colleges and universities, the Bachelor of Science in Nursing (BSN) programs prepare new graduates to practice across all healthcare settings and assume the widest variety of RN roles. BSN programs encompass all of the course work taught in ADN and diploma programs plus a more in-depth treatment of the physical and social sciences, nursing research, public and community health, nursing management, and the humanities. The additional course work enhances the student's professional development, prepares the new nurse for a broader practice, and provides the foundation for progression to advanced practice roles in nursing. With 606 entry-level baccalaureate programs enrolling students nationwide, approximately 31% of nurses in the workforce received their basic education in baccalaureate programs (HRSA, 2007).

Considerations in Selecting a Nursing Entry Route

Choosing the most appropriate entry point depends on a variety of factors including what the future nurse hopes to achieve in his/her career, a student's opportunities for college entrance, and family and work obligations. Financial considerations are also important. Diploma and associate degree programs typically cost less annually than baccalaureate degree programs. Students choosing to attend schools locally and to live at home based on personal preferences or family obligations may also have lower costs than students who attend schools at a distance or who live on campus. Before making a decision about costs, students are advised to consider all factors including available financial aid at various institutions and the costs of additional education required beyond the various entry points to meet career goals.

At present, nurses entering the profession with a baccalaureate degree are four times more likely to pursue a graduate degree in nursing than other entry-level clinicians (HRSA, 2007). Yet nurses entering the profession today with an ADN or diploma have an increasing number of opportunities to advance their education to the graduate level. In addition to the more traditional path of entering and completing a bachelor's degree after earning an associate degree in nursing, there are now programs that provide a more direct path to master's degrees for these students. Currently, there are 153 programs available throughout the U.S. to prepare these RNs in master's degree programs where they can earn a Master's of Science in Nursing (MSN) degree. RN to MSN programs generally take about three years to complete with specific requirements varying by institution and based on the student's previous course work. The baccalaureate level content not included in diploma and ADN programs is built into the front end of these degree completion programs. Mastery of this upper level, basic, nursing content is necessary for students to move on to graduate study. Upon completion, many programs award both the baccalaureate and master's degrees. Though the majority of these programs are offered in traditional classroom settings, some RN to MSN programs are offered largely online or in a blended classroom/online format.

Finally, those considering which entry point to choose must also pay attention to the issues of accreditation and articulation. Nursing programs accredited by the profession's two, nationally recognized, accrediting bodies—the Commission on Collegiate Nursing Education and the National League for Nursing Accrediting Commission—have demonstrated that they meet professional standards and are quality programs. Nursing students planning to continue their education beyond their entry point at some point in their career are strongly encouraged to complete their basic education in an accredited program since credits from unaccredited programs are not generally accepted as transfer credits at four-year institutions.

Entry-level students interested in pursuing a degree-completion program in the future should also inquire about articulation (or transfer) agreements between ADN or diploma programs and four-year institutions. These agreements ensure the smooth transfer of credits between higher education institutions and often specify how many credits can travel from program to program. Hundreds of articulation agreements have been forged by schools nationwide, including some statewide agreements that apply to all public institutions. Students graduating from programs without articulation agreements and those seeking to complete a nursing program in another state may run the risk of having fewer credits transfer between schools. Students are encouraged to contact program administrators to see what articulation agreements exist and determine which courses yield transferable credit.

EMERGING ENTRY POINTS

Beyond the traditional entry routes to a career as a registered nurse, a number of additional pathways are emerging and proving effective at attracting new audiences into the nursing profession. These alternative routes include entry-level master's programs; accelerated programs for graduates of non-nursing disciplines; community college-based baccalaureate programs; and RN completion programs for Licensed Practical Nurses and other allied health providers.

Entry-Level Master's Programs

Interest in entry-level or generic master's programs is running high among career changers wishing to enter nursing at an advanced level. Designed for individuals with undergraduate degrees in fields other than nursing, these 28–36 month programs build on previous learning experiences and prepare graduates for teaching, research, and specialty nursing roles. According to AACN's 2007 survey of baccalaureate and graduate nursing programs, 56 entry-level master's programs are enrolling students at nursing schools in the U.S., and 13 new programs are under development. Enrollments in and graduations from these programs are on the rise. In 2007, 4,303 students were enrolled and 1,032 students graduated from entry-level master's programs. By comparison, in 2006, there were 3,854 students enrolled and 870 graduates from these programs.

Exciting new options among entry-level master's degrees are programs that prepare nurses for advanced generalist roles, including the Clinical Nurse Leader (CNL®). Gaining in prominence, CNLs are lateral integrators of care who put evidence-based practice into action to ensure that patients benefit from the latest innovations in care delivery. Evidence-based nursing practice integrates the best research available with clinical expertise and patient values for optimum care (Institute of Medicine, 2003). The CNL role combines expert clinical practice with microsystems-level advocacy, centralized-care coordination, outcomes management, risk assessment, and quality improvement. AACN is facilitating the efforts of more than 90 education-practice partnerships around the country to integrate this new role into a variety of practice settings. The Department of Veterans Affairs (VA), the nation's largest employer of RNs, is a strong supporter of the CNL. The VA is among the early adopters of this role and is moving to introduce CNLs into all VA healthcare facilities.

Accelerated Programs for Graduates of Non-Nursing Disciplines

Accelerated baccalaureate programs offer the quickest route to licensure as a registered nurse for adults who have already completed a bachelor's or graduate degree in a non-nursing discipline. These programs generally take between 11 and 18 months to complete, including prerequisites. Accelerated baccalaureate programs accomplish programmatic objectives in a shorter time by building on prior learning. Instruction is intense with courses offered full-time with no breaks between sessions. Students receive the same number of clinical hours as their counterparts in traditional entry-level nursing programs.

Over the past five years, the number of accelerated baccalaureate nursing programs has expanded rapidly, and these programs are now available in 43 states plus the District of Columbia and Puerto Rico. In 2007, there were 205 accelerated baccalaureate programs enrolling students, compared to 90 programs that were available in 2002 (AACN, 2008). In addition, 37 new accelerated baccalaureate programs are in the planning stages. This number of new programs far outpaces all other types of entry-level nursing programs currently being considered at four-year colleges and universities. In terms of enrollment growth, AACN's 2007 annual survey found that 9,938 students were enrolled in accelerated baccalaureate programs, up from 8,493, 7,829 and 6,090 students in 2006, 2005 and 2004, respectively. The number of program graduates has also increased with 5,881 graduates in 2007 as compared to 5,232, 3,769 and 2,422 graduates in 2006, 2005 and 2004, respectively.

Community College-Based Baccalaureate Programs

In response to the calls . . . to increase the production of baccalaureate-prepared nurses, community colleges across the country are offering BSN programs on-site at these institutions. In response to the calls by the American Organization of Nurse Executives (2005) and other authorities to increase the production of baccalaureate-prepared nurses, community colleges across the country are offering BSN programs on-site at these institutions. Given their commitment to serving local needs, these community colleges are working to provide a cost-effective solution for bringing more baccalaureate nurses into the profession and meeting community demands.

In October 2005, AACN members endorsed a position statement in support of community college-based baccalaureate programs that meet the same standards as traditional baccalaureate programs offered at four-year institutions. The emergence of baccalaureate nursing programs at community colleges underscores the national need to increase the number of accessible and affordable pathways to raise the education level of the nursing workforce. Sixteen states have changed regulations to allow community colleges to offer baccalaureate programs, with four states specifically moving to offer the BSN degree: Florida, Indiana, Nevada and Washington. Community colleges in Florida have made the most progress in offering the BSN through its statewide systems with programs now available at five institutions, including St. Petersburg College and Miami Dade College (Community College Baccalaureate Association, 2008).

RN Completion Programs for Licensed Practical Nurses and Other Allied Health Providers

. . . LPN to ADN programs were credited with . . . bringing the highest number of ethnic minority students . . . into the student population. Community colleges and four-year institutions also offer bridge programs for Licensed Practical Nurses/Licensed Vocational Nurses (LPNs/LVNs), Emergency Medical Technicians (EMTs), and other allied health professionals who wish to transition into the Registered Nurse role. In California, for example, eight community colleges offer LVN to ADN programs which account for 4.2% of the nursing students enrolled in the state's RN programs (Waneka & Spetz, 2008). Though this percentage is relatively small, the LPN to ADN programs were credited with having the lowest attrition rate (2.9%) among all entry-level programs and were successful at bringing the highest number of ethnic minority students (68.9%) into the student population. These data underscore the importance of developing these pipeline programs even further.

In four-year colleges and universities, the number of LPN to BSN programs reached 155 in 2007 with an additional 12 programs opening over the next few years. Although the majority of these programs are presented using a traditional, in-class format, 18 programs are offered completely online. Schools are working collaboratively to ensure that credits transfer between institutions and students have the support needed to succeed at this new level of academic rigor.

MOVING ALONG THE EDUCATION CONTINUUM

. . . too few nurses choose to advance their education to the graduate level, despite . . . need for nurse practitioners, clinical nurse specialists, nurse anesthetists, nurse midwives, researchers, faculty, administrators, and other roles requiring expert level preparation. Entering the nursing profession is only the first step for professionals wishing to advance in the field and maintain the competency needed in this ever-evolving, practice discipline. The NLN and AACN are both strong supporters of academic progression through formal, degree-granting programs and lifelong-learning experiences to enhance nursing knowledge. Unfortunately, too few nurses choose to advance their education to the graduate level, despite the great need for nurse practitioners, clinical nurse specialists, nurse anesthetists, nurse midwives, researchers, faculty, administrators, and other roles requiring expert level preparation. Nurses looking to move into baccalaureate and/or graduate study may choose from a variety of program options. These options include BSN degree-completion programs for RNs; direct baccalaureate to doctoral programs leading to either a research-focused, terminal degree (PhD, DNSc, DSN) or a practice-focused, terminal Doctor of Nursing Practice (DNP) degree in nursing; master's degree programs to progress to the highly complex and specialized-practice roles; and programs providing additional preparation for faculty positions. Many of these options are offered online. These first two options will be discussed in depth below.

RN to BSN Programs

In addition to the growing number of RN to MSN programs, RN to BSN programs provide an efficient bridge for diploma and ADN-prepared nurses who wish to expand and enhance previous knowledge and advance in their careers. In fact, most RNs who advance their formal education beyond their initial preparation choose to complete a baccalaureate nursing program (HRSA, 2007). RN to BSN programs build on initial nursing preparation with course work to enhance professional development, prepare for a broader scope of practice, and provide a better understanding of the cultural, political, economic, and social issues that affect patients and influence care delivery. These programs are growing in importance since many professional practice settings, including Magnet hospitals and academic health centers, now require or prefer the baccalaureate degree for specific nursing roles.

With a growing awareness about the positive outcomes associated with advancing to higher levels of education (Aiken et al., 2003 & 2008; Estabrooks et al., 2005; Ridley, 2008; Tourangeau et al., 2007) and increasing encouragement from employers who provide tuition support for RN to BSN programs, more and more nurses are returning to school to complete a baccalaureate degree. Currently, 50,963 nurses are enrolled in 559 RN to BSN programs offered at schools throughout the U.S. From 2006 to 2007, enrollments in RN to baccalaureate programs increased by 11.5% or 5,188 students, which makes this the fifth consecutive year of enrollment increases in these degree completion programs (AACN,

2008). As more and more graduates of associate degree and diploma programs enter RN-BSN programs nationally, greater numbers of nurses will be prepared to enter graduate programs in nursing, in order to inform and support evidence-based practice in a wide variety of practice and educational settings.

Baccalaureate to Doctoral Programs

In terms of doctoral preparation, nursing schools nationwide are moving to open more programs leading directly from the baccalaureate degree to doctoral degrees in response to the profession's dire need for more nurse faculty and researchers. These programs allow graduates of baccalaureate nursing programs to move quickly into graduate study. A great benefit of these programs is that they encourage strong BSN students to continue their education without long gaps between degree completions. In nursing, the average time it takes to complete a doctoral program is 15.9 years from the time a student first enrolls in a master's program. By comparison, the average completion time for a doctorate in other fields is 8.5 years from the first enrollment in a master's program (Berlin & Sechrist, 2002).

The "fast-track" nature of a baccalaureate to doctoral program is derived from a sequencing of course work that eliminates the need for students to enroll first in a master's program and then a doctoral program. These programs take four to five years to complete and provide intense clinical instruction and specialized experiences throughout the course of study. This new level of clinical education builds on the experiences these students have already completed in their BSN programs and becomes progressively more complex as students demonstrate mastery in their graduate studies.

The nation's first baccalaureate to doctoral program, a BSN to PhD program, was offered in 1995 by the University of Texas Health Science Center–San Antonio. Since then, the number of fast-track doctoral programs has grown steadily from one program in 1995, to eight programs in 1999, to 63 programs in 2007. According to AACN's latest annual survey (2008), ten new baccalaureate to doctoral programs are under development.

Fast-track doctoral programs are also gaining in popularity with the arrival of Doctor of Nursing Practice programs. Since the passage of AACN's position statement in October 2004, which called for transitioning specialty nursing programs at the master's level to the doctoral level by the year 2015, nursing schools nationwide have been moving in this direction at a rapid pace. Today, 65 DNP programs are admitting students at institutions located in 30 states plus the District of Columbia. In addition, 63 new practice doctorates are being developed at both large and mid-sized nursing schools in the U.S.

DNP curricula build on current master's programs by providing education in evidence-based practice, quality improvement, and systems thinking among other key areas. The DNP is designed for nurses seeking a terminal degree in nursing practice and offers an alternative to a research-focused, doctoral program. DNP-prepared nurses are well-equipped to fully implement the science developed by nurse researchers prepared in PhD, DNSc and other research-focused nursing doctoral programs.

With the emergence of the Doctor of Nursing Practice degree, more nursing schools are moving to offer a BSN to DNP option. Of the 65 DNP programs now enrolling students, 25 schools (38.4%) admit post-baccalaureate students while the majority only admit graduates of master's-level nursing programs. The number of post-baccalaureate DNP programs is expected to increase dramatically as new programs are opened, and master's programs are transitioned to the doctoral level.

In addition to hundreds of programs offered in traditional classroom settings, access to baccalaureate nursing and graduate education is further enhanced by the widespread availability of online programs. According to the 2008 edition of *Nursing Programs* published by Peterson's, there are currently 163 online baccalaureate degree completion programs offered in the United States as well as 109 master's programs and 16 doctoral programs in nursing. Most online degree-completion programs will accept graduates from accredited diploma or ADN programs which meet equivalent quality standards set for professional nursing programs.

CONCLUSION

Nursing as a profession is making great strides in attracting new recruits and increasing the education level of those already in the RN workforce. The latest National Sample Survey of Registered Nurses (2007) found that the greatest changes in education level of nurses between 2000 and 2004 were at the master's and doctoral degree levels. During this time period, the number of RNs with a graduate degree increase by 37.0%. Further, the National League for Nursing's latest data report (2008) found that the overall number of American institutions offering nursing programs expanded by 6.4% between 2005 and 2006. During that time frame, graduations from all pre-licensure programs grew by 8.5%, with graduations from baccalaureate programs showing the largest increase of almost 20%. Clearly these are signs that nurses are moving to become more highly educated in response to the evolving needs of the profession.

Moving nurses further along the educational continuum will take a shared commitment among nurse educators and stakeholders that is fueled by innovation and collaboration (Bednash & Lancaster, 2008; NLN, 2005). Together nursing's academic leaders are working to prepare a strong and well-educated nursing workforce, which is in the best interest of both patients and the healthcare system. Research confirms what nurses have always known: that RNs are the key to patient safety; they play a central role in lowering mortality rates, preventing medical errors, and ensuring quality outcomes. Nurse educators must continue to work together to ensure that nursing remains an attractive career choice, that graduates from all types of nursing education programs are well prepared to enter the workforce, and that these graduates have access to multiple pathways for academic progression, in order to meet the challenges of contemporary nursing practice.

REFERENCES

Agency for Healthcare Research and Quality. (2007). Nurse staffing and quality of patient care. Evidence Report/ Technology Assessment Number 151. Accessed May 9, 2008 at www.ahrq.gov/downloads/pub/evidence/pdf/ nursestaff/nursestaff.pdf.

Aiken, L. H., Clarke, S. P., Sloane, D. M., Lake, E. T., & Cheney, T. (2008). Effects of hospital care environment on patient mortality and nurse outcomes. *Journal of Nursing Administration, 38*(5), 223–229.

Aiken, L.H., Clarke, S.P., Cheung, R.B., Sloane, D.M., & Silber, J.H. (2003). Educational levels of hospital nurses and surgical patient mortality, *Journal of the American Medical Association, 290,* 1617–1623.

American Association of Colleges of Nursing (2008). *2007–2008 enrollment and graduations in baccalaureate and graduate programs in nursing.* Washington, DC: Author.

American Association of Colleges of Nursing. (2008). Accelerated Programs: The fast track to careers in nursing. Issue Bulletin. Accessed May 15, 2008 at www.aacn.nche.edu/Publications/Issues/Aug02.htm.

American Organization of Nurse Executives. (2005). Practice and education partnership for the future. Accessed May 10, 2008 at www.aone.org/aone/resource/practiceandeducation.html.

Berlin, L., & Sechrist, K. (2002). The shortage of doctorally prepared nursing faculty: A dire situation. *Nursing Outlook, 50*(2), 50–56.

Buerhaus, P., Staiger, D.O., & Auerbach, D.I. (2008). *The future of the nursing workforce in the United States: Data, trends and implications.* Boston: Jones and Bartlett Publishers.

Community College Baccalaureate Association. (2008). Baccalaureate conferring locations. Accessed May 10, 2008 at www.accbd.org/colleges_areas.php.

Dohm, A., & Shniper, L. (2007). Occupational employment projections to 2016. Washington, DC: U.S. Department of Labor, Bureau of Labor Statistics.

Donley, R., & Flaherty, M.J. (2002). Revisiting the American Nurses Association's first position on education for nurses. OJIN: *The Online Journal of Issues in Nursing. 7*(2). Accessed August 29, 2008 from http://www.nursingworld.org/MainMenuCategories/ANAMarketplace/ANAPeriodicals/OJIN/TableofContents/Volume72002/No2May2002/RevisingPostiononEducation.aspx.

Estabrooks, C.A., Midodzi, W.K., Cummings, G.C., Ricker, K.L., & Giovanetti, P. (2005). The impact of hospital nursing characteristics on 30-day mortality. *Nursing Research, 54*(2), 72–84.

Health Resources and Services Administration. (2007). The registered nurse population: Findings from the March 2004 National Sample Survey of Registered Nurses. Washington, DC: U.S. Department of Health and Human Services. Accessed May 10, 2008 at ftp://ftp.hrsa.gov/bhpr/nursing/rnpopulation/theregisterednursepopulation.pdf.

Institute of Medicine (2003). *Health professions education: A bridge to quality.* Washington, DC: National Academies Press.

Lancaster, J., & Bednash, P. (2008). AACN Commentary on Professional Polarities in Nursing. *Nursing Outlook, 56*(2), 50–51.

Mahaffey, E.H. (2002). The relevance of associate degree nursing education: Past, present, future. OJIN: *The Online Journal of Issues in Nursing. 7*(2). Accessed August 29, 2008 from http://www.nursingworld.org/MainMenuCategories/ANAMarketplace/ANAPeriodicals/OJIN/TableofContents/Volume72002/No2May2002/RelevanceofAssociateDegree.aspx.

Mee, C.L. (2006). Nursing2006 salary survey. *Nursing*, 56(10), 46–51.

National Council of State Boards of Nursing. (2008). 2007 number of candidates taking NCLEX examination and percent passing, by type of candidates. Accessed May 10, 2008 at www.ncsbn.org/1237.htm.

National League for Nursing. (2008). Nursing data review academic year 2005–06. New York City: Author.

National League for Nursing. (2005). Transforming nursing education. Position statement. New York City: Author.

National Organization for Associate Degree Nursing. (2007). Position statement on ADN as entry level nursing degree. Accessed May 10, 2008 at www.noadn.org.

Ridley, T.R. (2008). The relationship between nurse education level and patient safety: an integrative review. *Journal of Nursing Education, 47*(4), 149–157.

Tourangeau, A.E, Doran, D.M., McGillis Hall, L., O'Brien Pallas, L., Pringle, D., Tu, J.V., & Cranley, L.A. (2007). Impact of hospital nursing care on 30-day mortality for acute medical patients. *Journal of Advanced Nursing, 57*(1), 32–41.

U.S. Bureau of Labor Statistics, (2007). Occupational employment and wages for 2006. Accessed May 10, 2008 at www.bls.gov/news.release/pdf/ocwage.pdf.

Waneka, R., & Spetz, J. (2008). California board of registered nursing 2006–2007 annual report. Accessed May 10, 2008 at www.rn.ca.gov/pdfs/schools/0607prelicensure.pdf.

NURSING THE GREAT SOCIETY: THE IMPACT OF THE NURSE TRAINING ACT OF 1964

JOAN E. LYNAUGH

EDITORS' NOTE

The 1964 Nurse Training Act provided the first substantive and ongoing federal support for the development of the nursing workforce. This article describes the history of the act and its relevance to today's nursing workforce. Without this federal support, the shortage of nurses would be far worse than it is.

■ ■ ■

This article, first presented as the Kate Hurd-Mead Lecture, is one aspect of my exploration of twentieth-century transformations in American nursing practice and education. At times I am tempted to argue that there are two distinct eras in the history of nursing; a ninety-year history from about 1860 to 1950, followed by a fifty-year history from 1950 to the turn of the present century. Of course, I won't pursue that, because it is a kind of nonsense. But I am fascinated by the busy decades after World War II. Indeed, the period between 1950 and 1980 was a time of erratic but fundamental change in every arena of nursing.

What we see by 1950 is a public and professional consensus about two things related to the nursing profession in the United States. Most nurses were not well enough educated for the demands of their work. And, in any case, nurses were too scarce to meet the rising health care expectations of Americans. These complaints about nursing were not new. What *was* new was both the political energy and an emerging set of public/private coalitions willing to do something about it. I will return to this later. First, though, I want to look briefly at two influences inside nursing that I think helped channel reform; we can see these influences at work beginning in the 1930s.

INFLUENCES INSIDE NURSING

The more obvious of the two internal influences was the gradual development of staff nursing in hospitals. Fully trained but poorly paid nurses ultimately replaced the pupil nurses who, since the inception of organized nursing, had been the main caregivers for hospital patients. As hospitals hired graduate nurses, the orientation of nursing practice changed from the earlier entrepreneurial private duty model, where the patient paid the nurse, to an institutional model, where the patient or insurance company paid the hospital for the work of the graduate nurse on its staff.

This transition from entrepreneur to employee might have worked out all right for nursing. Unfortunately, for the first twenty years or so, the design of staff nursing in hospitals mimicked the inhibiting style of the traditional nurse training school. The early conception of staff nursing placed heavy emphasis on supervision, hierarchical relations, and procedural conformity. It stifled the investigation of problems and certainly did not encourage innovation in nursing practice. In turn, such an unsatisfying and inadequate nursing system led to an incessant turnover of nurses in hospital work and severe quality problems in patient care. Thus, a system of top-down control originally designed to manage pupils caring for the sick and intended to ensure safety for patients became more and more dysfunctional. The strains and shortages of World War II effectively prevented attention from being given to these problems, and they remained to plague the nursing and hospital leaders of the 1950s. In spite of the problems in staff nursing, however, the field slowly abandoned its largest work group, private duty nurses, in favor of hospital-paid staff work.

The other influence on nursing dating from the 1930s was a nascent challenge to the traditional, authoritative teaching of nursing commonly found in the hospital-based training schools that dominated nursing education. The traditional curriculum emphasized learning standard methods of doing the work: ward management, medical diagnosis and treatment, and sanitation. Challenges to this tradition came from a few nurse faculty members such as Martha Ruth Smith at Simmons College and Virginia Henderson at Teachers College, Columbia University (later at Yale University).

There seem to be two faces to their critique of education for nurses. First, they argued that nursing education should be about studying nursing practice and changing the way nurses cared for patients, not about preserving a traditional, authoritative standard of care. That is to say, for them, learning nursing meant developing the ability to give a provable reason for taking nursing action in a particular instance. Second, they began to conceptualize nursing around major problems, each of which, they argued, must be defined by the individual situation and grounded in science.

Henderson and her likeminded colleagues insisted that nurses must think of and adjust their care to the individual person, one patient at a time. This idea and teaching flew in the face of routine, efficiency, and control, to say nothing of interfering with the unvarying, perfect procedures that made up the bulk of clinical training in nursing. During the 1940s, more critics appeared: for example, Faye Abdellah, Dorothy Smith, Hildegard Peplau, Irene Beland, Thelma Ingles, and Frances Reiter began to exhort nurses to know and develop more science and to perceive their patients as individuals instead of bed numbers or diagnoses.

By the 1950s it is possible to see, in nursing journals and conference proceedings, a change in self-image. Nurses began to see themselves as holding a unique therapeutic place in the care of patients, a place that involved more than the perfect execution of a series of delegated tasks. Moreover, some nurses began to insist on nurses' rights to make decisions about the care they gave patients. One tangible piece of evidence for the universality of this change was the removal of any reference to physician supervision of nurses in the revised definition of nursing adopted by the International Council of Nurses in 1960. But, in state after state, the legal debates set off by these ideas would go on for more than twenty years, as nurse practice acts were challenged and revised.

INFLUENCES OUTSIDE NURSING

While nurses struggled with problems of quality of practice, turnover, self-image, and demand for more nurses, the context in which they were operating was changing fast. When World War II ended, Americans began to focus on domestic problems. High on the list of work to be done was building larger and better systems of higher education and of health care. Nursing found itself at the intersection of these concerns in 1946; its future would be markedly affected by local and national decision making regarding both higher education and an expanding health care system.

The GI Bill of 1944 virtually guaranteed the rapid growth of America's colleges and universities. Then, in 1946, President Harry Truman appointed the President's Commission on Higher Education, which advocated universal access to higher education for people who combined interest with ability to do the work. Among the commission's many recommendations was the expansion of the country's two-year junior colleges, which came to be called community colleges. Over the next thirty years, in response to the goals of the Truman Commission, the number of students enrolled in higher education would increase tenfold and the number of faculty sixfold, and the number of educational institutions would double. When we consider that before World War II only about one in four Americans completed high school, it is easier to appreciate how dramatic an educational change was under way by 1950.

At virtually the same time, the Hospital Survey and Reconstruction Act (usually called Hill-Burton), also signed by Truman in 1946, began to provide money to states and local communities to develop and expand hospitals and other health facilities. Contributions by employers to health insurance as a form of nontaxable wage benefit became common, and health care insurance via employment boomed. In 1946, only about one-third of Americans held some form of health insurance. Fifteen years later, three-quarters of Americans had health care insurance. This gave them unprecedented access to medical and hospital care. The combination of expanding hospitals under Hill-Burton and expanding citizens' access to hospital care via insurance created a heavy and persistent demand for hospital nurses and ratcheted up the pressure to address nursing's problems.

In the late 1940s, 1,100 hospital-based schools of nursing educated almost all the nation's nurses. Most programs were three years in length; successful completion entitled the graduate to sit for a state licensing exam leading to certification as a registered nurse. There was no college credit attached to most of these programs. A handful of hospital programs were associated with colleges; there, students who completed two years of liberal arts study along with their three years of nursing training earned baccalaureate degrees from the college.

The hospital school domination of the nursing educational system did not satisfy many in the postwar nursing leadership. But the hospital school began to be seen as a problem by hospital leaders, too. They complained that the schools burdened the hospitals with unrecoverable costs. A coalition of interests began to grow. Study after study recommended relocating the education of nurses from hospital-owned schools to colleges and universities.

PUBLIC AND PRIVATE ACTIVISM

This article is primarily focused on federal involvement in the nursing problems of the mid-twentieth century, but it is important, I think, to recognize the active interplay between public and private interests. Just one example, which I have written about elsewhere, is the activism of the W. K. Kellogg Foundation during the 1950s and later. The Kellogg Foundation developed its own postwar plan for nursing under the leadership of Mildred

Tuttle, a public health nurse who directed Kellogg's Nursing Division for twenty-three years. The Kellogg plan was based on the postwar goals developed by the National Council for War Service, a wartime consortium of nursing and hospital leaders. Its two main goals were to expand university-based nursing programs by improving their faculties and to set up university-based programs to provide continuing education for nurses on the job. Kellogg funded ten universities with modest but otherwise unattainable grants to hire or retrain faculty and teach clinically focused courses to improve the skills of their graduates. The foundation spent about a million dollars on the project, which lasted from 1948 to 1953.

Throughout the 1950s and through most of the 1960s, Kellogg convened a Nursing Advisory Committee to help oversee foundation initiatives in the field. There were always some nurses from the federal government as well as deans of schools of nursing and leaders in public health on the advisory committee, which met annually or more often at foundation headquarters in Battle Creek, Michigan. Members gave advice and answered staff questions. The minutes of the advisory committee reflect the concerns and agenda of one important segment of the nursing leadership of the time. By 1960, it is easy to see the outlines of their preferred course of action.

First, they said, the hospital school must be phased out. The wording of the minutes implies that hospital schools were finished; in fact, as we know, it would be another fifteen years before that happened. Next, they agreed that some sort of assistant to the professional nurse was essential, and they agreed that nurses with two years of preparation at the new community colleges should be those assistants. And, finally, they agreed that the baccalaureate degree should be the main route of entry into professional nursing and also the basis for specialization at the master's level.

Meanwhile, in Washington, DC, Lucile Perry Leone, chief nurse officer of the Public Health Service, urged the surgeon general to appoint a commission to investigate nursing problems. A distinguished panel of health professionals, educators, and philanthropists made their report in 1963. Leone, Rozella Schlorfeldt, Faye Abdellah, and Eleanor Lambertsen, all longtime members of Mildred Tuttle's Nursing Advisory Committee at Kellogg, served or consulted on the panel. Titled *Toward Quality in Nursing,* the surgeon general's report called for tripling the number of nurses graduating each year, including a fourfold increase in the number of baccalaureate graduates, and expanding the number of nurses with master's degrees by a factor of ten by 1970. Its many other recommendations included funding for nursing research, building new schools and improving existing ones, and providing direct money for higher education to nurses seeking advanced degrees.

All this was to be overseen by the Division of Nursing of the Public Health Service. Let me give a very brief introduction to the Division of Nursing, since it will play a large role in this Great Society story. Its origins date to the 1930s, when some nurses were brought into government to implement the provisions of the Social Security Act of 1935. But the main impetus for growth in the division dates from the Bolton Act of 1943, which established the Cadet Nurse Corps. Representative Frances Payne Bolton sponsored the Cadet Corps idea as a means of addressing the acute shortage of nurses during the war. The money went to schools of nursing to enable them to admit more students. About 120,000 nurses completed the very popular program before it terminated five years later.

Leone led the Cadet Nurse Corps program during the war and became chief of the new Division of Nursing when the Public Health Service was reorganized in 1946. The impact and favorable image of the Cadet Nurse Corps and a growing consensus that a vigorous nursing workforce would be essential to postwar planning for health helped establish the division as the face of nursing in the federal government.

As we will see, the Nurse Training Act of 1964 (NTA), signed by President Lyndon Johnson after John Kennedy's assassination in 1963, pretty much mandated the recommendations in *Toward Quality in Nursing*. The 1964 legislation meant that the preparation of nurses was acknowledged as central to the nation's health agenda. The federal government's approach to nursing fitted in with its other broad interventionist programs in civil rights, poverty, and social welfare.

HOW A PRIVATE AGENDA BECAME PUBLIC POLICY

I would like to explore briefly how the NTA, a remarkable piece of legislation, came to be. How did it happen that money was reappropriated to sustain it in various forms for the next fifteen years?

Kennedy's health message to Congress in February 1963 listed a long menu of health priorities; among its details were new programs of financial assistance to modernize and replace hospitals under the Hill-Burton Act, build nursing homes, and increase the number of professional nurses. Kennedy's message on nursing was taken directly from the surgeon general's report, which was published and distributed that same month. And, indeed, by September 1963, Kennedy signed the Health Professions Educational Assistance Act, a program of construction grants for teaching facilities and student loans to physicians, dentists, and nurses.

Wilbur Cohen, an old Washington hand going back to the Social Security era, was an assistant secretary in the Department of Health, Education, and Welfare (HEW) in the early years of the Johnson administration. In an interview ten years later, Cohen recalled his thinking in 1963 and 1964. "Once you had the 1963 Act," he said, "it was easy for me to take the next step. . . . Once you break the back of the ideological opposition, then all you are arguing about is money and so on. But the first thing you had to do, you couldn't start with nurses. You had to start with physicians and dentists because they are elite, they had the political power. Once we broke their back, the nurse legislation in 1964 was relatively easy."

And so, in February 1964, Lyndon Johnson said that "the rapid development of medical science places heavy demands on the time and skill of the physician. Nurses must perform many functions that were once done only by doctors. . . . The nursing profession, too, is becoming more complex and exacting. The longer we delay, the larger the deficit grows, and the harder it becomes to overcome it." He recommended raising enrollment in schools of nursing by 75 percent in five years, building new schools of nursing, removing financial barriers to studying nursing, and encouraging nurses to study for higher degrees to enable them to teach and manage care.

Hearings on the legislation were held in April; witnesses reminded the legislators that the recommendations of the surgeon general called for federal involvement and stressed the success of previous funding for nursing education. In other words, the NTA was proposed to Congress as the next logical step in solving the problems of supply and quality of nurses.

Representative Claude Pepper from Florida, a longtime supporter of nursing in Congress, urged that educational aid be in the form of grants rather than loans, arguing that nurses would have trouble paying off loans since their salaries were so low. He was right: nurses' average annual salaries were about $1,000 less than those of the average factory worker and included no sick leave, no health insurance, no pension, and minimal vacation time in return for a forty-eight-hour week.

The American Hospital Association (AHA) supported the bill in principle. But James Howell, MD, chair of the AHA committee on nursing, and Ruth Sleeper, chief nurse at Boston's Massachusetts General Hospital, complained that the money for construction was available only to collegiate schools. They both argued for similar support for hospital-owned diploma schools. The argument about hospital schools continued in further hearings. Finally, to keep the AHA on board, $41 million was authorized for "special" grants to hospital schools.

When President Johnson signed the bill in August 1964, it called for $283 million for five programs for five years and an additional $4.6 million to administer the act. First, it authorized $90 million in construction grants, $55 million for hospital schools and associate's degree programs, and $35 million for college programs. Second, another $17 million was designated for special projects. Third, as noted above, $41 million in grants to hospital schools was added. Fourth, the traineeship program, which gave money directly to students, got $50 million. And, fifth, $85 million was set aside to provide loans, not grants, to students. However, the bill also provided that graduates who worked in nursing for five years would be forgiven 50 percent of their loan.

The NTA was a very big event for nursing and health care. As we will see, it launched significant changes in both education and practice. As we will also see, however, it sustained long-standing ambivalence about higher education for nurses by supporting three different levels of schools.

Indeed, the surgeon general's report, on which the legislation was built, contained that same ambivalence, compromise, and inability to acknowledge what was by then the precipitous decline of hospital-based diploma programs. For example, on page 54 the report calls for a major expansion of both diploma and collegiate programs to increase the number of professional nurse graduates. But on page 57 it recommends traineeship support for up to two years full-time study toward the baccalaureate but prohibits graduates of diploma and associate's degree programs from applying. One can only imagine the across-the-table arguments that led to such peculiar recommendations.

As it turned out, one of the major facts of life for nurses throughout this period was constant pressure on graduates of associate's degree and hospital programs to upgrade their educational credentials in order to hold or advance in their jobs. Thus political pressure to keep supporting all schools led to expensive and inefficient career experiences, by preparing nurses in a way that created a need for constant reeducation.

So this Great Society program, the Nurse Training Act, would change higher education in nursing, but it was an incremental not a radical change. It was, as it came to be called in the hearings and recommendations, "a balanced approach" to funding nursing education. The coalition that prepared and put through the 1964 NTA, a coalition of legislators, bureaucrats, the AHA, the American Nurses Association (ANA), educators, and private philanthropists agreed to prioritize huge increases in the number of nurses. The decision to pledge big increases in numbers in a short period of time trumped any moves to get rid of hospital-based schools in order to put the focus on baccalaureate and associate's degree programs. Moreover, in the first NTA, there was little attention to upgrading quality n the nursing workforce.

As we know, the Democratic majority gave the Johnson administration a firm grip on Congress, and during 1965 and 1966 a total of 55 health bills were passed. The NTA was operating in a very supportive environment. In fact, even Republicans helped out. Senator Jacob Javits of New York introduced a bill to expand nurse scholarships, build more nursing schools, and increase teaching improvement grants for the schools. This was a $25 million program with an interesting twist, as it allowed transfers of money earmarked for hospital schools to go to college programs if the money was unused by the hospital schools. At least seven colleges benefited from this stealth legislation.

In 1968, an extension of the Nurse Training Act was incorporated into the broader Health Manpower Act. This time the discussion included an intense debate about who should accredit nursing programs; accreditation was necessary to be eligible for assistance under the act. Much of the energy for the debate came from associate's degree nursing programs in community colleges. They felt that the National League for Nursing, the voluntary body responsible for accreditation, did not serve them well. In the end, accreditation from any recognized accrediting body was deemed sufficient to qualify a school for participation. Funding for the NTA was extended through fiscal year 1971.

By January 1970, there were 700,000 registered nurses in practice, 150,000 more than in 1964. Also, between 1963 and 1970, the number of nurses with bachelor's degrees increased by 84 percent and those with master's degrees by 63 percent. Nurses holding doctorates doubled, so there were more than 700 by 1970. Falling enrollments in hospital diploma programs were more than compensated for by huge increases in community college enrollment and a substantial growth in baccalaureate enrollment. The profession was expanding rapidly, but still the demand for more nurses remained insatiable.

THE POLITICAL CLIMATE CHILLS

It is worth mentioning here that the American Nurses Association appointed its first ever lobbyist in 1971. Constance Holleran, who had worked in the Division of Nursing for about four years, took the ANA lobbying job and launched an aggressive effort to represent the ANA more forcefully on Capitol Hill. The next year, Nurses for Political Action was incorporated. The first national organization of nurses to work in political action, it soon affiliated with the ANA. It seems clear that nurses were gearing up to cope with a changed environment in Washington.

The Nixon administration was not enthusiastic about the NTA but did not mount strong objections in 1971. In fact, the 1971 bill did not differ materially from its 1964 and 1968 predecessors; it authorized $855 million to be spent through 1974. And the bill encouraged the growth of nurse-practitioner programs.

But something new happened in 1972, when the administration budget for 1973 asked for less than half the amount authorized by the 1971 NTA. The House and Senate put most of the money back in the budget; Nixon promptly vetoed the legislation that housed the restored funds. Congress could not override his veto, but instead worked the funding up again, this time by about $50 million. Nixon again vetoed the bill. So Congress was forced to keep the Division of Nursing going through 1973 via continuing resolutions.

Nixon won with 61 percent of the vote in 1972. Under the new HEW secretary, Caspar Weinberger, the administration turned openly hostile toward nursing NTA funding was impounded by the president's Office of Management and Budget (OMB). In response, the National League for Nursing filed suit against the OMB and HEW to compel the release of the money, claiming that their acts violated the intent of Congress. After six months of legal activity, a federal judge ordered the release of almost $74 million to nursing. This was a modest victory in what would be a long struggle through the 1970s.

In his 1976 interview, Wilbur Cohen explained what he thought was going on in HEW:

My view is that Nixon . . . brought people who were designed to cut back on the federal government's role, and the federal government's expenditures. He, Erlichman, Haldeman, and Weinberger were of that persuasion. . . . And, when Nixon saw that Weinberger was doing it so well at OMB, he says take over HEW and get rid of [Elliot] Richardson who won't do it. We will put Richardson in Defense and put Weinberger in HEW. . . . Weinberger's instructions were to cut the guts out of all these [Great Society] programs, including nursing.

Friends of nursing in Congress, Senators Warren Magnuson and Jacob Javits and Representatives Paul Rogers and Silvio Conti, vigorously defended the NTA programs. At the same time, an intense lobbying effort cranked out information so that nurses around the country could try to influence their legislators. But still, looking at the early 1970s, one could say that nursing initiatives at the federal level seemed on the verge of extinction. In fact, it looks as though the Division of Nursing was saved only by the Watergate affair.

After Nixon finally left office, a weakened Gerald Ford continued to oppose the NTA appropriations for 1976 through 1978 and sent a veto message to Congress. The Senate voted 67 to 15 to override and the House crushed Ford's veto by 384 to 43. Republican Javits summed up Congress's prevailing attitude by declaring how essential nursing was to operate the health system and maintain its quality.

Things looked bright in 1975, and the election of 1976, which brought Jimmy Carter and a Democratic majority to office, offered hope to some for a return to the generous days of the Great Society. But by the end of the 1970s, both the Great Society and regular reappropriations of money for nursing were things of the past. An era of conservatism in spending on health was emerging.

Nurses and their supporters would continue campaigning and would have success in some quarters. But the arguments and priorities of the 1980s and 1990s are the subject of some future article. For now, I would like to stop and consider what all that money really meant. Sources indicate that about 4 billion federal dollars were spent on nursing in the 1960s and 1970s. As I said at the outset, it seems to me that the money, given the preferences of the succession of administrations and legislators, given the direction and management of the bureaucrats at the Division of Nursing, and given the priorities of leaders in nursing and health care, manifestly affected the course of nursing in those years and up to the present day.

Of course, these events are rather recent, so we are denied the perspective of time from which to witness and assess their importance. Still, I would like to point out four avenues of change that seem to me to be lasting in importance and meaningful for the present and future. First, of course, is the impressive growth in the actual numbers of nurses and the definition of at least two levels of nurses. Second is the funded decision to broaden the scope of practice of nurses by supporting the rapid development of specialized, now called advanced, nursing practice. Third is the investment in systematic investigation of nursing care problems and the development of an infrastructure for nursing research. And fourth is the firming up of nursing as a middle-class occupation with reasonable aspirations for self-direction, legal independence, expectations of affluence, and an individualistic self-image. I will deal with each of these areas briefly.

GROWTH ON TWO LEVELS

As we have seen, the dominant argument for federal support of nursing was the public's desire for more nurses. This didn't begin with the Great Society programs, of course; it dates from the Cadet Corps of World War II. The tenor of the argument is best captured in a quotation from Thomas Parran, surgeon general during the war. Speaking to Lucile Perry Leone, the nurse in charge of the Cadet Corps, he said, "More and better is all right, but first, it has to be more." That was the idea, more nurses, and that view prevailed until 1980. And, indeed, we got more nurses. In 1960 there were 279 nurses for every 100,000 people; by 1980 there were 560. That is twice as many in a single generation. Today, there are very close to three million nurses in the United States.

A striking aspect of this growth is the rapidly changing context in which it took place. In 1960, more than 80 percent of nursing students were enrolled in hospital-based diploma schools; by 1980, only about 16 percent were in hospital-based schools and the number was dropping fast. In 1960, fewer than 5 percent of nursing students were enrolled in two-year associate's degree programs in community colleges; by 1980, 40 percent were in associate's degree programs. In 1960, about 20 percent of nursing students were enrolled in baccalaureate programs; by 1980, slightly more than 40 percent were in baccalaureate programs. Thus, in twenty years the main location of education for nurses moved from hospitals to colleges.

But something else happened too. For the first time, an acknowledged level of difference prevailed in entry-level education for nurses. The graduate of the two-year program earns an ADN degree and becomes eligible to sit for the exam for state registration. So does the graduate of the four-year program, who earns a BSN. But the graduate of the two-year program cannot move up in nursing toward a specialty practice job or management or teaching unless he or she continues his or her education through the baccalaureate and probably a master's degree. This is a remarkable escalation of the educational criteria for advancement. It is comparable to the escalating demands for residency training and certification when the era of medical specialization began. There may well be a permanent debate among nurses and others about the wisdom and validity of the choices made, but the fact is, the implementation of the NTA underwrote the multitier educational system we have now.

Expanding the Scope of Practice in Nursing

In the 1960s there was a strong, prevailing idea that America's citizens had a right to health care. The 1965 passage of Medicare and Medicaid, as well as the extension of health insurance to much of the population, gave people access to that ideal. The idea of the nurse-practitioner as a means to address demands for care from a financially enabled population was driven forward by federal support. Right from the beginning, the Division of Nursing assisted nursing in its efforts to define the expanded role of the nurse and to develop a place for the nurse practitioner in the health care system. In fact, in the early 1970s, it is most likely that federal enthusiasm for the nurse-practitioner idea exceeded that of the nursing leadership. Beginning in about 1969 and continuing through the 1980s, the federal government spent about $175 million on various aspects of the nurse-practitioner idea. At first, the Nursing Division supported short programs of continuing education to train nurse-practitioners; after about ten years, however, most federal support was going to master's level programs.

At the same time, the traineeship money that was reappropriated every two years stoked the development of master's programs in nursing all across the country. Applicants to master's programs began to focus on clinical specialties in midwifery, critical care, oncology, maternal and child health, anesthesia, and gerontology, as well as the nurse-practitioner programs. Between 1965 and 1980, graduations from master's programs in nursing quadrupled. After fifteen years of traineeship support, about 67,000 nurses held a master's or doctoral degree. It is worth noting that the steady influx of federal dollars into schools of nursing on college campuses made the schools much more attractive to college presidents and trustees.

Investigating Nursing Problems and Creating an Infrastructure for Research

Actually, the federal government sponsored research in nursing via its Research Grants and Fellowship Branch well before the NTA was passed in 1964. Some $625,000 to support research training and research projects became available beginning in 1955. From 1958 to 1966, with a focus on training faculty, some money went to further education for those who either were not trained in research or needed to upgrade their skills. Other funds went to fund offices and centers to facilitate research productivity in schools of nursing. The Nurse Scientist Graduate Training Program, established in 1964, made it possible for schools of nursing to get their students into other departments of the university where they could earn doctorates. Departments in the basic sciences, sociology, anthropology, and other fields trained nurses in research. In turn, these newly minted researchers could compete for research funding and qualify for faculty appointments. The 1974 National Research Service Award Act was designed to provide both institutional and individual pre- and post-doctoral awards to nurses aspiring to become scientists. One way or another, using the federal money I have mentioned here, private sources, and philanthropic support, some schools of nursing found ways to carry out research projects and develop doctoral programs. Looking at the chronology of federal research grants, one can see a gradual trend in studies, from how to teach nursing, to examining nursing theories, and on to more clinically focused studies of nursing practice.

NURSING'S ASPIRATIONS

Throughout the Great Society days of the NTA there was a sense of optimism and promise. At the same time, great unrest and ongoing rejection of traditional norms and organizations kept the field in turmoil. Nurses stopped wearing caps and white uniforms; some became very active in the social movements of the time. Undoubtedly, this was partially due to the fluid social situation generated by the women's movement, the civil rights movement, and, of course, the hot debate over Vietnam. But some of it, I think, grew from tearing down nursing's old educational system and building up something quite new. It often seemed that no one was in charge and, in some sense, that didn't seem to matter.

When my colleague Julie Fairman and I were interviewing nurses for our history of the development of the critical care nursing specialty, we were both struck by the pioneer critical care nurses' joy in just striking out on their own, learning and doing as much as they could in patient care. Those who longed to change their work were in no mood to be held back by traditional organizational constraints, whether those constraints came from hospital management or the American Nurses Association. A rash of new specialty organizations in nursing sprang up in the 1970s—organizations for oncology nurses, critical care nurses, nurse-practitioners, and many others—and these likeminded nurses began to gather power unto themselves.

Across the country, in state after state, nurses campaigned for changes in the state laws governing their practice. A key target was the legal stipulation for physician supervision of nursing practice, a component often found in laws governing nursing. Another target was the stipulation in state laws that prohibited nurses from diagnosing anything, even death. Throughout the 1970s, the laws were changed, sometimes in the direction sought by nurses and sometimes not. But, overall, the constraints on nursing weakened, effectively making the practice of nurse-practitioners and other specialty practitioners legal.

As I noted at the outset, there was a major influx of working- and middle-class Americans into our colleges and universities after World War II. Nurses got their chance to change their status through education in the late 1950s and, most dramatically, during the 1960s and 1970s. Nurses began to see themselves as knowledge workers and sought the chance to move up in the world through education.

An expert nurse is one who, through education and demonstration of special knowledge, is capable of recognizing and solving unique, important clinical problems and showing good results. This kind of performance attracts recognition and grants social authority. For many nurses, professional achievement became a means to social mobility. And, as salaries began to rise toward the end of the 1970s, a new kind of financial stability and even affluence helped secure that new image.

AFTERWORD

So, by 1980, the legacy of the Great Society initiatives in nursing could be summed up as many more nurses doing more and specialized work; an entirely new system of education and new avenues of research in health care; and a generation of women and men who found entirely new opportunities in an old profession.

ACKNOWLEDGMENTS

This article was first presented as the Kate Hurd-Mead Lecture at the College of Physicians of Philadelphia, March 15, 2006.

NOTES

Congressional Quarterly (Washington, DC), 1964, 1971, 1978.

Connolly, Cynthia A., and Joan E. Lynaugh, *Fifty years at the Division of Nursing, United States Public Health Service.* Washington, DC: American Nurses Association, April 1997.

Kalisch, Philip A., and Beatrice J. Kalisch. "Nurturer of Nurses: A History of the Division of Nursing of the U.S. Public Health Service and Its Antecedents, 1798–1977," Final Report of PHS Contract NO1-NU-44129, unpublished manuscript, division of Nursing, Washington, DC, 1977. Material in quotations was drawn from this report.

Lynaugh, Joan E., and Barbara L. Brush. *American Nursing: From Hospitals to Health Systems.* Cambridge, MA: Blackwell, 1996.

ADVANCED PRACTICE NURSING

Reprints of Key Articles

Connie Mullinix and Dawn P. Bucholtz, "Role and Quality of Nurse Practitioner Practice: A Policy Issue"

Mary O. Mundinger, Robert L. Kane, Elizabeth R. Lenz, Annette M. Totten, Wei-Yann Tsai, Paul D. Cleary, William T. Friedewald, Albert L. Siu, and Michael L. Shelanski, "Primary Care Outcomes in Patients Treated by Nurse Practitioners or Physicians: A Randomized Trial"

Donna Diers, "Nurse-Midwives and Nurse Anesthetists: The Cutting Edge in Specialist Practice"

Dorothy Brooten, Mary D. Naylor, Ruth York, Linda P. Brown, Barbara Hazard Munro, Andrea O. Hollingsworth, Susan M. Cohen, Steven Finkler, Janet Deatrick, and JoAnne M. Youngblut, "Lessons Learned from Testing the Quality Cost Model of Advanced Practice Nursing (APN) Transitional Care"

Joan M. Stanley, "Reaching Consensus on a Regulatory Model: What Does This Mean for APRNs?"

10

ROLE AND QUALITY OF NURSE PRACTITIONER PRACTICE: A POLICY ISSUE

CONNIE MULLINIX

DAWN P. BUCHOLTZ

EDITORS' NOTE

Advanced practice registered nurses are providing care to myriad populations in all clinical settings. They continue to struggle for the right to practice in accordance with their educational preparation and to be paid equitably for their services. Mullinix and Bucholtz provide a contemporary analysis of the factors that stand in the way of full utilization of these practitioners who have demonstrated that they can deliver on the clinical and financial outcomes that our nation now expects.

■ ■ ■

Many nurse practitioners (NPs) would like to practice independently, but, currently, some degree of physician supervision is required in 24 states.[1-3] Twenty-three states, including the District of Columbia, require no physician involvement.[3] As the healthcare delivery system treats an increasingly chronically ill, aging population, more practitioners are needed, creating an opportunity for NPs to expand their role in the system.[4] By the year 2020, an estimated 85,000 additional practitioners will be needed.[5] Expanded use of advanced practice nurses is being advocated as a solution to this growing shortage.[4] The Institute of Medicine has recommended eliminating restrictions on NPs that impact their ability to provide care.[6] In primary care, NPs can give up to 90% of the care provided to children and 80% of the care provided to adults.[7,8]

In the 1990s, the managed care environment exacerbated economic competition between physicians and non-physician providers. Physicians recognized that, in a capitated environment, NPs could make primary care economically viable.[9] In an article advising MDs how to strengthen their practices' profitability, Terry pointed out that NPs could "devote extra attention to patients whose insurance pays less, such as those on Medicare, leaving physicians free to see more patients who are commercially insured."[10] Medical Doctors have realized considerable economic gain from lower-paid non-physician providers. In states that require physician supervision and restrict direct third-party reimbursement, NPs perform services and procedures for which the physicians who employ them are reimbursed. The MD may pay the NP a salary and pocket the difference.[11] When NPs are directly reimbursed by third-party payers, the rate is often lower than the MD rate for the same services, and undercompensating NPs for their skills. Because this is accepted practice, limited and unequal reimbursement for services is a significant barrier to NP's ability to practice independently.[4]

However, the biggest obstacle NPs face in their struggle for independence remains the "unsubstantiated concerns for public safety."[12] The issue of quality of care, clothed in the guise of concern for public safety, continues to be raised as a political tool to limit non-physician healthcare provider expansion. The American Medical Association's (AMA)

House of Delegates proposed resolutions to "strongly push for patient education on the education and competency of nurse practitioner . . . and the necessity of physician-lead care."[13]

The struggle for NP autonomy has increasingly politicized the debate over quality of care and has made establishing the capabilities of NPs more important than ever. The essential debate now centers on collaboration with a physician, as opposed to independence or strict supervision, and clearly on the ability of NPs to establish that the care they provide is adequate. Collaboration (working together) has been advocated as a means to enhance primary care by those who note that physicians and nurses complement each other's primary care skills.[14] While medicine largely integrates knowledge from the biochemical and physical science, nursing pulls from the social sciences and focuses on the person-environment interaction.[15] When practice is complementary and based on competence, the patient's best interests are served.[12] Opponents of collaboration consider it a means of creating NP dependence on physicians. In this view, when collaboration is taken as an opportunity for physicians to supervise NPs (a position of traditional dominance defended by the AMA), the ability of NPs to practice becomes dependent on MD sanction.[16] Further, those who argue that NPs should be under the supervision of MDs say that they are concerned that patients receive the highest quality of care available.

The dialogue over "quality of care" can become a substitute for meaningful debate about the maintenance of medical dominance over primary health care. The real issue at stake may be "turf." As early as 1993, Roy Schwarz, the AMA's senior vice president for medical education and science said, "We're always accused of this being a turf and money issue. And I'm sure that, for some doctors, it is. But for the AMA, it's a quality issue, a patient-protection issue, a do-no-harm issue."[10] Patient protection arguments center on the training and education of the NP, asserting that NPs are not trained to handle complex medical problems and an MD is necessary for support and consultation.[17] They raise the concern that nurses' limited education in diagnostic reasoning means that they may not appreciate the seriousness of a clinical problem and may fail to refer the patient to someone more expert.[18] The research, however, has shown that NPs provide safe and effective care within their scope of practice, which is governed by protocols, and that they seek consultation appropriately.[19] Still, a battle for independent practice rights is waged in state legislatures, and the AMA publication *American Medical News (AMNews),* chronicles it. A December 1999 article on the AMA push for organized opposition to legislation expanding the scope of practice for non-physicians stated, "Although the AMA supports collaborative arrangements with physician assistants (PAs) and nurse practitioners, it long has opposed non-physicians who seek independent practice rights that stray into the realm of medicine."[20] A January 2000 article on the Health Care Financing Administration's decision to recognize NPs (along with PAs and certified nurse specialists) as independent practitioners reported, "As another century turns, physicians are enraged over how non-physicians continue to creep into the practice of medicine in many specialties, from optometrists with laser surgery rights to psychologists who can prescribe medicine to nurse anesthetists who seek even more practice rights. Medicare's acceptance of the expanded scope of practice for non-physician practitioners, specifically nurse practitioners, is of particular concern because the lack of physician supervision could jeopardize patient care."[21]

Since their profession was initiated in 1966, an ample body of literature has evolved demonstrating that NPs are capable of providing quality care.[6] This research has been essential to counter opposition to advanced nursing by physicians, whose stated objection to NP care has always been the issue of quality while the real issue is the role and independence of the NP.[22] Despite the weight of evidence indicating that NPs provide quality care, this issue continues to be fiercely debated.[16,18] Therefore, we have examined the literature from the 1970s to the present. At least 3 major reviews, as well as a number of smaller reviews, have been published. By far the most definitive study was Mundinger and colleagues' randomized controlled trial comparing NPs' and physicians' delivery of primary care, which found no differences.[23,24] An early review of 21 studies comparing NPs and PAs to physicians found that the "new professionals" provided primary care that was "indistinguishable from physician care."[25] At the time of that study, physician care was generally understood to be the most acceptable standard for comparison.

A major review of NP quality of care was included in a 1986 policy analysis conducted by the Office of Technology Assessment (OTA).[26] After examining the research, the OTA concluded that "within their area of competence, NPs, PAs, and CNMs [certified nurse midwives] provide care whose quality is equivalent to that of care provided by physicians."[26] The authors used physician care as the standard for comparison because it was not possible to examine quality of care directly. However, the OTA also found that these practitioners were more adept at communicating with patients and at conducting preventive actions. While comparisons with physicians may have been necessary, said the OTA, "Comparison studies are biased against NPs, PAs, and CNMs because the studies assume the medical model as the standard—physician care is considered the standard for care."[26]

Another, more rigorous review in 1987 by Ventura, Feldman, and Crosby synthesized the literature on NP effectiveness, including quality.[27] The authors conducted a comprehensive information search, then engaged an expert panel to rate the literature on the basis of content, findings, and the type and strength of the research methods. Of 350 documents on the topic of effectiveness, they found 248 to be relevant and, using expert agreement, judged 56 to be of sufficient validity to warrant full analysis. Upon examination of these documents, the authors found support for NP effectiveness, and concluded that, "When NPs were compared to other providers, they were typically equal and occasionally superior in performance to other providers."[28-30]

Nevertheless, the issue of quality of care has not been settled for NPs. The debate continues despite well-executed research. Some argued that comparisons with physicians did not adequately account for the different type of care that NPs provide.[22] The difficulty of defining and measuring quality through research may be a central reason for NPs' inability to establish the quality of care that they provide. Quality has been defined as a property of care present in some measurable degree in the way a practitioner manages a specific episode of illness in a given patient.[31] Quality is assessed by looking at structure (the facilities and management of the healthcare organization), process (the behavior of the provider in diagnosing and treating illness), and outcome (the resulting change in health status, as well as the satisfaction of the patient with care). Although quality of care is complex and difficult to measure in any provider group, process and outcome measures have been used to assess physician quality of care, and the same measures have been applied to NP quality of care.[32-34]

Defining quality of care in terms of process and outcome, however, becomes even more complicated when care is further divided into the technical and the interpersonal.

Outcome measures that attempt to describe the technical aspect of care are categorized in the literature as patient-focused, provider-focused, and organization-focused. Choosing a mix of indicators across categories provides a more comprehensive understanding of care. Outcome measures are operationalized in the research as concretely numerical clinical test results and health status measures, but these may not provide the mix of indicators necessary.[35] Process measures, used to evaluate the "art" or how the practitioner manages social and psychological interactions with the patient, as well as the diagnosis and treatment of illness, have been less valued in the research on physician quality of care. Patient satisfaction has not been employed as an outcome measure until recently because it has more to do with patient perceptions of care than with the technical, measurable aspects of care. The art of care has been assumed to be the particular strength of the NP, yet assumptions about the NP's unique contributions to the art of care have not been conceptualized in the research and, therefore, a major component of NP care has been entirely neglected in the research literature.[36] Instead, process measures of provider behavior have compared the NP's ability to diagnose and treat with the physician's ability to do so. Only a few studies have captured those facets of care that arise from the nursing perspective. These include more psychosocial concern for the patient, greater attention to the history of the patient, and less reliance on immediate prescribing of medication.[37–39]

Another reason why the debate about NP quality of care has not been settled may be that the research has been flawed.[26,40,27] While randomized trials on the clinical outcomes of care have been conducted (the most notable being Spitzer et al., 1974, and Mundinger et al., 2000), the process-of-care studies have been primarily correlational or descriptive in design.[41,23] Some studies have used retrospective chart reviews, but the charts were not always standardized. Often, patient case mix was not controlled in terms of vital statistics, such as gender, or in terms of health status and acuity. Studies may have been conducted by parties with an interest in advancing the practice of the NP, potentially biasing the study in favor of the NP.[26] Other studies appear to have been conducted with an inherent bias against the NP, in that they compared NP practice to standards or statistical models without showing how other practitioners, such as MDs, would fare against such criteria.[42,43] Despite these problems, however, a number of sound, scientifically rigorous studies have been conducted.

Brown and Grimes conducted a meta-analysis of the literature on NPs that provided a quantitative assessment of the impact of primary care NPs' roles on the health outcomes of the people they served.[44] Rigorous criteria were used to select 38 key NP studies for analysis. The studies had to involve an NP intervention; be controlled with patient data from physician-managed care; provide a process-of-care or clinical outcome measure; be experimental, quasi-experimental or ex post facto; and permit calculation of effect sizes or direction of effects. In addition, the authors examined a subset of 12 studies that controlled for patient acuity in case mix. The strict selection criteria employed by Brown and Grimes should put to rest concerns about the rigor of the research upon which their conclusions were based.

The meta-analysis demonstrated that NPs do indeed provide quality care. Brown and Grimes found that NPs provided more health promotion activities than did physicians. NPs also scored higher on quality-of-care measures, such as diagnostic accuracy and completeness of the care process (i.e., taking a comprehensive medical/health history). Rates of drug prescription were equivalent, but nurses ordered more laboratory tests.

In terms of clinical outcomes, NPs achieved higher scores than physicians on resolution of pathological conditions and on the functional status of their patients, as well as on patient satisfaction and patient compliance. NPs and physicians demonstrated equivalent patient knowledge.

A more recent study, which received much media attention, was Mundinger et al.'s randomized trial comparing outcomes of physician and NP independent practice at 5 primary care clinics in New York.[23] Favorable state and institutional policies for independent practice of NPs provided a unique situation that allowed for comparison of separate independent practice outcomes of NPs and MDs. The patient outcomes measured in the study included health service utilization, health status, and patient satisfaction. Health service utilization information was obtained by computer records at 6 months and 1 year after the initial appointment with the clinician. No statistically significant differences were found between patients seeing NPs and MDs. Health status was measured using the Medical Outcomes Study Short-Form 36 at the initial visit and at 6 months, with accompanying physiologic tests. The health status scores were not significantly different. However, while there were no differences in physiologic indicators for patients with diabetes and asthma, patients with hypertension seeing NPs had a lower diastolic pressure than those seeing physicians (82 vs. 85 mm Hg, $P = .04$). A questionnaire used to measure patient satisfaction at the initial appointment and at 6 months showed no significant difference after the initial appointment. Ratings at 6 months, however, were higher for MDs, at 4.2 vs. 4.1 for NPs on a scale of 5 being excellent ($P = .05$).[23] The comparable outcomes seen in NP and MD practices add to the evidence of the quality of NP care. While future studies on the process of care may illuminate the different approaches between disciplines, the strength of this study's design made its contribution particularly important to the examination of outcomes and quality. A 2-year follow-up confirmed the findings of the original study.[24]

Although the study was accepted as well-designed and significant in the discourse on practice, there were varied responses within the medical community. Its publication in the *Journal of the American Medical Association* (*JAMA*) is evidence of openness to objective evaluation of practice by some in the medical community. In an accompanying editorial in the same *JAMA* issue, H. C. Sox described the piece as, "An important article about primary health care," and described the study as "well-designed" and "well-executed." While accepting its internal validity, however, Sox called for further study to make up for "weak" external validity due to the short study period (6 months), and the unique characteristics of the study population, clinicians, and healthcare facilities.[45] An article in Clinician News that included interviews with Mundinger and Sox as well as N. Dickey, president of the AMA, implied that organized medicine as a whole did not have the same enthusiasm for the study.[46] And a January 2000 issue of *AMNews* emphasized *JAMA's* controversial publication of the piece in their profile of the journal's new editor, Catherine D. DeAngelis.[46]

Mundinger et al.'s study, and the Brown and Grimes meta-analysis, taken in conjunction with the OTA study of NP quality of care, provide ample support for the position that NPs provide high-quality primary care in their areas of competence, and their role in the healthcare system should be expanded. With evidence concluding that NPs provide quality care, there is no recent research on this subject except for studies on specific disease entities. For example, the 2005 study by Wilson and colleagues uses 8 quality indicators to compare care given by NPs, PAs, infectious disease specialists, and generalist HIV experts when caring for HIV patients. This study concludes that NPs provide quality care.[47] Future research may examine NP quality of care for specific diseases though the question of overall quality has been resolved. Despite factors such as the need for more primary care providers and cost control, NPs continue to be thwarted in their ability to practice and to operate more autonomously. The issue of whether NPs should be allowed to practice independently should be decided with the understanding that they provide, and will continue to provide, quality care with clearly defined guidelines and adequate training. There is an increasing need for primary care providers; therefore, NPs are unlikely to displace physicians as primary care providers. Rather, they can provide services where a need exists. They should be given the respect they have earned and supported in their efforts to engage in high-quality health care. Without question, the research supports this approach.

Recommendations to allow full participation of NPs, and for patients to accrue the benefit of this care, the following are suggested:

1. NPs should be confident in their abilities despite criticism and questions about quality from organized medicine.

2. Researchers should focus on the quality of care received by patients regardless of provider.

3. Funders of research should, likewise, focus on the quality of care received by patients rather than the comparison of NPs with MDs.

4. Policymakers should eliminate legislative restrictions on the NP's practice and ignore the cautions of organized medicine about quality of care provided by NPs since such arguments are not grounded in evidence.

5. State legislators should lift requirements for MDs to review care provided by NPs.

6. Boards of nursing and nursing associations should push for the expanded role of the NPs collaborating with, but not controlled by, physicians so that patients benefit from the expertise of both professionals.

7. Boards of medicine and organized medical associations should focus on providing care to patients who need their services and collaborating with NPs.

In summary, the NP has much to offer but, to practice fully, policy must change to make fewer restrictions, and organized medicine should embrace the NP's role as a valued member of the healthcare team.

REFERENCES

1. Pearson L. The Pearson Report: A national overview of nurse practitioner legislation and healthcare issues. *Am J Nurse Pract* 2007;11:10–101.

2. Jones DC, Mullinix CF, Pearson L, Gara N, Spock K. *Characteristics of the Practice Environment for Nurse Practitioners and Physician Assistants.* Washington, DC: Bureau of Health Professions (US), Health Resources and Services Administration; 1994.

3. Pearson L. The Pearson Report: A national overview of nurse practitioner legislation and healthcare issues. *Am J Nurse Pract* 2008;12:9–80.

4. Mezey M, McGivern D, Sullivan-Marx E, Greenberg SA. *Nurse Practitioners: Evolution of advanced practice.* (4th ed). New York, NY: Springer; 2003.

5. Council on Graduate Medical Education (COGME). Recommendations to Improve Access to Health Care through Physician Workforce Reform. Fourth Report. Washington, DC: Health Resources and Services Administration; 1994.

6. Institute of Medicine (US). *Primary Care: America's Health in a New Era.* Washington, DC: National Academy Press; 1996.

7. Aiken L, Fagin C. More nurses, better medicine: They need more authority for primary care. *The New York Times* 1993, Mar 11; Sect.A:19, A:23.

8. Knickman JR, Lipkin M, Finkler SA, Thompson WG, Kiel J. The potential for using non-physicians to compensate for the reduced availability of residents. *Acad Med* 1992;67:429–38.

9. Kelley T. 'Mid-level providers' can ease your capitation crunch. *Manag Care* 1994;3:19–24,26.

10. Terry K. How 'physician extenders' can strengthen your practice. *Med Econ* 1993;70:57–72.

11. Safriet DJ. Health care dollars and regulatory sense: The role of advanced practice nursing. *Yale J Regul* 1992;9:417–88.

12. Henderson T, Chovan T. *Removing Practice Barriers of Non-physician Providers: Efforts by States to Improve Access to Primary Care.* Washington, DC: Intergovernmental Health Policy Project, George Washington University; 1994.

13. American Medical Association Resolution 5 (A-07): A call to Improve the Physician Image and Solidify the Role of the Physician Amongst Alternative Health Care Providers. Available at: http://www.ama-assn.org/ama1/pub/upload/mm/15/a-0_mss_refcom.pdf. Accessed September 22, 2007.

14. Mundinger MO. Advanced-practice nursing—good medicine for physicians? *N Engl J Med* 1994;330:211–4.

15. Baer ED. Philosophical and Historical Bases of Advanced Practice Nursing Roles. In: *Nurses, Nurse Practitioners: Evolution to Advanced Practice.* Mezey MD, McGivern DO, editors. New York, NY: Springer Publishing Company, Inc.; 1999. p72–91.

16. AMA policy H-160.950 Guidelines for Integrated Practice of Physicians and Practitioners. Available at: http://www.ama-assn.org/ama1/pub/upload/mm/15/a-0_mss_refcom.pdf. Accessed January 23, 2008.

17. DeAngelis CD. Nurse practitioner redux. *JAMA* 1994;271:868–71.

18. Kassirer JP. What role for nurse practitioners in primary care? *N Engl J Med* 1994;330:204–5.

19. Cruikshank BM, Clow TJ. Physician supervision/collaboration as reported by PNPs in practice settings. *Pediatr Nurs* 1984;10:13–8.

20. Greene J. Concern raised over increasing role of nonphysicians. *American Medical News* 1999; Dec 6:8, 11.

21. Butler L. Nonphysicians gain clout. *Am Med News* 2000; 43:1,26.

22. Stone PW. Nurse practitioners' research review: Quality of care. Letter to the Editor. *Nurse Pract* 1994;19:17,21,27.

23. Mundinger MO, Kane RL, Lenz ER, et al. Primary care outcomes in patients treated by nurse practitioners and physicians: A randomized trial. *JAMA* 2000;283:59–68.

24. Lenz ER, Mundinger MO, Kane RL, Hopkins SC, Lin SX. Primary care outcomes in patients treated by nurse practitioners or physicians: Two year follow-up. *Med Care Res Rev* 2004;61:332–51.

25. Sox HC. Quality of patient care by nurse practitioners and physician's assistants: A ten-year perspective. *Ann Intern Med* 1979;91:459–68.

26. Office of Technology Assessment. *Nurse Practitioners, Physician Assistants, and Certified Nurse-Midwives: A Policy Analysis.* Health Technology Case Study 37. Washington; 1986.

27. Ventura MR, Feldman MJ, Crosby F. Information Synthesis: Effectiveness of Nurse Practitioners. Technical Report. Report No. IIR-82–005. Washington, DC: Veterans Administration Central Office; 1987.

28. Ventura MR, Crosby F. An information synthesis to evaluate nurse practitioner effectiveness. *Mil Med* 1991;156:286–91.

29. Crosby F, Ventura MR, Feldman MJ. Future research recommendations for establishing NP effectiveness. *Nurse Pract* 1987;12:75–9.

30. Feldman MJ, Ventura MR, Crosby F. Studies of nurse practitioner effectiveness. *Nurs Res* 1987;36:303–8.

31. Donabedian A. *The Definition of Quality and Approaches to Its Assessment. Explorations in Quality Assessment and Monitoring, Vol. 1.* Ann Arbor, MI: Health Administration Press; 1980.

32. Greenfield S. The state of outcome research: Are we on target? *N Engl J Med* 1989;320:1142–3.

33. Kassirer JP. The quality of care and the quality of measuring it. *N Engl J Med* 1993;329:1263–5.

34. Epstein A. Performance reports on quality–prototypes, problems, and prospects. *N Engl J Med* 1995;333:57–61.

35. Jennings BM, Staggers N, Brosch LR. A classification scheme for outcome indicators. *J Nurs Scholarsh* 1999;31:381–8.

36. Stanford D. Nurse practitioner research: Issues in practice and theory. *Nurse Pract* 1987;12:64–75.

37. Campbell JD, Niekirk HJ, Hosokawa MC. Development of a psychosocial concern index from videotaped interviews of nurse practitioners and family physicians. *J Fam Pract* 1990;30:321–6.

38. Avorn J, Everitt DE, Baker MW. The neglected medical history and therapeutic choices for abdominal pain: A nationwide study of 799 physicians and nurses. *Arch Intern Med* 1991;151:694–8.

39. Mahoney DF. Appropriateness of geriatric prescribing decisions made by nurse practitioners and physicians. *J Nurs Scholarsh* 1994;26:41–6.

40. LaRochelle DR. Research studies on nurse practitioners in ambulatory health care: A review 1980–1985. *J Ambul Care Manage* 1987;10:65–75.

41. Spitzer WO, Sackett DL, Sibley JC, et al. The Burlington randomized trial of the nurse practitioner. *N Engl J Med* 1974;290:251–6.

42. Rosenthal GE, Mettler G, Pare S, Riegger M, Ward M, Laudefeld CS. Diagnostic judgments of nurse practitioners providing primary gynecologic care: A quantitative analysis. *J Gen Intern Med* 1992;7:304–11.

43. Fain JA, Melkus GD. Nurse practitioners practice patterns based on standards of medical care for patients with diabetes. *Diabetes Care* 1994;17:879–81.

44. Brown SA, Grimes DE. *Nurse Practitioners and Certified Nurse-Midwives: A Meta-Analysis of Studies on Nurses in Primary Care Roles.* Washington, DC: American Nurses Publishing; 1993.

45. Sox HC. Independent primary care practice by nurse practitioners. *JAMA* 2000;283:106–8.

46. Herrick T. JAMA reports patient outcomes comparable for NPs, MDs: Study may signal shift in physician attitudes. *Clinician News* 2000 Jan; 1, 6–7.

47. Wilson IB, Landon BE, Hirschborn LR, et al. Quality of HIV care provided by nurse practitioners, physicians assistants and physicians. *Ann Intern Med* 2005;143:729–36.

11

PRIMARY CARE OUTCOMES IN PATIENTS TREATED BY NURSE PRACTITIONERS OR PHYSICIANS

A RANDOMIZED TRIAL

MARY O. MUNDINGER

ROBERT L. KANE

ELIZABETH R. LENZ

ANNETTE M. TOTTEN

WEI-YANN TSAI

PAUL D. CLEARY

WILLIAM T. FRIEDEWALD

ALBERT L. SIU

MICHAEL L. SHELANSKI

EDITORS' NOTE

This article reports on a rigorous study comparing the clinical outcomes of nurse practitioners and physicians in primary care by the former dean of the school of nursing at Columbia University, who opened a nurse-practitioner practice in midtown Manhattan where it competed with some of the leading medical practices in the nation. The study's conclusion was that the outcomes of care provided by nurse practitioners and physicians are comparable, supplying evidence to support removing barriers to the use of nurse practitioners in primary care. Its publication in the *Journal of the American Medical Association* enhanced the study's credibility and visibility.

■ ■ ■

The many pressures on the U.S. health care system and greater focus on health promotion and prevention have prompted debates about primary care workforce needs and the roles of various types of health care professionals. As nurse practitioners seek to define their niche in this environment, questions are often raised about their effectiveness and appropriate scope of practice. Several studies conducted during the last 2 decades[1-4] suggest the quality of primary care delivered by nurse practitioners is equal to that of physicians. However, these earlier studies did not directly compare nurse practitioners and physicians in primary care practices that were similar both in terms of responsibilities and patient panels.

Over time, payment policies and state nurse practice acts that constrained the roles of nurse practitioners have changed. In more than half the states, nurse practitioners now practice without any requirement for physician supervision or collaboration, and in all states nurse practitioners have some level of independent authority to prescribe drugs.[5] Additionally, nurse practitioners are now eligible for direct Medicaid reimbursement in every state, direct reimbursement for Medicare Part B services as part of the 1997 Balanced Budget Act,[6] and commercial insurance reimbursement for primary care services within limits of state law. Finally, state law determines whether nurse practitioners are eligible for hospital admitting privileges, either by regulating access at the state level or by allowing local hospital boards to decide. The combination of authority to prescribe drugs, direct reimbursement from most payers, and hospital admitting privileges creates a situation in which nurse practitioners and primary care physicians can have equivalent responsibilities. The present study is a large randomized trial designed to compare patient outcomes for nurse practitioners and physicians functioning equally as primary care providers.

The opportunity to compare the 2 types of providers was made possible by several practice and policy innovations at the Columbia Presbyterian Center of New York Presbyterian Hospital in New York City. In 1993 when the medical center sought to establish new primary care satellite clinics in the community, the nurse practitioner faculty were asked to staff 1 site independently for adult primary care. This exclusively nurse practitioner practice was to be similar to the clinics staffed by physicians. All are located in the same neighborhood, serve primarily families from the Dominican Republic who are eligible for Medicaid, and follow the policies and procedures of the medical center. The nurse practitioner practice, the Center for Advanced Practice, opened in the fall of 1994.

New York State law allows nurse practitioners to practice with a collaboration agreement that requires the physician to respond when the nurse practitioner seeks consultation. Collaboration does not require the collaborating physician to be on site and requires only quarterly meetings to review cases selected by the nurse practitioner and the physician. The state also grants nurse practitioners full authority to prescribe medications, as well as reimbursement by Medicaid at the same rate as physicians. The medical board granted nurse practitioners who were faculty members in the school of nursing hospital admitting privileges, thereby making the basic outpatient services, payment, and provider responsibilities the same in the nurse practitioner and physician primary care practices. Additionally, nurse practitioners and physicians in the study were subject to the same hospital policy on productivity and coverage, and a similar number of patients were scheduled per session in each clinic.

While it has been posited that nurse practitioners have a differentiated practice pattern focused on prevention with lengthier visits,[7] this study was purposely designed to compare nurse practitioners and physicians as primary care providers within a conventional medical care framework in the same medical center, where all other elements of care were identical. Nurse practitioners provided all ambulatory primary care, including 24-hour call, and made independent decisions for referrals to specialists and hospitalizations. The Spanish language ability of the nurse practitioners and physicians was similar, although the physicians had somewhat better Spanish facility on average. All of the nurse practitioners ($n = 7$) and most of the physicians ($n = 11$) had limited knowledge of Spanish, and 6 physicians were either fluent or bilingual. Staff who served as interpreters were available at each study site. The central hypothesis was that the selected outcomes would not differ between the patients of nurse practitioners and physicians.

METHODS

Participants and Randomization

Between August 1995 and October 1997, adult patients were recruited consecutively at 1 urgent care center and 2 emergency departments that are part of the medical center. Patients who reported a previous diagnosis of asthma, diabetes, and/or hypertension, regardless of the reason for the urgent visit, were oversampled to create a cohort of patients for whom primary care would have an impact on patient outcomes, as has been postulated in previous studies.[8,9] Patients were screened by bilingual patient recruiters and asked to participate if they had no current primary care provider at the time of recruitment and planned to be in the area for the next 6 months. The study was approved by the institutional review board of Columbia Presbyterian Medical Center. After an oral explanation of the consent form, written informed consent was obtained from each patient (both English and Spanish explanations and forms were available).

Those who provided informed consent were randomly and blindly assigned to either the nurse practitioner or 1 of the physician practices. Different assignment ratios were used during the recruitment period. Initially the ratio was 2:1, with more patients assigned to the nurse practitioner practice, because it opened after the physician practices and was able to accept more new patients. Subsequently, the ratio was changed to 1:1 as the nurse practitioner practice's patient panel increased. Despite this change, the mean number of days between the urgent visit at which patients were recruited and the follow-up appointments was similar (8.6 days for patients assigned to nurse practitioners compared with 8.9 days for patients assigned to physicians).

Recruited patients were then offered the next available appointments at the assigned clinic, and project staff made reminder calls the day before the appointments. Patients who missed their appointment were offered another appointment at the assigned practice. After patients kept their initial appointments, they were considered enrolled in the study and eligible for follow-up data collection.

Patients were told which provider group they were assigned to after randomization, and the type of provider could not be masked during the course of care. Patients who refused to participate or were deemed ineligible for the study were given follow-up primary care appointments by the study recruiters to the same practices. Additionally, during the study period, all practices received new patients from usual sources such as hospital discharges, recommendations from friends and family, referrals from other physicians, direct access by the patients themselves, and advertising. The study did not require a different process of care or documentation for enrolled patients.

At the initial visit, the patients became a part of the nurse practitioner or physician practices' regular patient panel, and all subsequent appointments, care, and treatments were arranged through the practice site of the assigned primary care nurse practitioner or physician. The primary care nurse practitioners and physicians had the same authority to prescribe, consult, refer, and admit patients. Furthermore, they used the same pool of specialists, inpatient units, and emergency departments. No attempt was made to differentiate study patients from other patients in the practice or to influence the practice patterns of the participating nurse practitioners and physicians. However, patients were free to change their source of medical care during the study. Medicaid in New York is currently fee-for-service and patients could go to other providers, go to a specialist directly, or use the emergency department without notifying their primary care provider. Approximately 3% of patients (n = 43) went to another clinic after keeping the first randomly assigned appointment, and 9% (n = 116) went to multiple primary care clinics during the 6-month period.

Data Collection

At the time of recruitment, patients provided demographic and contact information and completed the Medical Outcomes Study 36-Item Short-Form Health Survey (SF-36). After the initial primary care visit, interviewers contacted the enrolled patients either by telephone or in person, if necessary, to administer a satisfaction questionnaire. Six months after this initial appointment, the enrolled patients were again contacted and asked to complete a second, longer interview. The decision to interview patients 6 months after the initial primary care visit was based on prior survey experience with this patient population.[10]

The primary care patients served by the medical center are primarily immigrants and frequently change residences, travel between New York and their countries of origin, and have interruptions in telephone service. Attempts were made to locate all enrolled patients for this follow-up, including those who could not be located for the initial satisfaction interview. At the 6-month interview, the SF-36 and the satisfaction questionnaire were repeated, and additional questions were asked about health services utilization. A research nurse accompanied the interviewers, and for patients who reported a diagnosis of asthma, diabetes, or hypertension, physiologic data were collected.

Data on all health services utilization at the assigned practice and all other medical center sites were obtained from the medical center computer records for both the 6 months prior to recruitment and for 6 months and 1 year after the initial primary care appointment. These data were collected for all patients who were enrolled, including those who could not be located for the 6-month follow-up interview. Utilization data were also available for patients who were recruited but who did not keep their initial primary care appointment and therefore were not enrolled in the study. For these patients, the data were collected for the 6 months prior to recruitment and 6 months and 1 year after the date of the missed appointment they were given at recruitment.

Main Outcome Measures

The SF-36 was used as a baseline and follow-up measure of health status. This instrument elicits patient responses to 36 questions designed to measure 8 health concepts (general health, physical function, role-physical, role-emotional, social function, bodily pain, vitality, and mental health)[11] or to create 2 summary scores (physical component summary and mental component summary).[12] The origin and logic of the item selection, as well as the psychometrics and tests of clinical validity, have been reported by the survey's developers.[13,14] Additionally, the survey's utility for monitoring general and specific populations, measuring treatment benefits, and comparing the burden of different diseases has been documented in 371 studies published between 1988 and 1996.[15,16] For example, the SF-36 has been used to measure differences in function between chronically ill patients with and without comorbid anxiety disorder;[17] has demonstrated that it can detect changes in health status that correspond to clinical profiles for 4 common conditions;[18] and has shown that it reflects changes in health status that correspond to a predicted clinical course for elective surgery patients.[19]

Patient satisfaction was measured by using "provider-specific" items from a 15-item satisfaction questionnaire used in the Medical Outcomes Study.[20] Three items related to clinic management were included in the survey to provide the medical center administration with information about patients' perceptions of the clinic, but those items were not intended for use in the comparison of providers.

The survey instruments used in the study were written in English and then translated into Spanish. The bilingual members of the study team reviewed the Spanish versions to ensure that the meaning had not been changed. Approximately 80% (78.8% at recruitment and 83.7% at 6 months) of the interviews were conducted in Spanish.

Physiologic measures included disease-specific clinical measurements taken by a research nurse at the time of the 6-month follow-up interview. Blood pressure was determined for patients with hypertension, peak flow for those with asthma, and glycosylated hemoglobin for those with diabetes.

Utilization data included hospitalizations, emergency department visits, urgent care center visits, visits to specialists, and primary care visits within the Columbia Presbyterian Medical Center system. Only visits with a nurse practitioner or physician at a primary care site were counted as primary care. Specialty visits were defined as visits to a medical specialty clinic or specialist physician office. Emergency department and urgent care center visits were combined before analysis.

Sample Size

Recruitment and enrollment goals were established based on estimates of the sample size needed to detect a difference of 5 points on a 100-point scale for the SF-36 scores on all scales when comparing 2 groups with repeated measures. As the randomization ratio was projected to change during the course of the study with availability of appointments, it was projected that the final ratio between the 2 groups would be 1 patient in the physician group for every 1.5 patients in the nurse practitioner group. The sample size estimates for unequal groups were extrapolated from those presented by the instrument's developer for equal groups, assuming $\alpha = .05$, 2-tailed t test, and power of 80%. Differences of more than 5 points are considered clinically and socially relevant, according to the guidelines for the interpretation of the survey.[11]

Analysis

Baseline demographics and health status for the nurse practitioner and physician groups at randomization and following enrollment were compared using χ^2 and t tests. Ten of the 12 satisfaction questions were factor analyzed (the 11th question that asks whether the patient would recommend the clinic to family and friends was left as a separate item; an item about medication instructions was dropped, as it was not applicable to the majority of respondents who were not prescribed any medications at their first visit). There were 3 factors with eigenvalues greater than 1, indicating that they represented reasonable constructs. The first, "provider attributes" (Cronbach $\alpha = .80$) rated the provider on technical skills, personal manner, and time spent with the patient on a 5-point scale from poor to excellent. "Overall satisfaction" (Cronbach $\alpha = .86$) was the factor created from 2 items addressing the quality of care received and overall satisfaction with the visit. The "communications" factor (Cronbach $\alpha = .59$) combined 5 areas in which patients may have had problems understanding the provider's assessment and advice. Mean scores were computed for each factor.

Using the data collected at recruitment, mean baseline scores on the SF-36 for the scales and summary scores were used to establish the comparability of the nurse practitioner and physician groups in terms of health status. Four types of analyses were conducted using the SF-36 as an outcome measure. The first 2 included t tests to compare mean scores for nurse practitioner and physician patients at 6-month follow-up (both unadjusted and adjusted for baseline demographics and health status) and baseline to 6-month change scores. The third was a subgroup analysis designed to compare the sickest patients. Patients whose baseline score on the physical component summary of the SF-36 was in the bottom quartile (sickest) of the study sample were selected, and 6-month follow-up SF-36 scores were compared using the same analyses used for the total sample.

The fourth analysis classified patients into categories according to the change from baseline to follow-up in each patient's individual scores on the summary measures. This analysis was modeled on a comparison of patients treated in health maintenance organization and fee-for-service systems.[21] The SE of measurement was used to create 3 categories: "same" (change not greater than what would be expected by chance), "better" (improved more than expected), and "worse" (declined more than expected).[12] While these definitions are based on a statistical construct, they provide results that may be more clinically relevant than mean scores or mean change in scores over time. A χ^2 test was then used to compare the distribution of the nurse practitioner and physician patients among these groups. In addition, the change from baseline to follow-up for the entire sample was compared using paired t tests.

Ranges and mean values for the physiologic measures were obtained, and mean values for the 2 groups were compared using t tests.

For the analyses of health services utilization, data were obtained for 6 months prior to the date of recruitment, 6 months after, and 1 year after the first primary care visit. Neither the recruitment visit nor the assigned primary care visit was included. Comparisons between the nurse practitioner and physician patients' health services utilization after enrollment were made using χ^2 tests (unadjusted) and Poisson regression (adjusted). To compare the utilization prior to recruitment with that following, signed rank tests were used.

The 159 patients (12.1%) who, after the first visit, either went to a clinic other than the one assigned or to multiple primary care clinics were maintained in the initially assigned group for the analyses, consistent with an intent-to-treat analysis. All analyses were repeated without these 159 patients, and the results were the same.

RESULTS

Recruitment, Enrollment, and Loss to Follow-up

Of the 3397 patients screened and given follow-up appointments, 41.6% were not randomized because they either refused to participate (11.2%) or did not meet the screening criteria (30.4%). Of the 1981 patients who were randomized, 1181 (59.6%) were assigned to the nurse practitioner clinic and 800 (40.4%) to the physician clinics. The average age of the randomized patients was 44.4 years and 74.6% were female; 84.9% were Hispanic, 8.8% were black, and 1.1% were white. There were no statistically significant differences in the demographics or health status of the patients randomized to nurse practitioners or physicians (Table 1).

The 1316 patients (66.4%) who kept their initial primary care appointments following randomization were considered enrolled in the study. This rate is comparable to the normal rate of appointments (65%) kept at the participating clinics (P. Craig, MA, RN, e-mail message, August 4, 1999). Compared with the 665 patients (32.4%) who did not keep their appointments, those who did (the enrolled patients) differed significantly at baseline in several respects. Enrolled patients were older (45.9 vs. 41.3 years); a higher

TABLE 11.1. Randomized and Enrolled Patient Characteristics at Baseline*

	Randomized Patients				Enrolled Patients			
	Nurse Practitioner Group (n = 1181)	Physician Group (n = 800)	Comparison	P Value	Nurse Practitioner Group (n = 806)	Physician Group (n = 510)	Comparison	P Value
Mean age, y	44.0	44.9	$t = 1.347$	.18	45.5	46.7	$t = 1.324$	.19
Female sex, %	74.2	75.3	$\chi^2 = 0.291$	.59	75.9	78.2	0.932	.33
Race, %								
Hispanic	88.2	87.3			91.0	89.3		
Black	8.3	10.4	$\chi^2 = 6.853$	.14	5.5	8.1	$\chi^2 = 5.675$	.23
White	1.3	0.9			1.5	0.8		
Other	1.8	1.4			1.7	1.8		
Unknown	0.4	0.0			0.3	0.0		
Mean No. of days between recruitment and initial appointment	8.6	8.9	$t = 0.478$	.63	7.9	7.5	$t = -0.709$	.48
Prevalence of selected chronic conditions, % of patients reporting each condition								
Asthma	20.2	17.6	$\chi^2 = 2.10$	.15	17.9	16.1	$\chi^2 = 0.702$	.40
Diabetes	10.2	11.8	$\chi^2 = 1.25$	.26	11.5	14.3	$\chi^2 = 2.183$	.14
Hypertension	30.0	34.1	$\chi^2 = 3.79$	.05	33.9	38.0	$\chi^2 = 2.371$	.12
MOS SF-36 subscale scores, mean								
Physical functioning	63.1	61.5	$t = -1.27$	.21	61.4	59.2	$t = -1.347$	.18
Role-physical	40.1	39.0	$t = -0.554$	.58	38.0	34.5	$t = -1.402$	.16
Bodily pain	44.5	44.6	$t = 0.032$	.98	44.0	43.2	$t = -0.416$	.68
General health	44.5	45.8	$t = 1.097$	.27	43.7	43.4	$t = -0.211$	.83
Vitality	48.4	48.3	$t = -0.016$	.99	47.8	46.7	$t = -0.827$	.41
Social functioning	60.0	60.0	$t = -0.074$	.94	59.3	57.8	$t = -0.979$	.33
Role-emotional	48.5	47.4	$t = -0.505$	.61	46.9	42.3	$t = -1.694$	.09
Mental health	55.0	55.7	$t = 0.603$	.55	54.6	53.7	$t = -0.608$	.54
Summary scores								
Physical component	38.4	38.0	$t = -0.637$	.52	37.9	37.2	$t = -1.041$	.30
Mental component	41.3	41.4	$t = 0.222$	.83	41.1	40.2	$t = -1.135$	.26

*MOS SF-36 indicates Medical Outcomes Study Short-Form 36.

proportion were female (76.8% vs. 70.2%) and Hispanic (90.3% vs. 82.9%); a higher percentage reported a history of 1 or more of the selected chronic conditions (53.7% vs. 45.0%); and they had to wait fewer days for their follow-up appointments (7.8 vs. 10.7). These findings are consistent with other studies of patient behavior relative to keeping or missing appointments.[22–24]

Our analysis of the data available on patients who did not keep their primary care appointments found no differences in health services utilization after 1 year among the patients assigned to the nurse practitioner group and physician group.

The difference in the retention rates between recruitment and enrollment for the nurse practitioner group (68.2%) and the physician group (63.8%) was statistically significant ($\chi^2_1 = 4.3$, $P = .04$). However, neither the patients who enrolled nor those who failed to keep their appointments differed significantly between the nurse practitioner and physician groups in terms of baseline demographics, SF-36 scores, or patient-reported prior diagnosis of the selected chronic conditions (Table 11.1).

Among the nurse practitioner patients, 59% saw the same provider for all primary care visits in the first year after the initial visits compared with 54% of the physician patients, and this difference was not statistically significant ($\chi^2_1 = 2.7$, $P = .11$).

Initial satisfaction interviews were completed for 90.3% (n = 1188) of all patients who made a first clinic visit (90.8% of the nurse practitioner group and 89.4% of the physician group). Almost 92% of all completed interviews took place within 6 weeks of the initial appointment.

Six-month interviews were completed for 79% of all enrolled patients (80.5% of the nurse practitioner group and 76.7% the physician group). This completion rate is considered high for a transient immigrant population and is comparable to or better than that achieved by other studies in the area served by the medical center. The majority of completed interviews (91.4%) took place between 180 and 240 days after the initial appointment. The most common reasons for loss to follow-up were the inability to locate the patient (65.9%) or that the patient had moved out of the area (17%). A small number of patients (23 [2.8%] in the nurse practitioner group and 16 [3.1%] in the physician group) refused to complete the interview when they were contacted. Five patients (2.9%) were located but were unable to complete the interview due to physical limitations or mental illness, and 3 patients (1.1%) were deceased. The Figure summarizes the participation rates at each major stage in the study.

Satisfaction

There were no significant differences in the scores between nurse practitioners and physicians for any of the satisfaction factors after the first visit (Table 11.2). At the 6-month interview there were no statistically significant differences in "overall satisfaction" or "communications" factors or in willingness to refer the clinic to others. The difference in mean score for the "provider attributes" factor, however, was significant, with the physician group rating providers higher than the nurse practitioner group (4.22 vs. 4.12 out of a possible 5; $P = .05$). The provider attribute consists of patients' ratings of the providers' technical skill, personal manner, and time spent with the patient. The clinical significance of a 0.1 difference on a 5.0 scale is unlikely.

FIGURE 11.1. *Study Profile*

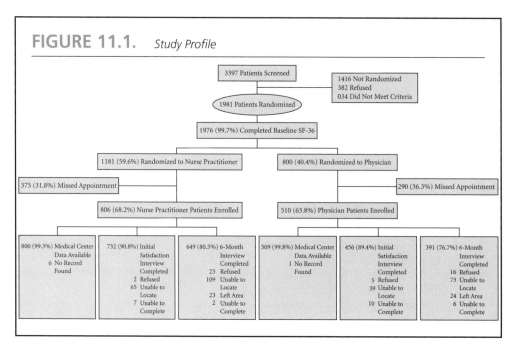

SF-36 indicates Medical Outcomes Study 36-item Short-Form Health Survey.

Self-reported Health Status

Overall, the health status of the study group improved from baseline to follow-up, and the improvement was statistically significant on every scale (Table 11.3).

There were no significant differences between the nurse practitioner and physician patients on any scale or summary score at 6 months. This is true for both the unadjusted scores and scores adjusted for demographics and baseline health status. The additional analysis (not shown) of the summary scores, using the change categories of "same," "better," and "worse" to characterize the clinical course of each patient, also revealed no significant differences between provider types.

Finally, 152 nurse practitioner patients and 103 physician patients were defined as the sickest (health status scores in the bottom quartile of the sample at baseline) and their scores analyzed separately. Again, there were no differences between nurse practitioner and physician patients in scale scores or summary measures at 6 months (both unadjusted and adjusted), nor did the change in scores from baseline to follow-up differ between nurse practitioner and physician patient groups.

Physiologic Measures

The physiologic measures taken at the time of the interview for patients who reported 1 of the selected chronic illnesses were not statistically significantly different between the nurse practitioner and physician patients for asthma and hypertension. The mean peak flow

TABLE 11.2. Patient Satisfaction: Initial Visit and 6-Month Follow-up Interviews

	Initial Visit				6-Month Follow-up			
	Nurse Practitioner Group (n = 726)	Physician Group (n = 453)	Comparison	P Value	Nurse Practitioner Group (n = 644)	Physician Group (n = 389)	Comparison	P Value
Provider attributes mean score*	4.16	4.19	t = 0.815	.42	4.12	4.22	t = 1.963	.05
Overall satisfaction mean score*	4.59	4.60	t = 0.144	.89	4.45	4.46	t = 0.161	.87
Problems, % of patients reporting [†]								
0	74.4	70.2			59.1	62.7		
1	15.4	18.7	χ^2 = 2.605	.46	25.1	23.5	χ^2 = 2.146	.54
2	6.5	7.2			10.2	7.8		
3–5	3.7	3.9			5.6	5.9		
% of patients who would recommend clinic to others	98.7	98.2	χ^2 = 0.544	.46	95.0	95.1	χ^2 = 0.000	.99

*Calculated from items rated on a 5-point scale, in which 5 is the most positive response.
[†]Percentages may not add to 100% due to rounding.

217

TABLE 11.3. Health Status Based on MOS SF-36 Results*

	Comparison of Baseline and 6-Month Scores for Entire Sample (n = 1040)			6-Month Scores for Nurse Practitioner Group (n = 649) and Physician Group (n = 391)					
				Unadjusted Mean Scores			Adjusted Mean Scores†		
	Baseline	6 mo	Change (Paired t tests)‡	Nurse Practitioner Group	Physician Group	Comparison	Nurse Practitioner Group	Physician Group	Comparison§
Physical functioning	60.30	64.26	$t = 4.631$	64.94	62.90	$t = -1.126$ $P = .26$	64.21	63.78	$t = 0.394$ $P = .77$
Role-physical	36.06	53.31	$t = 10.519$	53.74	52.62	$t = -0.375$ $P = .71$	52.92	53.38	$t = -0.192$ $P = .85$
Bodily pain	42.74	53.01	$t = 9.133$	53.66	52.07	$t = -0.748$ $P = .45$	52.91	52.73	$t = 0.092$ $P = .93$
General health	42.94	48.75	$t = 7.662$	48.79	48.67	$t = -0.070$ $P = .95$	48.42	49.04	$t = -0.454$ $P = .65$
Vitality	47.02	53.45	$t = -7.771$	53.86	52.79	$t = -0.635$ $P = .53$	53.27	53.38	$t = -0.072$ $P = .94$
Social functioning	58.51	70.47	$t = 12.507$	70.39	70.59	$t = 0.114$ $P = .91$	70.25	70.70	$t = -0.279$ $P = .78$
Role-emotional	44.70	56.26	$t = 7.105$	56.71	55.24	$t = -0.488$ $P = .63$	55.81	56.34	$t = -0.192$ $P = .85$
Mental health	53.51	60.17	$t = 8.177$	60.75	59.45	$t = -0.742$ $P = .46$	60.37	59.63	$t = 0.491$ $P = .62$
Physical component summary	37.46	40.63	$t = 8.706$	40.83	40.29	$t = -0.728$ $P = .47$	40.53	40.60	$t = -0.102$ $P = .92$
Mental component summary	40.56	44.58	$t = 9.438$	44.64	44.29	$t = -0.398$ $P = .69$	44.55	44.48	$t = 0.103$ $P = .92$

*MOS SF-36 indicates Medical Outcomes Short-Form 36.

†Adjusted for age, sex, baseline MOS subscale scores, and each selected chronic condition.

‡P values for change are all $<.001$.

§Adjusted t test is based on a regression model, with age, sex, baseline MOS subscale scores, and each condition entered as covariates.

measurements for the 64 physician patients with asthma was 292 L/min, compared with 297 L/min for the 107 nurse practitioner patients (t test = –0.29, P = .77). Glycosylated hemoglobin mean value for the 46 physician patients with diabetes was 9.4% vs. 9.5% for the 58 nurse practitioner patients (t test = –0.22, P = .82).

For patients with hypertension, there was no statistically significant difference in the systolic reading: 139 mm Hg for the 145 physician patients and 137 mm Hg for the 211 nurse practitioner patients (t test = 1.08, P = .28). The mean diastolic reading, however, was statistically significantly lower for the nurse practitioner patients at 82 mm Hg compared with 85 mm Hg for the physician patients (t test = 2.09, P = .04).

Utilization

For our comparison of outcomes we analyzed utilization of health care services for nurse practitioner and physician patients who enrolled in the study by keeping their initial primary care appointment. There were no statistically significant differences between the nurse practitioner and physician patients for any category of service during either the first 6 months or the first year after the initial primary care visit for either unadjusted or adjusted use rates (Table 11.4). When the utilization analyses were repeated for the subsets of "sickest" patients as defined in the "Self-reported Health Status" section above, no differences were found in the health care services utilization between the nurse practitioner and physician patients (Table 11.5). In the 6 months and 1 year after the initial primary care visit, enrolled patients in both groups made significantly more primary care and specialty visits and fewer emergency/urgent visits than in the 6 months prior to recruitment. The percentage of enrolled patients hospitalized was not significantly different for either 6 months or 1 year after the initial primary care appointment.

COMMENT

This study was designed to compare the effectiveness of nurse practitioners with physicians where both were serving as primary care providers in the same environment with the same authority. The hypothesis predicting similar patient outcomes was strongly supported by the findings of no significant differences in self-reported health status, 2 of the 3 disease-specific physiologic measures, all but 1 of the patient satisfaction factors after 6 months of primary care, and in health services utilization at 6 months and 1 year.

The difference between the nurse practitioner and physician patients' mean ratings of satisfaction with provider attributes was small but statistically significant. It may be attributable to the fact that the nurse practitioner practice was moved to a new site after 2 years and before recruitment and data collection were completed; the physician practices were not moved during the study period. When the "provider attribute" subscale scores for the nurse practitioner and physician patients whose 6-month follow-up period overlapped this move were compared, the ratings by nurse practitioner patients were significantly lower than those of the corresponding physician patients (4.16 vs. 4.36; P = .04). There was no significant difference in ratings among patients not affected by the move. Additional research will be needed to determine whether this is a persistent difference or if it results from conditions unique to this study.

TABLE 11.4. Health Services Utilization*

	Change for Entire Sample, %			6 Months After Initial Primary Care Visit, %			1 Year After Initial Primary Care Visit, %		
	6 mo Prior (N = 1309)	6 mo After (N = 1309)	Change, z Score†	Nurse Practitioner Group (n = 800)	Physician Group (n = 509)	Comparison	Nurse Practitioner Group (n = 800)	Physician Group (n = 509)	Comparison
Primary care visits									
0	88.8	21.2	-26.809	20.6	22.2	$\chi^2 = 0.059$ $P = .81$	18.0	19.1	$\chi^2 = 1.033$ $P = .31$
1	5.7	22.4		22.6	22.0		18.4	16.1	
2	2.9	17.3		18.0	16.3		13.8	13.4	
3	2.6	13.8		14.5	12.8		10.3	8.8	
4	0	9.8		9.6	10.0		9.3	8.8	
5	0	6.1		5.3	7.5		7.5	6.1	
≥6	0	9.3		9.4	9.2		22.9	27.7	
Specialty visits									
0	89.1	62.3	-15.578	61.8	63.1	$\chi^2 = 0.678$ $P = .41$	54.5	54.8	$\chi^2 = 0.265$ $P = .61$
1	5.6	14.2		13.3	15.7		13.9	16.5	
2	2.3	9.3		10.8	7.1		8.9	6.3	
≥3	3.1	14.2		14.3	14.1		22.8	22.4	
ED and urgent care									
0	58.1	76.5	-12.937	77.4	75.0	$\chi^2 = 0.428$ $P = .51$	65.8	66.2	$\chi^2 = 0.286$ $P = .59$
1	16.4	16.2		15.3	17.7		20.4	17.7	
2	16.4	4.0		4.3	3.7		7.4	8.6	
≥3	9.1	3.3		3.1	3.5		6.5	7.5	
Hospitalizations									
0	94.5	95.3	-0.884 $P = .38$	95.9	94.3	$\chi^2 = 1.703$ $P = .19$	91.5	90.2	$\chi^2 = 0.664$ $P = .42$
≥1	5.5	4.7		4.1	5.7		8.5	9.8	

*Percentage may not add to 100% due to rounding. ED indicates emergency department.
†Except for hospitalizations, $P < .001$ for column.

TABLE 11.5.   **Subgroup Analyses***

SF-36 Subscales	Nurse Practitioner Group (n = 152)	Physician Group (n = 103)	Comparison
**6-Month MOS SF-36 Scores for the Sickest Patients, Mean (SD)[†]**			
Physical functioning	46.69 (27.05)	48.17 (27.46)	$t = 0.425$ $P = .67$
Role-physical	33.55 (42.88)	32.28 (43.53)	$t = -0.231$ $P = .82$
Bodily pain	38.10 (29.72)	39.25 (29.36)	$t = 0.306$ $P = .76$
General health	38.06 (23.02)	37.08 (23.48)	$t = -0.333$ $P = .74$
Vitality	43.06 (25.21)	42.43 (25.14)	$t = -0.197$ $P = .84$
Social functioning	62.67 (28.87)	60.56 (29.33)	$t = -0.568$ $P = .57$
Role-emotional	42.39 (47.25)	43.04 (47.06)	$t = 0.109$ $P = .91$
Mental health	52.56 (28.11)	50.92 (52.47)	$t = -4.77$ $P = .63$
Physical component summary	23.71 (3.12)	23.84 (3.58)	$t = 0.293$ $P = .77$
Mental component summary	39.57 (13.35)	40.39 (12.70)	$t = 0.490$ $P = .63$

Health Services Utilization for the Subgroup of "Sicker Patients " No. (%)

	(n = 151)	(n = 101)	
Primary care visits			
0	30 (19.9)	17 (16.8)	
1	31 (20.5)	21 (20.8)	$\chi^2 = 0.144$
2	27 (17.9)	21 (20.8)	$P = .71$
≥3	63 (41.7)	42 (41.6)	
Specialty visits			
0	82 (54.3)	56 (55.4)	$\chi^2 = 0.390$
1	23 (15.2)	21 (20.8)	$P = .53$
2	20 (13.2)	8 (7.9)	
≥3	26 (17.2)	16 (15.8)	

(continued)

TABLE 11.5.   **Continued**

SF-36 Subscales	Nurse Practitioner Group (n = 152)	Physician Group (n = 103)	Comparison
Health Services Utilization for the Subgroup of "Sicker Patients " No. (%)			
	(n = 151)	(n = 101)	
ED and urgent care center visits			
0	108 (71.5)	79 (78.2)	
1	28 (18.5)	17 (16.8)	$\chi^2 = 1.81$
2	9 (6.0)	2 (2.0)	$P = .18$
≥3	6 (4.0)	3 (3.0)	
Hospitalizations			
0	142 (94.0)	99 (96.1)	
1	7 (4.6)	3 (2.9)	$\chi^2 = 0.542$
2	1 (0.7)	1 (1.0)	$P = .46$
3	1 (0.7)	0 (0)	

*Percentages may not add to 100% due to rounding. MOS SF-36 indicates Medical Outcomes Study Short-Form 36; ED, emergency department.
†Selection of "sickest patients" was determined using MOS SF-36 scores using the bottom quartile of the baseline physical component summary. Patients with a score below 28.16 were included.

A statistically significant, but small, difference was discerned in the mean diastolic blood pressure of patients with hypertension, with the nurse practitioner group having a slightly lower average reading at 6 months. Given the size of this change and the lack of differences in self-reported health status, there does not seem to be an obvious reason for this difference.

Although insufficient statistical power to discern differences has been a problem in much of the previous research comparing nurse practitioners and physicians, the sample size in this study was adequate to test the hypothesized similarity of nurse practitioner and physician groups. At the end of the study, power calculations were repeated using final sample size and the means and SDs from these data. These revealed that the sample size was adequate to detect differences from baseline to follow-up between the 2 patient groups of less than 5 points for 6 of the 8 scales (3.2 for general health; 3.3 for vitality; 3.4 for mental health; 3.4 for social function; and 4.2 for bodily pain) and less than 6 points on 2 scales (5.9 on role-physical and role-emotional). This magnitude of difference is similar to differences commonly reported in studies comparing groups[21,25] and in studies of change over time within 1 group.[17,26]

There is evidence that the outcome measures chosen were sensitive enough to discern any important differences. The SF-36 is a widely used outcome measure and its sensitivity has been documented in several studies.[11,18,27] In this study, there were sizable and statistically significant changes for both nurse practitioner and physician patients in all scale scores and summary measures from baseline to follow-up. Some improvement would be expected, even over a 6-month period with or without primary care, following the urgent care visits at which subject recruitment occurred; the SF-36 did detect improvement. The utilization indicators are in widespread use in cross-sectional and longitudinal studies. With the exception of number of hospitalizations, which stayed the same in both groups, these measures also changed significantly over time.

Strengths of this study included adequate sample size and the ability to randomize patients to equivalent clinical settings and to providers with equal responsibilities. However, there were also several limitations.

Patients could not be randomized at the point of initial contact with the provider. Because the nurse practitioner and physician practice sites were geographically separate, patients had to be randomized when they were recruited in the emergency department or urgent care center to give them follow-up appointments at various locations with different appointment schedules. This time and location gap likely contributed to the loss of almost one third of the sample between randomization and enrollment. Although this is substantial, it is within the range reported in similar randomized trials.[28]

While the loss rate was significantly different for the nurse practitioner and physician groups, there is no reason to suspect that this represents a systematic violation of the protocol or any compromise of randomization. Patients dropped out before receiving care, and the dropout rate was higher for those assigned to the traditional model of physician care. This suggests that assignment to the new model of nurse practitioner care did not negatively influence patient behavior. There is no evidence of selection bias in that there were no significant differences in demographics, baseline health status, or prerecruitment health services utilization patterns between nurse practitioner and physician randomized patients, for either those who enrolled or those who did not keep their appointments.

A 1-year follow-up for SF-36 and patient satisfaction would have been more useful than taking these measures at 6 months. In part, we believed a population with limited access to health care would show changes in these measures in 6 months. But more influential in the decision regarding follow-up was the knowledge that this population is difficult to track because of changing addresses, changing eligibility for Medicaid, and frequent extended trips out of the country. Although we do have service utilization data for both 6 months and 1 year, data on satisfaction and self-perceived health status were not collected for 1 year.

Finally, the study had some characteristics that limit the generalizability of results. It was conducted in medical center–affiliated, community-based primary care clinics, which may differ from individual providers or small group practices. The providers were faculty from a university medical center, hence were not necessarily typical of those in nonacademic practice settings. The patients were predominantly immigrants from the Dominican Republic who were eligible for Medicaid and many did not speak English. This differs from the setting in which many commercially insured patients receive primary care but does resemble other academic, public and safety net providers, and the Medicaid populations they serve. While the setting and patient population are limitations, they are also what permitted randomized assignment and an environment in which nurse practitioners and physicians were able to function equally as primary care providers. The ability to do this type of study, even in a setting atypical for some patients, adds significant weight to the results from prior studies that have demonstrated the competence of nurse practitioners.

Who provides primary care is an important policy question. As nurse practitioners gain in authority nationally with commercially insured and Medicare populations now accessing nurse practitioner care, additional research should include these populations. As cost and quality issues pervade the public debate on managed care, those who are the first-line health care providers become pivotal resources in the emerging health care system. Nurse practitioners have been evaluated as primary care providers for more than 25 years, but until now no evaluations studied nurse practitioners and physicians in comparable practices using a large-scale, randomized design. The results of this study strongly support the hypothesis that, using the traditional medical model of primary care, patient outcomes for nurse practitioner and physician delivery of primary care do not differ.

Funding/Support: Grant support for this study was received from the Division of Nursing, Health Resources and Services Administration, U.S. Department of Health and Human Services; The Fan Fox and Leslie R. Samuels Foundation; and the New York State Department of Health.

NOTES

1. Spitzer WO, Sackett DL, Sibley JC, et al. The Burlington randomized trial of the nurse practitioner. *N Engl J Med.* 1974;290:251–256.

2. Brown SA, Grimes DE. A meta-analysis of nurse practitioners and nurse midwives in primary care. *Nurs Res.* 1995;44:332–339.

3. US Congress, Office of Technology Assessment. *Nurse Practitioners, Physician Assistants, and Certified Nurse-Midwives: A Policy Analysis.* Washington, DC: US Government Printing Office; 1986. Health Technology Case Study 37.

4. Safriet BJ. Health care dollars and regulatory sense. *Yale J Regul.* 1992;9:417–488.

5. Pearson LJ. Annual update of how each state stands on legislative issues affecting advanced nursing practice. *Nurse Pract.* 1999;24:16–19, 23–24, 27–30.

6. The Balanced Budget Act of 1997, Pub L No. 105–33.

7. Mundinger MO. Advanced-practice nursing—good medicine for physicians? *N Engl J Med.* 1994; 330:211–214.

8. Bindman AB, Grumbach K, Osmond D, et al. Preventable hospitalizations and access to health care. *JAMA.* 1995;274:305–311.

9. Billings J, Anderson GM, Newman LS. Recent findings on preventable hospitalizations. *Health Aff (Millwood).* 1996;15:239–249.

10. Garfield R, Broe D, Albano B. The role of academic medical centers in delivery of primary care 1995. *Acad Med.* 1995;70:405–409.

11. Ware JE Jr, Snow K, Kosinski M, Gandek B. *SF-36 Health Survey: Manual & Interpretation Guide.* Boston, Mass: New England Medical Center; 1993.

12. Ware JE Jr, Snow K, Kosinski M, Gandek B. *SF-36 Physical and Mental Health Summary Scales: A User's Manual.* Boston, Mass: The Health Institute, New England Medical Center; 1994.

13. Ware JE Jr, Sherbourne CD. The MOS 36-Item Short-Form Health Survey (SF-36), I: conceptual framework and item selection. *Med Care.* 1992;30:473–483.

14. McHorney CA, Ware JE Jr, Raczek AE. The MOS 36-Item Short-Form Health Survey (SF-36), II: psychometric and clinical tests of validity in measuring physical and mental health constructs. *Med Care.* 1993; 31:247–263.

15. Shiely JC, Bayliss M, Keller S, Tsai C, Ware JE Jr. *SF-36 Health Survey Annotated Bibliography: First Edition* (1988–1995). Boston, Mass: The Health Institute, New England Medical Center; 1996.

16. Tsai C, Bayliss M, Ware JE Jr. *SF-36 Survey Annotated Bibliography: 1996 Supplement*. Boston, Mass: New England Medical Center; 1997.

17. Sherbourne CD, Wells KB, Meredith LS, Jackson CA, Camp P. Comorbid anxiety disorder and the functioning and well-being of chronically ill patients of general medical providers. *Arch Gen Psychiatry*. 1996; 53:889–895.

18. Garratt AM, Ruta DA, Abdalla MI, Russell IT. SF-36 health survey questionnaire, II: responsiveness to changes in health status in four common clinical conditions. *Qual Health Care*. 1994;3:186–192.

19. Mangione CM, Goldman L, Orav EJ, et al. Health-related quality of life after elective surgery. *J Gen Intern Med*. 1997;12:686–697.

20. Rubin HR, Gandek B, Rogers WH, Kosinski M, McHorney CA, Ware JE Jr. Patients' ratings of outpatient visits in different practice settings: results from the Medical Outcomes Study. *JAMA*. 1993;270:835–840.

21. Ware JE Jr, Bayliss MS, Rogers WH, Kosinski M, Tarlov AR. Differences in 4-year health outcomes for elderly and poor, chronically ill patients treated in HMO and fee-for-service systems. *JAMA*. 1996;276:1039–1047.

22. Deyo RA, Inui TS. Dropouts and broken appointments: a literature review and agenda for future research. *Med Care*. 1980;18:1146–1157.

23. Vikander T, Parnicky K, Demers R, Frisof K, Demers P, Chase N. New-patient no-shows in an urban family practice center. *J Fam Pract*. 1986;22:263–268.

24. Dockerty JD. Outpatient clinic nonarrivals and cancellations. *N Z Med J*. 1992;105:147–149.

25. Kusek JW, Lee JY, Smith DE, et al. Effect of blood pressure control and antihypertensive drug regimen on quality of life. *Control Clin Trials*. 1996;17(suppl 4):40S–46S.

26. Temple PC, Travis B, Sachs L, Strasser S, Choban P, Flancbaum L. Functioning and well-being of patients before and after elective surgical procedures. *J Am Coll Surg*. 1995;181:17–25.

27. Kopjar B. The SF-36 health survey: a valid measure of changes in health status after injury. *Inj Prev*. 1996;2:135–139.

28. Bertakis KD, Callahan EJ, Helms LJ, Azari R, Robbins JA, Miller J. Physician practice styles and patient outcomes. *Med Care*. 1998;36:879–891.

ACKNOWLEDGMENT

This study would not have been possible without the cooperation of the management, site administrators, patient representatives, and providers (nurse practitioners and physicians) of the Ambulatory Care Network Corporation at New York Presbyterian Hospital. Members of the faculty at the School of Nursing participated in the early development of both the Nurse Practitioner Practice and the Evaluation Study. These include Richard Garfield, DrPH; Theresa Doddato, EdD; Patrick Coonan, EdD; Mary Jane Koren, MD; and Julie Sochalski, PhD. We also gratefully acknowledge the contributions of the staff of the Evaluation of Primary Care in Washington Heights project: data managers Susan Fairchild, MPH, and Susan Xiaoqin Lin, MPH; project coordinator Monte Wagner, BSN; assistant coordinators Hussein Saddique, BA, and Selene Wun, BS; patient recruiters and interviewers Delmy Miranda, BA, Niurka Suero, Hendricks Vanderbilt, Eddy Spies, Ana Sanchez, Tamara Ooms, BSN, Eileen Coloma, BSN, Maricruz Polanco, BA, Hector Caraballo, BS, and Carlos Tejada; research nurses Michele Megregian, MS, Carina Ryder, MS, Jennifer Cotto, MS, Milan Gupta, MS, Patricia McGovern, MS, Joshua Vendig, MS, FNP, and especially Kate Hogarty, MS.

12

NURSE-MIDWIVES AND NURSE ANESTHETISTS: THE CUTTING EDGE IN SPECIALIST PRACTICE

DONNA DIERS

This chapter originally appeared as Diers, D. (1992). Nurse-midwives and nurse anesthetists: The cutting edge of a specialist practice. In L. H. Aiken, & C. M. Fagin (Eds). *Charting nursing's future: An agenda for the 1990s.* Philadelphia: J. B. Lippincott. Copyright © 1992 J. B. Lippincott Co. All rights reserved. Reprinted with permission.

EDITORS' NOTE

Nurse-midwives and nurse anesthetists have long histories that are complicated by questions of whether they are part of nursing practice, their relationship to obstetricians and anesthesiologists, equitable payment for services, and the continuing efforts by organized medicine to control these advanced practice registered nurses. Diers provides an historical look at these two roles and related intra- and inter-professional issues that persist to this day.

■ ■ ■

Midwifery is the oldest role for women healers. Nurse anesthesia is the oldest specialty *within* the nursing profession. Midwifery was in existence before obstetrics, and although surgeons created anesthesia, nurse anesthetists existed before anesthesiologists. The history and development of nurse-midwifery and nurse anesthesia provide the screen upon which to project current and future issues common to both professional groups: are nurse-midwives and nurse anesthetists nurses or not? complement or substitute? money and power. The same issues confront newer nursing specialties, and there are lessons to be learned from these pioneers.

BRIEF HISTORY

In the beginning, there were midwives:

> And it came to pass, when she was in hard labour, that the midwife said unto her, Fear not . . . (Genesis 35:17)

The king of Egypt tried to compel Hebrew midwives to kill all male children, but they did not obey. When called to task, the midwives dissembled: "And the midwives said unto Pharoah, 'the Hebrew women are not as the Egyptian women, for they are lively and are delivered ere the midwives come unto them'" (Exodus 1:19). Their actions pleased God, who "dealt well with the midwives . . ." and "made them houses" (Exodus 1:21–22), although one interpreter wrote, "their disobedience herein was lawful, but their dissembling evil" (*Geneva Bible,* 1560, p. 244). One of the male children saved was Moses.

In ancient Greece, some women were designated midwives (obstetrice), but many women assisted each other in birthing without official designation. The practice of medicine and surgery was restricted to men: if the work could be done equally well by women, the status of males and hence their fees would be reduced (Donnison, 1988). One Athenian woman, Agnodice, passed herself off as a male and was trained in surgery. She became such a popular birth attendant that physicians accused her of seducing her patients. To counter the charge, she revealed her true gender and was condemned to death for practicing medicine without a license. But Athens' principal matrons, many of whom she had assisted in childbirth, rallied around her, and the law was amended to allow women to practice medicine and surgery (Donnison, 1988).

International midwifery does not require training as a nurse, and contemporary efforts to move midwifery into nursing in the United Kingdom are controversial (Clay, 1987). Midwives first came to the United States with the slave trade in 1619, bringing the histories, traditions, art, and folklore from the mother country and handing them down to their daughters (Robinson, 1984). Midwives also came to this country later with the waves of European immigration. Bridget Lee Fuller traveled on the *Mayflower* and probably aided in three births on the voyage (Litoff, 1982). Anne Hutchinson, a rebellious colonist midwife, held meetings with women to discuss, among other things, opposition to the established church. She was tried as a witch and banished from Massachusetts to be massacred in what later became New York (Williams, 1981). The Hutchinson River Parkway is named for her. Until the 17th century, the personal experience of childbirth was considered an essential prerequisite for practicing midwifery (Donegan, 1978).

Midwifery gave a little-known gift to early scientific medicine. Ignatz Semmelweiss is justly credited with making parturition safer by insisting that medical students and faculty wash their hands between cases. What is not often discussed is how he got this idea. There were two services in the Allegemeinne Krankenhaus in Vienna, one in which midwives gave care to the poor and the other the teaching service for the school of medicine. Semmelweiss noticed that the incidence of puerperal fever in women who were delivered in the midwifery service was a great deal lower than the incidence in the medical school ward. Midwives did not perform autopsies, and it was the germs from autopsy material that were being carried back to the wards by the physicians' hands.

By the early 1900s, the appalling rate of infant mortality (124 out of 1000 births) was attributed in part to the fact that half the births were attended by traditional midwives. After World War I, "the government began insuring itself for future wars by ploughing money into public health. For the first time children were recognized as future members of the military . . ." (Tom, 1982, p. 7), and women were producers of future fighting men. The Sheppard-Towner Act of 1921 supported public health nurses to train midwives, state laws requiring registration of births and licensing of midwives were passed, and very soon, statistics began to document lowered maternal and infant mortality rates and eradication of neonatal ophthalmia at quite low cost. Organized medicine withdrew its support of the federal legislation, however, because the programs were not under physician direction nor control, and the legislation was allowed to lapse.

Nurse-midwifery began with the Frontier Nursing Service in Kentucky, under Mary Breckinridge, a nurse and British-trained midwife, in 1925. In 1931, the Lobenstine School of Midwifery, affiliated with the Maternity Center Association in New York City, began its formal training program for nurses. Formal preparation of nurse-midwives was thought by some to be a stopgap between traditional midwives and total control of birthing by obstetricians. In 1932, there were 3 million births and only 600 obstetricians, which made the American Medical Association's intended plan to eliminate nurse-midwives "impractical" (Hemschemeyer, 1943).

As of 1990, there were 26 nurse-midwifery programs, most of which are located within or affiliated with schools of nursing; 16 provided the master's degree and 10 are certificate programs. About 4000 nurse-midwives have been certified by the American College of Nurse-Midwives in the United States (Adams, 1989) since it began offering certification in 1971. In recent years, there has been a resurgence of lay midwives ("direct-entry mid-wives," "traditional midwives"), who are recognized by law in ten states and prohibited by law in ten others (Butter & Kay, 1988).

Before Crawford Long, M.D., removed two tumors from James Venable's neck under the influence of inhaled ether in 1842, whatever assistance people were given to control the pain of surgery or injury came from alcohol, sometimes champagne. In the wild days of the expanding American frontier, snake oil salesmen entertained mining camp audiences with demonstrations of nitrous oxide gas, and ether-sniffing was recreational. Long knew Venable liked to sniff ether (Long did too) and suggested this application in surgery. Long himself both administered the anesthesia and performed the surgery (Thatcher, 1953).

Lister's discovery of asepsis, published in 1867, and the later discovery of antisepsis made it possible for surgeons to cure something, but not without pain (and also not with-out the attendance of Florence Nightingale's trained nurses, who kept the environment clean and healthy, but that is another story). Long's use of ether as anesthesia, Horace Wells' and William T. G. Morton's experiments with nitrous oxide for dental extractions, and Morton's public demonstration of ether anesthesia at Massachusetts General Hospital in 1846 (Thatcher, 1953) made it possible for surgeons to invade the body cavity. Surgeons began to need help.

"Anesthizers" were surgeons in training, often more interested in observing the surgery and learning technique than in monitoring the anesthesia. As students, anesthizers were not paid; "the surgeon took whatever fee was paid, considering that the privilege of assisting him and seeing how he did his work was ample reward . . ." (Galloway, 1899, p. 1173 in Bankert, 1989). If the anesthizer was paid at all, it was a trivial portion of the surgeon's fee, perhaps $5 for a $200 operation—an early example of fee-splitting. There was no incentive for new physicians to take on anesthesia as a full-time job, since it was neither lucrative nor visible.

But surgeons needed help, and so they turned to nurses and trained them. In the begin-ning, they were religious sisters, who also did not have to be paid. The first identifiable nurse anesthetist was Sister Mary Bernard at St. Vincent's Hospital in Erie, Pennsylvania in 1877 (Bankert, 1989). The Sisters of the Third Order of St. Francis established a com-munity and hospitals throughout the Midwest and contracted with the Missouri Pacific Railroad to manage hospitals for railroad employees. One of the hospitals was St. Mary's in Rochester, Minnesota. The Sisters' explicit condition was that Dr. William Worrell Mayo take charge of it (Bankert, 1989). The Mayo Clinic had no interns in the beginning; there-fore anesthesia was administered by nurses. "And when the interns came, the brothers [Mayo] decided that a nurse was better suited to the task because she was more likely to keep her mind strictly on it . . ." (Bankert, 1989, p. 39).

One of the first two nurse anesthetists married Dr. Charles Mayo, and her place was taken by the "mother of anesthesia," the amazing Alice Magaw. She collected and reported her work in a series of papers beginning in 1899, which were published privately by the Mayo Clinic, since nurses could not be published in the medical literature. By 1906, she had participated in over 14,000 cases without a single death directly attributable to the anesthesia (Thatcher, 1953, p. 59).

The need for nurses to administer anesthesia was so widespread that Isabel Hampton Robb devoted a chapter to it in her first textbook (1893). Alice Magaw and early nurse anesthetists used both ether and chloroform, although Magaw preferred ether. The popularity of chloroform was greatly enhanced when Queen Victoria used it in delivering two of her children (Thatcher, 1953, p. 17).

The first formal course in anesthesia was organized at one of the Sisters' hospitals in 1912; it admitted secular nurses in 1924. By the beginning of World War I, there were five postgraduate schools of anesthesia, the most important of which was at Lakeside Hospital in Cleveland. There, George Crile, a surgeon, recruited Agatha Hodgins to become a nurse anesthetist, and they experimented together on animals with nitrous oxide gas and oxygen. They were also apparently the first to use morphine and scopolamine as adjuncts to anesthesia (Crile, 1947). The Lakeside program trained both physicians and nurses.

Hospital-sponsored units such as the Lakeside Unit, which were not part of the military, made anesthesia available near World War I battlefields, thereby greatly decreasing mortality. The enthusiasm for nurse anesthetists during and after the war did not escape the attention of physician anesthetists, and a long campaign began "to legislate her [*sic*] out of existence" (Thatcher, 1953, p. 108). World War II also helped to establish nurse anesthesia, since the military clarified the standing of nurse anesthetists in the service. Immediately after that war, the American Association of Nurse Anesthetists began to offer certification (1945). Men were admitted to membership in the association in 1947, and special programs for men nurse anesthetists (who could double as stretcher bearers) began. During the Vietnam War, a special draft of male professional nurses was issued; nurses who were women were specifically excluded (Redman, 1986). Of the ten nurses killed in Vietnam, two were male nurse anesthetists.

As of 1989, there were about 23,000 certified registered nurse anesthetists, 40 percent of whom were men. However, there were also 22,100 physician anesthesiologists. Nurse anesthetists administer over 65 percent of the anesthesia given in this country (American Association of Nurse Anesthetists, 1989) and 70 percent or more in rural areas (Bankert, 1989, p. 175).

NURSES OR SOMETHING ELSE

Nurse-midwives describe themselves as being educated in two disciplines—nursing and midwifery.

> The *nurse* part of the term . . . acknowledges that being a registered nurse is prerequisite to being a certified nurse-midwife. It also emphasizes the primary focus of the professional nurse on the . . . individual patient as well as on patient education, counseling and supportive care (Varney, 1987, p. 3).

Midwifery, however, is a profession in its own right, which in other countries does not require nursing as a base. Three legal cases in the United States have dealt with the practice of registered nurses whose preparation for midwifery was not obtained in a nurse-midwifery program (*Leggett v. Tennessee Board of Nursing,* 1980; *Leigh v. Board of Registration in Nursing,* 1984; *Smith v. State of Indiana ex rel. Medical Licensing Board of Indiana,* 1984). In all three, but for different reasons, the courts have held essentially that the nurse has to make a choice; if she holds herself as practicing midwifery, she is not practicing nursing; if she holds herself as practicing nursing, that is not midwifery and certainly not nurse-midwifery if she is not certified. The wording of state practice acts is crucial to these interpretations. Nurse-midwifery is the only advanced nursing specialty that is regulated in some states outside the nurse practice act, sometimes even by the board of medicine (Kelly, 1987). There has never been a case of nurse-midwives being sued for practicing medicine without a license. Such a case would be difficult to prosecute because midwifery existed before medical obstetrics and because it is often specifically excluded from definitions of the practice of medicine (*Leggett v. Tennessee Board of Nursing,* 1980; Harlow, 1988).

Anesthesia was a natural role for nurses to perform as they assisted the surgeon. Nurses were recruited into a field shunned by physicians after it was determined that interns lacked the "deftness and tender touch which patients required for a successful anesthetic" (Olsen, 1940, p. 4). The nurse's gender was important too: ". . . just as soon as the patient lies down to take his ether, if he is a man he gives up to the nurse, but if a man is going to administer that ether the feeling of resistance and fight is in him . . ." (Truesdale, 1913, p. 283).

Ira Gunn is perhaps the most articulate spokesperson for nursing within nurse anesthesia. "By rendering the patient incapable of providing care for himself, the anesthetist must become the care provider—and this care is basically nursing" (Gunn, 1975, p. 136). She argues that the practice of anesthesia does not fit medicine's defined turf—to diagnose, treat, prescribe, or operate in order to cure—since it is rarely administered as a diagnostic or therapeutic regimen. Rather, anesthesia "facilitates" cure just as nursing and dietetics do (Gunn, Nicosia, & Tobin, 1987, p. 97). Anesthesia is a comfort measure, in this view, and thus within the sphere of nursing.

Agatha Hodgins at Lakeside Hospital became a leader in nurse anesthesia practice and education, and she was the founder and first president of what became the American Association of Nurse Anesthetists. She was committed to the notion that the anesthesia service (which at this time was *only* nurse anesthetists) should be separate from the nursing service in hospitals (Thatcher, 1953, p. 132; Bankert, 1989, p. 68) because it was a special field requiring special education and recognition not possible if it were contained within the nursing department.

Both professional groups have danced around the relationship with organized nursing (and medicine; see later on) with a certain amount of dissembling. For both, the official relationship with the American Nurses' Association (ANA) was definitive for how they evolved as professional organizations.

At their very first meeting in 1931, the nurse anesthetists' new association decided "to affiliate with the American Nurses' Association" (Thatcher, 1953, pp. 184–185). (Note: They did not "seek" affiliation.) A long period of correspondence and negotiation ensued. At first, the ANA's issue was that the *International* Association, as they then called themselves, could not be accommodated because ANA's membership was only "American." The nurse anesthetists then changed the name to the *National* Association. Agatha Hodgins wrote: "In regard to being a section, as the work is not nursing . . .," she proposed an affiliate relationship with ANA, not quite in, not quite out (Hodgins to Marie

Louis, February 15, 1932, cited in Bankert, 1989, p. 70). According to Thatcher, there were several reasons why the ANA refused to accept the application for affiliation. The ANA argued that individual membership was already open to anesthetists as nurses.

> It was considered that, since in some states the administration of an anesthetic was regarded as a medical activity, the question could arise of nurse anesthetists' practicing medicine. Furthermore, if the [nurse anesthetists] were to be accepted as an affiliated group, it might bring upon the ANA some legal responsibility for them (Thatcher, 1953, p. 196).

The nurse-midwives' dealings with the ANA started in the 1950s, when the three nursing organizations were sorting themselves out. The nurse-midwives (not yet an official organization) asked, as did the nurse anesthetists, for a special interest group. Nurse-midwives had had a section in the National Organization of Public Health Nursing and published the first descriptive data about nurse-midwives (Hemschemeyer, 1947). But when it merged with what became the National League for Nursing, that section fell out. The ANA simply invited the nurse-midwives to be part of a study of maternal-child health. The new National League for Nursing assigned midwives to the Interdivisional Council, which encompassed pediatrics, orthopedics, crippled children, and school health, too broad a constituency to serve nurse-midwifery's interests (Varney, 1987, p. 8). Therefore the nurse-midwives organized their own association, incorporated in 1955. By then, the nurse anesthetists had an organization that was over 20 years old. Some leaders of the American Association of Nurse Anesthetists still wistfully wished to come under the ANA umbrella, but the ANA was not disposed to consider special interests.

Rebuffed by the ANA, and not wanting to affiliate with the anesthesiologists' organization (even had they been welcomed), the nurse anesthetists accepted the offer of the American Hospital Association to provide space, money, and moral support. Since anesthesia services were a hospital service, this affiliation made some sense.

Things came full circle in 1973 with the formation of the National Federation of Nursing Specialty Organizations and the ANA, when the ANA belatedly tried and failed to generate enthusiasm for a specialist forum under its own umbrella. The ANA and the American Association of Nurse Anesthetists, among others, were founding members of the Federation, and the American College of Nurse-Midwives also joined. Perhaps as payment for ANA support of the efforts of the American Association of Nurse Anesthetists to become the accrediting arm for nurse anesthesia educational programs, the American Association of Nurse Anesthetists supported the ANA's credentialing study and subsequent activities; the American College of Nurse-Midwives declined membership on the committee, although it sent observers (Fullerton, 1982). Nurse anesthetists took the leadership in 1989 by creating the Specialty Nursing Forum, Inc. It publishes a newsletter edited by Ira Gunn, which reports on specialist practice, legal or legislative issues such as prescriptive authority, and National Federation of Nursing Specialty Organizations news.*

Specialty Nursing Forum, published by Specialty Nursing Forum, Inc., 216 Higgins Road, Park Ridge, Illinois 60068–5790; (708) 692–7050.

Nurse-midwives seized the opportunity to build their new organization and the profession of nurse-midwifery and essentially backed away from organized nursing. Although the American College of Nurse-Midwives requires licensure as a registered nurse for initial certification by the association, it does not require continuing licensure (individual states may, however); continuing competency assessment is required every 5 years. By 1984, all states, as well as the District of Columbia, Guam, Puerto Rico, and the Virgin Islands, had recognized nurse-midwifery by name in law or regulation (Varney, 1987). The American College of Nurse-Midwives began to establish criteria for the approval of nurse-midwifery education programs in 1962, and its Division of Accreditation is recognized as the accrediting body for nurse-midwifery programs by the Office of Education. Not satisfied with being contained within the nursing literature, the official journal of the American College of Nurse-Midwives, the *Journal of Nurse-Midwifery*, fought for 156 years to be included in *Index Medicus*.

Just prior to World War II, the nurse anesthetists challenged the military nurse corps on whether nurse anesthetists would be considered nurses with the same pay and privileges but also with the obligation to perform staff nursing if no surgery was scheduled. At first the military waffled, but when war was declared and nurse anesthetists became necessary, they came to have a special place in military nursing—a clinical nursing specialty (Bankert, 1989).

The American College of Nurse-Midwives testified in favor of the American Association of Nurse Anesthetists' becoming the accrediting body for nurse anesthesia education in 1975 (Bankert, 1989, p. 158), but other than this activity, there has apparently been little communication between the two groups. Both have evolved independently of each other and of organized nursing.

COMPLEMENT OR SUBSTITUTE?

The relationship between professions is not only a political question but is also an economic one (Griffith, 1984). However, challenges to the practice of nurse-midwives and nurse anesthetists from organized medicine are more often phrased as matters of safety and control, thus concealing their economic basis.

In production economics, complements are either jointly used in the production process or consumed with each other as a good or service. Thus bread and butter are consumed together. An increase in the demand for one will cause an increase in the demand for the other. A decrease in the price of one (bread) will cause an increase both in the demand for it and for its complement (butter). But if the two are total substitutes for one another, an increase in the price of one (butter) will cause an increase in demand for the other (margarine).

Nurse-midwifery never grew up as a complement to medical obstetrics, nurse-midwives were not there to help out, except in the most remote sense of an increased demand for obstetric care that exceeded the supply of hands. But nurse anesthesia was a complement to surgery, necessary to its performance. Nurse-midwifery is a complete substitute for medical obstetrics in the care of the "essentially normal" patient, in family planning, and in well-woman gynecology. Nurse anesthesia is a complete substitute for anesthesiology, to the limits of its scope of practice. The political battles center on substitutability.

The legal authority to practice is a property right—a way to make a living—and thus interference with it is subject to litigation. This was the basis for early physician challenges to the legality of nurse anesthesia: nurses were stealing their property right.

The series of incursions against nurse anesthesia began in 1911, when the New York State Medical Society took it upon itself to declare that the administration of anesthetic by a nurse was a violation of state law (Thatcher, 1953, p. 108). This went nowhere. The following year the Ohio State Medical Board passed a resolution that no one other than a registered physician could administer an anesthetic (Thatcher, 1953, p. 110). This provoked nothing more serious than some editorials. But in 1916, the Ohio Medical Board was asked to take action against the Lakeside program as the "chief source of the nurse-anesthetist abuse" ("Use of nurses as anesthetists," 1916). A "spirited" hearing before the Board took place, and the upshot was that the edict against Lakeside was withdrawn (Thatcher, 1953, p. 113). After the complaint was withdrawn, Crile got an amendment to the Medical Practice Act passed to prevent the Act from applying to or prohibiting the administration of anesthetic by a registered nurse "under the direction of and in the immediate presence of the licensed physician" and also provided that the nurse had taken a prescribed course in anesthesia (Thatcher, 1953, pp. 116–117). He was taking no more chances in Ohio.* But next door in Kentucky, upon the request of the Louisville Society of Anesthetists, the attorney general delivered an opinion to the effect that the administration of an anesthetic is "unquestionably the practice of one of the branches of medicine and surgery" (Thatcher, 1953, p. 117). The Kentucky State Medical Association passed a similar resolution.

With what was to become a pattern of assertiveness, a Louisville surgeon, Louis Frank, and Margaret Hatfield, his nurse anesthetist, insisted on a court test; they sued the State Board of Health. The trial court ruled in favor of the defendants, but the case was appealed and reversed in 1917. In an opinion so strongly worded and memorable it is still quoted among nurse anesthetists, the judge wrote:

> . . . [These] laws have not been enacted for the peculiar benefit of the members of . . . professions, further, than they are members of the general community, but they have been enacted for the benefit of the people (*Frank et al. v. South et al.,* 1917).

Miss Hatfield was "not engaged in the practice of medicine."

The increasingly hostile climate for nurse anesthetists in California set another stage. To shorten a long and interesting story, Dagmar Nelson had been recruited from the Mayo Clinic to work as a nurse anesthetist for Dr. Verne Hunt in Los Angeles, at St. Vincent's hospital. The Anesthesia Section of the Los Angeles County Medical Association asked the Superior Court to permanently enjoin Nelson from giving anesthesia. Hunt hired lawyers, who argued that the Medical Association had no standing to sue. The politics got really dirty

---

*Ohio is relevant here. The fight against nurse anesthetists was led by Francis Hoeffer McMechan, M.D., of Cincinnati, just across the river from Louisville. McMechan took on this cause as a personal vendetta apparently, explicitly protecting the property right, and pursued it for years, often using his position as editor of the annual *Anesthesia Supplement* to the surgery journal as a personal platform. He had personal reasons apart from the public political ones. After he died, his wife continued to support this losing cause. His odd role is colorfully discussed in both Thatcher (1953) and Bankert (1989).

after the court sustained this argument. The Medical Society's *Bulletin* incorrectly reported that an injunction had indeed been granted. A furious blast from Hunt's lawyers made the *Bulletin* print a retraction with a curious introduction: ". . . the information . . . which appeared in the *Bulletin* was sent to the Editor's Desk from what appears to be an authentic source ..." (Thatcher, 1953, p. 144).

Since the Medical Society could not sue, one physician, William Chalmers-Frances, took up the cudgels on their behalf. He argued that because the surgeon was separated from the anesthetist by a screen, he could not supervise the actual administration of anesthesia; that an anesthetic was a drug and the anesthetist was using medical judgment in deciding the amount and thus was treating the patient; and that the anesthetist was observing the physical signs of patients and acting on them, thus diagnosing and practicing medicine (*Chalmers-Frances v. Nelson,* 1936).

Hunt's lawyers presented expert testimony and other evidence to the effect that giving drugs upon direct or *understood* instruction of a physician was a recognized practice within the definition of nursing and that supervision by a physician could be direct or *understood* (Thatcher, 1953, p. 146, emphasis in Thatcher). The trial took 12 days; 3 days later, the judge ruled that since Miss Nelson was under the direction and supervision of surgeons, her work did not constitute practicing medicine or surgery.

The ruling was appealed at the instigation of the Anesthesia Section, and the newly formed National Association of Nurse Anesthetists filed an amicus brief. Two years later, the Supreme Court of California stated: ". . . it is the legally established rule that they [nurse anesthetists] are but carrying out the orders of the physicians to whose authority they are subject . . ." (Thatcher, 1953, p. 148); the original judgment was upheld. The Anesthesia Section could not let it die, and they asked the county Medical Association to help pay the lawyers' fees ($2500). The Association declined.

Frank et al. v. South et al. (1917) and *Chalmers-Frances v. Nelson* (1936) provide the legal basis for nurse anesthesia practice as nursing and are still cited if the need arises. Although the right of certified registered nurse anesthetists to practice anesthesia has apparently been sealed by these two decisions, further attempts have been made to hack off portions of their anesthesia practice. The American Society of Anesthesiologists has issued proclamations stating that regional anesthesia (e.g., spiral blocks, epidurals and caudals) should be administered only by physicians and intra-arterial lines should be placed only by physicians (Bankert, 1989). Physician-owned malpractice insurance companies have taken these resolutions to heart and have written into the malpractice insurance policy for nurse anesthetists that they would not be covered for administering regional anesthesia (Blumenreich & Wolf, 1986). As the malpractice insurance crisis has heated up, some surgeons have attempted to distance themselves from "supervision" of anesthesia and have editorialized that somehow surgeons are more liable if anesthesia is administered by a certified registered nurse anesthetist than if it is administered by an anesthesiologist. Actually, courts have determined that the surgeon's supervision does not mean control, and therefore the liability is not automatically the surgeon's (Blumenreich, 1989).

A landmark case, *Oltz v. St. Peter's Hospital* (1986), established nurse anesthetists' standing to sue for anticompetitive strategies when anesthesiologists conspire to restrict or revoke their practice privileges. Another case has established their capacity to be awarded damages for illegal economic discrimination through exclusive contracts

(*Bhan v. NME Hospitals, Inc. et al.,* 1985). The issue of exclusive contracts is a difficult one for nurse anesthetists because they may well profit from being part of a practice group with anesthesiologists who have such a contract. One case has gone all the way to the Supreme Court on this issue (*Jefferson Parish Hospital v. Hyde,* 1984). In a split vote, the Court ruled that exclusive contracts are not illegal on their face ("per se"). Justice Sandra Day O'Connor suggested a more subtle standard of "adverse economic effects and potential economic benefits" (Blumenreich, 1984).

Antitrust and restraint of trade are extraordinarily difficult and time-consuming cases to mount and prove, depending, as the federal law does, on evidence of conspiracy. The full case of two nurse-midwives in Tennessee who could not obtain hospital practice privileges and whose collaborating obstetrician's malpractice coverage was cancelled has yet to be heard in court nearly 10 years after the incident in question. In the one part of the case that has been heard, the court ruled against the physician owners of the insurance company, reasoning that their activity was not "the business of insurance" but was actually anticompetitive (*Nurse-Midwifery Associates v. Hibbert,* 1983). The Federal Trade Commission also ruled against the insurance company, which filed a consent decree to terminate the practice of denying coverage to physicians who were in practice with nurse-midwives.

The Federal Trade Commission also obtained a consent order against the medical staff of Memorial Medical Center in Savannah, Georgia, where the obstetricians argued that a nurse-midwife, Rebecca Almand, should not be granted hospital privileges because "there was no shortage of obstetricians in the Savannah area" (*In Re Medical Staff of Memorial Medical Center,* 1988). The Federal Trade Commission order explicitly states, "Because nurse-midwifery services can substitute for certain kinds of obstetrical services . . ." nurse-midwives offer "a greater range of choices for consumers and increase competition in the provision of obstetrical care" (*In Re Medical Staff of Memorial Medical Center,* 1988). Time-consuming as the process of appealing to the Federal Trade Commission and obtaining a consent decree is (Almand's case took 5 years), the appellant does not have to pay for lawyers—the Federal Trade Commission's lawyers bring the case to the Commission.

Nurse-midwives have generally faced challenges to their practice in legislative hearings or local forums rather than in the courts. Organized physician groups have tried to prevent legal authorization of nurse-midwifery, prescriptive authority, licensure of out-of-hospital birthing centers, and third-party reimbursement. Nurse-midwives have also encountered attempts to restrict their practices by specifying that they may not conduct deliveries anywhere but in a hospital or that there must be a physician present at all deliveries. In the unfortunate situation at Boston City Hospital, the physicians unilaterally ruled that women with previous cesarean sections who desired a vaginal birth and women with minor chronic medical problems were too "high risk" for nurse-midwifery care. In addition, women with any meconium staining were to be delivered in the delivery room in stirrups, and a nothing-by-mouth policy was established for all women on the labor and delivery unit, even if they were in early labor or just there for a nonstress test. Finally, certified nurse-midwives were deemed unqualified to carry out initial prenatal history taking and physical examinations. These and other more blatant attacks on the nurse-midwifery service, which at its zenith in Boston had eleven nurse-midwives and seven physicians delivering services in two hospital-based clinics and nine neighborhood health centers, compromised the nurse-midwifery service in favor of residents and attending staff (Breece, Israel, & Friedman, 1989).

Nurse-midwives were at the center of the malpractice insurance issue, caught up in the same tort liability crisis that hit circuses, restaurants, and the Boy Scouts. The company that had covered nurse-midwives through the American College of Nurse-Midwives abruptly withdrew that coverage. The American Nurses' Association negotiated with their own insurance carrier to cover nurse-midwives, but that carrier withdrew support and in addition called into question its coverage of nurse practitioners and others in expanded roles. Eventually the American College of Nurse-Midwives was able to put together a consortium of insurance carriers to issue coverage, but it is a great deal more expensive than the previous coverage, and the policy stipulates that nurse-midwives must be "employees," which confuses practice quality issues with employment relationships.

The malpractice insurance situation has also affected obstetricians. In 1986, there were approximately 31,400 obstetricians; 35 percent of the 35,000 family practice physicians included obstetrics in their practices and an unknown number of general practitioners did so as well (Scholle & Klerman, 1988). One estimate indicated that 12.4 percent of obstetricians gave up obstetric practice (but continued their gynecologic practice), with considerable variation from state to state (8.3 percent in New York, 25.1 percent in Florida). Nearly half of general-family practice physicians have given up obstetrics (Scholle & Klerman, 1988). What effect this will have on nurse-midwife practices is not yet known.

In an exhaustive review of the legislation, Hadley argues that prescriptive authority makes nurses in expanded roles less complementary and more substitutable (Hadley, 1989). The economic analysis helps explain the resistance of organized medicine (and organized pharmacy too, to the extent that they wish to move beyond "dispensing" to "prescribing") to granting prescribing privileges to nurses. In general, prescriptive authority has been less of an issue for nurse-midwives than for nurse anesthetists, partly because the need of the former for access to pharmaceuticals is relatively limited. Nurse-midwives function under mutually agreed-upon medically approved standing orders that specify particular drugs for particular symptoms or conditions. Nurse-midwives, however, have had an interest in the authority to prescribe birth control devices (e.g., intrauterine devices) and to order laboratory tests and procedures (ultrasonography, for instance), which may be covered in the same laws or local policies.

Nurse anesthetists' issues regarding prescriptive authority have had to do with how the range of medications is limited by law or regulation; they need access to controlled drugs in all of the five Schedules of the Federal Controlled Substance Act (1981). Many of the 26 states that at present have some form of prescribing authority for nurses in advanced practice limit it to formularies or only Schedule II drugs.

Nurse anesthesia has formulated a unique argument about prescriptive authority. Gene Blumenreich, General Counsel of the American Association of Nurse Anesthetists, opines that since most surgery cannot be performed without anesthesia, scheduling a patient for surgery, which only a physician can do, is "generally equivalent to the prescription for anesthesia" (Blumenreich, 1988, p. 91). Thus, the physician prescribes "anesthesia" and leaves it up to the nurse anesthetist to determine the specifics (*Kamalyan v. Henderson,* 1954). A nurse anesthetist is obliged, as is any other nurse, to carry out the physician's order unless it is unlawful, the wrong medication, the wrong dose, or the wrong time, or if the nurse is not qualified to carry out the order or manage the potential (more immediate) complications and other providers are not sufficiently close to help (Ira Gunn, personal communication, April 11, 1990).

Both nurse-midwives and nurse anesthetists have used published statements about their practice to advantage, but quite differently. The American College of Nurse-Midwives, the American College of Obstetricians and Gynecologists, and the Nurses' Association of the American College of Obstetricians and Gynecologists issued their first joint statement in 1971, recognizing and supporting the development and utilization of nurse-midwives in teams "directed by a physician." A later supplementary statement made it clear that neither physical presence nor employment by physicians was intended. The most recent joint statement (American College of Nurse-Midwives, 1983) still stands. Nurse-midwives have been able to wave these statements in the faces of physicians or legislators who might question the working relationship and to hold obstetricians to the published words of their association. Negotiating such statements obviously requires that the participants communicate. The American Society of Anesthesiologists will not even meet to negotiate contemporary troubling issues with the American Association of Nurse Anesthetists. Thus, the American Association of Nurse Anesthetists has issued its own statements.

The anesthesia standards of the Joint Commission on the Accreditation of Health Care Organizations specify that an independent licensed practitioner is responsible for the determination of the patient's physical status and capacity to undergo anesthesia even though she or he need not perform these functions directly. To establish firmly that the certified registered nurse anesthetist is the *independent* licensed practitioner and perhaps to head off future battles, the American Association of Nurse Anesthetists has issued a position statement on "Relationships Between Health Care Professionals," which states that as independent licensed practitioners, certified registered nurse anesthetists function with the *consent* of another licensed provider who "supervises" but does not "control" the practice (American Association of Nurse Anesthetists, 1987). The statement has been distributed widely to hospitals, departments of anesthesiology, and government agencies. The American Association of Nurse Anesthetists and the American Society of Anesthesiologists have accepted editors' invitations to argue in publication, since they cannot talk in private, on who should train and supervise nurse anesthetists (Ditzler, 1979; Gunn, 1979) and in response to a policy analysis of anesthesia payment (Beutler, 1988; Weiss, 1988).

Linguists might find amusing research opportunities in tracing the changing language in the interprofessional statements, court cases, and legal arguments: from "direction" or "medically directed team" to "supervision" to "understood supervision" to "consent" and whatever comes next. The choice of the word "direction" (even when modified in nurse-midwifery to provide for "consultation, collaboration, and referral") in position statements contrasts with the efforts of other nursing groups to get out from under such terminology when nurse practice acts are revised. The landmark case, *Sermchief v. Gonzales* (1983), turned in part on just such a change in legislative language (Wolff, 1984). But in the political context in which both groups evolved, that terminology probably helped, and as the practices have matured, the "direction" has become more and more pro forma.

Whether there is truly a shortage of a surplus of physicians, a point that is hotly debated (Schwartz et al., 1988, 1989; Ginsberg, 1989), the American Medical Association has made its agenda all too clear. In 1985, the American Medical Association's House of Delegates passed a resolution "to combat legislation authorizing medical acts by unlicensed individuals" (American Medical Association, 1985). It commits state medical societies to fight off all attempts to expand the practice of "unlicensed" individuals (the license to practice *medicine* as the property right is the only one that counts). The American Medical Association will provide funds, speakers, position papers, and reviews of state legislation to any medical society facing a challenge [sic], as well as contributing financially to the political campaigns of sympathetic legislators.

The rhetoric of the American Medical Association emphasizes safety and physician authority, but the issue is really something else: money.

MONEY

Nurse-midwives and nurse anesthetists pursued third-party reimbursement in the same period, and eventually with the same success, but apparently without joining forces. Nurse-midwifery was written into third-party reimbursement legislation first in the Civilian Health and Medical Program of the Uniformed Services for military dependents who receive care outside military hospitals, and in 1980, in Medicaid, with the support of Senator Daniel K. Inouye (D-Hawaii), who is proud to announce that he was delivered by a midwife. The American College of Nurse-Midwives was able to effectively use the considerable literature on the success of nurse-midwifery with poor and underserved people (Diers & Burst, 1983). The Medicaid provision said that reimbursement for nurse-midwifery services was mandated in all jurisdictions with "legal authorization" for nurse-midwifery. In states without clear authorization in law or regulation, nurse-midwives worked to make sure language appeared using the Medicaid carrot to political advantage. Senator Inouye also got nurse-midwifery included in Medicare coverage where certified nurse-midwife services are available to handicapped women; certified nurse-midwives are also moving into the area of postmenopausal gynecology. Reimbursement for nurse-midwifery is also available under the Federal Employees Health Plan. These programs require only one act of one central government, which is a great deal easier than going through every state's insurance laws. Senator Inouye, alerted by the American College of Nurse-Midwives that some states were dragging their feet, asked the General Accounting Office to find out how many states had complied with the Medicaid provisions (Medicaid, 1987). By then, 44 states had amended their Medicaid programs and the General Accounting Office report signaled the Health Care Financing Administration to get after the others, who had lame excuses. As a mandated benefit under these federal plans, the government had the possibility of exercising punishment— withdrawal of all of the Medicaid funds for noncompliance.

The first (unsuccessful) efforts of the American Association of Nurse Anesthetists to obtain direct reimbursement targeted Medicare in 1976–1977, when Congress first expressed concern about the growing Part B Medicare payments for anesthesia, pathology, and radiology (Ira Gunn, personal communication, April 11, 1990). In 1982, under the Tax Equity and Fiscal Responsibility Act (TEFRA), which set the stage for diagnosis-related group (DRG)-based prospective payment, certain constraints were placed on billing of anesthesiologists. The Prospective Payment System threw a wrench in the works for certified registered nurse anesthetists, creating major reimbursement disincentives for hospitals to use them.

First, all nonphysician services provided within the hospital were considered to be covered by the DRG-based payment under Medicare Part A. Given an adequate number of anesthesia providers in the area, it was not in a hospital's interest to employ certified registered nurse anesthetists and bundle their services in the DRG-based Part A payment, when anesthesiologists could be paid under Part B, outside the hospital billing system. The law prohibited unbundling services previously provided as a package. Further, the DRG-based payment was a composite of costs reported by hospitals, some of which employed certified registered nurse anesthetists and some of which did not. If hospitals had not employed certified registered nurse anesthetists, their zero contribution to this composite had the effect of lowering the base for the rate calculation (the American Association of Nurse Anesthetists estimated that 17 percent or more of hospitals fell into this category, enough to make a difference [Garde, 1988]).

The American Association of Nurse Anesthetists developed a comprehensive strategy with two explicit agendas: to constrain costs and to create a level playing field in any competitive market (no inherent incentives or disincentives to use particular providers, and with all providers being paid out of the same pot—Part A or Part B—under the same constraints but not necessarily on the same payment rate). They sought and obtained a temporary 3-year cost pass-through for hospital-employed certified registered nurse anesthetist services. Then, in a rare show of support, some groups within the American Society of Anesthesiologists joined the successful proposal of the American Association of Nurse Anesthetists for a single exception from the unbundling provision for certified registered nurse anesthetists employed by anesthesiologists. Finally, the American Association of Nurse Anesthetists sought direct reimbursement for certified registered nurse anesthetists under Medicare, crafting the proposal to be budget neutral and guaranteeing acceptance of the assignment (to take the Medicare payment as full payment). Trying to move anesthesiologists into Medicare Part A proved too politically troublesome for Congress; therefore, nurse anesthetists were moved into Part B in legislation implemented in January, 1989.

The payment method for anesthesia services amounts to a pork barrel for anesthesiologists. In brief, there are pre-established "base units" that reflect the difficulty of a particular care. Then one time unit is added for every 15 minutes the patient is under anesthesia. The rationale here is that the length of the case is not under the control of the anesthesia provider. The sum of these units is multiplied by an allowable conversion factor in order to arrive at a payment rate. Those anesthesiologists who "medically direct" certified registered nurse anesthetists bill for the medical direction under two schedules: if they employ the certified registered nurse anesthetist, they bill for 15-minute time units; if they "direct" hospital-employed certified registered nurse anesthetists, they may only bill for 30-minute time units (assuming they are physically in the hospital), whereas the hospital bills for the certified registered nurse anesthetists' services. Anesthesiologists are the only physicians allowed under Medicare to bill a medical direction fee. The President's FY 1990 budget called for reductions in anesthesia Medicare fees of 25 percent, paying certified registered nurse anesthetists and anesthesiologists that same amount. Only one fee would be permissible. For the hospital-employed certified registered nurse anesthetist where the anesthesiologist "medically directs" the service, the hospital and anesthesiologists would have to negotiate who gets what portion of the fee. It has occurred to nurse anesthetists, as it has to nurse-midwives, that the sensible thing to do would be to hire physician anesthesiologists or obstetricians as consultants, paying them out of fees billed in the certified registered nurse anesthetist's or certified nurse-midwife's name.

In a Health Care Financing Administration contracted policy analysis, Cromwell and Rosenbach (1988) analyzed anesthesia payments. The report ends with an unusually forthright statement:

> Any maldistribution of anesthesiologists should not be solved by raising the reimbursement bridge in rural areas, but rather by lowering the reimbursement river in overdoctored cities. With an annual net income in excess of $140,000 . . . it seems extravagant for society to be offering extra bonuses to anesthesiologists . . . [U]nless some real reform is initiated soon, the opportunity to achieve an efficient anesthesiologist/CRNA mix could be lost, program outlays will remain unnecessarily high, and another occupation providing valuable care at low cost will be put on the endangered list (p. 17).

Insurance coverage in the private sector varies from state to state. Some states mandate reimbursement for nurse anesthetists if they are not practicing as another reimbursable health provider's employee or as a contractor. All states permit direct reimbursement to certified registered nurse anesthetists, but some Blue Cross/Blue Shield plans do and some do not. In 1982, Haire surveyed third-party payers and found that the vast majority of private insurance companies covered nurse-midwifery services directly even when the written policy did not mention nurse-midwifery. But the rate of coverage under Blue Cross/Blue Shield was much lower, reflecting the fact that the policy boards of many of these organizations are heavily weighted with physicians (Haire, 1982). Nurse-midwives have made considerable headway in health maintenance organizations, which are, after all, insurers as well as providers. Health maintenance organizations have found certified nurse-midwives to be cost-effective and highly marketable. Since health maintenance organizations do not employ anesthesia providers, this has not been an option for certified registered nurse anesthetists, although there is no particular reason why such groups could not contract to deliver anesthesia to a health maintenance organization's patients. Medicaid permits certified registered nurse anesthetists to be directly reimbursed, but allows states to make the decision; they are reimbursed under Medicaid in 22 states. Certified registered nurse anesthetists are eligible to seek direct reimbursement from the Civilian Health and Medical Program of the Uniformed Services.

The confusion of the employment relationship with professional supervision calls into question the notions of "supervision," "direction," and "control" of practice, which are holdovers from history. Nurse-midwifery has been more successful in separating the employment and economic issues. Nurse-midwifery has also made more coin out of data on the effectiveness of nurse-midwifery for underprivileged clientele, in effect painting a political picture of willingness to go where others will not. Nurse anesthetists have more often used the cost-effectiveness argument and have played upon politicians' and bureaucrats' charge to promote equity (the "level playing field").

Value—societal or otherwise—is money. Nurse-midwives have successfully argued their place as caregivers having different values and practices, relieving the high technology, pregnancy-as-a-disease orientation of physicians. Nurse anesthetists do not have as many opportunities to argue for the specialness of nursing, although an outsider reading their literature and the anesthesiology literature might detect a clear difference that parallels the difference between nurse-midwifery and obstetrics. Nurse anesthesia's rhetoric emphasizes care, comfort, use of distraction and other low technology interventions, communication and nurse-patient relationships, easy induction, and natural levels of sleep consistent with the surgical procedures. Anesthesiology's rhetoric conceptualizes anesthesia as a technical service necessary to keep the body's functions in balance while surgery is performed. More could be made of these parallels.

While nurse anesthetists may enjoy unconventional employment relationships, nurse-midwives also have moved into nontraditional or alternative settings for practice, such as out-of-hospital birthing centers. There is no equivalent opportunity for nurse anesthetists, who must practice where surgeons, dentists, or obstetricians do.

A large national study (N = 11,814) of out-of-hospital birth centers (Rooks et al., 1989) showed that the patient outcomes—complications, transfer rates, mortality—were in the same range as outcomes from earlier studies of low-risk women delivering in hospitals. An editorial that accompanies the report of the birth center study generally agrees with the conclusion that birth centers offer lower cost, greater availability of service, a high degree of patient satisfaction, and comparable safety; however, it still proposes that proximity to a hospital is the factor most to be adhered to in the future (Lieberman & Ryan, 1989). How close is close (in miles, attitudes, collaboration) is central to considering the relative independence of practice of nurse-midwives in these or traditional settings. The same issue is explicit in anesthesiology, phrased as the extent to which nurse anesthetists are a "close substitute" (Weiss, 1988). Here, the reference is to scope of practice, safety, and money. Is physician presence always required? If knowing the limits of one's ability or training is the "hallmark of the professional," as Michael Wolff argued in *Sermchief v. Gonzales* (Wolff, 1984), would it not seem that the appropriate practice relationship for both nurse-midwives and nurse anesthetists would be consultative, with the nurse specialists determining when consultation should occur? That, of course, makes the nurses gatekeepers . . . (Diers & Molde, 1983).

CONCLUSIONS

As specialist practice has matured through experience, education, regulation, accreditation, licensure, and economic independence, nurse specialists have drifted away from the tight relationship with medicine and traditional practice sites, and this is exactly what physicians worry about.

In spite of early resistance to primary care by nurses (Ford, 1982), the climate for nurse specialization has changed considerably since nurse-midwives and nurse anesthetists had their disappointing negotiations with the American Nurses' Association. However, other nursing specialties, notably oncology nurses and emergency department nurses, have also created their own organizations and literature, in the first instance deliberately outside the structure of the American Nurses' Association and in the second instance because they, too, were put off by the professional organization (Kelleher, 1990). Although psychiatric nurses have stayed within the American Nurses' Association, the fact that they have been swept up into a generic "therapist" title in many settings suggests an ambivalence about nursing, similar to nurse-midwives, and nurse anesthetists. Primary care nurse practitioners have created new organizations and journals outside the professional organization. Nurse-midwives, nurse anesthetists, psychiatric nurses, and nurse practitioners are the substitutable roles. The more complementary roles of the medical-surgical subspecialties and community health nursing may find a more sympathetic home within the professional organization.

Complementarity and substitutability are perhaps not as distinct as once was thought. And the different, sometimes overlapping, roles should surely not create the newest divisiveness within the profession. Nurse anesthesia might provide an interesting model for how a specialist practice can evolve wearing two hats. Practices do not have to be substitutable to be autonomous or powerful.

Nurse anesthesia profited from having friends in high places. Surely the early work of nurse anesthetists in the Mayo Clinic and Lakeside Hospital brought the specialty both influence and power and a high profile. Nurse-midwifery also had distinguished connections (Diers & Burst, 1983), and Mary Breckinridge herself was the daughter of an ambassador. Nurses in other kinds of expanded roles have found highly placed colleagues, and this is a helpful strategy to remember.

Nurse anesthesia has more often fought its battles through the courts than through legislation, and nurse anesthetist practice is most often contained within Nurse Practice Acts. The American Association of Nurse Anesthetists hires lawyers. Nurse-midwifery has more often turned to public forums such as the legislature and has sought legal authorization outside Nursing Practice Acts. The American College of Nurse-Midwives hires lobbyists. Nurse-midwifery has been able to generate consumer enthusiasm and rely on attention to mothers and babies for public exposure and pressure. Nurse-midwives' natural political constituency is families. Nurse anesthetists hardly have such a satisfied customer relationship, since their clients, even if they know their anesthesia was administered by a nurse, are asleep. Outpatient surgery may provide nurse anesthetists with more patient contact and more public presence because the surgery is shorter and the patients more often are awake, at least for part of the time. Careful analysis of natural constituencies for other nursing specialists is clearly in order. The hospice and oncology nurses have made good use of their poignant patient stories; the emergency nurses have natural allies in physicians, patients, and possibly the police.

Nurse anesthetists and nurse-midwives have leap-frogged over organizational, legislative, and legal issues—a success here for certified nurse-midwives, a success there for certified registered nurse anesthetists—yet there is scant evidence that they have studied one another's roles and activities. Their successes are remarkably consistent, requiring heroic effort. Perhaps nursing is now mature enough to learn from the lessons of those who have gone off in new directions so that we no longer have to reinvent the wheel.

It would be naïve to think that competition with organized medicine is over for nurse-midwives, nurse anesthetists, or any other nurse specialists. The fact that there are now so many definable nursing specialties is a strength rather than a weakness for nursing. The shared experience suggests that the natural constituency for nursing is nursing itself.

Despite the American Medical Association's declaration of war on advanced practice nursing, there are signs of some easing of tensions between medicine and nursing as the Association's membership declines and ages and newer physicians have learned to respect nursing's contributions. If the United States health care system ever moves to making access to health care universal, the need for nurses in all specialties will far exceed the available supply. A recently released federal report projects the need for 40 percent more nurse anesthetists by 2010, despite the growing number of anesthesiologists (Health Economics Research, 1990). We should be prepared to take advantage of this new desirability to help us, among other things, understand interprofessional relationships.

Substitutable practices are alternatives. The more fully substitutable the practice, including prescribing authority and payment for service, the more real is the choice for patients, hiring institutions, and third-party payers. Alternatives must not only prove themselves but also of necessity must *improve* to remain viable. Nurse-midwifery and nurse anesthesia have made enviable progress on quality control through accreditation and competency assessment, which might be a lesson for other specialties.

The final implication of this analysis is the critical power of data. Both specialty groups began early to record the results of their practices, long before data were needed politically. In effect, the data established the legitimacy of the practices, which were then embedded in legislation or court decisions. As nurse-midwifery and nurse anesthesia have no longer needed data for defense of quality or right to practice, their information has become increasingly sophisticated and tuned to policy issues. This direction should be a more general agenda for nursing. If nursing practices can be demonstrated to produce quality outcomes and to preserve natural and normal processes as much as possible, at a competitive cost, their future is assured.

REFERENCES

Adams, C.J. (1989). Nurse-midwifery practice in the United States, 1982–1987. *American Journal of Public Health, 79*(8), 1038–1039.

American Association of Nurse Anesthetists (1987). *Guidelines for nurse anesthesia practice.* Park Ridge, IL: American Association of Nurse Anesthetists.

American College of Nurse-Midwives, American College of Obstetricians and Gynecologists (1983). *Joint statement on maternity care.* Washington, DC: The College.

American Medical Association (1985). *Resolution: To combat legislation authorizing medical acts by unlicensed individuals.* Chicago: The Association.

Bankert, M. (1989. *Watchful CARE—A history of America's nurse anesthetists.* New York: Continuum.

Beutler, J.M. (1988). Perspectives: A nurse anesthetist. *Health Affairs, 7*(3), 26–31.

Bhan v. NME Hospitals, Inc. et al. (1985). 772 F. 2nd 1467 (9th Cir.).

Blumenreich, G.A. (1984). Jefferson Parish Hospital v. Hyde—The last chapter. *Journal of the American Association of Nurse Anesthetists, 52*(4), 462–463.

Blumenreich, G.A. (1988). Nurse anesthetists and prescriptive authority. *Journal of the American Association of Nurse Anesthetists, 56*(2), 91–93.

Blumenreich, G.A. (1989). Surgeons' responsibility for CRNAs. *Journal of the American Association of Nurse Anesthetists, 57*(1), 6–8.

Blumenreich, R.A., & Wolfe, B.L. (1986). Restrictions on CRNAs imposed by physician-controlled insurance companies. *Journal of the American Association of Nurse Anesthetists, 54*(6), 538–539.

Breece, C., Israel, E., & Friedman, L. (1989). Closing of the nurse-midwifery service at Boston City Hospital—What were the issues involved? *Journal of Nurse-Midwifery, 34*(1), 41–48.

Butter, I.H., & Kay, B.Y. (1988). State laws and the practice of lay midwifery. *American Journal of Public Health, 78*(9), 1161–1169.

Chalmers-Frances v. Nelson (1936). 6 Ca. 2nd 402.

Clay, T. (1987). *Nurses—power and politics.* London: William Heinemann Medical Books.

Crile, G.W. (1947). *George Crile: An autobiography.* Philadelphia: Lippincott.

Cromwell, J., & Rosenbach, M.L. (1988). Reforming anesthesia payment under Medicare. *Health Affairs, 7*(3), 6–18.

Diers, D., & Burst, H.V. (1983). The effectiveness of policy related research: Nurse-midwifery as case study. *Image Journal of Nursing Scholarship, 15*(3), 68–74.

Diers, D., & Molde, S. (1983). Nurses in primary care. The new gatekeepers? *American Journal of Nursing, 83,* 742–745.

Ditzler, J.W. (1979). Nurse anesthetists should be trained and supervised by anesthesiologists. In J.E. Eckenhoff (Ed.), *Controversy in anesthesiology* (pp. 205–210). Philadelphia: W.B. Saunders.

Donegan, J.B. (1978). *Women & men midwives: Medicine, morality and misogyny in early America.* Westport, CT: Greenwood Press.

Donnison, J. (1988). *Midwives and medical men—A history of the struggle for the control of childbirth* (2nd ed.). London: Historical Publications Ltd.

Federal Controlled Substance Act of 1981. 21 U.S.C.A. at 801–971 (West 1981 and Suppl. 1989).

Ford, L. (1982). Nurse practitioners: History of a new idea and predictions for the future. In L.H. Aiken (Ed.), *Nursing in the '80s* (pp. 231–248). Philadelphia: J.B. Lippincott.

Frank et al. v. South et al. (1917). *Kentucky Reporter 175:*416–428.

Fullerton, J.D.T. (1982). The ACNM and the NCHCA: The significance of membership . . . the evolution of the health credentialing agency, the National Commission for Health Certifying Agencies. *Journal of Nurse-Midwifery, 27*(3), 27–30.

Galloway, D.H. (1899, May 27). The anesthetizer as a specialist. *The Philadelphia Medical Journal,* 1173.

Garde, J.F. (1988). A case study involving prospective payment legislation, DRGs, and certified registered nurse anesthetists. *Nursing Clinics of North America, 23*(3), 521–530.

Geneva Bible: A facsimile of the 1560 edition (1969). Madison, Milwaukee, and London: University of Wisconsin Press.

Ginzberg, E. (1989). Physician supply in the year 2000. *Health Affairs, 8*(2), 84–90.

Griffith, H. (1984). Nursing practice: Substitute or complement according to economic theory . . . working relationships between physicians and nurses. *Nursing Economics, 2*(2), 105–110.

Gunn, I.P. (1975). Nurse anesthetist-anesthesiologist relationships: Past, present and implications for the future. *Journal of the American Association of Nurse Anesthetists, 43*(2), 129–139.

Gunn, I.P. (1979). Nurse anesthetists should control the teaching and practice of their profession. In J.E. Eckenhoff (Ed.), *Controversy in anesthesiology* (pp. 211–220). Philadelphia: W.B. Saunders.

Gunn, I.P., Nicosia, J., & Tobin, M. (1987). Anesthesia: A practice of nursing [editorial]. *Journal of the American Association of Nurse Anesthetists, 55*(2) 97–100.

Hadley, E. (1989). Nurses and prescriptive authority: A legal and economic analysis. *American Journal of Law and Medicine, 15*(2–3), 245–300.

Haire, D. (1982). Health insurance coverage for nurse-midwifery services: Results of a national survey. *Journal of Nurse-Midwifery, 27*(6), 35–36.

Harlow, M.O. (1988). Midwifery: State regulation. 59 *ALR* 4th 929–948.

Health Economics Research (1990). *Nurse anesthetists: Supply and demand.* Report to the National Center for Nursing Research and the Division of Nursing, U.S. Public Health Service. Washington, DC: U.S. Government Printing Office.

Hemschemeyer, H. (1943). The nurse-midwife is here to stay. *American Journal of Nursing, 43*(10), 916.

Hemschemeyer, H. (1947). Obstetrical nursing today and tomorrow. *Public Health Nursing, 39*(2), 35–39.

In Re Medical Staff of Memorial Medical Center (1988, June 10. Federal Trade Commission Docket No. C-3231, Decision and Order.

Jefferson Parish Hospital v. Hyde (1984). U.S. Supreme Court, March 26.

Kamalyan v. Henderson (1954). 277 P. 2nd 372.

Kelleher, J.C. (1990). When dreams come true [editorial]. *Journal of Emergency Nursing, 16*(1), 1–2.

Kelly, M.E. (1987). Control of the practice of nurse practitioners, nurse-midwives, nurse anesthetists and clinical nurse specialists. In C. Northrup & M.E. Kelly (Eds.), *Legal issues in nursing* (pp. 469–486). St. Louis, C.V. Mosby.

Leggett v. Tennessee Board of Nursing (1980). 612 South Western Reporter, 2nd, 476.

Leigh v. Board of Registration in Nursing (1984). 481 N.E. 2nd 401 (Ind. App.).

Lieberman, E., & Ryan, K.H. (1989). Birth-day choices. *New England Journal of Medicine, 321*(26), 1824–1825.

Litoff, J.B. (1982). The midwife throughout history. *Journal of Nurse-Midwifery, 27*(6), 3–11.

Medicaid: Use of certified nurse-midwives (1987, November). Report to the Honorable Daniel K. Inouye, U.S. Senate, U.S. General Accounting Office (GAO/HRD-88–25). Washington, DC: Government Printing Office.

Nurse Midwifery Associates v. Hibbert (1983). 577 F. Supp. 1273.

Olsen, G.W. (1940). The nurse anesthetists: Past, present and future. *Bulletin of the American Association of Nurse Anesthetists, 8*(4), 298.

Oltz v. St. Peter's Community Hospital (1986, November). CV 81–271–H–Res, Montana District Court.

Redman, R. (1986). The nurse and the draft in the Vietnam War. *Bulletin of the American Association for the History of Nursing, 10*(2), 2–3.

Robb, I.H. (1893). *Nursing: Its principles and practice for hospital and private use.* New York: E.C. Koechert.

Robinson, S.A. (1984). A historical development of midwifery in the black community: 1600–1940. *Journal of Nurse-Midwifery, 29*(4), 247–250.

Rooks, J.P., Weatherby, N.L., Ernst, E.K.M., Stapleton, S., Rosen, D., & Rosenfield, A. (1989). Outcomes of care in birth centers—the National Birth Center Study. *New England Journal of Medicine, 321*(26), 1804–1811.

Scholle, S.H., & Klerman, L.V. (1988, August). *The actual and potential impact of medical liability issues on access to maternity care.* Paper prepared for the Committee on the Effects of Medical Liability on the Delivery of Maternal and Child Health Care. Washington, DC: Institute of Medicine, National Academy of Sciences.

Schwartz, W.B., Sloan, F.A., & Mendelson, D.N. (1988). Why there will be little or no physician surplus between now and the year 2000. *New England Journal of Medicine, 318*(14), 892–897.

Schwartz, W.B., Sloan, F.A., & Mendelson, D.N. (1989). Debating physician supply: The authors respond. *Health Affairs, 8*(2), 91–95.

Sermschief v. Gonzales (1983). 660 SW. 2nd 683.

Smith v. State of Indiana ex rel. Medical Licensing Board of Indiana (1984). 459 NE. 2nd 401 (In. App. 2 Dist).

Thatcher, V. (1953/1984). *History of anesthesia with emphasis on the nurse specialist.* Philadelphia: J.B. Lippincott.

Tom, S.A. (1982). The evolution of nurse-midwifery: 1900–1960. *Journal of Nurse-Midwifery, 27*(4), 4–13.

Truesdale, P.E. (1913). *Transactions of the American Hospital Association, 15*, 283.

"Use of nurses as anesthetists in Ohio hospitals in violation of State law is charged; Medical Board acts" (1916). *Ohio State Medical Journal, 12*(12), 679.

Varney, H. (1987). *Nurse-midwifery* (2nd ed.). Boston: Blackwell Scientific.

Weiss, J.B. (1988, Fall). Perspectives: An anesthesiologist. *Health Affairs, 7*(3), 20–25.

Williams, S.R. (1981). *Divine Rebel—The life of Anne Marbury Hutchinson.* New York: Holt, Rinehart & Winston.

Wolff, M.A. (1984, February). Court upholds expanded practice roles for nurses. *Law, Medicine & Health Care,* 26–29.

ACKNOWLEDGMENTS

The author is extremely grateful to Ira P. Gunn, R.N., C.R.N.A., F.A.A.N., Consultant, Nurse Anesthesia Affairs, and Helen Varney Burst, R.N., C.N.M., M.S.N., Professor, Yale University School of Nursing, the acknowledged experts in their respective fields, who gave generously of their time and insight to provide information and interpretation. Sarah D. Cohn, R.N., C.N.M., J.D., Counsel, Medico-Legal Affairs, Yale New Haven Hospital, pointed out references in the legal literature, and her unique insights as a nurse-midwife and attorney were very helpful. The Reverend Rowan E. Greer, III, Walter H. Gray Professor of Anglican Studies, Yale Divinity School, donated an important piece of biblical scholarship. Susan Molde, R.N., M.S.N., made valuable editorial suggestions.

13

LESSONS LEARNED FROM TESTING THE QUALITY COST MODEL OF ADVANCED PRACTICE NURSING (APN) TRANSITIONAL CARE

DOROTHY BROOTEN

MARY D. NAYLOR

RUTH YORK

LINDA P. BROWN

BARBARA HAZARD MUNRO

ANDREA O. HOLLINGSWORTH

SUSAN M. COHEN

STEVEN FINKLER

JANET DEATRICK

JOANNE M. YOUNGBLUT

This article originally appeared as Brooten, D., Naylor, M. D., York, R., Brown, L. P., Munro, B. H., Hollingsworth, A. O., Cohen, S. M., Flinkler, S., Deatrick, J., & Youngblut, J. M. (2002). Lessons learned from testing the quality cost model of advanced practice nursing (APN) transitional care. *Journal of Nursing Scholarship, 34*(4), pp. 369–375. Copyright © 2002 John Wiley and Sons, Inc. All rights reserved. Reprinted with permission.

EDITORS' NOTE

Transitional care is gaining attention as an important approach to reducing hospital readmissions and improving other clinical outcomes and health care costs for Medicare beneficiaries. But the first test of a transitional care model that uses advanced practice registered nurses was on very low birthweight infants. The authors of the research on applying the model to both populations have described what they've learned from this work.

■ ■ ■

Dramatic changes in health care have occurred over the past 2 decades resulting in merged health systems, shortened hospital stays, rapid growth of outpatient and home care services and changed systems of reimbursement (Lesser & Ginsburg, 2001). The goal is to provide the most effective health care services at the lowest cost. Examining the effectiveness of health care providers has accompanied these changes. Today's data-driven health care systems require that provider practices are based on evidence and that provider time and number of patient contacts be justified (Delaney, Reed, & Clarke, 2000).

In 1980, responding to changes occurring in health care, a team of researchers at the University of Pennsylvania developed a model of transitional care delivered by advanced practice nurses (APNs) that could serve as a safety net for vulnerable patient groups being discharged early from hospitals; this approach might maintain quality care and reduce health care costs (Brooten, Brown, et al., 1988). Since 1980 research with this model of care has been conducted in two phases. The first phase, which remains ongoing, focused on testing, refining, and modifying the model for use with different patient groups. Consistent success in improving patient outcomes and reducing health care costs in patient groups in which the model has been tested led to the second phase of research. This second phase is focused on delineating the reasons for the model's success by linking patient outcomes and costs of care with the process of care. This ongoing research includes examination of patient problems that require more APN time and contacts, profiles of individual patients who require more APN time and contacts, and APN interventions used in providing transitional care (Brooten, Youngblut, Deatrick, Naylor, & York, 1997–2001). The purpose of this article is to describe the development, testing, modification, and results of this model of APN transitional care on patient outcomes and health care costs, and to delineate what has been learned for nursing education, practice, and further research.

THE QUALITY COST MODEL OF APN TRANSITIONAL CARE

The Quality Cost Model of APN Transitional Care was designed initially to promote early discharge of high-risk, high-cost, high-volume groups of patients by substituting a portion of hospitalization with a comprehensive program of transitional care delivered by APNs whose clinical specialty preparation matched the patient groups they followed (Brooten, Brown, et al., 1988). Transitional care was defined as comprehensive discharge planning designed for each patient group plus APN home follow-up through the period of normally expected recovery or stabilization. The intervention included a series of home visits, daily telephone availability of the APN specialists, and physician backup. In this model, quality of patient outcomes and health care costs are compared; research data include patient problems, APN interventions, type and number of patient contacts, and total time for each contact.

Development of the model was guided by the three-variable framework of quality of care including outcome, patient satisfaction, and cost (Doessel & Marshall, 1985). Cost and outcomes are the main variables, and satisfaction is viewed as an outcome of the health service. Master's-prepared APNs (clinical nurse specialists or nurse practitioners) were used for both quality and cost. Use of a master's-prepared APN specialist was based on the assumption that nurses with advanced knowledge and skill in the care of the specific patient groups they follow avoids the variability in preparation (Diploma, ADN, BSN) of nurse generalists. Master's-prepared APN specialists with advanced knowledge and skills can individualize care and function under general protocols needing less detailed procedures, protocols, and direct supervision than can personnel with less preparation. Whether APN specialists are needed for all patient populations has yet to be determined.

Components of the Intervention

The model was tested in a series of randomized clinical trials. Control groups received care that was standard for the group at the study site. In the original development of the model, patients in intervention groups were discharged early provided they met a standard set of discharge criteria agreed upon by the physicians and APN specialists (Brooten, Brown, et al., 1988), including physical, emotional, and informational readiness for discharge and an environment supportive of convalescence at home. Specifically, discharge criteria included: (a) general physiologic stability and absence or control of complications; (b) ability to assume self-care or having a support person in the home able and willing to assist in care; (c) no overt major emotional problems; (d) demonstrated knowledge of reportable signs and symptoms, medication administration, diet, activity limitations, and other group specific therapies and skills; and (e) a home environment supportive of convalescence with basic services such as heat and telephone (or ready access to one), the opportunity for rest, and available food and transportation.

The APNs prepared patients for discharge and coordinated discharge planning with patients, physicians, caregivers, hospital nursing staff, social service staff, community resource groups, equipment vendors, and others. The APNs also coordinated or provided patient and caregiver teaching, helped establish the day of discharge, coordinated plans for medical follow-up, and made referrals to community agencies. When problems were encountered, the APNs consulted with physicians and other health care providers.

Following discharge, the APN specialists conducted a series of home visits and were in contact with patients and their families by telephone. The number and timing of home visits varied with the patient group. Operating within broad protocols, the APNs used their clini-cal judgment regarding the number and length of contacts (telephone or home visits). The APNs were available to patients and families by telephone from 8 a.m. to 10 p.m. Monday through Friday and from 8 a.m. to noon on Saturday and Sunday. After 10 p.m. on week-days and noon on weekends, patients were asked to call their private physicians or hospital emergency room if immediate care was needed.

The APNs assessed and monitored the physical, emotional, and functional status of patients, provided direct care where needed, assisted in obtaining services or other resources available in the community, and provided group-specific as well as individual teaching, counseling, and support during convalescence. If complications arose, APN spe-cialists consulted with the backup physicians to determine the most effective immediate treatment.

Testing the Model

Testing provided data on the quality of care as reflected in patient outcomes and cost of care with thorough documentation of APN interventions. Patient physical and psychosocial out-comes included mortality, morbidity (e.g., rehospitalizations, acute care visits), functional status, affect, patient satisfaction with care, and outcomes important to specific patient groups. Cost of care included charges for initial hospitalization, rehospitalizations, and physician and other postdischarge health services, and in the APN intervention groups, cost of the services of the APN specialists. In the early testing of the model, costs also included time lost from employment by family members caring for patients. When shortened hos-pital stays became the norm for all patients, the focus on early discharge and the need to include this cost were eliminated. Each intervention group patient also had an interaction log created and maintained by the APNs. These logs documented each interaction between the patient and APN almost verbatim and included patient problems, APN interventions, type and time of patient contact (Brooten, Brown, et al., 1988).

Findings for Patient Outcomes and Health Care Costs

The model was initially developed and tested with very low birthweight (VLBW) infants (Brooten et al., 1986) through grants from the Division of Nursing at the Department of Health and Human Services. The model was subsequently refined, modified, and tested with women with unplanned cesarean deliveries (Brooten et al., 1994), women with high-risk pregnancies (York et al., 1997), and women after abdominal hysterectomy (Hollingsworth & Cohen, 2000), supported by a research program grant from the National Institute of Nursing Research (NINR; Brooten et al., 1989). With two NINR-funded grants, Naylor and colleagues tested the model with elders with cardiac medical and surgical DRGs (Naylor et al., 1994) and with elders with common DRGs at risk for poor outcomes follow-ing hospital discharge (Naylor et al., 1999). In a subsequent NINR-funded study using the model with women with high-risk pregnancies (preterm labor, diabetes, and hypertension),

Brooten and colleagues modified the antenatal portion. Antenatal APN home visits and telephone follow-up were substituted for half of the routine antenatal care provided by physicians in the clinic or physicians' office (Brooten et al., 2001). Findings from these studies are summarized in Table 13.1.

Widespread dissemination of the research in nursing and interdisciplinary journals led to public attention and effects on practice. Study findings have been presented in testimony to Congress and state legislatures and have been cited in the Congressional record. Protocols from several of the studies have been used by nurses in public health agencies. Physicians have adopted study discharge criteria. Clinicians in a major U.S. West Coast health care system used the findings on infant birthweight to change infant feeding practices. A neonatologist in Texas used the study's findings to establish a similar infant follow-up program. Nurses on the West Coast used the findings to establish a business to follow-up high-risk infants and children. To date, the body of work has resulted in 14 doctoral dissertations, 3 Doctor of Nursing (ND) theses, and well over 50 undergraduate, masters', and doctoral students publishing with the various research teams. In addition, other researchers have used the model as a framework for their research.

Work with the model is continuing. With a grant from the NINR, Naylor and colleagues are using it with elders with congestive heart failure (Naylor et al., in review). Also funded by the NINR, Brown and colleagues (1995–2001), using a modification of the model, are comparing maternal and infant outcomes and costs of care between two groups of women who breastfed their low birthweight infants: a control group that received routine care for breastfeeding and an intervention group that received a structured program of breastfeeding support services provided by perinatal APNs. Pilot studies have been conducted using the model with HIV positive infants and their families (Thurber & DiGiamarino, 1992).

Each test of the model was built on knowledge gained from previous trials, changes in health care, and specific needs of the study population. Length of APN follow-up changed based on recovery times from previous study groups and the clinical realities resulting from managed care penetration. Some measures, such as self-esteem, were dropped in subsequent trials because of little variability in scores, and others, such as functional status, were tailored to the study population. When testing with one study group was successful, data were analyzed to identify (a) those patients for whom the intervention did not yet show a difference, and (b) what modifications were needed to achieve greater improvements in patient outcomes and health care cost savings. For example, although we had achieved considerable improvements in outcomes and costs with the additive model in high-risk pregnancy, we realized the stressors of attending prenatal care remained and that we could reduce them by substituting APN care delivered in homes for half of traditional physician antenatal care delivered in clinics or physicians' offices. The reality of making health care improvements for elders with many co-morbidities necessitated a much broader team of health care specialists. Thus the intervention was continuously refined and more specifically targeted for subsequent testing.

TABLE 13.1. Randomized Clinical Trials of APN Transitional Care Model

Study group	APN intervention	Measures	Patient outcomes: APN intervention group	Health care costs: APN intervention group
VLBW infants (<1500 gms) (N = 79; 39 intervention, 40 control)	• Comprehensive discharge teaching • Home visits and telephone follow-up through 18 months after discharge	• Hospital length of stay • No. rehospitalizations • No. acute care visits • Hospital and outpatient charges • Infant growth & development • Infant immunization • Infant morbidity • Maternal affect	• Discharged mean of 11 days earlier, 200 gms less in weight, 2 weeks younger in age • No differences in rehospitalizations and acute care visits, physical or mental growth of infants • No differences in maternal affect	• Mean 27% reduction in hospital charges • Mean reduction of 22% in physician charges • Mean cost savings of $18,000 per infant
Unplanned cesarean birth (N = 122; 61 intervention, 61 control)	• Enrolled at delivery • Comprehensive discharge planning • Home visits and telephone follow-up for 8 weeks postpartum	• Hospital length of stay • No. rehospitalizations • No. acute care visits • Hospital and outpatient charges • Complications • Patient satisfaction • Maternal affect • Maternal self-esteem • Maternal functional status • Infant immunization	• Discharged mean of 30.3 hours earlier postpartum • Significantly greater patient satisfaction • Significantly greater number of infants immunized • No maternal rehospitalization vs. 3 in control group • No differences in maternal affect, self esteem, functional status	Mean 29% reduction in health care charges
High-risk pregnancy: Additive (N = 97; 44 intervention, 52 control)	• Antenatal home visits & telephone follow-up in addition to routine prenatal care • Comprehensive discharge planning • Home visits & telephone follow-up through 8 weeks postpartum	• No. antenatal rehospitalizations • Hgb A1c (women with diabetes) • Fetal & neonatal deaths • Infant birth weight • Infant gestational age • No. postpartum rehospitalizations • No. postpartum acute care visits • Hospital and outpatient charges • Complications • Maternal affect • Maternal self-esteem • Maternal functional status • Patient satisfaction • Infant immunization	• Significantly fewer antenatal rehospitalizations (women with diabetes) • LBW three times more prevalent in control women with diabetes • No differences in affect, self-esteem, return to function, satisfaction with care, infant immunizations	Mean 44% reduction in total hospital charges

Sample	Intervention	Outcomes Measured	Results	Cost Outcomes
Hysterectomy (N=109; 53 intervention, 56 control)	• Comprehensive discharge planning • Home visits and telephone follow-up for 8 weeks after discharge	• Hospital length of stay • No. rehospitalizations • No. acute care visits • Hospital and outpatient charges • Complications • Patient satisfaction • Affect • Self-esteem • Sexual function	• Significantly greater satisfaction with care • Mean rehospitalization costs $1500 less than controls • No differences in affect, self esteem, sexual function	• Mean 6% reduction in total hospital charges
High-risk pregnancy: Substitution (N=173; 85 intervention, 88 control)	• Antenatal APN home visits & telephone follow-up substituted for half of physician antenatal care in clinic • Comprehensive discharge planning • Home visits & telephone follow-up through 8 weeks postpartum	• No. antenatal rehospitalizations • Fetal & neonatal deaths • Infant birth weight • Infant gestational age • No. postpartum rehospitalizations • No. postpartum acute care visits • Hospital and outpatient charges • Complications • Maternal affect • Patient satisfaction	• Lower fetal and infant mortality (2 vs. 9) • 11 fewer preterm infants • More multiple pregnancies carried to term (77% vs. 33%) • Fewer prenatal hospitalizations (41 vs. 49) • Fewer infant rehospitalizations (18 vs. 24) • Savings of 750 hospital days	• 39% reduction in prenatal hospital charges • Total savings of $2,496,145 in health care costs for mothers and infants
Elderly: Cardiac medical & surgical DRGs (N=276; 139 intervention, 137 control)	• Hospital visits • Comprehensive discharge planning • 2-week telephone follow-up	• No. rehospitalizations • No. hospital days • No. acute care visits • Charges • Functional status • Mental status • Patient satisfaction • Perception of health • Self-esteem • Affect	• Fewer rehospitalizations, fewer total rehospitalized days in medical cardiac group from initial hospitalization to 6 weeks after DC only • No differences in surgical cardiac group • No differences in satisfaction and other patient and family outcomes	• Medical intervention group charges $170,248 lower at 2 weeks after DC and $137,508 lower from 2–6 weeks after DC • Charges similar for medical intervention and control groups from 6–12 weeks • Charges similar for surgical intervention and control groups
Elderly: Common medical & surgical DRGs (N=363; 177 intervention, 186 control)	• Comprehensive discharge planning • Home visits and telephone follow-up for 4 weeks after discharge	• No. rehospitalizations • No. hospital days • No. acute care visits • Medicare reimbursement • Functional status • Depression • Patient satisfaction	• From initial hospitalization through 2 weeks: • Fewer rehospitalizations • Fewer patients with multiple rehospitalizations • Fewer hospital days per patient • No significant differences in acute care visits, functional status, depression, or patient satisfaction	• Medicare reimbursements for control group double that for intervention group ($1.2 million vs. $0.6 million)

WHAT HAS BEEN LEARNED

Developing and testing the model across the life span with various groups of high-risk, high-cost, high-volume patients has made many important points clear, including the use of APN specialists, very different patterns of morbidity by patient group, a "dose effect" of APN care as well as points specific to patient groups.

The use of APN specialists, where the advanced knowledge and skills of the APNs are matched to the patient groups followed, was a key factor in improved patient outcomes and reduced health care costs. The APNs' content expertise provided credibility, legitimacy, and a level of trust when working with physicians, nursing staff, pharmacists, vendors, and other health care providers. The APNs' interpersonal skills and knowledge of systems and community resources were important to their success. Enacting the role successfully required constant interacting and negotiating with patients, families, physicians, nursing staff, research team members, various health care service providers, vendors, and others. Knowledge of systems and the ability to work within them to negotiate changes or to obtain needed resources for patients or families was equally important. This skill was apparent in the trials with women with high-risk pregnancies when, for example, the WIC worker did not work on the days when these women were seen in clinic. This situation required that the women return to the clinic on additional days to register for the program and the food important to their own and their fetus' health. Many similar situations occurred in working with the elder groups. Negotiating to alter staff's schedules or patients' schedules to decrease stress on the patients or to obtain needed resources occurred in several studies.

Testing the model among many patients' groups showed differing patterns of morbidity by group (Brooten, Naylor, et al., 1996). For the women with surgical procedures (cesarean and hysterectomy), almost all rehospitalizations occurred within the first 3 weeks after discharge (Donahue et al., 1994). In the VLBW infant group, more than 75% of the rehospitalizations occurred in the first 6 months after discharge (Termini, Brooten, Brown, Gennaro, & York, 1990). For elders with cardiac surgical conditions, rehospitalizations were most frequent in the 1st month after discharge, and patients with cardiac medical conditions had about equal numbers of rehospitalizations in the 1st and 2nd months after discharge (Naylor & McCauley, 1999). Although acute care visits were most numerous in the 1st month after discharge, a substantial number of acute care visits occurred throughout the follow-up period, unlike the pattern of rehospitalizations.

The reasons for rehospitalizations and acute care visits reflect the problems of each group. The VLBW infant group, with immature organ systems, was rehospitalized most frequently for respiratory difficulties, particularly pneumonia, and for surgery and general infections (Termini et al., 1990). Women in the cesarean and hysterectomy groups were rehospitalized most frequently for infections or complications associated with surgery including ileus and thromboembolism (Brooten, Naylor et al., 1996). Glucose control and preterm labor were major reasons for antenatal rehospitalizations for women with diabetes in pregnancy (Brooten et al., 1998; York, Brown, & Miovech, 1995). In the substitution high-risk pregnancy study, half of the rehospitalizations in the first 8 weeks postpartum were directly related to complications from the pregnancy (Hamilton, Brooten, & Youngblut, in press).

Problems of arrhythmias, unstable angina, myocardial infarction, and heart failure were the primary reasons for rehospitalizations in the elderly with medical and surgical cardiac DRGs (Happ, Naylor, & Roe-Prior, 1997). Profiles of rehospitalizations and acute care visits are important information for discharge planning and contacts after discharge. They also are important for researchers examining postdischarge patient outcomes. Most importantly, using the model reduced rehospitalizations across APN-followed groups. Where the reduction in rehospitalizations did not reach a level of statistical significance compared to controls, the trend was noted. Patient problems were detected earlier in the APN-followed groups resulting in shortened hospitalizations at less cost.

A dose effect of APN care became clear in testing the model across groups. When Naylor and colleagues (1994) used only the discharge planning portion of the model with APNs visiting patients in the hospital and contacting them by telephone for 2 weeks after discharge without home visits, reductions in rehospitalizations occurred only in the cardiac medical group and only for 6 weeks after discharge. When Naylor and colleagues (1999) strengthened the APN dose by adding home visits, the APN-followed group had significantly fewer readmissions and total hospital days than did patients in the control group 24 weeks after the initial hospitalization.

To achieve improved outcomes, APNs spent more time with subgroups of patients. Preliminary analysis demonstrated the cesarean birth group required a mean of 20 minutes more APN time during hospitalization and a mean of 40 minutes more in home visits with women who had morbidity (infections) compared to women without morbidity (Brooten, Knapp, et al., 1996). We also have noted large amounts of APNs' time spent with nonmorbid women who had problems with spousal abuse and parenting. While APN intervention into these issues might be regarded as beyond the concern of an insurer in a system of managed care, the potential social costs and benefits must be considered. What is the cost of APN time spent intervening compared to the financial and human costs of potential physical abuse of a woman or infant, intervention by the police, court costs, and possible foster placement of a child?

Optimal number and timing of postdischarge home visits and telephone contacts varied by patient group. In the elder and VLBW infant groups, APNs found that the effects of the first home visit were maximized when done 24 to 48 hours after discharge. This allowed time in the VLBW group, for example, for infant adjustment to the new environment and for the family to gather their questions. A telephone contact within the first 24 hours of discharge was important, however, to answer questions and concerns. Results of the intervention in the cesarean and hysterectomy group indicated that one home visit in the 1st week plus a telephone call in each of the first 2 weeks was sufficient for most women as long as the APNs were available by telephone for consultation. For women with diabetes during pregnancy, three antenatal home visits would have sufficed for most women if APN telephone consultation was available (Brooten et al., 1995).

Much was learned regarding discharge planning, including identification of periods of high anxiety in order to provide the most effective teaching. For all patient groups, the model protocols included patient teaching for postdischarge care plus return demonstration of basic knowledge and skills and printed take-home materials needed to promote recovery and maintain health after discharge. Teaching and return demonstration was begun as soon as possible during hospitalization and was repeated often to ensure patient learning.

Despite this comprehensive approach, many mothers of VLBW infants who had successfully demonstrated basic infant caretaking skills before discharge telephoned the APNs shortly after discharge to have the APNs review caretaking skills such as temperature taking (Brooten, Gennaro, Knapp, Brown, & York, 1989; Butts et al., 1988). The mothers apparently had not retained sufficient knowledge to act upon it or they were too anxious to try. Analysis of the data on maternal anxiety (Brooten, Gennaro et al., 1988) showed that maternal anxiety was highest the week the infant was born and the week of infant discharge when much of the discharge teaching and return demonstration had occurred. The effect of high anxiety on retention of information helped to explain the problem these mothers were experiencing. This same phenomenon was found in the first test of the model with elders (discharge planning only, no APN home visits; Naylor et al., 1994). These findings showed the importance of identifying points of highest anxiety in each patient group and avoiding these times whenever possible in conducting discharge teaching and return demonstrations.

Across groups we found that the most reliable and valid information on environmental supports was gained during home visits (Armstrong, Brown, York, & Robbins, 1991; Robbins, Armstrong, York, Brown, & Swank, 1991) and that patients tended to under-report or minimize environmental difficulties during hospital interviews. Coordination of the discharge plan and participants must begin as early after admission as possible if postdischarge services are to be in place at the time of discharge. This need was clearly demonstrated with the elder and VLBW groups. Both groups required multiple health and social services after discharge that needed to be obtained from several sources (Brooten, Youngblut, Deatrick, Naylor & York, in press).

We have learned much about measuring health care costs such as hospital, emergency room, and physician charges. Obtaining health care charges has become very difficult over the past 20 years, particularly following the advent of managed care. Fees are now required for obtaining such data from most health care systems, after patient permission, and often a delay of 6 months or more to receive the data. Obtaining health care costs from patients is also resource intensive. The costs of APN services were calculated as actual costs in our randomized sample trials and were converted to a charge that equaled the cost. Other methods that can be used include cost-adjusted charges, use of resource units (e.g., number of emergency room visits, postdischarge services), and microcosting. The costs of micro-costing analysis were prohibitive and were beyond the scope of our studies. However, our goal was not to determine the true costs for any patient, but rather, to determine whether patients in the APN intervention groups had lower costs than did patients in the control groups, and, if so, relatively how much lower. Charge data are adequate for making such proportional estimates, Similar proportional estimates would be needed if resource units or cost-adjusted charges were used (Brooten, 1997).

Based on our 20 years of working with this model of care delivery with high-risk populations and recent changes in the health care market, several implications for the education of APNs are clear. To keep people well over an extended period (e.g., 1 year), APNs must have in-depth understanding of how care is delivered across settings and the opportunity to provide care across settings. APNs must possess depth of knowledge and excellent clinical skills that are the hallmark of specialist practice. Knowledge and skills are necessary to individualize care and to anticipate and prevent problems to keep people well over the contract period and beyond. APNs must be able to: negotiate health and social systems to provide people with the supports necessary to stay healthy or minimize the effects of illness; collaborate effectively with physicians, families, and other providers; coordinate complex therapeutic regimens; develop strong patient advocacy skills and skills in teaching and counseling.

QUESTIONS REMAINING TO BE ANSWERED

Ongoing work (phase 2) includes analyzing data from 675 subjects, half of who have had the APN intervention, from 5 of the randomized trials using the Omaha system (Brooten et al., 1997–2001). The data set contains information about costs, patients' sociodemographic data and data on patients' problems and outcomes, APN interventions, and time per contact and per patient. Common instruments and costing methods have been used across studies. In each trial, the number of APN visits and telephone contacts was determined by protocol and provider judgment rather than by health care reimbursement plans. Results of this work will yield profiles of patients' problems and APN interventions by patient group and individual patient; patients who require more APN time or contacts; patients with higher health care costs and those with poorer outcomes. This work is beginning to link patient problems, APN interventions, costs, outcomes and APN resources consumed. Such data are essential to develop targeted, effective nursing interventions to improve the health of vulnerable, high-volume high-cost patient groups while maintaining reasonable health care costs—data important in evolving nursing practices and in systems of managed care.

Further work is needed in testing the model with APNs in supervisory or consultative versus direct care roles, the use of APN specialists versus registered nurse generalists, and testing with other vulnerable patient groups with frequent hospitalizations, rehospitalizations, or very high costs. The samples of the randomized trials to date have consisted of predominantly African American and White participants, reflecting national statistics for the relevant diagnoses and the demographic make-up of the recruitment sites. Applications of the model with other cultural groups are necessary. Continuing work in profiling patients' problems and APN interventions by group and individual patient, profiling high and low users of APN time and contacts, and linking them with outcomes and cost will allow more effective and efficient targeting of APN time and health care dollars toward optimal patient outcomes.

REFERENCES

Armstrong, C.L., Brown, L.P., York R., Robbins, D., & Swank, A. (1991). From diagnosis to home management: Nutritional considerations for women with gestational diabetes. *The Diabetes Educator, 17,* 455–459.

Brooten, D. (1997). Methodological issues linking costs and outcomes. *Medical Care, 35,* N587–N595.

Brooten, D., Brown, L., Munro, B., York, R., Cohen, S., Roncoli, M., et al. (1988). Early discharge and specialist transitional care. *Image: Journal of Nursing Scholarship, 20,* 64–68.

Brooten, D., Gennaro, S., Brown, L., Butts, P., Gibbons, A., Bakewell-Sachs, S., et al. (1988). Maternal anxiety, depression and hostility in mothers of preterm infants. *Nursing Research, 37,* 213–216.

Brooten, D., Gennaro, S., Knapp, H., Brown, L., & York, R. (1989). Clinical specialist pre and post discharge teaching of parents of very low birthweight infants. *Journal of Obstetric, Gynecologic and Neonatal Nursing, 18,* 316–322.

Brooten, D., Kaye, J., Poutasse, S., Nixon-Jensen, A., McLean, H., Brooks, L., et al. (1998). Frequency, timing and diagnosis of antenatal hospitalizations in women with high risk pregnancies. *Journal of Perinatology, 18,* 372–376.

Brooten, D., Knapp, H., Borucki, L., Jacobsen, B., Finkler, S., Arnold, L., et al. (1996). Early discharge and home care after unplanned cesarean birth: Nursing care time. *Journal of Obstetric, Gynecologic and Neonatal Nursing, 25,* 595–600.

Brooten, D., Kumar, S., Brown, L., Butts, P., Finkler, S., Bakewell-Sachs, S., et al. (1986). A randomized clinical trial of early discharge and home follow-up of very low birthweight infants. *The New England Journal of Medicine, 315,* 934–939.

Brooten, D., Munro, B., Roncoli, M., Arnold, L., Brown, L., York, R., et al. (1989). Developing a program grant for use in model testing. *Nursing and Health Care, 10,* 314–318.

Brooten, D., Naylor, M., Brown, L., York, R., Hollingsworth, A., Cohen, S., et al. (1996). Profile of postdischarge rehospitalizations and acute care visits for 7 patient groups. *Public Health Nursing, 13,* 128–134.

Brooten, D., Naylor, M., York, R., Brown, L., Roncoli, M., Hollingsworth, A., et al. (1995). Effects of nurse specialist transitional care on patient outcomes and cost: Results of five randomized trials. *The American Journal of Managed Care, 1,* 45–51.

Brooten, D., Roncoli, M., Finkler, S., Arnold, L., Cohen, A., & Mennuti, M. (1994). A randomized trial of early hospital discharge and nurse specialist home follow-up of women having cesarean birth. *Obstetrics and Gynecology, 84,* 832–838.

Brooten, D., Youngblut, J.M. Brown, L., Finkler, S.A., Neff, D.F., & Madigan, E. (2001). A randomized trial of nurse specialist home care for women with high risk pregnancies: Outcomes and costs. *American Journal of Managed Care, 7*(8), 793–803.

Brooten, D., Youngblut, J.M., Deatrick, J., Naylor, M.D., & York, R. (1997–2001). *Nurse practice functions: Patient problems and outcomes.* Grant No. R01-NR04102. Bethesda, MD: National Institute for Nursing Research, NIH.

Brooten, D., Youngblut, J.M., Deatrick, J., Naylor, M., & York, R. (in press). Patient problems, advanced practice nurse (APN) interventions, time and contacts across five patient groups. *Journal of Nursing Scholarship.*

Brown, L.P. (1995–2001). *Breastfeeding services for LBW infants—Outcomes and cost.* Grant No. R01-NR003881. Bethesda, MD: National Institute for Nursing Research, NIH.

Butts, P., Brooten, D., Brown, L., Bakewell-Sachs, S., Gibbons, A., & Kumar, S. (1988). Concerns of parents of low birthweight infants following hospital discharge: A report of parent initiated telephone calls. *Neonatal Network, 7*(2), 37–42.

Delaney, C., Reed, D., & Clarke, M. (2000). *Describing patient problems and nursing treatment patterns using nursing minimum data sets (NMDS & NMMDS) & UHDDS repositories.* Proceedings of the American Medical Informatics Association Symposium, 176–179.

Doessel, D., & Marshall, J. (1985). A rehabilitation of health outcomes in quality assessment. *Social Science in Medicine, 21,* 1319–1328.

Donahue, D., Brooten, D., Roncoli, M., Arnold, L., Knapp, H., Borucki, L., et al. (1994). Acute care visits and rehospitalizations in women and infants after cesarean birth. *Journal of Perinatology, 14*(1), 36–40.

Hamilton, M.S., Brooten, D., & Youngblut, J.M. (in press). High risk pregnancy: Postpartum rehospitalization. *Journal of Perinatology.*

Happ, M.B., Naylor, M.D., & Roe-Prior, P. (1997). Factors contributing to rehospitalization of elderly heart failure patients. *Journal of Cardiovascular Nursing, 11*(4), 75–84.

Hollingsworth, A., & Cohen, S. (2000). Outcomes of early hospital discharge of women undergoing abdominal hysterectomy. In M.T. Nolan & V. Mock (Eds.), *Measuring patient outcomes* (pp. 155–167). Thousand Oaks, CA: Sage.

Lesser, C.S., & Ginsburg, P.B. (2001). Back to the future? New cost and access challenges emerge. Initial findings from HSC's recent site visits. *Issue Brief – Center for Studies of Health System Change, 35,* 1–4.

Naylor, M., Brooten, D., Campbell, R., Jacobsen, B.S., Mezey, M., Pauley, M., et al. (1999). Comprehensive discharge planning and home follow-up of hospitalized elders: A randomized controlled trial. *JAMA, 281,* 613–20.

Naylor, M., Brooten, D., Jones, R., Lavizzo-Mourey, R., Mezey, M., & Pauley, M. (1994). Comprehensive discharge planning for the hospitalized elderly: A randomized clinical trial. *Annals of Internal Medicine, 120,* 999–1006.

Naylor, M., & McCauley, K. (1999). The effects of a discharge planning and home follow-up intervention on elders hospitalized with common medical and surgical conditions. *Journal of Cardiovascular Nursing, 14*(1), 44–54.

Naylor, M., McCauley, K., Brooten, D., Campbell, R., Jacobsen, B.S., Mezey, M., et al. (in review). Comprehensive discharge planning and home follow-up of elders hospitalized with heart failure: A randomized clinical trial. Manuscript submitted for publication.

Robbins, D., Armstrong, C., York, R., Brown, L.P., & Swank, A. (1991). Home visits for pregnant diabetic women: Environmental assessment as a basis for nursing intervention. *Clinical Nurse Specialist, 5,* 12–16.

Termini, L., Brooten, D., Brown, L., Gennaro, S., & York, R. (1990). Reasons for acute care visits and rehospitalizations in very low birthweight infants. *Neonatal Network, 8*(5), 23–26.

Thurber, F., & DiGiamarino, L. (1992). Development of a model of transitional care for the HIV positive child and family. *Clinical Nurse Specialist, 6*(3), 142–46.

York, R., Brown, L.P., & Miovech, S. (1995). Pregnant women with diabetes: Antepartum and postpartum morbidity. *Diabetic Educator, 21,* 211–213.

York, R., Brown, L.P., Samuels, P., Finkler, S., Jacobsen, B., Armstrong, C., et al. (1997). A randomized trial of early discharge and nurse specialist transitional follow-up care of high risk childbearing women. *Nursing Research, 46,* 254–261.

REACHING CONSENSUS ON A REGULATORY MODEL: WHAT DOES THIS MEAN FOR APRNS?

JOAN M. STANLEY

EDITORS' NOTE

Nursing practice is regulated by the states through their boards of nursing, but advanced practice registered nurses may be the purview of both nursing and medical boards, or a midwifery board, for example. These boards have differing requirements for regulating these nurses. In 2004, a group of national nursing organizations that included the National Council of State Boards of Nursing began to develop a consensus approach to this regulation that could be adopted by all states. This document provides a blueprint for how the profession sees the future of regulating advanced practice registered nurses.

■ ■ ■

Meeting regularly for the past 4 years, nursing's leading professional organizations have crafted a new model for future advanced practice registered nurse (APRN) regulation, certification, and education, commonly known as LACE. This APRN regulatory model, the product of the Advanced Practice Nursing Consensus Work Group, comprised of organizations representing each of these regulatory entities, and the National Council of State Boards of Nursing (NCSBN) APRN Committee, will shape future APRN practice and establish clear expectations for each of the components of LACE.[1]

APRNs, numbering over 240,000, play an essential role in meeting the nation's burgeoning health care needs.[2] The growing demand for health care services, the changing population, demographics, and growing shortages of health professionals, particularly primary care physicians, all demand an increased number of APRNs that are expertly prepared, are allowed to practice to the full extent of their knowledge and skills, and are readily accessible to patients in all settings. The changing landscape of health care and population demographics provides APRNs the opportunity to assume a more prominent role in care delivery and demonstrate the impact of APRN practice on patient outcomes. Currently, however, there is no uniformity across states in defining what an APRN is, what advanced practice nursing and education encompasses, and licensing and credentialing requirements. These realities lead to potential confusion among the public, weakens the APRN position in the public policy arena and health care community, and limits access to APRNs across states and settings.

HOW DID THIS HISTORIC AGREEMENT COME ABOUT?

As far back as 1993, NCSBN adopted a position paper on the licensure of advanced practice nursing, which included model legislation and administrative rules. In 2003, the NCSBN APRN Advisory Committee (known then as the APRN Advisory Panel) began work on a draft APRN vision paper, which was completed and disseminated in 2006 to a broad audience of stakeholders for feedback. Response from boards of nursing, national organizations, and individual APRNs was sizeable and varied. The NCSBN APRN Advisory Panel continued to work to respond to the concerns of the APRN community and to craft a future vision for APRN regulation.

In March 2004, in response to the growing concern and dialogue surrounding the lack of uniformity across the country regarding how advanced practice nursing was defined, what constituted an APRN specialty or subspecialty, and varied credentialing requirements from state to state, the American Association of Colleges of Nursing (AACN) and the National Organization of Nurse Practitioner Faculties (NONPF) proposed that the Alliance for APRN Credentialing (The Alliance for APRN Credentialing, comprised of 14 organizations, was convened by AACN in 1997 to discuss issues related to nursing education, practice, and credentialing.) convene a national consensus process to address these and other issues surrounding APRN regulation. In June 2004, an invitation to participate in a national APRN consensus conference was sent to 50 organizations, identified as having an interest in advanced practice nursing. Based on the recommendations from this first APRN Consensus Conference, a smaller representative work group was charged with the development of a future model for APRN Regulation. The Alliance APRN Consensus Work Group, made up of 23 organization designees, met regularly from 2004 to 2008 to craft a national consensus statement on APRN regulation.

Despite the tremendous amount of work to develop consensus around what the future of APRN regulation should look like, at a fourth APRN Consensus Conference in fall 2006, co-hosted by the American Nurses Association (ANA) and AACN, agreement was reached that future APRN practice would best be served if the parallel work of the APRN Consensus Process and the NCSBN APRN Advisory Committee could come together and, at a minimum, produce complementary recommendations that would guide future regulation. To achieve this goal, seen as a somewhat daunting task at the time, the APRN Joint Dialogue Group, a subgroup of the APRN Work Group and the NCSBN Advisory Committee, began meeting in January 2007. As this Joint Group continued to meet, agreement in many significant areas was reached, and it was finally decided that one joint paper, which reflected the work of both groups could and would be developed.

WHAT IS THE NEW APRN REGULATORY MODEL?

The new APRN Regulatory Model sets forth requirements for future APRN licensure, certification, education, and accreditation of APRN education programs. Under this regulatory model, 4 APRN roles are recognized: certified registered nurse anesthetist (CRNA), certified nurse-midwife (CNM), clinical nurse specialist (CNS), and certified nurse practitioner (CNP). These four roles are given the title Advanced Practice Registered Nurse (APRN), which is protected and can legally only be used by individuals licensed in 1 of these 4 roles. Under the new model, all APRNs will be educated in 1 of these 4 roles in addition to at least 1 of 6 population foci: individual across the lifespan/family, adult-gerontology, pediatrics, neonatal, women's health/gender-related, or psych/mental health. Nurse practitioners (NPs) will be licensed solely by the state board of nursing as an APRN, CNP and in one population. This will be the designation on one's license and what individuals will be required to use as the legal credential (for example, Jane Smith, APRN, CNP). The individual has the option and may indicate the population-focus as well.

In the model, key defining characteristics of an APRN include the completion of a graduate-level education program in 1 of the 4 roles; successful passage of a national certification examination that tests the APRN, role, and population-focused competencies; knowledge and skills to provide direct care to individuals as well as a component of indirect care; and educational preparation to assume responsibility and accountability for health promotion, assessment, diagnosis, and management of patient problems, including the use and prescription of pharmacologic and non-pharmacologic interventions.

The definition of an APRN stipulates that all APRNs must have the educational preparation to assume the management of patient problems including the prescription of pharmacologic agents. This means that all APRN education programs must provide the necessary content and experiences to prepare the graduate to prescribe pharmacologic agents. It does not mean that all APRNs must assume the responsibility for prescribing pharmacologic agents in their practice after graduation.

Under this new model, APRN education consists of broad-based graduate education, including 3 separate comprehensive, graduate-level courses in advanced physiology/ pathophysiology, health assessment, and pharmacology known as the APRN core, as well as appropriate clinical and didactic experiences that prepare the graduate with the specific nationally recognized APRN role and population-focused competencies. All APRN education programs, including master's and doctoral degree-granting programs and post-master's and post-doctoral certificate programs, will be accredited. In addition, all APRN education programs will be pre-approved by the accrediting body prior to admitting students.

Graduates of all APRN education programs must be eligible for national certification and will sit for a certification examination recognized by state licensing bodies. Certification examinations will assess the nationally recognized competencies of the APRN core, role, and at least one population-focus area of practice. APRN certification programs will continue to be accredited by a national certification accrediting body (the American Board of Nursing Specialties (ABNS) or the National Commission for Certifying Agencies (NCCA) and will require a continued competency mechanism.

APRNs will be licensed as independent practitioners for practice in 1 of the 4 APRN roles within at least 1 of the 6 population foci. APRNs may specialize in a more narrowly focused area within the population-focus but cannot be educated, certified, and licensed solely within that more narrow area of practice. In addition, this specialized preparation cannot expand the individual's practice beyond the role and population in which they are educated and certified. For example, a CNP educated as an adult-gerontology NP could obtain additional specialty knowledge and skills either as part of their original APRN education program or through additional education or experiences in an area such as adult oncology or cardiovascular health, but could not specialize in an area involving the care of children. Competence in the specialty will be regulated by the professional organizations, not boards of nursing; however, professional certification to demonstrate competence in the specialty is strongly recommended.

WHAT DOES THIS MEAN TO CURRENTLY LICENSED APRNS?

This new model, once fully implemented, has significant and exciting implications for all APRN practice, including independent practice, regulation solely by boards of nursing, and standardization of licensure requirements. More specifically, this new regulatory model will allow APRNs licensed in one state to move to any other state and obtain a license to practice if certain criteria are met. A grandfathering clause in the model allows practicing APRNs to continue to practice in the state of their current license. In addition, the model allows an APRN to practice through endorsement in another state if the APRN maintains an active practice in the APRN role and population, maintains current and active certification or recertification in the role and population, has met the educational requirements that were in effect in that state when the APRN completed his/her education program, and any other criteria established by the state. This means that if the other criteria for licensure are met, the APRN seeking licensure in another state will not have to meet these new educational criteria, which include the 3 separate APRN courses if they graduated from an APRN program prior to the adoption of this new model in that state. For example, if this new model with these comprehensive, broad-based education requirements is adopted by a state board in 2010 and an individual had graduated from an NP master's degree program prior to 2010, he or she would not have to meet the new education requirements. However, if an NP graduates in 2011 from a program that does not meet the new education requirements and seeks a license to practice in that state, he/she would not be eligible.

As of 2007, 7 states did not require national NP certification to practice, and an additional 3 states required national certification, but not in all cases.[3] Therefore, one significant implication for practicing NPs, or all APRNs, is that if an NP who is not nationally certified moves to another state and seeks a license to practice, that NP would have to obtain certification in the role and population to be eligible for a license in the new state. For this reason, all NPs are strongly encouraged to obtain national certification from one of the certification entities recognized by state boards. In the future, all NPs will be required to sit for national certification prior to becoming licensed.

HOW WILL THE MODEL IMPACT NP EDUCATION, CERTIFICATION, AND LICENSURE?

In addition to the implications for currently practicing NPs, other key elements of the model will have significant impact on NP education, certification, and NP practice. One of the most notable is the educational preparation and certification of NPs across the entire adult population. Preparation and certification of the Adult-Gerontology CNP must include care of the young to the older adult, and across the continuum of care from the well adult to the frail elderly adult. This broadened focus will require education programs to provide students with the necessary didactic and clinical experiences to ensure they are prepared with the depth of knowledge and skills of the current Adult and Gerontology NP. Likewise, certification bodies will expand assessment across this broadened focus and scope of practice. After extensive national dialogue, the decision to define the population as Adult-Gerontology was made to increase the number of NPs and other APRNs highly prepared to care for the growing older population. (AACN, in collaboration with the NYU

Hartford Institute, has received funding from the John A. Hartford Foundation to oversee a national consensus-process to validate competencies for this new Adult-Gerontology NP and for the Adult-Gerontology CNS.)

Faculty in an NP education program will need to assess the current curriculum to ensure that the 3 comprehensive courses included in the APRN Core (health assessment, physiology/pathophysiology, and pharmacology) meet the criteria described in the model. In addition, faculty must ensure that graduates are broadly prepared with the nationally defined role and population-focused competencies. Programs may continue to provide more specialized education preparation; however, this must be done only in addition to the broader preparation in the role and population. Didactic and clinical experiences must prepare the graduate to provide care across the entire scope of the identified role and population. Education programs must also ensure that graduates are eligible to sit for national certification in the role and population-focused area of practice. Under the new model, the APRN's education, certification, and license must all be congruent and in the same role and population-focused area of practice.

Another area of the model that received extensive attention and dialogue was the scope of NP practice from well care to acute care. Scope of practice is not defined by setting but by patient care needs. Pediatric and Adult/Gerontology CNPs will continue to be prepared with acute care and/or primary care competencies. Significant overlap exists between the competencies delineated for the acute care and primary care NP. Under the model, a CNP can be prepared with either or both of these sets of competencies. If prepared across both the acute care and primary care NP roles, the CNP must be prepared with the nationally recognized competencies of those roles and must obtain certification in both the acute and primary care CNP roles. However, a CNP should not be restricted from practicing in a setting, such as an outpatient setting or an acute care setting, based on the type of setting, but rather the CNP should be allowed to practice across settings and should be based on the needs of the individual patient.

As nursing practice evolves and health care needs of the population change, provisions are made in the model for the emergence of new roles or population foci. However, the emergence of a new role or population must be carefully considered, and a national process and criteria for this to occur are clearly delineated in the model.

IMPLEMENTATION OF THE MODEL

The targeted timeline for full implementation of the model is 2015. All involved in the development of this new regulatory model recognize, however, that implementation will be sequential and will require changes by all LACE entities. Some of the changes will be implemented immediately while others, such as changes in state laws and regulations governing APRN practice will, by necessity, occur over time.

Endorsement by APRN organizations is currently under way. Names of endorsing organizations will be listed in the report beginning November 2008. Due to varying processes and meeting schedules, additional organization's names will be added on a rolling basis after that date. Currently, endorsing organizations include AACN; ANA; NCSBN, NONPF; Academy of Medical-Surgical Nurses; American Academy of Nurse Practitioners; American Academy of Nurse Practitioners certification Program; American

Association of Critical-Care Nurses; American Association of Critical-Care Nurses Certification Corporation; American Association of Legal Nurse Consultants; American Board of Nursing Specialties; American College of Nurse Practitioners; American Holistic Nurses Association; American Nurses Credentialing Center; American Psychiatric Nurses Association; Association of Faculties of Pediatric Nurse Practitioners; Commission on Collegiate Nursing Education; Dermatology Nursing Certification Board; Emergency Nurses Association; Gerontological Advanced Practice Nurses Association; Hospice and Palliative Nurses Association; National Association of Clinical Nurse Specialists; National Association of Orthopedic Nurses; National Association of Pediatric Nurse Practitioners; National Board for Certification of Hospice and Palliative Nurses; National Certification Corporation; National Gerontological Nursing Association; National League for Nursing; National League for Nursing Accrediting Commission, Inc.; Nurse Practitioners in Women's Health; Nurses Organization of Veterans Affairs; Oncology Nursing Certification Corporation; Oncology Nursing Society; Orthopedic Nurses Certification Board; Pediatric Nursing Certification Board; Wound Ostomy and Continence Nurses Society; and the Wound Ostomy and Continence Nursing Certification Board. In addition to these organizational endorsements, at the 2008 NCSBN Annual Meeting held August 2008, delegates overwhelmingly adopted a new APRN Model Act and Rules and new Education Model Rules that are consistent with the *Consensus Model for APRN Regulation.*

The Joint Dialogue Group continues to meet to discuss the formation of a permanent LACE structure that will provide guidance for implementation. Critical characteristics of this structure include inclusiveness, transparency, and flexibility that will allow timely decision making, representation of all components of LACE and all 4 APRN roles, and ongoing communication among all entities.

In addition to the development of a national LACE structure, each individual state board of nursing, school of nursing, certification entity, and accrediting body will need to examine what changes are needed and what actions they specifically need to undertake to make this model a reality. Reluctance to make necessary changes by any of these entities of LACE will create undo barriers to obtaining desirable outcomes.

HOW WILL A UNIFORM REGULATORY MODEL IMPACT APRNS?

One of the most significant outcomes realized through the creation of a uniform regulatory model and through the creation of a permanent LACE structure is the increased transparency and communication among all 4 regulatory components. The outcome from this change will be an increased understanding of each others' roles, standards, and processes, which also should lead to decreased duplication in efforts, e.g., the setting of education standards and education program review.

Setting clear, common standards for APRN education, certification, and licensure across all states will protect the individual APRN from being denied a license to practice because his/her education program did not provide the necessary clinical experiences or coursework. This will also protect the APRN who becomes certified by one national certification body from being denied a license to practice when he/she moves to another state.

The Consensus Model for APRN Regulation also creates added protection for the public by ensuring that all APRNs are educated broadly with comprehensive preparation to provide care to a population of patients. One of the current concerns expressed by many state-licensing bodies has been that when individuals are prepared in a narrow area of practice can they (the state board) be assured that the APRN is prepared to provide a broader scope of services or care to that patient population when needed. Establishing standardized education and certification requirements for APRN licensure eliminates this uncertainty and concern.

A common definition for advanced practice and for regulatory requirements across all states has the potential to have a significant impact on APRN utilization and practice. A uniform definition makes the collection of workforce data possible. Without common licensing and credentialing requirements, obtaining accurate counts of all APRNs and identifying practice settings is difficult. This is particularly true for NPs due to the multiple certifications, specialties, licensing requirements, and titles used. Health professions workforce data are used by policy makers to craft national health care policy and make federal and state funding allocations.

Acting as a unified front strengthens the APRN community's opportunity to attain the goals set forth in the APRN Regulatory Model, including independent APRN practice, licensure solely under the regulation of state boards of nursing, uniformity of licensure/ certification/education requirements across all states, increased flexibility to practice to the full scope of the APRN knowledge and skills, and increased accessibility to APRN services.

The outcomes and implications for APRN education, certification, accreditation, and licensure described here are based on the assumption that the model will be fully implemented over time. The impact of the model and the individual requirements outlined will also be dependent upon the interpretation by the many individuals and organizations that will be tasked with their implementation. The members of the APRN Consensus Work Group, the NCSBN APRN Advisory Group and the organizations they represent worked diligently to craft a model and language that clearly delineates the consensus vision and specific requirements for this vision. LACE will provide an ongoing mechanism for communication among all of the components as they work towards full implementation.

For additional information or to download a copy of the *Consensus Model for APRN Regulation: Licensure, Accreditation, Certification & Education* (July 2008), go to http:// www.aacn.nche.edu/Education/pdf/APRNReport.pdf.

NOTES

1. APRN Consensus Work Group & National Council of State Boards of Nursing APRN Advisory Committee (2008). *Consensus model for APRN regulation: licensure, accreditation, certification & education.* Available at: http://www.aacn.nche.edu/ 2008; Accessed October 6, 2008.

2. U.S. Department of Health and Human Services Health Resources and Services Administration. In: *The registered nurse population findings from the March 2004 national sample survey of registered nurses.* Washington, DC: U.S. Department of Health and Human Services Health Resources and Services Administration; 2006;32.

3. Pearson LJ. The Pearson Report: a national overview of nurse practitioner legislation and healthcare issues. *Am J Nurse Pract.* 2007;11(2):10–101.

THE NURSING WORKFORCE/ NURSING SHORTAGES

Reprints of Key Articles

Peter I. Buerhaus, Douglas O. Staiger, and David I. Auerbach, "Implications of an Aging Registered Nurse Workforce"

Barbara L. Nichols, Catherine R. Davis, and Donna R. Richardson, "Global Nurse Migration"

IMPLICATIONS OF AN AGING REGISTERED NURSE WORKFORCE

PETER I. BUERHAUS

DOUGLAS O. STAIGER

DAVID I. AUERBACH

EDITORS' NOTE

One of the factors that undergirds the predictions of a persistent shortage of nurses is the aging of this workforce. Buerhaus and colleagues have examined the trend in the age of nurses, factors that contribute to it, and how to ameliorate its impact.

■ ■ ■

Registered nurses (RNs) comprise the largest group of health care professionals in the United States, with more than 2.0 million RNs employed in health care organizations in 1998.[1] This profession has experienced substantial changes during the last decade.[2–8] However, little attention has been given to the change in the age structure of the RN workforce. Data from the Census Current Population Survey (CPS) show that between 1983 and 1998 the average age of working RNs increased by more than 4 years, from age 37.4 to 41.9 years.[1] During the same time period, the proportion of the RN workforce younger than 30 years decreased from 30.3% to 12.1%, and the actual number of working nurses younger than 30 years decreased by 41%. In hospitals, the average age of RNs increased by 5.3 years between 1983 and 1998.[9] In contrast, the average age of the U.S. workforce as a whole increased by less than 2 years during this period (age 37.4 to 39.0 years), while the total labor force in the United States younger than 30 years decreased by less than 1%.

Explanations for the increasing average age of RNs involve a combination of demographic, social, and educational forces. Although the proportion of men in nursing has been increasing, explanations focus on women, who continue to make up more than 90% of the RN workforce. The size of the cohort of women aged 15 to 19 years from which nurse education programs drew students during the 1960s and 1970s declined in the 1980s, thereby decreasing the number of younger prospective nursing students in the U.S. population. Also, the recent expansion of career opportunities and rising wages for women relative to men[10] may have further reduced the pool of prospective nursing students because many women entered other careers. Similar aging trends have occurred in other professions and occupations traditionally dominated by women (e.g., teachers, social workers, secretaries, and hair dressers). In addition, the aging of the RN workforce has been attributed to the expansion of 2-year associate degree nursing programs during the 1980s, which apparently attracted individuals in their mid to late 30s interested in a second career.[11] Currently, 59% of entry-level nursing students graduate from associate-degree programs (Theresa M. Valiga, RN, EdD, National League for Nursing, 2000, unpublished data for 1998).

The nursing profession has been increasingly concerned about the ramifications of its aging workforce. In a survey of health care executives in 1995, the aging of the RN workforce was among the most frequently identified problems.[12] In 1996, the Institute of

Medicine noted that older RNs have a reduced capacity to perform certain physical tasks and warned that the aging of the workforce presents serious implications for the future.[13] A 1999 survey administered to nurse executives during a national conference found that 83% believed that the aging of the RN workforce will result in serious shortages of RNs in the next 10 to 15 years (P.I.B., unpublished data, 1999).

Despite this concern within the nursing profession, there has been little empirically based analysis of the causes and implications of an aging RN workforce. In this article, we investigate the quantitative contribution of various factors to the aging of the RN workforce. Using annual data from the past 25 years, we analyze the employment patterns of successive cohorts of RNs during their lifetimes to identify and assess key sources of observed changes in the age distribution and total supply of RNs, project the future age distribution and total RN supply to the year 2020, and compare projections to estimated requirements for RNs over the same period.

METHODS

Data

Data on employment of RNs were obtained from the CPS, which is a household-based survey administered monthly by the Bureau of the Census that covers a nationally representative sample of more than 100000 individuals.[1] In addition to demographic information collected in each month of the survey, detailed questions about employment (including occupation and hours worked) have been asked since 1973. Between 1973 and 1978, these questions were asked of all respondents to the May survey. From 1979 through 1998 (the latest year for which complete data were available), 25% of the sample in every month was asked the employment questions. The sample in each year was a representative cross-section of individuals, but each housing unit appears in the sample twice (exactly 1 year apart). Thus, some individuals may appear twice in the sample. Data from the CPS are used extensively by researchers and by the U.S. Department of Labor to estimate current trends in unemployment, employment, and earnings.

Data from the CPS were obtained for all individuals aged 23 to 64 years employed as RNs in the week of the survey (N = 60386). Because individuals aged 65 years and older comprise less than 2% of the RN workforce, they were excluded from the analysis. Registered nurses who worked less than 30 hours in a typical week were considered part-time workers. These data were used to estimate the number of RNs of each single year of age who were working in each year. We estimated the number of working RNs on a full-time equivalent (FTE) basis (i.e., as the number of fulltime employees plus one-half the number of part-time employees). All estimates were weighted by sampling weights provided by the CPS, making them representative of the U.S. noninstitutionalized population.

To ensure confidence that estimates based on CPS data reflect the population of RNs in the United States, CPS estimates were compared with data reported in the National Sample Survey of Registered Nurses (NSSRN).[14] This survey, conducted by the Bureau of Health Professions approximately every 4 years since the late 1970s, is the principal source of national data on RNs. As shown in the Table, CPS estimates of the average age and total

TABLE 15.1. **Comparison of Estimates of Total RN FTEs and Average Age of RNs***

	Total FTEs, No.		Average Age, y	
	NSSRN	CPS	NSSRN	CPS
1977	785,060	812,217	38.9	38.9
1980	985,788	1,090,232	38.0	37.9
1984	1,196,839	1,195,262	38.5	37.7
1988	1,345,915	1,342,641	39.2	38.4
1992	1,545,699	1,566,003	40.6	39.9
1996	1,777,151	1,743,191	41.9	40.8

*Data from the National Sample Survey of Registered Nurses (NSSRN)[15] and the Current Population Survey (CPS) for individuals between age 23 and 64 years.[1] RN indicates registered nurse; FTEs, full-time equivalents.

number of RNs are similar to NSSRN estimates from corresponding years. Beginning in 1984, the NSSRN changed from asking age (as is done in the CPS) to asking year of birth, and the difference in the survey question appears to have generated a slight increase in the average age estimated by the NSSRN as compared with CPS. For our analysis, we relied solely on the CPS data because the CPS is available annually and has asked a consistent set of questions over a longer time period than the NSSRN.

Additional data on the U.S. population by year and age between 1970 and 1998 were obtained from U.S. Bureau of the Census.[15] Forecasts of the U.S. population through 2020 by age were obtained from the "middle series" projections prepared by the U.S. Bureau of the Census.[16]

Statistical Analysis

Model. The analysis relies on a simple statistical model, commonly used by demographers and economists, that decomposes observed changes in the size and age of the RN workforce over time into 3 distinct components: population, cohort, and age effects.[17] The term *population* refers to the size of the total U.S. population of a given age in a given year. Population effects are expected to play an important role because the overall age distribution in the United States has changed recently with the aging of the baby boom generation. The term *cohort* refers to all the individuals born in any given year. Likewise, the term *cohort effect* refers to the propensity of individuals born in any given year to work as RNs. Cohort effects are expected to be important because women born in recent years have much broader career opportunities and, therefore, are less likely to choose nursing over other professions. Finally, the term *age* refers to a person's age in a given year. Age effects reflect the relative propensity of RNs to work at any given age and are expected to capture the tendency of RNs to work less during their childbearing years and as they approach retirement age.

More formally, the number of FTE RNs of a given age (a) that were born in a given year (b) can be described by the following equation:

$$(1) \text{ No. of FTE RN}_{a,b} = (\text{POPULATION}_{a,b})(q_b)(\alpha_a),$$

$$\text{for } a = 23, \ldots, 64 \text{ and } b = 1909, \ldots 1975.$$

The observed cohorts, born between 1909 and 1975, correspond to the cohorts that were between age 23 and 64 years at some point in the CPS sample years (1973–1998). The first term on the right-hand side of equation 1 captures population effects, with $\text{POPULATION}_{a,b}$ referring to the total U.S. population of a given birth cohort (b) at a given age (a). The second term captures cohort effects, with q_b representing the propensity of individuals from a given cohort to work as RNs. The final term captures age effects, with α_a representing the relative propensity of RNs to work at a given age. Thus, the total number of FTE RNs of a given age that are working in a given year is the product of the size of the population, the propensity of that cohort to choose nursing as a career, and the propensity of RNs to be working at that age.

Estimation. Both the cohort effects (q_b) and the age effects (α_a) are parameters that must be estimated. Rearranging Equation 1 and taking logs yields the following estimation equation:

$$(2) \ln(\text{No. of FTE RN}_{a,b} / \text{POPULATION}_{a,b}) = \log(q_b) + \log(\alpha_a),$$

$$\text{for } a = 23, \ldots, 64 \text{ and } b = 1909, \ldots, 1975.$$

Analysis of variance (ANOVA) was used to estimate the parameters of this equation. The unit of observation was an age-cohort group (e.g., the 1955 cohort at age 30 years). The dependent variable was the logged fraction of a given birth cohort at a given age that is working as RNs (defined on an FTE basis). The data cover 42 age years (23–64 years) and 26 calendar years (1973–1998) for a total of 1092 observations. The ANOVA model estimated main effects for cohort (birth year) and age. These parameter estimates were exponentiated to yield estimates of q_b and α_a. Standard errors for these estimates were calculated by the bootstrap method in a manner that accounted for the existence of multiple observations in the sample for some individuals and households.[18]

It is important to note that the ANOVA model in Equation 2 does not include main effects for the year in which the RNs were working (i.e., year effects). If year effects were included, then age and cohort effects would no longer be uniquely identified because year, cohort (or birth year), and age are linearly related to each other (year = birth year + age).[17] Thus, in the context of our model, a major change to conditions facing the entire RN workforce in a given year may be manifested via the cohort effect for future cohorts but not via a uniform effect on RNs of all ages working in a given year. For example, a sudden jump in RN wages may make nursing more attractive to new cohorts of RNs entering the labor market but would not encourage older cohorts to work more. This assumption is supported by findings from many studies showing that variation in RN wages has small effects on labor supply,[19-21] suggesting that year effects are likely to be small and may be safely ignored. In addition, year effects were not found to be jointly statistically significant at the 5% level ($P = .08$) when added to the model.

Forecasting. Forecasts of the total number of FTE RNs of each age in the years 2000–2020 were constructed based on Equation 1. The FTE forecasts were summed by year and age to produce aggregate forecasts. Constructing forecasts for a given age group in a given year required estimates of the population by age in future years, along with estimates of the cohort (q_b) and age (α_a) effects for the age group in that year. Population estimates were obtained from the U.S. Census "middle series" projections. The ANOVA model in Equation 2 provides estimates of age effects (α_a) for each age (23–64 years). The model also provides estimates of cohort effects (q_b) for cohorts born between 1909 and 1975. However, the model does not provide estimates of cohort effects for cohorts that were born after 1975 (not yet age 23 years by 1998, the last year of our data). Therefore, to construct forecasts of the cohort effect (q_b) for cohorts born after 1975, we used the average cohort effect from the 5 most recent cohorts observed in the estimation period (the cohorts born from 1971–1975). If future cohorts behave like recent cohorts, then this will yield accurate forecasts. We also investigated the sensitivity of forecasts to this assumption. Standard errors on the forecasts were estimated using the bootstrap method in a manner that accounted for the existence of multiple observations for some individuals and households.[18]

RESULTS

Estimates of Age and Cohort Effects

Estimates of age effects (α_a) from the model described in Equation 2 were jointly statistically significant ($P < .001$). Figure 15.1 plots the estimates relative to the effect at age 45 years (i.e., α_a/α_{45}). Thus, if population and cohort are fixed, Figure 1A shows the expected size of the RN workforce at each age as a percentage of the size of the workforce at age 45 years.

RN indicates registered nurse; FTEs; full-time equivalents. Estimates are based on the model described in Equation 2, "Statistical Analysis" subsection. Figure 15.1 shows

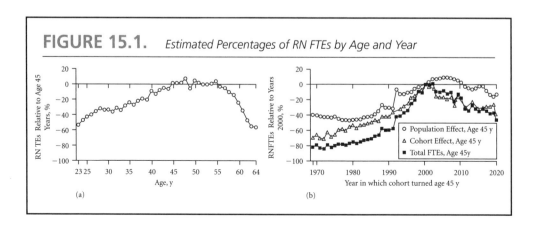

FIGURE 15.1. *Estimated Percentages of RN FTEs by Age and Year*

expected percentage of RN FTEs for a given cohort at each age relative to age 45 years (open circles). Standard errors for these estimates are 5%–10%. Figure 1B shows RN FTEs at age 45 years relative to 1955 birth cohort at age 45 years (in 2000) by population effect (open circles), cohort effect (open triangles), and total FTEs (closed squares). Standard errors are 5%–8% for estimates between 1978 and 2011 and 5%–15% for all other estimates.

The overall pattern of the age effects is consistent with expectations of how work effort varies over the life cycle. There is at first a rapid, and then more gradual, rise in FTEs through age 45 years, as many RNs finish nursing education and enter the labor force while others increase labor force activity as they pass out of their child-rearing years. Total FTEs are relatively stable from approximately age 45 to 55 years, followed by a rapid decline as RNs approach the usual retirement age of 65 years. Note that the age effects reflect both the number of RNs in the labor force at any given age and the average hours worked among those RNs in the labor force. Thus, while average hours worked among RNs in the labor force generally peaks prior to age 40 years,[21] total FTEs peak somewhat later because of an increased number of RNs in the labor force at older ages.

Estimates of cohort effects (q_b) from the model were jointly statistically significant ($P < .001$). Figure 15.1.B plots the estimates relative to the cohort of individuals born in 1955—or equivalently, relative to the cohort that is age 45 years in the year 2000. The estimates are reported according to the year in which each cohort turned age 45 years (rather than the cohort's birth year). Figure 15.1.B also shows estimates of the relative cohort effects (q_b/q_{1955}) and relative population effects (Population$_b$/Population$_{1955}$). In addition, we plot the product of these 2 effects, which is an estimate of the size of the RN workforce at a given age, relative to the 1955 birth cohort at the same age (total FTEs, age 45 years). Thus, Figure 15.1.B shows the estimated size of the RN workforce that was or will be aged 45 years in each year, relative to the year 2000, and how much of the relative difference is due to population vs. cohort effects.

The estimated differences across years are dramatic and consistent with expectations of how population and the attractiveness of a nursing career have changed over time. We estimate that the number of 45-year-old RNs will peak around the year 2000, reflecting both the effects of the baby boom (i.e., a large overall population aged 45 years) and the high propensity of women born around 1955 to choose nursing as a career (i.e., a large cohort effect). Prior to 1990, there were less than half as many 45-year-old RNs because of both a smaller overall population aged 45 years and a lower propensity of these earlier cohorts to choose nursing as a career. However, after the year 2000, most of the estimated decline in 45-year-old RNs will be due to the lower propensity of cohorts born after 1955 to choose nursing as a career (cohort effects). For example, in 2015 there will be about as many individuals aged 45 years in the population as there are in the year 2000, but the number of 45-year-old RNs will be about 35% lower because the cohort born in 1970 was much less likely to choose nursing as a career than the cohort born in 1955.

Evaluating the Validity of the Model

One criterion for evaluating the validity of our approach is the model's ability to predict the size and age distribution of the RN workforce within the estimation sample. The overall fit for the model was relatively good, with an adjusted R^2 of 0.82. The model's ability to fit the

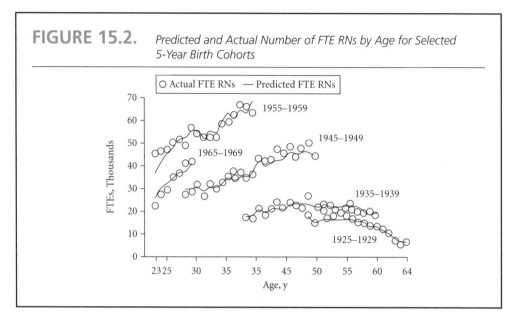

FIGURE 15.2. *Predicted and Actual Number of FTE RNs by Age for Selected 5-Year Birth Cohorts*

Each data point represents an average over 5 birth-year cohorts. FTE indicates full-time equivalent; RNs, registered nurses.

data is apparent in Figure 15.2, which plots the predicted and actual number of FTERNs for selected 5-year birth cohorts. Each data point represents an average over 5 birth-year cohorts. For example, the curve marked "1945–1949" traces out the predicted average annual FTEs supplied by RNs born in 1945–1949 at age 28 through 49 years. The actual number of average annual FTEs supplied by RNs in these cohorts lies quite close to the predicted values. Moreover, as predicted by the model, each cohort appears to follow a similar trajectory of FTE production as the cohort ages. Yet while the curves follow roughly the same shape with age, each cohort tends to provides a different level of FTEs throughout its lifetime. This is best illustrated by the 1955–1959 cohort, which has supplied more FTEs at every age than other cohorts.

The implications of Figure 15.2 for the size of the future RN workforce are profound. The number of FTE RNs supplied by the largest cohorts (e.g., 1955–1959) are likely to remain stable for another 10 to 15 years, before declining as these cohorts reach retirement age. However, the number of RNs supplied by younger cohorts (e.g., 1965–1969) are likely to remain well below the number supplied by cohorts born in the 1950s. Thus, in the short term we can expect an aging workforce (as the largest cohorts grow older), while in the longer term the workforce will shrink (as the largest cohorts retire and are replaced by much smaller cohorts of RNs).

To evaluate the model's ability to forecast RN supply beyond the estimation sample, we conducted a split-sample forecast. The model was estimated using data from 1973–1988 only, and the results were then used to forecast FTE RN supply for the years 1989–1998 (see "Methods" section for details). We show the results in Figure 15.3 aggregated in 2 ways: the upper curve shows total annual RN FTEs of all birth cohorts and ages and the

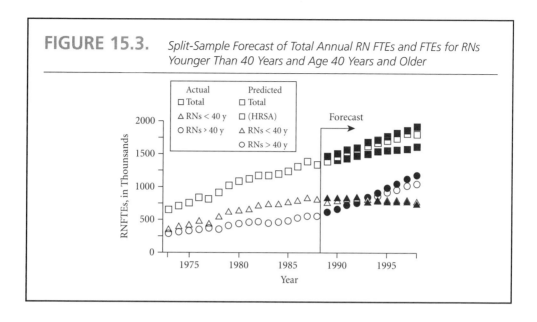

FIGURE 15.3. *Split-Sample Forecast of Total Annual RN FTEs and FTEs for RNs Younger Than 40 Years and Age 40 Years and Older*

lower curves show a similar comparison of forecasts for RNs younger than 40 years and for RNs aged 40 years and older. The forecast from our model tracks the actual number of FTEs quite well. In contrast, a Health Resources and Services Administration (HRSA) projection, based on data from 1988, underpredicted the number of FTEs throughout the 1990s, with a mean squared error more than 5 times as large as that for the forecast from our model.[22] In addition, our model accurately forecast a decline in the number of RNs younger than 40 years (and an accelerating growth aged 40 years and older) despite the fact that there was little evidence of this trend prior to 1988. Overall, the split-sample forecasts support the validity of our model: the model correctly predicted both the continued growth in FTEs, and the changeover in predominance from younger to older RNs that occurred in the 1990s.

The upper curve (shown in squares) is the total annual full-time equivalents (FTEs) produced by registered nurses (RNs) of all birth cohorts and ages in a given year. In lower curves (shown in triangles and circles), the FTEs are split into those produced by RNs aged 40 years and older and younger than 40 years. Closed symbols represent forecast for the years 1989 through 1998. Projections made by the Health Resources and Services Administration (HRSA) in 1988 of total FTE RN supply for the years 1990–1998 are provided for comparison.[22]

Projection to 2020

Using the same methods as in the split-sample forecast, we estimated the model by using all years of data (1973–1998) and projected the size of the RN workforce for the years 2001–2020. These projections, along with 90% confidence intervals, are shown in Figure 15.4. Our projections suggest that, following years of steady growth, the overall number of FTE RNs per capita will reach a peak in the year 2007 and will thereafter decline for the

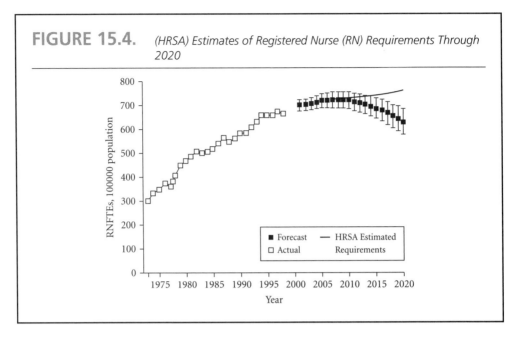

FIGURE 15.4. *(HRSA) Estimates of Registered Nurse (RN) Requirements Through 2020*

For comparison, the most recent (1995) estimates of RN requirements made by HRSA are plotted.[23] The HRSA estimates are based on models of demand in each major employment sector that take into account changes in demographic variables, health insurance coverage, income and affluence levels, and the impact of managed care. Error bars represent 90% confidence intervals. FTEs indicates full-time equivalents.

remainder of the forecast period. The absolute size of the RN workforce (not per capita) begins declining in 2012, and by 2020 will be approximately the same size as it is today. Based on these projections, the size of the RN workforce will be near HRSA-estimated requirements during the first decade of the new millennium, but will fall nearly 20% below requirements by the year 2020.

In addition to a decline in overall labor supply, the projections indicate a continued aging of the RN workforce. Figure 15.5 shows the actual and projected age distribution of the RN workforce every 10 years from 1980–2020. After increasing by roughly 3 years between 1990 and 2000, the average age of working RNs is projected to increase another 3 years before peaking at age 45.4 years in 2010 and declining slowly thereafter. Here again, the large 1950s cohorts dominate past and future trends in RN labor supply. In 1980 and 1990, when these large cohorts were in their 20s and 30s, the RN workforce was dominated by young RNs, with more than half the workforce younger than 40 years. By the year 2000, however, this distribution changes substantially. The 1950s cohorts are in their 40s, and RNs of this age dominate the workforce, outnumbering RNs in their 20s by nearly 4 to 1 (compared with 1980, when RNs in their 20s actually outnumbered RNs in their 40s). By 2010, the age distribution will have shifted as far as it will go (just before the 1950s RNs begin to retire), and more than 40% of RNs are projected to be older than 50 years. Only when the 1950s cohorts are reaching retirement age in 2020 does the projected distribution begin to shift back toward younger RNs.

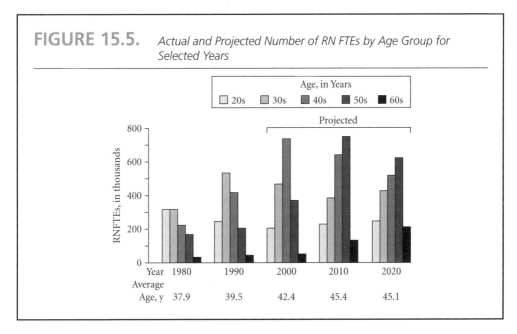

FIGURE 15.5. *Actual and Projected Number of RN FTEs by Age Group for Selected Years*

Standard errors for the estimates are 2% to 5%. Dates after 1990 are projected. RN indicates registered nurse; FTEs, full-time equivalents.

Forecast Assumptions

These forecasts depend importantly on 2 assumptions. First, we have assumed that future cohorts will enter nursing at a rate similar to cohorts that are currently in their mid-20s. Of course, future cohorts could be more likely to enter nursing (e.g., if wages or work conditions improve) or less likely to enter nursing (e.g., if the trend toward better career opportunities for women in other occupations continues). If we assumed that all future cohorts would be 10% more (less) likely to enter nursing, then the model would forecast an RN workforce in 2020 that was roughly 4.5% larger (smaller) and half a year younger (older). Thus, while the magnitude of the projected aging and future shortage is somewhat sensitive to what we assume about future cohorts, our basic conclusions are not. For example, for there to be no shortage by the year 2020, we would have to assume that all future cohorts (beginning with the cohort entering the labor market this year) entered nursing at a rate similar to that seen among the cohorts born in the 1950s. In other words, the size of the RN workforce during the next 20 years is largely determined by the size of cohorts that have already entered the labor market, and changes in the size of entering RN cohorts will be felt only gradually.

A second important assumption of our model is that changes over time in the size of the workforce for any given cohort depend only on the age of the cohort, and not factors that are specific to a given year. Thus, for a given cohort, any increase in the number of FTEs over time is interpreted as an age effect and not the result of economy-wide factors such as increasing wages. Of course, some of the increase in FTEs seen over the 1980s may have been in part caused by rising wages. We investigated this possibility by estimating alternative models that incorporated these year effects in various ways (results available from authors). These alternative models yielded estimates of age effects that increased less with age. The resulting forecasts of total FTEs were roughly similar in shape but 10% lower by 2020. Forecasts based on these alternative models were not robust to small changes in specification but consistently imply a workforce that is aging and shrinking even more rapidly than indicated by our base analysis.

COMMENT

Our analysis suggests that a fundamental shift occurred in the RN workforce during the last 2 decades. As opportunities for women outside of nursing have expanded, the number of young women entering the RN workforce has declined. This decline in the propensity of younger cohorts to choose nursing as a career has resulted in a steadily aging RN workforce. Over the next decade this aging will continue as the largest cohorts of RNs will be in their 50s and 60s, after which the RN workforce will contract as these cohorts begin to retire. As a result, the size of the RN workforce is forecast to be nearly 20% below projected requirements by 2020.

The continued aging of the RN workforce has important implications for employers. Efforts to restructure patient care delivery must be more ergonomically sensitive to older RNs, who are more susceptible to neck, back, and feet injuries and have a reduced capacity to perform certain physical tasks compared with younger RNs who once dominated the workplace.[24] Also, older and more experienced RNs may have higher expectations of working conditions and require greater autonomy and respect than has typically been accorded.

The RN shortages we foresee are in stark contrast to the oversupply expected by the Pew Health Professions Commission in 1995.[25] Moreover, unlike past shortages, the coming RN shortage will be driven by fundamental, permanent shifts in the labor market that are unlikely to reverse in the next few years. As shortages develop during the next 20 years, it can be expected that RN wages will rise, and employers will have little choice but to substitute other personnel for RNs. In anticipation of these developments, employers and nursing leaders should begin working together now to plan how best to use increasingly scarce RNs to deliver patient care in the future.

Long-term strategies to increase RN supply are needed to avoid a shortage. Although higher wages and better working conditions may attract more women and men to choose nursing as a career, these effects will occur only slowly and will be limited by the continued expansion of career opportunities for women outside of nursing. Alternatively, immigration of RNs educated outside the United States may provide the most feasible strategy. However, eliminating the projected shortage would require immigration on an unprecedented scale, and such a policy would not be without controversy.

Finally, the impending decline in the supply of RNs will come at a time when the first of 78 million baby boomers begin to retire and enroll in the Medicare program in 2010. Because RNs are vital in ensuring access to and quality of health care, it is critical that policymakers understand, and develop appropriate responses to, the implications of a rapidly aging RN workforce.

NOTES

1. Bureau of Labor Statistics. US Bureau of the Census Current Population Survey Technical Paper 63: Design and Methodology. Available at: http://www.bls.census.gov/prod/2000pubs/tp63.pdf. Accessed May 8, 2000.

2. Buerhaus PI, Staiger DO. Managed care and the nurse labor market. *JAMA*. 1996;276:1487–1493.

3. Buerhaus PI, Staiger DO. Trouble in the nurse labor market? recent trends and future outlook. *Health Aff (Millwood)*. 1999;18:214–222.

4. Aiken LH, Sochalski J, Anderson GF. Downsizing the hospital nursing workforce. *Health Aff (Millwood)*. 1996;4:88–92.

5. Gillilan M. Workforce reductions: low morale, reduced quality care. *Nurs Econ*. 1997;6:320–322.

6. Peter D Hart Research Associates Inc. *Health profession's view of quality: A national survey presented to the President's Advisory Commission on Consumer Protection and Quality*. Washington, DC: Peter D Hart Research Associates Inc; 1998.

7. Kaiser Family Foundation and Harvard School of Public Health. *1999 Survey of physicians and nurses*. July 28, 1999. Available at: http://www.kff.org/content/1999/1502. Accessed May 4, 2000.

8. Greene J, Nordhaus-Bike AM. Nurse shortage: where have all the RNs gone? *Hosp Health Netw*. 1998;72:78, 80.

9. Buerhaus PI, Staiger DO, Auerbach DI. Why are storages of hospital RNs concentrated in speciality care units? *Nurs Econ*. In press.

10. Blau FD, Ferber MA. *The economics of women, men and work*. 2nd ed. Englewood Cliffs, NJ: Prentice-Hall; 1992.

11. McBride A. Professional nursing education—today and tomorrow. In: Wunderlich G, Sloan F, Davis C, eds. *Nursing staff in hospitals and nursing homes: Is it adequate?* Washington, DC: National Academy Press; 1996:333–360.

12. Buerhaus PI, Staiger DO. Future of the nurse labor market in the view of health executives in high managed care states. *Image J Nurs Sch*. 1997;29:313–318.

13. Wunderlich G, Sloan F, Davis C, eds. *Nursing staff in hospitals and nursing homes: Is it adequate?* Washington, DC: National Academy Press; 1996:72–74.

14. Moses E. *The registered nurse population: Findings from the National Sample Survey of Registered Nurses*. Rockville, Md: US Government Printing Office; 1977, 1980, 1984, 1988, 1992, 1996.

15. Population Estimates Program, Population Division, US Census Bureau. US Population estimates by age, sex, race, and Hispanic origin: 1980 to 1998 (with extension to July 1, 1999). Available at: http://www.census.gov/population/www/estimates/uspop.html. Accessed October 1, 1999.

16. Population Division, Bureau of the Census. Population projections of the United States by age, sex, race, and Hispanic origin: 1995 to 2050 [machine-readable data file]. Washington, DC: US Bureau of the Census; May 1996.

17. Deaton A. *The Analysis of Household Surveys*. Baltimore, Md: Johns Hopkins University Press; 1997: chap 2.

18. Efron B, Gong G. A leisurely look at the bootstrap, the jacknife and cross-validation. *AmStat*. 1983; 37:36–48.

19. Bognanno M, Hixson J, Jeffers J. The short-run supply of nurses' time. *J Hum Resources*. 1974;9:80–94.

20. Link C, Settle R. Labor supply responses of married professional nurse: new evidence. *J Hum Resources*. 1979;14:256–266.

21. Buerhaus PI. Economic determinants of the annual number of hours worked by registered nurses. *Med Care*. 1991;12:1181–1195.

22. Division of Nursing, Bureau of Health Professionals, Health Resources and Services Administration, US Department of Health and Human Services. Health Personnel in the United States, 8th Report to Congress, 1991. Rockville, Md: Division of Nursing; 1991.

23. Division of Nursing, Bureau of Health Professionals, Health Resources and Services Administration, US Department of Health and Human Services. Basic Workforce Report: National Advisory Council on Nurse Education and Practice. Rockville, Md: Division of Nursing; 1996.

24. Rogers B. Nursing injury, stress, and nursing care. In: Wunderlich G, Sloan F, Davis C, eds. *Nursing staff in hospitals and nursing homes: Is it adequate?* Washington, DC: National Academy Press; 1996:503–532.

25. Pew Health Professions Commission. *Critical challenges: Revitalizing the health professions for the twenty-first century.* San Francisco: University of California, San Francisco, Center for the Health Professions; 1995.

ACKNOWLEDGMENTS

Funding/Support: This study was funded by the Robert Wood Johnson Foundation, Princeton, NJ.

16

GLOBAL NURSE MIGRATION

BARBARA L. NICHOLS

CATHERINE R. DAVIS

DONNA R. RICHARDSON

The chapter originally appeared as Nichols, B. L., Davis, C. R., & Richardson, D. R. (2011). Global nurse migration. In D. J. Mason, J. K. Leavitt, & M. W. Chaffee (Eds). *Policy & Politics in Nursing in Health Care,* 6th edition (pp. 401–408). St. Louis: Elsevier Saunders. Copyright © 2011 Elsevier. All rights reserved.

EDITORS' NOTE

The recruitment of foreign nurses to shore up the American nursing workforce has been controversial both within the United States and abroad. Barbara Nichols and her colleagues at the Commission on Graduates of Foreign Nursing Schools (CGFNS) provide a contemporary view of these controversies, relevant public policies, and potential policy responses that could provide a more reasoned, ethical approach to the recruitment and use of these nurses.

■ ■ ■

Migration is one of the defining issues of the 21st century. It is now an essential, inevitable and potentially beneficial component of the economic and social life of every country and region.

—Brunson McKinley, Director General,
International Organization for Migration

Migration within and between countries is commonplace and is expected to grow. The growing shortage of health care workers in developed countries drives migration, fuels aggressive recruitment, and is being temporarily resolved with migrant workers from developing countries. Since the domestic source of nurses in many countries is not keeping up with the increased demand, the gap will continue to be filled by foreign-educated nurses. This chapter discusses key nurse migration trends and challenges, and their policy implications.

MIGRATION AND THE GLOBAL HEALTHCARE WORKFORCE

General Trends in Migration

Migration is the movement of people from one country to another (international or external migration) or from one region of a country to another (internal migration). In general, five main trends characterize migration in the twenty-first century:

1. The number of international migrants is increasing; it is estimated that 1 in 35 individuals, worldwide, is an international migrant (Kingma, 2006).

2. There has been growth in the migration of skilled and qualified workers (Organization for Economic Co-operation and Development, 2002), with female migrants accounting for an increasing proportion of all migrants.

3. Women are reported to be migrating without partners or families (Kingma, 2007).

4. Violence against health care workers and gender-based discrimination persist in many countries.

5. Migration affects both developed and developing countries.

Almost all countries are affected by migration in one way or another, but developing countries are disproportionately affected because of their much smaller workforces and greater health care needs. Some countries provide the world with needed goods and services and are considered source countries for migration. Other nations accept the goods and services provided and are considered receiving countries. The United States is predominantly a receiving country and a prime destination for international migration.

As of 2008, immigrants made up 12.5% (38 million) of the total U.S. population. Mexican-born immigrants accounted for 30.1% of all foreign-born individuals living in the U.S., followed by immigrants born in the Philippines (4.4%), India (4.3%), and China (3.6%). These four countries, combined with Vietnam, El Salvador, Korea, Cuba, Canada, and the Dominican Republic, made up 57.7% of all foreign-born living in the U.S. in 2008 (Terrazas and Batalova, 2009). This pattern of Asian and Mexican immigration is quite different from the migration of Europeans in the previous century.

The Global Nurse Workforce

A number of "push" factors (reasons for leaving one's own country) and "pull" factors (reasons for choosing a receiving country) motivate nurses to migrate. Some countries, despite their own domestic health care needs cannot create enough jobs to employ the nurses they educate. Policies and restrictions related to pay and career structure, retention, recruitment, deployment, transfer, promotion, and the planning framework are other factors that "push" nurses to leave (Vujicic, Ohiri, & Sparkes, 2009).

Governmental policies on return migration and remittances also encourage nurses to seek employment in other countries. Return migration enables the source country to benefit from the skills acquired by the nurse while working in another country and thus provides an incentive for nurse migration. Remittance refers to the portion of an immigrant's income that returns to the source country in the form of either funds or goods. The World Bank estimates that global remittances reached $328 billion in 2008 (Orozco & Ferro, 2009). Nurses are more likely to be remitters than other migrants, remitting $8 billion to the Philippines and $5 billion to India in 2008. Remittances, which are the second most important source of external funding for developing countries (after direct investment), are generally used to provide financial support, decrease poverty, and improve education and health for families back home (Focus Migration, 2006).

Factors that "pull" nurses to developed countries include higher wages, improved living and working conditions, and opportunities for advancing their education and clinical skills. The continuing existence of gender-based discrimination in many cultures and countries, with nursing being undervalued as "women's work" relative to other professions, also encourages nurses to migrate. Table 16.1 presents the common push/pull factors that precipitate global nurse migration.

TABLE 16.1. **Common Push/Pull Factors That Precipitate Global Nurse Migration**

Push Factors	Pull Factors
• Low salary	• Higher salaries
• Limited career opportunities	• Career opportunities
• Lack of professional respect/autonomy	• Professional autonomy
• Violence in the workplace	• Better way of life
• Poor retirement benefits and practices	• Families already in the receiving country
• Poor working conditions	• Better working conditions/adequate supplies and staffing
• Tradition of migration	• Better resourced health systems
• Rise of HIV/AIDS in the workplace*	• Provision of post–basic education
	• Political stability
	• Improved standard of living

*Particular to African and Caribbean countries.

A migration-related issue that has received increasing attention is the effect of international nurse recruitment on local and global health care needs. When the U.S. nursing shortage exploded, so did the shortages in Canada, the United Kingdom (UK), and Australia. More troubling, many developing countries were experiencing nursing and physician shortages concomitantly with critical health challenges, such as HIV disease, infant mortality, and other public health problems. The developed countries encountered global criticism because they were accepting foreign-educated nurses from countries that needed nurses to meet their own health care needs. The question of how to balance the right of nurses to migrate for their own personal and professional reasons and the needs of people in both the source and receiving countries is still unanswered. Some receiving countries, such as the UK, have issued agreements with source countries, such as South Africa, to limit their recruitment in that country. Others have provided scholarships and educational funding with the intent to replenish the source countries' supply of nurses. Return migration upgrades a country's nursing workforce.

Trends in U.S. Nurse Migration

The U.S. is one of the top receiving countries for migrating nurses. Foreign-educated nurses entering the U.S. workforce tend to be female, 30 to 35 years of age and educated in baccalaureate programs. Generally, they have worked for 1 to 5 years in their home countries prior to migrating. When practicing in the U.S., the majority work in hospital settings (critical care and adult health), with long-term care being the second venue of choice (CGFNS, 2002).

Source countries that traditionally have provided nurses to the U.S. are the Philippines, Canada, and India. This pattern continues today and is augmented by emerging suppliers such as China, South Korea, Sub-Saharan Africa, and the Caribbean. Foreign-educated nurses can be found in all areas of the country; however, five states receive the majority of migrating nurses (California, New York, Texas, Florida, and Illinois), though other states have begun seeing an increase—most notably Georgia and North Carolina.

In 1994, "foreign-born" nurses made up 9% of the U.S. workforce, but, by 2008, this percentage had increased to 16.3% (Buerhaus, Auerbach, & Staiger, 2009). It should be noted that "foreign-born" does not mean that the individual also was educated outside the U.S. Many foreign-born students enter the U.S. on a student visa to attend nursing schools and then either return home or adjust their visa status to permanent and become part of the U.S. workforce. Initial findings from the 2008 National Sample Survey of Registered Nurses (NSSRN) indicate an increase in foreign-educated nurses in the workforce, from 3.7% in 2004 to 5.6% in 2008, despite periods of retrogression implemented by the U.S. State Department (Health Resources and Services Administration [HRSA], 2010).

Retrogression

Retrogression, the procedural delay in issuing visas when more visa applications have been received than visa slots exist, has limited the number of foreign-educated nurses that can obtain occupational visas to practice in the U.S. The Department of State determines when it is necessary to impose limits on the allocation of immigrant visas and to which countries retrogression will apply. Under retrogression, visa applications are not processed until the backlog is completed (Richardson & Davis, 2009). When retrogression was ordered in 2004, it applied only to China, India, and the Philippines and lasted for several months. The most recent retrogression (November 2006) was for all countries and continues as of 2010, causing a major decrease in the recruitment and visa certification of foreign-educated nurses (Richardson & Davis, 2009). A source country's economy may be dependent on how many of its citizens work overseas—a fact that fuels the push for changes in U.S. immigration and economic policies, which are needed to open the doors closed by retrogression and the downturn in the U.S. economy.

POLICY IMPLICATIONS FOR THE U.S. NURSING WORKFORCE

Imbalances in nurse staffing vary among nations, regions, states, levels of care, specialties, and organizations. The dynamics of supply and demand driven by an aging population, increasing demands for health care, and migration are out of balance with the growing global shortage. Nursing shortages are often a symptom of wider health system and societal elements. For sustainable solutions, it is not about just numbers of nurses but whether or not the health system enables nurses to use their skills effectively. Aiken and colleagues (2004) argued that "developed countries growing dependence on foreign trained nurses is largely a symptom of failed policies and underinvestment in nursing."

Receiving countries have the following four major policy challenges:

1. Determining the relative contribution of foreign-educated nurses to their in-country nursing workforce
2. Assessing credentials and improving regulatory mechanisms for licensure/registration
3. Providing initial periods of supervised practice as well as language training, health system orientation, cultural orientation, and social support
4. Developing ethical policies regarding recruitment (Buchan, Parkin, & Sochalski, 2003).

The U.S. historically has viewed foreign-educated nurses as a "quick-fix option" to meet U.S. nursing shortages and escalating patient care demands. Although the U.S. has the world's largest nursing workforce, Buerhaus and colleagues (2009) predict that U.S. dependence on foreign nurses is going to be a reality for the foreseeable future, thus the previously mentioned policy challenges must be addressed.

Determining the Relative Contribution of Foreign-Educated Nurses

Similar to many countries, the U.S. needs to enhance, reorient, and integrate its workforce-planning capacity across occupations and disciplines to identify the workforce skills and the roles required to meet service needs. It also needs to improve day-to-day matching of nurse staffing with workload.

A systems perspective is required to achieve priority of roles and a better balance of registered nurses to other health professionals and support workers. Data on skill mix are limited, and studies need to be done to highlight the nature of effective utilization of nurse specialists and nurse practitioners in advanced roles for improving the effectiveness of skill mix across the continuum of nursing care. To ensure that the nursing care needs of the public are met, a broader U.S. workforce policy is needed that balances foreign nurse recruitment and domestic needs. Table 2 presents a snapshot of the policy issues and strategic challenges that must be considered when migration policies are developed.

Keeping Track

Although foreign-educated nurses have been coming to the U.S. for over 50 years, there are no monitoring mechanisms in place to accurately report how many arrive, if and where they work (geographically and in what specialty), and how long they stay. The U.S. Citizenship and Immigration Service (USCIS) can tell us how many occupational visas they have issued, but neither by occupation nor by where the permanent visa holders are located. The only nurses the USCIS can accurately document are those on the temporary H-1C visa because it is limited to 500 per year. Trade NAFTA (TN) nurses, who also are on temporary status, are difficult to document because they may enter the U.S. on a daily basis if they are commuting from Canada to work in border states. This daily counting skews the tracking of the number of TN nurses.

Tracking by Nursing Organizations

Nursing organizations also are limited in their ability to document the number of foreign-educated nurses entering the U.S. The National Council of State Boards of Nursing (NCSBN) can provide data on the number of foreign-educated nurses taking the U.S. licensure examination, but this exam is given in regions around the world, and taking it does not ensure that the nurse is in or coming to the U.S.

CGFNS conducts a federal screening program called *VisaScreen®: Visa Credentials Assessment,* which is one of the requirements for an occupational visa; however not all nurses who complete the program will migrate in a given year. In addition, some nurses do not require an occupational visa, such as spouses or family of U.S. residents or citizens.

TABLE 16.2.   **Policy Issues and Strategic Challenges That Must Be Considered When Migration Policies Are Developed**

Policy Issue	Strategic Challenges
Demographics of workforce	Maldistribution of workers Aging nursing workforce Shrinking supply pool Variable retention Aging faculty Lack of prepared faculty
Poor or limited system planning for nursing workforce	Increasing RN supply Underfunding education programs for nurses Managing retention Improving recruitment Ameliorating effects of international recruitment/migration
Work/organizational environment	Opportunities for: • Career advancement • Continuing education • Professional development Reduction of occupational risks: • Reducing violence in the workplace • Taking protective measures regarding HIV/AIDS Job satisfaction: • Supportive supervision • Ability to use professional knowledge and skills Salary and wage structure Improving wage differentials between/among health professionals Workload/staffing Improving utilization and productivity of the health workforce
General governance governmental administrative and bureaucratic policies	Human resource planning and management Managing the role of bilateral and multilateral development partners Lack of data and valid information Managing the change process Policy and health sector reform

State boards of nursing also do not track the numbers of foreign-educated nurses. A few boards are beginning to collect aggregate data, but there is no universal data set. A major challenge for such data collection is that foreign-educated nurses may take one state's licensure exam to enter the U.S. but then apply for licensure by endorsement in a second state or even multiple states, depending on their work plans.

Monitoring Systems

The U.S. needs to establish a monitoring and tracking system for nurses who have immigrated to work in response to the nursing shortage. Such a system is essential to determine whether or not the recruiting of foreign-educated nurses does in fact contribute to a decrease in the shortage—especially as employers continue to demand increased visas for nurses, and as governments and professions attempt to establish effective workforce development and nursing education policies and funding.

Assessing Credentials and Improving Regulatory Mechanisms for Licensure

The migration of nurses and other health professionals is not a new phenomenon, but one that is growing each year—fueled by such factors as in-country shortages of health professionals, the desire for a better way of life, and opportunity for personal and professional advancement. The immigration of foreign-educated nurses and other health professionals varies by profession and is regulated by law in the U.S.

U.S. Illegal Immigration Reform and Immigrant Responsibility Act

The 1996 Illegal Immigration Reform and Immigrant Responsibility Act (IIRIRA) resulted in significant changes to existing U.S. immigration laws. Although the IIRIRA was promoted as an illegal immigration bill, its provisions have had a serious impact on legal immigration as well (Whitehouse & Gale, 2009). Section 343 of the IIRIRA requires that all health professionals, except physicians, who come to the U.S. for the purpose of performing labor as health care workers on either a permanent or temporary basis must undergo a federal screening program before obtaining an occupational visa.

CGFNS was named in the legislation to conduct the screening program for all named health professions, including nurses (registered and practical), occupational therapists, medical laboratory technologists, medical laboratory technicians, physical therapists, physician assistants, speech-language pathologists, and audiologists. The regulations implementing the law became final in 2003.

VisaScreen®: Visa Credentials Assessment

The CGFNS program that meets Section 343 requirements is known as VisaScreen®. It includes an assessment of the health professional's education to ensure that it is comparable to that of a U.S. graduate in the same profession; verification that licenses are valid and unencumbered; demonstration of written and oral English language proficiency; and, in the case of registered nurses, verification that the nurse has passed a test of nursing knowledge, either the CGFNS Qualifying Exam® or the NCLEX-RN® examination. Once all of these elements are successfully completed, the applicant is awarded a VisaScreen® certificate that must be presented to a consular office or, in the case of adjustment of status, the Attorney General as part of the visa application.

Educational Credentials

The International Council of Nurses (ICN) has guidelines and advocates for educational standards for general nurses. Foreign-educated, first-level (Registered) nurses are generally diploma or baccalaureate prepared. However, the largest number of immigrant nurses is from the Philippines, a country that has required the baccalaureate for entry into nursing practice since the 1980s. Diploma programs are on the decline in the United Kingdom and India, where the country is phasing out diploma programs. Most provinces in Canada require that those entering nursing be prepared at the baccalaureate level. The U.S. will have to accelerate its conversion to the BSN entry level for registered nurses, or it will lag behind the global community in preparing nurses to meet global health care needs.

Providing Supervised Practice, Language Training, Health System Orientation, Cultural Orientation, and Social Support

With the increase in global nurse migration, clinical competency becomes critical as nurses transition to practice in receiving countries. The more similar the nurse's health care system is to that of the receiving country, the more closely matched are the nurse's clinical skills. Employers identify clinical proficiency as vital to a safe transition to practice in the U.S.— second only to English language proficiency (Davis & Kritek, 2005). However, for many foreign-educated nurses, clinical experiences in their home country do not prepare them for nursing practice in the U.S.

Receiving institutions should have policies in place that support formal transition programs that incorporate orientations tailored to the needs of the foreign-educated nurse and assign a preceptor for as long as needed. Because most errors are made within the first 6 months of practice (Davis & Kritek, 2005), preceptors should be assigned for as long as needed, but not less than 6 months. Preceptors not only provide clinical support for foreign-educated nurses, but also enable their integration into the workforce, promote social networking, and help to create positive practice environments.

Language

In the U.S. written and spoken language proficiency for those seeking an occupational visa is mandated by law. However, the portion of English language testing that many foreign-educated nurses find most challenging is spoken English. This raises concerns because so much of nursing practice requires good verbal communication skills—interacting with patients and their families, physicians, nursing colleagues, and other health professionals.

Receiving institutions need to create policies on the use of language and programs that enable mastery of the language of practice—not only the formal language but also the slang, idioms, and abbreviations. Foreign-educated nurses must attempt to use the formal language of the workplace—English in the case of the U.S.—rather than fall back on use of their native language, especially when working with colleagues from their own countries.

Acculturation

The acculturation of foreign-educated nurses to a new setting in a host or receiving country can take up to 12 months. During this time the nurse goes through a number of stages. First there is initial excitement about working in a new environment. Then there is anxiety and a sense of isolation. In the next stage, the nurse feels a part of two cultures and explores his or her own beliefs and values about care as well as those of the institution. Finally, the nurse reaches the integration stage, in which there is a renewed enthusiasm for work and a reconciliation of the differences between personal and institutional values.

Receiving institutions should adopt policies that ensure that foreign-educated nurses work in an environment that is free from oppression and that promote integration of cultural competence into the daily practice of care. This might include an educational component that focuses on cultural awareness and increases staff knowledge of the most common cultures of their colleagues as well as their patients (Douglas et al., 2009).

Developing Ethical Policies Regarding Recruitment

In the 1970s, there were many reported instances of unethical recruitment practices and no international, national, or industry oversight of the recruitment of nurses. The unethical practices included usurious fees for immigration services and travel, substandard housing, misrepresented charges, inequitable salaries and benefits, broken contracts, harassment, and threats of legal action and deportation.

CGFNS International was established in 1977 to create a program of credentials evaluation that not only ensured the competency of foreign-educated nurses but also was professionally ethical and responsible to both the foreign-educated nurses and the U.S. public. The need for such an entity was a novel and controversial idea at the time. Nevertheless, CGFNS was created at the behest of the U.S. Departments of State, Labor and Health, Education, and Welfare (HEW)—later known as the Department of Health and Human Services (DHHS)—and the Immigration and Naturalization Service (INS), later to be absorbed by the Department of Homeland Security (DHS).

Many of the unethical recruitment practices declined as the federal government and state boards of nursing began requiring education and licensure screening of foreign-educated nurses. Nevertheless, they have not disappeared entirely. As nursing shortages have increased and recruitment has become a lucrative business, such practices are recurring—often with new, inexperienced recruitment businesses located both in the United States and abroad.

In the 1989 Immigration Nursing Relief Act (INRA), which provided temporary visas (H-1A) for registered nurses, Congress included language for the protection of foreign-educated nurses who experienced discrimination in salaries, assignments, and benefits. It also imposed penalties and fines for employers who engaged in such practices. Although the legislation sunsetted in 1995, these protections are still in place and have been used to challenge unethical and illegal practices by health care employers.

Ethical recruitment practices have become a priority of the international and U.S. nursing communities, as well as human rights organizations. The World Health Organization (WHO) has developed a Code of Practice on the International Recruitment of Health Care Personnel, which was adopted at the 63rd World Health Assembly in May 2010. The International Council on Nursing (ICN) issued a Code of Ethics for recruitment of nurses in 2007. National nursing organizations in the U.S. also have issued statements in support of ethical recruitment.

In 2008, the MacArthur Foundation funded the development of a U.S. Code of Ethics for Recruitment of Foreign-Educated Nurses that was issued in 2009 as a voluntary code. It was developed by an advisory council of stakeholders that was convened by AcademyHealth, a private sector health policy organization, and included representatives from unions, hospitals, nursing organizations, regulatory bodies, credentials evaluators, recruiters, staffing agencies, and immigration attorneys. The goal was to reduce the harm and increase the benefits of international nurse recruitment for source countries, receiving countries, U.S. patients, and migrant nurses. The Council evolved into the Alliance for Ethical International Recruitment Practices. Subscribers to the Code will agree to abide by it. Nurses will be able to refer possible violations of the Code to the Alliance, which will assist in resolution of the infractions or refer them to advocacy or government bodies. This work is essential as it focuses on the actual practices of greatest concern—aggressive, predatory recruitment practices that are abusive to nurses seeking a better life for themselves and their families. Nursing leaders in the U.S. will need to proactively implement these guidelines and continue to monitor abuses that may emerge, and that could negatively impact the recruitment and retention of foreign-educated nurses.

All of these codes stress the need for informed consent and transparency to ensure that the nurse knows and understands the content of work contracts, requirements for immigration, and his or her rights and responsibilities.

SUMMARY

The impact of global nurse migration on developed and developing countries has fueled a worldwide nursing shortage. "The issues surrounding nursing shortages and global nurse migration are inextricably linked. Global nurse migration has become a major phenomenon impacting health service delivery in both developed and developing countries. The phenomenon has created a global labor market for health professionals and has fueled international recruitment. International migration and recruitment have become dominant features of the international health policy debate" (Nichols, 2007).

The loss of human resources through migration of professional health staff to developed countries usually results in a loss of capacity of health systems in developing countries to deliver health care equitably. Migration of health workers also undermines the ability of countries to meet global, regional, and national commitments, such as the health-related United Nations Millennium Development Goals (MDG). Data on the extent and impact of migration are often anecdotal and fail to shed light on the multiple, interrelated causes, and multifaceted dynamics related to this complex phenomenon.

Without effective and sustained policy interventions, the global nursing shortage will persist, undermining global attempts to improve care outcomes and the health of all nations. In short, U.S. planning efforts should require the establishment of a national system that monitors the inflow of foreign nurses, their country of origin, the states and settings in which they work, and their impact on the nursing shortage.

For a list of related websites, please refer to your Evolve Resources at http://evolve .elsevier.com/Mason/policypolitics.

REFERENCES

Aiken, L., Buchan, J., Sochalski, J., Nichols, B., & Powell, M. (2004). Trends in international migration. *Health Affairs, 23(3),* 69–77.

Buchan, J., Parkin, T., & Sochalski, J. (2003). *International nurse mobility: Trends and policy implications.* Geneva: World Health Organization. Retrieved March 10, 2010, from http://whqlibdoc.who.int/hq/2003/WHO_EIP_OSD_2003.3.pdf.

Buerhaus, P. I., Auerbach, D. I., & Staiger, D. O. (2009). The recent surge in nurse employment: Causes and implications. Building a high-value nursing workforce. *Health Affairs Supplement, 28(4),* w 657–668.

CGFNS International (2002). *Characteristics of foreign nurse graduates in the United States workforce.* Philadelphia: Author.

Davis, C.R., Kritek, P.B. (2005). Foreign nurses in the U.S. workforce. *Healthy work environments: Foreign nurse recruitment best practices.* Washington, DC: American Organization of Nurse Executives. Retrieved December 3, 2009, from http://www.aone.org/anoe/pdf/ForeignNurseRecruitmentBestPracticesOctober2005.pdf.

Douglas, M.K., Pierce, J.U., Rosenkoetter, M., Callister, L.C., Hatter-Pollara, M., Lauderdale, J., et al. (2009). Standards of practice for culturally competent nursing care: A request for comments. *Journal of Transcultural Nursing 20(3),* 257–269.

Focus Migration. (2006). *Remittances: A bridge between migration and development.* Retrieved February 16, 2010, from http://www.focus-migration.de/Remittances_A_Brid.1200.0.html?&L=1.

Health Resources and Services Administration (HRSA). (2010). *The registered nurse population: Initial findings from the 2008 National Sample Survey of Registered Nurses.* Retrieved March 17, 2010, from http://bhpr.hrsa.gov/healthworkforce/rnsurvey/initialfindings2008.pdf.

Kingma, M. (2006). *Nurses on the move.* Ithaca, NY: Cornell University Press.

Kingma, M. (2007). Nurses on the move: A global overview. International Migration of Nurses [Special issue]. *Health Services Research, 42(3).* June 2007, Part II, 1281–1298.

Nichols, B. (2007). *The impact of global nurse migration on health services delivery (a white paper).* Philadelphia, Pennsylvania: CGFNS International, Inc.

Organization for Economic Co-operation and Development. (2002). *International mobility of the highly skilled.* Paris: Author.

Orozco, M., & Ferro, A. (Eds.). (2009). Worldwide trends in international flows. *Migrant Remittances, 6(2),* August 2009. Retrieved December 3, 2009, from http://www.microlinks.org/ev_en.php?ID=13069_201&ID2=DO_TOPIC.

Richardson, D.R., & Davis, C.R. (2009). Entry into the United States. In B.L. Nichols & C.R. Davis (Eds.), *The official guide for foreign-educated nurses: What you need to know about nursing and health care in the United States* (pp. 43–70). New York: Springer.

Terrazas, A., & Batalova, J. (2009). *Frequently requested statistics on immigrants and immigration to the United States,* October 27, 2009. Retrieved March 10, 2010, from http://www.migrationinformation.org/USfocus/print.cfm?ID=747.

Vujicic, M., Ohiri, K., & Sparkes, S. (2009). *Working in health: Financing and managing the public sector health workforce.* Washington, DC: World Bank.

Whitehouse, D., & Gale, D. (2009). Foreign-educated healthcare professionals in the United States healthcare system. In B.L. Nichols & C.R. Davis (Eds.), *The official guide for foreign-educated allied health professionals: What you need to know about health care and the health professions in the United States* (pp. 1–39). New York: Springer.

QUALITY, SAFETY, AND COST

Reprints of Key Articles

Jack Needleman, Peter I. Buerhaus, Soeren Mattke, Maureen Stewart, and Katya Zelevinsky, "Nurse-Staffing Levels and the Quality of Care in Hospitals"

Linda H. Aiken, Sean P. Clarke, Douglas M. Sloane, Jule Sochalski, and Jeffrey H. Silber, "Hospital Nurse Staffing and Patient Mortality, Nurse Burnout, and Job Dissatisfaction"

Jack Needleman, Peter I. Buerhaus, Maureen Stewart, Katya Zelevinsky, and Soeren Mattke, "Nurse Staffing in Hospitals: Is There a Business Case for Quality?"

17

NURSE-STAFFING LEVELS AND THE QUALITY OF CARE IN HOSPITALS

JACK NEEDLEMAN

PETER I. BUERHAUS

SOEREN MATTKE

MAUREEN STEWART

KATYA ZELEVINSKY

This article originally appeared as Needleman, J., Buerhaus, P. I., Mattke, S., Steward, M., & Zelevinsky, K. (2002). Nurse-staffing levels and the quality of care in hospitals. *New England Journal of Medicine, 346,* pp. 1715–1722.

EDITORS' NOTE

In the mid-1990s when hospitals were coping with the surge of managed care by replacing nurses with cheaper non-nurses, the Institute of Medicine released a report on the link between nurse staffing and clinical outcomes. One conclusion in the report was that there was insufficient evidence documenting a link between nursing staffing in acute care facilities and patient outcomes. Researchers responded to the challenge for rigorous research on this matter. This study by Needleman and colleagues was one of the first to be published. Its appearance in a top-tier medical journal brought media attention to the researchers' conclusion that adequate nurse staffing is associated with lower rates of complications and shorter lengths of stay among hospitalized medical and surgical patients.

■ ■ ■

Hospitals, wrote Lewis Thomas in *The Youngest Science,* are "held together, glued together, enabled to function . . . by the nurses."[1] More than 1.3 million registered nurses work in hospitals in the United States. As hospitals have responded to financial pressure from Medicare, managed care, and other private payers, registered nurses have become increasingly dissatisfied with the working conditions in hospitals. They report that they are spending less time taking care of increasingly ill patients and believe that the safety and quality of inpatient care are deteriorating.[2-7] Although the number of hours of care per patient-day provided by registered nurses rose through the mid-1990s,[8-12] some question whether the staffing of nurses has increased rapidly enough to keep pace with the increasing severity of illness among hospitalized patients and thus to ensure safe and high-quality care.[13]

Research on the relation between the level of staffing by nurses in hospitals and patients' outcomes has been inconclusive. Whereas some studies have reported an association between higher levels of staffing by nurses and lower mortality,[14-20] as well as lower rates of other adverse outcomes,[21-30] others have found no such relations.[30-39] Previous studies have assessed only a limited number of outcomes that are sensitive to the extent or quality of nursing care, such as falls by patients and errors in medication. Many studies have used small samples of hospitals, controlled only to a limited extent for the patient's initial risk for the outcomes under study, failed to include nurses' aides as part of the nursing staff, and used inconsistent measures of staffing levels. We examined the relation between the levels of staffing by nurses in hospitals and the rates of adverse outcomes among patients, using administrative data from a large multistate sample of hospitals.

METHODS

Measures of Adverse Outcomes

The study was approved by the Harvard School of Public Health Human Subjects Committee. On the basis of published[21,27,28,30,39–47] and unpublished materials, we identified 14 adverse outcomes during hospitalization (11 for both medical and surgical patients and 3 for surgical patients only) that could be coded on the basis of hospital-discharge abstracts and that are potentially sensitive to staffing by nurses. Building on previous studies,[30,48–50] we developed coding rules to construct risk groups of patients and to identify patients with each outcome (listed in the Appendix).

Study Population

We obtained data on hospital discharges and the staffing by nurses from 11 states that collect both types of data: Arizona, California, Maryland, Massachusetts, Missouri, Nevada, New York, South Carolina, Virginia, West Virginia, and Wisconsin. We estimated 1997 staffing as the weighted average of staffing in the hospital's fiscal years 1997 and 1998, except in Virginia, for which only fiscal 1997 data were available. We obtained data on discharges for the 1997 calendar year (for Virginia, we obtained data for the four calendar quarters matching each hospital's fiscal year). The initial sample was 1041 hospitals. We then excluded hospitals with an average daily census of less than 20, an occupancy rate below 20 percent, or missing data on staffing, as well as those reporting extremely low or high levels of staffing per patient-day (below the 7.5th percentile or above the 92.5th percentile). The final sample included 799 hospitals, which together accounted for 26 percent of the discharges from nonfederal hospitals in the United States in 1997.

Measures of Staffing

The levels of staffing by registered nurses, licensed practical nurses, and nurses' aides were estimated in hours. For states reporting staffing as full-time equivalents, we used a standard year of 2080 hours (52 weeks at 40 hours per week). In California, the levels of staffing of nurses for inpatient and outpatient care are calculated directly from financial data reported by the California Office of Statewide Health Planning and Development. Using these data, we found that the standard measure, "adjusted patient-days," that was used to adjust total hours of nursing care to reflect the number of both inpatients and outpatients treated at the hospital (hospital volume)[51] underestimated staffing for inpatient care and overestimated staffing for outpatient care. To adjust for this bias, we constructed a regression model, using data from California, that predicted staffing for inpatient care per inpatient-day on the basis of the level of staffing per adjusted patient-day and the number of outpatients treated; we used this model to estimate staffing for inpatient care from the staffing levels per adjusted patient-day reported in the other 10 states.

    For easier comparison of the levels of staffing by nurses in different hospitals, we adjusted the hours of nursing care per day for differences in the nursing care needed by the patients of each hospital. We used estimates of the relative level of nursing care needed by patients in each diagnosis-related group [28,52] to construct a nursing case-mix index for each hospital. We divided hours of nursing care per inpatient-day by this index to calculate the adjusted number of hours of nursing care per day.

RISK ADJUSTMENT AND CHARACTERISTICS OF THE HOSPITALS

To control for differences among hospitals in the relative risk of the outcomes as a result of variations in the mix of patients, we used patient-level logistic-regression analyses to predict each patient's probability of having each adverse outcome. Patient-level variables in these analyses included the rate of the outcome in the patient's diagnosis-related group, the state of residence, age, sex, primary health insurer, whether or not the patient was admitted on an emergency basis, and the presence or absence of 13 chronic diseases.[48] The regression analyses also included interactions between the specific rate of each outcome in each diagnosis-related group and all the other variables, as well as interactions between age and the variables related to chronic disease. We added the predicted probabilities for patients in each hospital to obtain the expected number of patients in that hospital who would have each outcome. We used the same variables in an ordinary least-squares regression analysis to estimate the expected length of stay. We obtained information on the other characteristics of the hospitals (number of beds, teaching status, state, and metropolitan or nonmetropolitan location) from the American Hospital Association's Annual Survey of Hospitals for 1997[51] and 1998.[53]

Statistical Analysis

The unit of analysis was the hospital. We calculated the length of stay, the rates of adverse outcomes, the hours of nursing care per inpatient-day, and the proportion of hours of nursing care provided by each category of nursing personnel.

For each outcome, we performed regression analyses with the use of nurse-staffing and control variables. In all analyses, the control variables included the state, number of beds, teaching status, and location of the hospital. We used ordinary least-squares regression to analyze the difference between the actual and expected length of stay. We report regression coefficients for these analyses. For other outcomes, we included the number of patients with the adverse outcome as the dependent variable in a negative binomial regression model (the appropriate model for this type of data[53]) and the expected numbers for each adverse outcome as the measure of exposure required by the model. We report incidence-rate ratios from these analyses.

We tested each coefficient for statistical significance using t-tests in the ordinary least-squares regression analyses and z statistics in the negative binomial regression analyses.[54] After controlling for other variables, we estimated the differences in the outcomes between hospitals with staffing levels of registered nurses at the 75th percentile and hospitals with staffing levels of registered nurses at the 25th percentile (the "decrease" in outcomes with higher levels of staffing). The 95 percent confidence intervals for the decreases were calculated with the use of Huber-White standard errors.[55] All P values are based on two-tailed tests. Statistical analysis was performed with the use of Stata software.[55]

To examine whether the mix of skills or the number of hours of nursing care was more important in influencing patient outcomes, we analyzed 10 models involving nurse-staffing variables and compared the results. We present results from the two models that most closely match those used in previous published studies. Model 1 examines the mix of skills and includes the proportion of hours of care by licensed nurses (registered-nurse–hours plus licensed-practical-nurse–hours) that were provided by registered nurses, plus aide-hours and the total hours per day provided by licensed nurses. Model 2 measures all staffing of nurses—by registered nurses, aides, and licensed practical nurses–in hours per day. Results obtained with the other models we analyzed have been reported elsewhere.[56]

RESULTS

Rates of Adverse Patient Outcomes and Length of Stay

The patient outcomes and characteristics of the hospitals are summarized in Table 17.1. Complications that are common in hospitalized patients, such as urinary tract infection, pneumonia, and metabolic derangement, were the most frequent. The highest rates were for "failure to rescue," defined as the death of a patient with one of five life-threatening complications—pneumonia, shock or cardiac arrest, upper gastrointestinal bleeding, sepsis, or deep venous thrombosis—for which early identification by nurses and medical and nursing interventions can influence the risk of death. The mean death rates were 18.6 percent among medical patients with one of these complications and 19.7 percent among surgical patients with one of these complications. Rates for outcomes were similar in all 11 states. The low rates of deep venous thrombosis—0.4 percent among surgical patients and 0.5 percent among medical patients—may reflect underreporting of this common complication.

TABLE 17.1. **Patient Outcomes and Characteristics of the 799 Hospitals***

Variable	Medical Patients (N = 5,075,969)[†]	Surgical Patients (N = 1,104,659)[†]
Outcome		
Length of stay (days)	5.0 ± 2.0	4.7 ± 1.4
Urinary tract infection (%)	6.3 ± 2.3	3.3 ± 2.1
Pressure ulcers (%)	7.2 ± 4.5	5.8 ± 6.6
Hospital-acquired pneumonia (%)	2.3 ± 1.2	1.2 ± 2.2
Shock or cardiac arrest (%)	0.6 ± 0.8	0.5 ± 0.6
Upper gastrointestinal bleeding (%)	1.0 ± 0.6	0.5 ± 0.5
Hospital-acquired sepsis (%)	1.3 ± 0.9	1.0 ± 0.8
Deep venous thrombosis (%)	0.5 ± 0.3	0.4 ± 0.4
Central nervous system complications (%)	0.6 ± 0.4	0.3 ± 0.4
In-hospital death (%)	3.2 ± 1.2	1.6 ± 1.6
Failure to rescue (%)	18.6 ± 5.9	19.7 ± 13.3
Wound infection (%)[‡]	—	0.8 ± 0.6

(continued)

TABLE 17.1. **Continued**

Variable	Medical Patients (N = 5,075,969)[†]	Surgical Patients (N = 1,104,659)[†]
Pulmonary failure (%)[‡]	—	1.2 ± 2.0
Metabolic derangement (%)[‡]	—	6.8 ± 7.2
	All Hospitals	
Hospital characteristic		
No. of beds	226.6 ± 198.9	
Teaching status (%)		
Major teaching hospital	10.3 ± 30.3	
Other teaching hospital	19.0 ± 39.3	
Nonteaching hospital	70.7 ± 45.5	
Location (%)		
Large metropolitan area	53.9 ± 49.9	
Small metropolitan area	25.7 ± 43.7	
Nonmetropolitan area	20.4 ± 40.3	

*Plus-minus values are means ±SD. The number of hospitals is smaller than 799 for some outcomes because hospitals with expected counts of zero were excluded. For medical patients, one hospital was excluded from the analysis of upper gastrointestinal bleeding and one from the analysis of shock or cardiac arrest. For surgical patients, 2 hospitals were excluded from the analysis of urinary tract infection; 9 from the analyses of pressure ulcer and pneumonia; 1 each from the analyses of shock or cardiac arrest, sepsis, central nervous system complications, deep venous thrombosis, in-hospital death, pulmonary failure, and wound infection; and 14 from the analyses of failure to rescue (defined as in-hospital death of a patient with hospital-acquired pneumonia, shock or cardiac arrest, upper gastrointestinal bleeding, sepsis, deep venous thrombosis, or pulmonary failure). For both groups of patients, two hospitals were excluded from the analysis of length of stay.
[†]Numbers shown are the number of patients discharged.
[‡]This outcome was assessed in surgical patients only.

Variations in Staffing Levels and Mix of Skills

The mean (±SD) numbers of hours of nursing care are shown in Table 17.2. Hours per inpatient-day averaged 7.8 for registered nurses, 1.2 for licensed practical nurses, and 2.4 for aides. Hours of care by licensed nurses per day averaged 9.0. The mean proportion of total hours of nursing care provided by registered nurses was 68 percent; aides provided 21 percent of total nurse-hours.

Association Between Adverse Outcomes and Staffing by Nurses

The relations between adverse outcomes and the levels of staffing by registered nurses are shown in Table 17.3 for medical patients and in Table 17.4 for surgical patients. The ordinary least-squares–regression coefficients (for length of stay) or the incidence-rate ratios (for other outcomes) are given for both registered-nurse–hours as a proportion of total

TABLE 17.2. Hours of Nursing Care*

Variable	Value
No. of hours of nursing care per patient-day	
Registered-nurse–hours	7.8 ± 1.9
Licensed-practical-nurse–hours	1.2 ± 1.0
Aide-hours	2.4 ± 1.2
Total	11.4 ± 2.3
Proportion of total hours of nursing care (%)	
Registered-nurse–hours	68 ± 10
Licensed-practical-nurse–hours	11 ± 8
No. of hours of care by licensed nurses per patient-day	9.0 ± 2.0
Registered-nurse–hours as a proportion of licensed-nurse–hours (%)	87 ± 10

*Plus–minus values are means ±SD. Licensed nurses are registered nurses and licensed practical nurses.

hours of care by licensed nurses and the number of registered-nurse–hours per patient-day. A negative regression coefficient or an incidence-rate ratio of less than 1.00 indicates that the frequency of the outcome declines as the staffing level increases. The estimated percent decreases in the rates of the outcomes associated with increasing nurse-hours from the 25th to the 75th percentile are also listed. We report results for death and outcomes for which a greater number of registered-nurse–hours or a higher proportion of licensed-nurse care provided by registered nurses was associated with lower rates of the outcome. Additional results are reported elsewhere.[56]

Registered Nurses and Adverse Outcomes

Among medical patients, we found an association between registered-nurse staffing and six outcomes. Both a higher proportion of licensed-nurse care provided by registered nurses (model 1) and more registered-nurse–hours per day (model 2) were associated with a shorter length of stay and lower rates of urinary tract infections and upper gastrointestinal bleeding. A higher proportion of registered-nurse–hours (model 1), but not a greater number of registered-nurse–hours per day (model 2), was associated with lower rates of three other adverse outcomes: pneumonia, shock or cardiac arrest, and failure to rescue. The association for failure to rescue was not as strong as the associations for the other five outcomes, and it was more sensitive to the specifications of the models.[56]

Among surgical patients, a higher proportion of registered-nurse–hours (model 1) was associated with a lower rate of urinary tract infection. A greater number of registered-nurse–hours per day (model 2) was associated with a lower rate of failure to rescue; a greater number of licensed-nurse–hours per day was also associated with a lower rate of failure to rescue (incidence-rate ratio, 0.98; 95 percent confidence interval, 0.97 to 1.00; P = 0.02). Because most licensed-nurse–hours are provided by registered nurses, these associations are consistent. Among both medical and surgical patients, we found no evidence of an

TABLE 17.3. **Relation Between Adverse Outcomes Among Medical Patients and the Levels of Staffing by Registered Nurses (RNs)***

Outcome	Regression Coefficient or Incidence-Rate Ratio (95% CI)†	Decrease in Rate of Outcome Associated with Increasing Staffing of RNs from 25th to 75th Percentile % (95% CI)	P value
Length of stay			
Proportion of RN-hours	−1.12 (−2.00 to −0.24)	3.5 (1.4 to 5.7)	0.01
No. of RN-hours per patient-day	−0.09 (−0.13 to −0.05)	5.2 (3.4 to 7.1)	<0.001
Urinary tract infection			
Proportion of RN-hours	0.48 (0.38 to 0.61)	9.0 (6.1 to 11.9)	<0.001
No. of RN-hours per patient-day	0.99 (0.98 to 1.00)	3.6 (1.2 to 6.0)	<0.003
Upper gastrointestinal bleeding			
Proportion of RN-hours	0.66 (0.45 to 0.96)	5.1 (0.5 to 9.7)	0.03
No. of RN-hours per patient-day	0.98 (0.97 to 0.99)	5.2 (1.4 to 8.9)	<0.007
Hospital-acquired pneumonia			
Proportion of RN-hours	0.59 (0.44 to 0.80)	6.4 (2.8 to 10.0)	0.001
No. of RN-hours per patient-day	0.99 (0.98 to 1.00)	2.7 (−0.4 to 5.8)	0.08
Shock or cardiac arrest			
Proportion of RN-hours	0.46 (0.27 to 0.81)	9.4 (2.6 to 16.3)	0.007
No. of RN-hours per patient-day	0.98 (0.96 to 1.01)	4.1 (−2.5 to 10.8)	0.22
Failure to rescue			
Proportion of RN-hours	0.81 (0.66 to 1.00)	2.5 (0.0 to 5.0)	0.05
No. of RN-hours per patient-day	1.00 (0.99 to 1.01)	0.1 (−2.5 to 2.4)	0.96
In-hospital death			
Proportion of RN-hours	0.90 (0.74 to 1.09)	1.4 (−1.1 to 3.8)	0.27
No. of RN-hours per patient-day	1.00 (0.99 to 1.01)	0.3 (−2.1 to 2.7)	0.83

*There were a total of 799 hospitals, but hospitals were excluded from the analysis of any outcome for which their expected count was zero. Two hospitals were excluded from the analysis of length of stay, one was excluded from the analysis of upper gastrointestinal bleeding, and one was excluded from the analysis of shock or cardiac arrest. The proportion of licensed-nurse–hours provided by registered nurses ("proportion of RN-hours") was measured by model 1; the number of RN-hours per patient-day was measured by model 2. Model 1 also included measures of aide-hours per patient-day and licensed-nurse–hours per patient-day. None of these other variables showed a consistent association with the rates of outcomes. The models are described further in the Methods section. No association was found between the measures of registered-nurse staffing and the following adverse outcomes among medical patients: sepsis, deep venous thrombosis, central nervous system complications, and pressure ulcers. CI denotes confidence interval.

†Data for length of stay are regression coefficients; data for all other outcomes are incidence-rate ratios. A negative regression or an incidence-rate ratio of less than 1.00 indicates that the frequency of the outcome declines as staffing increases. Confidence intervals have been rounded.

TABLE 17.4.   **Relation Between Adverse Outcomes Among Surgical Patients and the Levels of Staffing by Registered Nurses (RNs)***

Outcome	Incidence-Rate Ratio (95% CI)[†]	Decrease in Rate of Outcome Associated with Increasing Staffing of RNs from 25th to 75th Percentile % (95% CI)	P value
Urinary tract infection			
Proportion of RN-hours	0.67 (0.46 to 0.98)	4.9 (0.3 to 9.5)	0.04
No. of RN-hours per patient-day	1.00 (0.98 to 1.02)	0.0 (–4.2 to 4.2)	1.00
Failure to rescue			
Proportion of RN-hours	0.73 (0.49 to 1.09)	3.9 (–1.1 to 8.8)	0.12
No. of RN-hours per patient-day	0.98 (0.96 to 0.99)	5.9 (1.5 to 10.2)	0.008
In-hospital death			
Proportion of RN-hours	0.99 (0.67 to 1.47)	0.1 (–4.7 to 4.9)	0.97
No. of RN-hours per patient-day	1.00 (0.99 to 1.01)	0.0 (–3.9 to 3.8)	0.98

*There were a total of 799 hospitals, but hospitals were excluded from the analysis of any outcome for which their expected outcome was zero. Two hospitals were excluded from the analysis of urinary tract infection, 14 from the analysis of failure to rescue, and 1 from the analysis of in-hospital death. The proportion of licensed-nurse–hours provided by registered nurses ("proportion of RN-hours") was measured by model 1; the number of RN-hours per patient-day was measured by model 2. Model 1 also included measures of aide-hours per patient-day and licensed-nurse–hours per patient-day, and model 2 also included measures of aide-hours per patient-day and licensed-practical-nurse–hours per patient-day. None of these other variables showed a consistent association with the rates of outcomes. The models are described further in the Methods section. Only results showing a consistent association with the rates of outcomes are presented. No association was found between the measures of registered-nurse staffing and the following outcomes among surgical patients: length of stay, pneumonia, sepsis, deep venous thrombosis, shock or cardiac arrest, gastrointestinal bleeding, pressure ulcers, metabolic derangement, central nervous system complications, pulmonary failure, and wound infection. CI denotes confidence interval.
[†]An incidence-rate ratio of less than 1.00 indicates that the frequency of the outcome declines as staffing increases.

association between in-hospital mortality and the proportion of registered-nurse–hours, the number of registered-nurse–hours per day, or the number of licensed-nurse–hours per day.

Measures of Staffing by Other Nurses

In addition to the association with a lower rate of failure to rescue among surgical patients, a greater number of licensed-nurse–hours per day was associated with a shorter length of stay among medical patients (regression coefficient, –0.08; 95 percent confidence interval, –0.12 to –0.05; P < 0.001). Measures of staffing by aides and licensed practical nurses had either nonsignificant associations with lower rates of the adverse outcomes we studied or significant associations with higher rates of the adverse outcomes (data not shown). Thus, whereas there was evidence that greater numbers of registered-nurse–hours or licensed-nurse–hours were associated with a shorter length of stay among medical patients and lower rates of failure to rescue among surgical patients, there was no evidence of an association between lower rates of the outcomes we studied and a greater number of licensed-practical-nurse–hours or aide-hours per day or a higher proportion of aide-hours.

DISCUSSION

In a large sample of hospitals from a diverse group of states, after controlling for differences in the nursing case mix and the patients' levels of risk, we found an association between the proportion of total hours of nursing care provided by registered nurses or the number of registered-nurse–hours per day and six outcomes among medical patients. These were the length of stay and the rates of urinary tract infections, upper gastrointestinal bleeding, hospital-acquired pneumonia, shock or cardiac arrest, and failure to rescue (the death of a patient with one of five life-threatening complications—pneumonia, shock or cardiac arrest, upper gastrointestinal bleeding, sepsis, or deep venous thrombosis). The evidence was weaker for failure to rescue than for the other five measures. As in other studies,[32,57] higher levels of staffing by registered nurses were associated with lower rates of failure to rescue among surgical patients, among whom we also found an association between a higher proportion of registered-nurse–hours and lower rates of urinary tract infections.

The fact that fewer outcomes among surgical patients than among medical patients were found to be associated with the level of staffing by registered nurses may have several explanations. Surgical patients may be healthier than medical patients and therefore have a lower risk of adverse outcomes. The smaller size of the samples of surgical patients may also have made it more difficult to detect associations.

Our findings clarify the relation between the levels of staffing by nurses and the quality of care. We found consistent evidence of an association between higher levels of staffing by registered nurses and lower rates of adverse outcomes, but no similar evidence related to staffing by licensed practical nurses or aides. Our findings may reflect the actual contribution of these different members of the nursing staff to patients' outcomes in general, or they may be specific to the outcomes we examined. It is possible that the outcomes for which we found significant associations may be more sensitive to the contribution that the skills and education of registered nurses, in particular, make to patient care.

A higher proportion of total hours of nursing care provided by registered nurses was more frequently associated with lower rates of adverse outcomes than was a greater number of registered-nurse–hours per day. This difference may reflect a real effect, or it may simply indicate that we could measure differences in the mix of staff among hospitals with greater precision than we could nurse-hours adjusted for case mix.

We tested the association between staffing levels and 25 outcomes in medical and surgical patients and found an association for 8 of these outcomes. With the exception of failure to rescue among medical patients, these results were consistent across alternative regression models. Because of the large number of comparisons, however, it is possible that some of the associations we found may be false positive findings. In addition, differences among hospitals may be caused not by the staffing level of nurses per se but by other unmeasured factors associated with higher levels of staffing by registered nurses or other unmeasured characteristics of the hospitals' nursing work force. The level of staffing by nurses is an incomplete measure of the quality of nursing care in hospitals. Other factors, such as effective communication between nurses and physicians and a positive work environment, have been found to influence patients' outcomes.[58,59]

Other limitations of our study arise from weaknesses of currently available data. Constructing a data base on the staffing levels of nurses for inpatient care from the diverse data sets of multiple states required substantial efforts to standardize the data and to determine what proportion of a hospital's nursing staff was allocated to inpatient care. Because of the absence of reliable coding indicating whether secondary problems were present when the patient was admitted or developed later, constructing measures of quality from discharge abstracts involved defining appropriate coding and exclusion rules for each adverse outcome. These outcomes are likely to be underreported, and the degree of underreporting may be higher where staffing levels are low. Each of these limitations weakened our ability to observe associations between outcomes and staffing levels. We studied only adverse outcomes. Furthermore, not all outcomes among patients that are important to examine (for example, falls or medication errors) can be studied on the basis of discharge data. The outcomes for which we found associations with the levels of staffing by nurses should be viewed as indicators of quality rather than as measures of the full effect of nurses in hospitals.

Further research is needed to refine the measurement of the nursing case mix on the basis of discharge data and to elucidate the factors influencing the staffing levels of nurses and the mix of nursing personnel in hospitals. Given the evidence that such staffing levels are associated with adverse outcomes, as well as the current and projected shortages of hospital-based registered nurses,[60,61] systems should be developed for the routine monitoring, in large numbers of hospitals, of hospital outcomes that are sensitive to levels of staffing by nurses. Beyond monitoring, hospital administrators, accrediting agencies, insurers, and regulators should take action to ensure that an adequate nursing staff is available to protect patients and to improve the quality of care.

ACKNOWLEDGMENTS

Supported by a contract (230–99–0021) with the Health Resources and Services Administration, Department of Health and Human Services, with funding from the Health Resources and Services Administration, the Agency for Healthcare Research and Quality, the Centers for Medicare and Medicaid Services, and the National Institute of Nursing Research; by a grant (R01 HS09958) from the Agency for Healthcare Research and Quality; and by a Dissemination and Development Grant from Abt Associations (to Dr. Mattke). The views expressed in this article are those of the authors and not necessarily those of the funding agencies or the organizations that provided data.

Presented in part at the annual meeting of the Academy for Health Services Research and Health Policy, Atlanta, June 10–12, 2001.

We are indebted to Carole Gassert, Evelyn Moses, Judy Goldfarb, Tim Cuerdon, Cheryl Jones, Peter Gergen, Carole Hudgings, Pamella Mitchell, Donna Diers, Chris Kovner, Mary Blegen, Margaret Sovie, Nancy Donaldson, Ann Minnick, Lisa Iezzoni, Leo Lichtig, Robert Knauf, Alan Zaslavsky, Lucian Leape, Sheila Burke, Barbara Berney, Gabrielle Hermann-Camara, and the Harvard Nursing Research Institute for advice and recommendations; to the California Office of Statewide Health Planning and Development and the State of Maryland for providing data at no cost; and to the staffs of the agencies in each state from which we obtained data for their assistance.

APPENDIX   Coding Rules for Adverse Outcomes*

Outcome	Definition	
	Included	Excluded
Length of stay	Length of stay as reported on discharge abstract	None
Urinary tract infection	ICD-9-CM: 599.0, 996.64	Primary diagnosis, MDC 11–15; ICD-9-CM: 646.60646.64, 639.8
Pressure ulcers	ICD-9-CM: 682, 707.0	Primary diagnosis, hemiplegia,[†] quadriplegia,[†] paraplegia,[†] IV drug abuse[†]
Hospital-acquired pneumonia	ICD-9-CM: 507.0, 997.3, 514, 482.0–482.2, 482.4–482.9, 485, 486	Primary diagnosis—ICD-9-CM: 480–487, 507.0, 514, 997.3; secondary diagnosis—ICD-9-CM: 480, 481, 483, 484, 487; MDC 4, AIDS,[†] immunocompromised states[†]
Shock or cardiac arrest	ICD-9-CM: diagnoses—427.5, 785.5, 785.50, 785.51, 785.59, 799.1; procedures—93.93, 99.6, 99.63	Primary diagnosis, MDC 4, MDC 5, hemorrhage,[†] trauma[†]
Upper gastrointestinal bleeding	ICD-9-CM: 531.00–531.31, 531.9, 532.00–532.31, 532.9, 533.00–533.31, 533.9, 534.00–534.31, 534.9, 535.01, 535.4, 578.9, 530.82	Primary diagnosis, MDC 6–7, trauma,[†] burn,[†] alcoholism,[†] ICD-9-CM: 280.0, 285.1
Hospital-acquired sepsis	ICD-9-CM: 038, 790.7	Primary diagnosis, immunocompromised states,[†] AIDS,[†] length of stay <3 days, DRG: 20, 68–70, 79–81, 89–91, 126, 238, 242, 277–279, 320–322, 415–417, 423
Deep venous thrombosis	ICD-9-CM: 415.1, 415.11, 451.11, 451.19, 451.2, 451.81, 453.8	Primary diagnosis, ICD-9-CM: 673.2
Central nervous system complications	ICD-9-CM: 780.0, 293.0, 298.2, 309.1–309.9	Primary diagnosis, MDC 1, MDC 19, MDC 20
Death	Discharge status—death	None
Failure to rescue	Discharge status—death, with sepsis, pneumonia, upper gastrointestinal bleeding, shock or cardiac arrest, or deep venous thrombosis	Absence of sepsis, pneumonia, upper gastrointestinal bleeding, shock or cardiac arrest, or deep venous thrombosis
Wound infection	ICD-9-CM: 958.3, 998.5	Primary diagnosis

(continued)

APPENDIX **Continued**

	Definition	
Outcome	Included	Excluded
Pulmonary failure	ICD-9-CM: 514, 518.4, 518.5, 518.81, 518.82	Primary diagnosis, MDC 4, MDC 5, trauma[†]
Metabolic derangement	ICD-9-CM: 250.10, 250.11 (excluding diabetes as primary diagnosis), 998.0 (excluding those without operation or procedure during hospital stay), 788.5 (excluding acute myocardial infarction,[†] cardiac arrhythmia, cardiac arrest, or gastrointestinal hemorrhage† as primary diagnosis), 276 (excluding MDC 5, MDC 7, MDC 10, MDC 11), 251.0	Primary diagnosis, trauma

*ICD-9-CM denotes *International Classification of Diseases, 9th Revision, Clinical Modification;* MDC major diagnostic category; AIDS acquired immunodeficiency syndrome; and DRG diagnosis-related group.
†The condition was as defined in Iezzoni,[49] updated to match the 1997 codes.

NOTES

1. Thomas L. *The youngest science: notes of a medicine-watcher.* New York: Viking Press, 1983.

2. Wunderlich GS, Sloan FA, Davis CK, eds. *Nursing staff in hospitals and nursing homes: is it adequate?* Washington, D.C.: National Academy Press, 1996.

3. President's Advisory Commission on Consumer Protection and Quality in the Health Care Industry. *Quality first: better care for all Americans.* Washington, D.C.: Government Printing Office, 1997. (Accessed May 6, 2002, at http://www.hcqualitycommission.gov/final.)

4. Lake E. *The organization of hospital nursing.* Philadelphia: University of Pennsylvania, 1999. (Dissertation.)

5. Schultz MA, van Servellen GA. A critical review of research on hospital mortality among medical-surgical and acute myocardial infarction patients. *Nurs Health Sci* 2000;2:103–12.

6. Aiken LH, Clarke SP, Sloane DM, et al. Nurses' reports on hospital care in five countries. *Health Aff (Millwood)* 2001;20(3):43–53.

7. Buerhaus PI, Donelan K, DesRoches C, Lamkin L, Mallory G. State of the oncology nursing workforce: problems and implications for strengthening the future. *Nurs Econ* 2001;19:198–208.

8. Buerhaus PI, Staiger DO. Managed care and the nurse workforce. *JAMA* 1996;276:1487–93.

9. Buerhaus PI, Auerbach D. Slow growth in the United States of the number of minorities in the RN workforce. *Image J Nurs Sch* 1999;31:179–83.

10. Kovner CT, Jones CB, Gergen PJ. Nurse staffing in acute care hospitals, 1990–1996. *Policy Politics Nurs Pract* 2000;1:194–204.

11. Spetz J. Hospital employment of nursing personnel: has there really been a decline? *J Nurs Adm* 1998;28:20–7.

12. Anderson GF, Kohn LT. Hospital employment trends in California, 1982–1994. *Health Aff (Millwood)* 1996;15(1):152–8.

13. Aiken LH, Sochalski J, Anderson GF. Downsizing the hospital nursing workforce. *Health Aff (Millwood)* 1996;15(4):88–92.

14. Hartz AJ, Krakauer H, Kuhn EM, et al. Hospital characteristics and mortality rates. *N Engl J Med* 1989;321:1720–5.

15. Manheim LM, Feinglass J, Shortell SM, Hughes EFX. Regional variation in Medicare hospital mortality. *Inquiry* 1992;29:55–66.

16. Krakauer H, Bailey RC, Skellan KJ, et al. Evaluation of the HCFA model for the analysis of mortality following hospitalization. *Health Serv Res* 1992;27:317–35.

17. Scott W, Forrest W, Brown B. Hospital structure and postoperative mortality and morbidity. In: Shortell SM, Brown M, eds. *Organizational research in hospitals*. Chicago: Blue Cross, 1976:72–89.

18. Flood AB, Scott WR, Ewy W. Does practice make perfect? II. The relation between volume and outcomes and other hospital characteristics. *Med Care* 1984;22:115–25.

19. Flood AB, Scott WR. *Hospital structure and performance*. Baltimore: Johns Hopkins University Press, 1987.

20. Silber J, Rosenbaum PR, Ross RN. Comparing the contributions of groups of predictors: which outcomes vary with hospital rather than patient characteristics? *J Am Stat Assoc* 1995;90:7–18.

21. Kovner C, Gergen PJ. Nurse staffing levels and adverse events following surgery in U.S. hospitals. *Image J Nurs Sch* 1998;30:315–21.

22. Flood SD, Diers D. Nurse staffing, patient outcome and cost. *Nurs Manage* 1988;19:34–5, 38–9, 42–3.

23. Neidlinger SH, Bostrom J, Stricker A, Hild J, Zhang JQ. Incorporating nursing assistive personnel into a nursing professional proactive model. *J Nurs Adm* 1993;23:29–37.

24. Fridkin SK, Pear SM, Williamson TH, Galgiani JN, Jarvis WR. The role of understaffing in central venous catheter-associated bloodstream infections. *Infect Control Hosp Epidemiol* 1996;17:150–8.

25. Archibald LK, Manning ML, Bell LM, Banerjee S, Jarvis WR. Patient density, nurse-to-patient ratio and nosocomial infection risk in a pediatric cardiac intensive care unit. *Pediatr Infect Dis J* 1997;16:1045–8.

26. Pronovost PJ, Jenckes MW, Dorman T, et al. Organizational characteristics of intensive care units related to outcomes of abdominal aortic surgery. *JAMA* 1999;281:1310–7.

27. Blegen MA, Goode CJ, Reed L. Nurse staffing and patient outcomes. *Nurs Res* 1998;47:43–50.

28. Lichtig LK, Knauf RA, Milholland KD. Some impacts of nursing on acute care hospital outcomes. *J Nurs Adm* 1999;29:25–33.

29. Robert J, Fridkin SK, Blumberg HM, et al. The influence of the composition of the nursing staff on primary bloodstream infection rates in a surgical intensive care unit. *Infect Control Hosp Epidemiol* 2000;21:12–7.

30. Iezzoni LI, Daley J, Heeren T, et al. Using administrative data to screen hospitals for high complication rates. *Inquiry* 1994;31:40–55.

31. al-Haider AS, Wan TTH. Modeling organizational determinants of hospital mortality. Health Serv Res 1991;26:303–23.

32. Silber JH, Rosenbaum PR, Schwartz JS, Ross RN, Williams SV. Evaluation of the complication rate as a measure of quality of care in coronary artery bypass graft surgery. *JAMA* 1995;274:317–23.

33. Taunton RL, Kleinbeck SVM, Stafford R, Woods CQ, Bott MJ. Patient outcomes: are they linked to registered nurse absenteeism, separation, or work load? *J Nurs Adm* 1994;24:Suppl:48–55. [Erratum, *J Nurs Adm* 1994;24:72.]

34. Iezzoni LI, Ash AS, Schwartz M, Daley J, Hughes JS, Mackiernan YD. Judging hospitals by severity-adjusted mortality rates: the influence of the severity-adjustment method. *Am J Public Health* 1996;86:1379–87.

35. Iezzoni LI, Ash AS, Schwartz M, Mackiernan YD. Differences in procedure use, in-hospital mortality, and illness severity by gender for acute myocardial infarction patients: are answers affected by data source and severity measure. *Med Care* 1997;35:58–71.

36. Silber JH, Rosenbaum PR. A spurious correlation between hospital mortality and complication rates: the importance of severity adjustment. *Med Care* 1997;35:Suppl:OS77–OS92.

37. Bradbury RC, Stearns FE Jr, Steen PM. Interhospital variations in admission severity-adjusted hospital mortality and morbidity. *Health Serv Res* 1991;26:407–24.

38. Zimmerman JE, Shortell SM, Rousseau DM, et al. Improving intensive care: observations based on organizational case studies in nine intensive care units: a prospective, multicenter study. *Crit Care Med* 1993;21:1443–51.

39. Wan TTH, Shukla RK. Contextual and organizational correlates of the quality of hospital nursing care. *QRB Qual Rev Bull* 1987;13:61–4.

40. Bryan YE, Hitchings KS, Fuss MA, Fox MA, Kinneman MT, Young MJ. Measuring and evaluating hospital restructuring efforts: eighteen-month follow-up and extension to critical care. *J Nurs Adm* 1998;28:21–7.

41. Czaplinski C, Diers D. The effect of staff nursing on length of stay and mortality. *Med Care* 1998;36:1626–38.

42. CONQUEST: overview. Rockville, Md.: Agency for Health Care Policy and Research, 2001. (Accessed May 6, 2002, at http://www.ahrq.gov/qual/conquest/conqovr1.htm.)

43. Iezzoni LI, Mackiernan YD, Cahalane MJ, Phillips RS, Davis RB, Miller K. *Screening quality of care using administrative data.* Boston: Beth Israel Deaconess Hospital, 1999.

44. Karon SL, Sainfort F, Zimmerman DR. Stability of nursing home quality indicators over time. *Med Care* 1999;37:570–9.

45. Keyes MA. CONQUEST 2.0: an emerging clinical performance measurement tool. *J Healthc Qual* 2000;22:29–36.

46. Palmer RH, Lawthers AG, Banks NJ, et al. *CONQUEST 1.0: overview of final report and user's guide.* Rockville, Md.: The Agency, 1996.

47. Silber JH, Williams SV, Krakauer H, Schwartz JS. Hospital and patient characteristics associated with death after surgery: a study of adverse occurrence and failure to rescue. *Med Care* 1992;30:615–29.

48. Iezzoni LI, Foley SM, Heeren T, et al. A method for screening the quality of hospital care using administrative data: preliminary validation results. *QRB Qual Rev Bull* 1992;18:361–71.

49. Iezzoni LI. Complications screening program for the Health Care Financing Administration (CSP-HCFA): CSP updated to FY 1993 coding guidelines. Boston: Beth Israel Hospital, 1994.

50. Healthcare cost and utilization project quality indicators (HCUPQIs). Rockville, Md.: Agency for Healthcare Research and Quality, 2000. (Accessed May 6, 2002, at http://www.ahrq.gov/data/hcup/qifact.htm.)

51. The AHA annual survey database: fiscal year 1997 documentation. Chicago: American Hospital Association, 1998.

52. Ballard KA, Gray RF, Knauf RA, Uppal P. Measuring variations in nursing care per DRG. *Nurs Manage* 1993;24:33–6, 40–1.

53. The AHA annual survey database: fiscal year 1998 documentation. Chicago: American Hospital Association, 1999.

54. Greene WH. *Econometric analysis.* 4th ed. Upper Saddle River, N.J.: Prentice-Hall, 2000.

55. Stata reference manual: release 6. College Station, Tex.: Stata, 1999.

56. Needleman J, Buerhaus P, Mattke S, Stewart M, Zelevinsky K. *Nurse staffing and patient outcomes in hospitals.* Boston: Harvard School of Public Health, 2001. (Accessed May 6, 2002, at http://bhpr.hrsa.gov/dn/staffstudy.htm.)

57. Silber JH, Kennedy SK, Even-Shoshan O, et al. Anesthesiologist direction and patient outcomes. *Anesthesiology* 2000;93:152–63.

58. Knaus WA, Draper EA, Wagner DP, Zimmerman JE. An evaluation of outcome from intensive care in major medical centers. *Ann Intern Med* 1986;104:410–8.

59. Aiken LH, Smith HL, Lake ET. Lower Medicare mortality among a set of hospitals known for good nursing care. *Med Care* 1994;32:771–87.

60. The hospital workforce shortage: immediate and future. *TrendWatch.* Vol. 3. No. 2. Washington, D.C.: American Hospital Association, June 2001:1–8.

61. Buerhaus PI, Staiger DO, Auerbach DI. Implications of an aging registered nurse workforce. *JAMA* 2000;283:2948–54.

18

HOSPITAL NURSE STAFFING AND PATIENT MORTALITY, NURSE BURNOUT, AND JOB DISSATISFACTION

LINDA H. AIKEN

SEAN P. CLARKE

DOUGLAS M. SLOANE

JULIE SOCHALSKI

JEFFREY H. SILBER

This article originally appeared as Aiken, L. H., Clarke, S. P., Sloane, D. M., Sochalski, J., & Silber, J. H. (2002). Hospital nurse staffing and patient mortality, nurse burnout, and job dissatisfaction. *Journal of the American Medical Association, 288*(16), pp. 1987–1993. Copyright © 2002 American Medical Association. All rights reserved. Reprinted with permission.

EDITORS' NOTE

This was the second major study on nurse staffing and clinical outcomes published after the 1996 IOM report on nurse staffing, following the Needleman et al. study (reprint 17) by a mere six months. This one was published in another leading American medical journal, and, like the Needleman study, garnered wide public and industry media attention. This study found that adequate nurse staffing lowers mortality rates and is key to retaining nurses. "The 7% solution" was a phrase that emerged to summarize this study's finding that, for every increase of one patient to the average caseload of a surgical nurse, the mortality rate increases by 7%.

■ ■ ■

The past decade has been a turbulent time for U.S. hospitals and practicing nurses. News media have trumpeted urgent concerns about hospital understaffing and a growing hospital nurse shortage.[1–3] Nurses nationwide consistently report that hospital nurse staffing levels are inadequate to provide safe and effective care.[4–6] Physicians agree, citing inadequate nurse staffing as a major impediment to the provision of high-quality hospital care.[7] The shortage of hospital nurses may be linked to unrealistic nurse workloads.[8] Forty percent of hospital nurses have burnout levels that exceed the norms for health care workers.[4] Job dissatisfaction among hospital nurses is 4 times greater than the average for all U.S. workers, and 1 in 5 hospital nurses report that they intend to leave their current jobs within a year.[4]

In 1999, California passed legislation mandating patient-to-nurse ratios for its hospitals, which goes into effect in July 2003. The California legislation was motivated by an increasing hospital nursing shortage and the perception that lower nurse retention in hospital practice was related to burdensome workloads and high levels of job-related burnout and job dissatisfaction. Stakeholder groups advocated widely divergent minimum ratios. On medical and surgical units, recommended ratios ranged from 3 to 10 patients for each nurse.[9–11] In early 2002, California's governor announced that hospitals must have at least 1 licensed nurse for every 6 medical and surgical patients by July 2003, a ratio that will move to 1 to 5 when the mandates are fully implemented.[12]

This study reports on findings from a comprehensive study of 168 hospitals and clarifies the impact of nurse staffing levels on patient outcomes and factors that influence nurse retention.[13] Specifically, we examined whether risk-adjusted surgical mortality and rates of failure-to-rescue (deaths in surgical patients who develop serious complications) are lower in hospitals where nurses carry smaller patient loads. In addition, we ascertained the extent to which more favorable patient-to-nurse ratios are associated with lower burnout and higher job satisfaction among registered nurses. We also estimated excess surgical deaths associated with the different nurse staffing ratios vigorously debated in California. Finally, we estimated the impact of nurse staffing levels proposed in California on nurse burnout and dissatisfaction, 2 precursors of turnover.[13] Our findings offer insights into how more generous registered nurse staffing might affect patient outcomes and inform current debates in many states regarding the merits of legislative actions to influence staffing levels.

METHODS

Patients, Data Sources, and Variables

Our study combines information about hospital staffing and organization obtained from nurse surveys with patient outcomes derived from hospital discharge abstracts and hospital characteristics drawn from administrative databases.[14] The study protocol for linking anonymized nurse data and handling denominalized patient data was approved by the institutional review board of the University of Pennsylvania.

Hospitals. Data were collected on all 210 adult general hospitals in Pennsylvania. Information about hospital characteristics was derived from the 1999 American Hospital Association (AHA) Annual Survey and the 1999 Pennsylvania Department of Health Hospital Survey.[15,16] Ultimately, 168 of the 210 acute care hospitals had discharge data for surgical patients in the targeted Diagnosis Related Groups (DRGs) during the study period, as well AHA data, and survey data from 10 or more staff nurses. Six of the excluded hospitals were Veterans Affairs hospitals, which do not report discharge data to the state. Twenty-six hospitals were excluded because their administrative or patient outcomes data could not be matched to our surveys because of missing variables, primarily because they reported their characteristics or patient data as aggregate multihospital entities. In 10 additional small hospitals, the majority of which had fewer than 50 beds, fewer than 10 nurses responded to the survey.

A nurse staffing measure was calculated as the mean patient load across all staff registered nurses who reported having responsibility for at least 1 but fewer than 20 patients on the last shift they worked, regardless of the specialty or shift (day, evening, night) worked. This measure of staffing is superior to those derived from administrative databases, which generally include registered nurse positions that do not involve inpatient acute care at the bedside. Staffing was measured across entire hospitals because there is no evidence that specialty-specific staffing offers advantages in the study of patient outcome[17] and to reflect the fact that patients often receive nursing care in multiple specialty areas of a hospital. Direct measurement also avoided problems with missing data common to the AHA's Annual Survey of hospitals, which imputed staffing data in 1999 for 20% of Pennsylvania hospitals.

Three hospital characteristics were used as control variables: size, teaching status, and technology. Hospitals were grouped into 3 size categories: small ($\leq$100 hospital beds), medium (101–250 hospital beds), and large ($\geq$251 hospital beds). Teaching status was measured by the ratio of resident physicians and fellows to hospital beds, which has been suggested as superior to university affiliations and association memberships as an indicator of the intensity of teaching activity.[18] Hospitals with no postgraduate trainees (nonteaching) were contrasted with those that had 1:4 or smaller trainee:bed ratios (minor teaching hospitals) and those with ratios that were higher than 1:4 (major teaching hospitals). Finally, hospitals with facilities for open heart surgery and/or major transplants were classified as high-technology hospitals and contrasted with other hospitals.[19]

Nurses and Nurse Outcomes. Surveys were mailed in the spring of 1999 to a 50% random sample of registered nurses who were on the Pennsylvania Board of Nursing rolls and resided in the state. The response rate was 52%, which compares favorably with rates seen in other voluntary surveys of health professionals.[20] Roughly one-third of the nurses who responded worked in hospitals and included the sample of 10184 nurses described here. No special recruiting methods or inducements were used. Demographic characteristics of the respondents matched the profile for Pennsylvania nurses in the National Sample Survey of Registered Nurses.[21] Nurses employed in hospitals were asked to use a list to identify the hospital in which they worked, and then were queried about their demographic characteristics, work history, workload, job satisfaction, and feelings of job-related burnout. Questionnaires were returned by nurses employed at each of the 210 Pennsylvania hospitals providing adult acute care. To obtain reliable hospital-level estimates of nurse staffing (the ratio of patients to nurses in each hospital), attention was restricted to registered nurses holding staff nurse positions involving direct patient care and to hospitals from which at least 10 such nurses returned questionnaires. In 80% of the 168 hospitals in the final sample, 20 or more nurses provided responses to our questionnaire. There were more than 50 nurse respondents from half of the hospitals. We examined 2 nurse job outcomes in relation to staffing: job satisfaction (rated on a 4-point scale from very dissatisfied to very satisfied) and burnout (measured with the Emotional Exhaustion scale of the Maslach Burnout Inventory, a standardized tool).[22,23]

Patients and Patient Outcomes. Discharge abstracts representing all admissions to nonfederal hospitals in Pennsylvania from 1998 to 1999 were obtained from the Pennsylvania Health Care Cost Containment Council. These discharge abstracts were merged with Pennsylvania vital statistics records to identify patients who died within 30 days of hospital admission to control for timing of discharge as a possible source of

BOX 18.1: SURGICAL PATIENT DIAGNOSIS RELATED GROUPS INCLUDED IN THE ANALYSES OF MORTALITY AND FAILURE-TO-RESCUE

General Surgery
    146–155, 157–162, 164–167, 170, 171, 191–201, 257–268, 285–293, 493, and 494
Orthopedic Surgery
    209–211, 213, 216–219, 223–234, 471, 491, and 496–503
Vascular Surgery
    110–114, 119, and 120

variation in hospital outcomes. We examined outcomes for 23,2342 patients between the ages of 20 and 85 years who underwent general surgical, orthopedic, or vascular procedures in the 168 hospitals from April 1, 1998, to November 30, 1999. Surgical discharges were selected for study because of the availability of well-validated risk adjustment models.[24–29] The number of patients discharged from the study hospitals ranged from 75 to 7,746. Only the first hospital admission for any of the DRGs listed in Box 18.1 for any patient during the study period was included in the analyses.

In addition to 30-day mortality, we examined failure-to-rescue (deaths within 30 days of admission among patients who experienced complications).[24–29] Complications were identified by scanning discharge abstracts for *International Classification of Diseases, Ninth Revision, Clinical Modification* (*ICD-9-CM*) codes in the secondary diagnosis and procedure fields that were suggestive of 39 different clinical events. Distinguishing complications from previously existing comorbidities involved the use of rules developed by expert consensus and previous empirical work, as well as examination of discharge records for each patient's hospitalizations 90 days before the surgery of interest for overlap in secondary diagnosis codes.[27–29] Examples of complications included aspiration pneumonia and hypotension/shock. Patients who died postoperatively were assumed to have developed a complication even if no complication codes were identified in their discharge abstracts.

Risk adjustment of mortality and failure-to-rescue for patient characteristics and comorbidities was accomplished by using 133 variables, including age, sex, surgery types, and dummy variables indicating the presence of chronic preexisting health conditions reflected in the *ICD-9-CM* codes in the discharge abstracts (e.g., diabetes mellitus), as well as a series of interaction terms. The final set of control variables was determined by a selection process that paralleled an approach used and reported previously.[27–29] The C statistic (area under the receiver operating characteristic curve) for the mortality risk adjustment model was 0.89.[30]

Data Analysis

Descriptive data show how patients and nurses in our sample were distributed across the various categories of hospitals defined by staffing levels and other characteristics. Logistic regression models were used to estimate the effects of staffing on the nurse outcomes (job dissatisfaction and burnout) and 2 patient outcomes (mortality and failure-to-rescue). We computed the odds of nurses being moderately or very dissatisfied with their current positions and reporting a level of emotional exhaustion (burnout) above published norms for medical workers and of patients experiencing mortality and failure-to-rescue under different levels of registered nurse staffing, before and after control for individual characteristics and hospital variables. For nurse outcomes, we adjusted for sex, years of experience in nursing, education (baccalaureate degree or above vs. diploma or associate degree as highest credential in nursing), and nursing specialty. For analyses of patient outcomes, we controlled for the variables in our risk adjustment model, specifically, demographic characteristics of patients, nature of the hospital admission, comorbidities, and relevant interaction terms. For analyses of both patient and nurse outcomes, we adjusted for hospital size, teaching status, and technology.

All logistic regression models were estimated by using Huber-White (robust) procedures to account for the clustering of patients within hospitals and adjust the SEs of the parameter estimates appropriately.[31,32] Model calibration was assessed with the Hosmer-Lemeshow statistic.[33] We used direct standardization to illustrate the magnitude of the effect of staffing by estimating the difference in the numbers of deaths and episodes of failure-to-rescue under different staffing scenarios. Using all patients in the study and using the final fully-adjusted model, we estimated the probability of death and failure-to-rescue for each patient under various patient-to-nurse ratios (i.e., 4, 6, and 8 patients per nurse) with all other patient characteristics unchanged. We then calculated the differences in total deaths under the different scenarios.[34] Confidence intervals (CIs) for these direct standardization estimates were derived with the δ method described by Agresti.[35] All analyses were performed using STATA version 7.0 (STATA Corp, College Station, Tex), and $P<.05$ was considered statistically significant in all analyses.

RESULTS

Characteristics of Hospitals, Nurses, and Patients

Distributions of hospitals with various characteristics, distributions of nurses surveyed, and patients whose outcomes were studied are shown in Table 18.1. Fifty percent of the hospitals had patient-to-nurse ratios that were 5:1 or lower, and those hospitals discharged 65.9% of the patients in the study and employed 64.4% of the nurses we surveyed. Hospitals with more than 250 beds accounted for a disproportionate share of both patients and nurses (45.5% and 43.4%, respectively). Although high-technology hospitals accounted for only 28.0% of the institutions studied, more than half (55.3%) of the patients discharged and 53.8% of nurses surveyed were from high-technology hospitals. A majority of the patients studied and nurses surveyed were drawn from the 61 hospitals (36.3%) that reported postgraduate medical trainees in 1999.

As shown in Table 18.2, 94.1% of the nurses were women and 39.6% held a baccalaureate degree or higher. The mean (SD) work experience in nursing was 13.8 years (9.8). Thirty-one percent of the nurses in the sample worked on medical and surgical general units, while 19.6% and 9.8% worked in intensive care and perioperative settings, respectively. Forty-three percent of the nurses had high burnout scores and a similar proportion were dissatisfied with their current jobs.

Of the 232,342 patients studied, 53,813 (23.2%) experienced a major complication not present on admission and 4,535 (2.0%) died within 30 days of admission. The death rate among patients with complications was 8.4%. The surgical case types and clinical characteristics of the patient cohort are shown in Table 18.3. Slightly more than half of patients (51.2%) were classified in an orthopedic surgery DRG, with the next largest group of patients (36.4%) undergoing digestive tract and hepatobiliary surgeries. Chronic medical conditions, with the exception of hypertension, were relatively uncommon among these patients. Patients who experienced complications and were included in our analyses of failure-to-rescue were similar to the broader group of patients in our mortality analyses with respect to their comorbidities, but orthopedic surgery patients were less prominently represented among patients with complications than in the overall sample.

TABLE 18.1.   **Study Hospitals, Surgical Patients Studied, and Nurse Respondents in Hospitals***

	No. (%)		
Characteristic	Hospitals (N = 168)	Patients (N = 232 342)	Nurses (N = 10 184)
Staffing, patients per nurse			
≤ 4	20 (11.9)	41 414 (17.8)	1741 (17.1)
5	64 (38.1)	111 752 (48.1)	4818 (47.3)
6	41 (24.4)	48 120 (20.7)	2114 (20.8)
7	29 (17.3)	21 360 (9.2)	1106 (10.9)
≥ 8	14 (8.3)	9696 (4.2)	405 (4.0)
Size, No. of beds			
≤ 100	41 (24.4)	16 123 (6.9)	842 (8.3)
101–250	95 (56.6)	110 510 (47.6)	4927 (48.4)
≥ 251	32 (19.1)	105 709 (45.5)	4415 (43.4)
Technology			
Not high	121 (72.0)	103 824 (44.7)	4706 (46.2)
High	47 (28.0)	128 518 (55.3)	5478 (53.8)
Teaching status			
None	107 (63.7)	98 937 (42.6)	4553 (44.7)
Minor	44 (26.2)	80 127 (34.5)	3435 (33.7)
Major	17 (10.1)	53 278 (22.9)	2196 (21.6)

*Percentages may not add up to 100 because of rounding.

TABLE 18.2.   **Characteristics of Nurses (N = 10 184) in the Study Hospitals***

Characteristic	No. (%)
Women	9425 (94.1)
BSN degree or higher	3980 (39.6)
Years worked as a nurse, mean (SD)	13.8 (9.8)
Clinical specialty	
Medical and surgical	3158 (31.0)
Intensive care	1992 (19.6)
Operating/recovery room	998 (9.8)
Other	4026 (39.6)
High emotional exhaustion	3926 (43.2)
Dissatisfied with current job	4162 (41.5)

*Sample size for individual characteristics varied because of missing data. BSN indicates bachelor of science in nursing. High emotional exhaustion refers to levels of emotional exhaustion above the published "high" norm for medical workers.[20] Dissatisfied with current job combines nurses who reported being either very dissatisfied or a little dissatisfied.

TABLE 18.3.   **Characteristics of the Surgical Patients Included in Analyses of Mortality and Failure-to-Rescue***

Characteristic	No. (%)	
	All Patients (N = 232 342)	**Patients With Complications (n = 53 813)**
Men	101 624 (43.7)	25 619 (47.6)
Age, mean (SD)	59.3 (16.9)	64.2 (15.7)
Emergency admissions	63 355 (27.3)	21 541 (40.0)
Deaths within 30 days of admission	4535 (2.0)	4535 (8.4)
Major Diagnostic Categories (MDCs)		
General surgery		
Diseases and disorders of the digestive system (MDC 6)	54 919 (23.6)	19 002 (35.3)
Diseases and disorders of the hepatobiliary system (MDC 7)	29 660 (12.8)	6804 (12.6)
Diseases and disorders of the skin, subcutaneous tissue, and breast (MDC 9)	12 771 (5.5)	3010 (5.6)
Endocrine, nutritional, metabolic diseases, and disorders (MDC 10)	4853 (2.1)	1535 (2.9)
Orthopedic surgery		
Diseases and disorders of the musculoskeletal system (MDC 8)	118 945 (51.2)	17 403 (32.3)
Vascular surgery		
Diseases and disorders of the circulatory system (MDC 5)	11 194 (4.8)	6059 (11.3)
Medical history (comorbidities)		
Congestive heart failure	11 795 (5.1)	5735 (10.7)
Arrhythmia	3965 (1.7)	1765 (3.3)
Aortic stenosis	2248 (1.0)	848 (1.6)
Hypertension	79 827 (34.4)	20 648 (38.4)
Cancer	28 558 (12.3)	9074 (16.9)
Chronic obstructive pulmonary disease	19 819 (8.5)	7612 (14.2)
Diabetes mellitus (insulin and noninsulin dependent)	31 385 (13.5)	9597 (17.8)
Insulin-dependent diabetes mellitus	3607 (1.6)	1755 (3.3)

*Patients who died postoperatively were assumed to have developed a complication even if no complication codes were identified in their discharge abstracts.

Staffing and Job Satisfaction and Burnout

Higher emotional exhaustion and greater job dissatisfaction in nurses were strongly and significantly associated with patient-to-nurse ratios. Table 18.4 shows odds ratios (ORs) indicating how much more likely nurses in hospitals with higher patient-to-nurse ratios were to exhibit burnout scores above published norms and to be dissatisfied with their jobs. Controlling for nurse and hospital characteristics resulted in a slight increase in these

TABLE 18.4. **Patient-to-Nurse Ratios with High Emotional Exhaustion and Job Dissatisfaction Among Staff Nurses and with Patient Mortality and Failure-to-Rescue***

	Odds Ratio (95% Confidence Interval)					
	Unadjusted	P Value	Adjusted for Nurse or Patient Characteristics	P Value	Adjusted for Nurse or Patient and Hospital Characteristics	P Value
Nurse outcomes						
High emotional exhaustion	1.17 (1.10–1.26)	<.001	1.17 (1.10–1.26)	<.001	1.23 (1.13–1.34)	<.001
Job dissatisfaction	1.11 (1.03–1.19)	.004	1.12 (1.04–1.19)	.001	1.15 (1.07–1.25)	<.001
Patient outcomes						
Mortality	1.14 (1.08–1.19)	<.001	1.09 (1.04–1.13)	<.001	1.07 (1.03–1.12)	<.001
Failure-to-rescue	1.11 (1.06–1.17)	.004	1.09 (1.04–1.13)	.001	1.07 (1.02–1.11)	<.001

*Odds ratios, indicating the risk associated with an increase of 1 patient per nurse, and confidence intervals were derived from robust logistic regression models that accounted for the clustering (and lack of independence) of observations within hospitals. Nurse characteristics were adjusted for sex, experience (years worked as a nurse), type of degree, and type of unit. Patient characteristics were adjusted for the patient's Diagnosis Related Groups, comorbidities, and significant interactions between them. Hospital characteristics were adjusted for high technology, teaching status, and size (number of beds).

ratios, which in both cases indicated a pronounced effect of staffing. The final adjusted ORs indicated that an increase of 1 patient per nurse to a hospital's staffing level increased burnout and job dissatisfaction by factors of 1.23 (95% CI, 1.13–1.34) and 1.15 (95% CI, 1.07–1.25), respectively, or by 23% and 15%. This implies that nurses in hospitals with 8:1 patient-to-nurse ratios would be 2.29 times as likely as nurses with 4:1 patient-to-nurse ratios to show high emotional exhaustion (i.e., 1.23 to the 4th power for 4 additional patients per nurse = 2.29) and 1.75 times as likely to be dissatisfied with their jobs (i.e., 1.15 to the 4th power for 4 additional patients per nurse = 1.75). Our data further indicate that, although 43% of nurses who report high burnout and are dissatisfied with their jobs intend to leave their current job within the next 12 months, only 11% of the nurses who are not burned out and who remain satisfied with their jobs intend to leave.

Staffing and Patient Mortality and Failure-to-Rescue

Among the surgical patients studied, there was a pronounced effect of nurse staffing on both mortality and mortality following complications. Table 18.4 also shows the relationship between nurse staffing and patient mortality and failure-to-rescue (mortality following complications) when other factors were ignored, after patient characteristics were controlled, and after patient characteristics and other hospital characteristics (size, teaching status, and technology) were controlled. Although the ORs reflecting the nurse staffing effect were somewhat diminished by controlling for patient and hospital characteristics, they remained sizable and significant for both mortality and failure-to-rescue (1.07; 95% CI, 1.03–1.12 and 1.07; 95% CI, 1.02–1.11, respectively). An OR of 1.07 implies that the odds of patient mortality increased by 7% for every additional patient in the average nurse's workload in the hospital and that the difference from 4 to 6 and from 4 to 8 patients per nurse would be accompanied by 14% and 31% increases in mortality, respectively (i.e., 1.07 to the 2nd power = 1.14 and 1.07 to the 4th power = 1.31).

These effects imply that, all else being equal, substantial decreases in mortality rates could result from increasing registered nurse staffing, especially for patients who develop complications. Direct standardization techniques were used to predict excess deaths in all patients and in patients with complications that would be expected if the patient-to-nurse ratio for all patients in the study were at various levels that figure prominently in the California staffing mandate debates. If the staffing ratio in all hospitals was 6 patients per nurse rather than 4 patients per nurse, we would expect 2.3 (95% CI, 1.1–3.5) additional deaths per 1000 patients and 8.7 (95% CI, 3.9–13.5) additional deaths per 1000 patients with complications. If the staffing ratio in all hospitals was 8 patients per nurse rather than 6 patients per nurse, we would expect 2.6 (95% CI, 1.2–4.0) additional deaths per 1000 patients and 9.5 (95% CI, 3.8–15.2) additional deaths per 1000 patients with complications. Staffing hospitals uniformly at 8 vs. 4 patients per nurse would be expected to entail 5.0 (95% CI, 2.4–7.6) excess deaths per 1000 patients and 18.2 (95% CI, 7.7–28.7) excess deaths per 1000 complicated patients. We were unable to estimate excess deaths or failures associated with a ratio of 10 patients per nurse (one of the levels proposed in California) because there were so few hospitals in our sample staffed at that level.

COMMENT

Registered nurses constitute an around-the-clock surveillance system in hospitals for early detection and prompt intervention when patients' conditions deteriorate. The effectiveness of nurse surveillance is influenced by the number of registered nurses available to assess patients on an ongoing basis. Thus, it is not surprising that we found nurse staffing ratios to be important in explaining variation in hospital mortality. Numerous studies have reported an association between more registered nurses and lower hospital mortality, but often as a by-product of analyses focusing directly on some other aspect of hospital resources such as ownership, teaching status, or anesthesiologist direction.[19,27,36–42] Therefore, a simple search for literature dealing with the relationship between nurse staffing and patient outcomes yields only a fraction of the studies that have relevant findings. The relative inaccessibility of this evidence base might account for the influential Audit Commission in England concluding recently that there is no evidence that more favorable patient-to-nurse ratios result in better patient outcomes.[43]

Our results suggest that the California hospital nurse staffing legislation represents a credible approach to reducing mortality and increasing nurse retention in hospital practice, if it can be successfully implemented. Moreover, our findings suggest that California officials were wise to reject ratios favored by hospital stakeholder groups of 10 patients to each nurse on medical and surgical general units in favor of more generous staffing requirements of 5 to 6 patients per nurse. Our results do not directly indicate how many nurses are needed to care for patients or whether there is some maximum ratio of patients per nurse above which hospitals should not venture. Our major point is that there are detectable differences in risk-adjusted mortality and failure-to-rescue rates across hospitals with different registered nurse staffing ratios.

In our sample of 168 Pennsylvania hospitals in which the mean patient-to-nurse ratio ranged from 4:1 to 8:1, 4,535 of the 232,342 surgical patients with the clinical characteristics we selected died within 30 days of being admitted. Our results imply that had the patient-to-nurse ratio across all Pennsylvania hospitals been 4:1, possibly 4,000 of these patients may have died, and had it been 8:1, more than 5,000 of them may have died. While this difference of 1,000 deaths in Pennsylvania hospitals across the 2 staffing scenarios is approximate, it represents a conservative estimate of preventable deaths attributable to nurse staffing in the state. Our sample of patients represents only about half of all surgical cases in these hospitals, and other patients admitted to these hospitals are at risk of dying and similarly subject to the effects of staffing. Moreover, in California, which has nearly twice as many acute care hospitals and discharges and an overall inpatient mortality rate higher than in our sample in Pennsylvania (2.3% vs. 2.0%), it would be reasonable to expect that the difference of 4 fewer patients per nurse might result in 2,000 or more preventable deaths throughout a similar period.

Our results further indicate that nurses in hospitals with the highest patient-to-nurse ratios are more than twice as likely to experience job-related burnout and almost twice as likely to be dissatisfied with their jobs compared with nurses in the hospitals with the lowest ratios. This effect of staffing on job satisfaction and burnout suggests that improvements in nurse staffing in California hospitals resulting from the new legislation could be accompanied by declines in nurse turnover. We found that burnout and dissatisfaction predict nurses' intentions to leave their current jobs within a year. Although we do not know how many of the nurses who indicated intentions to leave their jobs actually did so, it seems reasonable to assume that the 4-fold difference in intentions across these 2 groups translated to at least a similar difference in nurse resignations. If recently published estimates of the costs of replacing a hospital medical and surgical general unit and a specialty nurse of $42,000 and $64,000, respectively, are correct, improving staffing may not only save patient lives and decrease nurse turnover but also reduce hospital costs.[44]

Additional analyses indicate that our conclusions about the effects of staffing and the size of these effects are similar under a variety of specifications. We allowed the effect of nurse staffing to be nonlinear (using a quadratic term) and vary in size across staffing levels (using dummy variables and interaction terms) and found no evidence in this sample of hospitals that additional registered nurse staffing has different effects at differing staffing levels. Limiting our analyses to general and orthopedic surgery patients and eliminating vascular surgery patients (who have higher mortality and complication rates) did not affect our conclusions and effect-size estimates. Also, our findings were not changed by restricting attention to inpatient deaths vs. deaths within 30 days of admission. Results were unaffected by restricting analyses to patients who were discharged after our staffing measures were obtained, rather than to the patients who were discharged from 9 months before to 9 months following the nurse surveys that produced our staffing measures. They were also unchanged by restricting the sample of nurses from which we derived our staffing measures to medical and surgical nurses, as opposed to all staff nurses. Finally, they were neither altered by adjusting for patient-to-licensed practical nurse ratios and patient-to-unlicensed assistive personnel ratios (neither of which were related to patient outcomes) nor affected by excluding the hospitals in our sample with smaller numbers of patients or nurses. One limitation of this study is the potential for response bias, given a 52% response rate. We find no evidence that the nurses in our sample were disproportionately dissatisfied with their work relative to Pennsylvania staff nurses from the National Sample Survey of Registered Nurses (a national probability-based sample survey performed in 2000).[21] Furthermore, with respect to demographic characteristics (sex, age, and education) included in both surveys, our sample of nurses also closely resembles those participating in the National Sample Survey of Registered Nurses. We are confident that these results are not specific to this particular sample of nurses. Ultimately, longitudinal data sets will be needed to exclude the possibility that low hospital nurse staffing is the consequence, rather than the cause, of poor patient and nurse outcomes.

Our findings have important implications for 2 pressing issues: patient safety and the hospital nurse shortage. Our results document sizable and significant effects of registered nurse staffing on preventable deaths. The association of nurse staffing levels with the rescue of patients with life-threatening conditions suggests that nurses contribute importantly to surveillance, early detection, and timely interventions that save lives. The benefits of improved registered nurse staffing also extend to the larger numbers of hospitalized patients who are not at high risk for mortality but nevertheless are vulnerable to a wide range of unfavorable outcomes. Improving nurse staffing levels may reduce alarming turnover rates in hospitals by reducing burnout and job dissatisfaction, major precursors of job resignation. When taken together, the impacts of staffing on patient and nurse outcomes suggest that by investing in registered nurse staffing, hospitals may avert both preventable mortality and low nurse retention in hospital practice.

NOTES

1. Stolberg SG. Patient deaths tied to lack of nurses. *New York Times.* August 8, 2002:A18.
2. Parker-Pope T. How to lessen impact of nursing shortage on your hospital stay. *Wall Street Journal.* March 2, 2001:B1.
3. Trafford A. Second opinion: less care for patients. *Washington Post.* August 20, 2002:HE01.
4. Aiken LH, Clarke SP, Sloane DM, et al. Nurses' reports on hospital care in five countries. *Health Aff (Millwood).* 2001;20:43–53.
5. Henry J. Kaiser Family Foundation. Survey of physicians and nurses. Available at: http://www.kff.org/content/1999/1503. Accessed March 22, 2002.
6. Shindul-Rothschild J, Berry D, Long-Middleton E. Where have all the nurses gone? final results of our Patient Care Survey. *Am J Nurs.* 1996;96:25–39.
7. Commonwealth Fund. Doctors in five countries see decline in health care quality. *Commonwealth Fund Quarterly.* 2000;6:1–4.
8. Joint Commission on Accreditation of Healthcare Organizations. *Health care at the crossroads: strategies for addressing the evolving nursing crisis,* 2002. Available at: http://www.jcaho.org/news+room/news+release+archives/health+care+at+the+crossroads.pdf. Accessed September 17, 2002.

9. Spetz J. What should we expect from California's minimum nurse staffing legislation. *J Nurs Adm.* 2001;31:132–140.

10. Seago JA. The California experiment: alternatives for minimum nurse-to-patient ratios. *J Nurs Adm.* 2002;32:48–58.

11. Friedman L. Nurse ratios are still too high. *San Francisco Chronicle.* January 30, 2002:A19.

12. Governor Gray Davis announces proposed nurse-to-patient ratios [press release]. Sacramento, Calif: Office of the Governor; January 22, 2002.

13. Lake ET. Advances in understanding and predicting nurse turnover. *Res Sociol Health Care.* 1998;15:147–171.

14. Aiken LH, Clarke SP, Sloane DM. Hospital staffing, organizational support,andquality of care: cross-national findings. *Int J Qual Health Care.* 2002;14:5–13.

15. AHA *annual survey database*. 1999 ed. Chicago, Ill: American Hospital Association; 1999.

16. Commonwealth of Pennsylvania. Hospital questionnaire: Reporting period July 1, 1998-June 30, 1999. Harrisburg, Pa: Department of Health, Division of Statistics.

17. Needleman J, Buerhaus PI, Mattke S, Stewart M, Zelevinsky K. *Nurse staffing and patient outcomes in hospitals.* Available at: http://bhpr.hrsa.gov/nursing/staffstudy.htm. Accessed August 6, 2002.

18. Ayanian JZ, Weissman JS, Chasan-Taber S, Epstein AM. Quality of care for two common illnesses in teaching and nonteaching hospitals. *Health Aff (Millwood).* 1998;17:194–205.

19. Hartz AJ, Krakauer H, Kuhn EM, et al. Hospital characteristics and mortality rates. *N Engl J Med.* 1989;321:1720–1725.

20. Asch DA, Jedrziewski MK, Christakis NA. Response rates to mail surveys published in medical journals. *J Clin Epidemiol.* 1997;50:1129–1136.

21. *The registered nurse population.* Rockville, Md: US Dept of Health and Human Services; 1996.

22. Maslach C, Jackson SE. Burnout in health professions: a social psychological analysis. In: Sanders GS, Suls J, eds. *Social Psychology of Health and Illness.* Hillsdale, NJ: Lawrence Erlbaum Associates; 1982:227–251.

23. Maslach C, Jackson SE. *Maslach Burnout Inventory manual.* 2nd ed. Palo Alto, Calif: Consulting Psychologists Press; 1986.

24. Silber JH, Williams SV, Krakauer H, Schwartz JS. Hospital and patient characteristics associated with death after surgery: a study of adverse occurrence and failure to rescue. *Med Care.* 1992;30:615–629.

25. Silber JH, Rosenbaum PR, Ross RN. Comparing the contributions of groups of predictors: which outcomes vary with hospital rather than patient characteristics? *J Am Stat Assoc.* 1995;90:7–18.

26. Silber JH, Rosenbaum PR, Schwartz JS, Ross RN, Williams SV. Evaluation of the complication rate as a measure of quality of care in coronary artery bypass graft surgery. *JAMA.* 1995;274:317–323.

27. Silber JH, Kennedy SK, Even-Shoshan O, et al. Anesthesiologist direction and patient outcomes. *Anesthesiology.* 2000;93:152–163.

28. Silber JH, Rosenbaum PR, Trudeau ME, et al. Multivariate matching and bias reduction in the surgical outcomes study. *Med Care.* 2001;39:1048–1064.

29. Silber JH, Kennedy SK, Even-Shoshan O, et al. Anesthesiologist board certification and patient outcomes. *Anesthesiology.* 2002;96:1044–1052.

30. Hanley JA, McNeil BJ. The meaning and use of the area under a receiver operating characteristic (ROC) curve. *Radiology.* 1982;143:29–36.

31. Huber PJ. *The Behavior of Maximum Likelihood Estimates Under Non-standard Conditions: Proceedings of the Fifth Berkeley Symposium on Mathematical Statistics and Probability.* Berkeley: University of California Press; 1967:221–233.

32. White H. Maximum likelihood estimation of misspecified models. *Econometrica.* 1982;50:1–25.

33. Hosmer DW, Lemeshow S. *Applied logistic regression.* New York, NY: John Wiley & Sons Inc; 1989.

34. Bishop YM, Fienberg SE, Holland PW. *Discrete Multivariate Analysis: Theory and practice*. Cambridge, Mass: MIT Press; 1975.

35. Agresti A. *Categorical data analysis*. New York, NY: John Wiley & Sons Inc; 1990.

36. Shortell SM, Hughes EFX. The effects of regulation, competition, and ownership on mortality rates among hospital inpatients. *N Engl J Med.* 1988;318:1100–1107.

37. Institute of Medicine. *Nursing staff in hospitals and nursing homes*: Is *it adequate*? Washington, DC: National Academy Press; 1996.

38. Aiken LH, Sloane DM, Lake ET, Sochalski J, Weber AL. Organization and outcomes of inpatient AIDS care. *Med Care.* 1999;37:760–772.

39. Mitchell PH, Shortell SM. Adverse outcomes and variations in organization of care delivery. *Med Care.* 1997;35(suppl 11):NS19–NS32.

40. Moses LE, Mosteller F. Institutional differences in postoperative death rates. *JAMA.* 1968;203:492–494.

41. Pronovost PJ, Jenckes MW, Dorman T, et al. Organizational characteristics of intensive care units related to outcomes of abdominal aortic surgery. *JAMA.* 1999;281:1310–1317.

42. Needleman J, Buerhaus P, Mattke S, Stewart M, Zelevinsky K. Nurse-staffing levels and the quality of care in hospitals. *N Engl J Med.* 2002;346:1715–1722.

43. Audit Commission. *Acute hospital Portfolio: Review of national findings: Ward staffing*. London, England: The Audit Commission; 2001:3.

44. Nursing Executive Committee. *Reversing the flight of talent: Nursing retention in an era of gathering shortage*. Washington, DC: Advisory Board Co; 2000.

ACKNOWLEDGMENTS

Funding/Support: This study was supported by grant R01 NR04513 from the National Institute of Nursing Research, National Institutes of Health.

Acknowledgment: We thank Paul Allison, PhD, from the University of Pennsylvania for statistical consultation, and Xuemei Zhang, MS, Wei Chen, MS, and Orit Even-Shoshan, MS, from the Center for Outcomes Research at the Children's Hospital of Philadelphia for their assistance.

19

NURSE STAFFING IN HOSPITALS: IS THERE A BUSINESS CASE FOR QUALITY?

JACK NEEDLEMAN

PETER I. BUERHAUS

MAUREEN STEWART

KATYA ZELEVINSKY

SOEREN MATTKE

This article originally appeared as and is copyrighted and published by Project Hope/*Health Affairs* as Needleman, J., Buerhaus, P. I., Stewart, M., Zelevinsky, K., & Mattke, S. (2006). Nurse staffing in hospitals: Is there a business case for quality? *Health Affairs, 25*(1), pp. 1715–1722. The published article is archived and available online at www.healthaffairs.org.

EDITORS' NOTE

As the evidence mounted on the connection between nurse staffing and clinical outcomes of care, questions arose regarding the cost of improving staffing. Could hospitals afford to achieve these improved outcomes? Needleman and colleagues addressed this question by examining the clinical and financial outcomes of three comparisons: increasing the overall hours of nursing care, increasing the percentage of total nursing care hours that are provided by RNs, or doing both. Their conclusion: holding total nursing care hours constant but increasing the proportion of those hours that are provided by RNs improves outcomes and *lowers* costs.

■ ■ ■

Patient safety and quality improvement efforts have grown impressively in recent years. Despite these gains, though, questions remain about the value of improving quality from both societal and hospital perspectives. From the societal perspective, the question is whether gains from improving quality reduce costs to patients, hospitals, and payers or, if they increase costs, whether the value of the quality improvement to patients justifies spending more on care. From the hospital perspective, the question is whether cost savings or revenue gains from improving quality offset the costs of quality initiatives—that is, whether there is a business case for quality. Sheila Leatherman and colleagues, in language relevant to both perspectives, recently wrote, "There is a compelling need to understand better the economic implications for all stakeholders of implementing quality improvement."[1]

The growing body of evidence linking hospital workforces to patient outcomes suggests that one way to improve quality is to increase nurse staffing.[2] Because nurses are a large portion of hospital labor costs, the cost of increasing staffing would not be insignificant. The additional costs of having more nurses, however, should be offset to some extent by the monetary and nonmonetary benefits of reducing adverse outcomes.

There are many ways to improve quality and patient safety in hospitals (for example, equipping hospitals with new technology, investing in training and education, imposing regulations, and increasing nurse staffing). Whether there is a business case for any particular option depends on many factors, and each hospital will have to make its own assessment. In instances where there is not a clear business case for increased nurse staffing, there might be a "social case"; thus, it would be socially beneficial to have policy intervention.

In this study we provide data to help hospitals and policymakers consider both the business and social cases for investing in nurse staffing by estimating the costs of increasing staffing and cost savings resulting from avoided deaths, reduced lengths-of-stay, and decreased adverse patient outcomes associated with higher nurse staffing levels.

STUDY DATA AND METHODS

In an earlier study we analyzed data from 799 nonfederal acute care general hospitals in eleven states. Discharge abstracts and nurse staffing data were obtained from the states; data on hospital size, location, teaching status, from the American Hospital Association (AHA) annual survey; and cost-to-charge ratios, from Medicare cost reports.

In regression analyses we found an association of nurse staffing and (1) lengths-of-stay, urinary tract infections, upper gastrointestinal bleeding, hospital-acquired pneumonia, shock, or cardiac arrest among medical patients and (2) "failure to rescue," defined as the death of a patient with one of five life-threatening complications—pneumonia, shock or cardiac arrest, upper gastrointestinal bleeding, sepsis, or deep vein thrombosis—among surgical patients. Details of that study are described elsewhere.[3] Exhibit 19.1 presents rates of these outcomes and descriptive statistics for the 799-hospital sample.

In this study we simulated the effect of three options to increase nurse staffing: raise the proportion of hours provided by registered nurses (RNs) to the seventy-fifth percentile for hospitals below this level; raise the number of licensed (that is, RNs and licensed practical/vocational nurses, or LPNs) nursing hours per day to the seventy-fifth percentile; and raise staffing to each of these levels in hospitals where each is below the seventy-fifth percentile. This percentile was chosen based on our judgment that attaining this level of staffing is feasible for most hospitals (Exhibit 19.2).

The required number of additional nurse hours to meet the seventy-fifth-percentile levels was estimated from the original sample. Estimates of avoided adverse outcomes and days of care were simulated from the regression models from the earlier study, and estimates of avoided costs and deaths were made with additional regression modeling in the original data. Costs of avoided adverse outcomes were estimated from patient-level regressions of costs per case on patient diagnosis and other characteristics and variables for each adverse outcome. Costs of avoided days were estimated by multiplying average costs per day by regression-based estimates of reduced days net of the days associated with adverse outcomes.

Because many hospital costs are fixed in the short run, hospitals might not fully recover the average costs of avoided days or avoided complications. Based on a review of studies of hospital fixed and variable costs, we estimated variable costs of hospitals to be 40 percent of average costs, and we multiplied calculated costs by this amount to estimate the short-term cost impact of reduced hospital patient days and avoided adverse outcomes.[4] Over time, hospitals should be able to adjust their fixed costs to reflect the change in volume. We present estimates of cost savings assuming short-term savings of 40 percent of average costs and with full recovery of fixed costs.

We projected the results from the sample to all nonfederal U.S. acute care hospitals and updated the estimates of needed staffing, avoided adverse outcomes and days, and costs to reflect hospital costs, admissions, and lengths-of-stay in 2002. Specifically, our sample had 26 percent of the discharges from U.S. nonfederal acute care hospitals in 1997. We constructed national estimates of adverse outcomes, nursing full-time equivalents (FTEs), and costs by multiplying estimates from the sample by 100 divided by 26. We used data on RN wages from the 1997 and 2002 Current Population Surveys (CPS) and the change in admissions, lengths-of-stay, spending per admission, and spending per day between 2002 and

EXHIBIT 19.1. Mean and Standard Deviation (SD) of Patient Outcomes and Hospital Characteristics, Hospital Sample

Outcomes	Mean	SD
Length-of-stay (days)	5.02	1.98
Urinary tract infection	6.30%	2.34%
Hospital-acquired pneumonia	2.34%	1.15%
Shock/cardiac arrest	0.57%	0.81%
Upper GI bleeding	1.04%	0.63%
Failure to rescue[a]	19.69%	13.30%

Hospital characteristics	Mean	SD
Mean number of beds	226.58	198.86
Teaching status		
Major teaching hospital	10.26%	30.37%
Other teaching hospital	19.02	39.27
Nonteaching hospital	70.71	45.54
Location		
Large metro area	53.94%	49.88%
Small metro area	25.66	43.70
Nonmetro area	20.40	40.32

Source: J. Needleman et al. (2002). Nurse-staffing levels and quality of care in hospitals. *New England Journal of Medicine 346*(22), pp. 1415–1422.
Notes: All outcomes except "failure to rescue" are analyzed for medical patients; "failure to rescue" is analyzed for surgical patients. The sample had 799 hospitals, with 5,075,969 medical and 1,104,659 surgical discharges. Because they had no patients in the pool for the event, one hospital was excluded from the analysis of upper gastrointestinal (GI) bleeding, one from the analysis of shock and cardiac arrest, and fourteen from the analysis of failure to rescue. Two were excluded from the analysis of length-of-stay because of outlying predictions. Percentages may not add up to 100 percent because of rounding.

[a] "Failure to rescue" is defined as hospital mortality among patients with hospital-acquired pneumonia, shock or cardiac arrest, upper GI bleeding, sepsis, deep vein thrombosis, or pulmonary failure.

EXHIBIT 19.2. **Proportion of Registered Nurses (RNs) and Number of Licensed Nursing Hours at the 25th and 75th Percentiles of Hospitals Studied**

	Mean	Standard Deviation	25th Percentile	75th Percentile	Minimum	Maximum
Proportion of RNs	0.87	0.10	0.81	0.94	0.49	1.00
Number of licensed hours	8.99	2.05	7.58	10.23	4.07	16.75

Source: J. Needleman et al. (2002). Nurse-staffing levels and quality of care in hospitals. New England Journal of Medicine 346(22), pp. 1415–1422.

1997 from the AHA annual survey to update the estimates of avoided adverse outcomes, avoided days, deaths, and costs. In aggregate, between 1997 and 2002, licensed hours per day and the proportion of licensed hours provided by RNs reported to the AHA, and average case-mix, measured by the Medicare case-mix index, did not change substantially; thus, no adjustments were made to the staffing variables.[5]

Because neither our prior work nor other studies capture all of the effects of nurse staffing on patient care, and because we do not have direct measures of patient-reported quality, we do not attempt a cost-effectiveness analysis of the impact of raising nurse staffing. We do present estimates of the cost per avoided death.

Study Results

- **Cost of increasing nurse staffing.** In 2002, U.S. short-term acute general hospitals employed 942,000 FTE RNs and 120,000 FTE LPNs.[6] Increasing the proportion of RNs to the seventy-fifth percentile (option 1) would require hospitals below this level to replace more than 37,000 FTE LPNs with RNs at an estimated cost of $811 million.

Increasing nurses in hospitals with licensed hours below the seventy-fifth percentile (option 2) requires an increase in FTE RNs of 114,456, and FTE LPNs of more than 13,000, costing $7.5 billion. If hospitals below either of these staffing levels increased staffing to the seventy-fifth percentile (option 3), FTE RNs would increase by nearly 158,000 and FTE LPNs would fall, changes that would cost $8.5 billion (Exhibit 19.3).

- **Reduced adverse outcomes and avoided hospital days.** Increasing nurse staffing is associated with fewer adverse outcomes under all options (Exhibit 19.4), with 70,000 fewer adverse outcomes if hospital nurse staffing met both seventy-fifth-percentile thresholds (option 3).

Decreases in urinary tract infections, pneumonia, and shock or cardiac arrest are associated most with increasing the proportion of RNs. Failure to rescue in surgical patients is more sensitive to the number of licensed nursing hours per day. Upper gastrointestinal bleeding appears equally sensitive to changes in both staffing measures. We believe that urinary tract infections, pneumonia, and shock or cardiac arrest are more sensitive to

EXHIBIT 19.3.   Costs of Hiring Additional Registered Nurses (RNs) and Licensed Practical Nurses (LPNs) to Increase Nurse Staffing to the 75th Percentile of Hospitals Studied, National Estimates Updated to 2002

	Option 1: Raise proportion of RNs to 75th percentile without changing number of licensed hours	Option 2: Raise number of licensed hours to 75th percentile without changing proportion of RNs	Option 3: Raise both proportion of RNs and number of licensed hours to 75th percentile
Change in FTE RNs	37,089	114,456	157,894
Change in FTE LPNs	–37,089	13,093	–30,345
Total cost (in millions)	$811	$7,538	$8,488

Source: Authors' estimates using data from J. Needleman et al. (2002). Nurse-staffing levels and quality of care in hospitals. New England Journal of Medicine 346(22), pp. 1415–1422, updated to 2002 based on 1997 and 2002 American Hospital Association annual survey data and on wage data for nurses employed in hospitals from the Current Population Survey.
Note: Full-time equivalent (FTE) estimates were derived by dividing change in total hours by 2,080.

the RN/LPN mix than hours at the bedside because preventing these complications draws heavily on the skills and education of RNs in patient assessment and intervention, not just increased time to observe and treat patients.

Hospital days would be lower by 1.5 million under option 1, almost 2.6 million under option 2, and 4.1 million under option 3. The larger reduction in length-of-stay (and corresponding reduction in cost) associated with option 2 compared with option 1 reflects our earlier finding that length-of-stay is associated more with hours of nursing care than with the RN/LPN mix.

Short-term cost savings associated with reducing adverse outcomes and hospital days are substantial (Exhibit 19.4). Because the costs of changing the RN/LPN mix without changing licensed hours are relatively low (option 1), short-term cost savings exceed the cost increases by $242 million. While options 2 and 3 are associated with substantial avoided costs, these are not enough to offset the costs of increased nurse staffing. The net short-term cost increase associated with options 2 and 3 would be $5.8 and $5.7 billion, respectively. Although large, these amounts are approximately 1.5 percent of annual hospital expenditures.

Over time, hospitals can adjust fixed costs to reflect reduced volume or replace these days and services with other, higher-value services or programs to which the fixed costs would be allocated. For some hospitals, this adjustment would be speedy; for others, slow. If fixed costs were fully recaptured, the net costs of increased nurse staffing would be much lower (Exhibit 19.4).

Decreases in length-of-stay associated with higher nurse staffing generate more than 90 percent of our projected cost savings. We examined four other studies finding an association of either hours of nurse staffing or the proportion of nursing staff that is RNs and lengths-of-stay in either medical-surgical units or hospitals in general, to determine whether using results from these studies would generate higher or lower estimates than ours.[7] Although most are not directly comparable to our study, when we reanalyzed these results, we found that our estimates of the association of staffing and lengths-of-stay are approximately equal to those that would be constructed from two of the studies, and approximately half those that would be estimated from two others.[8] Two additional studies assessing the association of nurse staffing and lengths-of-stay in intensive care units (ICUs) found that moving nurse staffing below a one-to-two ratio was associated with 30–50 percent longer stays.[9] In light of these comparisons, our estimates of cost offsets appear conservative.

• **Avoided in-hospital deaths.** Increased staffing under all options is associated with fewer in-hospital deaths (Exhibit 19.4). We examined results from two recent studies that reported an association of staffing and mortality, to determine whether applying results from these studies would generate higher or lower estimates of avoided deaths than ours. Applying the results of Barbara Mark and colleagues, we would increase our projected avoided deaths by 60–80 percent.[10] Applying the finding of Linda Aiken and colleagues for surgical patients, our projected number of postsurgical deaths would be three times larger and, if we extrapolated this result to all patients, medical and surgical—which we do not believe is justified based on our and others' research—the estimate of avoided deaths would be more than three times larger than we present.[11]

Discussion

There is an unequivocal business case for hospitals to improve nurse staffing under one option we examined: raising the proportion of RNs without changing licensed hours. This option also was the least costly—$811 million—and would achieve a net reduction in short-term costs of $242 million. We note that these are aggregate estimates, and some hospitals might not realize the expected savings, such as those where RNs' wages are relatively high compared with LPNs' wages. Although these hospitals might not experience a net cost savings, patients treated in them would likely still benefit from reduced lengths-of-stay and fewer adverse outcomes.

Although the increase in nurse staffing under option 2 yields a smaller reduction in both adverse outcomes and their associated costs compared with option 1, it results in a much larger reduction in hospital days because of unmeasured complications and delays in care, with sizable cost savings. Nevertheless, the costs of this approach are not offset by cost savings associated with the reduction in adverse outcomes and the increase in avoided hospital days.

Changing nurse staffing to meet both thresholds (option 3) results in an increase in RN employment but a decrease in LPNs. Although this option would achieve the greatest reduction in adverse outcomes and hospital days, estimated staffing costs would be highest and not totally offset by estimated savings.

Our cost estimates of short-term savings are based on an assumption that hospitals' variable costs are 40 percent of average costs. Over time, hospitals should be able to reduce fixed costs in response to changes in use, and long-term savings are likely to be much higher than in the short term, although options 2 and 3 still do not pay for themselves (Exhibit 19.4). The speed of this adjustment depends on whether the hospital can scale

EXHIBIT 19.4. Avoided Adverse Outcomes, Hospital Days, Costs, and Deaths If Proportion of Registered Nurses (RNs) or Number of Licensed Nursing Hours Were Increased to the 75th Percentile of Hospitals Studied, National Estimates Updated to 2002

	Option 1: Raise proportion of RNs from 75th percentile without changing number of licensed hours	Option 2: Raise number of licensed hours to 75th percentile without changing proportion of RNs	Option 3: Raise both proportion of RNs and number of licensed hours to 75th percentile
Number of avoided adverse outcomes			
Failure to rescue (major surgery pool)	354	597	942
Urinary tract infection	40,770	4,174	44,773
Hospital-acquired pneumonia	11,761	1,372	13,093
Upper GI bleeding	4,145	4,129	8,182
Shock or cardiac arrest	2,908	540	3,426
Total avoided outcomes	59,938	10,813	70,416
Hospital days avoided	1,507,493	2,598,339	4,106,315
Cost impacts (in millions)			
Cost savings assuming that 40% of hospital costs are variable			
Cost savings of avoided outcomes	$73	$17	$89
Cost savings of avoided days	980	1,702	2,683
Total avoided costs	1,053	1,719	2,772
Net cost of increasing nursing	-242	5,819	5,716
Net cost as percent of hospital expenses	-0.1%	1.5%	1.4%

Cost savings assuming that fixed hospital costs are recovered (in millions)			
Cost savings of avoided outcomes	$183	$42	$224
Cost savings of avoided days	2,450	4,256	6,707
Total avoided costs	2,633	4,298	6,930
Net cost of increasing nursing	−1,821	3,240	1,558
Net cost as percent of hospital expenses	−0.5%	0.8%	0.4%
Avoided deaths	4,997	1,801	6,754

Source: Authors' estimates using data from J. Needleman et al. (2002). Nurse-staffing levels and quality of care in hospitals. New England Journal of Medicine 346(22), pp. 1415–1422, updated to 2002 based on 1997 and 2002 American Hospital Association annual survey data and on wage data for nurses employed in hospitals from the Current Population Survey.

Note: Urinary tract infection, hospital-acquired pneumonia, upper gastrointestinal (GI) bleeding, and shock or cardiac arrest and change in length-of-stay were analyzed for medical patients only. Failure to rescue was analyzed for surgical patients only. Cost savings of avoided outcomes and days are initially reduced by 60 percent based on research that only 40 percent of hospital costs are variable in the short run. Over time, fixed costs should be reduced to reflect changed volume. Estimates based on recovery of 40 percent of average costs and all average costs are presented. Net cost of increasing nurse staffing was calculated by subtracting total estimated cost savings due to avoided outcomes and days from cost of increasing nurse staffing reported in Exhibit 19.3.

back operations or replace the lost volume with other services to which the fixed costs can be allocated.

• **Reduction in patient deaths.** We estimated that more than 6,700 in-hospital patient deaths could be avoided by raising nurse staffing and that approximately three-quarters (4,997) of these could be achieved by increasing the proportion of RNs (option 1). To provide context for this finding, we estimated the cost per avoided death by dividing the net cost of increased nurse staffing by the number of avoided deaths associated with each staffing option. Under option 3, in which both staffing thresholds are met, estimated short-term costs per avoided death are $846,000. Under option 2, in which only licensed nursing hours are increased, short-term costs per avoided death are $3.23 million, which approximates the marginal cost per avoided death of moving from option 1 to option 3. Estimated costs of avoided deaths, assuming full recovery of fixed costs, would be $231,000 for option 3 and $1.8 million for option 2.

In estimating the benefits of increased nurse staffing, we did not consider the value to patients and their families of reduced morbidity (such as decreased pain and suffering, and days lost from work), the economic value to hospitals of lower liability and improved reputation and image from reducing adverse nursing-related morbidity and mortality, or the positive effects of increased nurse staffing in reducing adverse outcomes not considered in this analysis but observed in other studies, including patient falls, bloodborne infections, decubitus ulcers, and medication errors.[12] Similarly, increased patient satisfaction, good discharge planning, and patients' increased ability to perform self-care were not included in this study, yet they, too, have both economic and noneconomic value.[13] Nor did we estimate potential cost savings from reducing nurse turnover through increased nurse staffing.[14] Given this undercounting of the cost offsets from increased nurse staffing, our estimates of the cost per avoided death should be viewed as upper-bound estimates. The costs per avoided death that we estimated are below the values of a statistical life used by federal agencies in their rule making on health and safety, which range from $3 million to $6 million.[15] By these standards, investing in additional licensed nursing hours is worth doing.

• **Implications for hospitals and policymakers.** Pressures are mounting for hospitals to control costs at the same time patient volume is increasing and the demand to improve patient safety and quality is gaining momentum. Our analysis examines the costs of responding to this demand by raising hospital nurse staffing, and it estimates the cost offsets and economic value associated with avoided hospital days, morbidity, and mortality. These estimates can inform discussions and influence judgments about nurses' contribution to improving the quality of care.

From a hospital's perspective, increasing nurse staffing is costly. Nevertheless, greater use of RNs in preference to LPNs appears to pay for itself. Improved patient outcomes and reduced days associated with more hours of nurse staffing would only partially offset the costs to achieve them, and, depending on the reimbursement systems in use, cost savings could be shared with payers instead of accruing solely to the hospital. This creates a strong disincentive to increase nurse staffing. From a patient's perspective, however, using standard measures of value, the additional costs to increase nurse staffing appear justified.

Policymakers and public and private payers should focus on finding ways to reconcile patient and hospital perspectives. For example, when Medicare was established in 1965 and hospitals faced a large shortage of nurses, Congress included extra payments to help hospitals raise wages and increase staffing. Might providing payment supplements to hospitals to increase nurse staffing bridge the gap between public and private valuation of increased staffing?

The central questions that emerge from this study for public and private payers, patient advocates, hospitals, accreditation agencies, and others involved in setting policy are as follows: How important is the goal of improving patient quality? Should increasing nurse staffing be encouraged as a means for pursuing this goal? Should funds be made available to hospitals to help realize this goal? And finally, What assurances are needed that any funds provided to hospitals are actually used to increase nurse staffing?

NOTES

1. S. Leatherman et al., "The business case for quality: Case studies and an analysis," *Health Affairs 22,* no. 2 (2003): 17–30.

2. See, for example, Institute of Medicine, *Keeping patients safe: Transforming the work environment of nurses* (Washington: National Academies Press, 2003); M.W. Stanton and M.K. Rutherford, "Hospital nurse staffing and quality of care" (Rockville, Md.: Agency for Healthcare Research and Quality, 2004); and J. Needleman and P. Buerhaus, "Nurse staffing and patient safety: Current knowledge and implications for action," *International Journal for Quality in Health Care 15,* no. 4 (2003): 275–277. See also R.J. Blendon et al., "Views of practicing physicians and the public on medical errors," *New England Journal of Medicine 347,* no. 24 (2002): 1933–1940; and D.E. Altman, C. Clancy, and R.J. Blendon, "Improving patient safety—Five years after the IOM report," *New England Journal of Medicine 351,* no. 20 (2004): 2041–2043.

3. J. Needleman et al., "Nurse-staffing levels and the quality of care in hospitals," *New England Journal of Medicine 346,* no. 22 (2002): 1715–1722 and J. Needleman et al., "Nurse staffing and patient outcomes in hospitals" (Boston: Harvard School of Public Health, 2001).

4. The studies reviewed include B. Friedman and M.V. Pauly, "A new approach to hospital cost functions and some issues in revenue regulation," *Health Care Financing Review 4,* no. 3 (1983): 105–114; J.R. Lave and L.B. Lave, "Hospital Cost Functions," *Annual Review of Public Health 5* (1984): 193–213; M.V. Pauly and P. Wilson, "Hospital output forecasts and the cost of empty hospital beds," *Health Services Research 21,* no. 3 (1986): 403–428; and T.W. Grannemann, R.S. Brown, and M.V. Pauly, "Estimating hospital costs: A multiple-output analysis," *Journal of Health Economics 5,* no. 2 (1986): 107–127.

5. Methods are described in greater detail in an online Technical Appendix, http://content.healthaffairs.org/cgi/content/full/25/1/204/DC1.

6. American Hospital Association, Annual Survey of Hospitals, 2002.

7. K.G. Behner et al., "Nursing resource management: Analyzing the relationship between costs and quality in staffing decisions," *Health Care Management Review 15,* no. 4 (1990): 63–71; S.D. Flood and D. Diers, "Nurse staffing, patient outcome, and cost," *Nursing Management 19,* no. 5 (1988): 34–43; L.K. Lichtig, R.A. Knauf, and D.K. Milholland, "Some impacts of nursing on acute care hospital outcomes," *Journal of Nursing Administration 29,* no. 2 (1999): 25–33; and M.A. Schultz et al., "The relationship of hospital structural and financial characteristics to mortality and length of stay in acute myocardial infarction patients," *Outcomes Management for Nursing Practice 2,* no. 3 (1998): 130–136.

8. Our findings were approximately equal to those found by Lichtig and Schultz. They were half those estimated by Flood and Diers and by Behner.

9. R.K. Amaravadi et al., "ICU nurse-to-patient ratio is associated with complications and resource use after esophagectomy," *Intensive Care Medicine 26,* no. 12 (2000): 1857–1862; and P.J. Pronovost et al., "Organizational characteristics of intensive care units related to outcomes of abdominal aortic surgery," *Journal of the American Medical Association 281,* no. 14 (1999): 1310–1317.

10. B.A. Mark et al., "A longitudinal examination of hospital registered nurse staffing and quality of care," *Health Services Research 39,* no. 2 (2004): 279–300.

11. L.H. Aiken et al., "Hospital nurse staffing and patient mortality, nurse burnout, and job dissatisfaction," *Journal of the American Medical Association 288,* no. 16 (2002): 1987–1993.

12. The other studies are cited in Note 2.

13. P.H. Mitchell, S. Ferketich, and B.M. Jennings, "Quality health outcomes model: American Academy of Nursing expert panel on quality health care," *Image—The Journal of Nursing Scholarship 30,* no. 1 (1998): 43–46.

14. See, for example, T.W. Tai, S.I. Bame, and C.D. Robinson, "Review of Nursing Turnover Research, 1977–1996," *Social Science and Medicine 47,* no. 12 (1998): 1905–1924; S.J. Cavanagh, "Nursing Turnover: Literature Review and Methodological Critique," *Journal of Advanced Nursing 14,* no. 7 (1989): 587–596; C.B. Jones, "Staff Nurse Turnover Costs, Part I: A Conceptual Model," *Journal of Nursing Administration 20,* no. 4 (1990): 18–23; and C.B. Jones, "Staff Nurse Turnover Costs, Part II: Measurements and Results," *Journal of Nursing Administration 20,* no. 5 (1990): 27–32.

15. W.K. Viscusi, "The value of risks to life and health," *Journal of Economic Literature 31,* no. 4 (1993): 1912–1946; U.S. Environmental Protection Agency, Office of the Administrator, "Guidelines for preparing economic analyses" (Washington: EPA, 2000); U.S. Department of Transportation, Office of the Secretary of Transportation, "Revised departmental guidelines: Treatment of value of life and injuries in preparing economic evaluations" (Washington: DOT, 2002); and DOT, "Revision of departmental guidance on treatment of the value of life and injuries," 2002, http://ostpxweb.dot.gov/VSL_background.htm (accessed 18 October 2005).

ACKNOWLEDGMENTS

This study was supported by the Commonwealth Fund, a New York City–based private, independent foundation. The views presented here are those of the authors and not necessarily those of the Commonwealth Fund, its directors, officers, or staff. The authors thank the reviewers for their helpful suggestions on an earlier version of this paper.

SPECIALTY PRACTICE IN NURSING

Reprints of Key Articles

Charlene Harrington, "Long-Term Care Policy Issues"

Karen Buhler-Wilkerson, "The Future of Home Care"

Kristine M. Gebbie, "Follow the Money: Funding Streams and Public Health Nursing"

Katherine Boo, "Swamp Nurse"

American Academy of Pediatrics Council on School Health, "Role of the School Nurse in Providing School Health Services"

LONG-TERM CARE POLICY ISSUES

CHARLENE HARRINGTON

The chapter originally appeared as Harrington, C. (2011). Long-term care policy issues. In D. J. Mason, J. K. Leavitt, & M. W. Chaffee (Eds). *Policy & Politics in Nursing in Health Care,* 6th edition (pp. 206–213). St. Louis: Elsevier Saunders. Copyright © 2011 Elsevier. All rights reserved.

EDITORS' NOTE

Long-term care is largely nursing care, whether provided by licensed nurses (including advanced practice registered nurses) or nurses aides. Nurse researcher Charlene Harrington has been a leader in examining the factors that influence the quality of long-term care, particularly in nursing homes. In this piece, she takes a comprehensive look at the quality of care in long-term care facilities, the relevant public policies and their enforcement, and workforce issues.

■ ■ ■

He who wants to warm himself in old age must build a fireplace in his youth.
—German Proverb

The population of the United States is aging with the number of adults aged 65 and older almost doubling (from 37 million to over 70 million between 2005 and 2030) from 12% to almost 20% of the population by 2030 (Institute of Medicine [IOM], 2008). With the aging of the population, the demand for long-term care (LTC) and the need for nurses and other personnel to provide services is growing rapidly. The IOM predicts a major shortage of health workers with geriatric training to address the growing needs of the aging population. With total LTC expenditures of $190 billion in 2007 (Hartman et al., 2009), LTC is a critical sector (9% of total health spending), but one that receives little attention from the nursing profession.

This chapter focuses on some of the policy and political issues facing nursing in LTC. First, it reviews the problems with the quality of nursing home care, the poor enforcement of federal quality regulations, and a lack of ownership transparency (intelligibility). Second, it examines nursing home staffing and reimbursement policies. Third, it discusses the need for expanding home and community-based service (HCBS) programs. Finally, nurses are urged to become advocates for older and disabled people who need LTC services.

POOR QUALITY OF CARE AND WEAK REGULATORY ENFORCEMENT

Poor nursing home quality has been documented since the early 1970s and culminated in passage of the Omnibus Budget Reconciliation Act (OBRA) of 1987 to reform nursing home regulation (IOM, 2001). Although it was expected that OBRA 1987 would improve the survey and enforcement system and ultimately improve quality, these expectations have yet to be realized. A number of studies and reports have described the poor quality of some nursing homes (IOM, 1996, 2001, 2003). In 2008, over 90% of nursing homes received about 150,000 deficiencies for failure to meet federal regulations, for a wide range of violations of quality standards that result in unnecessary resident weight loss, pressure ulcers, accidents, infections, decline in physical functioning, and many other problems (Harrington et al., 2009). Almost 65,000 formal complaints were made to state regulatory agencies about poor nursing home quality, and 26% of nursing homes received deficiencies for causing harm or jeopardy to nursing home residents in the U.S. in 2008. Many studies during the past decade have documented the serious quality problems related to ongoing problems with the federal and state survey and enforcement system, including the complaint investigation process (U.S. General Accounting Office [U.S. GAO], 1999a, 1999b, 2002; 2003; U.S. Government Accountability Office [GAO], 2007, 2008).

State surveyors are often unable to detect serious problems with quality of care and allow most facilities to correct deficiencies without penalties (U.S. GAO, 2002; GAO, 2008). Some state survey agencies downgrade the scope and severity of deficiencies, and many states do not refer cases for intermediate sanctions (U.S. GAO, 2003; GAO, 2008). State surveys are problematic for reasons including the continued predictability of standard surveys and the inadequacy and lack of timeliness of consumer complaint investigations (U.S. GAO, 2003; GAO, 2008). Problems with poor state investigation and documentation of deficiencies and large numbers of inexperienced state surveyors in some states also occur, and federal oversight of state activities continues to be inadequate.

When violations are detected, few facilities have follow-up enforcement actions or sanctions taken against them (Harrington et al., 2004; Harrington, Tsoukalas, et al., 2008). The continued widespread variation in the number and type of deficiencies issued by states shows that states are not using the regulatory process consistently and are not following federal guidelines (U.S. GAO, 2003). Some state officials admit they are unable or are unwilling to comply with federal survey and enforcement requirements (Harrington et al., 2004). State enforcement problems are related in part to inadequate federal and state resources for regulatory activities, which have declined by 9% between 2002 and 2007 when adjusted for inflation (Harrington et al., 2004; GAO, 2009). U.S. Senate committees have held many hearings about nursing home survey problems and have repeatedly urged the Centers for Medicare and Medicaid (CMS) to improve the survey and enforcement process (U.S. GAO, 1999a, 1999b, 2002, 2003; GAO, 2007, 2008).

The federal-state nursing survey and certification process give the appearance that the government is doing something about the quality of care problems, but in reality the process does little to change or improve care. To ensure the safety of residents, strong improvement and increased funding for the survey and certification program are needed, and poor performing facilities should be terminated from Medicare and Medicaid.

INADEQUATE NURSING HOME STAFFING LEVELS

Low nurse staffing levels are the single most important contributor to poor quality of nursing home care in the U.S. Over the past 25 years, numerous studies have documented the important relationship between nurse staffing levels and the outcomes of care (IOM, 1996, 2001, 2003; Harrington, Zimmerman, et al., 2000). The benefits of higher staffing levels, especially RN staffing, can include lower mortality rates; improved physical functioning; fewer pressure ulcers, catheterized residents, and urinary tract infections;

lower hospitalization rates; and less antibiotic use, weight loss, and dehydration (IOM, 1996, 2001, 2003). Three separate IOM reports have recommended increased nurse staffing in nursing homes, particularly RN staffing.

The average U.S. nursing home provides a total of 3.7 hours per resident day (hprd) of total RN and Director of Nursing, licensed vocational or practical nurse (LVN/LPN), and nursing assistant (NA) time (Harrington et al., 2009). Of the total time, most (62% or 2.3 hours) is provided by NAs, who have an average of 11 residents for whom to provide care with only 2 weeks of training. RNs provide only 36 minutes (0.6 hour) of time per patient day and must care for about 34 to 40 residents, although nurses usually have many more residents on nights, weekends, and holidays (Harrington et al., 2009). The most disturbing finding is that average RN staffing hours in nursing homes has declined by 25% since 2000, with RNs having been replaced by NAs (Harrington et al., 2009). This has reduced the quality of care at a time when nurse staffing levels are already inadequate to protect the health and safety of residents (CMS, 2001).

One study found widespread quality problems in most nursing homes: inadequate assistance with eating (only 4 to 7 minutes of assistance); verbal interactions during mealtime only 28% of the time; false charting (inaccurate documentation of feeding assistance, toileting, and repositioning); toileting assistance only 1.8 times on average in 12 hours; residents not turned every 2 to 3 hours; over one half of residents left in bed most of the day; walking assistance only one time a day on average; and widespread untreated pain and untreated depression (Schnelle et al., 2004). Comparing the results of the staffing study findings with studies of eight separate quality indicators (weight loss, bedfast condition, physical restraints, pressure ulcers, incontinence, loss of physical activity, pain, and depression), Schnelle and colleagues (2004) concluded that staffing levels were a better predictor of high-quality care processes than the eight quality indicators that were examined.

To ensure safe care, minimum staffing thresholds have been identified and need to be established in regulations. Schnelle and colleagues (2004) studied differences in the quality of care processes among selected California nursing homes with different staffing levels. They found that nursing homes in the top 10th percentile on staffing (4.1 hprd or higher) performed significantly better on 13 of 16 care processes implemented by NAs, compared with homes with lower staffing. Residents in the highest-staffed homes were significantly more likely to be out of bed and engaged in activities during the day and receive more feeding assistance and incontinence care.

A Centers for Medicare and Medicaid Services (CMS) (2001) report found that staffing levels for long-stay residents that are below 4.1 hprd result in harm or jeopardy for residents (if below 1.3 hprd for licensed nurses and 2.8 hprd of NA time). NA time should range from 2.8 to 3.2 hprd, depending on the care residents need, just to carry out basic care activities (CMS, 2001). This amounts to 1 NA per 7 or 8 residents on the day and evening shifts and 1 NA per 12 residents at night. When actual staffing levels were compared with the target goals recommended by the CMS report (2001), 97% of all facilities were found to be operating below the desired level in 2001. The recommended nurse staffing level in the CMS (2001) report was similar to the 4.5 hprd level recommended by experts (Harrington, Kovner, et al., 2000).

Unfortunately, CMS has not agreed to establish minimum federal staffing standards that would ensure that nursing facilities meet the 4.1 hprd, mostly because the potential costs were estimated to be at least $7 billion in 2000 dollars (CMS, 2001). Most nursing homes are for-profit entities and are unlikely to voluntarily meet a reasonable level of staffing with regulatory requirements. If staffing levels are to improve, minimum federal staffing standards are needed, along with additional government funding to pay for the staffing. Some states have begun to raise their minimum staffing levels since 1999. California (3.2 hprd) and Delaware (3.29 hprd) have established high standards for direct care, and Florida established a 3.9 hprd total minimum standard (Harrington, 2008). These standards are improvements but are still well below the 4.1 hprd level recommended by the CMS 2001 report. Efforts to increase the minimum staffing standards that take into account resident acuity (case mix) should continue to have the highest priority at the state and federal levels.

NURSING FACILITY REIMBURSEMENT REFORM

Nursing home reimbursement methods and per diem reimbursement rates influence the cost of providing care. In 2007, Medicaid paid for 44% of the nation's total $131 billion nursing home expenditures; Medicare paid for 18%; consumers paid for 27%; and private insurance and other payers paid for 11%. Overall, the federal and state government paid for 62% of nursing home expenses (Hartman et al., 2009).

State Medicaid reimbursement policies have focused primarily on cost containment at the expense of quality and have established very low payment rates. The majority of states have adopted Medicaid prospective payment systems (PPSs) for nursing homes that set rates in advance of payments, which are successful in controlling reimbursement growth rates, but facilities tend to respond by cutting the staffing and quality levels (Grabowski et al., 2004).

To make matters worse, Congress passed Medicare PPS reimbursement for implementation starting in 1998 to reduce overall payment rates to skilled nursing homes (Medicare Payment Advisory Commission [MedPAC], 2009). Under PPS, Medicare rates are based in part on the resident case mix (acuity) in each facility to take into account the amount of staffing and therapy services that residents require. Skilled nursing homes, however, do not need to demonstrate that the amount of staff and therapy time actually provided is related to the payments allocated under the PPS rates.

As a result of Medicare PPSs, nursing home professional staffing decreased and regulatory deficiencies increased, showing the negative effect of Medicare PPSs (Konetzka et al., 2004). As noted previously, the level of RN staffing in U.S. nursing homes has declined by 25% since 2000 (Harrington et al., 2009). The average hours for licensed practical or vocational nurses held steady during the period, whereas the hours for NAs increased to replace the lost RN hours.

One policy option is to revise the Medicaid and Medicare PPS formulas to specify the minimum proportion of the payments that must be used for nurse staffing and therapy services. If the minimum amount of payments for nursing and therapy services were regulated, nursing homes would be prevented from cutting nurse staffing and using the funds for profit-making.

Despite the Medicare PPS rate cuts, excess profits have grown because Medicare does not limit the profit margins of nursing homes. A recent study showed that Medicare skilled nursing profit margins have exceeded 10% for the past 7 years and were 17.5% for

for-profit facilities in 2007 (MedPAC, 2009). The median total margins for all payers were less (primarily because of low Medicaid payment rates). Facilities with very high profits appear to be taking profits at the expense of quality. Nursing homes with net income profit margins greater than 9% were found to have higher deficiencies and poorer quality of care, apparently because they were taking excess profits (O'Neill, et al., 2003). Strict limits on administrative costs and profit margins under Medicare and Medicaid PPS could be instituted to reduce the excess profit-taking by nursing homes.

Poor quality of care in nursing homes has been associated with low wages and benefits and high employee turnover rates (Harrington & Swan, 2003). Nursing home wages and benefits are substantially lower than those of comparable hospital workers (and lower than those in many jobs in the fast food industry and other unskilled jobs) and are generally well below the level of a living wage (CMS, 2001; Kaye et al., 2006). A CMS study (2001) found that NA wages and benefits need to be raised by 17% to 22% in order to retain employees and stabilize the workforce in long-stay facilities. Congress and CMS should ensure that state Medicaid rates include adequate amounts for nursing wages and benefits.

CORPORATE OWNERSHIP TRANSPARENCY

For-profit companies have owned the majority of the nation's nursing homes for many years and operate 66% of facilities compared to non-profit (28%) and government-owned facilities (6%) in 2007 (Harrington et al., 2009). Many studies have shown that for-profit nursing homes operate with lower costs and staffing, compared to non-profit facilities, which provide higher staffing and higher-quality care, and have more trustworthy governance (Harrington et al., 2001; Harrington, Zimmerman, et al., 2000; O'Neill et al., 2003; Schlesinger & Gray, 2005).

For-profit corporate chains emerged as a dominant organizational form in the nursing home field during the 1990s, promoted with the idea that they would be more efficient and have access to capital through the stock market. The proportion of chain-owned facilities increased from 39% in the 1990s to 52.5% of all nursing homes in 2008 (Harrington et al., 2009). The largest nursing home chains have been publicly-traded companies with billions in revenues. Research shows that shareholder value is pursued by such companies by using three interlinked strategies at the expense of quality: (1) debt-financed mergers, which place a burden on facilities to pay off their debts; (2) labor cost constraints including low nurse staffing levels and low wages/benefits to increase net income; and (3) noncompliance with regulatory requirements where regulatory sanctions are considered to be a normal cost of business (Kitchener et al., 2008). Many large nursing home chains own a number of related companies including residential care/assisted living facilities, home health agencies, hospices, pharmacies, staffing organizations, and other related companies. These related companies refer patients to each other and use their corporate interrelationships to maximum net revenues.

By 2007, private equity companies had purchased six of the largest chains with about 9% of nursing home beds; these companies have few reporting requirements (Duhigg, 2007). Shielded by private equity companies, the ownership of nursing homes has become so complex that it is increasingly difficult to identify the owners of nursing homes. Many large chains have multiple investors, holding companies, and multiple levels of companies involved, where property companies are separated from the management of facilities, largely designed to avoid litigation. The lack of transparency in the ownership responsibilities makes regulation and oversight by state survey and certification agencies problematic.

The new health care reform law begins to address these concerns. Nursing facilities receiving Medicare and Medicaid funding will have to disclose information regarding ownership, accountability requirements, and expenditures. This information must be made available to the public on the Medicare nursing home compare website (Kaiser Family Foundation, 2010). This provision was sponsored by the National Citizens Coalition for Nursing Home Reform (NCCNHR) and other advocacy organizations.

HOME AND COMMUNITY-BASED SERVICES

LTC services that are needed for long periods (more than 90 days) are focused on providing assistance with limitations in activities of daily living and supporting those with cognitive limitations and mental illness. About 13 million individuals (over half under age 65) living in the community in the U.S. received an average of 31.4 hours of personal assistance per week in 1995 (LaPlante et al., 2002). More recent data show that about 11 million living in the community receive assistance with activities of daily living and 92% of those individuals received informal help from family and friends, and only 13% received paid help (Kaye, Harrington et al., 2009).

The cost of nursing home care was almost six times as much as home- and community-based services (Kaye, Harrington et al., 2009). One reason for the high institutional spending is the oversupply of institutional LTC beds and the undersupply of HCBS. Although the number of nursing home beds grew and the aged population increased over the past decade, it is surprising to note that the average certified nursing facility occupancy rates in states declined from 90% in 1995 to only 85% in 2008, creating an excess supply of nursing home beds in many states (Harrington et al., 2009). The reductions in nursing home facility occupancy rates are probably related to the growth in residential care and assisted living facilities as substitutes and to the rapid growth of HCBS.

There are increased pressures to expand HCBS, especially in the Medicaid program. The public increasingly reports a preference for LTC provided at home over services in institutions, and this is encouraged by reports of serious nursing home quality problems (Kitchener et al., 2005). In addition, the 1990 Americans with Disabilities Act (ADA) and the subsequent legal judgment in the 1999 Olmstead Supreme Court decision require that states must not discriminate against persons with disabilities by refusing to provide community services when these are available and appropriate.

In response to the increased demand, Medicaid HCBS programs increased by 46% and expenditures increased by 104% from 1999 to 2005 (Ng et al., 2008). Combined Medicaid home health and personal care services, and home- and community-based waiver programs served 2.8 million participants, and expenditures were $35 billion in 2005 (Ng et al., 2008).

The Affordable Care Act (ACA) of 2010 includes some important provisions regarding long-term care, specifically for HCBS. First, it establishes a national, voluntary self-funded insurance program for purchasing community living assistance services and supports (CLASS program), an initiative that was sponsored by Senator Edward Kennedy. The program is established through the workplace, and premiums would be paid through payroll reductions on a voluntary basis. After paying into the system for five years, individuals with functional limitations could receive a cash benefit of not less than an average of $50 per day to purchase the non-medical services and supports necessary to maintain community residence. The program becomes effective January 1, 2011 (Kaiser Family Foundation, 2010).

Second, the law extends the Medicaid Money Follows the Person Rebalancing Demonstration program through September 2016 and allocates $10 million per year for five years to continue the Aging and Disability Resource Center initiatives. In addition, it gives states new options for offering home- and community-based services through a Medicaid state plan rather than through a waiver. The program allows states to provide Medicaid coverage for individuals with incomes up to 300% of the Supplemental Security Income payment level to receive home- and community-based services after October 1, 2010 (Kaiser Family Foundation, 2010).

Third, it establishes the Community First Choice Option in Medicaid to provide community-based attendant supports and services to individuals with disabilities who require an institutional level of care. This provision would offer states an enhanced federal matching rate of 6 percentage points more than their current federal funds. In addition, it creates the State Balancing Incentive Program to provide enhanced federal matching payments to eligible states to increase the proportion of non-institutionally–based long-term care services for five years starting in October 2011 (Kaiser Family Foundation, 2010). These provisions to expand home- and community-based services under Medicaid were sponsored by ADAPT, an advocacy organization for individuals with disabilities, and a coalition of consumer advocacy groups.

But there is strong evidence that the current supply of HCBS is inadequate to meet current and future need. State Medicaid program directors report that many disabled groups are not served by existing HCBS programs and that state programs lack adequate funding and have waiting lists (Ng et al., 2008). In 2007, only 30 states had Medicaid personal care attendant programs, and many states have limited services under their HCBS waiver programs. The waiting lists for HCBS have increased from 192,447 reported in 2002 to 331,689 in 2007, with waiting periods of 9 to 26 months to access services (Ng et al., 2008).

Some states have rapidly expanded their HCBS programs, but others lag behind, relying heavily on institutional services. In spite of the steady growth in HCBS spending, the Medicaid program reported spending $58.99 billion (58.5% of total LTC) on institutional LTC services and $41.8 billion (41.5% of total LTC) on HCBS services in 2007 (Burwell et al., 2008). Medicaid HCBS programs urgently need more funding to expand access to care at home and to prevent institutionalization.

The main opposition to expanding HCBS is the potential costs if additional Medicaid participants request new LTC services. One study showed that states offering extensive HCBS had spending growth comparable to states with low HCBS spending (Kaye, LaPlante et al., 2009). States with well-established HCBS programs had much less overall LTC spending growth compared with those with low HCBS spending because these states were able to reduce institutional spending. There appeared to be a lag of several years before institutional spending declined. In contrast, states with low levels of HCBS expenditures had an increase in overall costs, as their institutional costs increased. Thus, states that expanded their HCBS programs have not had increased costs or have had a reduction in their total LTC costs over time.

PUBLIC FINANCING OF LONG-TERM CARE

As of 2010, the only segment of the U.S. population whose cost of LTC is covered consists of individuals who live below the poverty threshold and are enrolled in Medicaid. Except for short-term postacute care, the rest of the population must either pay for care out of pocket or resort to privately-purchased LTC insurance. The financially crippling cost of LTC (as much as $90,000 per year) is one of the great fears confronting persons who are otherwise self-supporting, and few persons have either the means or motivation to insure themselves privately. Only about 7 million private LTC policies were in force, covering 3% of the population aged 20 and older in 2005 (Feder et al., 2007). Thus, this does not appear to be a viable financing mechanism for the future (Wiener, 2009). If individuals "spend down" to the poverty threshold, they can become Medicaid-eligible, making LTC a means-tested program. The spend-down requirements constitute a hardship to the patient, a social stigma, and dependence on public assistance that would be unnecessary if the entire population were insured.

A mandatory social insurance program for LTC offers distinct advantages over the current U.S. means-tested system. If everyone paid into the system, individuals would have access to coverage when they are chronically ill or disabled without the humiliation of having to become poor to receive services. By expanding the Medicare program to include LTC, the payment of LTC contributions early in a worker's life could "prefund" relatively affordable LTC services that generally are required late in life. Thus, the financial risk could be spread across the entire population so that individual premium costs or taxes would be relatively manageable, in comparison with the costs of insurance purchased when individuals are older and at high risk of needing LTC. Countries in Scandinavia, Germany, and Japan have adopted mandatory public long-term insurance systems that can serve as models for the U.S. These countries generally provide protection and coverage for persons who need LTC (Wiener, 2009). The area of greatest concern for any type of new public LTC program is cost. The nation should focus on the public financing of LTC insurance that would ensure that all citizens have adequate, high-quality LTC when they need such services. The CLASS provision of the ACA may have limited success because it is voluntary.

SUMMARY

These policy changes for LTC that are embedded in ACA would not have happened without major grassroots advocacy activities and a coalition of organizations supporting reforms for individuals with disabilities and those who are aged over a long period of time. This advocacy work did make a difference. Nurses and nursing organizations need to join forces with consumer groups to accomplish large-scale policy changes. These new long-term care reforms are major steps forward to the eventual goal of obtaining a comprehensive mandatory public long-term care insurance system for everyone in the U.S. who needs long-term care and supports.

But more needs to be done. We need a vision for advocacy in LTC that is multidimensional and long-range. Political efforts are needed at the local, state, and national levels. Community mobilization, public education, legislative reform, and legal actions are all needed to bring about policy changes to ensure access to high-quality LTC services. Consumer advocates and organizations, such as the National Citizens Coalition for Nursing Home Reform, ADAPT for disability rights, and the AARP, have taken a lead in reform efforts, but they need help to make progress. Nurses should join these organizations to work closely with consumer advocates.

REFERENCES

Burwell, B., Sredl, K., & Eiken, S. (2008). Medicaid LTC expenditures in FY 2007. Thomson Medstat, September.

Centers for Medicare & Medicaid Services (CMS). (2001). Appropriateness of minimum nurse staffing ratios in nursing homes. Report to Congress: Phase II Final. Volumes I to III. Baltimore: CMS (prepared by Abt Associates).

Duhigg, C. (2007). At many homes, more profit and less nursing. *New York Times.* September 23, A1-A20, A21.

Feder, J., Komisar, H. L., & Friedland, R. B. (2007). Long-term care financing: Policy options for the future. Washington, D.C.: Georgetown University. Retrieved from http://ltc.georgetown.edu/forum/ltcfinalpaper061107.pdf

Grabowski, D. C., Angelelli, J. J., & Mor, V., 2004. Medicaid payment and risk-adjusted nursing home quality measures. *Health Affairs, 23*(5):243–252.

Harrington, C. (2008). Nursing home staffing standards in state statutes and regulations. San Francisco, CA: University of California. Retrieved on August 17, 2010, from http://www.pascenter.org/documents/Staffing _regulations_1_08.pdf

Harrington, C., Carrillo, H., & Woleslagle Blank, B. (2009). Nursing facilities, staffing, residents, and facility deficiencies, 2003–08. San Francisco: University of California. Retrieved from www.pascenter.org/nursing _homes/nursing_trends_2008.php

Harrington, C., Granda, B., Carrillo, H., Chang, J., Woleslagle, B., Swan, J. H., Dreyer, K., et al. (2008). State data book on LTC, 2007: Program and market characteristics. Report prepared for the U.S. Dept. of Housing and Urban Development. San Francisco: University of California. Retrieved from www.pascenter.org/documents/ PASCenter_HCBS_policy_brief.php

Harrington, C., Kovner, C., Mezey, M., Kayser-Jones, J., Burger, S., Mohler, M., Burke, R., & Zimmerman, D. (2000). Experts recommend minimum nurse staffing standards for nursing facilities in the United States. *Gerontologist, 40*(1), 5–16.

Harrington, C., Mullan, J., & Carrillo, H. (2004). State nursing home enforcement systems. Journal of Health Politics, Policy and Law, 29(1), 43–73.

Harrington, C. & Swan, J. H. (2003). Nurse home staffing, turnover, and casemix. *Medical Care Research and Review, 60*(2), 366–392.

Harrington, C., Tsoukalas, T., Rudder, C., Mollot, R. J., & Carrillo, H. (2008). Study of federal and state civil money penalties and fines. *The Gerontologist, 48*(5): 679–691.

Harrington, C., Woolhandler, S., Mullan, J., Carrillo, H., & Himmelstein, D. (2001). Does investor-ownership of nursing homes compromise the quality of care? *American Journal of Public Health, 91*(9), 1452–1455.

Harrington, C., Zimmerman, D., Karon, S. L., Robinson, J., & Beutel, P. (2000). Nursing home staffing and its relationship to deficiencies. *The Journals of Gerontology. Series B, Psychological Sciences and Social Sciences, 55*(5):S278–S287.

Hartman, M., Martin, A., McDonnell, P., Catlin, A., and the National Health Expenditure Accounts Team. (2009). National health spending in 2007: Slower drug spending contributes to lowest rate of overall growth since 1998. *Health Affairs, 28*(1), 246–261.

Institute of Medicine [IOM], Committee on Improving Quality in Long-Term Care, Division of Health Care Services, (Wunderlich, G. S., & Kohler, P. [Eds.]). (2001). *Improving the quality of long-term care.* Washington, D.C.: National Academies Press.

Institute of Medicine [IOM], Committee on the Adequacy of Nurse Staffing in Hospitals and Nursing Homes. (Wunderlich, G. S., Sloan, F. A., & Davis, C. K. [Eds.]). (1996). *Nursing staff in hospitals and nursing homes: Is it adequate?* Washington, D.C.: National Academies Press.

Institute of Medicine [IOM], Committee on the Future Health Care Workforce for Older Americans. (2008). *Retooling for an aging America: Building the health care workforce.* Washington, D.C.: National Academy of Science Press.

Institute of Medicine [IOM], Committee on the Work Environment for Nurses and Patient Safety. (Page, A. [Ed.]). (2003). *Keeping patients safe.* Washington, D.C.: National Academies Press.

Kaiser Family Foundation. 2010. Focus on health: Summary of new health reform law. Washington, D.C.: March 26, 2010. Retrieved on April 23, 2009, from www.kff.org/healthreform/upload/finalhcr.pdf

Kaye, H. S., Chapman, S., Newcomer, R. J., & Harrington, C. (2006). The personal assistance workforce: Trends in supply and demand. *Health Affairs, 25*(4), 1113–1120.

Kaye, S. H., Harrington, C., & LaPlante, M. P. (2009). Long-term care in the United States: Who gets it, who provides it, who pays, and how much does it cost? *Health Affairs, 29*(1), 11–21.

Kaye, S. H., LaPlante, M. P., & Harrington, C. (2009). Do noninstitutional long-term care services reduce Medicaid spending? *Health Affairs, 29*(1), 262–272.

Kitchener, M., Ng, T., Miller, N., & Harrington, C. (2005). Medicaid home and community-based services: National program trends. *Health Affairs, 24*(1), 206–212.

Kitchener, M., O'Meara, J., Brody, A., Lee, H. Y., & Harrington, C. (2008). Shareholder value and the performance of a large nursing home chain. *Health Services Research, 43*(3), 1062–1084.

Konetzka, R. T., Yi, D., Norton, E. C., & Kilpatrick, K. E. (2004). Effects of Medicare payment changes on nursing home staffing and deficiencies. *Health Services Research, 39*(3), 463–487.

LaPlante, M., Harrington, C., & Kang, T. (2002). Estimating paid and unpaid hours of personal assistance services in activities of daily living provided to adults living at home. *Health Services Research, 37*(2), 387–415.

Medicare Payment Advisory Commission. (2009). *A data book: Health care spending and the Medicare program.* Washington, D.C. Retrieved on April 23, 2009, from www.medpac.gov/june-0DataBook.pdf

Ng, T., Harrington, C., & O'Malley, M. (2008). Medicaid home and community based service programs: Data update. (Report prepared for the Kaiser Commission on Medicaid and the Uninsured, August.) Washington, D.C.: Kaiser Commission on Medicaid and the Uninsured. Retrieved on April 23, 2009, from www.kff.org/medicaid/upload/7720_02.pdf

O'Neill, C., Harrington, C., Kitchener, M., & Saliba, D. (2003). Quality of care in nursing homes: An analysis of the relationships among profit, quality, and ownership. *Medical Care, 41*(12), 1318–1330.

Schlesinger, M., & Gray, B. H. (2005). *Why nonprofits matter in American medicine: A policy brief.* Washington D.C.: Aspen Institute.

Schnelle, J. F., Simmons, S. F., Harrington, C., Cadogan, M., Garcia, E., & Bates-Jensen, B. (2004). Relationship of nursing home staffing to quality of care? *Health Services Research, 39*(2), 225–250.

U.S. General Accounting Office (GAO). (1999a). Nursing homes: Additional steps needed to strengthen enforcement of federal quality standards. Report to the Special Committee on Aging, U.S. Senate. GAO/HEHS-99-46. Washington, D.C.: GAO.

U.S. General Accounting Office (GAO). (1999b). Nursing homes: Complaint investigation processes often inadequate to protect residents. Report to Congressional Committees. GAO/HEHS-99-80. Washington, D.C.: GAO.

U.S. General Accounting Office (GAO). (2002). Nursing homes: Quality of care more related to staffing than spending. Report to Congressional Requestors. GAO/HEHS-02-431R. Washington, D.C.: GAO.

U.S. General Accounting Office (GAO). (2003). Nursing home quality: Prevalence of serious problems, while declining, reinforces importance of enhanced oversight. Report to Congressional Requesters. GAO-03-561. Washington, D.C.: GAO.

U.S. Government Accountability Office (GAO). (2007). Nursing home reform: Continued attention is needed to improve quality of care in small but significant share of homes. GAO-07–794T, Washington, D.C.: GAO, May 2, 2007.

U.S. Government Accountability Office (GAO). (2008). Nursing homes: Federal monitoring surveys demonstrate continued understatement of serious care problems and CMS oversight weakness. GAO-08–517, Washington, D.C.: GAO, May 9, 2008.

U.S. Government Accountability Office (GAO). (2009). Medicare and Medicaid participating facilities: CMS needs to reexamine state oversight of health care facilities. GAO-09–64, Washington, D.C.: GAO, February 13, 2009.

Wiener, J. M. (2009). *Long-term care: Options in an era of health reform.* Washington, D.C.: RTI International.

21

THE FUTURE OF HOME CARE

KAREN BUHLER-WILKERSON

This epilogue originally appeared as Buhler-Wilkerson, K. (2001). *No place like home: A history of nursing and home care in the United States.* Baltimore: The John Hopkins University Press. Copyright © 2001 The Johns Hopkins University Press. Reprinted with permission of The Johns Hopkins University Press.

EDITORS' NOTE

Home nursing care has its roots in nursing's beginnings, before hospitals were available. Its history is complicated, reflecting changes in nurses' roles and public policies. The late nurse historian Karen Buhler-Wilkerson documented this evolution. This epilogue to her book, *No Place Like Home: A History of Nursing and Home Care in the United States,* discusses the implications of this history for contemporary practices and policies.

■ ■ ■

In November 1999, after a decade of research for this book, I faced a difficult task. During those years of research and writing, I had often stared at the message on an orange index card posted above my desk: "To the visiting nurses of Boston who for fifty years have cared for the city's sick with an unchanging purpose in a changing world." The message is from a plaque presented to the Boston Visiting Nurse Association in November 1936. I had titled this index card "The Problem?" suggesting to myself the hypothesis that failure to change had relegated an essential and sensible method of caring for the sick at home to the margins of our health care system. As I was bringing this project to a close, I found my hypothesis was wrong and my conclusion, at best, disheartening. Home care both held fast to its original purpose and responded to a changing world; care providers retained definitions and objectives while simultaneously making necessary compromises and adjusting methodologies. Despite this clarity of vision and resourcefulness, home care never lost its vulnerability. Nor has it yet found its place in modern health care.

THE LEGACY OF HOME CARE

As chronicled in this book, organized home care in the United States began in the antebellum South. The ladies of Charleston, South Carolina, developed a system of caring that was compatible with the needs of the poor and the southern way of life at that time. Domestic expertise and antebellum notions of civic and religious duty came together to produce an enduring set of themes central to home care: mission and money. The ladies of Charleston were also the first to document home care's "vexing" predicaments of family circumstances, race relations, and chronic disease. As they quickly learned, families and their home lives were unpredictable and often uncontrollable, yet they were vital determinants of the outcomes of care. From the beginning, this was a women's story, since both patients and caregivers were almost exclusively women.

Sporadic efforts by social reformers and religious groups followed, but it was entry of the trained nurse into the homes of the poor in the 1880s that transformed caring for the sick at home. Home nursing care of the poor was financed by philanthropists and provided by a visiting nurse. The ailments encountered by these nurses were often acute, frequently complex, and almost always complicated by difficult social and economic circumstances. The visiting nurse's mission was to care for the sick, to teach the family how to care for its sick family member, and to protect the public from the spread of disease through forceful yet tactful lessons in physical and moral hygiene. Medical care of the urban poor varied with the circumstances of the patient, ranging from visits to dispensaries or folk healers (or both) for most ailments to house calls from private physicians in times of acute crisis. Hospital care was sought only in the absence of all other alternatives.

From its inception, home-based care differed for the rich and the poor. For the middle and upper classes, those who could afford to purchase care, illnesses were usually supervised at home by the family physician. Even the most seriously ill were often treated at home; the patient's bedroom was the workplace for most nurses and physicians. Nursing care was provided by a private-duty nurse who remained with the family for the duration of the illness and received fee-for-service payments. One of the greatest difficulties with this approach to privately purchased care was its unpredictable, individually driven system of distribution. Demand for these nurses was sporadic and seasonal. By the beginning of the twentieth century, the supply of private-duty nurses exceeded demand.

As knowledge of the work of visiting and private-duty nurses spread, the number of organizations providing such services rapidly expanded. In many U.S. cities, this expansion was characterized by an idiosyncratic mix of government, voluntary, and entrepreneurial initiatives. Despite tremendous growth overall, most organizations remained small undertakings. Isolated and uncoordinated, these fragile organizations were vulnerable to shifts in community support and perceptions of need. With health departments, visiting nurse associations (VNAs), other voluntary organizations, and private-duty nursing registries providing an uncoordinated assortment of curative and preventive nursing services, gaps and duplication were inevitable. Despite three decades of experiments, demonstrations, and studies attempting to establish comprehensive coordinated home care, little changed.

By the 1930s, home care reached a turning point. For VNAs and for most communities, the circumstances that had originally created a demand for services no longer seemed to exist. Urban death rates declined dramatically, and chronic disease replaced infection as the leading cause of death. Importantly, chronic disease did not frighten the public or stimulate philanthropic responses. The original mission of the VNAs became increasingly elusive, and support gradually declined. Simultaneously, medical, surgical, and even some obstetrical patients of all classes began to seek hospital care. With more middle- and upper-class patients using hospitals, private-duty nurses predictably followed them into these institutions. For family caregivers, the trend toward hospitalization became a partial solution to the endless obligations of caring for the sick at home. At a time when home care offered a less expensive alternative to institutional care, the home was nevertheless perceived as a less desirable locus of care. Throughout the 1940s, the ascendancy of chronic illness and the growing stature of the hospital dominated the nation's health care agenda. The work and financing of home care continued to be overshadowed and recast by these realities.

For VNAs in the 1950s, the number of home visits dwindled, costs spiraled, and deficits expanded. While many hoped that the growing availability of health insurance would relieve financial worries, home care programs struggled to survive. Amazingly, by the end of the decade, home care was being reinvented. This "back-to-the-home movement" provided the groundwork for federal policy on home care that would follow in the 1960s.

MEDICARE: HOME CARE'S SECOND COMING

Across the United States, implementation of the Medicare program on 1 July 1966 marked the beginning of a new era for home care. Almost overnight, Medicare redefined home care as an alternative to hospital care. What resulted was a narrowly defined, fragmented, and uncoordinated set of acute-care services poorly adapted to the needs of the chronically ill at home. Although expenditures grew, many families of the elderly and their physicians found home care unfeasible and institutional care much less trouble. Policymakers and third-party payers who regarded home care of little intrinsic value continued to search for evidence of cost effectiveness. As always, the majority of care at home was provided by informal support systems—family, friends, or neighbors, mostly women.

By the 1970s, home care became part of the debate about long-term care for the elderly. This time, it was examined as a cost-effective substitute for nursing-home care. Confronted with a growing number of elderly people in need of care, a variety of research studies and federal demonstration projects examined the impact of home care on the total cost of care. After a decade of study, the findings were not encouraging. It was generally agreed that home care did not significantly reduce hospitalization or nursing-home use. It also became clear that patients did not have the same goals for home care as did payers or policymakers. They simply sought relief—as caregivers, paying consumers, and managers of care.[1]

Throughout the 1980s, a variety of legislative and judicial actions and revisions of Health Care Financing Administration policies produced expansion of home care coverage and removed disincentives for home care use. Changes in hospital reimbursement resulting in earlier hospital discharge, combined with new portable technologies, also moved services such as intravenous nutrition, chemotherapy, respiratory therapies, dialysis care, and other high-tech therapies into the home setting. Rapid growth combined with frenetic transfer of technology to the home immediately became home care's next challenge.

As in the hospital, the marvels of technology came with a price. This new technological challenge created substantial gaps between technical prowess and the humane, just, and efficient use of technology. Questions of access, equity, standards of quality, and consequences for families were quickly raised. Over time, it became clear that sending patients home to manage and monitor complicated equipment and materials that required special knowledge, skill, and composure could cause them harm.[2]

By 1994, as the result of a 22 percent growth in the over-sixty-five population in the 1980s, high-tech advancements, changing financial incentives, and consumer preference for care at home, both the number of agencies providing home care and Medicare home health care spending increased dramatically. Reluctantly, policymakers acknowledged the necessity of planning for the acute, primary, and long-term care needs of an aging population and its projected epidemic of disability and dependency. Simultaneously, rising home care use and expenditures created the demand for tighter management of the costs, quality, and outcomes of care at home. The challenge remained to create an affordable model of coordinated and integrated care.[3]

By 1996, the National Health Policy Forum concluded that it was the lack of consensus on definition and objectives that made development of public policy for home care so difficult. The forum cautioned, "Home care is at once both a formal service provided by paid staff and assistance furnished by such informal supporters as families and relatives, a medical and a nonmedical intervention, acute and long-term care, and a service with merits of its own and one whose value is assessed in terms of reductions in institutional care. These dichotomies affect the principal goals of home care, its component elements, and its place within an overall continuum of health care."[4]

This contemporary summary reflects the entire history of home care. Once again, policymakers are revisiting its costs and benefits. Providers of home care are adaptive and persistent, adjusting case mix and patterns of care to match available reimbursement and somehow offering services needed or desired by the sick and vulnerable. It is no surprise, however, that home care is not always a thrifty substitute for costly institutional care—it is simply care at home![5] The effectiveness of home care is difficult to quantify, but the large reservoir of need makes growth difficult to curtail. As one group of authors has suggested, home care may be our one way to institutionalize "caring."[6]

REINING IN A BENEFIT OUT OF CONTROL

By 1996, Medicare coverage for home care was described as a benefit out of control. The milestones in this evolution are well documented in the literature and have been examined endlessly by legislators, policymakers, and health services researchers. Regardless of its pros and cons, home care was the fastest growing component of the Medicare program during the 1990s. Representing 10 percent of all Medicare costs, home care accounted for $16 billion in spending annually.[7]

Over a thirty-year period, a program designed to meet the needs of people with short-term acute illness was also providing long-term care to the chronically ill. Ambiguity over the interpretation of benefits had created the opportunity for providers of home care to recast the Medicare regulations. Just like the Metropolitan Life Insurance Company in earlier years, the government suddenly found it could not manage or control home care. While presumed reasonable, necessary, and medically appropriate, the expansion of home care was deemed unsustainable; policymakers' demands for reform were heard once again.[8]

For policymakers faced with the potential insolvency of the Medicare program, the growth of care at home raised the all too familiar questions of how much and what kind of home care we are willing to pay for, who should receive that care, who should provide it, and for how long. A century of experimentation in home care had clearly outlined the parameters of the controversy and its likely outcome. As disenchantment with home care's assumed ability to reduce the costs of health care grew, the debate was further politicized by charges of overutilization, fraud, and abuse. Politicians and the public were reminded of the impossibility of policing what happens in the privacy of the patient's home.[9]

In this threatening climate, thousands of small, competitive, vulnerable, and disjointed home care agencies were called upon to unite. The National Association for Home Care served as the focal organization for these efforts. Founded in 1982, this organization is the largest trade association serving the interests of home care, hospice, and home health aide organizations nationally. Its chosen sound bite for the 1997 federal budget debates was

"Home Care: It Works, It Saves Money, and It Keeps Families Together." As the 1997 federal budget debates raged on, however, home care's message was not marketable politically.[10]

On 1 October 1997, the Medicare home care benefit enacted in 1965 was for all practical purposes discontinued without public discussion. This time, home care's threatened demise was the result of cost-containment efforts to reduce the federal deficit and to ensure the solvency of the Medicare program. Predictably, policymakers once again failed to confront home care's peculiar, reverberating, and fundamental underlying ambiguities. Not addressed were the really tough political issues: Is caring for the sick at home a private family obligation or a responsibility shared with a caring society? Should home care be provided only under the most restrictive of circumstances, or whenever it can help? Or should we simply not decide and just keep muddling along?

The outcomes of this so-called reform were swift and dramatic: more than three thousand home care agencies closed, the number of visits per patient decreased, and public funding for home care was significantly reduced. The greatest impact was in the reduction of home health services for persons with medically complex chronic illnesses. It appeared that home care in the twenty-first century would be characterized by fewer services, more family caregiving, and new technologies such as tele–home care.[11] Concerned with short-sighted economic and political attacks, home care's proponents were once again forced to reinvent their purpose, mission, and goals.

The combination of an aging population and a decline in available family caregivers only emphasizes an expanding need for home care services currently not covered by any form of third-party coverage. At present, one third of home care services are purchased out-of-pocket by families. Most of these services are obtained from organizations reminiscent of private-duty registries of the past, with an estimated ten thousand agencies offering some form of home care, from brief visits to twenty-four-hour live-in care.[12]

Today, a significant but largely invisible group of "informal caregivers" provides most care for the sick at home. Despite an estimated at-market value for their work of $196 billion, there is little support to sustain the efforts of these family caregivers. As in the past, this obligation falls disproportionately on women. For these women, "caring" remains inconvenient and challenging and interrupts daily patterns of living and working. In our culture, the demands of home care are grossly undervalued and codified as housework, family obligation, or perhaps a voluntary charitable responsibility. During the nearly two centuries examined in this book, the circumstances of patients and families in need of home care have changed very little—women manage on their own as best they can. In a society that has never confronted our inability to "value" women's work, it is not surprising that we have such difficulty measuring, quantifying, and paying for "home care." Instead of acknowledging the home as the preferred site of caregiving, we see it as a repository of unmet need.

Sickness and injury are not congruent with a production-oriented and worker-dependent society. Assistance from family, benevolent volunteers, or paid caregivers is generally required (although not always available) and transcends class, race, ethnicity, age, gender, place, and time. The fear of "failure to die or get well" remains a central concern in any discussion of home care; whatever the configuration of services, long-term care is a particular cause of uneasiness. How to determine the appropriate recipients and payers is a fundamental and unresolved problem, after years of inconclusive debate. The open-ended and private nature of care at home has spawned endless worry and a general unwillingness to pay for the home care of others.

Predictably, home care survived at the margins of the health care system while the hospital was transformed into the uncontested site for giving birth, receiving treatment for illness, and dying. The prominence of the hospital obscured the unseen yet steady and competent visits sustaining the sick at home.[13] While we are willing to invest in "scientific" advancements and hospital care, ours is not a caring society that routinely asks families in need how we can help.

HOME CARE'S FUTURE

On 14 November 1999, the front page of the *New York Times* announced that, for the first time ever, annual spending for Medicare had dropped. This reversal in spending actually surprised many health policy experts. Given the hopes that the Balanced Budget Act of 1997 would simply slow the growth of Medicare, the *decline* in spending was declared a phenomenal development. While the *Times* acknowledged that reductions in home care contributed to this dip in spending, it failed to mention the personal consequences of this policy decision.[14]

By April 2000, *New York Times* headlines proclaimed "Medicare Spending for Care at Home Plunges by 45%." This article described how, in just one year, the number of people receiving home care shrank by six hundred thousand, making the consequences of limiting payments for home care inescapable. The facts were clear: home care agencies simply could no longer stay in business if they accepted elderly patients requiring long-term or complex care. Most disturbing was the news that some agencies now accept only those patients who have "a close relative who can provide some of the care." As government bureaucrats publicly expressed their surprise at the extent of reductions and health policy experts predicted longer and costlier stays in hospitals and nursing homes, advocates for the elderly declared alarm at reports that our most vulnerable elderly were unable to get "home care help." Politicians, hoping to be reelected and eager to allay voters' concerns, declared the cuts "far deeper and more wide-reaching than Congress ever intended" and promised a bipartisan remedy. Declaring this an incident of "good intentions . . . gone awry," a *Times* editorial suggested that it would be prudent for Congress to cancel future reductions and give serious attention to "what the payment system [for home care] ought to be." Perhaps this time an analysis of how we pay for home care should be preceded by a serious consideration of what kind of "home care help" we as a society want to purchase. Hopefully, this time we can get past our ambiguities about what our neighbors deserve and our fear that somehow we will end up paying for someone else's "housework."[15]

For those home care providers who survived the first wave of draconian cuts, proposed rules for Medicare's new home care prospective payment system promise a better future for providers and recipients of home care. As in the past, changes in financing mean yet another reinvention of care at home. While long-range planning awaits publication of the final regulations in July 2000, dramatic changes in visiting patterns, case mix, provision of therapies, and length of service are expected. Once again, the promise is for clinical needs to determine the level and amount of care received at home.

Simultaneously, the implications of a June 1999 Supreme Court ruling (*Olmstead v. L.C.*) were being declared "deep and profound" by state officials across the country. By mandating the redirecting of state spending from institutions to community-based care, the Court had created the opportunity for people of all ages with all types of disabilities to be cared for at home. Then, in February 2000, the Clinton administration directed states to evaluate hundreds of thousands of people in nursing homes, mental hospitals, and state institutions for the possibility of care at home. Finally, by declaring unnecessary institutionalization of individuals with disabilities discriminatory under the Americans with Disabilities Act, Donna Shalala, Secretary of Health and Human Services, essentially extended a vast array of home care services to those currently cared for in institutions, as well as to underserved disabled people already living at home. Compliance with these federal mandates could potentially cost more than $2 billion a year nationwide. While state officials predict that the *Olmstead* decision will "bust the bank," it is likely to lead to dramatic changes for thousands of people living with disabilities.[16]

Thus, in a few short months, the future of home-based care for persons who are acutely or chronically ill has been completely rewritten. In the final analysis, the problem is not the unwillingness of providers to change patterns of care in a changing world. More to the point, the story of caring for the sick is one in which the problems are keenly understood and the solutions do exist.[17] We certainly know how to provide and finance community-based care in this country. An outstanding example is PACE (Program of All-inclusive Care for the Elderly), a comprehensive service delivery and financing model of acute, primary, and long-term interdisciplinary care.

As this final (for now) chapter attests, the money can always be found when sufficient public will exists to change the status quo. In a recent *New England Journal of Medicine* letter to the editor, Anne Somers, noted health care expert and experienced family caregiver, described her personal experiences with the callousness of a prosperous society that turns its back on this devastating problem of caring for those with chronic illnesses. She concludes that decent care at home is entirely possible. "It is not cheap, but it is feasible. The lack of such relief is primarily a problem of public policy and political will."[18] The inability of the public to visualize the elements, outcomes, or value of home care only compounds the difficulty of deciding whether care of the sick at home is our civic duty or a private family responsibility. Perhaps it is the gendered and private nature of home care that makes commitment to this "institutionalization of caring" so difficult. On this point of divergence, we are left to this day with the unanswered question, "Who pays, for whom, for what, and how much?"

NOTES

1. William Weissert, "Home Care Dollars and Sense: A Prescription for Policy," in Daniel Fox and Carol Raphael, eds., *Home-Based Care for a New Century* (Malden, Mass.: Blackwell Publishers, 1997), 121–33.

2. J. D. Arras, ed., *Bringing the Hospital Home: Ethical and Social Implications of High-Tech Home Care* (Baltimore: Johns Hopkins University Press, 1995); J. B. Wood and Carol Estes, "The Impact of DRG's on Community-based Service Providers: Implications for the Elderly," *AJPH* 80 (1990): 840–43.

3. Fox and Raphael, *Home-Based Care,* 1–4; C. M. Tauber, *Sixty-five Plus in America* (Washington, D.C.: U.S. Government Printing Office, 1992); A. E. Benjamin, "An Historical Perspective on Home Care Policy," *Milbank Quarterly* 71 (1993): 129–66; Virginia Conley and Mary Walker, "National Health Policy Influence on Medicare

Home Health," *Home Health Care Services Quarterly* 17 (1998): 1–15; Richard Hegner, "Medicare Coverage for Home Care: Reining in a Benefit out of Control" (National Health Policy Forum Issue Brief No. 694, 1996), 2–7.

4. Hegner, "Medicare Coverage for Home Care," 3.

5. Ibid., 1–10; Fox and Raphael, *Home-Based Care;* Edward M. Campion, "New Hope for Home Care?" *New England Journal of Medicine* 333 (November 1995): 1213–14; W. G. Weissert, "Home and Community-Based Care: The Cost-Effectiveness Trap," *Generations* 10 (1985): 47–50; Christine Bishop and Kathleen Carley Skwara, "Recent Growth of Medicare Home Health," *Health Affairs* 13 (fall 1993): 106.

6. H. Gilbert Welch, David E. Wenneberg, and W. Pete Welch, "The Use of Medicare Home Health Care Services," *New England Journal of Medicine* 335 (August 1996): 324–29.

7. Ibid.; Benjamin, "Historical Perspective"; Fox and Raphael, *Home-Based Care;* Karen Buhler-Wilkerson, "Home Care the American Way: An Historical Analysis," *Home Health Care Services Quarterly* 12 (1991): 5–18.

8. Nora Super Jones, "Access to Home Health Services under Medicare's Interim Payment System" (National Health Policy Forum Issue Brief No. 744, 1999).

9. Ibid.; William A. Sarraille, "The Home Health Industry Faces Mounting Allegations of Fraud," *Journal of Long-Term Health Care* 17 (summer 1998): 10–18; Mary Mundinger, *Home Care Controversy: Too Little, Too Late, Too Costly* (Rockville, Md.: Aspen Publications, 1983).

10. See, for example, the National Association for Home Care Web site: http://www.nahc.org. See also David Hess, "U.S. Cost-Savings Moves in Home Health Care Seem Off Target," *Philadelphia Inquirer,* 21 February 1998, A3; Alice Ann Love, "Medicare Warns Agencies on Home Health Cutbacks," *Philadelphia Inquirer,* 4 February 1998, C1–2.

11. Jones, "Access to Home Health Services." The National Association for Home Care has issued numerous news releases on this topic; see, for example, "Medicare Home Health Care Interim Payment System Is Inherently Unfair to Patients and Providers," 15 July 1998. The theme for the September issue of the association's magazine, *Caring,* was "Medicare Today, Tomorrow—Forever?" See Judith Feder and Marilyn Moon, "Can Medicare Survive Its Saviors?" *Caring* (September 1999): 30–33; Dayle Berke, "The Balanced Budget Act of 1997—What It Means for Home Care Providers and Beneficiaries," *Journal of Long-Term Health Care* 17 (summer 1998): 2–9.

Typical of home care's resiliency, the VNA of Greater Philadelphia kept its mission alive in an environment made extremely difficult by the Balanced Budget Act of 1997. During 1998 and 1999, its nurses made five hundred thousand visits to 15,588 patients and their families. Its comprehensive array of services included hospice, infusion, pharmacy, adult day care, meals on wheels, community outreach, and health-promotion programs. In addition, the association opened VNA House Calls, a collaborative primary care practice in which a team of nurse practitioners and physicians provide care in patients' homes. "Making Strides and Meeting Challenges Marked Year at the VNA," 1999 Annual Report, VNSP Collection.

12. National Association for Home Care, *Basic Statistics about Home Care, 1999* (Washington, D.C.: National Association for Home Care, 1999); Peter Arno, Carol Levine, and Margaret M. Memmott, "The Economic Value of Formal Caregiving," *Health Affairs* 18 (March/April 1999): 182–88; Carol Levine, "The Loneliness of the Long-Term Care Giver," *New England Journal of Medicine* 340 (May 1999): 1587–90. The National Association for Home Care is once again using the term *private-duty;* see, for example, *Caring Magazine* 18 (October 1999): 51.

13. Charles Rosenberg, *The Care of Strangers: The Rise of America's Hospital System* (New York: Basic Books, 1987); Rosemary Stevens, *In Sickness and in Wealth: American Hospitals in the Twentieth Century* (New York: Basic Books, 1989); David Rosner, *A Once Charitable Enterprise: Hospitals and Health Care in Brooklyn and New York, 1885–1915* (Princeton: Princeton University Press, 1982).

14. Robert Pear, "Annual Spending on Medicare Dips for the First Time," *New York Times,* 14 November 1999, 1, 26.

15. Robert Pear, "Medicare Spending for Care at Home Plunges by 45%," *New York Times,* 21 April 2000, A1, A20. The editorial appeared four days later: "The Plunge in Home Care," *New York Times,* 25 April 2000, A22.

16. Michael Vitez, "A Challenge to Where the Disabled May Receive Long-Term Care," *Philadelphia Inquirer,* 14 June 1999, A1; Robert Pear, "U.S. Seeks More Care for Disabled outside Institutions," *New York Times,* 13 February 2000, A24.

17. C. Eng, J. Pedulla, G. P. Eleazer, R. McCann, and N. Fox, "Program of All-inclusive Care for the Elderly (PACE): An Innovative Model of Geriatric Care and Financing," *Journal of the American Geriatrics*

Society 45 (1997): 223–32; Mary Naylor and Karen Buhler-Wilkerson, "Creating Community-Based Care for the New Millennium," *Nursing Outlook* 47 (May/June 1999): 120–27. These issues are constantly being brought to the attention of the public. The *Philadelphia Inquirer* ran a four-part series during the spring of 1998 examining the high cost of living longer. The conclusion was that America must now face the cost of care for millions. Sara Rimer has written several front-page articles in the *New York Times;* see, for example, "Blacks Carry Burden of Care for the Elderly," *New York Times,* 15 March 1998, A1.

18. Anne Somers, "Long-Term Care at Home," *New England Journal of Medicine,* 341 (September 1999): 1005.

FOLLOW THE MONEY: FUNDING STREAMS AND PUBLIC HEALTH NURSING

KRISTINE M. GEBBIE

This article originally appeared as Gebbie, K. M. (1995). Follow the money. A commentary on funding streams and public nursing. *Journal of Public Health Management and Practice, 1*(3), pp. 23–28. Copyright © 1995. All rights reserved. Reprinted with permission.

EDITORS' NOTE

Lillian Wald founded public health nursing in the late 1800s on the Lower East Side of Manhattan. Despite the rich history of nurses' essential roles in public health, nurse Kristine Gebbie, former commissioner of health in Oregon and Washington states, explains why many health departments have reduced their nursing workforce.

■ ■ ■

The world of health and illness care is undergoing major change, both in the way services are organized and the way services are financed. While the basic structure of public health agencies has not changed, these agencies are being affected by changes going on around

PUBLIC HEALTH IN AMERICA

Vision:
Healthy People in Healthy Communities

Mission:
Promote Physical and Mental Health and Prevent Disease, Injury, and Disability

Public Health

- Prevents epidemics and the spread of disease
- Protects against environmental hazards
- Prevents injuries
- Promotes and encourages healthy behaviors
- Responds to disasters and assists communities in recovery
- Assures the quality and accessibility of health services

Essential Public Health Services

- Monitor health status to identify community health problems
- Diagnose and investigate health problems and health hazards in the community
- Inform, educate, and empower people about health issues
- Mobilize community partnerships to identify and solve health problems
- Develop policies and plans that support individual and community health efforts
- Enforce laws and regulations that protect health and ensure safety

them. As is almost always the case, change in the environment surrounding any workplace brings change in the environment of that workplace, if only the change in time invested in questioning what is occurring. In the present situation, the changes in the public health workplace are far more than conversation; programs are being dramatically reorganized, funding sources are shifting, new terminology is being introduced, and the resource base for any governmental activity seems to be shrinking. This commentary focuses on how previous changes in funding streams have affected public health nursing and on how that might change over time.

THE PERSPECTIVE OF PUBLIC HEALTH

Public health is set apart from other components of health and illness care by its attention to population groups. The official public health agency of any jurisdiction has the responsibility to the governing structure of that jurisdiction (city council, county commission, governor and legislature, president and Congress) for all persons within the jurisdiction, with the stated or presumed goal of raising the level of health of the whole population over time. The historical record is full of examples of the dramatic impact of such attention: the

- Link people to needed personal health services and assure the provision of health care when otherwise unavailable
- Assure a competent public health and personal health care workforce
- Evaluate effectiveness, accessibility, and quality of personal and population-based health services
- Research for new insights and innovative solutions to health problems

Source: Essential Public Health Services Work Group of the Core Public Health Functions Steering Committee

Membership:

American Public Health Association
Association of State and Territorial Health Officials
National Association of County and City Health Officials
Institute of Medicine. National Academy of Sciences
Association of Schools of Public Health
Public Health Foundation
National Association of State Alcohol and Drug Abuse Directors
National Association of State Mental Health Program Directors
U.S. Public Health Service
Centers for Disease Control and Prevention
Health Resources and Services Administration
Office of the Assistant Secretary for Health
Substance Abuse and Mental Health Services Administration
Agency for Health Care Policy and Research
Indian Health Service
Food and Drug Administration, Fall 1994

assurance of safe sewage disposal virtually eliminating many epidemic diseases previously accounting for many illnesses and deaths; the fluoridation of drinking water reducing dental caries; the combination of education and regulation reducing the use of tobacco products.

It is sometimes difficult to identify the precise line between public health services and personal care; the administration of a vaccine to an infant is both a personal protection for that child and a step toward an adequate herd immunity for the community as a whole. Both the provider of personal care and the public health practitioner should be attentive to the timely provision of immunizations to children, and there is no exactly correct answer to who should administer the dose. In a world in which there was no system of primary medical care available, the public health agency could successfully organize immunization clinics and campaigns and achieve the necessary targets. In a world in which every child had a personal caregiver practicing clinical preventive services, all children would be immunized without the intervention of a health department. Today's world fits neither extreme, and in most areas of the country the process of moving toward full immunization of all children is a partnership among health departments, medical centers and clinics, family practitioners, and pediatricians.

The purest public health roles are those of fact finder and system builder, educator, and connector. The box provides a framework for understanding the mission, vision, and essential services of public health today. The direct provision of a care service might be part of a response to an epidemic or outbreak (as in provision of directly observed tuberculosis treatment or prophylaxis) or a means of assuring at least some level of care to the otherwise unserved. Even where providing care to some portion of the population for which it is responsible, the public health agency would be expected to distinguish itself from other care providers by the population focus of its approach.

CHANGES OVER TIME

Casual conversations with members of a community often reveal the perception that public health means the practice of medicine in a public clinic open to serve the poor or the medically indigent. One reason for this is the relative invisibility of a well-functioning and effective health department. When epidemics are being prevented, when risk reduction programs are effective, when partnerships to promote health are widely based in the community, the health department is a part of the background, calling no attention to itself and in fact giving public visibility and credit to its many partners. The occasional outbreak of disease may jolt a community into a brief period of awareness, as we are aware of the fire department when a truck races by, sirens wailing. There may be periods of publicity when standards for risk-reducing regulations regarding water systems or tobacco are adopted or revised, though at that point attention may focus less on the public health agency than on its governing body.

The visibility of the medical care system, partly because of its expense, and partly because of the high level of media interest in the technology of modern illness care, also means that health equals medical care in the minds of many. The fact that only about 10 percent of the improvement in health status over this century is attributable to medical intervention is lost in the maze of attention to diagnostic equipment, surgical procedures, and pharmaceutical developments. Public health agencies and associations have increased their efforts to make communities aware of all that public health encompasses through such activities as Public Health Week, the first full week in April, now noted by observances in at least 20 states. If successful, such visibility may overcome this first reason for public ignorance of public health.

The second reason for the misperception that publicly financed care for the poor is what public health is all about is that such activities have occupied a growing share of public health agency activities. The assurance of access to needed personal health and illness care services is one of the essential services of public health. When there are no providers of personal health care services, the only way to assure access to those services is to provide them. As the number of those uninsured and underinsured grows, lack of access may be due not only to a limited number of practitioners in a community, but also to the lack of a way to pay, or absence of means of payment acceptable to the provider community (as Medicaid often has not been). The inflation in the cost of providing personal care has meant that even if the amount of personal care provided by a health department has not grown, as measured by number of caregivers or number of patients, the cost will have steadily increased as a proportion of the agency's budget. Given the limits on spending imposed on most units of government, this may well mean that growth in the cost of personal care services has come at the expense of population-based services.

FINANCING PUBLIC HEALTH

In an understanding of public health as an activity undertaken for the common good, general tax revenues are the logical base of support. The fiscal support for most health departments is much more complex than that, however. Funds come from general tax dollars, from special tax revenues assigned to health (as tobacco taxes have been in some instances), from fees charged for specific activities (licenses to operate restaurants, or clinic visit charges), and from grants or contracts from other governmental units, foundations, or entities. Local health agencies are often the recipients of grants from the state health department (much of which may be funded in turn by grants to the state from the federal health agencies), and from one or more of the many foundations interested in the health of the public. In the push to tighten local public health budgets and avoid increasing local tax rates, health departments have been encouraged to seek even more revenue from other levels and units of government and required to charge fees for services previously considered a service free to anyone.

Among those services previously offered at no point-of-service charge are laboratory services such as the testing of private well water for contaminants and the personal visits associated with the treatment of sexually transmitted diseases, reproductive health, or immunization. In all of the personal care examples, agencies generally have policies that assure that those who are unable to pay still receive service. This is done through the use of a mechanism such as a sliding fee scale, which has a no-pay provision at the lowest income levels.

Around the limited set of personal care services identified in the previous paragraph, many local health departments have established full primary medical care programs. These offer the same range of services that might be found in any general practice clinic. These programs assure that the child too ill to be seen in a well-child clinic is evaluated and treated, or that the adult with a noninfectious disease receives appropriate services. In many communities, this expansion has been in response to the gradual overloading of emergency departments with individuals unable to find any other source of primary care services.

As mentioned previously, many of the services offered in pursuit of protecting the general health of the public are identical with those offered for the direct service of specific individuals. This list would include family planning, immunization, well-child care, and pre- and post-natal care. To the extent that those seeking these services from the health agency are eligible for Medicaid benefits, the services are ones generally covered by Medicaid, services for which a private medical practitioner or clinic would be reimbursed if provided. Health departments providing increasing amounts of personal care for those unable to find care elsewhere in the community identified Medicaid billing as one source of revenue to allow continuation of services. Local health departments worked together to identify ways of improving their billing systems and worked with state Medicaid agencies and the federal Health Care Financing Administration to develop policies that made this billing more effective. (While the same logic would apply to maximizing revenue from other insurance coverage, the limited number of persons using health departments as primary caregivers insured by non-Medicaid sources has meant this has not been pursued as vigorously.)

THE IMPACT ON NURSING

Nurses are one of the largest components of the public health work force and are most visible in those services requiring contact with individuals about their personal state of health or illness. This includes immunizations, treatment and investigation of sexually transmissible diseases and tuberculosis, all reproductive health services, school health services, and programs screening for previously undetected/untreated noninfectious conditions such as hypertension, breast cancer, or cervical cancer. As these personal contacts have more and more become part of a network of personal primary care, for which bills are filed with a payment source, the investment of nursing time is seen in a different light.

The early models of public health nurses in the community involve very unstructured blocks of time, invested in getting to know the population of a neighborhood and working with them over time to improve their health. The stories told always included personal care (teaching a new mother how to feed and bathe her infant, immunizing a school population) but care was co-mingled with the more diffuse interactions described in the essential public health services taxonomy as "inform, educate and empower people about health issues," "mobilize community partnerships and action to identify and solve health problems," and "link people to needed personal health services." These latter services have longer cycles between the investment of professional energy and the result of a healthier community, and are difficult to quantify.

The confluence of tighter public budgets, increased use of Medicaid (or other insurance) generated revenue, and an increased interest in the efficient professional management of public health can lead to a very different approach to nursing in the public health agency than that described previously. Where the nursing staff are seen primarily as clinicians serving individual clients, their time investment will be monitored for maximum number of billable contacts per day or week. The increasingly limited general fund revenue available to the health department may be tied up entirely with response to outbreaks of communicable disease and other emergencies. There may be no support for general nursing time that cannot be supported by revenues associated with care for specific individuals. And while specific individuals may be cared for in any setting, office or clinic settings allow for the maximum number of persons to be seen in the available hours.

The increasing use of management models translated from personal care settings may well exacerbate this tendency to minimize the amount of time available for the more diffuse community interactions. A county commission reading literature on bringing private sector management approaches into government, and not well informed on the difference between public health and medicine, will be inclined to assume that a good hospital or clinic manager is a good public health manager, that a computer-based records and billing system tested in private practice will work just fine in the health department. And to the extent that the health department is the "private medical clinic" for those unable to find care elsewhere, these translations are appropriate, and useful. Those nurses employed as clinicians to provide primary (or specialty) personal care in health departments may find the record keeping, billing and management systems useful, appropriate and effective.

But, the provision of personal care in the absence of other caregiving resources is only one half of one of the ten essential public health services. Singular attention to this one does dramatic disservice to the others. Public health nurses have the capacity to contribute to all of them, working in collaboration with the other disciplines of public health. They have done so historically, and should do so in the future. For this to happen, public health nurses must understand and expect to use their full potential, and the funding sources must be available. Making this happen will take substantial effort.

HEALTH REFORM AND MANAGED CARE

While the last Congress did not enact major changes in the health system, the system is continuing to undergo major shifts. The most notable of these is the increasing use of various forms of what is called managed care. Without getting into the details of the multiple definitions of that term, it can be fairly captured as approaches to insurance coverage that attempt to control the costs of care and limit the use of unusually expensive interventions, through capitated payments, provider risk-sharing, or use of primary care gatekeepers. Not only are various private insurers and self-insured companies moving to these approaches, but so are public programs such as Medicaid. This means that health services previously billable as individual care events may not be reimbursable unless specifically prescribed by a primary caregiver, or unless provided within a planned network that is offering all levels of care including hospitalization.

The public health department that has become reliant on billing Medicaid for primary care services has several options when Medicaid moves to managed care as the principal approach to payment. If the shift in payment makes Medicaid-financed patients more attractive, and there is sufficient private caregiving capacity in the community, the health department may simply shut down its clinics. (If there is not sufficient private capacity and the health department is large enough, it may assume full managed care responsibility for some population groups. It is unlikely that this will be a very large proportion of the 3,000 plus local health departments in the nation.) This allows the health department to take seriously its full mission, and invest more resources in the complete range of public health services, working in collaboration with all personal care providers, environmental health agencies, and other relevant groups in the jurisdiction.

WHAT ABOUT NURSING?

A great many of the nurses currently employed in public health settings have only known public health in this era of primary care practice. As the money for primary care shifts into managed care, those nurses may need to follow it in order to continue a clinical career that has been satisfying and has provided needed service to many. Presentations by those associated with large managed care networks would indicate that they are interested in employing practitioners who think of the community as well as, or even before, the hospital, and who are interested in prevention as well as treatment. It would be to the benefit of managed care organizations to seek out and employ experienced nurses from public health agencies, especially if enrollment includes large numbers from population groups considered hard to reach or having complex problems. The potential of this shift out of public employment is leading to high anxiety levels in many nurses, and not only because of the uncertainty of finding employment. There has been some "bashing" of the private sector by those in public health over the years, and it can be difficult to see yourself changing sides in the process.

The other option for nurses is to stay with public health. Nurses are needed if an agency is to fulfill all of the essential public health services. The number of nurses may be smaller, however, it takes fewer individuals to develop an immunization education campaign for a town of 50,000 than to actually administer vaccine to all of the children in that town. It takes fewer individuals to develop a comprehensive injury prevention program than to staff an emergency clinic for children. The examples are numerous. The day-to-day activities are different, and the time lines for feedback and evaluation of progress are lengthened.

The lines will be blurred, and it is essential that public health agencies continue to employ individuals from those disciplines that understand personal health and illness care and can effectively work in both personal care and population-based settings. The nurse choosing to develop more fully skills in epidemiology, community organization and mobilization, health education and outreach, policy development, and research will be challenged as never before.

That nurse will also have the immense challenge of helping find the money needed. There was not room in this commentary to deal with the concerns about funding raised by the changes in primary care. Available documentation from state and local health departments indicates severe under-funding for public health services. Achieving a stable funding base for population-based public health as a necessary complement to personal health care should be a central goal in all reforming efforts. In choosing to follow the money to personal care, important though that was, we have neglected the information systems, research, and policy development that could assist us in assuring that there were sufficient dollars to support effective public health activities in every community in the country.

That will happen only with a great deal of effort and extremely clear communication about population-based public health. Effective communication with the community is the hallmark of all public health; nursing can and should be there in the future, as it has been in the past.

23

SWAMP NURSE

KATHERINE BOO

EDITORS' NOTE

This *New Yorker* article brought new visibility for the Nurse-Family Partnership, a two-decades-old home visitation program for reducing risk for vulnerable, first-time mothers and their newborns. The program uses registered nurses for the home visits and has rigorously demonstrated short-term and long-term outcomes for mothers and their children that speak to its success. This article follows one of the nurses who works in the program in Louisiana. It shows how small gains are important to nurse and mother, as well as the challenges both face in achieving these gains. The program is spreading across the country with local, state, and federal support.

■ ■ ■

In the swamps of Louisiana, late autumn marks the end of the hurricane and the sugarcane seasons—a time for removing plywood from windows and burning residues of harvest in the fields. Then begins the season of crayfish and, nine months having passed since the revelry of Mardi Gras, a season of newborn Cajuns. Among the yield of infants in the autumn of 2004 was a boy named Daigan James Plaisance Theriot, and, on the morning of Daigan's thirtieth day of life, he was seated next to a bag of raw chickens in the back of an Oldsmobile Cutlass. His mother, a teen-ager named Alexis, was in front, squeezed between her younger sister and her sister's latest beau, a heavily tattooed man who had just been released from maximum-security prison. The car came down a road that begins with a bayou and ends in dented trailers, and stopped at a small wooden house.

When Alexis's sister leaned into the back seat to fetch the poultry, the young man, grinning, slipped a hand down the back of her jeans. Alexis stared at the couple for a moment, then pushed them aside to pick up Daigan. Alexis's hair was long and streaked with pink, and her face was a knot of frustration. As Daigan began to cry, she crossed the yard denouncing in absentia his father, whom she called Big Head: "If I see him, I will hurt him—Big Head asking for it now." When she reached the porch, which was crammed with auto parts and porcelain toilets, she fell silent, then forced a smile. Amid the fixtures stood a tall black nurse.

The nurse, Luwana Marts, holds one of the stranger jobs in the Louisiana state bureaucracy: she is a professional nurturer in a program called the Nurse-Family Partnership, which attempts to improve the prospects of destitute babies. A few months earlier, Alexis, eighteen and pregnant, had arrived at a local government office seeking Medicaid for her impending delivery. She ended up with both the Medicaid and Luwana. As a rule, Cajun families don't welcome government intervention, especially when it occurs inside their homes, involves their infants, and means the presence of a dark-skinned person. To some parents, Alexis among them, Luwana was a spy in the house of maternity, and so she now and again had to lie in wait for reluctant beneficiaries.

Alexis maneuvered herself and Daigan past the toilets, from which cacti had started to grow, and pushed open the front door with her hip. She entered a combined living room, dining room, kitchen, laundry, and storage facility that was home to five people, a dying cockatoo named Tweety, and multitudes of flat silver bugs. Luwana followed Alexis, Daigan, little sister, and boyfriend inside. That morning, feeling the onset of flu symptoms, Luwana had decided to avoid contact with the infants she called her "little darlings." In the field, though, calculations of risk were subject to change. She dropped her satchel, slathered her hands with Purell disinfectant, and reached out. Alexis handed over Daigan and wrapped her arms tightly around herself. "So, tell me," the nurse began with practiced tranquility as she scanned a body in a playsuit for damage. "Not the happiest day of your life?"

Alexis and nineteen other girls in Luwana's caseload call her their "nurse-visitor," a term whose genteel ring seldom comports with the details of her job. She is one of eight nurses, all mothers themselves, who work the parishes of Terrebonne and Lafourche, persuading poor first-time mothers-to-be to accept assistance. The Nurse-Family Partnership model is currently being tried in Louisiana and nineteen other states on the basis of promising preliminary results—results achieved in the face of the nurses' preposterously difficult assignment. In regular visits until a baby is two years old, they try to address, simultaneously, the continual crises of poverty and the class—transcending anxiety of new maternity: this creature is inexplicable to me. Despite its ambition, the program is rooted in a pessimistic view of the future that awaits an American child born poor—a sense that the schools, day-care centers, and other institutions available to him may do little to nurture his talents. Shrewder, then, to insulate him by an exercise of uncommon intrusion: building for him, inside his home, a better parent.

Thus, no matter how chaotic the scene—no matter that Alexis's sister had taken a break from hacking chicken parts by the kitchen sink in order to satisfy the ex-inmate's sexual needs in the next room—Luwana's first task is to create an aura of momentousness around the new baby. As she moves through a household, giving advice about routine building, breast-feeding, and storing shotguns out of reach, she attempts to win over not just a young mother but a typically unwieldy cast of supporting players, from the baby's father to the great-grandmother getting high in a tent behind the house. What Luwana tells each family may seem, on the face of it, fiction: that in this infant enormous possibilities inhere. But such fictions can be strategic, especially in cultures in which the act of becoming a mother is honored far more than what the mother subsequently does for her child.

Alexis, who wore a tight red T-shirt, would have been striking even without the pink improvements she'd made to her caramel-colored hair, and since fifth grade, when she'd lost interest in schoolwork, most of her opportunities had come from men who'd taken note of her looks. Lately, she'd been wishing that she'd had a longer, simpler childhood, but, in the childhood that she had, full hips and breasts and lips had served her well. They served her less well now. To Luwana's questions about Daigan's feeding schedule, she responded monosyllabically while studying her manicured fingers. She'd received the manicure, plus some blue balloons and a chocolate-chip cake, on what she called the "heartful" occasion of Daigan's birth. The days preceding his arrival had not been happy. Alexis lived with her mother and father, a grocery clerk and a construction worker who were in constant conflict. When Alexis was eight months pregnant, the fights grew so fierce that she fled the household altogether. Her recent return testified less to domestic reconciliation than to the impact that a squalling baby has on the sleepover invitations a girl receives.

As Luwana tried to draw Alexis out, the phone rang, and Alexis covered her ears. "I'm guessing this is Daigan's dad who keeps on calling," Luwana said, after the third round of unanswered rings. Alexis met her eyes for an instant, then burst into tears. "O.K., now," the nurse said, "spell it out for Miss Luwana." Between sniffles, the proximate cause of distress became clear. Daigan's father, a sturdy twenty-six-year-old named James, worked on a tugboat on the Mississippi River. That weekend, he would be returning to shore and expected to have sex with Alexis, though she was not healed from childbirth, nor was she using contraception.

"No way!" Luwana said. "Keep your legs closed: embed that in your brain. Tell him to keep his hands to himself. And if you can't stand up for yourself, stand up for Daigan. You've got a lot of work ahead, giving him what he needs. Look around, Alexis. You need another baby in this picture?"

"No," Alexis said dully. Then she brightened: "Miss Luwana, maybe you can write me an excuse note, like for gym?"

Luwana's church friends smiled knowingly when they learned that she worked for the state. They pictured cubicles, potted plants, and cushy hours. She seldom corrected this impression, nor did she say that some mornings, driving her six-year-old Maxima toward some difficult case, she wanted to turn north and spend the rest of her working life in more high-minded quarters. But Luwana's efforts were invigorated by the fact that twenty years ago she was herself a poor, pregnant teen-ager in these swamps. "I know now that there were government programs on the books designed to help girls in my situation, but back then, especially if you were black, you didn't hear about them," she said. She is now thirty-eight, with two sons and a husband who has spent most of his working life in a mill that makes paper cups. It took her fourteen years, between child-rearing and stints as a nurse's aide, to earn a bachelor's degree in nursing. Her state job pays thirty-five thousand dollars a year, half of what she'd make in the emergency room of a private hospital. "Oh, I have my material longings—every so often I'll throw a pity party for the house I'll never have," she said. "But quite a few of us nurses are working, you could say, in the context of our own memories."

"How he doing?" Alexis asked uneasily, as Luwana's fingers explored Daigan's soft spot.

"You're the mama," Luwana responded. "You tell me."

"He's got a big head like his father," Alexis said under her breath. Then she rallied: "He's not as cranky as he was. And one thing I learned already is how he cries different when he's hungry than when he's wet." Luwana bestowed on Alexis a dazzling smile that she had thus far reserved for Daigan. "Making that distinction is important," she said. "You're listening to him, and in his own way he's explaining what he needs. Pretty soon now he'll be making other sounds, and when he does you'll want to make that noise right back. He'll babble, and then you'll talk to him, and that's how you'll develop his language. Now, what you may also find, around five to eight weeks, is that he'll be crying even more—it's a normal part of his development, but it can also stress out the mom, so we'll want to be prepared for it. The main thing will be keeping calm. And if you just can't keep calm—if you find yourself getting all worked up and frustrated—well, then what?"

"Put him down? So I don't hurt him, shake him, make him brain-dead?"

"Put him down and . . .?" Luwana drilled her girls hard on this particular point.

"Call someone who isn't upset? Let the baby be, and get help."

Luwana turned to Daigan and clapped. "See, your mama is getting it," she said, using the high-frequency tones that babies hear best. "She's surely going to figure you out."

There was a trick that Luwana relied on to stave off dejection: imagining how a given scene would unfold if she weren't in it. In Alexis's case—one that, in terms of degree of difficulty, fell roughly in the middle of her caseload—she knew that slight improvements had already been made. At Luwana's urging, Alexis had stopped drinking and smoking when she was pregnant and had kept her prenatal appointments. So she wasn't incapable of changing her life on Daigan's behalf; the odds were just long.

Sitting cross-legged on the floor now, Luwana sang "Clementine" and made faces at Daigan, and for a moment Alexis studied this demonstration of engagement with her child. But then her gaze drifted over to her sister and the ex-con, who had emerged from the bedroom to chop the rest of the chicken. The young man, whose tattoos included white supremacist ones, put on mirrored sunglasses for this task, a fashion choice that made Alexis giggle. Luwana's primary subject that day was infant attachment, a topic she tailored to fit Alexis's limited attention span. "A funny thing about the axe murderers," she said casually. "Usually something missing in the love link." And, indeed, axe-murdering seemed to register with both Alexis and the former prisoner, who set down his knife and came over. "I need to hear, too—mines is horrible," he said. "We whup him but since he turned two he don't do nothing we say, probably 'cause his mama on drugs and sleeping around and getting locked up—well, she's a whore."

"You hit a two-year-old?" Luwana asked, her eyes narrowing. "You teach him how to fight and are surprised when he turns around, starts fighting you?" She then fixed her stare on Alexis, who began examining the brown linoleum floor.

"The love link," Luwana began again. Now the room was still. "It's a cycle. When there's no safe base for the baby—when you're not meeting his basic needs, satisfying his hunger, keeping him out of harm's way—there will be no trust, no foundation for love. And that's when you might just get the axe murderer. Maybe sometimes we have a baby and expect that baby to comfort us? Well, sorry, it works the other way around. It's on you now to comfort him, earn his trust, because that's how Daigan is going to learn how to love."

Infant-development strategies, like other forms of social capital, are perversely distributed in America-fetishized in places where babies are fundamentally secure and likely to prosper, undervalued in places where babies are not. The nurse-visiting program aims, in a fashion, at equalization. The territory that Luwana and her colleagues cover begins an hour's drive southwest of New Orleans, down fog-prone highways lined with cypress trees which lead to the Gulf of Mexico. On the shoulders, turkey vultures pause, flicking mud from their wings. Mississippi River sediment shaped this marshy delta, to which eighteenth-century French Acadians, expelled by the British from Nova Scotia, laid a claim not hotly contested. The terrain now occupied by the exiles' descendants is muggy, heavily wooded, and visited so often by hurricanes that Katrina, which made landfall near here, failed to register as a main event. Residents have another, steadier battle with nature, because they've built their lives on one of the fastest-sinking landmasses on earth.

The social demographics are almost as fragile. Louisiana literacy rates are among the nation's lowest; infant mortality and child-poverty rates—thirty per cent of all children are poor—are among the very highest; and almost half of all births are to single mothers. Historically, the swamp region's topography isolated it from the rest of the state, but drawbridges and thoroughfares have been erected in recent years, and cane fields now give way to Wal-Marts. Still, idiosyncratic child-rearing beliefs endure: a baby will become constipated if held by a menstruating woman; formula is healthier than breast milk; giving an infant a haircut before his first birthday will stunt his growth and hurt his brain.

The cases that Luwana and her fellow-nurses take typically begin with a referral from a public-health or prenatal clinic: a form indicating the age and address of an expectant mother and the baby's due date. Occasionally, a nurse shows up at the given address to find a mother-to-be converting Sudafed to methamphetamine on a hot plate. Other times, a pregnant girl's father is hostile because he's the probable father of his daughter's child. But the nurse's typical commission is to work with what she finds. And while Luwana believes that some aspects of mothering are instinctual, what she teaches is more like applied science. Her tools include a polystyrene demonstration baby named Dionne, picture books, a raft of developmental checklists, and, above all, her trade's bleak knowledge: babies can get used to almost anything—as many of those babies' mothers had.

The Nurse-Family Partnership program began twenty-eight years ago as the obsession of a developmental psychologist named David Olds. He is fifty-seven years old, with clear blue eyes and a tendency to fidget not unlike that of Luwana's adolescent mothers. He grew up in a working-class household and as a young man taught in an inner-city day-care center, an experience that led him to suspect that by age four or five some children are already gravely damaged. In the nineteen seventies, after earning a Ph.D. at Cornell under the late child psychologist Urie Bronfenbrenner, he began working with colleagues to translate this grim view into an elaborate scheme of prevention. At the time, scientific knowledge about early brain development and the importance of a child's first years of learning was more limited than it is now. But for Olds, who has one biological child and two adopted children, intuition as much as evidence suggested that the rescue effort should begin before birth, and unfold in the setting where an infant would spend most of his time. As for what sort of person a low-income young woman might trust inside her home, he and his colleagues settled on nurses, who in poor communities have high status and medical expertise that many pregnant women want. In 1978, Olds used a federal grant to test his idea in Elmira, an economically depressed, mostly white community in New York's Southern Tier, which had the highest rates of child abuse and neglect in the state.

"Some policymakers look for cure-alls, which this isn't," said Olds, who continues to study his protocol's effects as the director of the Prevention Research Center for Family and Child Health, at the University of Colorado, in Denver. "We keep refining how we do this as the nurses report back on their experiences, because there's still a lot that we don't know—for instance, how best to help mothers who are battered or mentally ill." Nonetheless, when he conducted random-assignment evaluations (among the most strenuous tests of a social program's effect) to gauge how the Elmira mothers and children were faring at the completion of the program, he found more improvement than he had expected. One of his chief concerns had been child abuse, and it turned out that children whose mothers had finished the nurse-visiting program were far less likely to be abused or injured than their counterparts in a control group. He also discovered that by the time the nurse-visited children were four, their mothers were more likely to be employed, off public assistance, and in stable relationships with their partners. Evaluations of two subsequent pilot programs—with primarily black families in Memphis and a racially diverse group in Denver—showed less dramatic results against control groups but suggested additional possibilities. By age six, for instance, the nurse-visited Memphis children had larger vocabularies, fewer mental-health problems, and slightly higher I.Q.s. In all three sites, the mothers had fewer subsequent children and longer spaces between them. An economic analysis of the Olds experiment commissioned by the state of Washington concluded that the approach—which currently costs around four thousand dollars per year per family—was cost-effective as well, because the children aided by the nurses had required fewer expensive social services such as foster care and hospitalization.

The early optimism surrounding programs meant to help poor children is often dispelled by the rigorous assessments that come later. Children may make startling intellectual and functional gains in the hothouse of a model program—say, a preschool run by skilled and idealistic teachers—but those gains tend to vanish when the children move on to their communities' less hospitable institutions. This phenomenon, known as "fade-out," is one of the great frustrations of antipoverty policy, and I was first drawn to Olds's work because his long-term findings seemed to defy the regressive trend. By the time the Elmira children turned fifteen, they were still demonstrably better off than their control group peers. For instance, they'd been arrested far fewer times, one of several findings that inspired the U.S. Department of Justice to cite Olds's infant intervention program as a model for the prevention of juvenile crime. I wondered, however, about the objectivity of the Olds studies, since, regardless of acceptance by peer-reviewed publications like the *Journal of the American Medical Association*, he is essentially grading his own work. When I raised specific questions about the long-term outcomes in Elmira, Olds decided to recalculate his data using seven different evaluation methodologies, grasping that such a test might undercut his life's work. He later reported that some of the original findings—for instance, those about Elmira teen-agers drinking and running away less than their counterparts—weren't holding up under a preliminary analysis. He was so dismayed by these results that he seemed oblivious of the fact that other evidence of the improved futures of nurse-visited children and their mothers was now about as solid as findings can be when the subject is social policy's impact on human behavior.

The nurse-visitor approach makes some liberals uneasy, because they fear that its focus on good parenting will undermine the fight for decent schools, quality day care, and other institutional supports for poor children. Libertarians recoil at a government-funded program that meddles in private lives, and child-welfare advocates have been frustrated by Olds's restraint. In their view, a "scientifically proven" approach like nurse visiting could have attracted bipartisan support and been widely implemented years ago, if its creator had more emphatically promoted it.

Olds's cautiousness is based not just on a sense of personal fallibility but on what he considers the faltering of Head Start in the late sixties and seventies. A rapid, politically driven expansion inflated public expectation while diluting program standards; by the eighties, conservative policymakers were using Head Start's modest results to justify the rejection of other government antipoverty programs. Olds wants his protocol to expand incrementally, as he fine-tunes it. Currently, thanks to a hodgepodge of public and private funders, nurse visitors in places as diverse as Los Angeles, Fargo, Allentown, Tulsa, and Bedford Stuyvesant serve an annual twenty thousand of the United States' 2.5 million low-income children under the age of two.

Louisiana, where I decided to watch Olds's ideas at work over the course of a year, is one of nurse-visiting's most difficult settings. Legislators there have been sufficiently impressed with the program to more than double its size in four years, with the help of federal Medicaid dollars. But, in a state where nurses often run out of breath when recounting the disadvantages of their clients ("The mom I'm working with now is a sixteen-year-old unmedicated, bipolar rape victim and crack-addicted prostitute with a pattern of threatening to kill her social worker, who recently abandoned her baby at her ex-boyfriend's sister's, and who has an attempted murder charge in another situation—well, I think I've got all the risk factors," a colleague of Luwana's said one day), nurse-visiting is unlikely to be mistaken for a cure-all.

In the bayou, every schoolchild knows that a shrimp's heart is in its head, and that now it's cheaper to buy that shrimp from China. So last winter, in a neighborhood called Upper Little Caillou, people who once worked on the water were trawling for a service sector niche. On homemade signs in yards, the inventory of salable goods continually evolved: "Shrimp/Alterations/Vinyl Blinds"; "Turtle Meat, Adult Novelties & Bail Bonds." Maggie Lander, a seventeen-year-old client of Luwana's, was among the residents hawking what she imagined rich people might want, such as her mother's cache of Harlequin novels. In the interest of clarity of message, though, the front of her home bore just one sign—"No smoking"—on behalf of her one-year-old daughter.

In a few years, Maggie figured, her daughter would perceive the deficiencies of her home, as Maggie did—understanding, for instance, that a sheet stapled to the ceiling wasn't what people usually meant by an interior wall. But she chose to believe what Luwana had told her: that babies didn't care about the surface of things. Their standards were deeper, Maggie believed, than those of some grownups she knew.

In addition to selling secondhand goods, Maggie worked for a janitorial service. She has a lisp, a vulpine face, and auburn hair that she parts down the middle and often lets fall over her eyes. When Luwana came around, though, Maggie tucked the strands behind her ears, revealing the sallow beauty of a Victorian consumptive. For a half-Mexican, half-Native American schoolmate named José Hernandez, the sexual attraction had been intense. It wasn't entirely an accident when, after a year and a half of courtship, she got pregnant.

In the bayou region, which is traditionally Catholic, no doctors admit to performing abortions. Home remedies, though, are highly evolved: blue cohosh root, a belly flop from bed to floor, the placenta-rupturing magic of cocaine. ("Is the baby shaking yet?" practitioners of this late-stage strategy asked when they entered the local emergency room; they knew the drill better than the doctors did.) But most pregnancies here were not terminated; as Maggie's mother liked to say, "God doesn't make mistakes." Maggie concurred with this theory. Still, when Luwana first appeared on her broken front porch, she was relieved to have a fresh pair of eyes on her life.

David Olds and his researchers like findings that can be quantified, and Luwana has learned to report her experiences accordingly. The forms she filled out, however, didn't always capture the extent of a family's despair. The first time she'd come to Maggie's house, she had found an intelligent, underfed tenth grader in her second trimester who was sick with untreated hepatitis B and was also trying to care for her mother, who was bedridden and weighed eighty-two pounds. "I was in another world then, wanting to die," Maggie's mother, whose name is Tammy, recalled. "I'd been played the fool by a man I thought wanted a wife." Though mother and daughter shared malnourishment, depression, and very close quarters, they seemed to exist in separate spheres.

One afternoon before Christmas, the effects of Luwana's yearlong campaign against hopelessness were easy to see. The baby, whose name is Maia, was an exuberant babbler, with a paunch so magisterial that her patchwork jeans were left unbuttoned. Maggie's mother was rounder, too, thanks to antidepressants, and she was working alongside Maggie at the cleaning company. Maggie was buoyed by her recent engagement to José, whom Maia plainly adored. He had moved into the house shortly before his daughter's birth, and he, Maggie, and Maia now occupied a sweltering room in the rafters.

As Maggie discussed her low-budget wedding plans with Luwana, she bounced her dark-skinned daughter gently, while her fingers traced shapes on the baby's thigh. Maggie had become a diligent student of child-development technique, reading aloud so often from the parenting handouts Luwana had given her that she got on José's nerves. "She's, 'Listen to this on early brain development,' and I'm like 'O.K., I was here when Luwana went over it, I know,'" he said. "But she has to memorize this stuff." Luwana, of course, found the habit agreeable, and privately gave Maggie her highest praise: "The girl's an overcomer." But, in the swamps, a massively improved life is not the same as a good one.

Maggie was now weak from the interferon that Luwana pressed her to take for her hepatitis. Maggie didn't know whether she had caught the disease from the twenty-five-year-old to whom she lost her virginity, at age thirteen, or whether she had been born with it. But the combined pressures of infirmity and maternity had led her to a decision with which Luwana took strong issue: dropping out of school after Maia was born.

"I'm just trying to see that we're taking logical steps here," the nurse said gently. A fiercer iteration of her argument—that bearing a child as an unmarried teen-ager and failing to finish high school were matchless predictors of lifetime poverty—had just brought tears to Maggie's eyes. "You have too much to lose, and I know you don't want to clean houses all your life. Remember when I met you? It was one of the first things you said—how adamant you were about finishing?"

"I will go back, Miss Luwana, I promise," Maggie replied. "It's just now, with my job and Maia doing so many new things—I don't know . . ." Luwana's concern with diplomas, career plans, and jobs with benefits wasn't shared by many people Maggie knew. In a sinking region, land and housing came cheap, and dinner could be yanked from the brown water, so uneducated people could in fact "work the odd one," "do for themselves," and get by.

Luwana, like many of her clients, is good at suppressing emotion. Among her cases were a young mother who had attempted suicide in her third trimester, two others who'd been violently abused, and one who was paraplegic and mentally disabled. Maggie's case troubled the nurse differently. She saw in the girl something of her younger self—"You know, that caged bird singing"—and feared the potential was going to be lost.

"I mean, I'm not going to be just some dropout," Maggie promised Luwana now, gathering conviction. She reminded the nurse of a pact she'd made with José, who worked nights with her on the cleaning crew and spent his days in high school. He'd get his diploma while she took care of Maia, then it would be her turn for school.

"So he's going to be the main one keeping Maia, is that what you're saying?" Luwana said skeptically. "You're going to trust him with her next year when you don't trust him now—when he doesn't wake up when she's crying?" In the year that Luwana and Maggie had spent together, Luwana had grown alert to the girl's romantic habits of mind.

When Maggie and José cleaned houses for lawyers and car dealers, José enjoyed discoveries of drug stashes and signs of affairs. "Wife large," he'd say with a broken-toothed smile, brandishing a find. "Panties behind the trash can in the bathroom, petite." Maggie preferred to dwell on other evidence. "I like dirty kitchens more than the fancy spotless ones," she said, "because in the dirty ones you can picture the homey wife and the father and kids all eating together and talking like a family." She hoped to replicate this scenario with José and Maia.

"Let's see," she said one day of the family life she had personally experienced. "In the last few years, we stayed in that trailer park we couldn't afford, then the little blue house we couldn't afford, either—had to give it back. Then a trailer park, then my auntie's trailer when we couldn't afford the trailer, then back to the trailer park, then straight to a little bitty camper behind my aunt's trailer—now, *that* was tiny, you walk in the door, there's a mattress and a table and that's it. Then we moved in with my uncle, then with my mom's boyfriend, then back to the trailer park, then back to the boyfriend, then back to my uncle, and then here."

Luwana had bettered her own circumstances with the help of caring teachers and strong parents, neither of which Maggie seemed to have. Her father, an illiterate as well as an addict, beat her mother when Maggie was young, and then his neck was broken in a car wreck. Afterward, he got sober, found religion, and separated from Tammy. Both parents are devoted to Maggie, but their leverage is minimal. "I hear Luwana saying to Maggie, 'It's not about you, you're making decisions for your daughter now,'" Tammy once said, "and I can almost see it on the tip of Maggie's tongue, 'But you didn't, Mom. You didn't look out for me.'" Tammy thought often about a day, shortly before Maggie got pregnant, when her daughter told her she was suicidal. "I didn't want to hear it," Tammy said. "I just wanted to believe that Maggie was the one thing in my lousy life I'd done right." Now Maggie considered Maia one thing that she was doing right.

Luwana crouched to study the teenager as she and Maia played with a set of plastic blocks. Some adolescents were reluctant to play with their babies because it violated their code of nonchalance. Maggie, though, played zealously until Maia lost interest and tried to crawl away. When Maggie picked her up, Luwana objected: "She's at an age where it's good for her to explore. You want to let her learn to be independent."

"House isn't safe," Maggie said, running her hand across a patch of rough plywood. "I gotta keep her in one place."

"Your authority is her safety, too," Luwana said, then whispered excitedly in Maia's ear, "Let's see you walk! You want to walk? I think you want to walk!"

"She doesn't want to, she's not ready," Maggie protested. Luwana raised an eyebrow, and then they both laughed. It was Maggie who wasn't ready. She said, "It's like, stop here where it's happy, because what if the rest ain't this good?"

Every December, Santa Claus comes down the bayou on a shrimp boat twinkling with lights, at which time bitterness begins to rise in a swamp nurse's heart. This is the season when families whose financial and emotional problems she's been working for months to unravel go deep into debt, drink themselves into oblivion, and beat each other up with more than usual frequency. On Christmas Day, their babies get "Lion King" DVDs that they can't watch, because the television has been repossessed. For Luwana, the rest of the winter is mop-up.

One morning in February, Luwana and six other nurses gathered at the Terrebonne Parish Health Unit, in a low-slung concrete building situated between a shabby neighborhood and an oil rig. A space shortage meant that the nurses conducted their weekly meetings in a storage area, but to Luwana the hours there were luxurious—a time of reassurance that she wasn't working alone.

Waiting for the late arrivals, the nurses discussed the deficiencies of the Atkins diet and the doings of their own adolescent children. Luwana's younger son was a smart and willful twelve-year-old, and the other nurses nodded knowingly at her assertion "I'm better with other people's kids than I am with my own."

The meeting came to order with the appearance of Claudette McKay, the unit's fifty-seven-year-old supervisor; she'd been one of the first nurse-visitors in the region—apparently a memorable one. At noon the day before, as she drove through Terrebonne Parish to a local diner, a young woman in a skullcap yelled in her open window, "I'm going to carjack you!" "You skipped your birth-control appointment!" Claudette barked back, unfazed, as the girl, a client from four years ago, smiled sheepishly and promised to return to the clinic. A few minutes later, as the nurse ate lunch, a little girl across the diner started gesturing wildly in her direction. "One of mine," Claudette said. "Interesting how, years later, they still react to the voice."

Now Claudette's bifocals slid down her nose as she ripped through orders of business, one item of which was the resignation of a nurse, who had taken a less stressful job. Then she turned to Luwana: "Which of your wonderful cases do you want to tell us about today?" Claudette could be hard on Luwana, whom she'd hired two years before. At the time, Luwana had envisioned a job that left time for her husband, children, and the teenagers she tutored and counseled at her church. But in a place where resistance to nurse-visiting was great, and sixty-four per cent of mothers abandoned the program before their children turned two, Claudette expected—and in Luwana's case eventually got—passionate commitment.

Although passion is tricky to sustain in the winter, Luwana took solace in two girls she called "my model moms" and in the unexpected stability of Alexis. On Valentine's Day, the teen-ager had accepted a marriage proposal from Daigan's father, who had a steady income from tugboat work. They'd moved into an apartment down the street from her parents, which Alexis planned to decorate in "purples and blues." Away from her parents' home, she seemed happier and marginally more attentive to Daigan; she was also, finally, on birth control. So today Luwana solicited her colleagues' advice on a different case: a household in which, as she worked with the mother and baby, a libidinous grandmother kept trying to feel her up. "I try not to make a big deal about it, because I don't want to lose the trust I've gained with the family," Luwana said. "But I have to say, Eeeeeee! I don't like it."

As the other nurses burst into laughter, Claudette, who happened to know the grandmother in question, suggested that a confrontation wouldn't be as counterproductive as Luwana feared. "Next time she tries, you just say, `Honey, back it up,' " she advised. "She'll get that sort of language, since she's all in your face herself."

The discussion moved on to several mentally retarded mothers who, inexplicably, had been cut from disability rolls. The nurses sometimes had to scramble to prevent retarded mothers and their children from being evicted while convincing the bureaucracy that the person who had an I.Q. of sixty last year had roughly the same I.Q. now. And then the nurses turned to a case that worried them all: a withdrawn seventh grader in a violent household who appeared, in her third trimester, to be starving her baby.

One of the nurses said, "I'm at that door every day, but they won't open it, and now she's not going to school. I'm afraid she'll try to abort the baby on her own." The nurses hoped to get the girl into a Baton Rouge home for expectant mothers—and quickly, because when last seen she had been bloody from a fight with her mother. This abuse had been reported to child-protection authorities, who concluded that the girl was safe where she was.

That week, state officials were vowing to reform the child-protection system, after a violent shaking left an eight-month-old boy in a nearby town brain-dead. But the nurses understood what was left unsaid: though state child-abuse deaths were rising, a shortage of child-protection workers, family services, and foster parents meant that at-risk children were often stuck in dangerous homes. The nurses eventually decided that the safety of the seventh grader necessitated what they called "the back-channel option," involving an appeal to a sympathetic local judge. Then the women grabbed their satchels and headed out down the bayous, to fresh troubles they would keep to themselves until they met the following week.

"How many centimetres?" Luwana said into her cell phone one day as she drove down the highway. "Well, baby, that's what the epidural is for, you don't feel it. Sometimes it also gives you chills, be ready for that. I'll be there as soon as I can." Luwana's niece was about to give birth after what the nurse called "the longest pregnancy, emotionally speaking, on record," and Luwana had been at the hospital most of the night. Her fatigue was exacerbated by the fact that her next client, Alexis, had just left a message telling her not to come. Luwana turned off the main road and drove down gravel paths in search of a cell-phone signal. First she called Alexis's sister, whom she had recently turned into an informant, and who reported that Alexis and James, her fiancé, had been brawling. "Look, Alexis, I'm not trying to get in your business," she was saying a few minutes later, "but Daigan is my business. O.K., O.K., can I see you tomorrow? No, I need to see you tomorrow." When she hung up, she said, "I don't feel good about this."

Although by now Alexis had mastered the good-mother script—"I can't stand leaving Daigan, he's developing so fine and I don't want to miss nothing"—the baby seemed, at six months, to contradict her. He was lethargic and close to obese, which Luwana attributed to Alexis's discovery that overfeeding a baby will make him sleep more. As she fretted, her cell phone rang again. "Eight centimetres?" she said in a voice considerably brighter than her mood. "Baby, I'll be there as soon as I can."

Her last visit of the afternoon was with an introverted young woman named Krystal. (Many teen-age mothers on the bayou are named either Krystle or Alexis, after feuding characters in the television show "Dynasty," which was popular when they were born.) Four months earlier, when Krystal's son was two weeks old, the young mother had seemed overwhelmed by her baby, and further rattled by a belief that, after a Cesarean, the obstetrician had left his instruments in her belly. Since then, Krystal had become improbably adept with her son. "My pa be saying, 'There's something wrong with your baby, all these noises he's making,'" she now told Luwana, laughing. "I told him, Pa, you ain't know about preverbal—my baby is talking." Krystal, like most of the literate mothers in Luwana's caseload, was now reading to her baby as well as talking to him, and had become obsessed with his developmental progress. That day was her son's four-month evaluation, and Krystal watched solemnly as the nurse explained the neurological, auditory, and visual cues she was looking for, and jotted estimations in a notebook. After several minutes, the nurse sat up straight. "Mama!" she announced.

"He's on task!" Relief flooded Krystal's face.

By the time Luwana left the house, another impoverished baby had joined the citizenry of Louisiana: her niece's six-pound-ten-ounce son. Outside Terrebonne General Hospital, the new father was waiting to dramatize the day's high points: "Man, I be getting sick with they snipping her little bits to get the baby out. But guess what," he added mischievously, "he got a hairy back just like his mama." In the recovery room, Luwana hugged her niece and dropped a gift bag on the table: condoms and contraceptive foam. "This is wonderful," Luwana told the couple, shaking her head. "And it's going to be a long, long time before you do it again."

Luwana waited again on Alexis's porch. "I knew she would do me like this," she said, rising on tiptoe to check a bedroom window. By now, she was expert in the ruses of the poor: although they couldn't afford to stay away long, they were often quite good at hiding. After a few minutes, she gave up and got back into her car, at which time something down the road caught her attention. She swallowed hard and hit the gas, overtaking a strapping, sunburned man on a motorcycle.

"James!" she yelled, leaning out the window. Daigan's father turned around, surprised.

He climbed off the bike, removed his helmet, and stared past the nurse toward Alexis's little wooden house. "Well," he said, "she broke my heart. And you know all what I did for her—you saw."

Luwana got to the point: "Where's my baby?"

"The new guy got no job, on drugs, on parole, got warrants out for his arrest. And"—James's tone suggested this failing was the greatest—"ain't got no car."

"And . . . Daigan? You know that's my main concern."

"My first thought is that Alexis is bringing that boy around people he shouldn't be around, you know, but ain't nothing I can do about it 'til I got definite proof. But, uh . . ." He hesitated for a minute, then told the nurse that he had caught Alexis and the young man together.

"You saw?" Luwana asked, uneasy.

"My own eyes."

"James, did you react? Maintain . . . composure?"

"I retained my composure, Miss Luwana, I did. It was hard but I did."

"Just get up, get out?"

He nodded.

"Takes a big man, James," she said, exhaling. "Takes a big man."

Tears filled the man's eyes. "I don't know what happened," he said. "I'm moving out today. Dude probably up in there so I got to go."

"But you have to work out some arrangements, James. Because whatever happens, Daigan still needs you to be the dad."

"I know, I will," he said, in a tone that said he wouldn't, and as he rode off Luwana shuddered. She tended to think of a given child's circumstances as the product of many generations; sometimes, though, the speed of change stunned her. In the time it took to smoke a cigarette, children could be stripped of their fathers. "And in the middle of this is the poor . . . Daigan," she said as she pulled back onto the roadway, "and I can't talk to Alexis, can't see where her head is at, I just . . ." She took a wrong turn, braked at a dead end, and rested her forehead on the steering wheel. "I don't know what I am doing."

Then she sat up straight, shifted into reverse, and repeated the word she'd just said to Daigan's father: "Composure. Composure."

Over the winter, Maggie had stopped taking her hepatitis medicine, as it made her too tired to work. José may have contracted the disease as well, but had decided that ignorance was preferable to treatment. Luwana had ruled out ignorance in the case of their daughter, however, and arrived at the house one stormy afternoon to hear the results of the toddler's test.

"It's all messed up," Maggie informed her. "We have to do the test over, but I don't know why—maybe they don't tell me stuff because they think I'm a kid."

"You are a kid," José snapped at Maggie. He was staring at her from the far end of the room, a black look in his eyes. When their one-year-old daughter ambled toward him, he scooped her up and began to sing a Metallica song into her ear:

> I have lost the will to live
> Simply nothing more to give
> There is nothing more for me
> Need the end to set me free.

"Look," Luwana said, temporarily ignoring the domestic drama. "You guys have got to step up, make the doctors explain. Never leave that office until you understand what's going on, even if you have to say, 'Let me see the records'—they're your records, because Maia is your baby. If she's sick, you're going to have to fight for her, and you're going to have to have the information down." Luwana wrote for a minute in her notebook, then looked up. "O.K., I'm all ears: What is up with you two? And Maggie, what's the deal with the hair?"

The deal with the hair was that Maggie had dyed it black with two platinum skunk-streaks, because skunky was how she was feeling. "It's over—we're not getting married," she told Luwana. "I just blew up my life, right there." José nodded, leaving Maggie to explain: how she and José had fought, and how she'd had sex with one of his friends; how the next day, José's high-school classmate tipped him off, and the guilty friend had proffered the details. José had promptly abandoned his cleaning-crew job, stopped his financial contributions to the household, and was moving out. Maggie's mother sat behind the couple, listening with her head in her hands. She'd been working sixteen-hour shifts to compensate for the lost income; still, her bank account was overdrawn.

"The pressures," Maggie said miserably. "The men come at you, and when they get what they want they don't like you for it. I mean, I know that's how it works. And I know that José is the person I want to marry—I wanted the three of us to grow up together."

"Well, I don't do forgiveness," José said. "And I don't do nice, either. Maybe logical, maybe even humane. But nice doesn't help for nothing in this world."

Luwana immediately set out to discourage José from doing what Daigan's father had done: abandon the baby along with the mother. "You can't take this anger out on Maia," she told him with some heat. "This girl has bonded hard with you—you see it, you hear her call you Daddy. And if she has hepatitis it's only that much more important that you keep the bond strong. She is going to need both of you for a long, long time."

"She's a smart girl," José said, rubbing his forearms and looking at his daughter, who now stood in an open cupboard blowing kisses around the room like a film star. "We're trying to keep it from her but I think she already knows. I mean, I'm not thinking straight, all

I can think about Maggie is bad names. But if I let myself get angry . . ." He paused, then concluded, "Well, that would be it."

"When we have a child, sometimes we feel like being a parent, and sometimes we don't," Luwana said. "And when we don't feel it we act our way through it, because Maia is no sweater you bought at Wal-Mart and change your mind about." There was a silence then, and Maggie looked away. Atop the cupboard was an old photo of Maggie in eyeglasses donated by the Lions Club—"back when I was ten and nerdfal and smart." If she had it to do over, she wouldn't have brought Maia into the world and tried to make a family with José. But this belated realization made her feel more ashamed than she already felt.

"So fake it," Luwana said, "starting now." She hugged them both, then ushered them out into the storm. "No point in postponing Maia's test," she said by way of goodbye. "Sooner we know if she's sick, the better we plan."

Maggie drove to the hospital, tense and wincing. Rain pummeled the wild irises that had come into bloom on the roadsides, traffic was slow, and other drivers were being hard on their horns. "You were the coolest," José hissed into her ear, mindful of what their daughter was overhearing. "You liked my sports, my music, my video games, and then you went and acted like any other stupid girl . . ." By the time they arrived, they were sick of the argument and each other, and they refocused their attention on Maia. As the baby had her blood drawn, they hovered over her, declared her brave, exclaimed over a Sesame Street Band-Aid. Then they went their separate ways: José with Maia to hang out at his parents' house, and Maggie to a week of double shifts at work.

In the month that followed, the girl's janitorial specialties, "garbage and floors," brought her almost unsettling comfort; it was only when she'd put up the mops that Metallica's "lost the will to live" song began to run at high speed through her mind. There was a chance that Luwana could help her get her head straight about sex and win José back. But there was little chance that their daughter was going to have a normal life. The test results had confirmed it: Maia's liver was already damaged by hepatitis, and the odds were one in four that she would develop potentially fatal complications.

When Maggie was seven months pregnant, Luwana had asked her to write down the qualities she hoped to pass on to her daughter. "How to be a lady," Maggie wrote first, and then "What love is." She wasn't thinking then about the worst parts of herself, and how those, too, could be transmitted.

In the summer of 2005, the Census Bureau reported that poverty had increased in the United States for the fourth straight year; and the Nurse-Family Partnership produced an empirical snapshot of the one thousand mothers and children in Louisiana who had finished the nurse-visiting program. By some measures, the nurses' efforts seemed to have been trumped by local custom: only a third of the mothers had forsaken formula to attempt breast-feeding, for instance. Other findings were more encouraging, though. By the time their children turned two, almost sixty per cent of mothers over twenty were working and forty-one per cent of those who had started the program without a high-school diploma or equivalency degree had one in hand. And though it was too soon to determine whether their children's intellectual capacities had been strengthened, one of the study's findings was suggestive. Thirty per cent of toddlers had scored in the top quartile of a national test of language development. But Luwana couldn't help thinking of the mothers and babies who hadn't flourished, and the battle of wills she was now losing with Alexis.

Luwana had pushed Alexis to support herself instead of counting on men, and in July this wish was realized. The teen-ager took a full-time job as a short-order cook, earning six dollars an hour. And while her latest lover didn't have a job, he didn't have a criminal record, either, and sometimes babysat while she worked. But then there was Daigan: a jolly ten-month-old with eyes that missed nothing and a body so large that he was unable to crawl.

As Luwana held him, her trusty mind-trick—would this scene have been worse without me in it—didn't provide the comfort it sometimes did. "I think she'll keep making small changes in the months ahead, but now I don't expect a transformation," Luwana said of Alexis. "She doesn't want for herself what I want for her, and that's something I have to make myself accept."

Alexis concurred with the nurse's forecast, and decided to quit the program. One evening in August, she sat on the couch and looked at Daigan, who was on the floor in a "Motor Speedway Heavy Duty" T-shirt, staring back. "Luwana really cares abut me," she said. "And she's helped me a lot—I learned stuff, like how old they gonna get and what they gonna go through and how they gonna grow. But what Luwana says to do—well, basically, I just do it my way." She had recently miscarried her new boyfriend's baby, she said as Daigan emitted a single high shriek. As she reflected on the miscarriage, sadness softened her face, until another thought hit her, and she broke into a beautiful smile. Her boyfriend was eager to try again, she said. "And next I want a little girl."

A few days later, Luwana arrived at Maggie's house to find that a tropical storm had blown off part of the roof. She scarcely noticed, as she had come to celebrate a battle that she'd won. The day before, Maggie had returned to high school. The girl spiritedly shared some newfound knowledge: "In Rome, the invaders came and tried to wipe out all the intelligent people—all the teachers and libraries—because they didn't want the competition, but then everyone ended up kind of stupid." José, who was with her, then took her hand. Together, they informed Luwana that decisions bigger than high school had also been made. José was joining the Marines, and he and Maggie had decided to marry. In the telling, their mouths were straight lines. Love and patriotism were not much on their minds.

"I'm less nervous about Iraq than I am about marrying Maggie," José told the nurse as he and Maggie took turns pushing the talkative eighteen-month-old Maia around in an empty diaper box. Since they lived in a community with a particularly high death rate in the war, Maggie saw the Marine Corps and marriage as equally distressing propositions. But the couple had made a hard calculation, and there were two things they wanted for their daughter that they didn't know another way to get: good, possibly life-extending medical care and a habitable dwelling in which she might grow up.

A few days later, Katrina came through the swamps, damaging homes but sparing lives. As Luwana cared for injured New Orleaneans in a triage unit, Maggie, José, and their families undertook a familiar ritual in this hurricane alley: taping together broken windows, eating from cans, and waiting for the electricity to return. One day, Maggie, whose skin was mottled with poison ivy after bundling up fallen branches, realized that there were just enough food stamps left to buy a wedding cake at Wal-Mart.

The ceremony would take place on a building site that Maggie's father mowed for pocket money. There was a gazebo on the field and, one rainy evening shortly before José left for boot camp, a silver cloud of mosquitoes as well. The wedding guests assembled, the shrimpers among them watching the sky as they slapped and scratched. Heat lightning flashed; somewhere, new storms were gathering, and Gulf waters felt to them weirdly warm. They sensed another hurricane, Rita, which would arrive the following week and obliterate thousands of fragile dwellings in Luwana's territory. Among the homeless would be Maggie and Maia.

But now the bride, waiting for her mother to find the tape with the wedding music on it, leaned into a mirror to see if her tube of lipstick had met its target despite her shakes. She'd seen enough movies to know that such trembling was normal, and that these moments before the vows were for dreaming. "Three bedrooms someday," she said as Luwana came to escort her across the field. "And two baths."

Afterward, Luwana tried to feel optimistic—to see, in the tough choices of two teenagers, real hope for an impoverished American child. And if the sacrifice and exertion required to secure that tenuous possibility struck her as outsized, well, she was a practical woman, and she had a fresh obligation in a hamlet named Cut Off—a newborn whose parents had met in court-ordered drug rehab and then broke up.

"So beautiful, Miss Alaysia, even when you cry," Luwana sang off-key to Cut Off's newest resident, a dark-haired girl in a soiled white dress. "Real tears already? Baby, you're quick! Now Mama, are you reading to her yet?"

ROLE OF THE SCHOOL NURSE IN PROVIDING SCHOOL HEALTH SERVICES

AMERICAN ACADEMY OF PEDIATRICS

COUNCIL ON SCHOOL HEALTH

EDITORS' NOTE

Nurses are often the first to be cut when school districts have to balance their budgets. But learning is impeded by poor health and nurses are key to health promotion, as pointed out in this consensus document by the American Academy of Pediatrics Council on School Health. It calls for a nurse in every school.

■ ■ ■

SCHOOL NURSE DEFINITION

The National Association of School Nurses defines school nursing as:

> A specialized practice of professional nursing that advances the well-being, academic success, and lifelong achievement of students. To that end, school nurses facilitate positive student responses to normal development; promote health and safety; intervene with actual and potential health problems; provide case management services; and actively collaborate with others to build student and family capacity for adaptation, self-management, self-advocacy, and learning.[1]

BACKGROUND

After the child's home, school represents the second most influential environment in a child's life. As more students enter schools with health or mental health problems, pediatricians face the challenge of managing their care throughout the school day. The school nurse is the health care representative on site. An understanding of the school nurse's role is essential to ensure coordinated care. There is a recognized relationship between health and learning, as there is between school nurse availability and student well-being and educational success.[2-4] The role of the school nurse encompasses both health and educational goals.[5-7] Students today may face family crises, homelessness, immigration, poverty, and violence, which increase both their physical and mental health needs. School nurses perform a critical role within the school health program by addressing the major health problems experienced by children. This role includes providing preventive and screening services, health education and assistance with decision-making about health, and immunization against preventable diseases. In addition, school nurses may provide interventions for acute and chronic illness, injuries and emergencies, communicable diseases, obesity, substance use and abuse, adolescent pregnancy, mental health, dental disease, nutrition, and sexually transmitted infections.[8-13] School nurses need to be physically present in schools to address these responsibilities appropriately. Improved student outcomes result where schools have a full-time school nurse.[3] Inadequate staffing threatens the school nurse's role as medical home extender.

School nurses are well positioned to take the lead for the school system in partnering with school physicians, community physicians, and community organizations. They facilitate access to Medicaid and the State Children's Health Insurance Program to help families and students enroll in state health insurance programs and may assist in finding a medical home for each student who needs one.

This policy statement has been endorsed by the National Association of School Nurses.

SCHOOL NURSE ROLE

The National Association of School Nurses identifies 7 core roles that the school nurse fulfills to foster child and adolescent health and educational success.[13] The roles are overarching and are applicable to school nurses at all levels of practice, in all geographic settings, and with all clients.

1. The school nurse provides direct care to students.[13] The school nurse provides care for injuries and acute illness for all students and long-term management of students with special health care needs. Responsibilities include assessment and treatment within the scope of professional nursing practice, communication with parents, referral to physicians, and provision or supervision of prescribed nursing care. An individualized health care plan is developed for students with chronic conditions, and when appropriate, an emergency plan is developed to manage potential emergent events in the school setting (eg, diabetes, asthma). Ideally, this health plan is aligned with the management plan directed by the child's pediatrician and regularly updated through close communication. The school nurse is responsible for management of this plan and communication about the plan to all appropriate school personnel.

The school nurse has a unique role in provision of school health services for children with special health needs, including children with chronic illnesses and disabilities of various degrees of severity. Children with special health needs are included in the regular school classroom setting as authorized by federal and state laws. As a leader of the school health team, the school nurse must assess the student's health status, identify health problems that may create a barrier to educational progress, and develop a health care plan for management of the problems in the school setting. The school nurse ensures that the student's individualized health care plan is part of the individualized education plan (IEP),[14] when appropriate, and that both plans are developed and implemented with full team participation, which includes the student, family, and pediatrician.

2. The school nurse provides leadership for the provision of health services.[13] As the health care expert within the school, the school nurse assesses the overall system of care and develops a plan for ensuring that health needs are met. Responsibilities include development of plans for responding to emergencies and disasters and confidential communication and documentation of student health information.

3. The school nurse provides screening and referral for health conditions.[13] Health screenings can decrease the negative effects of health problems on education by identifying students with potential underlying medical problems early and referring them for treatment as appropriate. Early identification, referral to the medical home, and use of appropriate community resources promote optimal outcomes. Screening includes but is not limited to vision, hearing, and BMI assessments (as determined by local policy).

4. The school nurse promotes a healthy school environment.[13] The school nurse provides for the physical and emotional safety of the school community by monitoring immunizations, ensuring appropriate exclusion for infectious illnesses, and reporting communicable diseases as required by law. In addition, the school nurse provides for the safety of the environment by participating in environmental safety monitoring (playgrounds, indoor air quality, and potential hazards). The school nurse also participates in implementation of a plan for prevention and management of school violence, bullying, disasters, and terrorism events. The school nurse may also coordinate with school counselors in developing suicide prevention plans. In addition, if a school determines that drug testing is a part of its program, school nurses should be included in school district and community planning, implementation, and ongoing evaluation of this testing program.[15]

5. The school nurse promotes health.[13] The school nurse provides health education by providing health information to individual students and groups of students through health education, science, and other classes. The school nurse assists on health education curriculum development teams and may also provide programs for staff, families, and the community. Health education topics may include nutrition, exercise, smoking prevention and cessation, oral health, prevention of sexually transmitted infections and other infectious diseases, substance use and abuse, immunizations, adolescent pregnancy prevention, parenting, and others. School nurses also promote health in local school health councils.

6. The school nurse serves in a leadership role for health policies and programs. As a health care expert within the school system, the school nurse is a leader in the development and evaluation of school health policies. These policies include health promotion and protection, chronic disease management, coordinated school health programs, school wellness policies, crisis/disaster management, emergency medical condition management, mental health protection and intervention, acute illness management, and infectious disease prevention and management.[16]

7. The school nurse is a liaison between school personnel, family, health care professionals, and the community.[14] The school nurse participates as the health expert on the IEP[17] and 504[18] teams. IEP teams identify the special education needs of students; 504 teams plan for reasonable accommodations for students' special needs that impact their educational programs.[18] As the case manager for students with health problems, the school nurse ensures that there is adequate communication and collaboration among the family, physicians, and providers of community resources. This is a crucial interface for the pediatrician and the school nurse to ensure consistent, coordinated care. The school nurse also works with community organizations and primary care physicians to make the community a healthy place for all children and families.

SCHOOL NURSE ACTIVITIES

The range of school health services varies by school district. The following health services are the minimum that should be offered, according to the American Academy of Pediatrics (AAP) manual *School Health: Policy and Practice.*[19]

- Assessment of health complaints, medication administration, and care for students with special health care needs;

- A system for managing emergencies and urgent situations;

- Mandated health screening programs, verification of immunizations, and infectious disease reporting; and

- Identification and management of students' chronic health care needs that affect educational achievement.

The AAP recognizes the need for appropriate management of student health conditions in its policy statement, "Guidelines for Administration of Medication in School."[20] It also recognizes the need for policies for emergency medical situations that can occur in school and the school nurse's role in developing and implementing these policies.[21,22] The school nurse serves as an extension of traditional community health services, ensuring continuity, compliance, and professional supervision of care within the school setting.

SCHOOL HEALTH SERVICES TEAM

The school nurse functions as a leader and the coordinator of the school health services team. The team may also include a school physician, licensed practical nurses, health aides and clerical staff, school counselors, school psychologists, school social workers, and substance abuse counselors. The health team may also expand to create a coordinated school health team that integrates health services, health education, physical education, nutrition services, counseling/psychological/social services, healthy school environment, health promotion for staff, and family/community involvement.[23] Occupational therapists, physical therapists, and speech-language pathologists may also be part of the school health team. A pediatrician often fills the school physician role, because pediatricians are knowledgeable about general pediatrics, school health, and adolescent health. School physicians review guidelines, policies, and programs related to health care in schools. In some schools, a pediatric or family nurse practitioner functions as the school nurse and may provide additional services. Unlicensed assistive personnel (unlicensed individuals who are trained to perform as an assistant to the licensed nurse) may be part of the school health services team. Although they may possess state certification in medication administration as a nursing assistant or other nursing tasks, they must be trained and supervised by the school nurse in accordance with state nurse practice laws to perform delegated nursing tasks. Under this approach, the school nurse has the responsibility to decide which nursing tasks may be delegated and to whom within the school setting, in accordance with state laws and regulations.

Some schools may have a school-based health center in or adjacent to the school, which may provide primary care and psychosocial services. The school nurse coordinates the activities of the school health services team with the child's primary care physician and/ or with the school-based health center to provide continuity of care and prevent duplication of services.

PROFESSIONAL PREPARATION FOR SCHOOL NURSES

The AAP supports the goal of professional preparation for all school nurses and recommends the use of appropriately educated and selected school nurses to provide school health services. The National Association of School Nurses has determined that the minimum qualifications for the professional school nurse should include licensure as a registered nurse and a baccalaureate degree from an accredited college or university. There should be a process by which additional certification or licensure for the school nurse is established by the appropriate state board. The AAP supports national certification of school nurses by the National Board for Certification of School Nurses.[24]

CONCLUSION

The AAP supports having a full-time school nurse in every school as the best means of ensuring a strong connection with each student's medical home. Interim steps toward achieving this ideal can be made by achieving the Healthy People 2010 goal, which states that districts should employ at least 1 nurse per 750 students, with variation, depending on the community and student population.[25] Schools with high percentages of students with special health needs would require more intensive ratios of nurse to students; for example, 1 nurse per 225 students when students require daily professional nursing services or interventions, and 1 nurse per 125 when students have complex health needs.[26] The presence of the school nurse in every school allows the school physician to work most efficiently in providing the coordinated care that each student requires.

The AAP recommends and supports the continued strong partnership among school nurses, school physicians, other school health personnel, and pediatricians. These partners serve the health of children and youth best by facilitating the development of a coordinated school health program, facilitating access to a medical home for each child,[27] and integrating health, education, and social services for children at the community level. School nurses, as part of a coordinated school health program, contribute to meeting the needs of the whole child and supporting their success in school.[28]

RECOMMENDATIONS

1. Pediatricians should establish a working relationship with the school nurses who care for their patients with chronic conditions to ensure that individual patients' health plans are executed effectively within the school. In addition, pediatricians' communications with school nurses concerning their patients should be sufficiently clear and detailed to guide school nurses in overseeing the care of individual children.

2. Pediatricians can offer direct support of school nurses by serving on school wellness policy committees, school health advisory committees, emergency preparedness

committees, or other school-related decision-making bodies. In addition, local physicians may be asked to consult on or assist in writing school health-related policies.

3. School-based screening for vision, hearing, or other conditions may require coordination between local physicians and the school nurse to ensure students are referred for additional evaluation and treatment, and for communication with students, families, school administration, and the community.

4. Pediatricians should play an active role in supporting the availability and continuing education of the school nurse. This role may encompass updates on new AAP recommendations and research findings that would keep the school nurse's practice as aligned as possible with current AAP policy.

NOTES

1. National Association of School Nurses. *Definition of School Nursing.* Silver Spring, MD: National Association of School Nurses; 1999. Available at: www.nasn.org/Default.aspx?tabid=57. Accessed April 16, 2007.

2. Telljohann S, Dake J, Price J. Effect of full-time versus part-time school nurses on attendance of elementary students with asthma. *J Sch Nurs.* 2004;20(6):331–334.

3. Allen G. The impact of elementary school nurses on student attendance. *J Sch Nurs.* 2003;19(4):225–231.

4. Guttu M, Engelke MK, Swanson M. Does the school nurse-to-student ratio make a difference? *J Sch Health.* 2004;74(1):6–9.

5. DeSocio J, Hootman J. Children's mental health and school success. *J Sch Nurs.* 2004;20(4):189–196.

6. Wolfe LC, Selekman J. School nurses: what it was and what it is. *Pediatr Nurs.* 2002;28(4):403–407.

7. Ross S. The clinical nurse specialist's role in school health. *Clin Nurse Spec.* 1999;13(1):28–33.

8. Denehy J. Thinking upstream about promoting healthy environments in schools. *J Sch Nurs.* 2001;17(2):61–63.

9. Schainker E, O'Brien MJ, Fox D, Bauchner H. School nursing services: use in an urban public school system. *Arch Pediatr Adolesc Med.* 2005;159(1):83–87.

10. Denehy J. Health education: an important role for school nurses. *J Sch Nurs.* 2001;17(5):233–238.

11. Taras H, Wright S, Brennan J, Campana J, Lofgren R. Impact of school nurse case management on students with asthma. *J Sch Health.* 2004;74(6):213–219.

12. Perry C, Toole K. Impact of school nurse case management on asthma control in school-aged children. *J Sch Health.* 2000;70(7):303–304.

13. National Association of School Nurses. *Issue Brief: School Health Nursing Services Role in Health Care: Role of the School Nurse.* Silver Spring, MD: National Association of School Nurses; 2002. Available at: www.nasn.org/Default.aspx?tabid=279. Accessed April 16, 2007.

14. Wolfe LC. Role of the school nurse. In: Selemank J, ed. *School Nursing: A Comprehensive Text.* Philadelphia, PA: F. A. Davis; 2006:111–127.

15. National Association of School Nurses. *Position Statement: The Role of the School Nurse Regarding Drug Testing in Schools.* Silver Spring, MD: National Association of School Nurses; 2003. Available at: www.nasn.org/Default.aspx?tabid=218. Accessed December 3, 2007.

16. Brener ND, Burstein GR, DuShaw ML, Vernon ME, Wheeler L, Robinson J. Health services: results from the School Health Policies and Programs Study 2000. *J Sch Health.* 2001;71(7):294–303.

17. US Department of Education, Office of Special Education and Rehabilitative Services. Assistance to states for the education of children with disabilities; preschool grants for children with disabilities; and service obligations

under special education: personal development to improve services and results for children with disabilities; proposed rule. *Fed Regist.* 2005;70(118):35782–35892.

18. American Academy of Pediatrics, Committee on Children With Disabilities. Provision of educationally related services for children and adolescents with chronic diseases and disabling conditions. *Pediatrics.* 2000;105(2):448–451.

19. American Academy of Pediatrics, Committee on School Health. *School Health: Policy and Practice.* 6th ed. Elk Grove Village, IL: American Academy of Pediatrics; 2004.

20. American Academy of Pediatrics, Committee on School Health. Guidelines for the administration of medication at school. *Pediatrics.* 2003;112(3 pt 1):697–699.

21. American Academy of Pediatrics, Committee on School Health. Guidelines for emergency medical care in school. *Pediatrics.* 2001;107(2):435–436.

22. Hazinski MF, Markenson D, Neish S, et al. The medical emergency response plan for schools: a statement for healthcare providers, policymakers, school administrators, and community leaders. *Pediatrics.* 2004;113(1 pt 1): 155–168.

23. Centers for Disease Control and Prevention. Promising practices in chronic disease prevention and control. 2003. Available at: www.cdc.gov/nccdphp/publications/PromisingPractices/pdfs/PromisingPractices.pdf. Accessed April 16, 2007.

24. National Association of School Nurses. *Position Statement: Education, Licensure, and Certification of School Nurses.* Silver Spring, MD: National Association of School Nurses; 2002. Available at: www.nasn.org/Default .aspx?tabid=219. Accessed April 16, 2007.

25. US Department of Health and Human Services. *Healthy People 2010: Understanding and Improving Health.* Washington, DC: US Public Health Service; 2000.

26. National Association of School Nurses. *Position Statement: Caseload Assignments.* Silver Spring, MD: National Association of School Nurses; 2006. Available at: www.nasn.org/Default.aspx?tabid=209. Accessed April 16, 2007.

27. American Academy of Pediatrics, Medical Home Initiatives for Children With Special Needs Project Advisory Committee. The medical home. *Pediatrics.* 2002;110(1 pt 1):184–186.

28. Cooper P. Life before tests. *The School Administrator.* Available at: www.aasa.org/publications/saarticledetail.cfm ?ItemNumber=3138&snItemNumber=950&tnItemNumber=951. Accessed April 16, 2007.

AFTERWORD

DONNA E. SHALALA AND LINDA BURNES BOLTON

The Robert Wood Johnson Foundation Initiative on the Future of Nursing at the Institute of Medicine was developed in the midst of a national debate on universal coverage. The Patient Protection and Affordable Care Act of 2010 focuses mostly on expansion of coverage. The Initiative on the Future of Nursing rethinks the role that nurses—the largest group of health care providers in the nation and the world—can play in improving the health of our people by improving the delivery of care.

The image that people often have of nurses as acute care handmaidens who wear white caps is so out of date and inaccurate that it may impede the nation's ability to harness the expertise and vision of these professionals in ways that can produce the needed improvements in the quality of health care. The report of the Initiative and this book provide a description of contemporary nursing practice and an analysis of the issues that impede taking advantage of this rich pool of talent.

The evidence is clear that we must shift our focus to the care that individuals and populations need to improve and protect their health, whether it means changing the way nurses are educated or addressing the interprofessional competition that results in resistance to the full utilization of nurses. Both the report and the book provide examples of nurses who are leaders in the development of innovative models of care that respond to the unmet health needs of individuals, families, and communities.

So while the report focuses on nursing, it is within the context of how to develop a transformed health care system that emphasizes health promotion, wellness, chronic care management, and care coordination.

After doing this work, we believe that there are three important points that people should keep in mind as the work moves forward:

1. Removing the system barriers that limit the contributions of nurses in the delivery and organization of health care services is essential. These barriers, which exist in both the public and private sectors, include unjustified limitations on nurses' scope of practice at the state and federal levels, as well as a reluctance on the part of insurers to credential and pay nurses appropriately in primary care. Although most nurses will continue to provide high-quality acute care in hospitals we must also ensure that we're using nurses for population- and community-based care and support payment for such care.

2. Funding for comparative effectiveness research needs to include studies of care delivery systems led by nurses in collaboration with consumers and other health professionals. Nurses have developed programs of care and interventions that focus on health promotion and chronic care management, as well as self-care. We

need rigorous research that can inform public and private policies on care models that promote access to affordable, quality, equitable care. For example, why is a nurse-midwifery-led childbirthing center in Washington, DC, able to reduce ethnic disparities in maternal-child outcomes? How do we scale-up such successful models of care and how will the model work in different communities? What are the essential elements of the model that are necessary to have consistent clinical and financial outcomes?

3. Community-based care must become the foundation of health care in our nation as we attempt to shift to an emphasis on health promotion and chronic care management. Whether as employees or independent practitioners, nurses are essential to achieving this aim. Nurses have already developed innovative models of care that could be scaled-up to help us refashion our care delivery system. But our focus on acute care has left us in the dark about how many nurses are needed to provide community-based care and what is acceptable in the variability of the outcomes of this care. The lack of quantitative evidence on the effect of nursing care in the community impairs our ability to plan for a nursing workforce that is educated and licensed to provide unrestricted health education, disease prevention, self care management, and coordination of care.

The report of the Initiative on the Future of Nursing is a call to action for all sectors of our nation. Keeping people healthy is in everyone's best interests.

Donna E. Shalala was the chair, and Linda Burnes Bolton the co-chair, of the Robert Wood Johnson Initiative on the Future of Nursing at the Institute of Medicine.

THE EDITORS

Diana J. Mason, RN, PhD, FAAN, is the Rudin Professor of Nursing at the Hunter College, City University of New York, where she codirects the Center for Health, Media, and Policy. For over 10 years, she served as editor-in-chief of the *American Journal of Nursing*, and continues in an emeritus capacity. For over 25 years, she has been coproducer and comoderator of "Healthstyles," an award-winning weekly, live radio program in New York City, and is a member of the National Advisory Committee of Kaiser Health News, a nonprofit news organization. A fellow in the American Academy of Nursing, she has served as co-chair of "Raise the Voice," an initiative of the Academy that was funded by the Robert Wood Johnson Foundation to identify and make visible to policymakers and journalists the innovative models of care and interventions developed by nurses that can help to transform health care in the United States. She is the lead coeditor of the award-winning book, *Policy and Politics in Nursing and Health Care,* now in its sixth edition. She is a graduate of West Virginia University (BSN), St. Louis University (MSN), and New York University (PhD), and holds honorary doctorates from Long Island University (DHL) and West Virginia University (DSc).

Stephen L. Isaacs, JD, is a partner in Isaacs/Jellinek, a San Francisco-based consulting firm, and president of Health Policy Associates, Inc. A former professor of public health at Columbia University and founding director of its Development Law and Policy Program, he has written extensively for professional and popular audiences. His book, *The Consumer's Legal Guide to Today's Health Care*, was reviewed as "the single best guide to the health care system in print today." His articles have been widely syndicated and have appeared in law reviews and health policy journals. He also provides technical assistance internationally on health law, civil society, and social policy. A graduate of Brown University and Columbia Law School, Isaacs served as vice president of International Planned Parenthood's Western Hemisphere Region, practiced health law, and spent four years in Thailand as a program officer for the U.S. Agency for International Development.

David C. Colby, PhD, the vice president of research and evaluation at the Robert Wood Johnson Foundation, leads a team dedicated to improving the nation's ability to understand key health and health care issues so that informed decisions can be made concerning the way Americans maintain health and obtain health care. His team also assesses how the Foundation is doing through evaluations, performance measures, and scorecards, and makes those assessments public. He came to the Foundation in January 1998 after nine years of service with the Medicare Payment Advisory Commission and the Physician Payment Review Commission, where he was deputy director. Earlier he taught at the University of Maryland Baltimore County, Williams College, and State University College at Buffalo. He was an associate editor of the *Journal of Health Politics, Policy and Law* from 1995 to 2002. He received his doctorate in political science from the University of Illinois, a master of arts from Ohio University, and a bachelor of arts from Ohio Wesleyan University.